PERSPECTIVES ON WRITING

Series Editor, Mike Palmquist

D1713751

PERSPECTIVES ON WRITING
Series Editor, Mike Palmquist

The Perspectives on Writing series addresses writing studies in a broad sense. Consistent with the wide ranging approaches characteristic of teaching and scholarship in writing across the curriculum, the series presents works that take divergent perspectives on working as a writer, teaching writing, administering writing programs, and studying writing in its various forms.

The WAC Clearinghouse and Parlor Press are collaborating so that these books will be widely available through free digital distribution and low-cost print editions. The publishers and the Series editor are teachers and researchers of writing, committed to the principle that knowledge should freely circulate. We see the opportunities that new technologies have for further democratizing knowledge. And we see that to share the power of writing is to share the means for all to articulate their needs, interest, and learning into the great experiment of literacy.

Existing Books in the Series

Charles Bazerman and David R. Russell, *Writing Selves/Writing Societies* (2003)
Gerald P. Delahunty and James Garvey, *The English Language: from Sound to Sense* (2009)
Charles Bazerman, Adair Bonini, and Débora Figueiredo (Eds.), *Genre in a Changing World* (2009)

GENRE IN A CHANGING WORLD

Edited by

Charles Bazerman
Adair Bonini
Débora Figueiredo

The WAC Clearinghouse
wac.colostate.edu
Fort Collins, Colorado

Parlor Press
www.parlorpress.com
West Lafayette, Indiana

The WAC Clearinghouse, Fort Collins, Colorado 80523-1052
Parlor Press, LLC, West Lafayette, Indiana 47906

Copyeditor, Designer: David Doran
Series Editor: Mike Palmquist
Printed in the United States of America

Library of Congress Cataloging-in-Publication Data

Genre in a changing world / edited by Charles Bazerman, Adair Bonini, Debora Figueiredo.
    p. cm. -- (Perspectives on writing)
  Includes bibliographical references.
  ISBN 978-1-60235-125-7 (pbk. : alk. paper) -- ISBN 978-1-60235-126-4 (alk. paper) -- ISBN 978-1-60235-127-1 (adobe ebook)
  1. English language--Rhetoric--Study and teaching. 2. Report writing--Study and teaching. 3. Language arts--Correlation with content subjects. 4. Interdisciplinary approach in education. I. Bazerman, Charles. II. Bonini, Adair. III. Figueiredo, Débora de Carvalho.
  PE1404.G399 2010
  808'.042--dc22
                                2009032938

The WAC Clearinghouse supports teachers of writing across the disciplines. Hosted by Colorado State University, it brings together scholarly journals and book series as well as resources for teachers who use writing in their courses. This book is available in digital format for free download at http://wac.colostate.edu.

Parlor Press, LLC is an independent publisher of scholarly and trade titles in print and multimedia formats. This book is available in paperback, cloth, and Adobe eBook formats from Parlor Press on the World Wide Web at http://www.parlorpress.com. For submission information or to find out about Parlor Press publications, write to Parlor Press, 816 Robinson St., West Lafayette, Indiana, 47906, or e-mail editor@parlorpress.com.

Contents

Editors' Introduction   ix
Charles Bazerman, Adair Bonini, and Débora Figueiredo

Part 1: Advances in Genre Theories   1

1   Worlds of Genre—Metaphors of Genre   3
   John M. Swales

2   From Speech Genres to Mediated Multimodal Genre Systems:
Bakhtin, Voloshinov, and the Question of Writing   17
   Paul Prior

3   To Describe Genres: Problems and Strategies   35
   Maria Antónia Coutinho and Florencia Miranda

4   Relevance and Genre: Theoretical and Conceptual Interfaces   56
   Fábio José Rauen

Part 2: Genre and the Professions   77

5   Accusation and Defense: The Ideational Metafunction of
Language in the Genre Closing Argument   78
   Cristiane Fuzer and Nina Célia Barros

6   The Sociohistorical Constitution of the Genre *Legal Booklet:*
A Critical Approach   97
   Leonardo Mozdzenski

7   Uptake and the Biomedical Subject   134
   Kimberly K. Emmons

8   Stories of Becoming: A Study of Novice Engineers
Learning Genres of Their Profession   158
   Natasha Artemeva

9   The Dissertation as Multi-Genre:
Many Readers, Many Readings   179
   Anthony Paré, Doreen Starke-Meyerring, and Lynn McAlpine

Part 3: Genre and Media   195

10   The Distinction Between News and Reportage in the
Brazilian Journalistic Context: A Matter of Degree   196
   Adair Bonini

11   The Organization and Functions of the Press *Dossier*:
The Case of Media Discourse on the Environment in Portugal   223
   Rui Ramos

12   Multi-semiotic Communication in an Australian Broadsheet:
A New News Story Genre   243
   Helen Caple

13   Narrative and Identity Formation: An Analysis of Media
Personal Accounts from Patients of Cosmetic Plastic Surgery   255
   Débora de Carvalho Figueiredo

Part 4: Genre in Teaching and Learning   277

14   Genre and Cognitive Development: Beyond Writing to Learn 279
   Charles Bazerman

15   Bakhtin Circle's Speech Genres Theory: Tools for a Transdisciplinary
Analysis of Utterances in Didactic Practices   295
   Roxane Helena Rodrigues Rojo

16   The Role of Context in Academic Text Production
and Writing Pedagogy   317
   Désirée Motta-Roth

17   Teaching Critical Genre Awareness   337
      Amy Devitt

18   Curricular Proposal of Santa Catarina State:
Assessing the Route, Opening Paths   352
      Maria Marta Furlanetto

19   Intertextual Analysis of Finnish EFL Textbooks:
Genre Embedding as Recontextualization   375
      Salla Lähdesmäki

Part 5: Genre in Writing Across the Curriculum   393

20   Exploring Notions of Genre in "Academic Literacies"
and "Writing Across the Curriculum":
Approaches Across Countries and Contexts   395
      David R. Russell, Mary Lea, Jan Parker,
      Brian Street, and Tiane Donahue

21   Genre and Disciplinary Work in French Didactics Research   424
      Tiane Donahue

22   Negotiating Genre: Lecturer's Awareness in
Genre Across the Curriculum Project at the University Level   442
      Estela Inés Moyano

23   The Development of a Genre-Based Writing Course for
Graduate Students in Two Fields   465
      Solange Aranha

24   Written Genres in University Studies:
Evidence from an Academic Corpus of
Spanish in Four Disciplines   483
      Giovanni Parodi

Author and Editor Institutional Affiliations   503

Genre in a Changing World
Editors' Introduction

Charles Bazerman, Adair Bonini, and Débora Figueiredo

It has been a decade since the Vancouver conference on genre, which resulted in the volume *The Rhetoric and Ideology of Genre* (appearing in 2002). Since then the world of genre studies and genre approaches to literacy instruction have continued to grow rapidly, gaining variety and complexity as the concept of genre has been examined through a widening variety of intellectual traditions, has been researched in the social histories of many countries, and has been creatively applied in many different educational settings internationally. Although there have been many conferences and publications on genre in the intervening years, this is the first volume since the one arising out of the Vancouver conference to represent the current range of work on genre. As you will see that range is now truly remarkable and puts us on the verge of another dynamic period of theoretical reformulation, research, and application.

The twenty-four papers in this volume were selected from the over 400 presentations at SIGET IV (the Fourth International Symposium on Genre Studies) held on the campus of UNISUL in Tubarão, Santa Catarina, Brazil in August 2007. Two special issues of journals have also been drawn from this conference: issue 3.1 of *Linguistics and Human Sciences* and a forthcoming issue of *L1: Educational Studies in Language and Literature*. At this conference two series of conferences were brought together. The first SIGET conference was in 2003 at Londrina, Paraná as a predominantly Brazilian event, meeting again in 2004 in Vitória, Paraná and in 2005 in Santa Maria, Rio Grande do Sul. In 2007 the organizing committee of SIGET in order to expand the international scope of the conference reached out to include the participants in a series of informally organized genre conferences in North America and Europe convening in Ottawa in 1992, in Vancouver in 1998, and in Oslo in 2001. Participants in SIGET IV came from all over the globe, and authors in this volume represent Argentina, Australia, Brazil, Canada, Chile, Finland, France, Portugal, the United Kingdom, and the United States.

Both the wide range of participation and Brazil as the venue of this remarkable conjunction were no accident. All regions of the world are increasingly aware that they are caught up in a global information economy. People of all nations need to be able to communicate in specialized professional realms to prosper and reap the benefits of new levels of knowledge-based professional and organizational practice. The pervasiveness, immediacy and interactivity of the new communicative media, including the World Wide Web, have further heightened awareness of the need to read and write in many rapidly evolving forms. The need to prepare the citizens to communicate in specialized ways (whether in a first language or a second international language) typically becomes evident in higher education, even at the post-graduate level. Genre is a useful concept to begin to understand the specialized communicative needs that go beyond the traditional bounds of literacy education.

Furthermore, higher education has been growing in most countries out of the same desire to prepare citizens to be part of knowledge-based economies. Students given new access to higher education need advanced literacy skills to succeed at university. Participation at higher levels of education puts greater demands on writing and production, as students need to go beyond reproducing received knowledge to gathering new information and data, developing critical judgment, engaging in discussions and decision making, and applying knowledge to new situations and problems. Students also need to grapple with the specialized languages of disciplines. Again, genre provides a useful way to understand the higher-level literacy demands of different academic disciplines and arenas of professional training.

The increasing recognition of the demands of writing for participating in higher education and beyond, along with the aspirations for more people in each nation to gain access to the benefits of advanced levels of education, has in turn led to a recognition of expanding writing education in primary and secondary schooling. This writing education is seen in more practical and worldly terms than the traditional view of letters as a purely humanities subject. Writing is seen more as a tool to participate in both professional and disciplinary worlds and in the worlds of everyday life. Again genre helps elaborate writing as a focused, purposive, highly differentiated task. Thus genre has become a more salient aspect of educational policies for primary and secondary schooling in many countries.

Brazil provides a striking case of educational interest in genre, as the National Curricular Parameters explicitly specify:

> Every text is organized within a specific genre according to its communicative purposes, as part of the conditions of discourse production, which generate social uses that determine any and every text. Genres are, therefore, historically determined, and constitute relatively stable forms of utterances available in a culture

(Brasil, 1988, p. 21).

Further, in the work with the contents that compose the practices of listening to oral text, reading written texts, producing oral
and written texts and doing linguistic analysis, the school must
organize a set of activities that allow the students to master oral
and written forms of expression in situations of public usage of
their language, keeping in mind the social and material situational
conditions of text production (the social place occupied by the
producer in relation to his/her addressee(s); the addressee(s) and
their social place; the author's intention or purpose; the time and
material location of the text production and its mode of circulation) and selecting, from this standpoint, genres appropriate for
text production, involving its pragmatic, semantic and grammatical dimensions. (Brasil, 1988, p. 49)

In addition to its genre based curriculum and its rapidly expanding higher
educational system, Brazil is an exciting locale for genre studies because it is a
meeting place of many intellectual traditions that are not in such close dialogue
in other parts of the world. Brazilian scholars draw on rich French and Swiss
traditions of genre and language education and European philosophic traditions
as well as on the Anglophone traditions of Systemic Functional Linguistics, English for Specific Purposes, and rhetorical and activity based genre theory (sometimes called North American genre theory). Within an open, dialogic intellectual climate, combined with its own Freirian concern for the empowerment of
individuals within real world practices, Brazil has developed creative approaches
to exploring the many dimensions of genre and bringing those understandings
to the classroom, making the implementation of the National Curricular Parameters a laboratory for developing genre-based language education.

The many intellectual and theoretical resources you will find in the essays
in this volume include rhetoric, Systemic Functional Linguistics, media and
critical cultural studies, sociology, phenomenology, enunciation theory, the Geneva school of educational sequences, cognitive psychology, relevance theory,
sociocultural psychology, activity theory, Gestalt psychology, and schema theory.
Some of these approaches are raised in the opening theoretical section, but others appear throughout, as all articles are theoretically, empirically, and practically
grounded.

The first section "Advances in Genre Theories" consists of four essays that
raise fundamental issues of how different kinds of genre theory may be seen in
relation to each other or can be supplemented by new perspectives. John Swales

in the opening chapter explores the complexity of genre by comparing how different metaphors guiding different theories illuminate different aspects of genre. Paul Prior directs our attention to the multimodality of genred interactions, not only in the textual content but in the very situations of text production, use, and attributing meaning. Antonia Coutinho raises the problematics of attributing genre by looking at the case of genres that are invoked within a fictionalizing frame of another genre, changing the interpretation and stance towards the original genre while necessarily still maintaining important aspects of its generic identity. In the final chapter of the opening section Fábio José Rauen draws on relevance theory to examine how genre is shaped by relevance considerations within situations and how genre then focuses relevance expectations of users, thereby leading to a more efficient alignment of writer and reader.

The second section on "Genre and the Professions" considers how the work of professions has been carried out through genres and how genres have become crucial in how we understand ourselves and our roles in a knowledge and profession based world. The first two chapters look at genre in the law. Cristiane Fuzer and Nina Célia Barros examine closing arguments in closing trials to show how the defendant is kept at the narrative center, while the legal practitioners who are the primary actors in the trial are backgrounded. Leonardo Pinheiro Mozdzenski traces the origins of lay legal primers in Brazil making the law accessible to all citizens back to religious instructions and historically transformed by political movements and changing socioeconomic arrangements. Kimberly Emmons turns our attention to the impact of mental health professions as she studies how people take up professional discourses of mental health to shape their subjectivities as depressed. The formation of professional communicative practice through students' learning of engineering genres is the subject of Natasha Artemeva's chapter. Finally, Anthony Paré, Doreen Starke-Meyerring, and Lynn McAlpine find how the process of writing dissertations inserts students into complex educational and professional sets of communicative relations, in which they must find their way.

The third section on "Genre and Media" considers how journalistic genres in the public sphere shape our view of the world. The first three essays in this section explore the complexity and novelty of newspaper genres, and the last considers how journalistic stories influence public subjectivities. Adair Bonini looking at Brazilian newspapers finds that news stories fall into a spectrum between report and reportage. Rui Ramos examines press dossiers, the thematic collection of stories in Portuguese newspapers. Helen Caple finds in an Australian newspaper a new genre of print news story responsive to the graphic culture fostered by internet culture. To close this section Débora de Carvalho Figueiredo analyzes how identities are formed through stories of plastic surgery experiences in women's magazines.

Since the great contemporary interest in genre has been motivated by the needs of language education, it is appropriate that the final two sections consider educational implications and applications of genre theory and research—the earlier devoted to an array of approaches and the latter specifically to programmatic applications, all of which could be considered Writing Across the Curriculum. The section on "Genre and Teaching/Learning" begins with Charles Bazerman's inquiry into how the writing of specific genres might be instrumental in cognitive development. Roxane Helena Rodrigues Rojo then considers how genre theory can be turned toward understanding classroom discourse. Desirée Motta-Roth describes the sophisticated design of a course in academic writing for masters and doctoral students, mixing theory and practice as students learn to participate in their professional world. Amy Devitt similarly describes and provides the theoretical rationale of a pedagogy aimed at increasing students' critical awareness of genre. Maria Marta Furlanetto describes the difficult process of initiating teachers into an understanding of genre so that they are better able to implement a state-wide genre-based curriculum. In the final study of this section Salla Lähdesmäki uses theories of genre and intertextuality to analyze how second-language textbooks incorporate other genres as part of learning activities.

The last section considers how genre theory has been used to help students learn to communicate within specialized disciplines and professions, in the kinds of programs that have been called Writing Across the Curriculum. This section provides comparisons of the way genre is being used in different educational settings, organized differently in different countries. The first chapter, collaboratively written by David Russell, Mary Lea, Jan Parker, Brian Street and Tiane Donahue presents and compares the British Academic Literacies approach with the US Writing Across the Curriculum movement. Next Tiane Donahue presents the French didactics approach to academic writing. Estela Inés Moyano presents a linguistically based initiative at an Argentinian University to increase faculty's genre awareness of student assignments so as to improve support for first language writing assignments in subject matter courses. Solange Aranha describes a second language genre-based disciplinary-focused writing courses for graduate students. The volume ends with Giovanni Parodi presenting a Spanish language corpus research project into genres used in disciplinary courses in a Chilean university.

A world tied together by communication and knowledge, enacting increasingly complex cooperations on many levels, puts an increasing demand on the genres that share our meanings and knowledge, that coordinate our actions, and that hold our institutions together. A world being transformed by new technologies and media as well as new social and economic arrangements creates the need for rapid and deep transformation of genres. In a world where pressing problems require increasing levels of coordination and mutual understanding, forging effective genres is a matter of global well-being. In a world where increasingly high degrees of literate participation are needed by citizens of all nations, advancing the communicative competence of all, making available the genres of power and cooperation, is a matter of social capacity and social justice. As committed educators and researchers, the contributors to this volume and the participants in SIGET draw strength from the importance of this work.

REFERENCES

Brasil. (1998). Ministério da Educação e do Desporto. Secretaria de Educação Fundamental. Parâmetros Curriculares Nacionais: língua portuguesa: Terceiro e quarto ciclo do ensino fundamental: língua portuguesa. Brasília, Distrito Federal, Brazil: MEC/SEF.

Coe, R., Lingard, L., & Teslenko, T. (Eds.). (2002). *The rhetoric and ideology of genre*. Cresskill, New Jersey: Hampton Press.

ADVANCES IN GENRE THEORIES

1   Worlds of Genre—Metaphors of Genre

John M. Swales

INTRODUCTION

More than a decade ago, Hyon (1996) published an influential article in *TESOL Quarterly* entitled "Genre in three traditions: Implications for ESL"; indeed, by April 2007, I note it had received 56 references in *Google Scholar*. In it, she argued that work on literary genres had been conceived of in three distinct ways by researchers and practitioners with different backgrounds and representing different parts of the world. As readers may know, she instances the international ESP Tradition, North American New Rhetoric, and the Australian Systemic-Functional School. On the first, she notes that "many ESP scholars have paid particular attention to detailing the formal characteristics of genres while focusing less on the specialized functions of texts and their surrounding social contexts" (p. 695). In contrast, New Rhetoric scholars "have focused more on the situational contexts in which genres occur than on their forms and have placed special emphases on the special purposes, or *actions*, that these genres fulfill within these situations" (p. 696). For SFL scholars, genre is one element in a complex social semiotic system, delineating and exploring the textual features of which is empowering for both learners and (disadvantaged) citizens.

In this 1996 paper, Hyon details some other differences among the three traditions: a broader, more rhetorical mode definition of genre for the Australians, and a greater interest in applying genre studies to high schools and workplaces; a concentration on post-secondary academic and professional genres for the other two traditions; a greater interest in ethnographic methods among the New Rhetoricians, perhaps especially those working in Canada; and a greater reluctance to commit to the pedagogical relevance of genre studies among these scholars. As Hyon notes, one possible explanation for these disparities lies in the target audiences of the three groups. For the systemicists, these are students who are either acquiring English as a second language or whose English L1 literacy skills need considerable scaffolding. For ESP specialists, the primary audiences are students in EFL situations or who need to acquire specialized EAP discourses as part of their professionalization. And for New Rhetoricians, a primary audience consists of undergraduates taking composition or rhetoric courses as part of a Liberal Arts education.

Hyon's paper was a valuable map-making exercise that made much sense in the mid- 1990s. As Berkenkotter observed in a web posting dated 27 January, 2006 and entitled "North American Genre Theorists," "Hyon's categories have stuck." However, by 2007, what had become known as the genre movement had coalesced somewhat, with the result that the divisions among the three traditions have become much less sharp—even if they have not entirely disappeared. This rapprochement can be seen in a number of recent books. Even a cursory reading of the following quartet shows trends toward assimilation of views and a shared appreciation of previous work by the likes of Bakhtin, Miller and Myers:

Bhatia (2004) *Worlds of Written Discourse: A Genre-based View*
Devitt (2004) *Writing Genres*
Frow (2006) *Genre*
Swales (2004) *Research Genres: Explorations and Applications*

Bhatia and Swales represent the ESP tradition, Devitt that of US composition/ rhetoric, and Frow is a systemic linguist, yet the following single quotations from each, despite this selectivity, will suffice to indicate something of this coming-together of views:

> *Discourse as genre,* in contrast, extends the analysis beyond the textual product to incorporate context in a broader sense to account for not only the way the text is constructed, but also the way it is often interpreted, used and exploited in specific institutional or more narrowly professional contexts to achieve specific disciplinary roles. (Bhatia, 2004, p. 20)

>> I propose, then, that genre be seen not as a response to a recurring situation but as a nexus between an individual's actions and a socially defined context. Genre is a reciprocal dynamic within which individuals' actions construct and are constructed by recurring context of situation, context of culture, and context of genres. (Devitt, 2004, p. 31)

>> And I try to stress that genres are not fixed and pre-given forms by thinking about texts as performances of genre rather than reproductions of a class to which texts belong, and by following Derrida in stressing the importance of edges and margins—that is, stressing the open-endedness of generic frames. (Frow, 2006, p. 3)

>> My current attempt [is] to see genres no longer as single—and perhaps separable—communicative resources, but as forming com-

plex networks of various kinds in which switching modes from speech to writing (and vice versa) can—and often does—play a natural and significant part. (Swales, 2004, p. 2)

Some of the consolidating trends that emerge from these volumes and from other publications would include (a) a balance between constraint and choice; (b) the role of local contextual coloring in the realization of genre exemplars, such as the Brazilian predeliction for using *Considerações Finais* for the final article section title; (c) a greater sense that genres and genre sets are always evolving in response to various exigencies; and (d) a consequent more nuanced approach to genre awareness-raising and genre acquisition. With regard to this last, Anthony has observed, "The proposed methods for teaching genres have changed from explicit approaches to those in which features of genres are 'negotiated' through classroom discussion or 'reinvented' through elaborate writing tasks" (2000, p. 18).

METAPHORS OF GENRE

Despite this consolidation, there remains the question of the definition of genre itself, especially when all those recent arrivals on the genre scene (the information scientists and documentarians) would seem to be crying out for a working and workable definition. I offered one such elaborated definition in *Genre Analysis* back in 1990. But when I came to revisit the topic a few years ago, I concluded that I could not basically reiterate a position espoused more than a decade previously but, true to the grand academic imperative, would have to offer something new. (Even though, I have to confess, in my heart of hearts, I felt that there was little actually wrong with that old earlier characterization, except for a mistaken emphasis on genres as distinct independent entities). My rationale for retreat was a little forced, or so it now seems to me. On definitional depictions, I wrote:

> For one thing they fail to measure up to the Kantian imperative of being true in all possible worlds and all possible times; for another, the easy adoption of definitions can prevent us from seeing newly explored or newly emerging genres for what they are. (2004, p. 61)

The first rationale looks impossibly demanding, while the second looks unlikely or, at the least, unproven. Instead I offered a suite of six metaphors, mostly borrowed or adapted from others, that I claimed would variously illuminate our understanding of genres. The resulting picture looked like this:

Frames of Social Action	→	Guiding Principles
Language Standards	→	Conventional Expectations
Biological Species	→	Complex Historicities
Families and Prototypes	→	Variable Links to the Center
Institutions	→	Shaping Contexts; Roles
Speech Acts	→	Directed Discourses

The first of these metaphors comes from Bazerman. Here is an edited extract:

> Genres are not just forms. Genres are forms of life, ways of being. *They are frames for social action.* . . . Genres shape the thoughts we form and the communications by which we interact. Genres are the familiar places we go to create intelligible communicative action with each other and the guideposts we use to explore the familiar. (1997, p. 19; my emphasis)

This is an inspiring and helpful characterization, this idea of a frame as a starting place or an initial orientation, and indeed is subtly different from Carolyn Miller's famous 1984 definition centered on the accomplished rhetorical action itself. The metaphor rightly focuses attention on the familiar and the quotidian. However, the metaphor is less helpful when we find ourselves on unfamiliar ground, as when we either have difficulty in discerning the frame for rhetorical action, or worse, in our ignorance, we choose the wrong frame. Often here we are dealing with what I called in a 1996 paper "occluded genres" (Swales, 1996), i.e., those that are hidden and out of sight to all but a privileged and expert few. For a first quick example, I was approached twice in the first half of 2007, once by a colleague in the US and once by a colleague in Europe, because for the first time in their academic lives they had been asked by an Australian university to write an external examiner's report on a PhD thesis. Would I be able send them a couple of examples to help them decide what to focus and, just as importantly, what not to focus on?

PERSONAL STATEMENTS/STATEMENTS OF PURPOSE

My second example is more extended and concerns a two-page document required of graduate student applications in the US called either *personal statement* (PS) or *statement of purpose* (SOP). This text is now part of a complex bunch of documents including a CV, a GPA transcript, various test scores such as those for GRE and TOEFL, letters of recommendation, and, increasingly, a writing sample. We thus see the forces of generification at work here; in contrast, when I applied for graduate school at a British university in the 1960s I hand-wrote a short application letter and then was invited for interview by the head of department. In the interview, he asked me what I read in the applied linguistics field (luckily I could mention Halliday, Mackintosh, & Strevens, 1964) and then asked me a couple of questions about Italian loan words in Libyan colloquial Arabic. After 20 minutes or so, the professor remarked "well, you seem a nice enough chap" and I was in.

The PS/SOP remains largely an occluded genre, except perhaps for those who can gain access to the special issue of *Issues in Writing* (15:1; Fall/Winter 2004) guest edited by Brown and Barton and which can be found at www.uwsp.edu/ english/iw. And this occlusion is problematic because a "wrong" PS/SOP could block initial entry to an academic career in the US. There are, in my estimation, four main problems:

- The misleading nature of the titles of the genre
- Balancing the past and the future
- Distinguishing yourself (i.e., going beyond the CV)
- For PhD programs, offering a believable long-term commitment

On the first problem, the *Personal Statement* label somewhat over-emphasizes the life story element, its *apologia pro sua vita* aspect; on the other hand, the *Statement of Purpose* label over-articulates the importance of specifying future research projects. In the same vein, there is a tension here between stressing the value of past achievements and the validity and credibility of future aspirations. The third problem raises the issue of somehow going beyond a potted biography that does little more than provide a narrative version of the details in the CV. As a number of the specialist informants in the *Issues in Writing* observed, they are looking for something memorable in the PS/SOP; in particular, something that they might remember an applicant by, something that they can "take away." Finally, there is the issue for applicants to PhD programs (typically a five-year journey in the US) of how to demonstrate that you have the intellectual resources and the academic persistence to endure a journey of that length. In my experience at the Department of Linguistics at Michigan, this exigency is particularly difficult for students who have recently completed a more practice-oriented MA degree. Members of this group need to reconstruct themselves toward addressing fundamental issues and theoretical concerns, so what might have worked for an MA application, such as "I want to make myself a more professional language teacher and so help improve international communications," is recognized as not resonating as well at the more advanced level.

In the special issue, Bekins, Huckin & Kijak (2004) offer a move analysis of graduate medical school Personal Statements, which they calculate is followed 60-70% of the time by the texts judged to be effective:

Move 1: **Hook** (a narrative to grab the reader's attention)
Move 2: **Program** (why this particular specialization/location)
Move 3: **Background** (evaluation of skills, landmarks of achievement)
Move 4: **Self-promotion** (distinctive individual qualities)
Move 5: **Projection** (personal professional goals/career trajectory)

Here is one of their winning hooks (from an application for medical residency in surgery):

> I remember hearing the loud snap resonating across the field and having no doubt it was broken. Looking down at my forearm during the high school football game, the distal end dangling as both the left radius and ulna had been broken at midshaft. I felt certain I had experienced my last football event . . . .

As you can doubtless imagine, the application goes on to say that this forearm was fully mended by brilliant surgical intervention and thus the young man was inspired to follow a career in surgery.

My second example comes from an undergraduate of my acquaintance who graduated last year in linguistics and is applying for an MA in applied linguistics at a leading British university. She opens with this rhetorically arresting minihook:

> The moment came on Friday, June 23rd, 2006, at precisely 5:25 pm. I was attending the conference . . . .

And her final paragraph concludes:

> As the conference went on, I set a challenge for myself: I would ask a question of one of the speakers about their presentation. When the final speaker stepped up to the podium, I knew this was my last chance. . . . And so the moment arrived, that Friday afternoon; I stood up, took a deep breath, and crossed the line from observer to participant in the professional world of applied linguistics.

The clever framing of her SOP doubtless contributed to the success of her application.

Nearly all applicants, of course, have to struggle with this genre. However, there is also considerable anecdotal evidence that these kinds of occluded text, those that involve both the personal and professional, and those that are both evaluative and self-evaluative, are more likely than more formal genres to be influenced by local cultural traditions and conventions, and thus give rise to cross-culturally diverse strategies. From my fairly extensive experience of reading Michigan's Statements of Purpose and occasionally teaching or tutoring this genre, I offer the following slightly tongue-in-cheek observations:

SOPs from Scandinavia: Much verbal modesty since "deeds speak louder than words"; a reluctance to boast.

SOPs from Africa/India: Appeals for pity and for special consideration, such as "I am the youngest of eight siblings, only two of whom have jobs."

SOPs from East Asia: Considerable early educational histories and particularly on ranking data: "My department is ranked as the fourth best out of 28, and in my final undergraduate year I was ranked third out of 73 civil engineering students."

SOPs from Britain: Because of traditional UK PhD student profiles, a preponderance of very specific research proposals, such as "I would like to analyze anti-accusative structures in serial verbs in Khmer, especially as they occur in personal narratives of those with only an elementary school education." These are sometimes taken as an affront by my colleagues, along the lines of this kind of reaction: "How can she decide on this particular topic before taking my course on the syntax of Southeast Asian languages?"

SOPs from the US: Often an attempt to show interest in everything: "I am interested in generative syntax, nasalization, Jamaican creoles, cross-cultural semiotics, and neurolinguistics. Also namedropping is common, as in "I took syntax with Chomsky."

In order to characterize rather more comprehensively what might be happening here, we need to invoke two additional metaphors. For the variation described above, we need to recognize that there are different degrees of approximation from various parts of the world to what experienced US gatekeeper-readers of this genre might come to expect. In other words, there are degrees of divergence from the prototypical center. This is not to say, of course, that unusual, idiosyncratic or creative SOPs cannot be successful—as Bhatia has noted on several occasions "genre-bending" can be a "high risk, high reward" option—but that there are prototypical expectations underlying the stylistic and linguistic surface. More generally, we also would do well to come to recognize that the PS/SOP is institutionalized. This becomes particularly clear when we read the interview statements made by the appointed readers of these documents. The reading protocol and interview data in the *Issues in Writing* volume indicate that the expert readers on admission committees rely to a considerable extent on first impressions—in effect, whether they are turned on or turned off by the opening paragraph. A wrong step here can be hard to recover from. Barton, Ariail and Smith found that "if the opening failed, either because it was not memorable or because it made no compelling connection to the profession, the readers skipped, skimmed, expressed criticism, and generally reacted negatively to the text" (2004, p. 109). We know that marketing research shows that those junk-mail solicitation letters have only a few seconds to catch the readers' attention if they are not to be immediately discarded in exasperation. The situation here is, of course, not so extreme, but there appear to be parallels.

More generally, the medical readers studied by Bekins, Huckin and Kijak "most wanted to see in a PS a clear statement of what the applicant had learnt from his or her life experiences" (2004, p. 65). The PS, they conclude, should be "a site for self-reflection on formative experiences" (p. 69). It would seem then that for the powerful and busy institutional gatekeepers this kind of projection is part of putting together over these two pages a convincing and compelling professional identity. I therefore suggest that the three genre metaphors of frame, prototype and institution help us understand these texts a little more clearly and a little more fully.

THE ART HISTORY MONOGRAPH

The other extended investigation into the roles of genre theory and metaphors of genre in understanding collectivities of documents takes as its subject an important and long-standing genre—that of the art history monograph. This type of monograph is a book-length study of the life, times and work of a single artist—almost exclusively a white male. Typically the volume contains many illustrations of the artist's work, and perhaps some of those other artists who had had a formative influence on him. It is widely agreed that the archetype for this genre is Vasari's *Lives of the Painters, Sculptors and Architects,* first published in Florence in 1550. Vasari laid down the foundation for the belief that the visual arts cannot be comprehended without taking their human origins into account; more specifically, there must exist a dialectic relationship between the biographical identity and the artistic identity of the chosen artist. The monograph, as it developed, also began to pay particular attention to the identified masterpieces and great works of the artist, evaluating and interpreting them in various ways so that their achievements became more easily recognizable to the non-specialist reader. A visit to any large bookshop today will reveal many exemplars of this genre, and there are a number of important and successful publishers in this area, such as the German firm Taschen.

I will first attempt to illustrate the recent evolution of the art history monograph by taking the case of the American painter Thomas Eakins (1844-1916) and his most famous painting *The Gross Clinic* completed in 1875; in fact this large work is arguably the most famous painting in the history of North American art.

The first full length study of Eakins' work was Lloyd Goodrich's 1933 *Thomas Eakins: His Life and Work.* (Note the traditional arrangement of the title.) Here is part of Goodrich's depiction of the picture:

> While the picture represents a whole scene, it is at the same time the portrait of one man. Dr Gross dominates it, with his silvery hair, fine brow, and strong features catching the full force of the light—an imposing figure, with the rugged force of a pioneer in his profession. Every detail in the picture contributes to the dramatic value of his figure and the subordinate drama of the group of assistants clustered round the patient. . . . The viewpoint is absolutely objective; the hand that guides the brush is as steady as the hand that guides the scalpel. But there is no lack of humanity; not the sentimentality that hides its eyes and shrinks from the less pleasant aspects of life, but the robust understanding of the scientist who can look on disease and pain, and record them truthfully. (p. 50)

As the above passage shows, Goodrich's focus here is on the affinities between the "scientific" surgeon and the "scientific" painter, as shown most tellingly by the phrase "the hand that guides the brush is as steady as the hand that guides the scalpel." Eakins, by choosing for this major work a scientific "drama of contemporary life," underscores, for Goodrich, both his modernity and his American individuality and originality.

We need to fast-forward 50 years to reach the next major study of the painter—Elizabeth Johns' *Thomas Eakins: The Heroism of Modern Life.* Johns' book was a flagship publication flying under the banner of the new "social art history." The traditional emphasis on the distinctive individual genius of the artist living in his private world is now replaced by closer attention to the material and social contemporary forces that impinged upon the artist. Her discussion, therefore, of *The Gross Clinic* focuses on the details of the medical setting and of medical science at that time. In a typical passage, she writes:

> Moreover, the surgery that defined Gross as a modern surgeon was not the heroic amputation or the bladder-stone removal that had been practiced by earlier surgeons for centuries, but a quiet surgical procedure that in its capacity to improve the life of a patient illustrated incisively the benefits of the evolution of surgery. Including the patient's mother to assure that his audience would not miss the youth of Gross's patient, Eakins makes a point that could only be made with his operation; the happy outcome of the surgery in Gross's clinic is a child with a whole leg instead of a stump. (1983, p. 75)

Four years later, leading art historian Michael Fried published a volume whose title indicates considerably higher aspirations: *Realism, Writing, Disfiguration: On Thomas Eakins and Stephen Crane*. In Fried's discussion of the painting, Eakins is no longer the meticulous if somewhat provincial super-realist of the Goodrich account, nor the precise documentarian characterized by Johns, but rather a master in the absorptive tradition of Vermeer and a dramatist worthy of comparison with Caravaggio. For Fried, Eakins achieves powerful *reality effects* by unreal disfigurations and distortions. Further, Fried projects a strongly Freudian interpretation on the painting:

> On the one hand, Gross the master healer is deeply reassuring, an exemplum of perfect calm and mature resource; on the other hand, his bloody right hand holding the scalpel may be read not only as threatening castration but as having enacted it, . . . the precise focus of menace would have been an actual channel of access for the painter's fantasmatic identification with the threatening paternal power and thus also for his confirmation of the latter's identification as healer. (1987, pp. 66-67)

Since the publication of Fried's monograph, some further papers have come to light and which are given prominent attention in the latest volume on Eakins—Henry Adams (2005), *Eakins Revealed: The Secret Life of an American Artist*. (Contrast this with Johns' title!) Fried's psychological reading is now reinforced by more details about Eakins' ambivalent relationship with his father, the mental illness of his mother and of other members of his family, and his exhibitionism, narcissism and his voyeurism. The darker story revealed by the Bregler papers allows Adams to compare literary scholars, who traditionally have no problem with discussing tragic aspects of writers' lives, with art history scholars:

> . . . art historians have always tended to impose idealizing notions that have little bearing or relevance. Their practice of polishing the artist's biography goes along with a tendency to prettify the art itself. But neither Eakins' art nor his life offers an ideal. The lessons they teach are of a very different kind. (2005, p. xiv)

The story I have recounted about a single painting shows, I hope, a complex historicity. The conventional expectations of the art history monograph that had remained relatively fixed from Vasari to Goodrich have evolved and diversified through social history, psychoanalysis and various post-modernist tropes. In the case of Eakins, the inspirational volume of 1933 had evolved by 2005 into one that is darkly tragic. A key work of art, *The Gross Clinic*, which started out as a new historicist demonstration of surgical advance and prowess in Philadelphia in the third-quarter of the 19th century has changed into a troubled and disfiguring depiction of highly conflicted, if largely suppressed, family relations. After 125 years, the great power of the painting remains, but the lesson it now teaches seems to be of a very different kind.

The larger context of the art monograph can also be illuminated by the metaphor of genre as institution, and here my arguments rely in part on a 2006 volume by Guercio entitled *Art as Existence: The Artist's Monograph and Its Project*. Despite the popularity of "life and works" monographs in bookshops and in libraries, it can be argued that this genre has lost a considerable part of its institutional status. For one thing, many of the leading art historians of the last century looked beyond individual artists and/or their schools to larger trends: Wöfflin's studies of general cultural zeitgeist allowed a contrastive analysis of the features dividing the classical and the baroque; Baxandall's explorations of the artistic consequences of theories of perception in 18th century France; Panovsky's pursuit of iconology in pictures from the Low Countries; and what we might describe as Gombrich's "viewer response theory."

In addition, the monographic tradition does not sit well with contemporary views of the individual human subject. Perhaps since Barthes' famous essay on "The Death of the Author" (1977), the stability of the person, both artistic and otherwise, has transmuted into plethoras of co-constructed and shifting identities. As Guercio states, "Under the influence of psychoanalysis and of philosophies weary of the burdens of metaphysics, the idea that a subject is a fundamental essence, consistent and unitary, was undermined and exposed as a vanishing illusion" (2006, p. 9). Feminism and post-colonialism also added their dissenting voices to the European tradition of the life and works of male artists; as Nochlin's (1971) famous essay title trenchantly put it, "Why have there been no great women artists?"

A further factor resides in a shift in the priorities of the leading graduate programs in art history or fine art. The traditional doctoral dissertation in the form of a so-called *catalogue raisonné* (a careful and heavily footnoted chronological list of all works properly attributed to an artist, accompanied by a biographical sketch) fell first out of favor, and, more recently, this fate, at least for the best students, has befallen the artist's monograph. One obvious reason is that these art departments are running out of individual artists worth devoting huge amounts of time and effort to; less obviously, interest has shifted to more interdisciplinary topics, involving literature, sociology, psychology or various kinds of complex scientific analyses, such as micrographs of paint layers. In consequence, the monograph output is no longer dominated by university departments but by museum curators, connoisseurs, fine art dealers, and specialists in major auction houses. This in turn has led to a considerable amount of commodification in the sense that publishing a monograph on a hitherto unmonographed artist very often leads to increased interest in and knowledge about that artist's life and works. This in turn often leads to a considerable appreciation in the value of those works.

The genre-as-institution and genre-as-species metaphors are also particularly helpful in the way they can elucidate the rise and fall of genres over time, from creative beginnings, to distinguished products, to tired replicas, and possibly on to various kinds of revival—from archetypes to divergences, to spin-offs, and to splits that might break the original central genre into several more specialized ones. And so it has been with the art history monograph. Further, the metaphor helps us in seeing the genre not only in terms of itself, but also in terms of its institutional ranking, where it stands in the world. Thus, what might seem on the surface to be a highly successful genre, may in reality turn out to be much less so.

FINAL CONSIDERATIONS

As I see it, the work of genre is to mediate between social situations and the texts that respond strategically to the exigencies of those situations. As Frow notes, when texts are well conceptualized and well constructed, they *perform* the genre. When these performances proliferate, genres tend to drift through time and geographical space, partly inherently and partly as a result of intertextual acceptances and rejections. The work of genre analysts is to track these textual regularities and irregularities and explain them in terms of the relevant and pertinent social circumstances and the rhetorical demands they engender. Part of the work of those genre analysts with applied aspirations would then be to refashion these findings so that, by comparison and contrast, by episodic dissection, by rhetorical consciousness-raising, and by task designs such as the systemic-functionalists' "wheel of genre," they can become more transparent to those who would wish or need to become better consumers or producers of textual exemplars in the targeted genre or genres. I have attempted to show how these latter developments might work out at least in part with the genre of the personal statement/statement of purpose.

But this is not the case with art-historical discourse. This type of discourse, as I have discovered to my cost, has so far proved recalcitrant in revealing its secrets. As Tucker (2003) has noted, discussions of art works show a stronger interdependence of description and evaluation than we customarily find. In addition, there are puzzling relationships between the verbal and visual, and between banal ostensive reference to some feature in the art object and highly allusive and symbolic commentary. It seems clear that this kind of discourse, in its more successful manifestations, succeeds in engaging the reader on many levels, and can do so with very different trajectories for handling the general and the particular, and for describing, invoking and evaluating. Untangling these layers or laminations in ways that would help aspiring readers and writers of such texts remains a task for the future.

REFERENCES

Adams, H. (2005). *Eakins revealed: The secret life of an American artist*. Oxford: Oxford University Press.

Anthony, L. (2000). Implementing genre analysis in a foreign language classroom. *TESOL Matters, 10,* 3-18.

Barthes, R. (1977). The death of the author. In *Image-Music-Text*. New York: Hill and Wang.

Barton, E., Aarail, J., & Smith, T. (2004). The professional in the personal: The genre of personal statements in residency applications. *Issues in Writing, 15,* 76-124.

Bazerman, C. (1997). The life of genre, the life in the classroom. In W. Bishop & H. Ostrum (Eds.), *Genre and writing* (pp. 19-26). Portsmouth, NH: Boynton/Cook.

Bekins, L., Huckin, T., & Kijak, L. (2004). The personal statement in medical school applications: Rhetorical structure in a diverse and unstable context. *Issues in Writing, 15,* 56-75.

Bhatia, V. (2004). *Worlds of written discourse: A genre-based view*. London: Continuum

Devitt, A. (2004). *Writing genres*. Carbondale: Southern Illinois University Press.

Fried, M. (1987). *Realism, writing, disfiguration: On Thomas Eakins and Stephen Crane*. Chicago: University of Chicago Press.

Frow, J. (2006). *Genre*. London: Routledge.

Goodrich, L. (1933). *Thomas Eakins: His life and work*. New York: Whitney Museum of American Art.

Guercio, G. (2006). *Art as existence: The artist's monograph and its project.* Cambridge, MA: MIT Press.

Hyon, S. (1996). Genre in three traditions: Implications for ESL. *TESOL Quarterly, 30*, 693-722.

Johns, E. (1983). *Thomas Eakins: The heroism of modern life*. Princeton, NJ: Princeton University Press.

Nochlin, L. (1988). Why have there been no great women artists? *Art News 69*(9), 22-39.

Swales, J. M. (1990). *Genre analysis: English in academic and research settings.* Cambridge: Cambridge University Press.

Swales, J. M. (1996). Occluded genres in the academy: The case of the submission letter. In E. Ventola & A. Mauranen (Eds.), *Academic writing: Intercultural and textual issues*. Amsterdam: John Benjamins.

Swales, J. M. (2004). *Research genres: Explorations and applications*. Cambridge: Cambridge University Press.

Tucker, P. (2003). Evaluation in the art-historical research article. *Journal of English for Academic Purposes, 2*, 291-312.

2 From Speech Genres to Mediated Multimodal Genre Systems: Bakhtin, Voloshinov, and the Question of Writing

Paul Prior

INTRODUCTION

Over the past 20 years, so much has been written on genre, so many astute analyses have been undertaken, so many important theoretical observations have been made (see, e.g., Bazerman, 1988; Berkenkotter & Huckin, 1995; Coe, Lingard, & Teslenko, 2002; Devitt, 2004; Freedman & Medway, 1994; Hyland, 2004; Russell, 1997; Swales, 2004), that it is challenging now to say something new that needs to be said, especially in the context of a volume dedicated to genre studies. It has been widely agreed for some time now that genres are not solely textual phenomena, that genres should be understood not as templates but as always partly prefabricated, partly improvised or repurposed. Over the last 15 years, in different terms and with somewhat different emphases, but with increasing clarity, genre analysts have been moving from a focus on genres as isolated phenomena to a recognition of how specific types of texts are formed within, infused by, and constitutive of systems of genres. Genres have been described in terms of chains (Swales, 2004; Fairclough, 2004), colonies (Bhatia, 2002), repertoires (Orlikowski & Yates, 1994; Devitt, 2004), sets and systems (Bazerman, 1994, 2004a; Devitt, 1991, 2004), and ecologies (Spinuzzi, 2004). Theorists have also begun to highlight ways that genre theory has privileged public texts whose primary functions are informational, rhetorical or aesthetic. For example, Swales (1996, 2004) has identified the category of *occluded* genres, and Spinuzzi (2004) has highlighted the way many workplace genres are designed primarily to mediate activity (e.g., to work as aids to thinking and action rather than as means of inter-office or external communication). Attention to modes other than writing has also grown. Räisänen (1999), for example, has examined the chains of written and oral genres involved in presenting at academic conferences. Analyzing topological and typological dimensions, Lemke (1998) has argued that scientific texts are, and long have been, routinely *multimedia genres*, whose mix of modalities plays a crucial role in the construction of meaning. Situated genre analyses in specific sites (e.g., Bazerman, 1999; Berkenkotter, 2001; Kamberelis, 2001; Prior, 1998) have also highlighted ways that literate activity involves multimodal chains of genres. For example, a group may engage in planning "talk" (which might include written notes, drawings, diagrams, and so on as well as presentational and conversational talk); that planning talk may lead to a series of written drafts that are perhaps reviewed through a series of oral and written responses (with annotational genres including textual editing, marginal comments, and extended comments); and all of this activity may culminate in a final written text that is then read in certain typified ways and prompts other responses. Many of the genres in such chains are both relatively occluded and more oriented to mediational or processual purposes of individuals or groups than to wider public exchange. More and more, we understand that the rhizomatic threads of genre spread just about everywhere we might look into human societies. What is there to add to these insights, or more to the point, what might this chapter contribute to genre studies?

Without claiming a unique perspective, I will identify and elaborate on several points that do not seem to me widely shared and agreed to at present. The points I am identifying relate to where I am looking from, specifically from my participation in Writing Studies, where attention to writing as a process was woven into the formation of the field and where the question of how writing relates to other modes has become a pressing concern. From this perspective, I will focus on four key issues (the nature of the Bakhtinian notion of *utterance*, the problem of the text, the question of writing, and the relationship of inner to outer semiotics) that lead in the end to the notion of *mediated multimodal genre systems*. All four of these issues derive from theoretical and empirical attention to writing or more broadly literate activity.

RECOVERING VOLOSHINOV'S THEORY OF THE UTTERANCE FROM BAKHTIN'S LATER DEFINITION

Bakhtin's (1986) account of *speech genres*, that is, of genres as typified forms of situated *utterance*, has profoundly altered genre theory in the past decades. However, that seminal essay also displays how thoroughly Bakhtin's approach to genre was grounded in literary issues, rather than the linguistic, semiotic, psychological, and sociological perspectives that we find in the work of Voloshinov (and to a lesser extent Medvedev)[1]. In fact, Bakhtin displays his limits in a prominent and repeated way: seriously undermining and confusing the fundamental unit of analysis in his theory, the utterance.

Let's turn to three quotations that illustrate the problem. In the following passages, Bakhtin (1986) is defining utterances (spoken and written) as the real unit of speech communication (in contrast to the abstract sentences of linguistic analysis):

The boundaries of each concrete utterance as a unit of speech communication are determined by a change of speaking subjects, that is a change of speakers. Any utterance—from a short (single-word) rejoinder to the large novel or scientific treatise—has, so to speak, an absolute beginning and an absolute end . . . . (p. 71)

Complexly structured and specialized works of various scientific and artistic genres, in spite of all the ways in which they differ from rejoinders in dialogue, are by nature the same kind of units of speech communication. They, too, are clearly demarcated by a change of speaking subjects, and these boundaries, while retaining their external clarity, acquire here a special internal aspect because the speaking subject—in this case, the author of the work—manifests his own individuality in his style, his world view, and in all aspects of the design of the work. (p. 75)

The work is a link in the chain of speech communication. Like the rejoinder in dialogue, it is related to other work-utterances: both those to which it responds and those that respond to it. At the same time, like the rejoinder in dialogue, it is separated from them by the absolute boundaries of the utterance. (p. 76)

Bakhtin's problem here is not subtle. In defining the utterance as the real unit of speech communication, he makes two claims that undermine the power of a dialogic approach. First, he equates utterances with externalized utterances. Second, he equates spoken utterance (talk) with works (texts). In effect, he is saying that a "Hi, Sally!" spoken on the street to a passing acquaintance and Tolstoy's *War and Peace* each count equally, each one utterance, each a move in a sequence of dialogue. Bakhtin does seem to sense the oddness of this claim, but he locates the difference in marks of individuality in texts, marks that index the vision and craft of the author (yet another indication of what a narrow literary canvas Bakhtin was painting on).

Bakhtin's departure from the earlier theory articulated by Voloshinov[2] could hardly be more plain:

The process of speech, broadly understood as the process of inner and outer verbal life, goes on continuously. It knows neither beginning nor end. The outwardly actualized utterance is an island arising from the boundless sea of inner speech, the dimensions and forms of the island are determined by the particular situation of the utterance and its audience. (Voloshinov, 1973, p. 96)

19

Where Bakhtin (1986) boasts of the absolute beginning and end of utterances (which he believes give the utterance scientific priority), Voloshinov argues that speech has neither beginning nor end, that utterance is an island rising from the sea of inner speech. Voloshinov (1973) initially articulates the point more generally as a semiotic rather than solely a linguistic issue (and Voloshinov does not mention signs only in passing).

> We repeat: every outer ideological sign, of whatever kind, is engulfed in and washed over by inner signs—by the consciousness. The outer sign originates from this sea of inner signs and continues to abide there, since its life is a process of renewal as something to be understood, experienced, and assimilated, i.e., its life consists in its being engaged ever anew into the inner context. (p. 33)

Voloshinov's (1973) attention to inner speech and consciousness needs to be placed in the broader context of his social (ideological) theory of the formation of consciousness itself: "Consciousness takes shape and being in the material of signs created by an organized group in the process of its social intercourse" (p. 13).

In another early, disputed text, Bakhtin/Medvedev (1978) locates utterance and genre firmly within as well as outside of the individual:

> It is the forms of the utterance, not the forms of language that play the most important role in consciousness and the comprehension of reality. . . . we do not think in words and sentences, and the stream of inner speech which flows within us is not a string of words and sentences. We think and conceptualize in utterances, complexes complete in themselves. . . . These integral, materially expressed inner acts of [people's] orientation to reality and the forms of these acts are very important. One might say that human consciousness possesses a series of inner genres for seeing and conceptualizing reality. (pp. 133-134)

Voloshinov (and it seems Medvedev) clearly had a robust notion of utterance as inner speech and inner genre that Bakhtin only fleetingly affirms and easily abandons. (When Bakhtin writes of inner speech, he is typically writing of the *representation* of inner speech for characters in a novel.) Many of the problems that I address in the next three sections flow from Bakhtin's definition of the utterance as externalized utterance and his clear equation of talk and text.

REVISITING THE PROBLEM OF THE TEXT: THE COMPOSED UTTERANCE

When Voloshinov and Bakhtin articulated their account of utterance and distinguished utterances from the specialized representation of "decontextualized" linguistic sentences, they aimed to put the study of language and, especially for Voloshinov, signs, firmly in the lived world, in concrete space and time. However, locating signs-in-use also called for a recognition of the complex temporalities of semiosis. Utterances do not achieve their sense and function in a moment. Their relevance, production, interpretation, and use all require attention to temporal trajectories—to the histories that lead to an utterance, the unfolding events of its use, the imagined projections of its future, and ultimately the way it is in fact understood, taken up, replayed and reused in near and perhaps more distant futures.

Writing Studies, which focused attention early (Emig, 1971) on the acts of composing that lead to a text, has argued for the need to see written utterances (the situated moment-to-moment production of texts) as historical acts exactly on a par with spoken utterances (the situated moment-to-moment production of talk). Collapsing years of written production across diverse events into a moment of publication (if such a moment ever arrives and for many, perhaps most, texts, it does not) is a high price to pay for "proving" that utterances are real units of communication[3].

However, the problem of the text, specifically of what I will call *composed utterances* (for reasons that should become clear shortly), remains. If online production of written utterances is equated to online production of spoken utterances, how do we understand texts that emerge out of long histories of production, texts that are composed and often lengthy? Such utterances not only have a history, as even a simple "Hey, Sally, what's up?" must have history; they have a history of focused composition. Composed utterances (and genres) call on us to analyze the chains of utterances that are woven together in a teleological project; the various ways that the composed document/performance overtly or covertly indexes its specific history of composition; and the ways that production, reception, and use take that history into account.

Interestingly, the problem of the composed utterance is not limited to written texts; it also applies to talk—to formally composed speech, repetition of memorized text, and even events that are worked out orally in advance. Judith Irvine's (1996) analysis of insult poetry at Wolof wedding ceremonies makes this point clear as she examines how the insults are co-composed prior to the event by sponsors, others in the community and a *griot* (a low-ranking female bard); how the *griot* delivers and leads the insults during the event; and how what Irvine calls *shadow conversations* (those conversations that are not here-and-now but are felt here-and-now) are critical to the production, uptake, and interpretation of the insults. Likewise, to understand an utterance by an actor on a stage or in a film—the way the utterance is delivered, the way the audience interprets it, the way it is re-used and re-presented—it is critical to understand the shadow conversations, writings, and texts that are at play. Kevin Roozen's (Prior, Hengst, Roozen, & Shipka, 2006) analysis of semiotic remediations in the historical trajectory of an amateur comedy skit offers us a detailed glimpse into the complexity of such composed performances, particularly the way compositional events can bring together multiple people who co-compose the text/performance in interaction. Such composed performances index not simply some authorial vision, but also the social identities and discourses represented; the interpretive work of the actor who is animating her lines; and the influence of the director, stage crew, and others who have shaped the contexts of the performed utterances[4]. Political speeches, film and stage drama, religious ceremonies, sales pitches, language drills, sermons—once we begin to look, a lot of talk fits into the category of composed utterance, sometimes with texts woven into the history (as in Roozen's comedy skits) but sometimes (as in Wolof insult poetry) without it.

Composed signs (whether material artifacts, enacted performances, or both) are not unique in having a history, but are special in the ways that histories are aligned and are sedimented into and impinge on the present. The presence of a history of composing activity bumps up against another problem: the need to recognize writing not only as activity, but also as activity that can happen face-to-face. If we conceptualize genres as involving production, reception, distribution, and representation, then it is important to *not* see these as separate stages, but as co-present dimensions of discourse with multiple and changing configurations over time.

ANIMATING WRITTEN UTTERANCES: LITERATE ACTIVITY AS CO-PRESENT PRODUCTION

Even in some of the richest theoretical and empirical work, there remains a tendency to freeze writing (as though it entered the world from some other realm), to see writing as a noun rather than a verb, to specifically not study writing as activity. For example, in what is otherwise a sophisticated account of dialogic theory and method, Linell (1998) devotes almost no space to the question of writing. When he does turn to writing, he touches briefly on the notion of writing as activity but clearly fills in the blanks with cultural assumptions rather than the kind of close research attention he offers talk:

> Written texts, being permanent records, encourage the view that the meanings of texts "are there" "in the texts themselves." But mean-

ings are of course assignments and accomplishments by human beings, writers and readers. The production of meaning takes place in
interactions, on the one hand in the writer's struggle with thoughts
and words in conceiving and formulating the text and in her interplay with the text so-far produced, and, on the other hand, in the
reader's efforts in assigning meaning to the text and in using the text
as a vehicle, as a means for activating semantic potentials of words
and text chunks, in the service of creating an understanding which
somehow fits the contexts given and purposes which are relevant for
him. (p. 268)

Linell usefully does invite us to consider text as a human product, to see writing and reading as acts, and also notes the role of in-progress text; however, he
imagines a culturally prototypical scene of writing (see Prior, 1998, for analysis
of such scenes) rather than studying actual scenes of writing. In Linell's scene,
the writer is always alone, the text is always permanent, the reader is always
somewhere else, making meaning on her own.

Scollon and Scollon (2003) also display this blind spot in current theorizing
of discourse. Their approach to mediated discourse and what they call *geosemiotics* offers a theoretically rich and empirically rigorous examination of semiotic practices in material worlds. They pay close attention to ways that texts are
handled, to the complex textures of texts, even to esoteric issues like text vectors.
Critically, however, writing does not appear as activity on their expansive map.
Consider the following quote:

. . . there are three ways in which language can be located in the
material world, the interaction order (including speech, movement, gesture), visual semiotics (including text and images), and
place semiotics (all of the other non-linguistic symbols that directly or indirectly represent language). Geosemiotics analyzes the
semiotic systems among which we take action in the world. (p. 13)

The point I want to draw attention to here is that the interaction order is glossed
as "speech, movement, gesture" but not as writing. Writing (or at least its products) only appears in the next item, visual semiotics. It is true that this glossing
of the interaction order is not presented as complete, yet writing as action does
not appear later. Farther down in the paragraph, Scollon and Scollon indicate
that their interest is in bringing together studies of the interaction order (talk,
movement and gesture) and textual analysis (study of the structures of text).

Writing must be done in particular times and places and it can be done in
face-to-face social interactions. Writing as a face-to-face activity has begun to

emerge in studies that look at people working around whiteboards and screens (see, e.g., Hall, Stevens, & Torralba, 2002; Heath & Luff, 2000; Prior, 2007) and in situated studies of writing processes across varied settings (see, e.g., Bazerman, 1999; Beaufort, 1999; Iedema, 2003; Kamberelis, 2001; Prior, 1994, 1998; Prior & Shipka, 2003). At first, examples of face-to-face writing and reading may seem esoteric, until we recognize that group invention/response and writing on boards in schools and workplaces routinely involve co-present writing and reading. Board texts, inventional texts (e.g., notes, outlines), written responses, and drafts are also typically temporary (not the permanent records Linell invoked), as are many other texts written on scraps of paper; on steamed or frosted windows; in the dirt, sand, or snow; and so on. It is also worth noting that many early literacy experiences involve face-to-face reading and writing, something we should expect from a Vygotskyan perspective where practices move from the social to the (relatively) individual.

VOLOSHINOV AND VYGOTSKY: THE CURRENTS OF INNER AND OUTER SEMIOTICS AS MULTIMODALITY

That writing is a process also means that writing is a stream within the broader flows of semiotic activity. Once we see genres as produced in processes that have histories, then we find that multimodality arises not only when a particular text/performance is realized materially in multiple media, but also when we consider the multimodal chaining that marks historical processes. More fundamentally, every text, every utterance, is multimodal as it must involve a mix of inner and outer semiotics.

Bakhtin (1981, 1986) does reach into inner semiotics when he defines utterance, but only in the arenas of planning (by the speaker or writer) and reception (the inner responses of people). It is important to recall that, for Bakhtin and Voloshinov, the utterance is not defined by what is produced only, but also by its reception. Bakhtin (1986) writes: "Still current in linguistics are such fictions as the 'listener' and 'understander' (partners of the 'speaker'), the 'unified speech flow,' and so on. These fictions produce a completely distorted idea of the complex and multifaceted processes of active speech communication" (p. 68). Voloshinov (1973) articulated this point as well:

> . . . there is no reason for saying that meaning belongs to a word as such. In essence, meaning belongs to a word in its position between speakers; that is, meaning is realized only in the process of active, responsive understanding. Meaning does not reside in the word or in the soul of the speaker or in the soul of the listener. Meaning is the effect of interaction between speaker and listener.

> . . . It is like an electric spark that occurs only when two different terminals are hooked together. (pp. 102-103)

Voloshinov (1976) argued that *"any locution actually said aloud or written down for intelligible communication* (i.e., anything but words merely reposing in a dictionary) *is the expression and product of the social interaction of three participants: the speaker* (author), *the listener* (reader), and *the topic* (the who or what) *of the speech* (the hero)" (p. 105; italics in original). If we took a Bible passage as an example, in one case it might be read reverently as part of a religious ritual, whereas in another case it might be read critically by an archeologist searching for clues for a dig. Such uptakes structure different situated utterances, not one utterance with two interpretations[5].

Voloshinov (1973), as noted above, articulates a much more robust and central notion of inner speech, inner genre, and inner semiotics. Complementing Bakhtin/Medvedev's notion (1978) that we possess inner genres to perceive and understand reality, Voloshinov (1973) suggests how ideological content, especially in the form of social evaluations, can be found even in inner feelings and emotions:

> . . . not even the simplest, dimmest apprehension of a feeling, say, the feeling of hunger not outwardly expressed—can dispense with some kind of ideological form. Any apprehension, after all, must have inner speech, inner intonation and the rudiments of inner style: one can apprehend one's hunger apologetically, irritably, angrily, indignantly, etc. (p. 87)

Vygotsky (1987) also saw the transitions between inner and external speech as complex:

> External speech is not inner speech plus sound any more than inner speech is external speech minus sound. The transition from inner to external speech is complex and dynamic. . . . (p. 280)

Prior and Shipka (2003; see also Prior, Hengst, Roozen, & Shipka, 2006) argue that Vygotsky's fundamental theory of human development and consciousness was very attuned to the semiotic transformations that link the inner semiotics of thought, perception, motivation and feeling to the outer semiotics of action (talk, writing, drawing, object production and manipulation, movement, stance).

When I presented an earlier version of this argument at the SIGET 4 conference in Turabão, Brazil on the morning of August 17, 2007, I wanted to illustrate some of the relations between inner and outer semiotics in the sea of signs. The utterance I chose that day as an illustration was: *"The camera is on the floor."* As a reader who knows English, you can make some meaning of this linear packaging of six words, but the meaning structure is skeletal and how you fill in the blanks is critical. Different readers might imagine different kinds of cameras (video or photographic, digital or film, different historical designs) placed in particular ways (lying, sitting upright, on a tripod, neatly or haphazardly) on different kinds of floors (concrete, wooden, carpeted; in a classroom or a home closet). Or perhaps, no particular camera-in-the-world is imagined and only the barest meaning is registered. As Voloshinov (1976) wrote:

> The concrete utterance is born, lives, and dies in the process of so-cial interaction between the participants of the utterance. Its form and meaning are determined basically by the form and character of this interaction. When we cut the utterance off from the real grounds that nurture it, we lose the key to its form as well as its import—all we have left is an abstract linguistic shell or an equally abstract semantic scheme. . . . (p. 105)

When I said *the camera is on the floor*, I was standing behind a table and podium on a raised platform in a large hemispherical auditorium talking to an audience of a few hundred people, mainly sitting in chairs lined up on the floor but some standing around the outer edges of the room. A large video camera on a tall tripod on the concrete floor below the platform was focused on the upper half of my body and its images were being projected on two large screens on the walls to the left and right of the platform. The externalized utter-ance was heard in English and (by simultaneous translation through headsets) in Portuguese. I noted in my talk that I used the definite article "the" although I had not yet mentioned a camera, because my utterance was accompanied by a pointing gesture and the camera was, I assumed, visible to the audience. Hence, the utterance was already multimodal (language accompanied by gesture and oriented to the perceptible visual-material space of the room and the audience). I noted that when we saw the camera on the floor our inner semiotics did not experience first the camera, then the floor, and only those two objects (as the linear sentence presents it)[6]. I also noted the importance of evaluation to inner semiotics. A foundation of Voloshinov's and Bakhtin's account of the utterance, *evaluation* points to the affective, motivated, socially indexed dimensions of the utterance as well as to stance/evaluation. For me, the camera on the floor oc-casioned a particular self-awareness and some discomfort as it was projecting a large (not necessarily flattering) image of my face on the screens left and right, an inner sense that I assumed might be understood but not felt by members of the audience. *The camera is on the floor* illustrated the gaps that exist between inner and outer semiotics, one of the reasons why as speakers and writers we so often experience a sense of loss when our words fail to capture the inner webs of meaning and feeling that we had meant them to convey.

The camera is on the floor also makes it plain that multimodality is a routine dimension of language in use, as utterances can only happen in embodied, material, multisensory, multi-semiotic worlds. Bakhtin (1981) did argue that utterances are fundamentally situated in time and space, fundamentally *chronotopic* (set in and indexing both representational and material-perceptible worlds). An understanding of genres as inner and outer, as semiotically remediated, and as central to socialization (the co-production of the person and the social) flows from Voloshinov's boundless inner sea of signs fed by the ideological streams of cultural-historical practice. In this light, multimodality is not some special feature of texts or certain kinds of utterance, and certainly is not a consequence of technologies (cf. Kress, 2003). Multimodality has always and everywhere been present as representations are propagated across multiple media[7] and as any situated event is indexically fed by all the modes present, whether they are focalized or backgrounded. In this sense, all genres are irremediably multimodal; the question then becomes what particular configurations of multimodality are at work in a particular genre system.

COMPOSED UTTERANCES AND SEMIOTIC ARTIFACTS: A MULTIMODAL ETHICS OF ANSWERABILITY

Composed utterances highlight the tension that emerges between historical flows and semiotic artifacts. Whereas all utterances have a history, the composed utterance has a history where a sequence of interactions and possibly a series of externalized inscriptions have been organized around the project of a final text/performance. Through composition, different moments of history, different persons, different voices, different addresses may become embedded in the composed utterance. The utterance may come to be crafted and polished through revision and response rounds. In my own research, I traced in one study (Prior, 1998), for example, how written and oral responses got embedded in composed utterances (seminar papers, conference papers, PhD exams, dissertation prospectuses) that emerged around a sociology seminar linked to funded research project, and in another study (Prior, 2007) how an art and design group engaged in talk, drawings (on paper and whiteboards; often with written annotation), gesture, computer programming, and data entry over eleven months to revise (and remediate) another type of composed semiotic artifact (an interactive, online art project). These long histories of intense collaboration were organized around the finalization of a semiotic artifact that could be shared with wider publics.

Bakhtin (1986) may have equated situated talk with published texts because these externalizations are presented as final, and hence might be supposed to have kinds of consequentiality, responsibility and affordance for uptake that differ from those of in-progress texts[8]. Attending to such factors, from practical as well as ethical perspectives, is important. However, consequentiality, responsibility and affordance for uptake are routine dimensions of discourse. Indeed, in his earliest ethical discussions of action and answerability, Bakhtin (1993) argued that it was the ongoing flow of deeds—not certain special deeds—that carry ethical dimensions. What degrees of responsibility, levels of care and attention, and scopes of consequence a multimodal text entails must be a question of a complexly situated ethical and political geometry, not a categorical question, not a question of whether a text is in-progress or final, or even for that matter externalized or interiorized.

CONCLUSION: MEDIATED MULTIMODAL GENRE SYSTEMS

Voloshinov and later Bakhtin articulated an expansive view of genres as concrete, historical phenomena. Their historical orientation is key not only to a dialogic, non-structuralist understanding of language (and more broadly signs), but also to the integration of semiotic mediation with a sociohistoric account of the formation of individuals and society. A dual orientation to genre as discourse and development has led North American versions of genre theory in particular to explore relations between genre theory and sociocultural theories of mediated activity and agency (e.g., in the work of Vygotsky, Engeström, Wertsch, Latour)[9]. Here I propose the notion of *mediated multimodal genre systems* as a framework for genre studies (see also Molle & Prior, 2008). This notion asks us to look for multimodality not only *in* specific texts, but also

- in the productive chains of discourse that make up the whole system (e.g., where a sequence of oral and embodied genres of discussion, inquiry, composing, response, and presentation may mix with written and visual inscribed genres—or, more to the point, where a set of differently configured multimedia genres are linked together in locally situated ways),
- in their use (e.g., a text may be written to be read; a speech may be transcribed), and
- in the consciousness (the situated inner semiotics) of people as well as in externalized artifacts and actions.

It argues for a semiotic perspective on genre systems, considering such systems as fundamentally constituted in the varied activities and artifacts involved in trajectories of mediated activity—that is, not only in the whole ensemble of discourse production, representation, distribution, and reception, but also in the activity and socialization that flow along with and form that ensemble[10].

NOTES

[1] Of course, to make such a comparision, it is first important to distinguish the work of Voloshinov from that of Bakhtin. Morson and Emerson's (1990) astute analysis of the authorship disputes around Voloshinov's texts comes down clearly for the distinct authorship of Voloshinov, in part (as is outlined in this chapter) because differences in the theories themselves suggest distinct authorship. Bazerman (2004b) has articulated the particularly strong resonances between Voloshinov's and Vygotsky's theories, which reflect Voloshinov's close attention to psychological, sociological, and linguistic theories.

[2] To understand the historical development of these theories, it is important to return to the original Russian dates of publication. Voloshinov began to articulate the notion of utterances and their typifications in a 1926 essay and in his 1927 monograph on Freudianism (both translated and published in English in 1976) and then most fully in his 1929 book (translated and published in English in 1973). Bakhtin takes up utterances in his essay, *Discourse in the Novel*, written in 1934-35, published in Russian in 1975 and in English in 1981 and then most fully in the essay "The problem of speech genres," written in 1952-53 published in Russian in 1979 and in English in 1986.

[3] Bakhtin may well have had other motivations for the equation of spoken utterances with works (written texts), particularly for example in light of his earlier work on the ethical grounds of action (see Bakhtin, 1993), a point I return to later in this chapter.

[4] Prior (1998) and Prior and Shipka (2003) consider this kind of heterogeneity and hybridity, not only in signs but also and especially in historical trajectories of representation and action, through the notion of *chronotopic lamination*.

[5] Bakhtin (1986) writes: "Two or more sentences can be absolutely identical (when they are superimposed on one another, like two geometrical figures, they coincide); moreover, we must allow that any sentence, even a complex one. . .can be repeated an unlimited number of times in completely identical form. But as an utterance (or part of an utterance) no one sentence, even if it has only one word, can ever be repeated: it is always a new utterance (even if it is a quotation)." (p. 69).

[6] Here I was alluding to Vygotsky's (1987) reflections on the transformations

that occur between thought and externalized speech:

> Thought does not consist of individual words like speech. I may want to express the thought that I saw a barefoot boy in a blue shirt running down the street today. I do not, however, see separately the boy, the shirt, the fact that the shirt was blue, the fact that the boy ran, the fact that the boy was without shoes. I see all this together in a unified act of thought. In speech, however, the thought is partitioned into separate words. . . What is contained simultaneously in thought unfolds sequentially in speech. Thought can be compared to a hovering cloud which gushes a shower of words. (p. 281)

Jody Shipka and I reflected on this example of inner and outer semiotics, noting:

> Beyond the shift from a holistic and multi-sensory semiotic to a linear-verbal semiotic, there is also the question of the observer's feelings about the scene, questions of tone and evaluative orientation. Is the barefoot boy celebrating with abandon a beautiful summer day, evoking perhaps a complex mix of joy and nostalgia? Or is the barefoot boy a starving and ragged child running from soldiers and explosions, producing quite different emotions and motives for action? In any case, squeezed into an externalizable form something is lost, not only the holistic world of inner representation, but also a world that is embodied, affect rich, and deeply dialogic. At the same time, the externalized form adds to and amplifies certain meanings, producing resonances not intended or felt by the writer. (Prior & Shipka, 2003, p. 215)

[7] Hutchins (1995) describes distributed cognition in terms of "the propagation of representational state across representational media" (p. 118), where one of these media is the brain. His work begins to suggest how the boundaries of inner and outer might be neither negated nor equated, but blurred and softened.

[8] I wish to acknowledge and thank Charles Bazerman for raising this interesting issue in response to my SIGET paper. His questions led me productively back to Bakhtin's earlier work on ethics and answerability.

[9] We might also begin to examine more seriously the consequences of seeing activity and genre systems as assemblages or actor-network rhizomes (Latour, 2005), as mycorrhizae formations (Engeström, 2006), or as flow architectures (Knorr-Cetina, 2005).

[10] I would like to thank Cory Holding for a chain of insightful responses to in-progress drafts of this chapter and Samantha Looker for a close, careful final reading of the text.

REFERENCES

Bakhtin, M. (1981). *The dialogic imagination: Four essays* (C. Emerson & M. Holquist, Trans.; M. Holquist, Ed.). Austin: University of Texas Press.

Bakhtin, M. (1986). *Speech genres and other late essays* (V. W. McGee, Trans.). Austin: University of Texas Press.

Bakhtin, M. (1993). *Toward a philosophy of the act* (V. Liapunov, Trans.; M. Holquist & V. Liapunov, Eds.). Austin: University of Texas Press.

Bakhtin, M., & Medvedev, P. (1978). *The formal method in literary scholarship: A critical introduction to sociological poetics* (A. J. Wehrle, Trans.). Baltimore: Johns Hopkins University Press.

Bazerman, C. (1988). *Shaping written knowledge: The genre and activity of the experimental article in science.* Madison: University of Wisconsin Press.

Bazerman, C. (1994). Systems of genres and the enactment of social intentions. In A. Freedman & P. Medway (Eds.), *Genre and the new rhetoric* (pp. 83-96). London: Taylor & Francis.

Bazerman, C. (1999). *The languages of Edison's light.* Cambridge: MIT Press.

Bazerman, C. (2004a). Speech acts, genres, and activity systems: How texts organize activity and people. In C. Bazerman & P. Prior (Eds.), *What writing does and how it does it: An introduction to analyzing texts and textual practices* (pp. 79-101). Mahwah: Lawrence Erlbaum.

Bazerman, C. (2004b). Intertextualities: Voloshinov, Bakhtin, literary theory, and literacy studies. In A. Ball & S. Freedman (Eds.), *Bakhtinian perspectives on language, literacy, and learning* (pp. 53-65). Cambridge: Cambridge University Press.

Bazerman, C., & Prior, P. (2005). Participating in emergent socio-literate worlds: Genre, disciplinarity, interdisciplinarity. In R. Beach, J. Green, M. Kamil, & T. Shanahan (Eds.), *Multidisciplinary perspectives on literacy research* (2nd ed.). (pp. 133-178). Cresskill: Hampton Press.

Beaufort, A. (1999). *Writing in the real world: Making the transition from school to work.* New York: Teachers College Press.

Berkenkotter, C. (2001). Genre systems at work: DSM-IV and rhetorical recontextualization in psychotherapy paperwork. *Written Communication, 18,* 326-349.

Berkenkotter, C., & Huckin, T. (1995). *Genre knowledge in disciplinary communication: Cognition/culture/power.* Mahwah: Lawrence Erlbaum.

Bhatia, V. (2002). Applied genre analysis: Analytical advances and pedagogical procedures. In A. Johns (Ed.), *Genre in the classroom: Multiple perspectives* (pp. 279-284). Mahwah, NJ: Erlbaum.

Coe, R., Lingard, L., & Teslenko, T. (2002). *The rhetoric and ideology of genre.* Cresskill: Hampton Press.

Devitt, A. (1991). Intertextuality in tax accounting: Generic, referential, and functional. In C. Bazerman & J. Paradis (Eds.), *Textual dynamics of the professions: Historical and contemporary studies of writing in professional communities* (pp. 336-357). Madison: University of Wisconsin Press.

Devitt, A. (2004). *Writing genres.* Carbondale: Southern Illinois University Press.

Emig, J. (1971). *The composing processes of twelfth graders.* Urbana: National Council of Teachers of English.

Engeström, Y. (2006). Development, movement, and agency: Breaking away into mycorrhizae activities. In K. Yamazumi (Ed.), *Building activity theory in practice: Toward the next generation* (pp. 1-43). Osaka: Center for Human Activity Theory, Kansai University.

Fairclough, N. (2004). *Analyzing discourse: Textual analysis for social research.* London: Routledge.

Freedman, A., & Medway, P. (Eds.). (1994). *Genre and the new rhetoric.* London: Taylor & Francis.

Hall, R., Stevens, R., & Torralba, T. (2002). Disrupting representational infrastructure in conversations across disciplines. *Mind, Culture, and Activity, 9,* 179-210.

Heath, C., & Luff, P. (2000). *Technology in action.* Cambridge: Cambridge University Press.

Hutchins, E. (1995). *Cognition in the wild.* Cambridge: MIT Press.

Hyland, K. (2004). *Genre and second language writing.* Ann Arbor: University of Michigan Press.

Iedema, R. (2003). *Discourses of post-bureaucratic organization.* Amsterdam: John Benjamins.

Irvine, J. (1996). Shadow conversations: The indeterminacy of participant roles. In M. Silverstein & G. Urban (Eds.), *Natural histories of discourse* (pp. 131-159). Chicago: Chicago University Press.

Kamberelis, G. (2001). Producing heteroglossic classroom (micro)cultures through hybrid discourse practice. *Linguistics and Education, 12,* 85-125.

Knorr-Cetina, K. (2005). How are global markets global? The architecture of a flow world. In K. Knorr-Cetina & A. Preda (Eds.), *The sociology of financial markets* (pp. 38-61). Oxford: Oxford University Press.

Kress, G. (2003). *Literacy in the new media age.* London: Routledge.

Latour, B. (2005). *Reassembling the social: An introduction to actor-network theory.* Oxford: Oxford University Press.

Lemke, J. L. (1998). Multiplying meaning: Visual and verbal semiotics in scientific text. In J. Martin & R. Veel (Eds.), *Reading science* (pp. 87-113). London: Routledge.

Linell, P. (1998). *Approaching dialogue: Talk, interaction, and contexts in dialogical perspectives.* Amsterdam: John Benjamins.

Molle, D., & Prior, P. (2008). Multimodal genre systems in EAP writing pedagogy: Reflecting on a needs analysis. *TESOL Quarterly, 42,* 541-566.

Morson, G., & Emerson, C. (1990). *Mikhail Bakhtin: Creation of a prosaics.* Stanford: Stanford University Press.

Orlikowski, W., & Yates, J. (1994). Genre repertoire: The structuring of communicative practices in organizations. *Administrative Science Quarterly, 39,* 541-574.

Prior, P. (1991). Contextualizing writing and response in a graduate seminar. *Written Communication, 8,* 267-310.

Prior, P. (1994). Response, revision, disciplinarity: A microhistory of a dissertation prospectus in sociology. *Written Communication, 11,* 483-533.

Prior, P. (1998). *Writing/disciplinarity: A sociohistoric account of literate activity in the academy.* Mahwah: Lawrence Erlbaum.

Prior, P. (2003). "Are communities of practice really an alternative to discourse communities?" Paper presented at the American Association of Applied Linguistics Conference, Arlington, Virginia. Available at https://netfiles.uiuc.edu/pprior/Prior/PriorAAAL03.pdf. Accessed 31 May 2007.

Prior, P. (2007). Remaking *IO*, remaking rhetoric: Semiotic remediation as situated rhetorical practice. In P. Prior, J. Solberg, P. Berry, H. Bellowar, B. Chewning, K. Lunsford, L. Rohan, K. Roozen, M. Sheridan-Rabideau, J. Shipka, D. Van Ittersum, D. & J. Walker (Contributors), Re-situating and re-mediating the canons: A cultural-historical remapping of rhetorical activity. Kairos 11.3. Available at http://kairos.technorhetoric.net/11.3/index.html. Accessed 25 May 2007.

Prior, P., Hengst, J., Roozen, K., & Shipka, J. (2006). "I'll be the sun:" From reported speech to semiotic remediation practices. *Text and Talk, 26,* 733-766.

Prior, P. & Shipka, J. (2003). Chronotopic lamination: Tracing the contours of literate activity. In C. Bazerman & D. Russell (Eds.), *Writing selves, writing societies* (pp. 180-238). Fort Collins: The WAC Clearinghouse. Available at http://wac.colostate.edu/books/selves_societies/. Accessed 21 May 2007.

Prior, P., Solberg, J., Berry, P., Bellowar, H., Chewning, B., Lunsford, K., Rohan, L., Roozen, K., Sheridan-Rabideau, M., Shipka, J., Van Ittersum, D., & Walker, J. (2007). Re-situating and re-mediating the canons: A cultural-historical remapping of rhetorical activity. *Kairos 11.3.* Available at http://kairos.technorhetoric.net/11.3/index.html. Accessed 25 May 2007.

Räisänen, C. (1999). *The conference forum as a system of genres.* Gothenberg: Acta Universitatis Gothoburgensis.

Russell, D. R. (1997). Rethinking genre in school and society: An activity theory analysis. *Written Communication, 14,* 504-554.

Scollon, R., & Scollon, S. (2003). *Discourses in place: Language in the material world.* London: Routledge.

Spinuzzi, C. (2004). *Four ways to investigate assemblages of texts: Genre sets, systems, repertoires, and ecologies.* ACM SIGDOC 2004 Conference Proceedings. New York: ACM. Available at http://portal.acm.org/citation.cfm?id=1026560&dl= &coll=&CFID=15151515&CFTOKEN=6184618 Accessed 31 May 2007.

Swales, J. (1990). *Genre analysis: English in academic and research settings.* New York: Cambridge University Press.

Swales, J. (1996). Occluded genres in the academy. In E. Ventola & A. Mauranen (Eds.), *Academic writing* (pp. 45-58). Amsterdam: John Benjamins.

Swales, J. (2004). *Research genres: Exploration and applications.* Cambridge: Cambridge University Press.

Wertsch, J. (1991). *Voices of the mind: A sociocultural approach to mediated action.* Cambridge: Harvard University Press.

Voloshinov, V. (1973). *Marxism and the philosophy of language* (L. Matejka & I. Titunik, Trans.). Cambridge: Harvard University Press.

Voloshinov, V. (1976). *Freudianism: A Marxist critique* (I. Titunik, Trans.; I. Titunik & N. Bruss, Ed.). New York: Academic Press.

Vygotksy, L. (1987). *Problems of general psychology: the collected works of L.S. Vygotsky, volume 1.* (N. Minick, trans.). New York: Plenum.

3   To Describe Genres: Problems and Strategies

Maria Antónia Coutinho
Florencia Miranda

INTRODUCTION

The relation between genre as an abstract category and text as an empirical object that is always an example of a certain genre raises epistemological and methodological questions. There seems to be a consensus in the literature on genre theory, the description of genres raises difficulties—taking into consideration, on the one hand, the multiplicity of facts and criteria that may intervene in this descriptive work, and on the other hand, the changing nature that characterizes genres (because they are theoretically in an infinite number). Simultaneously, it is accepted that any text is related to a genre, which may be more formally or more freely reproduced. Therefore, it is needed to think, methodologically, about the viability of the description of genres— mainly if we consider that, we can only have access to those through empirical texts that are an example of genre. How can we stably describe and analyze genres— that are only observed through texts that are actually produced? Which are the epistemological forms that can sustain effective work on genres? Which are the methodological specifications?

In this paper we are going to show some strategies for dealing with this problematic. On the one hand, it is important to be aware of the duality necessarily entangled in the production and interpretation of texts: on one side, the common plan that guarantees "a family pattern" (it must be underlined, without the inclusion of rules or universal ambitions) and on the other side the plan of singularity that makes any text unique. Within this scope, we must define the means of organized analysis recognizing the duality of genre and text—and supporting the specification of the genres (that, as we have underlined, are un-ontological entities). Besides, methodological procedures suitable to work with the genres must be considered – mainly, concerning the need to create differentiated conditions for observing the texts, without recourse to manipulations, more or less controlled.

On the following pages, we will start with a brief scenery of some expressive landmarks, concerning the possible analysis of the genres and the texts—highlighting some pertinent gaps in this context. Later on, some positive suggestions will be presented—on the one hand related to the separation of analysis plans, interfering with the notion of *parameters of genre* and *mechanisms of textual realization*; on the other hand, presenting *genre fictionalization* as a methodological strategy which, assuring the preservation of natural, text circulation conditions, offers up for analysis genres manipulated without the intervention of researchers. For analysis of genre fictionalization, we will further introduce the notion of *genre marker*.

GENRES AND TEXTS: PROBLEMS WITH DESCRIPTION

One of the arguments usually mentioned to justify the impossibility of descriptive work is the diversity and the mutability which characterize genres. Theoreticians and analysts seem to concur on these characteristics; however, these characteristics do not seem to prevent the genres from working. In other words, despite diversity and mutability, speakers and writers, when they speak or write (and when they listen or read) do not have difficulty in identifying and using genres they have experience with and which are part of their contemporary social world.

Another strong argument presented against description concerns the multiplicity of factors in interaction which mobilises each genre. That is why, it is obvious that the several typological attempts (situational, enunciative and functional), necessarily partial, are inevitably vowed to failure. Even if the typological attempt is rejected—taking into consideration that it contradicts the virtually unlimited expansion to which genres are subjected—the conviction remains strongly, that the quantity of potential criteria makes the description unfeasible.

Without questioning the validity of these arguments, nonetheless, methodologically, the impossibility of any exhaustive classification of genres does not necessarily correspond to a radical impossibility of description. The general methodological thesis important to resume work is the need to think out suitable methodological strategies and instruments of analysis to objects known as unstable.

Despite the problems of mutability and diversity, the literature has developed ways of describing literature. In agreement with Bakhtin, we may consider that the description of any genre has at least three components: the thematic subject, the composition and the style (Bakhtin, 1984, p. 265). It is not sure if these points are enough for complete description. Nonetheless, Bakhtin's proposal still seems to be a good suggestion for work in the sciences of language— which are slowly moving from a logical-grammatical approach to a rhetorical-hermeneutical approach (Rastier, 2001)[1]. Concerning the thematic subject, very little was advanced after Voloshinov's struggle (assigned to Bakhtin) to clarify the notions of *theme* and *meaning*, putting in perspective the energetic way the second is related to the first: "Meaning means nothing in and of itself, it is but potential, a possibility of signifying within a concrete theme" (Bakhtin, 1977, p. 145). Though as a simple suggestion, it is worthwhile to underline the way this concept shows perspectives for analysis that later studies on texts and genres have not completely developed: the relationship between theme and genre; the relationship between the theme and other facts involved in generic format; and the relationship between meaning (or language) and the genres.

In the following paragraphs, we are going to distinguish the contributions of Adam and Bronckart. To Adam, we owe a lengthy reflection on the regularities of elements of text composition, particularly text types and/or prototype sequences, with which Adam is most closely associated. We will also consider his work on other elements to be considered in textual composition: simple periods (which, unlike the sequences, are not typified) and text plans, which may be fixed (depending on the genre concerned) or occasional (Adam, 2002a, pp. 174-175).

Jean-Paul Bronckart (1997, 2006), within the theoretical-epistemological approach called socio-discursive interactionism (hereafter ISD), on the other hand approaches description of texts, not genres. Nonetheless, Bronckart does consider the general text substructure, which he proposes as having the following elements:

- the text plan (which organizes the theme);
- types of discourse, to be understood as modes of enunciation (interactive discourse and theoretical discourse, for the explanatory mode; interactive report and narration, for the narrative mode)[2];
- possibilities of articulation between types of discourse (embedding and fusion, among other possibilities);
- sequences (narrative, descriptive, injunctive, explicative, argumentative, dialogical);
- other planning means (the schematization, as the minimal form of the explanatory mode, where the object is presented in a purely explanatory manner, as in definitions, enumerations and in enunciating rules; and the script as the minimal form of the narrative mode, where the linear organization reproduces the chronological order of events, with no process of tension building).

Although we cannot develop here the problematic of style—that alone deserves a profound and up-to-date reflection—it is important to maintain the manner the theme has been put in perspective, namely by Adam (1999). As shown in Figure 1 (Adam, 1999, p. 93), the author distinguishes three different zones within the variation possibilities: a normative zone, defined by higher frequency constants; a zone of relative normativization, corresponding to grammar and genres (with more rigid rules for grammar, more flexible rules for genres); and the zone of system variation, where style and text are to be found.

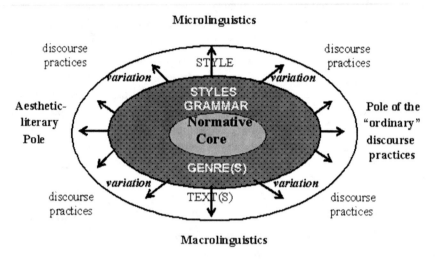

FIGURE 1: STYLE (ADAM, 1999, P. 93)

From the author's point of view, *style* (in the singular) corresponds to individual variation, while *styles* (in the plural) should be related to cases of "phraseology of a social group (being it juridical, medical, sportive, etc.) . . ." Besides being aware that *styles* correspond for true, only to those phraseologies, it is important to underline how the genre is an agent of stability and even of standardness, while texts are variation cases, related to genre.

After briefly considering some questions related to the three components mentioned by Bakhtin, we should return to the mentioned topic: what the authors say about the possibility of genre description.

Dominique Maingueneau (1996, p. 44) started to consider the following facts to define a genre ("contraintes définitoires"): the nature of the enunciators and the co-enunciators, the circumstances of space and time associated with enunciation, the support, the theme and the organizing method. In further works, the author has introduced insignificant changes, retaining the following components of genre: finality, place, temporality, nature of the interlocutors, material support/presentation and text organization/plan (Maingueneau, 1998, pp. 51-54; 2002, pp. 55-62). Clearing referring to the contribution of Maingueneau just mentioned, Jean-Michel Adam proposes an extension of the components, taking into consideration eight components: semantics, enunciative, pragmatic, stylistic and phraseological, compositional, material, peri-textual and meta-textual (Adam, 2001, pp. 40-41).

Our interest here is not in the number or the nature of the considered components, but in Adam's complete overlap of generic and textual plans, as he asserts that the components of genre correspond to the individual text organization[3] (2001, p. 28). The justification looks more than evident: admitting, as we have been doing, that the genre does not have ontological reality, the components of genre would be also, necessarily, textual components. Nonetheless the relation that unites the genre to the text effectively produced must be more clearly articulated. Jean-Michel Adam asserts genres regulate the textual practice through two apparently contradictory principles: a principle of identity, oriented for the repetition and the reproduction, and a principle of difference, oriented for the innovation and the variation (Adam, 2002, p. 38). Within this viewpoint, the deficiency of the previous hypothesis has to be recognized—that is, that the same components are not sufficient to analyze simultaneously the genres and the texts. How to give evidence, then, to the innovations that carry out (or are carried out in) concrete texts? How to know if they are still examples of the same initial genre?

Within the socio-discursive interactionism framework, Jean-Paul Bronckart describes the textual architecture through an organization in layers (similar to a puff paste): in the first place, the general substructure, that includes the text plan, types of discourse, sequences and other forms of planning (script and schematization); secondly, mechanisms of textualization (mechanisms of connection, on one side, of verbal and nominal cohesion, on the other); finally, enunciation mechanisms (enunciative responsibilities and modalities).

Jean-Paul Bronckart has underlined systematically that between an empirical text and the genre that it depends on is established a double relation of adoption and of adaptation, as the situation is realized by the producer. However, separating textual architecture from the notion of genre obscures where and how the adoption and the adaptation are done.

In synthesis, we will be able to say that any one of the indicated solutions (to describe the genres or to describe the texts) leaves unresolved the central questions in this problematic—the inter-relation between these categories. Therefore, a repertoire of components of genre does not assure the effective description of any text depending on that same genre; and inversely, a model of architecture of the texts leaves us without any capacity of relation with the formats that those depend on (a more or less strict or more or less creative form).

In the following section, we will describe an assembly of notions/instruments of analysis that will help us bring together the concepts of genre and text architecture.

PARAMETERS OF GENRE, MECHANISMS OF TEXTUAL REALIZATION AND GENRE MARKERS

The starting point for the elaboration of the instruments of analysis[4] that we are going to describe is related to a conviction already referred to above: that the impossibility of any exhaustive classification of genres does not correspond necessarily and inevitably to a radical impossibility of description. This viewpoint situates itself in the same positioning of several authors, already referred to above, who all take into consideration the need to distinguish stability and variation, but without providing a means to make the distinction. Despite, as we already said, that it does not put in perspective the way each text adopts and/ or adapts the genre it depends—Bronckart refers to the "objective differences" in the interior of the architext (Bronckart, 2006, p. 146)—this may suggest the possibility of identifying contrasting aspects of the genres. Adam (1999) attributes to the genres a normative function—more flexible than the normative function of the language as Bakhtin had already mentioned (Bakhtin, 1984, p. 285). Subsequently, Adam formulated again and/or explained this same viewpoint, referring to two guiding principles: a principle of identity (centripetal), oriented for the repetition and the reproduction, performing a normative role; and a principle of difference (centrifugal), oriented for the innovation and the variation (Adam, 2001, p. 38).

So admitting the need to notice the movements of stability and of variation associated with the functioning of the genres, we add a last argument: if we exclude the possibility of description of the genres, we wind up with a model of organization of the texts that cannot describe the relations with the formats that they depend on (a more or less strict, more or less creative form).

Starting from this hypothesis, we propose that the same model of analysis will be able to, and must be applied to both individual empirical texts and to abstract genres. The instrument that we are presenting has been conceived using the frame of the socio-discursive interactionism. To this we have added some ideas of other linguists and discourse analysts, especially to analyze less explicit or less evident aspects[5]. Our intention here is not to focus on details of the model of analysis but to emphasize the hypothesis that any model must be able to function, simultaneously, for the analysis of texts and for the analysis of genres.

The same points of analysis (in general, concerned with the conditions of production and to the text architecture) are considered in relation to the plan of the generic shape and to the plan of the organization of the singular texts. In the first case, concerning the generic shape, the task is to identify the foreseeable characteristics that constitute the identity of the genre—those characteristics we assign as *parameters of genre*. Characteristics are not absolutely set or mandatory, but are only predictabilities. In the second case, the one of the singular texts, the task is to identify the way the text (each text) assumes the predictabilities that are determined by the genre. In other words, the parameters of genre are fixed as empirical texts through what we have assigned as *mechanisms of textual realization*. These mechanisms concern the management of the semiolinguistics resources of a text. The correspondence between parameters and mechanisms is not fully reciprocal. In fact, the same parameter will be able to be brought up to date through different mechanisms, and it is in the specificity of the mechanisms that the singularity of each text is rooted. The textual output does not reduce itself to the mechanical application of an assembly of strict parameters. Alternatively, the existence of generic parameters, while informing the text realization, does not reveal the active role of the subjects that are able to "play strategically with the conditionings of the genre," as emphasized by Charaudeau (1992, p. 15):

> The speaker always has the possibility to play with the genre constraints; he/she can comply with them, subvert or transgress them partly, according to what he/she considers to be the issue of his/her act of communication. At the same time, any text is the result of a confrontation between the genre constraints and the strategies carried out by the speaker.

As we are trying to show, these two notions (parameters of genre and mechanisms of textual realization) maintain the possibility to notice two kinds of different objects, despite their closeness: the genres that function like standards of (relative) stability and normatization; on the other hand, the empirical texts that, taking advantage of the possibilities of generic variation, constitute always singular cases in an ultimate analysis.

In what concerns the procedure of analysis, it should be underlined that the movement starts from the real texts—the only ones directly available for analysis, in our perspective (since, as we said, the genres do not have their own ontological reality); if the survey of the mechanisms of textual realization is going to identify the parameters of genre, these must be newly confronted with the plan of the texts, in a way to assure an analysis of control.

Figure 2 presents a global vision of the considered instruments and procedures of analysis.

As we already said, the interest of the model of the displayed analysis goes, in a great measure through the possibility to articulate the description of the texts and the description of the genres, without pretending any fixation of the malleability and the mutability that are a characteristic of the category of genre[6]. However, we still need another notion—*genre marker*—to notice the way the subjects recognize the identity of the genres they handle.

The notion of *genre marker* notices the functioning of the mechanisms of textual realization in the procedure of reception/interpretation of the texts (including the situations of criticism and/or text analysis). The mechanisms function like (or work like) genre markers as they are going to identify the lines that are associated specifically to a genre. Therefore, the marker is a semiotic mechanism (of any sort) that functions like any clue or indication of the updating of a generic parameter with distinctive value.

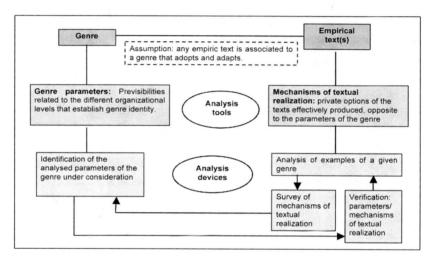

FIGURE 2: GETOC—INSTRUMENTS AND ANALYSIS DEVICES

It is possible to identify two big classes of genre markers: the *self-referential* and the *inferential*. The self-referential markers express in an explicit form the generic category of the text. Examples of this class of markers are the generic labels put in the peritext of examples of certain genres ("advertisement," "novel," "review," "interview," etc.), also the nominal syntagmas that, integrated in the body of the text, set out the genre in which the text participates ("I send *this email* for . . .", "the objective of *this paper* is . . .", "in the section X of *this written essay* . . .", "*in this class* I am going to analyze . . .", etc.). Already the inferential markers indicate implicitly genre parameters and for that reason, they need more interpretative work, where the interpreter's knowledge about the genre is activated from his experience with texts of the genre in question. In principle, any class of textual realization mechanism can turn out into a genre marker (the lexicon, the syntax, the enunciative organization, the mechanisms of material presentation as the typography and the chromatic variation, etc.). One of the most evident examples of this class of markers is the occurrence of ritual expressions as "*once upon a time* . . ." (short story), "I would like to request . . ." (formal letter) or *"mostly sunny/few showers"* (weather forecast).

Occasionally, the markers are able to function in an isolated or individual form (that is, it is possible that from the identification of only one mechanism we will be able to recognize the genre), but this verifies itself especially in the occurrence of self-referential markers. Contrarily, the inferential markers are indications that the receiver apprehends, in the majority of the cases, an interconnected form. This is so because the markers—as the parameters they indicate—are *specific* to a genre, but not *exclusive*.

For the study of the markers, we propose (following Miranda, 2007) to distinguish the following semiolinguistic dimensions of the text organization: thematic (or semantic/lexical), enunciative, compositional, dispositional/material presentation, strategic/intentional and interactive[7]. In each dimension, we will be able to identify different species of mechanisms with the function of markers. These aspects will be resumed further on—through the examples of fictionalized genres that will be analyzed in section 5. Before that, however, it will be necessary to set out the notion of fictionalization in the section to follow.

THE *FICTIONALIZATION* OF GENRES AS A METHODOLOGICAL STRATEGY

By fictionalization we mean the transformation of a nonfiction genre into a fictional, playful or aesthetic one. The notion of *fictionalization* that we are going to use corresponds to a conceptual re-elaboration that mobilizes several contributions of literary and linguistics order. In the first place, we draw on the notion of hypertext, defined by Genette (1982) and resumed by Adam (2005, p. 15) in the following:

> . . . retaking of a text A (hypotext) by a latter text B (hypertext) in the form of pastiche (imitation), parody (transformation), but also in the form of a simple continuation, as in translation; i.e., transposition or subversion of a text by another for humorous, satirical or serious purposes.

We also consider fundamental for the conception of fictionalization the notion of *intertextualization* proposed by Miranda (2004, 2007). This process can be defined as corresponding to the cases where a relation of co-presence is established among elements (or features) associated to parameters of textualization that are prominent of differentiated (two or more) genres in the space of only one text. In other words, a given text, inscribed in a specific genre, intertextually appeals to features associated with other distinct genres[8].

From a relational point of view, the genre of the text in question is a "summoned" genre that functions as a hypergenre, whereas the "called" genres constitute what we will be able to name hypogenres[9]. Therefore, it is a dominant relation where the hypogenres are integrated in a certain way, to serve the interests of the hypergenres.

The intertextualization can assume varied forms. The hypogenres can arise actualised or fictionalized and they can fill the totality of the text (in the case of a global pastiche of a genre) or they can be integrated as portions of a text. Either actualised or fictionalized, the hypogenres can participate in several discourse strategies (Miranda, 2004).

When studying the intertextualization, one of the central problems is the recognition of the generic crossing in a text. This is how the genres in interaction can be identified semiotically (we are not concerned here with the cognitive aspects of this recognition). A first answer is that it is not a matter of a true "crossing of genres" (that is the text itself is inscribed in more than a genre), but of an effect of crossing of genres. In other words, what is "crossed" are parameters associated with different genres. These parameters can be observed (or "recuperated") through the mechanisms that materialize them. In this way, the identification of the genres in interaction is possible through the occurrence of genre markers.

In principle, a text built by the intertextualization process will have markers of the hypergenre and markers of the hypogenre. However, and given that the markers are semiotic elements, it is possible that only the markers of the hypogenre occur and that the hypergenre is only identified through situational aspects (producer, material form, etc.) and not by semiotic aspects. This is particularly visible in cases of pastiche covering the totality of the text.

To follow, we are going to observe two texts where there is intertextualization, and the hypogenres are fictionalized (or simulated). Through these cases, we will be able to notice the paper of the markers for the identification of the game of fictionalization.

We use this last term—*fictionalization*—in a sense not far from the one we can see from Bernié (2001), when he claims that:

> . . . semantic variations observable among texts by the same researcher, and on the same type of scientific problem, are linked to genre variations which cannot be explained either by a simple adjustment of presentation techniques or even by the famous reflective virtues of the activity, but by a different "fictionalization" of contextual parameters of the writing activity, i.e., by the performing and staging of a different socio-discursive context. (p. 331)

As can be seen, the author speaks of fictionalization when referring to cases where there is a staging of the contextual parameters—considering them integrated in the broader scope of genre variations. Following the same direction, we establish the distinction between *genre actualization* and *genre fictionalization*—which notions are more fully developed and exemplified in Leal and Gonçalves (2007). Within the scope of this article, we will insist on the specificity of fictionalization as simulation, or pastiche, of genre. In other words: genre is used for purposes differing from those which are in principle associated with it—humorous or playful purposes in general, advertising, aesthetic. This means that at least some genre parameters will necessarily have to be maintained, in order to ensure that the genre is recognized—a *sine qua non* condition to achieve the desired (humorous or other) effect.

According to what we have just finished saying we assume that to deal with texts with fictionalization of genres obliges the same genres to be taken simultaneously into account in the actualized version (and not in a fictionalization). The process offers different conditions of observation: if natural text circulation conditions remain unchanged, this makes differentiated materials available for analysis whereby these would not result from a recourse to manipulations which, however controlled, could never avoid undoing the situationality inherent to each genre.

Of this viewpoint, the fictionalization of genres can constitute a very useful strategy in the work of description of the genres and the texts—as we expect that the following section can show, through the analysis of two examples.

EXEMPLIFICATION: THE ROLE OF THE MARKERS IN THE FICTIONALIZATION OF GENRES

Appendix 1 presents an advertising announcement of a service of connection to the internet. There is, indeed, an assembly of elements (that is, "markers") that indicate the actualization of this genre. For example in the composition plan, we see the occurrence of some characteristic sections of the advertising announcements: a slogan, a mark with the respective logo and an instructive segment with facts for the obtaining of the product. Therefore, these sections have the function of inferential markers of the (hyper) genre.

If this text actualizes the genre advertisement, there is also the "summons" of another genre: the instruction manual[10]. This hypogenre is called to serve the argumentative interests of the announcement and it occupies a restricted space in the entire text. Indeed, barely a section of the announcement (the body of the text) corresponds to the "instruction manual." The question is how (through which clues) we recognize the presence of the instructive genre. To answer this question, it is necessary to identify the generic markers.

It is probable that the assembly of markers identified in the first place in the process of reading, concerns the compositional, the dispositional and the interactive dimensions. Nevertheless, there are also markers of the thematic, the enunciative and the strategic dimensions that orient our interpretative work.

From among the **compositional markers**, we notice the text plan (Adam, 2002a) is composed of three big sections: the title, a series of figurative drawings and a series of propositions that barely function as legends. The verbal component of the text plan (title and "legends") conforms to an injunctive sequence (Bronckart, 1999, p. 237). This sequence characterizes itself by the construction of a chaining of actions (set out in the "legends"), that constitute necessary steps to reach a result (set out in the title). In a local level, there is the reiterated occurrence of imperative phrases, whose internal composition is a structure verb + complement.

The **dispositional** or **material markers** discriminate the sections of the text plan. Indeed, it is by means of the typographical variation and the pagination that, for example, it is possible to distinguish a title from a "legend." On the other hand, the arrangement of each element of the series (drawings or propositions), establishes a construction in chain that organizes the sequence of the actions. The organization column format permits that, in the mechanism of reading in Portuguese language (from the top to the bottom and from the left to the right), the actions are interpreted like successive steps, such that the first step will be the one that is introduced in the upper position and the last step will be in the lower position of the series.

The **interactive marker** that highlights the identification of the instructive genre is the redundant relation between the nonverbal and the verbal components. What is said is simultaneously shown in the images. It is partly thanks to this relation that the specification of definite expressions is justified (*the* packaging, *the* CD-ROM, *the* reader of CD, etc.).

We also find clues for the identification of the hypogenre in the lexicon. Indeed, the lexicon is one of the most significant **thematic markers**. In this case, there is, on one side, an assembly of technical words—in this case informatics (internet, CD-ROM, computer, CD reader)—and, on the other hand, an assembly of lexical items that assign actions (to catch, to open, to lay down, to put).

Concerning **enunciative markers**, we observe the absence of timing and space signs (deictic) and of marks of the first person. Beyond that, we see the occurrence of the second person in verbs (catch, open, lie down, put) and possessive adjectives (its).

Finally, we highlight, among the **strategic/intentional markers**, the reiterated occurrence of the speech act of instruction (which can be noted in each of the "captions"), the elimination of deictic linguistic structures, the lexical reiteration and the absence of subjective or valorizing elements.

The raised markers constitute semiotic clues that allow us to recognize the genre evoked in this text. In principle, all these markers actualize parameters of the hypogenre and, so, we would be able to assume that there is an actualization of the genre here. However, this segment of the advertising announcement does not function like the manual that it seems to be. If, as it is set out in the title, the actions enunciated and shown are going to instruct about the process of installation of the internet at home, such actions do not correspond to true specific steps of that process. Indeed, in a software installation manual—as this intends to be—it is not necessary to indicate what the subjects should do with the packaging of the CD-ROM. In this sense, the utterances "grab the packaging," "open the packaging," etc., do not correspond to possible or foreseeable formulations in this genre, as it functions in our society.

Still in the scope of the thematic contents, the occurrence of the closing sentence phrase "it is done" is also improbable in a text of this instructive genre. Then, two possible readings exist: either it is an actualization of genre with qualitative errors, or the "errors" are deliberate and controlled. The option for some of these interpretations, and given that this "instruction manual" is part of an advertising announcement, it is necessary to consider the argumentative strategy built in the announcement.

In this text, the central argument arises in the slogan: "fazer clix custa nix" (to do clix costs nix). This game of words between the name of the product (clix) and the ad hoc created neologism (nix) would be formulated again in the following words: "to do clix" = to link the computer to the internet and "costs nix" = does not cost or it is easy. Then, the main argument of the announcement is centred in the offered simplicity of installation of the product. Thus, it is not astonishing that the "manual" is shown to be a useless or unnecessary object: since the installation is easy, the "manual" barely indicates what should be done with the packaging of the CD and with the CD. Beyond that, the action of putting a CD-ROM in the computer reader is an obvious mechanical procedure for any user. The separation of this action in small actions that are, indeed, of automatic achievement, is therefore a strategic game of demonstration of the simplicity of the procedure. Thus, if it was a matter of a "true" software installation manual it would be necessary to enumerate the actions that should be carried out *from* the introduction of the CD-ROM in the reader and not the achievable actions *to* that step.

In short, the observation detailed of the genre markers in this segment of the announcement allows us to affirm that, although a big number of generic parameters are actualized, there is fictionalization in the plan of the thematic contents. This is verified in the kind of enunciated actions and in the occurrence of the final expression "and it is done." Later, after commenting on the second case, we will come back to this example.

Text 2 reproduced in the appendix is also a case of intertextualization. This example adds some other elements to the argument. It is a sample of the genre cartoon, as it is set out in the self-referential marker in peritextual position. In this genre, as well as in other similar genres (for example, the comics); the process of intertextualization is frequent and, perhaps still more necessary. Indeed, the nature of the cartoon is "to call" other genres inside itself. To this peculiarity, we will be able to give the name of "constitutive intertextualization"[11]. In that case, contrary to Text 1, the hypogenre fills the totality of the text.

A varied assembly of markers suggest the evoked genre. From the **compositional**, the **dispositional** and the **interactive** viewpoint, nonverbal and verbal units compose a text plan that is characterized by the following peculiarities: (1) the presence of an image in the central position and of a series of brief utterances distributed in the upper and the lower region of the text; (2) one of the utterances is noticeable graphically by the typography, by the colour and by the location in the page ("massive destruction"); (3) in the lower region there is a relatively long segment composed by an enumeration; (4) the relation between the image and the verbal segments is basically of an illustration (because the image does not complete, substitute or repeat the information given by the utterances).

Compositionally, we also observe the occurrence of an elevated number of noun clauses and the occurrence of participial small clauses. The developed verbal sentences are few in number. The identification of a sequential organization of descriptive kind corresponds also to the plan of the composition, where the *anchoring* operations ("massive destruction" in the function of subject-title) and the *aspectualization* operations (Adam, 1992) are carried out.

Thematically, we find a salient semantic field and lexicon associated with cinematography: original argument, film, director, main actor, assembly, visual effects, etc. Ritual expressions are also invoked: "nominated for X academy Oscars," "a production X" and "filmed in X." Beyond that, we should notice the reiterated occurrence of "best," preceding the nouns relative to the cinematographic field.

It is clear that these are not the only mechanisms of textual realization that function like genre markers in this text. However, these elements look sufficient for the identification of the called genre: the poster-advertising genre of a cinematographic film.

As in Text 1, in this example the markers actualize parameters of the hypogenre, but a fictionalization of genre is built. To arrive at this conclusion it is necessary to observe at least two aspects. The first aspect concerns the text situational dimension, specifically the producing entity and the support of circulation: someone signs this sample (which does not happen in advertising) and it is published in the section of a magazine entitled "recreational society," and is further labeled as a cartoon. The second aspect is the thematic organization: the nouns that occur in the text do not correspond to the world of the makers of the cinematographic fiction, but to the world of the makers (contemporary to the text) of the Anglo-American political reality: Tony Blair, George W. Bush, CIA and British Secret Service, etc. Then, this text relates in fiction an advertising poster of a film that does not exist nor would be able to exist. The fictionalization of a cinematographic advertising poster here accomplishes critical humor.

These two observed examples are different kinds of fictionalization of genres, but both coincide in the particular plan that establishes the fictionalization, i.e., in the organization of the thematic contents. Despite this coincidence, the two examples show that the occurrence of fictionalized thematic contents does not concern exclusively the mobilization of fictional contents, as in the case of the film that never existed referred to in Text 2. Indeed, we notice that in Text 1 there is no "fictional" contents, but there is an infringement on the norms (or parameters) of the genre. This is a thematic infringement, since it concerns, specifically, the propositional contents of the enunciated actions. Thus, to fictionalize parameters of a genre does not necessarily introduce imaginary elements. It rather subverts a genre, creating another reality where the infringements are not infringements anymore. This is a game of creation of an action where everything (in semiotics) is admissible. In practice: in Text 1, the enunciated actions are inappropriate in relation to the norms of the genre "instruction manual," according to the operation of this genre in our daily life; however, in the fiction created in the announcement (in another reality) this is a plausible manual.

Genre markers play an important role in the interpretation of the intertextualization and, particularly, of the fictionalization of genres. These examples demonstrate that the identification of the generic markers (self-referential or inferential) is an essential procedure in the process of reading or listening to the texts. By means of the recognition of these semiotic clues, the subjects are capable of interpreting the generic inscription of a text. This process of comprehension of the generic inscription of the text is fundamental to assure the communication (according to, among others, Bakhtin, 1992 and Maingueneau, 1998). Without doing that interpretative work, the subjects-receivers do not play the game proposed by the subjects-producers. From both the theoretical and applied viewpoint, the detailed observation of the hypogenres markers distinguishes the mechanisms of textual realization that respect the norms of the genre and the mechanisms subverting them.

FINAL CONSIDERATIONS

This work started from the need to answer two questions: on one side, to know in what measure the genres can be described, although by definition they are only accessible through the empirical texts that actualize them; on the other, to verify up to where there is or there is not a convergence in the work about genres and about texts.

To face these questions we have presented some instruments of analysis that, to our knowledge, make the distinction (but also the articulation) viable of near but not coincidental objects of analysis: the genres, while abstract categories, and the empirical texts that constitute always a sample of a determined genre. Thus, we assume that each genre can be described through an assembly of parameters—parameters that, to the empirical level of the text, can carry out a differentiated form, constituting what we assign as mechanisms of textual realization. As we also saw, those mechanisms can function like genre markers—in the measure that they are going to identify, or to make recognizable, the genre in question, in a situation of textual reception/interpretation.

We have identified the fictionalization of genres as a particular case of intertextualization (as a process which places in a co-presence relation two or more genres within a text) as we have shown the highlighting function that falls to the genre markers, in the cases of fictionalization. Enumerating these signs makes it possible to detect the semio-linguistic dimensions in which fictional or transgressive elements appear and, at the same time, makes it possible to point out the specific tools in which fiction/transgression materializes. This enumerating also allows the understanding that the fictionalization of a genre does not imply the total subversion of the generic parameters. Indeed, to recognize the fictionalized genre some parameters should be necessarily actualized without absolute infringements. This is the reason why the cases of fictionalization are going to constitute a privileged occasion of analysis for us: without the manipulated interference of the researcher, the genre shows itself in the double role of the actualization (or lineal adoption) and of the fictionalization (or simulation).

The two examples observed show different ways of fictionalization of genres and the markers' participation in this process. In one of the cases (Text 2), a fictional subject/object is built: the film spoken on the text does not exist. In another case (Text 1), there is an infringement on the thematic parameters of the genre, because topics not predicted by the genre in question are introduced.

Also worth underlining is that the fictionalization of genres (or the fictionalization or infringement of the parameters) is not carried out only in the plan of thematic content organization. This means that there may be texts in which enunciative or compositional mechanisms indicate the fictional convening of a genre other than that in which the texts are inscribed. That is why the choice of the two commented examples should not cause us to conclude that the thematic markers constitute the only possible clues for the identification of the phenomenon. Indeed, hypothetically, any class of marker would be able to fill that function.

To uncover cases that show this we need to continue to observe with curiosity the infinite textual world that surrounds us. And that necessary empirical work about texts of different genres will alone be able to show conclusively the operating efficiency of the proposals presented here.

APPENDIX A

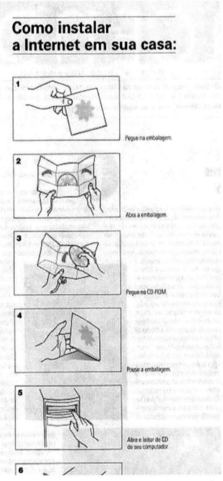

Como instalar a Internet em sua casa:

TEXT 1: PUBLISHED NOVEMBER 11, 2001 IN NOTÍCIAS MAGAZINE (PORTUGAL), P. 101

APPENDIX B

TEXT 2: PUBLISHED FEBRUARY 8, 2004, IN *REVISTA PÚBLICA*
(PORTUGAL), P. 4

NOTES

[1] As underlined by J. M. Adam, the three dimensions in Bakhtin (1984) are close to the ancient rhetorical triad—the *inventio*, the *dispositio* and the *elocutio*. (Adam, 1999, p. 92).

[2] In French: *discours interactif* and *discours théorique* (*ordre de l'exposer*); *récit interactif* and *narration* (*ordre du raconter*) (Bronckart, 1997).

[3] Those levels of text organization are previously referred, in the same article, in five blocks: phrastic and trans-phrastic, compositional structure (sequences and text plans), semantics (discourse representation), enunciation (situational anchoring and responsibility), speech acts (illocutionary) and argumentative orientation (Adam, 2001, p. 41).

[4] These notions are a product of the inquiry in Text Theory developed in the Faculdade de Ciências Sociais e Humanas of the Universidade Nova de Lisboa. Two of them (*parameters of genre* and *mechanisms of textual realization*) were developed within the framing of the sub-project Géneros Textuais e Organização do conhecimento—GeTOC (Textual Genres and Organization of the Knowledge), integrated in the project DISTEX (Linguistics Centre of the New University of Lisbon, 2003-2006). The third (*genre markers*) is an elapse of the study of Florencia Miranda, within her PhD research (Miranda, 2007).

[5] For more details, see Coutinho, Alves, Gonçalves, Miranda, & Pinto (2008, forthcoming); Leal & Gonçalves (2007).

[6] Indeed, the distinction between *parameters of genre* and *mechanisms of textual realization* is going to grasp the (synchronic) variation and, in that same measure, contribute to the possibility of the diachronic perspective (thus identifying the process of generic change).

[7] This proposal based itself in a critical reading of the contributions of authors such as Adam, Bronckart and Maingueneau. For a more detailed presentation, see Miranda (2007). For an approach to the proposals of these theoreticians, it is possible to see, among others, Adam (2001), Bronckart (1999) and Maingueneau (1998).

[8] It is important to highlight that, the way as it is here assumed (and it was proposed in Miranda, 2004 and 2007), this process should be differentiated from the "intertextuality" phenomenon (in the strict sense), whose specificity is to put in co-presence two or more empirical texts in the same textual space. Despite the proximity of the notion that is proposed here with the notion of "intergeneric intertextuality" that Marcuschi (2003, p. 31) utilizes in the sequence of the works of Ulla Fix, the term intertextualization is not limited to the cases where exists, as Marcuschi says, "a mixture of functions and forms of genre diverse in a given genre."

[9] The use of the prefixes "hyper-"and "hypo-"arises here in the sequence of

Gérard Genette (and of his studies about the transtextuality), but putting the focus of the problem in the genres and not alone in the texts. For the Genette perspective about the hypertextuality, see Genette (1982).

[10] We are going to underline that others can replace the generic "labels" that we are using without any prejudice to the analysis. In principle, for the characterization of the genres it is irrelevant that the genre be nominated socially by only a name or by multiple denominations. Therefore, it does not matter, as an example, if the genre of this text is called "advertising announcement" or "publicity."

[11] The *constitutive intertextualization* opposes itself to the *strategic intertextualization*. This distinction is also a proposal developed in Miranda, 2007.

REFERENCES
Adam, J.-M. (1992). *Les textes: Types et prototypes*. Paris: Nathan.
Adam, J.-M. (1999). *Linguistique textuelle: Des genres de discours aux textes*. Paris: Nathan.
Adam, J.-M. (2001). En finir avec les types de textes. In M. Ballabriga (Org.), *Analyse des discours. Types et genres: Communication et interprétation* (pp. 25-43). Toulouse, France: EUS.
Adam, J.-M. (2002a). De la période à la séquence: Contribution à une (trans) linguistique textuelle comparative. In H. L. Andersen & H. Nølke (Eds.), *Macro-syntaxe et macro-sémantique* (pp.167-188). Bern, Switzerland: Peter Lang.
Adam, J.-M. (2002b). Plan de texte. In P. Charaudeau & D. Maingueneau (Eds.), *Dictionnaire d'Analyse du Discours* (pp. 433-434). Paris: Seuil
Adam, J.-M. (2005). La translinguistique des textes à l'œuvre. In P. Lane (Dir.), *Des discours aux textes: modèles et analyses* (pp. 11-38). Rouen, France: Publication des Universités de Rouen et du Havre.
Bakhtin, M. (1992). *Estética da Criação Verbal*. São Paulo: Martins Fontes.
Bakhtin, M. (1977). *Le marxisme et la philosophie du langage*. Paris: Minuit.
Bernié, J. P. (2001). Les genres discursifs, des outils sociaux de transformation des connaissances. In M. Ballabriga (Org.), *Analyse des discours. Types et genres: Communication et interprétation* (pp. 331-355). Toulouse, France: EUS.
Bronckart, J. P. (2006). *Atividade de linguagem, discurso e desenvolvimento humano*. Campinas, São Paulo: Mercado de Letras
Charaudeau, P. (1992). *Grammaire du sens et de l'expression*. Paris: Hachette.
Coutinho, M. A., Alves, M., Gonçalves, M., Miranda, F., & Pinto, R. (in press). Parâmetros de géneros e mecanismos de realização textual—aspectos teóricos. *Diacrítica*. Braga, Portugal: Universidade do Minho
Genette, G. (1982). *Palimpsestes*. Paris: Seuil.
Leal, A., & Gonçalves, M. (2007). Gêneros ficcionalizados e identidade de

género. In A. Bonini, D. Figueiredo, & F. Rauen (Eds.), *Proceedings of the 4th International Symposium on Genre Studies* [CD] (pp. 696-707). Tubarão, Santa Catarina, Brazil: University of Southern Santa Catarina.

Maingueneau, D. (1996). *Les termes clés de l'analyse du discours.* Paris: Seuil.

Maingueneau, D. (1998). *Analyser les textes de communication.* Paris: Dunod.

Maingueneau, D. (2002). Un genre de discours. In C. Dardy, D. Ducard, & D. Maingueneau (Eds.), *Un genre universitaire: Le rapport de soutenance de thèse* (pp. 47-86). Lille, France: Presses Universitaires du Septentrion.

Marcuschi, L. A. (2003). Gêneros textuais: Definição e funcionalidade. In A. P. Dionísio, A. R. Machado, & M. A. Bezerra (Eds.), *Gêneros textuais e ensino* (pp. 19-36). Rio de Janeiro: Editora Lucerna.

Miranda, F. (2004). Aspectos do cruzamento de géneros como estratégia discursiva. In M. A. Marques, M. E. Pereira, R. Ramos, & I. Ermida (Eds.), *Práticas de investigação em análise linguística do discurso. Actas do II encontro internacional de análise linguística do discurso* (pp. 195-211). Braga, Portugal: Universidade do Minho

Miranda, F. (2007). *Textos e géneros em diálogo—uma abordagem linguística da intertextualização.* Unpublished doctoral thesis, Universidade Nova de Lisboa, Lisboa, Portugal.

Rastier, F. (2001). *Arts et sciences du texte.* Paris: PUF.

4   Relevance and Genre: Theoretical and Conceptual Interfaces

Fábio José Rauen

INTRODUCTION

Sperber and Wilson's (1986, 1995) relevance theory considers the relation between cognitive efforts and effects in such a way that the greater the benefits and the lower the costs, the more relevant is an input for cognitive mechanisms. A research program to be pursued can be the evaluating of the production and reception roles of specific genres in this equation. Processing effort, for instance, may be minimized by the reiteration of standard genre structures, so that these structures become transparent (automatic) to the user. Thus, in an increasingly more efficient way, relevant ostensive stimuli can be conveyed based on more transparent structures.

The aim of this text is to consider some theoretical and conceptual interfaces between relevance theory and Swales' genre analysis (1990, 1992, 1998) tradition. I argue that if genre structures are derived from something deeper, relevance relations between text and context, in turn genre structures provide a discursive context that cognitively focuses the attention of writer and reader, thereby setting relevance constraints and increasing communicative efficiency.

In order to develop this argument, I selected an example of a query letter from Simoni's (2004) M. Sc. L. dissertation. Section 2 presents this text and the genre moves and steps analyzed in Simoni's work. Section 3 shows a brief précis on relevance theory. Based on Wilson's (2004) Pragmatic Course, with some punctual adaptations of my own, this section argues that the human communication is guided by cognitive and communicative principle of relevance. Section 4 is concerned with Blass' (1990) perspective on textual analysis. The central claim of her work is that relevance relations are crucial to the textual connectiveness. Section 5 analyses the query letter text indicating how both relevance-oriented and genre-based analysts can improve the descriptive and explanatory level of their analysis by combining relevance and genre approaches. Section 6 is dedicated to the journalist's role, the query letter's first utterer, in the linguistic and structural choices of the text. I argue these choices are constrained not only by the genre structure, but also by relevance relations. Finally, section 7 is dedicated to concluding remarks.

THE QUERY LETTER GENRE: AN EXAMPLE TO GUIDE THE DISCUSSION

To illustrate the discussion, I use as an example a query letter selected from

Simoni's (2004) M. Sc. L. dissertation[1]. For her, query letters are a kind of reader's letter (published in newspaper sections), whose answer contains information or a problem resolution from experts.

The genre query letter is particularly interesting for relevance theory, because each of the three major sections is presented by a different utterer who carries out a different series of rhetorical moves. The journalist, the first utterer, is responsible for the text formatting and title assignment; the querier, the second utterer, is responsible for the letter; and the expert, the third utterer, is responsible for the answer. According to Bonini (2007), this fact shows that "the genre is not only a way to convey a message. Rather, it is a unifying principle of a set of actions and social practices." For him, not only the question/answer interaction fits into the query letter text, but also modes of editing and specific ways of reading come into play (to the newspaper reader, to the letter writer, to the section editor, to the specialist responsible for the answer, and so on).

For Simoni (2004), the query letter is composed of three rhetorical actions or moves (Swales, 1990): "identifying the text," "formulating a question" and "providing an answer." Each move presents a number of rhetorical sub-actions or steps. Her research found two standards for query letters: direct and indirect, as the experts' answers were quoted or reported in the third move "providing a response." Chart 1, below, refers to the rhetorical structure of a direct query letter.

MOVE 1: Identifying the text (Produced by U1)

Step 1: Giving the topic of the text—and/or
Step 2: Giving the subtopic of the text

MOVE 2: Formulating a question (Produced by U2)

Step 1: Outlining the scene—and/or
Step 2: Presenting the problem—or
Step 3A: Requesting information—or
Step 3B: Requesting positioning—or
Step 3C: Requesting information
Step 4: Providing data for identification

MOVE 3: Providing a response (Produced by U1 or U3)

Step 1: Describing the subject addressed by the letter writer—and/or

> Step 2: Positioning him/herself—and/or
> Step 3: Indicating a procedure—and/or
> Step 4: Providing general assessment of the problem—and/or
> Step 5: Providing credentials—or
> Step 6: Providing data for identification/credential

CHART 1: RHETORICAL STRUCTURE OF A DIRECT QUERY LETTER
(TRANSLATED FROM SIMONI, 2004, P. 51)

The text in Chart 2 is a direct query letter example. This text was collected from Simoni's (2004) corpus, and was rediscussed in Bonini (2007).

MOVES	TEXT	STEPS
Identifying the text (Produced by U1)	Drawer	Giving the topic of the text
Formulating a question (Produced by U2)	§ I have a drawer's contract registered in a notary's office in 1985[2]. In mid-1996, I paid off the property with the FGTS[3].	Outlining the scene
	Caixa informed me the owner of the property must now sign the payoff contract. But for years I have had no contact with her.	Presenting the problem
	What should I do?	Requesting solution
	§ Luiz Silva Rio de Janeiro	Providing data for identification

Providing a response (Produced by U1 and U3)	§ It is commonplace, when someone formalizes a drawer's contract, that the seller of the property grants, in the same act, a proxy which permits the buyer to represent him/herself in all actions related to the implementation of the negotiation.	Describing the subject addressed by the consulting
	We believe, in the reader's case, that there should be a proxy, which would solve the problem. Without this proxy, the reader may not even be able to effectuate the sale by public deed. In this case, the only solution would be to file a suit for the compulsory adjudication, in which the reader would use his document to get the final deed. Then, with the court's judgment, granting him the final deed, the reader should get the CEF payoff.	Reporting a procedure
	Luiz Wanis, Lawyer	Providing credentials

CHART 2: EXAMPLE OF A DIRECT QUERY LETTER GENRE (TRANSLATED FROM SIMONI, 2004, P. 93)

RELEVANCE THEORY

The interpretation of each utterance of a query letter results from the interaction of the linguistic properties of the sentences these utterances convey (their phonological, syntactic and semantic structure) with contextual factors of the utterance[4]. The central problem in a cognitive pragmatics is that the meaning handled by the speaker goes well beyond the linguistic meaning assigned by the grammar to the sentence which composes these utterances. Therefore, to comprehend utterances, a set of pragmatic processes must be used by the readers in order to complete, enrich and complement the schematic sentence meaning yielding a hypothesis about the writer's meaning[5].

Relevance theory is strictly concerned with overt intentional communication. In this kind of communication, there are two layers of intention for the reader to discover: the basic writer's intention to inform the readers about something—*informative intention*; and a higher-order intention that the readers should recognize that informative basic intention—*communicative intention* (Sperber & Wilson, 1986, 1995). So, comprehending an utterance is equivalent to obtaining an overtly intended interpretation: the one the writer wants the reader to recover, is actively helping the reader to recover, and would recognize if asked about it.

For relevance theory, human cognition is relevance-oriented. The basic claim is that new (or newly presented) information is relevant in a context when it interacts with the context yielding cognitive effects.

There are, according to Sperber and Wilson (1986, 1995), three cognitive effects of information in a context: (a) strengthening a contextual assumption; (b) contradicting and eliminating a contextual assumption; and (c) combining that information with a contextual assumption to yield contextual implications, that is, conclusions deducible from new information and context together, but neither from new information nor from the isolated context.

For example, take the title and the first utterance of the selected query letter text:

(1) Drawer.
(2) I have a drawer's contract registered in a notary's office in 1985.

Let's imagine a reader who supposes, because of the title, that the text is a query about a manufacturing defect of some purchased furniture. This assumption is contradicted by the first utterance of the text, where the second utterer refers to a drawer's contract. So, when this reader processes the second utterance, this first assumption is eliminated.

In a second version, let's imagine a reader who supposes, when he/she is reading the title, that the text was a query about a drawer's contract. In this second version, the textual processing of the first utterance strengthens this original hypothesis, making it more certain. In this case, there is a strengthening of an assumption.

Finally, let's imagine a reader who knows the Brazilian home mortgage system. In this case, the first utterance of the text combines with his/her memorized encyclopedic assumptions, yielding a conclusion that the querier's property is mortgaged, for example. This is a contextual implication.

Here is a possible chain of assumptions "S" for this inference[6]:

S_1—Drawer's contracts are related to mortgaged properties (implied premise from encyclopedic memory);

S_2—Someone has registered a drawer contract in a notary's office in 1985 (implied premise from linguistic input);

S_3—If S_1 and S_2, then S_5;

S_4—If S_1, then S_5 (by *and-elimination*);

S_5—Someone's property was mortgaged (implied conclusion by *modus ponens*)[7].

Information is relevant in a context if it has cognitive effects in that context, and the greater its cognitive effects the greater its relevance. However, it is crucial to consider the costs to get these cognitive effects. So, the smaller the processing effort required to derive these effects, the greater the relevance of the input. In order to see how this happens, let's compare two versions to the first utterance of the query letter:

(2a) I have a drawer's contract registered in a notary's office in 1985.

(2b) It is not true that I do not have a drawer's contract registered in a notary's office in 1985.

Here, utterance (2a) is easier to process, and other things being equal, by hypothesis, it is more relevant than utterance (2b). This occurs because utterance (2b) includes the logical form of utterance (2a) as a subpart of its own logical form.

According to Wilson (2004), the problem of a theory of human cognition is answering how human beings consciously or automatically select which inputs to deal with, which context in which to process them, and when to stop. If human cognition is relevance-oriented, then systems of perception, memory and inference are organized so that they automatically tend to allocate attention and processing resources to the most relevant accessible inputs, and to process them in a way that tends to maximize their relevance. This is the *Cognitive Principle of Relevance*: human cognition tends to be geared to the maximization of relevance (Sperber & Wilson, 1986, 1995).

In overt intentional communication, to communicate is to offer information, and offers create presumptions or expectations that will be justified or not. Therefore, the act of addressing someone automatically creates a *presumption of relevance*. In turn, as utterances may have a number of linguistically possible and potentially relevant interpretations, the actual interpretation is the one which best satisfies this presumption or expectation.

How much relevance is needed for the writer to satisfy the readers' expectations? According to Sperber and Wilson (1995), the utterance should have at least enough cognitive effects, at a low enough processing cost, to be worth dealing with. So, they have developed a notion of optimal relevance which involves two clauses: (a) the utterance should be at least relevant enough to be worth processing; and (b) the utterance should be the most relevant one compatible with the speaker's abilities and preferences.

What counts as "relevant enough," clause (a), varies individually and circumstantially. A query letter on drawer's contracts, for instance, can be more or less relevant. The query letter text as a whole will be interesting to readers who are experiencing or have experienced a similar problem recounted by the second utterer. The title and some passages of the query letter are sufficient to readers who haven't experienced those problems to understand them. Thus, relevance expectations differ in predictable ways from situation to situation, and it is expected that the utterances reach relevance in more or less specific ways on different circumstances.

Clause (b), in turn, is very important to describe and explain textual comprehension, because it rules out the readers' need to go on and consider other less accessible interpretations, after having recognized an acceptable interpretation. This suggests a concrete comprehension procedure which readers may use to discover the best hypothesis about the writers' meaning. The procedure predicts that the reader must follow a path of least effort in computing cognitive effects: (a) considering interpretations (e.g., reference assignments, contexts, etc.) in order of accessibility; and (b) stopping when his expectation of relevance is satisfied (or abandoned) (Wilson, 2004).

RELEVANCE AND TEXTUALITY

Blass (1990), in *Relevance relations in discourse*, proposes that the basis for judgments of textuality must be founded on relevance relations and not on traditional notions such as cohesion and coherence[8]. According to her, textual connectiveness is derived from something deeper, i.e., from relevance relations between text and context. Such relations are precisely what every reader automatically looks for while interpreting a text or every analyst automatically looks for when explaining and describing this text. Blass' central hypothesis is that relevance relations, based on the balance between contextual effects and processing efforts, are behind the judgments of good text formation.

Based on Blakemore (1987), Blass disagrees with the view according to which traditional cohesive mechanisms are markers of coherence. For her, these mechanisms function as restriction markers on semantic relevance. These restrictions are very important, because the writer indicates through these marks the direction which should be pursued to achieve relevance. This way, the reader's interpretation task is made easier.

It is worth mentioning that if the meaning of a sentence underdetermines the meaning of the utterance conveyed by this sentence, it is reasonable to generalize that the meaning of a text underdetermines the meaning of the discourse conveyed by the text. That is, the linguistic structure of the text underdetermines what is communicated. Precisely on the basis of the gap between the content of texts and discourses, and considering that the reader's task is interpreting the writer's intention through inferential strategies during the process of understanding, the role of context is crucial to this task.

Blass then highlights the importance of considering cognitive factors which are necessary for a discourse analysis. For her, if the concept of discourse is not primarily linguistic, under an approach to textuality with claims for plausibility and consistency, this concept cannot be dealt with in a purely linguistic way, as foreseen in a semiotic approach based on encoding and decoding.

For relevance theory, the reader's role is important in the processing of textual elaboration, because the writer's verbal behavior is limited by the reader's expectation of relevance. As part of the relation between writer and reader, these expectations of relevance should be considered as the basis for the analysis of the relation between text and discourse[9].

For Blass, the criterion of consistency with the principle of relevance selects and restricts the set of assumptions to be used by the reader in textual interpretation. Having said that, "textuality, as judgment of good textual formation and, *a fortiori*, as a condition for interpretation, is constructed in the course of verbal processing with contextual information, rather than with formal or semantic connectivity of linguistic-textual structures" (Silveira & Feltes, 1999, p. 78)[10].

GENRE AND RELEVANCE

Genre analysis is closely connected to the concept of language as social action. According to Bazerman (2004), much of this task is concerned with the analysis of how production, circulation and ordered use of these texts partially constitute the activity itself and the organization of the social groups. In other words, the task is to understand how, by using texts, human beings create realities of meaning, social relations and knowledge.

Insofar as texts become successful, they create social facts. They are significant social actions mediated by language—in fact, speech acts. These acts are carried out by means of standardized, typical and intelligible textual forms—genres. These genres, in turn, establish networks of relations with other neighborhood genres. As Bazerman (2004) said: "Together the text types fit together as genre sets within genre systems, which are part of systems of human activity" (p. 311).

Austin (1962), in *How to do things with words*, defended the idea that words do not only mean, but do things. His pioneering study progressed on the understanding of what he called performative verbs, opposed to constative verbs. Performative verbs could only be evaluated in terms of felicity, instead of truth conditions[11].

Even more important was Austin's speech acts classification as locutionary, illocutionary and perlocutionary. A locutionary act consists of a set of linguistic elements which can be subsumed by a proposition: what was literally said. An illocutionary act is what the writer wanted to say with what he/she said: his/her intentional or desired act. Finally, a perlocutionary act is the set of effects the speech acts causes in the reader, or its actual effects.

So, if speech acts are at the essence of social functioning, a deeper understanding of how someone comprehends these acts must be very important to genre analysts. Accordingly, it is worth noting that Austin's trichotomy can be reconsidered in a relevance-theoretical context. Taking account of how this happens, I must review how pragmatic interpretation is processed in terms of logical form, explicature and implicature concepts[12].

For relevance theory, an utterance is a structured set of concepts in a propositional or logical form. As Sperber and Wilson (1986, 1995) said, concepts are species of labels or addresses. By hypothesis, for each concept which makes up the logical form of the proposition conveyed by the utterance, it is possible to access logical, encyclopedic and lexical information[13]. In the case of an utterance to be processed (including by a genre analyst), the content assigned to the sentence consists of a proposition, or logical form, usually an incomplete representation, which is determined, according to Kempson (1988), by the concepts the individual expressions name and by the logical configuration associated with the syntactic structure of the sentence.

In order to understand the utterance, readers look for an interpretation that matches their expectation of relevance. Therefore, based on encoded language and following a path of least effort, they enrich the inputs of the logical form to get the explicit meaning and complete it in an implicit level until their interpretation is consistent with their expectation of relevance. In this case, the logical form is usually enriched by logical inferences to get the explicature, here understood as a semantically complete propositional logical form. According to Sperber and Wilson, "an assumption communicated by an utterance U is explicit if and only if it is a development of a logical form encoded by U" (1995, p. 182).

In relevance-theoretical terms, inferential understanding processes are installed as outputs of the decoding process. Inferential processes, which correspond to the development of the logical form communicated by the utterance, are an explicature of this utterance. In an explicature, many pragmatic operations happen, including reference assignment, indeterminacies resolution, disambiguation, metaphoric interpretation or ellipses enrichment. In this case, one can include high-level descriptions, containing, for example, the writer's attitude about the utterance, in other words, the subjacent speech act.

In addition, there are inferences which exceed the logical form development and constitute utterance implicatures. In such cases, the propositional logical form compounds an implied premise to deductively generate an implied conclusion, possibly the writer's intended last interpretation.

Take these representational levels in the excerpt below which compounds the first and second rhetorical actions or moves of the query letter example: "identifying the text" and "formulating a question," respectively.

(1) Drawer
(2) I have a drawer's contract registered in a notary's office in 1985.
(3) In mid-1996, I paid off the property with the FGTS.
(4) Caixa informed me the owner of the property must now sign the payoff contract.
(5) But for years I have had no more contact with her.
(6) What should I do?
(7) Luiz Silva
(8) Rio de Janeiro

In the excerpt, utterance (6), now (6a), contains, by hypothesis, the logical form (6b):

(6a) What should I do?
(6b) should do, someone, something.

The logical form (6b) is semantically incomplete, because two logical constituents are open: the noun phrases which perform subject and object function of "should do." This logical form must be developed to become a complete proposition likely to be true or false.

According to Sperber and Wilson (1986, 1995), there are two relations to be considered in an utterance: the relation between propositional form and the speaker's thought, and the relation between the speaker's thought and what the speaker's thought represents. Thus, utterances can be used descriptively and interpretively. They can be descriptions of states of affairs of the actual or fictional world, or descriptions of desirable states of affairs; or they can be interpretations of thoughts or attributed utterances, or interpretations of desirable thoughts[14].

In written questions, the propositional form of the utterance corresponds to an interpretation of the writer's thought, which may be an interpretation of a desirable thought. By hypothesis, the reader of an interrogative utterance recovers its logical form and integrates it into a high-level description, including the illocutionary act, with the logical form *The writer is asking Wh-P*, where *Wh-P* is an indirect question.

Sperber and Wilson distinguish *yes-no questions,* which have a logical form and a fully propositional form (e.g., "Do you like orange juice for breakfast?"), from *Wh-questions,* which have a logical form, but no fully propositional form (e.g., "What kind of juice do you like for breakfast?"). Utterance (6) is a *Wh-question.* It cannot constitute a fully propositional form, just because the second utterer, the querier, does not know what he should do to register the property. In this case, the reader is authorized to interpret that the answer will be relevant if it tells the querier what should be done.

In the excerpt of the query letter, according to Simoni (2004), the rhetorical move "formulating a question" has four rhetorical steps: "outlining the scene," "presenting the problem," "requesting a solution," and "providing data for identification." Among the steps, "requesting a solution" is high-ordered, since it mobilizes the rhetorical move "providing a response." This mobilization follows relevance relations.

For the second utterer, the answer to his query is the relevant dimension. Because of this, he produces a writing ostensive stimulus which, by explaining his doubt, reduces the reader's cognitive effort as best as possible, according to his preferences and abilities. At this point, his knowledge includes that the most economical way to get a solution is to ask a question. So he proceeds. However, this is part of the answer. Why did he send this question to the newspaper? Supposedly, it is because assumptions about the functioning of the genre in this hyper-genre come into play[15]. Accordingly, if the need for an answer is the most essential relevant dimension which catalyzes the text, the existence of the social practice of providing answers to questions in newspapers enables the interaction. The journalist, based on the background of the genre, processes the mediation.

The explicature of the relevant question is immersed in this interaction mediated by the first utterer, and configured by the standard structures of the genre. In this case, it is crucial to define the syntactic subject of "should do." This definition is gotten by the sender of the query, whose identification is the fourth rhetorical step of the second move, according to Simoni (2004). This is "Luiz Silva." Moreover, another requirement is to define the syntactic object of "should do." Precisely, this constituent is what "Luiz Silva" does not know—the relevant logical constituent, replaced by "WH" from now on.

This explicature can be developed, possibly, as follows:

(6b) should do, someone, something.

(6c) should do, Luiz Silva, WH.

As can be seen, utterance (6c) is still far from clear.

As argued before, we must fit this logical form into a high-level description which gives account of the speech act in scene. This is something very close to the rhetorical step "requesting a solution": *The second utterer is asking Wh-P.*
Here it is:

(6d) The second utterer is asking (should do, someone, something).
(6e) Luiz Silva is asking (should do, Luiz Silva, WH).

Supposedly, the logical form (6e) is closer to that which is at stake in this rhetorical step. However, this logical form does not capture the querier's doubt. This is only possible if the reader's cognitive context is rich enough with assumptions to complete the writer's meaning.

The first utterer, the journalist, does not give the query letter a title just to carry out the standard scheme of the genre. The lexical item "drawer" provides the assumption that this is a query about a drawer. The same happens with the rhetorical steps "outlining the scene" and "presenting the problem." Furthermore, the reading of these utterances triggers a set of assumptions from the reader's encyclopedic memory. Many of these assumptions are strange to readers who do not know the Brazilian home mortgage system. Whatever these assumptions, all of them are in service to the explicitness of the relevant logical constituent of Luiz Silva's query.

Take, by hypothesis, a set of assumptions for this event:

S_1—The text is a query (derived from the encyclopedic memory and the knowledge, even if intuitive, of the query letter genre);

S_2—The query is about a drawer's contract (derived from textual input);

S_3—Luiz Silva has a drawer's contract registered in a notary's office in 1985 (from textual input);

S_4—Luiz Silva's drawer's contract refers to some property (implied conclusion from the ambiance of S_3 in the reader's cognitive context);

S_5—Luiz Silva paid off the property with his FGTS (Fundo de Garantia por Tempo de Serviço) in 1996 (from textual input);

S_6—The FGTS (Fundo de Garantia por Tempo de Serviço) can be used for paying off properties (implied conclusion from the ambiance of S_5 in the reader's cognitive context);

S_7—Caixa [Econômica Federal] informed Luiz Silva that the owner of the property must now sign the payoff contract from 1996 (from textual input);

S_8—The mortgage of the property was made by CEF [Caixa Econômica Federal] (implied conclusion from the ambiance of S_7 in the reader's cognitive context);

S_9—For CEF [Caixa Econômica Federal], the owner of the property is not the owner of the drawer's contract (derived from encyclopedic memory, or implied conclusion from antecedent assumption).

Then, utterance (5) comes into the scene. It expresses the querier's problem, and serves as evidence to infer the reason for his query.

S_{10}—Luiz Silva has had no contact with the owner of the property for years (from textual input).

S_{11}—Drawer's contracts must be formalized (derived from encyclopedic memory);

S_{12}—If S_{10} and S_{11}, then S_{14};

S_{13}—If S_{11}, then S_{14} (implied conclusion by *and-elimination*);

S_{14}—Luiz Silva probably doesn't know how to formalize Luiz Silva's drawer's contract with the owner of the property (implied conclusion by *modus ponens*).

With this set of assumptions and inferences, it is possible to establish, by hypothesis, a complete proposition for utterance (6). This proposition is probably relevant enough to be worth processing by all readers of the text.

Here it is:

(6f) The second utterer is asking something (should do, someone, something, for any purpose).

(6g) Luiz Silva is asking (should do, Luiz Silva, WH, to formalize Luiz Silva's drawer's contract with the owner of the property).

Let's see now the third utterer's answer:

(9) It is commonplace, when someone formalizes a drawer's contract, that the seller of the property grants, in the same act, a proxy which allows the buyer to represent him/her in all actions related to the implementation of the negotiation.

(10)We believe, in the reader's case, that there should be a proxy, which would solve the problem.

(11) Without this proxy, the reader may not even effectuate the sale by public deed.

(12) In this case, the only solution would be to file a suit for the compulsory adjudication, in which the reader would use his document to get the final deed.

(13) Then, with the court's judgment, which grants him the final deed, the reader should get the CEF payoff.

(14) Luiz Wanis, Lawyer.

Luiz Wanis' answer turns around the relevant logical constituent of utterance (6): possibly, something like (15a). The lawyer sees two possible solutions: Luiz Silva has or has not a proxy to represent the owner of the property in all actions related to the implementation of the negotiation, in (15b) and (15c), respectively.

(15a) Luiz Silva should do something to formalize Luiz Silva's drawer's contract with the owner of the property.

(15b) Luiz Silva should do something to formalize Luiz Silva's drawer's contract with the owner of the property, if Luiz Silva has a proxy to represent the owner of the property in all actions related to the implementation of the negotiation.

(15c) Luiz Silva should do something to formalize Luiz Silva's drawer's contract with the owner of the property, if Luiz Silva doesn't have a proxy to represent the owner of the property in all actions related to the implementation of the negotiation.

So, the relevant logical constituent, in italics, can be completed in two versions, by hypothesis, as the logical forms (15d) and (15e):

(15d) Luiz Silva should *use a proxy from the owner to represent her in all actions related to the implementation of the negotiation* to formalize Luiz Silva's drawer's contract with the owner of the property, if Luiz Silva has a proxy to represent the owner of the property in all actions related to the implementation of the negotiation.

(15e) Luiz Silva should *file a suit for the compulsory adjudication by Luiz Silva using the document that Luiz Silva has in hand to get the final deed of the property, and then Luiz Silva must obtain the CEF payoff, and then Luiz Silva must register the property* to formalize Luiz Silva's drawer's contract with the owner of the property, if Luiz Silva doesn't have a proxy to represent the owner of the property in all actions related to the implementation of the negotiation.

It should be noticed that, to achieve these logical forms several assumptions have to be mobilized in the participants' minds, including, for example, the potential acts to formalize a drawer's contract, which include obtaining the deed, paying off the mortgage and registering the property. Here, it is worth mentioning Blass' argument that texts are only pieces of evidence or clues which constitute the input of the understanding processes, providing part of the data of logical and conceptual nature for the stage of inferential interpretation. That is, textuality is not a phenomenon necessarily and sufficiently explained in terms of the relations between linguistic and textual structures, but a processing phenomenon which is operated in the mind. In other words, textual interpretation does not solely derive from textual elements, but from a whole range of encyclopedic knowledge about the operational ways of property registration and mortgages, in addition, of course, to the knowledge, even if intuitive, of the genre operation in which the utterance (6) occurs.

THE ROLE OF THE QUERY LETTER'S FIRST UTTERER

Luiz Silva had to elaborate his query in such a way that the journalist would consider it relevant enough to be included in the newspaper. The journalist had to, constrained by newspaper production conditions or by his own expertise on the query letter genre, to format the query in such a way to make it relevant enough to get a specialist's answer, and for the readers to consider the question and the answer relevant enough to be worth reading. After all, as relevance theory argues, the journalist makes his/her best, according to his/her preferences and abilities.

The journalist has two objectives in producing an utterance: creating some change in the interlocutor's cognitive environment and reducing the processing cost of such change. As mentioned, an utterance is processed step by step. So the reader reaches some of its constituents, with its associated logical and encyclopedic inputs, before others. According to Sperber and Wilson (1995), exploring efficiently this temporal sequence is essential. The earlier disambiguation and the assigned references to lexical items are arrived at, the lower the processing effort. Conversely, the greater the number of possible interpretations which the reader has to pay attention to while processing the utterance, the greater the processing effort will be. Consequently, a writer who aims at optimal relevance should structure his/her utterance so as to make the reader's processing easier.

To interpret an utterance, individuals form top-down anticipatory hypotheses about the general logical structure, and solve ambiguities and ambivalences based on these assumptions. At a sentential level, anticipatory assumptions to be confirmed are logically related to one another. One hypothesis is implied by the other, forming a focal scale. In this scale, "each member analytically implies the immediately preceding member and is analytically implicated by the immediately succeeding member" (Sperber & Wilson, 1995, p. 208). Thus, in a successful communication, the reader confirms his/her anticipatory hypotheses during the interpretation process of the utterance.

If genres are relatively stable structures of ways of saying, which make up social activities, such stabilization should follow from arrangements which, following the principle of relevance, enlarge cognitive effects and reduce processing efforts. Thus, if the focal scale allows describing how the structural organization of a sentence reduces processing effort and enlarges cognitive effects, the same thing applies to syntactic arrangements which make up genre structures.

Accordingly, in the rhetorical move "formulating a question," the rhetorical steps "outlining the scene," "presenting the problem" and "providing data for identifying" present clues to the relevant dimension of the query. I argue that this occurs because the clues function as anticipatory assumptions to the matter which will be treated in the course of the query letter, precisely because they provide evidence of where relevance rests: the query of the second utterer.

Two questions can be highlighted based on this hypothesis. Firstly, a counter-argument for including the rhetorical step "providing data for identification" as an anticipatory hypothesis (and thus defining "Luiz Silva" as a logical constituent of the utterance) is that this step succeeds utterance (6), which textualizes the rhetorical step "requesting a solution."

I believe this is an interesting example to discuss cognition and social practices. Signing letters is an established social practice as the signature gives credibility to the interaction. Even in indirect query letters, where the specialist's answer is reported, the query respects the standards of a signed letter (Simoni, 2004)[16].

This practice constrains the anticipated presentation of the second utterer. The identification has a standard place in these cases. Moreover, it is crucial to think about hyper-genre constraints. Journalists are constantly struggling with the amount of space, always limited in newspapers. I argue that not only knowledge of the Brazilian home mortgage system operates in the construction of the explicature of the utterance (6), but knowledge of genre. The reader knows where to look for the logical constituent which defines the second utterer, because he/she also knows, even if intuitively, the genre. This suggests that the knowledge of genre theories can assist relevance-based researches, because such knowledge enables questions of social interfaces in the description and explanation of pragmatic interpretation processes.

Secondly, could the title of the query letter be a step of the rhetorical move "formulating a question"? Simoni (2004) classified the title "Drawer" as the rhetorical move "identifying the text" and also as the rhetorical step "giving the topic of the text." The fact that this move is standard in query letters is one of the arguments in her favor. Moreover, Luiz Silva's letter to the editorial staff supposedly did not have a title. Because of this, this move is solely the journalist's responsibility. However, which of the three rhetorical moves of the letter would not be mediated by the journalist? The title would be the only textual constituent where the journalist's authorship is more evident. Probably, other textual parts referring to both query and answer are, in certain degrees, paraphrases from the querier and the lawyer's original texts.

Fulfilling the function of the rhetorical step "giving the topic of the text," the title decreases the reader's cognitive effort, when it helps to contextualize the relevant question to Luiz Silva's query. If this perception is correct, a query letter could be formed by two main rhetorical moves: query and answer, something closer to a projection of the question/answer interaction in the newspaper medium. In this case, relevance theory could help genre analysts because this knowledge provides questions from a cognitive point of view to the description and explanation of the procedures of rhetorical moves and steps assignment.

CONCLUDING REMARKS

In this work, based on Simoni's (2004) query letter analysis, I discussed a possible application of the genre concept to a text comprehension theory, considering Sperber and Wilson's (1986, 1995) relevance approach, and, in the genre field, the works from Swales' (1990, 1992, 1998) tradition.

Based on the query letter analysis, I demonstrated how contextual cognitive processes intervene. Some of the essential elements to understanding come from the reader's encyclopedic knowledge about the way of mortgaging and registering properties in Brazil. The query letter is built from the completion of one of the logical constituents of the second utterer's question in utterance (6). Around this logical constituent, the series of rhetorical moves and steps of the text are arranged. As I discussed above, the generic structures which occur in texts are, I believe, at the service of something deeper and essential: relevance relations.

On the other hand, these generic structures set relevance restrictions and enlarge communicative efficiency, providing a discursive context that cognitively focuses the attention of writer and reader. As I argued above, the formatting of the text by the journalist was constrained not only by relevance relations but also by newspaper production conditions, including the query letter genre constraints. So, his relevance-oriented competence and abilities must include his expertise on the query letter genre. Relevance relations guide the generic structures; and generic structures, in turn, guide relevance relations. I think this two-way influence justifies a collaborative approach.

NOTES

[1] Simoni's (2004) work is part of the Newspaper Genres Project (Projeto Gêneros do Jornal) of the Graduate Program in Language Sciences of the University of Southern Santa Catarina.

[2] "Drawer's Contract" is an agreement between a person who is paying a mortgage, the seller, and another person, the buyer, who takes up the payment through a verbal combination or a particular contract. It is an agreement where the risk depends on the participants' confidence, because the contract belongs to the seller. The buyer is exposed to a risk in case the seller acts in bad faith, dies or moves to an ignored place (as in Luiz Silva's query). The seller is exposed to a risk when the buyer fails to pay off the mortgage or fails to pay condominium taxes. Brazilian jurisprudence considers that the buyer is entitled to claim the property possession when there is a contract or commitment of sale, even if this document is not registered. Contracts of this type should be kept in a drawer (hence the expression) until the mortgage is fully paid and officially formalized.

[3] FGTS (Fundo de Garantia por Tempo de Serviço/Assurance Fund for Period of Work) consists of the total of monthly payments employers deposit in accounts opened at the public bank Caixa Econômica Federal (CEF or Caixa) on behalf of their employees. CEF is the main agent for the Brazilian federal government's public policies, and so the major national agent for home financing programmes. The main purpose of FGTS is giving financial support to workers, in the event of dismissal without just cause. The resources of the FGTS can be used also for paying off mortgages, as is the case in Luiz Silva's query.

[4] This section is a summary of Wilson's (2004) Pragmatic Course with some adaptations of my own. For instance, I respectively used the lexical items "writer" and "reader," instead of Wilson's choices of "speaker" and "hearer."

[5] Here, context is understood as a range of mentally-represented assumptions the reader is capable of retrieving or deriving from memory, perception or inference (isolated, or in combination) in order to identify the writer's meaning. Thus, context is the set of assumptions (apart from the assumption that the utterance has been produced) which is applied in the interpretation, including assumptions achieved from the interpretation of preceding text(s) and physical circumstances.

[6] "S" designates "supposition."

[7] To know more about the relevance-theoretic deductive mechanism used in this chain of assumptions, see Sperber and Wilson (1986, 1995).

[8] According to Blass (1990), discourse is all acts of verbal communication, whether linguistic or not; text, in turn, is what is recorded from the discourses, i.e., it is a purely linguistic and formal object.

[9] According to Blass (1990), the way the language is interpreted is largely universal, so people of the most diverse cultures operate within a similar logic. For her, although background assumptions vary, the innate principle of relevance seems to be crucial in explaining the universality of the inferential processes characterizing human communication.

[10] In other words, Blass (1990) follows Sperber and Wilson's argument premises that the semantic representation of a sentence is recovered by a process of linguistic decoding, in general automatic and unconscious, and enriched through contextually accessible information, by the criterion of consistency with the principle of relevance. The nature of this operation explains, for example, why someone tries to build textual coherence before he/she immediately considers the text inconsistent.

[11] This is the case of "I baptize," whose analysis cannot be done in terms of truth-conditions, but in terms of felicity, if certain felicity conditions are appropriate (ritualistic words, actors and social circumstances).

[12] On representational levels, see Carston (1988), Silveira (1997), Silveira & Feltes (1999), and Sperber & Wilson (1986, 1995).

[13] Lexical information, of representational nature, has to do with the language counterpart of the concept. The encyclopedic information, also of representational nature, is the extension or denotation of the concept. The logic information, of computational nature, consists of a finite, small and constant set of deductive rules applied to the logical forms of which they are part. So, building the contents of an utterance simultaneously implies identifying the words that constitute this utterance, recovering their denotation and extension and applying deductive rules to their logic entries.

[14] According to Sperber and Wilson (1995, p. 231), the basic relation may be summarized as follows: "metaphor involves an interpretive relation between the propositional form of an utterance and the thought it represents; irony involves an interpretive relation between the speaker's thought and attributed thoughts or utterances; assertion involves a descriptive relation between the speaker's thought and a state of affairs in the world; requesting or advising involves a descriptive relation between the speaker's thought and a desirable state of affairs; interrogatives and exclamatives involve an interpretive relation between the speaker's thought and a desirable thought."

[15] On hyper-genre notion, see Bonini (2004).

[16] In requirements, this does not occur because the signature that follows the request for deferral does not identify the petitioner. That is why the sentence showing the relevant dimension explains the utterer: "Someone requires . . ."

REFERENCES

Austin, J. L. (1962). *How to do things with words.* Oxford: Clarendon Press.

Bazerman, C. (2004). Speech acts, genres, and activity systems: How texts organize activity and people. In C. Bazerman & P. Prior (Eds.), *What writing does and how it does it: An introduction to analyzing texts and textual practices* (pp. 309-339). Mahwah, New Jersey: Erlbaum.

Blakemore, D. (1987). *Semantic constraints on relevance.* Oxford: Blackwell.

Blass, R. (1990). *Relevance relations in discourse: A study with special reference to Sissala.* Cambridge: Cambridge University Press.

Bonini, A. (2004). Em busca de um modelo integrado para os gêneros do jornal. In M. M. Cavalcante & M. A. P. Brito (Orgs.), *Gêneros textuais e referenciação.* Fortaleza, Ceará, Brazil: PPGL/UFC.

Bonini, A. (2005). Os gêneros do jornal: Questões de pesquisa e ensino. In A. M. Karwoski, B. Gaideczka, & K. S. Brito (Orgs.), *Gêneros textuais: Reflexões e ensino.* União da Vitória, Paraná, Brazil: Kaygangue.

Bonini, A. (2007). A relação entre prática social e gênero textual: Questão de pesquisa e ensino. *Veredas (UFJF), 11*(2), 1-21.

Campos da Costa, J. (2005). A teoria da relevância e as irrelevâncias da vida cotidiana. [Special issue]. *Linguagem em (Dis)curso, 5,* 161-169.

Carston, R. (1988). Implicature, explicature, and truth-theoretic semantics. In R. Kempson (Ed.), *Mental representations: The interface between language and reality* (pp. 155-181). Cambridge: Cambrige University Press.

Karwoski, A. M., Gaideczka, B., & Brito, K. S. (Orgs.). *Gêneros textuais: Reflexões e ensino.* União da Vitória, Paraná, Brazil: Kaygangue.

Kempson, R. (Ed.). (1988). *Mental representations: The interface between language and reality.* Cambridge: Cambridge University Press.

Kinderman, C. A. (2003). *A reportagem jornalística: Desvendando as variantes de gênero.* Unpublished master's thesis, University of Southern Santa Catarina, Tubarão, Santa Catarina, Brazil.

Rauen, F. J. (2008). Sobre relevâncias e irrelevâncias. In Campos, J., & Rauen, F. J. (Eds.), *Tópicos em teoria da relevância.* Porto Alegre: Edipucrs. Retrieved December 15, 2005 from http://www.pucrs.br/edipucrs/teoriadarelevancia. pdf.

Silveira, J. R. C. (1997). *Teoria da Relevância: Uma resposta pragmático-cognitiva à comunicação inferencial humana.* Unpublished doctoral thesis, Pontifical Catholic University of Rio Grande do Sul, Rio Grande do Sul, Brazil.

Silveira, J. R. C., & Feltes, H. P. M. (1999). *Pragmática e cognição: A textualidade pela relevância e outros ensaios* (2nd ed.). Porto Alegre, Brazil: Edipucrs.

Simoni, R. M. S. (2004). *Uma caracterização do gênero carta-consulta nos jornais O Globo e Folha de S. Paulo.* Unpublished master's thesis, University of Southern Santa Catarina, Tubarão, Santa Catarina, Brazil.

Sperber, D., & Wilson, D. (1986). *Relevance: Communication & cognition.* Oxford: Blackwell.

Sperber, D., & Wilson, D. (1995). *Relevance: Communication & cognition* (2nd ed.). Oxford: Blackwell.

Swales, J. M. (1990). *Genre analysis: English in academic and research settings.* New York: Cambridge University Press.

Swales, J. M. (1992). Re-thinking genre: Another look at discourse community effects. In J. M. Swales, *Re-thinking genre colloquium.* Ottawa, Ontario, Canada: Carleton University.

Swales, J. M. (1998). *Other floors, other voices: A textography of a small university building.* Mahwah, New Jersey: Erlbaum.

Wilson, D. (2004). *Pragmatic Theory.* Retrieved March 15, 2005, from University College London, Linguistics Department: http://www.phon.ucl.ac.uk/home/nick/pragtheory/

GENRE AND THE PROFESSIONS

Accusation and Defense: The
Ideational Metafunction of Language
in the Genre Closing Argument

Cristiane Fuzer
Nina Célia Barros

INTRODUCTION[1]

"Few professions are as concerned with language as is the law." This idea from Tiersma (1993) may help us to understand the growing interest of legal professionals in the study of language, as well as the interest of linguists in the investigation of the language used in legal contexts. The complexity and technicality of the legal language presents a challenge to those involved with the education of legal practitioners. For this reason, a new branch of linguistics, which specializes in the study of legal language, has been growing lately: Forensic Linguistics. Its theorizations and practical applications indicate that linguists may contribute positively to the interpretation of laws and legal procedures. According to Gibbons (2003, p. 69), "whatever the technique used, the linguist would clarify and make more concrete and explicit the basis for [judicial] deciding, and in some cases might provide useful additional information."

There are researchers who are concerned with understanding the functioning of legal language and its technicalities as a way of familiarizing the ordinary citizen with legal practices that concern, in one way or another, all of us. In this sense, Rodrigues (2005, p. 20) argues that "if (almost) all aspects of our life in society are guided by rules, that is, organized in legal terms, it is urgent that we pay some attention to the analysis of this language which defines and structures our behaviors."

In this study, we intend to join this field of research,[2] searching for a better understanding of the functioning of legal practices and the ways social actors involved in criminal proceedings in the Brazilian context are represented in written texts.

Legal proceedings are crucial instruments in the judicial exercise and have the objective, according to Capez (2005), of providing an adequate solution for the conflict of interests between the State and the transgressor by following a specific sequence of acts: the elaboration of the accusation, the production of proof, the defense and the public accusation. The criminal proceedings, therefore, are defined as "a series or sequence of acts that are carried out and developed across a period of time, with the purpose of penal law application in the concrete case" (Capez, 2005, p. 527).

Criminal proceedings have the objective of judging different types of crimes, such as crimes against life (attempted and completed), against customs, against someone's physical and psychological integrity, against freedom, against properties (attempted or completed), against honor, against the affiliation to the State, etc. (Brasil, 1940). The crimes against life, in the Brazilian Penal Code (Brasil, 1940), are typified as: homicide, "when the agent wanted the result or assumed the risk of producing it" (art. 121); "the inducement, instigation or help to commit suicide" (art. 122); infanticide, "[for a woman] to kill, under the influence of the puerperal state, her own son/daughter, during the delivery or immediately after" (art. 123); abortion, either provoked by the pregnant woman, or with her consent (art. 124); or provoked by a third person (art. 125).

The proceedings of the Brazilian criminal justice system are based on the accusatory system, in which one party accuses, another defends and a third party judges. The accuser or prosecutor (who represents the State) and the defense (who represents the defendant) are situated at the same equity level; the representative who judges (the judge) keeps him/herself equally distant from both parties (Capez, 2005).

The Criminal Procedure Code (Brasil, 1941) is the law that rules who can or should take certain actions, allegations and decisions, for how long and in which place, and indicates what are the correct sequence of actions during the criminal proceedings. The Penal Code (Brasil, 1940) is the law that defines the types of crimes and establishes the penalties to be applied to their perpetrators.

In this essay we investigate the representation produced by the accusation and the defense in a type of text which instantiates one of the genres that is part of the judicial proceedings: the closing argument. The public prosecutor and the defense attorney in the genre of final arguments create different characterizations of actors to enlist the court in various representations of truth. The analysis has implications both for how we understand the realities created by various genres and the importance of those genres in creating institutional outcomes of material consequence in lives and social relations.

To do this, we will use the concepts of Systemic-Functional Grammar (SFG), described by Halliday & Matthiessen (2004), to characterize what grammatical roles are fulfilled by the accuser (public prosecutor) and by the defender (defense attorney). We will also use the categories proposed by van Leeuwen (1997) to verify how these social actors (public prosecutor and defense attorney) are represented, respectively, in the accusation and defense discourses at the sociosemantic level. After the presentation of the methodological guidelines, we will move to the description and analysis of the accusation and defense representations built in a closing argument that integrates a criminal case tried at the jurisdiction of Santa Maria, Rio Grande do Sul, Brazil, which followed the legal channels from 1997 to 2002.

CONTEXTUALIZING THE GENRE CLOSING ARGUMENT

Many of the activities that organize human society are only made possible through language. Bakhtin (2003) claimed that people, when communicating verbally, select the words according to the specific aspects of the genre they are participating in; certain types of utterances are generated by certain functions (scientific, technical, official, of the daily life, etc.) and by some conditions of communication, specific to each field.

These elements are revisited as foundations for the genre analysis currently developed by many authors, such as Meurer & Motta-Roth (2002). They claim that the awareness of these three aspects—what is said, who is saying it and how it is said—makes it possible for individuals to articulate themselves through the use of language so that they can reach their objectives through appropriating and expanding upon the relevant genres which are available in their culture.

This perspective is common to three theoretical approaches that focus on genre analysis: Australian Genre Theory, English for Specific Purposes (ESP) and Studies on New Rhetoric.[3]

For the researchers who work with Australian Genre Theory, as Christie and Martin (1997), language is considered a system of choices through which the speakers/writers may express their world experiences, interact with others and elaborate coherent messages in specific contexts. This conception is centered on the Systemic-Functional Linguistics developed by Halliday, who founded the Linguistics Department of the University of Sidney in 1975 and has had great influence on language theory and education in Australia. In this approach, emphasis is given to global text structure and characteristics at the clause level, associated with the field (the activity involved), the relation among the participants, and the manner (the communication channel) of the discursive event. Genres are seen, thus, as social processes directed to a purpose, structural forms that cultures utilize in certain contexts with the aim of achieving different objectives. People communicate using genres that provide expectations about a text (Hyon, 1996).

In the area of ESP, scholars such as Swales (1990) and Bhatia (1993) explore notions of dialogism and situations suitable for the utilization of a genre by one authorized participant. The focus of these scholars is more directed towards the knowledge of the text structure belonging to a genre than to the social aspects of the genre (Hyland, 2004). The objective is to explain how individuals can demonstrate their skills and abilities as members of groups they participate in. Therefore, genres are defined as "communicative events" characterized "by their communicative purposes and by their different patterns, structure, style, content and audience" (Swales, 1990, p. 58).

To explain how social contexts and how written and spoken texts come together to constitute social practices, ESP scholars have been adopting the notion of "genre systems" in relatively fixed sequences, originally discussed by Devitt (1991) and Bazerman (2004), who are followers of the New Rhetoric perspective. For Bazerman (2004) and Miller (1984, 1994), genres may incorporate interests and values of a particular social group and reinforce social rules and relations between writers and readers. This perspective is more directed at the social aspects of communities and less focused on text forms. Therefore, to understand the meanings of a text it is necessary to understand the relationship[4] between the participants of the social event of which the text is part. In this sense, the text is seen as a discourse that incorporates "speech acts," based on the theories of the philosophers John Austin and John Searle. The speech act (the text) is the result of words said in the appropriate time, the appropriate circumstances and by the appropriate person. According to Bazerman (2004, p. 316), "one way we can help coordinate our speech acts with each other is to act in typical ways, ways easily recognized as accomplishing certain acts in certain circumstances."

Within social groups, relatively stable patterns emerge as recognizable, familiar genres, seen as answers to recurrent social situations. Genres are, therefore, part of socially organized activities; they are part of the way human beings give form to social activities (Bazerman, 2004). For Miller (1984), comprehending genres under a social approach may help to explain how people find, interpret, react and create certain texts.

The collection of types of texts produced by the individual when performing a particular activity corresponds to what Bazerman (2004) denominates a set of genres. This set gathers all the genres used by an agent to exert his/her role in the group in which he/she participates. One may say that the set of genres used by a lawyer, for example, may include: power of attorney, petition, closing argument, etc.

The different sets of genres used by people who work together in an organized way (if one considers the patterned relations established in the production, flow and use of texts) are part of a system of genres. In a system of genres, the genre sets are linked and circulate in predictable temporal sequences and patterns. Therefore, the genre sets used by a lawyer, for example, will integrate the genre system used by the criminal institution. In this system, sets of genres produced

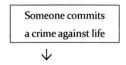

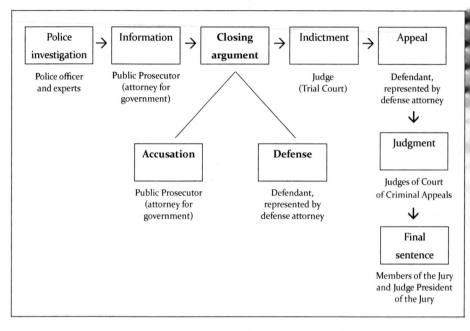

FIGURE 1: SYSTEM OF MAIN GENRES OF BRAZILIAN CRIMINAL PROCEEDINGS AND THEIR MAIN ACTORS

by other professionals (prosecutors [MP][5], police officers, justice clerks, judges) will be, in some ways, related (the inquiry report produced by the chief of police, for example, will serve as basis for the accusation text and, later, for the closing argument).

To locate the place of the genre closing argument in the Brazilian criminal proceedings, Figure 1 shows the sequence (in chronological order) of activities carried out by the social actors of the main genres that comprise the criminal proceedings. We also present the social actors who participate in each stage of the referred proceedings.

In the Brazilian legal system, after the police investigation (in which the author of the crime is charged) and the indictment, the parties present the closing argument. This genre is used in the instructional stage of the criminal proceedings, before the dispatch of the first judge's sentence[6] and, therefore, before directing the case to a jury trial. In the text, the parties should present all their considerations, report the facts in detail, and describe what happened from the opening of the police inquiry to the moment of the closing argument. According to Pimenta (2007), it is in this text that the legal argumentation operates well, once the parties have used all possible means to convince the judge of the "truth" of their versions of the facts, searching to influence the judge in his decision. In comparison to the other legal genres, the argument text (especially the defense one) is longer than the others.

The basic function of the closing argument is to request the defendant's conviction or acquittal and/or the reduction of the sentence. The parties should construct their thesis (of accusation and defense) according to the types of crimes defined by the Penal Code, because penalties will be applied according to this classification. The judge decides which request from the parties is more valid, taking into account their arguments. In the judicial proceedings analyzed in this article (the trial of a woman accused of killing her own son during delivery), the accusation claims that this was a homicide (in which there was the intention to murder); however, the defense argues that it was an involuntary manslaughter (no murder intention) or an infanticide (murder under the influence of the postpartum depression).

To determine how the roles of prosecutor and defense attorney are represented in a text that instantiates the genre closing argument in judicial proceedings, we studied the grammatical (Halliday & Matthiessen, 2004) and the semantic-social roles (van Leeuwen, 1997) attributed to these social actors in the discourse.

METHODOLOGICAL GUIDELINES

To identify the representation of the accusation and defense in texts that instantiate the closing argument genre, we carried out a qualitative analysis of the clauses in which the social actors public prosecutor and defense attorney participate. The texts are part of the judicial proceedings of the 1st Criminal Jurisdiction from the District Court of Santa Maria-RS, Brasil, in a case tried between 1997 and 2000. The judicial proceedings deal with a case of infanticide (later disqualified to homicide) which consists of "killing [performed by a woman], under the influence of the puerperal state, her own son/daughter during delivery or immediately after" (Brasil, 1940, Penal Code, art. 123).

The following guiding questions were raised:

(a) In which clauses do these social actors perform the acts of accusation and defense?

(b) How are these social actors represented according to the transitivity system?

SOCIAL ACTORS	INCLUDED	BACKGROUNDED
Public Prosecutor (N = 14)	35%	65%
Defense attorney (N = 15)	40%	60%
Other legal practitioners (judge, police officers, experts) (N = 20)	15%	85%
Defendant (N = 32)	68%	32%
Victim (N = 23)	78%	22%

TABLE 1: INCLUSION AND EXCLUSION BY BACKGROUNDING OF THE SOCIAL ACTORS REPRESENTED IN THE TWO TEXTS WHICH INSTANTIATE THE CLOSING ARGUMENT GENRE IN CRIMINAL PROCEEDINGS[7]

To delineate the answers to these questions, we started the analysis by identifying in which clauses the social actors of accusation and defense have been included and/or backgrounded, and then the verbal processes performed by these social actors. In Table 1, we introduce the terms used in the texts to refer to the social actors of accusation and defense and the ways they were represented. Discursive representations may include or exclude social actors according to their interests and purposes in relation to the audience to whom they are addressed. When there is no reference to the social actor in any part of the text, a process of exclusion is carried out by suppression. On the other hand, it is possible to exclude the social actor only partially, leaving it in the background, that is, it is excluded in relation to a given activity, but is mentioned somewhere else in the text and may be inferred by the reader (van Leeuwen, 1997).

As we can see in Table 1, the social actors most frequently included in the closing argument, both by the defense and the accusation, are the defendant and the victim. The social actors most frequently backgrounded are the legal practitioners. In the following section, we will describe and analyze the ways the social actors that perform the acts of accusation and defense are represented.

DESCRIPTION AND ANALYSIS

Starting with the classification of the clause components (participants, processes and circumstances) it is possible to recognize in which of them the representatives of the State (public prosecutor) and the defense (defense attorney) participate. We apply this analysis to the closing arguments in this section.

Representation of the accusation

In the closing argument produced by the accusation, the district attorney's office appears as Actor in processes related to the legal activity, as we can see in the clauses that open and close the text, respectively:

> *A PROMOTORIA DE JUSTIÇA* **ofereceu** *denúncia contra XXX* . . . .
> THE DISTRICT ATTORNEY'S OFFICE **has offered** accusation against XXX . . . .

> *ANTE O EXPOSTO,* <u>*a Promotoria de Justiça*</u> **requer** *a procedência parcial da denúncia* . . . .
> IN THE FACE OF THE EVIDENCE, <u>the District Attorney's Office</u> **requests** the partial granting of the indictment . . . .

In the first fragment, the district attorney engages in the process of "offering an accusation." The action of offering, more than to give or propose something, in the context of the criminal justice system, denounces somebody to the judicial institution. We can therefore classify "has offered" as a material process in this context.

In the second fragment, the process "requests" may generate different interpretations depending on the approach that the analyst adopts to study the text. It may at first be considered a mental process, expressing a desire. However, in the legal context, "to request" does not refer only to internal experiences in the world of consciousness of the text's author; rather, it builds the representation of a specific legal action performed by the district attorney's office in any text related to the genre closing argument. By the way, to request is a typical practice of this genre (the same is observed in the defense context). Therefore, it is possible to classify "to request," in the genre closing argument, as a material process.

In both fragments, the Actor is explicit, that is, the district attorney is represented as the agent of the legal activities by means of, in the terms of van Leeuwen's (1997) taxonomy, Inclusion by activation. This way of representing the accusation occurs only in the opening of the closing argument (in which the prosecutor's main activity is mentioned—to denounce) and in its closing (in which requests are directed to the judge—in this case, to indict the defendant).

Besides activation, it is possible to observe other categories of the public prosecutor's representation included in the discourse. The personalization of this social actor occurs only once, at the final part of the text, by means of nomination and functionalization, when the public prosecutor's signature is registered. In the other two times in which the prosecutor is included (in the first and last paragraph), as Actor and Senser (main participants of material and mental processes), according to Halliday's (2004) system of transitivity, this social actor is represented through reference to its institution ("attorney's office").

In the other passages, exclusion mechanisms backgrounding the social actor are used, since there are no marks of the district attorney's representation, with little visibility of the agent (van Leeuwen, 1997) of the accusation. This occurs in:

> . . . *Sem maiores detalhamentos da prova, basta* **ser salientado** *que a ré escondia a gravidez e logo após a morte do filho, também escondeu-lhe o cadáver* . . . .
> . . . Without more details about the proof, it is enough **to be stressed** that the defendant hid the pregnancy and immediately after her son's death, also hid the corpse . . . .

By means of the deletion of the passive agent, it is from the background that the prosecutor participates in the process of emphasizing certain actions practiced by the accused. This way, a saying that does not belong exclusively to the prosecutor (**to stress**) is built. The role of Sayer could be fulfilled either by the prosecutor or by the judge (to whom the text is directed initially) or by anyone familiar with the case. With this, a subtle co-participation is created for the reader, thus making the utterance part of a consensus.

Following the first clause ("Without more details about the proof"), the nominalization also operates as a mechanism for the backgrounding of the social actor "public prosecutor." This form of exclusion, associated with the idea of dispensing further proof, indicates that the proof will be neither further examined nor contested.

Exclusion by backgrounding is also observed in mental process clauses, as we can see in the fragments below:

> . . . *também escondeu-lhe o cadáver, para* **se concluir** *que o alegado proceder culposo não encontra respaldo seguro no contexto probatório e fático,* **podendo-se** *facilmente* **concluir** *ao contrário, ou seja, que, em vistas das circunstâncias apontadas, tenha agido com dolo direto de matar.*
> . . . also hid his corpse, **which allows one to conclude** that the alleged involuntary conduct is not supported safely in the probatory

and factic contexts, **making it** safe to **conclude** the contrary, that is, that, due to the circumstances pointed out, she had acted with intent to kill.

> . . . *as lesões provocadas, como se vê de fls. 48 e 49, são indicativos de padecimento intenso da vítima . . . .*
> . . . the provoked lesions, **as can be seen** on pages 48 and 49, indicate the intense suffering of the victim . . . .

Again the deletion of the agent leaves open who would be the social actors fulfilling the role of Senser of these mental processes (**allows one to conclude; being safe to conclude; can be seen**). In reality, these conclusions are drawn by the prosecutor, but it is not this that is represented discursively. Who concluded that the defendant had acted voluntarily? The judge, the prosecutor, the defense attorney, the jury—any of these social actors could have done it. When the public prosecutor builds this representation, he takes for granted that everyone will come to the same conclusion, that is, will accept the conclusion that he himself arrived at. This form of backgrounding that operates as an argumentative strategy for the thesis support is also used in the defense's closing argument (see section 4.2).

Besides the prosecutor, other social actors from the legal institution are represented in the text, as can be observed in these examples:

> Materialidade comprovada <u>pelo auto de fl. 10 e fotos de fls. 48/50</u>
> . . . .
> Materiality proved by <u>the proceedings on page 10 and pictures of pages 48/50</u> . . . .

> . . . <u>o alegado proceder culposo</u> não encontra respaldo seguro no contexto probatório e fático . . . .
> . . . <u>the alleged involuntary behavior</u> is not safely supported in the probatory and factic context . . . .

> *ANTE O EXPOSTO, a Promotoria de Justiça requer a procedência parcial da denúncia, para **pronunciar** a ré nos termos da inicial . . . .*
> DUE TO THE EXPOSED FACTS, the district attorney's office requests the partial granting of the accusation, **to indict** the defendant in the terms of the initial request . . . .

In the first fragment, "the proceedings on page 10 and pictures on pages

48/50" are Actors of the material process to prove. The "proceedings on page 10" correspond to the record of the necropsy, written by the medical experts who examined the body and attested the circumstances of death. The "pictures on pages 48/50" correspond to the photographic register done by the police officers who went to the crime scene. In both cases, these social actors are impersonalized, referred to neither by their names nor by their functions, but only by the pages in which the results of their activities (a medical report, photos) are found. Using van Leeuwen's (1997) terms, we may classify this representation as objectivation of the social actors by means of utterance autonomization. In this category, the social actor is represented by metonymic reference to his/her utterance—in these cases, texts that instantiate other genres integrating the judicial proceedings in which the utterances are found. Therefore, it is only possible to know who the referred actors are through recourse to these texts.

In the second fragment, although there is no indication of localization in the judicial proceedings, it is possible to infer that the Carrier of "the alleged involuntarily behavior" is related to the defense utterance. This can be explained by taking into consideration the classification given to the crime by the parties: for the accusation it is murder; for the defense, involuntary manslaughter or infanticide. Therefore, "the alleged involuntarily behavior" is a nominalization of the saying and requesting activity performed by the defendant's lawyer.

In the third fragment, there is the exclusion by backgrounding of the judge in the second clause ("to indict the defendant"). It is possible to infer that the judge is the Actor of the material process "to indict" because, in the Brazilian legal context, only the judge has the right to indict a defendant.

The examples analyzed above illustrate some of the ways by which the prosecutor represents himself in his closing argument text and how he represents other social actors involved in the criminal proceedings.

Representation of the defense

The closing argument by the defense has a particularity in relation to the accusation. While the accusatory discourse is built by a social actor—the prosecutor—the defense discourse is represented as if it were built by the defendant herself, as it is shown in the analysis of the transitivity of the clauses that are part of the first and the last paragraph of the text:

> *MATILDA, qualificada nos autos,* **vem** *perante V. Exa., por intermédio de seu defensor firmatário, no prazo do art. 406 do CPP,* **dizer** *e* **requerer** *o seguinte . . . .*
> MATILDA, qualified in the proceedings, **comes** before Your Excellency, through her authorized defense attorney, within the time

limits of art. 406 of the Criminal Procedures Code, **to say** and **request** the following . . . .

*POR TODO O EXPOSTO, **requer*** . . . .
DUE TO ALL THE EXPOSED, [she] **requests** . . . .

*N. Termos, P. [**Pede**] Deferimento.*
In these Terms, [she] A. [**Asks**] her request to be granted.

In the clause that introduces the text, "MATILDA" (the defendant) is represented as the Actor of "comes to say and request." In the same way, at the closing of the text the defendant is again the Actor of the processes "requests" and "asks" (considered material processes due to the same reasons specified in the analysis of "request" earlier). This strategy creates the idea that the defendant is the author of all that is being said and requested in the text.

However, in other passages there are marks of representation of the defense attorney as the real text author, as in:

*A defesa, por sua vez, **entende** que a ré deve responder por homicídio culposo, diante da circunstância do fato* . . . .
The defense, on its turn, **understands** that the defendant should be indicted for involuntary manslaughter, due to the circumstances of the fact . . . .

In this fragment, the defense attorney (who had already been represented in the introduction as the defendant's "authorized defense attorney") signals his participation as Senser of the mental process "**understands**," which projects the clause as Phenomenon. From this point on, the defendant is represented only as the author of a crime (who "should be indicted for involuntary manslaughter"). During the text development, the social actor who performs the legal activity of defense is the lawyer. This also takes place in other passages:

. . . *Assim sendo, a defesa **entende** que deve ser operada a desclassificação para homicídio culposo* . . . .
. . . Therefore, the defense **understands** that [the charges] should be disqualified to involuntary manslaughter . . . .

. . . *Apenas para **argumentar**, caso este juízo entenda em mandar a ré a júri popular pelo homicídio doloso, **entende** a defesa que deve ser afastada a qualificadora da crueldade, isto porque a ré não poderia,*

> *dentro do contexto, de querer ser cruel, de querer fazer a vítima (seu filho recém-nascido) padecer de sofrimento desnecessário . . . .*
>
> . . . Only **for argument's sake**, in case this court decides to try the defendant for homicide before a jury, the defense **understands** that the aggravating factor of cruelty should be left aside, because the defendant could not, in this context, have wanted to be cruel, have wanted to make the victim (her newborn child) undergo unnecessary suffering . . . .

Bearing in mind the description of the sociosemantic roles, one may say that, in the three fragments mentioned, the defense is represented by means of inclusion through activation (van Leeuwen, 1997).

Exclusion by backgrounding, as has occurred in the accusation's closing argument, is also observed in the defense's final argument:

> . . . ***Note-se*** *que em ambas as situações há necessidade da vontade livre e consciente de produzir o resultado morte . . . .*
>
> . . . **It should be noted** that in both situations there is the need of a free and conscious will of causing the death . . . .

> . . . *De outra banda,* ***deve-se examinar*** *a hipótese da ocorrência do delito de infanticídio . . . .*
>
> . . . On the other hand**,** the hypothesis of the crime of infanticide **should be examined** . . . .

The deletion of the passive agents makes it possible for the role of Senser of the mental processes "to notice" and "to examine" to be fulfilled either by the defense attorney, or by other social actors who had access to the text. If the participant had been made explicit (noted/examined "by the defense," "by the prosecutor" or "by the judge"), the agency would be defined and, thus, the ambiguity of meaning would have been avoided. So, at the same time that the agents of the mental processes are excluded, there are openings, in the reading context, for involving other social actors.

In another passage, this ambiguity of agency is softened, and the engaging effect is evident:

> *O comportamento de MATILDA, como já* ***vimos****, não revela que queria matar seu filho recém-nascido ou que assumiu o risco de produzir o resultado morte.*
>
> The behavior of MATILDA, as we **have** already **seen**, does not

reveal that she wanted to kill her newborn son or that she assumed the risk of causing his death.

In the clause "as we have already seen," the Senser is "we," which includes necessarily the utterer, besides other agents inserted in the legal proceedings. The defendant is excluded from this mental process, since she appears as participant of another clause, in which she is represented as agent of mental processes related to the intention to kill (wanted to kill; assumed the risk of causing his death). This way, the defendant is represented as someone who does not understand, does not observe, does not perceive the meaning of her actions; she is merely represented as someone who murdered somebody. This denies the impression, created at the opening of the text, that the defendant was speaking for herself, and had come "to say and request" things in her own defense. The one who really performs those actions, semantically speaking, is the lawyer.

Another typical feature of the closing argument, as a resource to appeal to the judge, is that the activities related to the decision are represented with the deletion of their agents, as it is indicated in the processes underlined in the following fragments:

> *Mandar a ré a julgamento popular por homicídio doloso é entender que a mesma agiu com dolo, ou seja, queria matar ou assumiu o risco de matar.*
> To send the defendant to a trial by jury for homicide **is** to consider that she has acted with malice, that she wanted to kill or assumed the risk of killing.

> *A qualificadora **deve ser afastada**.*
> The aggravating circumstance **should be dismissed**.

> *POR TODO O EXPOSTO, requer:*
> (1) **Seja operada** *a desclassificação para HOMICÍDIO CULPOSO, pois a ré não queria matar e nem assumiu o risco de matar seu filho recém-nascido . . . .*
> DUE TO ALL THE EXPOSED, [we] request:
> (1) That the charge **should be disqualified** to INVOLUNTARY MANSLAUGHTER, because the defendant did not want to kill and neither assumed the risk of killing her newborn son . . . .

In the first fragment, through the infinitive clause "To send the defendant to a trial by jury for homicide," an action that can only be executed by the judge is mentioned, in case he decides to classify the crime as homicide (thus granting the prosecutor's request). When the action of a social actor is transformed into a grammatical participant, the agent (in this case, the judge) is excluded by backgrounding.

This same way of representing judicial actions occurs in the other two fragments. By means of passivation without agent, the social actor whose role is to dismiss the aggravating circumstance and to operate the disqualification of the crime is pushed into the background, even though anyone familiar with criminal legal proceedings knows that such social actor can only be the judge.

FINAL COMMENTS

The analysis of the grammatical and sociosemantic roles present in the genre closing argument, part of the process which begins with the indictment and precedes the sentence, has shown how the social actors involved in judicial proceedings are represented in this specific genre.

Both the accuser and the defense lawyer are represented in active form as petitioners who operate in opposition. While the first requires that the accused person be indicted (judged by a jury), the second requires that the crime be classified as one of the types for which the law accepts attenuating circumstances and, consequently, gives more lenient penalties. This is one of the typical characteristics of the genre closing argument, that is, by means of this genre the activity of requiring something from the Court in the instructional phase of the criminal proceedings is performed.

In the case of the defense, there is a particularity as to the authorship of the text. In the introduction, the role of the Actor of the process "to require" is fulfilled by the accused person, as if she assumed the legal role of defending herself. However, as the text develops, she is only Actor of the processes related to the crime committed, while the processes related to the argument that are the basis for the initial request have as their agent the defense attorney. With this, the text creates, at its opening, the fiction that the accused presents her defense to the Court, but, at the same time, there are linguistic indications that the lawyer is the real utterer of the argument. After all, is the one who alleges something in a legal defense the accused or her lawyer? The effect of this ambiguity seems to bring the accused woman closer to the judge who is reading the request, which in a certain form contributes to the representation of the trial as a humane—and not solely a bureaucratic—process.

However, along the text, when the lawyer is represented as Actor, discursively he assumes his role instituted by the law. Therefore, the larger occurrence of representations of the defense attorney as the one who "understands" and "argues" makes this professional the main agent in the activities mentioned, leaving to the accused the role of author of a crime, not as a Sayer. So, in the closing argument the defendant has no voice, and all the things her accuser and defense attorney alleged about her are represented as facts, as the truth.

This analysis points out another characteristic of the genre closing argument: the use of exclusion by backgrounding of the main social actors due to the fact that it is assumed that the readers (especially the judge, the text's addressee) already know who these actors are. This strategy also avoids the identification of the legal practitioners involved in the trial, who are represented, when included, in an impersonal manner. While these actors are represented mainly by reference to their functionalization ("prosecutor," "district attorney's office," "defense attorney," "defense," "court," etc.), the defendant is represented generally by nomination (proper name) and categorization ("defendant," "accused").

In other genres present in judicial proceedings various linguistic means besides the name personalize the accused person with a unique identity. Legal practitioners, on the other hand, are rarely identified in detail, which, as it was observed by van Leeuwen (1997) in reference to bureaucratic language, backgrounds the responsibility for human activities "governed by impersonal procedures which, once put in place, are well-nigh impermeable to human agency" (p. 60).

The high representation of the defendant, coupled with the low inclusion of legal practitioners, emphasizes the role of the accused in the text, backgrounding the responsibility of the legal representatives. These social actors, when made explicit, are agents only of processes related to typical legal activities. In other words, the social actors of the
law do not act by themselves, they act in the name of their institution.

NOTES

[1] This paper integrates the doctoral thesis of the first author, developed at the Graduate Program in Languages and Linguistics of UFSM, with the support of CAPES (Coordination for the Improvement of Higher Education), under the supervision of the second author. We wish to thank Prof. Dr. Carlos Gouveia, from graduate program at Faculdade de Letras of the University of Lisbon (FLUL), for his contributions. We also thank Luciane Ticks and Sara Scotta Cabral for their readings and suggestions, and Vera Maria Xavier dos Santos for helping to review the text.

[2] Bhatia (1993, 1994), Cotterill (1992), Coulthard (1992, 2005a, 2005b), Eagleson (1994), Figueiredo (2004), Gibbons (2003), Goodrich (1987), Pimenta & Fuzer (2007), Shuy (1993), Tiersma (1993, 1999), among others.

³ For a more detailed comparative description of the three approaches, see Hyon (1996) and Hyland (2004).

⁴ According to Hyland (2004), when this relation is complex, many individuals may be excluded from the genres which comprise the social event (and this happens with some frequency in relation to the genres typical of the legal interaction).

⁵ MP (*Ministério Público*) is the acronym for the Brazilian Department of Justice, which is represented in the criminal proceedings by a district attorney (public prosecutor). This legal practitioner should examine the inquisition report (the text in which the police officers that investigated the case narrate the facts) and decide whether or not to criminalize the charges, if he/she understands that the materiality of the crime is proven and that there are clues that identifying somebody has committed, which requires eight testimonies (Oliveira, 2005).

⁶ Taking the closing argument as basis, the judge indicts the defendant. In a district court seven members representing the society compose the jury (Capez, 2005).

⁷ N corresponds to the number of occurrences of the social actor's participation in the two texts.

REFERENCES

Alcântara, H. R. (2006). *Perícia médica judicial* (2nd ed.). Rio de Janeiro: Guanabara Koogan.

Bakhtin, M. (2003). *Estética da criação verbal*. São Paulo: Martins Fontes.

Bazerman, C. (2004). Speech acts, genres, and activity systems: How texts organize activity and people. In C. Bazerman & P. Prior (Eds.), *What writing does and how it does it: An introduction to analyzing texts and textual practices* (pp. 309-337). Mahwah, New Jersey: Erlbaum.

Bhatia, V. K. (1993). *Analysing genre: Language use in professional settings*. Harlow: Longman.

Bhatia, V. K. (1994). Cognitive structuring in legislative provisions. In J. Gibbons (Ed.), *Language and the law* (pp. 136-155). London: Longman.

Brasil. (1940). *Presidência da República, código penal, decreto-lei n. 2.848, December 7, 1940*. Retrieved April 24, 2005, from http://www.planalto.gov.br/CCIVIL/Decreto-Lei/Del3689.htm

Brasil. (1941). *Presidência da República, código de processo penal, decreto-lei n. 3.689, October 3, 1941*. Retrieved April 10, 2005, from http://www.planalto.gov.br/CCIVIL/Decreto-Lei/Del2848.htm

Capez, F. (2005). *Curso de processo penal* (12th ed.). São Paulo: Saraiva.

Christie, F., & Martin, J. (1997). *Genre and institutions*. London: Continuum.

Cotterill, J. (2002). *Language in the legal process*. Hampshire, United Kingdom:

Palgrave.

Coulthard, M. (1992). Forensic discourse analysis. In R. M. Coulthard (Ed.), *Advances in spoken discourse analysis* (pp. 242-257). London: Routledge.

Coulthard, M. (2005a). *Some forensic applications of descriptive linguistics.* Retrieved October 14, 2007, from http://www.aston.ac.uk/lss/staff/profile/coulthardm.jsp

Coulthard, M. (2005b). *The linguist as expert witness.* Retrieved October 12, 2007, from http://www.aston.ac.uk/lss/staff/profile/coulthardm.jsp

Devitt, A. J. (1991). Intertextuality in tax accouting. In C. Bazerman & J. Paradis (Eds.), *Textual dynamics of the professions* (pp. 336-357). Madison: University of Wisconsin Press.

Eagleson, R. D. (1994). Forensic analysis of personal written text: A case study. In J. Gibbons (Ed.), *Language and the law* (pp. 362-373). London: Longman.

Figueiredo, D. C. (2002). Vítimas e vilãs, monstros e desesperados: Como o discurso judicial representa os participantes de um crime de estupro. *Linguagem em (Dis)curso, 3,* 135-156.

Figueiredo, D. C. (2004). Violência sexual e controle legal: Uma análise crítica de três extratos de sentenças em casos de violência contra a mulher [Special issue]. *Linguagem em (Dis)curso, 4.*

Gibbons, J. (2003). *Forensic linguistic: An introduction to language in the justice system.* London: Blackwell.

Goodrich, P. (1987). *Legal discourse.* London: Macmillan.

Halliday, M., & Matthiessen, C.M.I. (2004). *An introduction to functional grammar* (3rd ed.). London: Arnold.

Hyland, K. (2004). *Genre and second language writing.* Ann Arbor: University of Michigan Press.

Hyon, S. (1996). Genre in three traditions: Implications for ESL. *Tesol Quartely, 30*(4), 693-722.

Martin, J., & Rose, D. (2003). *Working with discourse: Meaning beyond the clause.* London: Continuum.

Meurer, J. L., Bonini, A., & Motta-Roth, D. (Eds.). (2005). *Gêneros: Teorias, métodos e debates.* São Paulo: Parábola.

Miller, C. (1984). Genre as social action. *Quaterly Journal of Speech, 70,* 151-167.

Miller, C. (1994). Rhetorical community: The cultural basis of genre. In A. Freedman & P. Medway (Eds.), *Genre and the new rhetoric* (pp. 67-68). London: Tylor & Francis.

Oliveira, M.V.A. (2005). *O julgamento em plenário do Júri Popular.* Retrieved April 15, 2005, from http://www1.jus.com.br/doutrina/texto.asp?id-1070

Pimenta, V.R. (2007). *Textos forenses: Um estudo de seus gêneros textuais e sua relevância para o gênero "sentença."* Unpublished doctoral dissertation, Federal

University of Uberlândia, Uberlândia, Minas Gerais, Brazil.

Pimenta, V.R., & Fuzer, C. (2007). O direito positivo brasileiro e suas heterotopias: mas esta é uma questão lingüística? *Proceedings of Seminário Internacional em Letras, Santa Maria, Brazil, 2007.*

Rodrigues, C.C.C. (2005). *Contributos para a análise da linguagem jurídica e da interacção verbal na sala de audiências.* Unpublished doctoral thesis, University of Coimbra, Coimbra, Portugal.

Shuy, R. (1993). *Language crimes: The use and abuse of language evidence in the courtroom.* Cambridge: Blackwell.

Swales, J. (1990). *Genre analysis: English in academic and research settings.* Cambridge: Cambridge University Press.

Tiersma, P.M. (1993). Linguistic issues in the law. *Language, 69,* 113-137.

Tiersma, P.M. (1999). *Legal language.* Chicago: University of Chicago Press.

Van Leeuwen, T. (1997). The representation of social actors. In C.R. Caldas-Coulthard & M. Coulthard (Eds.), *Texts and practices: Readings in critical discourse analysis.* London: Routledge.

6   The Sociohistorical Constitution of the Genre *Legal Booklet:* A Critical Approach

Leonardo Mozdzenski

INTRODUCTION[1]

This study aims at investigating the sociohistorical path of the Brazilian legal booklet (layman's law guide), from the appearance and propagation of those genres that contributed to its formation until the development of current educational booklets which explain law to layman readers. To fulfill this objective, we will observe three major historical and social events which influenced the development of this genre until it assumed its present form. First of all, however, it is important to clarify what "legal booklet" stands for, as well as which hypothesis could be applied to the comprehension and study of this genre.

Despite the countless possibilities of materialization, nowadays legal booklets can be understood as participants of the discursive constellation of *educational* or *informative booklets*, defined by Mendonça (2004, p. 1,278) as publications "destined to inform the population about their rights, duties, and the ways to prevent diseases, accidents, etc. They can mix comic book narratives and didactic and/or informative texts, and are part of the material of institutional advertising campaigns."

Starting from the theoretical framework first elaborated by Swales (1990) and later improved by Bhatia (1993), Gomes (2003, pp. 158-159) distinguishes four characteristics regarding the genre *educational booklet*:

(1) The communicative purpose which conducts this event is to explain, to teach and to instruct those who are interested in or affected by unknown, or even unavailable, social actions and practices.

(2) The genre "booklet" is a sociopolitical instrument, because it not only tries to describe and convey certain questions to the individuals, but also tries to turn them into citizens who are aware of their actions and the actions of others. These individuals are informed about the facts surrounding them so they can demand or approve of their rights.

(3) Booklets perform tutorial functions, for they instruct and explain how individuals must proceed and act as they confront specific issues.

(4) Finally, the fact is that booklets have not only the communicative purposes of informing and teaching, but mainly those of instructing, ordaining,

and recommending through precise, prescriptive orientations.

This last aspect of educational booklets—crucial for our sociohistorical critical analysis—can be related to the notion of genre as a "system of social coercion" proposed by Marcuschi (2003), based on the reflections of Fairclough (2001). As Marcuschi (2003, p. 2) asserts, "genres are socially stabilized discursive activities which operate the most varied types of social control and even the exercise of power. In a succinct formulation, I would say that genres are our way of social insertion, action and control."

So, if communicative activities are considered forms of social (and cognitive) organization and are conditions for a major part of the actions we practice, as Marcuschi (2003) highlights, it is possible to perceive that these actions are results of the values which constitute a genre and are responsible for the enactment of communicative activities. Moreover, Marcuschi (2003, p. 13) proposes that "it is possible to change genres of rhetorical instruments into political instruments in social actions. For genres are not only discursive artifacts or objects, but also social practices."

Thus educational booklets (in general)—and legal booklets (in particular)—cannot be conceived as merely neutral guides for the enactment of sociocommunicative activities. Instead, they are strongly charged with the coercive purpose of linguistic and social practices. Even though making it easier for laypeople to read norms written in hermetic legalese, legal booklets not only support but also strengthen the primary objectives of law, defining patterns of social behavior, and therefore guaranteeing the sustenance of the structured and well-established social-legal system.

Due to this scenario, I suggest that today's legal booklets originate from the formal and ideological confluence—and influence—of three genres:

(a) *Religious and school primers*, which gave birth to the idea that modern legal booklets refer to the "first rudiments" of some realm of knowledge—in this case, that of the legal realm. Similarly to their antecedents, modern legal booklets instruct laypeople, authoritatively, on how to think and act when confronted with specific unknown social (and legal) practices;

(b) *Illuminist political pamphlets*, evoking legal values and principles considered universal ("legal stereotypes" according to Warat, 1995; or "ideographs" according to McGee, 1980), such as *justice, human rights, social peace, equality*, etc., in the same way as current legal booklets do. In these publications, the true purposes of the institutionalized laws are not questioned; they just keep on (re)producing the myth that our legal system is neutral, democratic and equally focused on the safety and well-being of everyone;

(c) *Educational booklets produced in Brazil after the so-called Vargas Age*[2], working as an efficient instrument for the diffusion of the political-ideological propaganda in Brazil's New State (1937-1945). These political-legal booklets constitute, actually, the first publications with the format of contemporary legal booklets. Through simple language—often aided by beautiful illustrations—governmental ideas were widely promoted.

Thus, this investigation consists of a reconstitution of the main steps taken along this sociohistorical trajectory, in order to show how some genres in circulation since the 16th century formed the social basis for the modern Brazilian legal booklets. Moreover, I aim at explaining how those three genres mentioned above (religious/school primers, political leaflets, and "Vargist" educational booklets) were extremely significant to understand how the genre *legal booklet* has become a powerful sociopolitical instrument of tutelage and coercion in Brazil.

RELIGIOUS AND SCHOOL PRIMERS

Letters played a fundamental role in the appearance of several distinct genres. According to Bazerman (2005, p. 83), the letter—by establishing a direct communication between two people within a specific relationship and in given circumstances—could flexibly promote the formation and development of many institutional practices. As examples of genres that have letters as their social basis, Bazerman cites the scientific paper, the patent and the stockholders' report, among many others. To this list, we could add the legal and educational booklet.

Cartilha—the Portuguese term for both literacy/religious primers and informative/ educational booklets and brochures—is formally defined as "an elementary book for teaching children to read; the ABC book" and, by extension, "a book of elementary principles or any elementary compilation," as well as "a prayer-book or a small book which contains notions of the Christian doctrine" (Houaiss, 2004, p. 638). Note that "school book" and "prayer-book" were meanings not originally distinguished in the Middle Ages, as reading was taught from prayer-books and catechisms.

Etymologically, the Portuguese word *cartilha* is formed by two parts: "carta" (which means *letter*, as in a written or printed communication addressed to a person and usually transmitted by mail) + "ilha" (which is a diminutive suffix), from the Spanish *cartilla*, meaning originally "a small book which contains the letters of the alphabet and the first reading and writing lessons; diminutive for 'carta' (*letter*)" (Houaiss, 2004, p. 638).

Historically, religious primers were largely produced and spread around the world in the beginning of the 16th century—the Great Age of Discovery—when Christian missionaries propagated learning and religion beyond the boundaries of Europe; not rarely a large number of these missions were associated with imperialism and oppression through the Counter-Reformation or Catholic Reformation movement (Moisés, 1971, p. 17). The Brazilian Houaiss Dictionary (2004, p. 638) points out that the first known use of the word *cartilha* occurred in 1539, in the second volume of the missionary work *Monumenta Missionaria Africana*, which attempted to convert African villagers to Christianity. Thus the link between the letter and this emerging genre was direct. According to Gomes (2003, p. 157), this religious/literacy "primer was an instrument of communication between missionaries and the local population, who wanted to share their experiences, culture and knowledge."

Due to its close relations with the Catholic Church, Portugal tried, since early on, to follow the so-called "evangelizing and catechizing actions" of other European countries. At the end of the Middle Ages and in the early Renaissance, several European nations were making strong efforts to disseminate Christianity among the "infidels," especially outside their territorial space. Adopting an aggressively colonialist practice, the Portuguese conquerors tried not only to ensure that the dominating ideas of the European medieval culture were exported to the "gentiles" through the Jesuits' works, but also to guarantee the maintenance of political and economic public power in the hands of the representatives of the Portuguese Empire in the colonies (Romanelli, 2002, p. 33).

Matos (1987, p. 41) asserts that the "evangelization of the conquered territories thus constituted one of the main support strategies in the Portuguese age during the 15th and 16th centuries." Matos also mentions the important role played by the evolution of European printing technology in the Christianization of the conquered regions. The development of the press in Portugal made possible a much wider circulation of cultural goods and the "testimony of the technical and cultural Portuguese identity" in the colonies (p. 41). Around 1539-1540, the first printing of so-called "exotic languages" was done in Lisbon for the production of a grammar book and a catechism directed to the "Ethiopian, Persian, Indian, before and beyond the Ganges" children (Matos, 1987, p. 48).

According to Matos (1987, p. 54), in 1554, by order of John III[3], king of Portugal, the first great example of the method of bringing to "infidels and Godless barbarians" the testimony of the word of Jesus Christ was printed: the *Cartilha em Tamul e Português* [*Religious primer written in Tamul and Portuguese*] (Figures 1 and 2).

FIGURE 1 (LEFT): FRONT COVER OF THE *CARTILHA EM TAMUL E PORTUGUÊS*, LISBOA, 1554 (MATOS, 1987, P. 55)

FIGURE 2 (RIGHT): ONE OF THE INNER PAGES OF THE *CARTILHA EM TAMUL E PORTUGUÊS*, LISBOA, 1554 (MATOS, 1987, P. 56)

On its front cover (Figure 1), the *Cartilha em Tamul e Português* has its center decorated with the crowned Portuguese coat of arms, with the following text written in ancient Portuguese with gothic characters:

> Cartilha que contem brevemente / ho que todo christão deve apren-
> der / para sua salvaçam. A qual el Rey / dom Joham terceiro
> deste nome / nosso senhor mandor imprimir / em lingoa Tamul e
> portugues / com a decraraçam do Tamul por / cima de vermelho.
> [Primer which contains, briefly / what every Christian must learn
> / for their salvation. Which the King / John III by his name / our
> lord ordered to be printed / in Portuguese and Tamul language /
> with the Tamul statement in red, on top.]

Among the several religious primers, catechisms and other similar works cited by Matos (1987), we can highlight *Conclusiones Philosophicas* (1556), *Doutrina Christã* (1557), *Tratado em que se mostrava pela decisão dos concílios, e authoridade dos Santos Padres a Primazia da Igreja Romana contra os erros scismaticos dos Abexins* (1560), *Compendio Espiritual da vida Cristãa* (1561), *Iesus I Constityciones* (1568) and *Doctrina Christam* (1578) (Figure 3).

FIGURE 3: THE RELIGIOUS BOOK *DOCTRINA CHRISTAM*, 1578 (MATOS, 1987, P. 56)

Small publications like these religious primers were a very efficient form of teaching Christian prayers to colonized peoples, giving them the "opportunity" to know and use the religious and linguistic codes of the Metropolis[4]. According to Matos (1987, p. 57), such "primers became, thus, a starting (or an exit) point for the autochthonous beliefs and an arrival point to the religious ideology of the pan-tutelage of a unique, just and merciful God. It was, in short, a form of depersonalization."

Indeed, these Christian primers and prayer-books operated as a powerful instrument of sociopolitical and religious tutelage of Portugal over the "impious ethnicities" from the "barbaric world" through normative and eulogistic texts. The beliefs of the native peoples were simply disregarded or even execrated, and the dialogue with the Christian God implied obedience to proper, immutable rules and the recitation of official prayers.

Specifically in Brazil, by the end of the 17th century, these religious books gained importance in the colonial book market. In her detailed study called *Livros de Devoção, Atos de Censura* [*Devotion Books, Censorship Acts*], Algranti (2004) makes a careful study of the works in circulation during this period which had, among their objectives, the aim of "engaging the reader directly through spiritual exercises which would enhance devotion" (Algranti, 2004, p. 177). The author lists several written genres in this religious realm, classifying them into seven categories: (a) theology and moral theology; (b) holy scripture; (c) canons; (d) Catholic Church priests; (e) devotion books (saints' lives, prayer-books, spiritual exercises, mystical works), destined at first to be consulted, recited and read individually, but which could also be shared with other people; (f) liturgical books (mass books and other works dedicated to the cult and to the religious service); and finally, (g) holy history.

According to Mott (1997), many people in the colonies saw their own houses as a privileged *locus* for the exercise of their religiosity. Due to Brazil's spatial dispersion and large territorial extension, it was common that long periods of time would pass without the visit of a priest to celebrate public rituals. Hence, religious primers, catechisms and devotion books in general—as well as the private oratories and images of saints present in all colonial households—represented the expression of their religiosity and devoutness, not rarely constituting "the only interlocutors available to bring, ultimately, comfort to those who read or listened to them" (Algranti, 2004, p. 196).

Besides these religious books, colonial Brazil saw the arrival of another very productive genre, which survives today: the literacy or school primer. As Cagliari (1998, p. 19) affirms, with the Renaissance (15th and 16th centuries), as well as with the use of the press in Europe, it was possible to give greater attention to the readers of books that started to be produced for a much wider audience. The reading of classical works was no longer collective and was becoming more and more individual. According to Schlickmann (2001), there was a social need to share these "conventions" with other people, so they could become useful to society and contribute to interactive relationships. Thus the emphasis on literacy started to constitute an important concern and, as a direct consequence, the first school primers appeared.

This period is also marked by the appearance of the first Neolatin grammars. From then on, grammar scholars, etymologists and philologists started to dedicate their intellectual efforts to school literacy since it was necessary to establish an official writing/spelling for the vernacular languages and to teach ordinary people to read and write in their mother languages, increasingly leaving Latin aside.

However, it is worth noticing that mainly in the colonies these teachings were inseparable from religious instruction. "Grammar and catechism, or literacy primers and prayer-books often appear side by side, printed in the same book, as is the case of the *Cartilla y Dotrina Christina . . . en la lengua Chuchona* [*School primer and the Christian doctrine . . . in Chuchona language*]," as Daher (1998, p. 36) notes. The author concludes that there was a "coextension" between these two genres.

The school primers in Portuguese used to apply the classical "synthetic methodology" of teaching[5]. The very first of them, the *Cartilha de João de Barros* [*João de Barros' little primer*] (Figure 4), was published in 1540, together with the grammar by the same author, and is considered the first illustrated textbook in Brazil.

FIGURE 4: THE SCHOOL PRIMER *CARTILHA DE JOÃO DE BARROS,* 1540 (CAGLIARI, 1998, P. 23)

Other famous Brazilian school primers started to be produced, including the *Metodo Castilho para o ensino rápido e aprazível do ler impresso, manuscrito, e numeração e do escrever: Obra tão própria para as escólas para uso das familias* [*Castilho Method for the fast and pleasant teaching of the printed and handwritten reading, numbers, and writing: a work appropriate for schools and for the use of families*], by Antonio Feliciano de Castilho (Figure 5), published in 1850; the *Cartilha maternal ou arte de leitura* [*Maternal School Primer or the Art of Reading*], by João de Deus (Figure 6), in 1870; and the *Primeira leitura para crianças* [*First Reading for Children*], by A. Joviano (Figure 7), edited at the end of the 19th century.

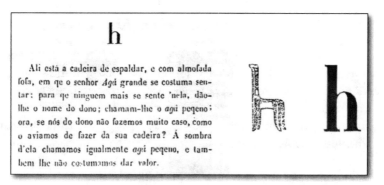

FIGURE 5: HOW TO WRITE THE LETTER "H" ACCORDING TO CASTILHO'S SCHOOL PRIMER, 1850 (CAGLIARI, 1998, P. 24)

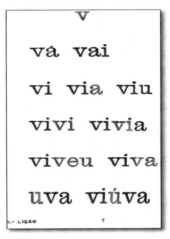

FIGURE 6: FRONT COVER AND THE "SECOND LESSON" OF JOÃO DE DEUS'S *CARTILHA MATERNAL*, 1870 (CAGLIARI, 1998, P. 24)

FIGURE 7: THIRD LESSON OF JOVIANO'S *PRIMEIRA LEITURA PARA CRIANÇAS*, END OF 19TH CENTURY (CAGLIARI, 1998, P. 25)

This brief explanation about the first literacy primers, as well as about colonial religious books, suggests that these genres had a wide and influential importance on the formation of Brazilian legal booklets. Today, educational or informative booklets—amongst them, we can mention laypeople's law guides—constitute what Gomes (2003, p. 157) calls a "hybrid genre of educational discourse, founded upon religious ideology, as well as upon school ideology."

As a "heritage" from the past primers, current educational booklets build a specific representation of "truth" by combining "informative credibility with the normative and regulative functions of showing individuals how they must act in social relations and events" (Gomes, 2003, p. 157). The message, then, is that, in order to achieve their goals—and, by extension, the text producers' goals—people *must* follow the norms and guidelines established in these booklets without questioning them.

In these modern educational/informative booklets, knowledge is merely "transmitted" or "transferred"—such as in the older religious and literacy primers—not in an active or interactive way or producing reflection or debate, but in an imposing, unquestionable way. This is what the Brazilian educator Paulo Freire (1987), in his most famous book, *Pedagogy of the Oppressed*, calls a "banking view of education as an oppressive tool," in which the student is viewed as an "empty account" to be filled by the teacher. According to Freire, in this banking view, "'knowledge' is a donation from those who see themselves as wiser to those who see themselves as ignorant, a donation founded upon one of the instrumental manifestations of the ideology of oppression—the absolutization of ignorance . . ." (Freire, 1987, p. 58).

As to the formal aspects current Brazilian legal booklets "inherited" from their preceding genres, we can mention, for example, the fact that catechism consists in a summary of the basic principles of Christianity in question-and-answer form, a linguistic strategy very common in present legal booklets; in addition, the use of pictures and short sentences typically used by school primers is another multimodal/linguistic resource we can observe nowadays in legal booklets.

POLITICAL PAMPHLETS

Besides religious and school primers, another genre that had a fundamental influence in the formation of Brazilian legal booklets was the political pamphlet. The first pamphlets came into being in modern Europe, at the beginning of the 15th century, consisting of publications that addressed contemporary public opinion issues and political news, examining several social, legal and religious matters. These themes, as Brown (1971, p. 19) asserts, were approached "from an acutely partial point of view," criticizing the government and clerical authorities, and not rarely were severely censored by the State.

According to Briggs and Burke (2004), it was during the Protestant Reformation in Germany, during the 1520s, that pamphlets began to be mass produced in order to reach a wide audience. Martin Luther wrote in vernacular—differently from other reformers, such as Erasmus, who used Latin—as a strategy to ensure that his message was understood by the highest possible number of common people.

Furthermore, the works of German Protestant reformers were available in great quantity and at affordable prices: 4,000 copies of Luther's first pamphlets, *An der christilichen Adel Deutscher Nation* [*To the noble Christians of the German nation*] and *Von der Freyheyt eyniß Christen menschen* [*Of the freedom of Christian men*], published in 1520 (Figure 8), were sold within a few days, and his *Little Catechism*, published in 1529, sold over 100,000 copies.

FIGURE 8: FIRST PAMPHLETS WRITTEN BY MARTIN LUTHER, 1520 (AVAILABLE AT HTTP://WWW.UNI-MUENSTER.DE)

Printed words became immensely important for these oppositional movements. Briggs and Burke (2004, p. 85) affirm that "printing converted the Reform into a permanent revolution." Like Germany in the 1520s, France, at the end of the 16th century, was also in the middle of the "pamphlet age" producing over 30 different texts a year between 1559 and 1572, featuring strong attacks on the Queen, Catherine de Medici—which made historian Donald Kelley declare that, in 1572, "the modern political propaganda was born" (cited by Briggs & Burke, 2004, p. 94). Other European nations also started to produce a high number of political pamphlets, such as the Dutch Republic (during the Eighty Years' War, from 1568 to 1648) and especially England, where several protest movements published many pamphlets questioning the British Monarchy.

From this turbulent political period, came the first ideas that would serve as a basis for Illuminism and, by extension, the French Revolution. The illuminist proposals which characterized European thought in the 18th century, particularly in France, were grounded on the belief in the power of reason to solve social problems. They opposed tradition—represented by the Absolute Monarchy and the Catholic Church—and fought for a new sociopolitical order, defending values such as democracy and liberalism. The French Revolution (1789-1799) was its principal expression in the political arena.

With the purpose of raising political awareness and engaging the involvement of ordinary people, inciting them to the revolutionary cause, pamphlets reached mass circulation, claiming the urgency of the construction of a new political culture and a new community of citizens. They used a "new 'revolutionary rhetoric' appealing to passion rather than reason, based in the 'magic' of words such as *liberté, fraternité, nation, patrie, peuple* and *citoyen*" (Briggs & Burke, 2004, p. 106).

The American rhetorical scholar Michael McGee, a renowned ideological critic, calls these magic words "ideographs." He defends that an "ideograph is an ordinary term found in political discourse" that "is a high-order abstraction representing collective commitment to a particular but equivocal and ill-defined normative goal" (McGee, 1980, p. 15). According to him, these words "constitute a vocabulary of public motives, which authorize and warrant public actions"; besides, it is "presumed that human beings will react predictably and autonomically" to the use of ideographs (p. 6). McGee also advocates the study of ideographs (such as *freedom* and *liberty*) to help identify the ideological position of a society.

It is worth mentioning that the use of the notion of ideographs—which make use of both stereotyped/idealized scenarios and values/principles considered universal (*justice, equality, human rights, citizenship*, etc.), called "legal stereotypes" by the eminent Argentinian jurist Luís Alberto Warat (1995)—represents one of the principal discursive resources used by current Brazilian legal booklets for the social construction of reality.

Regarding the use of language during this period, scholars observe that a "new language to serve the New Regime" was created, causing a huge linguistic revolution, once "writing changed hands" (Briggs & Burke, 2004, p. 107). The countless revolutionary pamphlets which spread the Age of Enlightenment to the "common men" despised the language used by the upper classes in the Old Regime—full of unnecessary technicalities and decorations—adapting it through the use of words and syntactic constructions that were close to everyday language. In addition, over 600 printings were produced, in an attempt to widen the political debate to illiterate people, with images occupying a key role in the process of meaning-making in pamphlets (Figure 9 represents one of the "sans-culotte" attacking the King).

FIGURE 9: A FRENCH REVOLUTION PAMPHLET, C. 1790 (SOURCE: "FRENCH REVOLUTION PAMPHLET COLLECTION," AVAILABLE AT HTTP://CHAUCER.LIBRARY.EMORY.EDU/FRENCHREVO)

It is also during this period that the *Declaration of the Rights of Man and of the Citizen* came into being. Approved by the French Constituent Assembly in 1789, this Declaration served as a preface for the Constitution of 1791, addressing the principles of the new world order, of the rights of nations and of the natural, inalienable and sacred rights of men. It condemned privileges and prejudices based on the widest possible application of liberty, equality and separation of powers. It is, however, a circumstantial work, written by and for the bourgeoisie, concerned with keeping the recently acquired power away from the hands of any absolutist monarch. Here "liberty" was conditioned by the obedience to bourgeois law, thus creating the belief—culturally institutionalized today—that only the established legal order is able to provide social security and balance. This general principle constitutes one of the most important contemporary legal stereotypes:

> Liberty consists in the freedom to do everything which injures no
> one else; hence the exercise of the natural rights of each man has
> no limits except those which assure to the other members of the
> society the enjoyment of the same rights. These limits can only
> be determined by law. (Article 4 of the *Declaration of the Rights*

of Man and of the Citizen, approved by the National Assembly of France, August 26, 1789.)

Captured by the illuminist ideals of the French Revolution, the English-born American writer and revolutionary politician Thomas Paine produced a text which would come to be a kind of remote precursor of the current legal booklet: the pamphlet *The Rights of Man*, published in two parts, in 1791 and 1792 (Figure 10 shows some excerpts from the beginning of the original work). The publication represents the first widely documented defense of the *Declaration of the Rights of Man and of the Citizen* and responds to the criticisms to the Revolution made by Edmund Burke in his book *Reflections on the French Revolution* (1790).

Paine confronted monarchy and heritability of power, and defended bourgeois legal values considering them as inherent to human nature as the "rights of men"—another recurrent legal stereotype. Paradoxically, the search for these rights, according to Paine, should not be centered on the history of Mankind—as Burke had done—but should transcend it, until reaching the moment of origin, when Men came into being through the hands of the Creator.

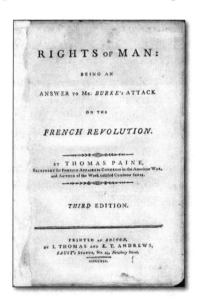 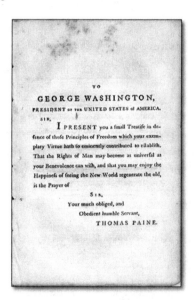

FIGURE 10: EXCERPTS FROM *THE RIGHTS OF MAN* BY THOMAS PAINE, 1791/1792 (AVAILABLE AT HTTP://WWW.EARLYAMERICA.COM)

In the beginning of the 19th century, Brazil also started to produce a series of pamphlets and periodicals of a political nature. Neves (1999, 2002) lists and analyzes several printings from that time, which in general reflected the French Revolution's illuminist and libertarian ideals, as well as the clash between the "hunchbacks" (absolute monarchists defending the Old Regime) and the "constitutionals" (liberal and intellectual politicians). Many of those political pamphlets and periodicals discussed legal matters and offered legal "counseling" to their readers in a way similar to our current legal booklets.

Among those periodicals, it is worth highlighting the *Revérbero Constitucional Fluminense* [*Rio de Janeiro Constitutional Reverberator*] (Figure 11), published in 1821/1822, which voiced a radical liberalism, concerned with "providing 'some ideas to guide and instruct the people about the major issue of today' . . . [which is] a liberal constitution" (Neves, 2002, p. 51).

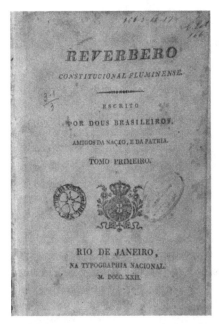 

FIGURE 11: THE PERIODICAL *REVÉRBERO CONSTITUCIONAL FLU-MINENSE*, 1821/1822 (SOURCE: "PRIMEIROS JORNAIS" COLLECTION OF BIBLIOTECA NACIONAL, AVAILABLE AT HTTP://WWW.BN.BR)

On the other hand, the conservative *Semanário Cívico* [*Patriotic Weekly*] (edited in 1821) defended loyalty and submission to the Portuguese Monarchy, intending to "instruct the citizens by using one of the commonest forms of the time: the political catechism" (Neves, 2002, pp. 51-52). In addition to these two periodicals, titles such as the *Constitucional* [*Constitutional*], the *Analisador*

Constitucional [*Constitutional Examiner*], the *Espreitador Constitucional* [*Constitutional Observer*] and the *Diário Constitucional* [*Constitutional Daily*] reveal the role that the discussion about political-legal issues—with the most diverse party-ideological orientation—played at that time. According to Lustosa (2000, pp. 25-26), this period marks "the Brazilian press being born, committed to the revolutionary process at a moment when just overnight we ceased to consider ourselves as Portuguese to assume our identity as Brazilian."

Specifically regarding political pamphlets and brochures—printed or even handwritten (Figure 12)—Neves (2002) emphasizes the important role played by the so-called "constitutional pamphlets" as efficient tools for the dissemination of the new political culture.

FIGURE 12: BRAZILIAN POLITICAL PAMPHLETS AND BROCHURES, BEGINNING OF THE 19TH CENTURY (SOURCE: "PRIMEIROS JORNAIS" AND "OBRAS RARAS" COLLECTION OF BIBLIOTECA NACIONAL, AVAILABLE AT HTTP://WWW.BN.BR)

Some of these leaflets—such as the *Constituição Explicada* [*Constitution Explained*], the *Constitucional Justificado* [*Constitution Justified*] and the *Catecismo Constitucional* [*Constitutional Catechism*] (this last one was organized in question-answer format)—tried to collect and explain the liberal political-legal vocabulary as their authors believed that new meanings were attributed to all political-legal terms, hence the need to reformulate their dictionary to clarify this "new language."

Other pamphlets—such as the *Diálogo entre o Corcunda Abatido e o Con-*

stitucional Exaltado [*Dialogue between the prostrated Hunchback and the exalted Constitutional*], the *Diálogo entre a Constituição e o Despotismo* [*Dialogue between the Constitution and Despotism*] and the *Alfaiate Constitucional* [*Constitutional Tailor*], which were usually illustrated—used dialogues through which the characters (people or personified objects) represented different sides or opposed political parties, and challenged each other to a word duel. Finally, aiming to reach a wider audience with the dissemination of those constitutional ideas, another group of pamphlets—among them, *A regeneração constitucional ou A guerra e disputa entre os Carcundas and Constitucionais* [*The constitutional regeneration or The war and the dispute between the Hunchbacks and the Constitutionals*]—followed the Brazilian tradition of parodying religious prayers and political speeches with a lot of humor and sarcasm.

The discursive strategies used by these political leaflets—called by Neves (2002) "the pedagogy of constitutionalism"—such as the glossary of technical terms, the question-answer sequences, the fictitious narratives with dialogues, as well as the use of humor and pictures, are extremely common in contemporary legal booklets.

A more focused analysis of these political pamphlets—predecessors of the modern layman's law guides—allows the conclusion that their producers were able to foresee the power of the word in promoting reforms by using efficient linguistic/discursive strategies for the dissemination of liberal ideals. Besides, they contributed to the foundation and diffusion of the ideological basis for the formation of the nation-state in Brazil.

However, fearing not only real popular participation in the country's destiny but also any abrupt changes in the Brazilian social organization, liberal politicians chose not to take into account the countless problems provoked by the "importation" of the European liberalism into a slave-based, newly-independent colony with continental dimensions. Finally, as Neves states (2002), only a "simulacrum" of the libertarian ideals was implanted. The political decisions continued to be restricted to a small elite who would later dominate the power structure in the Brazilian Empire. Moreover, notions such as *citizenship*, *liberty* and *human rights* resulted in an empty rhetoric, bringing back stereotyped legal principles with little or no concrete application.

This scenario remained relatively unaltered in the following stage of Brazilian politics, when the Monarchy was deposed by a military *coup d'etat*. The dictatorship installed during the so-called Old Republic (1889-1930) was also characterized by the maintenance of a political and social hierarchy, excluding the wider society.

LEGAL/EDUCATIONAL BOOKLETS PRODUCED DURING THE AGE OF VARGAS

From the so-called Vargas Age on, it is possible to observe a significant change in the way mass media started to be manipulated in order to function as the main propaganda tool for the government. Radio, cinema, books and newspapers broadcasted messages of a national-patriotic nature, praising and legitimizing the government, mainly through the image of its commander-in-chief, Getúlio Vargas. In this context, several types of educational booklets started to be produced and widely disseminated—among them, legal booklets.

Actually, this process began with the social and economic transformations Brazil was going through at the beginning of the 20th century. The frequent instability of the agro-export system—which culminated in the "Coffee Crisis" at the end of the 1920s—made evident how vulnerable the Brazilian economy was, always subjected to oscillations according to external facts or international policies which affected its development (such as the stock market crash in New York City in 1929).

Simultaneously it was possible to observe a representative urban-industrial growth, creating new social and economic forces in the country, and demanding new postures from the government. Popular dissatisfaction with that model of legitimizing the old political system, as well as with the dependency on international markets, was increasingly higher. The emerging industrial bourgeoisie was still marginalized by a federal policy focused on the production and exportation of coffee, where the decisions were made by a few oligarchies—families or political groups that perpetuated themselves in power.

Furthermore, under the influence of European avant-garde trends, a new generation of artists and intellectuals come into being, calling for a "consciousness raising" about the Brazilian reality. In February of 1922, the Modern Art Week took place, initiating the Brazilian Modernism: a movement that defended anti-liberal and nationalist ideals, often advocating "the typical, utopist and exaggerated nationalism, identified with the extreme right-wing political trends" (Nicola, 1987, p. 193).

In place of liberalism, the Brazilian government initiated a process of centralization of political power through an authoritative, interventionist State which aimed to serve their own interests presented as "national interests" to the people. Vargas appears strategically in this context, as fighting against external dependency and oligarchic domination, and defending "the national unity, the adaptation of our culture and institutions to the Brazilian reality, and the wide usage of national resources for a self-determined development" (Garcia, 1982, p. 56).

There were several strategies employed by the "Vargist" propaganda to control the crisis and neutralize conflicts and emerging social forces, demobilizing them politically. Vargas' principal objective was to ensure the concretization of the interests of the ruling classes through the reproduction of socially established dominant relationships. To do so, all efforts were directed at the adhesion of the unprivileged classes, in an attempt to persuade them that the structure of a totalitarian State would meet their own and the Nation's interests. At the same time, the previous government was disqualified with the excuse that it used electoral and political party systems for its own benefit and advantage and not for the "benefit of the Nation."

Thus countless patriotic messages started to be propagated, glorifying the Nation and awakening in its people pride in their nationality. A homogeneous, for-the-masses image of the Brazilian people was then created, characterizing them as orderly, tolerant and having a traditionally peaceful nature. The State's political and legal organizations started to be represented in the mass media as the only ones able to ensure *national security, justice, social peace* and the preservation of *human rights*, put into practice by a "neutral government" free of individual interests and under no influence of the elites. So, just the same as in those old political pamphlets cited above, stereotypical and socially crystallized values and principles were invoked by the mass media propaganda machine as a powerful persuasion mechanism—something that remains active in modern legal booklets.

Another recurring characteristic of this type of propaganda was the simplification of its messages. Due to the precarious education system and the high level of illiteracy in Brazil at that time, it was necessary to seriously reduce the complexity of economic, political, legal and ideological relationships, so the "common Brazilian" could understand and assimilate new ideas. According to Garcia (1982, p. 73), "the ideas to be propagated had to be extremely simplified and frequently repeated to be noticed, understood and memorized." The educational booklet *Quem foi que disse? Quem foi que fez?* [*Who said that? Who did that?*]— produced by Vargas' Department of Press and Propaganda—for instance, presents "important" Brazilian phrases and historical achievements, and it is stated in its introduction that

> [These words] are not directed to erudite people or to History scholars, but to the common man, the working man, the poor young man, who cannot buy books, to the soldier and the sailor who, because they defend the Country in times of danger and ensure peace for the workers, must know who the great men of Brazil

are; this is the land we must love with the same strength, ardor and enthusiasm as they have. (Cited by Garcia, 1982, p. 81)

Vargas was presented, on the one hand, as having exceptional qualities, a wise and active political leader; on the other, as the "father of the poor," "defender of the humble," personifying and acting in the people's interests. One of his recurring mottos was "The intermediation between Government and People is over" (cited by Garcia, 1982, p. 88). This strategically dichotomist image—simultaneously superior and accessible—can be observed, for example, in two examples. On one of the pages of the educational booklet *Getúlio Vargas para crianças* [*Getúlio Vargas for Children*] (Figure 13), published in 1941, a drawing of the President's face is inserted into the center of the Brazilian flag, which has the contours of the Brazilian map; and in the very title of the booklet *Comemorações do Estado Nacional na voz das classes e na palavra do chefe: 1937-1942* [*Celebrations of the National State in the voice of the classes and in the words of its Chief: 1937-1942*] (Figure 14), published in 1942, Vargas puts his "words" and the "people's voice" side by side, as if they composed a single chorus.

FIGURE 13: EXCERPTS FROM THE BOOKLET *GETÚLIO VARGAS PARA CRIANÇAS*, 1941 (SOURCE: FUNDAÇÃO GETÚLIO VARGAS,

AVAILABLE AT HTTP://WWW.FGV.BR)

FIGURE 14: FRONT COVER OF THE BOOKLET *COMEMORAÇÕES DO ESTADO NACIONAL,* 1942 (SOURCE: FUNDAÇÃO GETÚLIO VARGAS, AVAILABLE AT HTTP://WWW.FGV.BR)

Another strategy to consolidate the image of Vargas as an accessible and popular figure was to demonstrate his singular friendliness—very different from all previous political leaders—avoiding a solemn air and showing an "open, sincere smile, sometimes a "spontaneous" laugh, [which] weakened any obstacle which could come between himself and the masses" (Garcia, 1982, p. 91). The journalist Orígenes Lessa (1973, p. 67) went as far as affirming that "the President's smile distinguishes him from all other dictators." This is evidenced, for example, on the cover of the educational booklet *Getúlio Vargas, o amigo das crianças* [*Getúlio Vargas, friend of the children*] (Figure 15), published in 1940, where the President seems to smile openly at a cheerful child. Similar to Vargas' propaganda materials, the strategy of using images and drawings of happy, smiling people, where everything seems to be calm and harmonic, is also widely used in legal booklets today.

FIGURE 15: FRONT COVER OF THE BOOKLET *GETÚLIO VARGAS, O AMIGO DAS CRIANÇAS*, 1940 (SOURCE: FUNDAÇÃO GETÚLIO VAR-GAS, AVAILABLE AT HTTP://WWW.FGV.BR)

Actually, the joint manipulation of the verbal and non-verbal texts was one of the major persuasive instruments in these "Vargist" booklets. The producers of these texts showed a high level of control over the visual argumentation in the booklets, "orchestrating" word and image successfully. It is worth observing, for example, the booklet *A juventude no Estado Novo* [*The Youth in the New State*] (Figure 16), published around 1940:

FIGURE 16: EXCERPTS FROM THE BOOKLET *A JUVENTUDE NO ESTADO NOVO*, C. 1940 (SOURCE: FUNDAÇÃO GETÚLIO VARGAS, AVAILABLE AT HTTP://WWW.FGV.BR)

In this booklet, the images portray people's daily lives—school, family, work—through drawings with classical features, with sober, balanced colors, and the construction of a harmonic, homogeneous reality where order is respected and there is no conflict. Vargas appears smiling beside children ("people's man"), as well as working in his office ("serious, hard-working President"). Together with the pictures, there is always a message with the purpose of inciting the readers to fulfill their moral and civic duties.

Finally, with the publication of the booklet *A Constituição de 10 de novembro explicada ao povo* [*The Constitution of November 10th explained to the people*] (Figure 17), in 1940, written by Antônio Figueira de Almeida (a member of Vargas' Department of Press and Propaganda), the production, circulation and consumption of the genre "legal booklet" assumed a systematic and official turn. The rhetorical/ discursive strategy used then remains very frequent in current legal booklets: it consists in the citation of excerpts of the law (in this case, of the Constitution), followed by a "translation," that is, an explanation in an apparently simpler language.

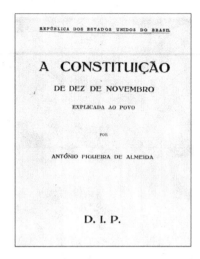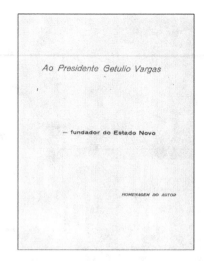

FIGURE 17: FIRST PAGES OF THE LEGAL BOOKLET *A CONSTITU-*
IÇÃO DE 10 DE NOVEMBRO EXPLICADA AO POVO, 1940 (ALMEIDA,
1940, PP. 2-4)

As in the other "Vargist" educational brochures, this legal booklet is full of patriotic and legal-political clichés, which obfuscate the repressive, totalitarian, and
interventionist character of the 1937 Constitution[6]: "The Republic is the government of the people, by the people, and for the people"; "The national flag, anthem
and coat of arms are symbols, artistic representations of the Nation itself. They aim
at elevating the heart and the spirit for the contemplation of the Nation's things.
This measure strengthens the bonds of national unity—congregating all citizens
in the same cult and the same patriotic love"; "While that one [*the 1891 Constitution*] allowed for an almost limitless autonomy, this one [*the 1937 Constitution*]
established a relative autonomy. And this is a highly beneficial providence as we
will see later" (Almeida, 1940, pp. 11-12).

From that point on, legal booklets started to be incorporated into the Brazil-
ians' daily lives, becoming a powerful "instrument of tutelage" (Gomes, 2003) of
those who produce them. In this sense, legal booklets educate laypeople, translating the legal terminology into everyday language and showing them their
rights and duties, with the aim of instructing them about how they *must* proceed
in the face of specific everyday situations, always respecting the established legal
order.

MODERN LEGAL BOOKLETS

During the last three or four decades, the Western world has been witnessing a significant change in the way texts which circulate socially are produced and read. Until a few years ago, the modes of communicative representation of verbal texts (spoken and written language) and non-verbal texts (images, sounds, gestures, etc.) were treated in an isolated manner according to their specificities. These boundaries, however, are becoming increasingly blurred.

Illustrations, photographs, graphics and diagrams, allied to composition and printing resources, such as type of paper, color, page layout, font, etc., are being systematically applied to written genres. According to Dionisio (2005, p. 159), "image and word maintain an increasingly closer, more integrated relationship." For Lemke (2002), verbal and visual representations co-evolved historically and culturally to complement and coordinate each other. With that, texts started to be perceived as *multimodal constructs* in which writing is only one of the ways of representing messages[7] (Jewitt & Kress, 2003; Kress & van Leeuwen, 1996, 2001).

It is also worth highlighting that the emergence of multimodal texts in the contemporary society started to demand, from the reader, an increasingly higher number of cognitive operations for understanding what is being read. Nowadays, the insertion of an individual into social practices of reading and writing surpasses the simple acquisition of the reading-and-writing technology. Instead, literacy—or *literacies*, as Dionisio prefers (2005)—must comprise different types of knowledge representation, making individuals able to "attribute meanings to messages coming from multiple language forms, as well as being able to produce messages, incorporating multiple language sources" (Dionisio, 2005, p. 159).

In the Brazilian realm of legal discourse, this phenomenon has been slowly observed, although the occurrences are still timid and isolated. On the one hand, legal institutions, with the objective of perpetuating the status quo, use the hermetic legal language as a powerful mechanism for the maintenance of hegemony, domination and discursive inequality (Mozdzenski, 2004). On the other hand, some isolated initiatives—from both public and private legal institutions—proposing to make the law more accessible to common citizens, have tried to turn the dull legal text into a more attractive, modern and (supposedly) uncomplicated genre. *Legal booklets* are an example of this trend, appearing from the confluence of three genres already addressed in the previous sections: (a) religious and school primers; (b) political pamphlets, particularly the illuminist revolutionary pamphlets; and (c) educational, political-legal booklets, published from the Vargas Age on.

As it is possible to observe from the images of many examples of the religious and school primers reproduced above, in these embryonic genres of legal booklets one can already perceive the importance of images for the construction of textual meanings. In a similar way, with the objective of translating legalese into common language, legal booklets use countless multimodal strategies of text-image interaction.

Figures 18a and 18b represent a clear example of this situation. Figure 18a consists of the reproduction of a part of the Brazilian Civil Code (Federal Law n. 10.406/2002) which includes the Brazilian intestacy law (i.e., the law of descent and distribution or intestate succession statutes) that determines who is entitled to the property from the estate under the rules of inheritance. Figure 18b, in turn, shows an excerpt of the legal booklet *Ao Encontro da Lei* [*Towards the Law*] (Netto, 2003), a part which also addresses the rules of inheritance.

In a general way, both treat the *same* subject: they describe how the Brazilian legal system regulates the norms of succession. Figure 18a, however, has little visual information: the Brazilian Civil Code follows rhetorical strategies very much crystallized in legal texts (in Brazil, law is divided into titles, sections, articles, paragraphs, etc.). Differently, Figure 18b explores many multimodal resources (drawings, diagrams, musical signs, a dynamic and colorful layout,

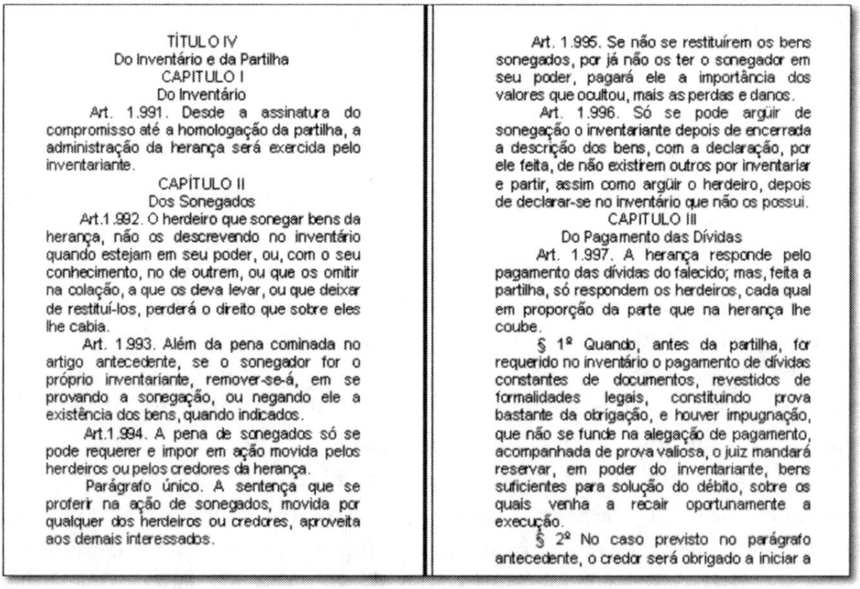

TÍTULO IV
Do Inventário e da Partilha
CAPITULO I
Do Inventário

Art. 1.991. Desde a assinatura do compromisso até a homologação da partilha, a administração da herança será exercida pelo inventariante.

CAPÍTULO II
Dos Sonegados

Art.1.992. O herdeiro que sonegar bens da herança, não os descrevendo no inventário quando estejam em seu poder, ou, com o seu conhecimento, no de outrem, ou que os omitir na colação, a que os deva levar, ou que deixar de restituí-los, perderá o direito que sobre eles lhe cabia.

Art. 1.993. Além da pena cominada no artigo antecedente, se o sonegador for o próprio inventariante, remover-se-á, em se provando a sonegação, ou negando ele a existência dos bens, quando indicados.

Art.1.994. A pena de sonegados só se pode requerer e impor em ação movida pelos herdeiros ou pelos credores da herança.

Parágrafo único. A sentença que se proferir na ação de sonegados, movida por qualquer dos herdeiros ou credores, aproveita aos demais interessados.

Art. 1.995. Se não se restituírem os bens sonegados, por já não os ter o sonegador em seu poder, pagará ele a importância dos valores que ocultou, mais as perdas e danos.

Art. 1.996. Só se pode argüir de sonegação o inventariante depois de encerrada a descrição dos bens, com a declaração, por ele feita, de não existirem outros por inventariar e partir, assim como argüir o herdeiro, depois de declarar-se no inventário que não os possui.

CAPITULO III
Do Pagamento das Dívidas

Art. 1.997. A herança responde pelo pagamento das dívidas do falecido; mas, feita a partilha, só respondem os herdeiros, cada qual em proporção da parte que na herança lhe coube.

§ 1º Quando, antes da partilha, for requerido no inventário o pagamento de dívidas constantes de documentos, revestidos de formalidades legais, constituindo prova bastante da obrigação, e houver impugnação, que não se funde na alegação de pagamento, acompanhada de prova valiosa, o juiz mandará reservar, em poder do inventariante, bens suficientes para solução do débito, sobre os quais venha a recair oportunamente a execução.

§ 2º No caso previsto no parágrafo antecedente, o credor será obrigado a iniciar a

FIGURE 18A: EXCERPTS FROM THE BRAZILIAN CIVIL CODE (FEDERAL LAW N. 10.406/2002)

etc.) and uses not only a less formal register of the language, but also several rhetorical strategies (characters dialoguing such as in comic books, song lyrics excerpts, fictional narratives which illustrate cases of law enforcement, etc.) with the purpose of making the norm comprehensible for the non-initiated.

FIGURE 18B: EXCERPTS FROM THE LEGAL BOOKLET *AO ENCON-TRO DA LEI* (NETTO, 2003, PP. 26-27)

Thus, it is clear why a *multimodal reading* of the genre legal booklet—or of any other genre—cannot be merely restricted to a conventional linguistic analysis nor to the cataloguing of its stable structures.

In current legal booklets, this intergeneric, multimodal hybridization is current and very productive, as it is possible to perceive through the various organizational forms taken. This heterogeneity can be observed right from the simple attribution of a name to this genre: in Brazil, most legal booklets are indistinctly and alternatively named *booklet, manual, guide, primer, guidelines*, etc. The rhetorical and discursive strategies also vary largely from issue to issue. Some booklets follow the question-and-answer scheme (similar to catechisms); others present directly a summary or the principal aspects of a certain law (similar to "Vargist" booklets). Others adopt diverse visual resources such as graphics, tables, diagrams, etc. And there is a frequent use of comic book stories, cartoons, or other pictorial elements—the same strategy used by those antecedent genres.

As mentioned before, the motivational principle of legal booklets is to make available the understanding of law and legalese to lay citizens through the retextualization of legal norms in a language that is closer to the users' daily lives, and which is, in general, visually more informative. However, it is worth emphasizing that, even though "facilitating" the comprehension of normative texts, legal booklets not only maintain but also reinforce the original purposes of law, establishing standards of conduct imposed by the State under the threat of organized sanctions, hence ensuring the maintenance of the institutionalized social order.

To achieve this, legal booklet producers conduct an effective process of "deconstruction" of legal language through countless multimodal resources and rhetorical strategies which try to enrich the visual information of the texts, making them more pleasant to read and supposedly easier to understand. In visually informative texts—such as the legal booklet I will analyze below—several factors are taken into consideration, such as target audience (their expectations, previous knowledge, familiarity—or lack thereof—with certain literacy practices, ideological orientation, etc.), the diverse possibilities of reading processing, the functionality of the contents presented and how they are presented, the use of images as a mechanism of organization, complementation, illustration, etc., among various other elements. With this, these booklets aim at creating an attractive and harmonious text, able to efficiently transmit information about their textual organization to readers through visible clues as we can observe in the following examples[8].

One of the most common configurations among legal booklets regards the use of a comic book format for the "translation" of legal text. As Mendonça (2003, p. 202) points out, "comic books may have a didactic function, being used to give instructions and to persuade, in educational campaigns." In these educational comic books, the "voices of the law"—that is, the voices from the power groups who have their interests guaranteed by legal norms and by the legal system as a whole—are presented in everyday speech, even though simulated and partially unreal. These powerful groups, even if not always explicitly "embodied" in the narratives, are represented as if they spoke in the language of the readers, forging a symmetrical relationship between the interlocutors and making the adoption of the proposed ideas easier.

We have here what Fairclough (2001, p. 166) calls a "contradictory stylistic configuration." On one side, the style is similar to a spoken, conversational interaction; on the other, the social hierarchic differences and the written formality of legal institutions establish asymmetrical subject positions for writers and readers of legal booklets. This "tension of voices" is often very evident in legal booklets, given that their self-declared function is to explain the legal text didactically, but at the same time to direct readers to a passive acceptance of their rights and duties in the terms strictly imposed by law.

Now observe Figure 19. It presents an excerpt from the *Cartilha da Justiça em Quadrinhos* [*Booklet of Justice Comic book*] (Association of Brazilian Magistrates, 1999), and reproduces the first two pages of the story "Nossos Direitos" [*Our rights*]. In this issue, the leading character Brasilzinho [*Little Brazil*] is a yellow-and-green-haired boy, wearing clothes in the colors of the Brazilian flag. His closest friends are three children: a black girl, a dark-skinned Native Indian boy and a white boy, alluding to the three ethnicities which are traditionally associated with Brazil's social formation.

The story in Figure 19 is told in two levels. On the first level, Little Brazil and his friends discuss the fact that many rights are not respected, because the masses do not always know about them. The landscape is idyllic—the sun is smiling, everyone is having ice cream and a yellow dog with a green tail and ears (!) runs around merrily. This apparent harmony is broken by the parallel narratives on the second level. Here, some situations where law has been disobeyed are shown—although in the end the law always "wins."

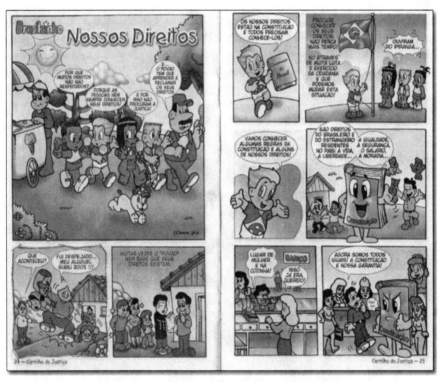

FIGURE 19: EXCERPTS FROM THE LEGAL BOOKLET *CARTILHA DA JUSTIÇA EM QUADRINHOS* (ASSOCIATION OF BRAZILIAN MAGISTRATES, 1999)

The excerpts above show a stereotyped view of law and justice, with the legal-legislative system always protecting the weakest, minorities and the unprivileged. In Figure 19, law enforcers assume a serious, authoritative air, and are construed invariably as pillars of justice and equality: pay attention, for example, to the last image where the Constitution, with a serious facial expression, reprehends a man who has made a sexist remark. Those who are disrespected never cease to count on legal support and, after the conflict is resolved, they are happy and contented. The notion is that a perfect, harmonic world is possible when the Constitution is followed.

The *Manual de Conduta do Preso* [*Manual of Conduct for the Inmate*] (Ferreira & Mesquita Neto, 2004) is an excellent example of how images are used together with the summary of the law. On its cover (Figure 20), the *Manual de Conduta do Preso* presents several images that describe forms of behavior expected of prisoners. In the main picture, the inmates greet one another smilingly, while a smiling prison warden watches. Their clothes are "casual" but very neat, and the place, besides spacious, seems to be clean and well-kept. It is, to sum up, a place of harmonic and pacific coexistence, where everyone is happy and cordial. In the smaller pictures on the right side of the cover, some undesired—and therefore, forbidden—behaviors (such as fights between prisoners and escape attempts) are represented with a red "X."

FIGURE 20: FRONT COVER OF THE LEGAL BOOKLET *MANUAL DE CONDUTA DO PRESO* (FERREIRA & MESQUITA NETO, 2004)

FIGURE 21: EXCERPTS FROM THE LEGAL BOOKLET *MANUAL DE CONDUTA DO PRESO* (FERREIRA & MESQUITA NETO, 2004)

The contents of the *Manual* (Figure 21) reproduce the imposing tone of the law through the recurring use of deontic modality, denoting obligation, as it is possible to observe on the pages reproduced here: "It is the duty of the condemned and of the temporary inmate to care for their personal hygiene . . ." (p. 16); "The condemned and the temporary inmate are obliged to conserve their objects of personal use . . ." (p. 17); etc.

We can firstly observe that the light, caricatured tone of those illustrations is in a striking contrast to the subtitles which accompany them. This is not the result of chance. These drawings build a social identity for the inmates that is significantly different from the one which would result if the producers of this booklet had chosen to complement their text, for example, with photographs of real scenes in Brazilian prisons, notorious for overcrowding, corruption, violence and torture. The inmates and the environment where they are confined are represented as if they were in a harmonic setting, where conflicts and problems are nonexistent, due to the obedience to the principles of the *Manual de Conduta* booklet and, by intertextual extension, to the prison laws. At any sign of disturbance of the institutionalized order, the obedient inmate must avoid confrontation and run away from the situation.

According to Kress and van Leeuwen (1996), the use of caricatures in the educational realm has the main purpose of attenuating the density of texts, as well as helping beginners to understand the information based on the emotional involvement of identification. In the specific case of this *Manual de Conduta do Preso*, however, the humorous trace with which the characters are drawn increases the "tension of voices" between the "voice of law" (embodied by the voice of the booklet's producer) and the voice of the "lifeworld" (in a Habermasian sense), creating a contradictory discourse and therefore compromising the veracity—or better, the "truth effect"—of the text.

FINAL REMARKS

In this brief study of the sociohistorical formation of legal booklets, my interest was to observe not only the main moments in the social history of the genres that gave birth to Brazilian legal booklets, but also their influence over the modern issues. In this context, our conclusion—based on Bazerman (2005), Algranti (2004), Neves (2002), Matos (1987), Garcia (1982), Marcuschi (2003), among others—is that today's legal booklets result from the formal and ideological confluence and influence of three other genres: religious/school primers, political leaflets, and "Vargist" educational booklets.

According to our investigation, the first moment begins with the appearance of the first religious and school (for literacy purposes) primers. After a brief incursion through the definition and etymological origin of the Portuguese word *cartilha*, this article showed how the historical circumstances—the Great Age of Discovery by European countries, as well as the Roman Catholic Church's Counter-Reformation movement—were crucial for the formation of religious prayer-books and catechisms. Literacy primers also appear in this context as a result of the "synthetic method" of learning used since Classical Antiquity which incorporated religious elements into the teaching of writing.

The next phase of this study consisted in analyzing the contribution of political leaflets and similar publications in the constitution of legal booklets, mainly those which divulged illuminist ideals during the French Revolution and the Independence of Brazil. Our analysis showed that this historical context consolidated some general legal ideals and principles—such as *justice, democracy*, and *human rights*—called "legal stereotypes" (Warat, 1995) or "ideographs" (McGee, 1980).

At last, we observed legal/educational booklets produced after the so-called Vargas Age, as a result of the historical and political moment Brazil was going through, which already presented many contact points with current booklets, and acted as a powerful tool for political and ideological propaganda during Vargas' New State dictatorship.

Having said that, the warning of Gomes (2003) regarding current booklets is clear, affirming that, in any form of discursive contestation, the use of educational booklets—and we can include legal booklets here—might be dangerous, since it operates with matters regarding evangelization, passivity, rules and tutelage. According to Gomes (2003, p. 157), the booklet

> is assumed as a hybrid genre of the educational discourse, founded upon religious as well as school ideology, as a teaching work seen as an example to be followed . . . bringing to the booklet a certain representation of truth or of something to believe, that is, bringing a certain informative credibility with normative and regulating functions, to show individuals how they must act in the face of social relations and actions.

Finally, as we have explained in more detail in Mozdzenski (2006), it is possible to observe that modern legal booklets use countless strategies to compose their texts, many of them mentioned in this article, directly inherited from their antecedent genres. These discursive and multimodal strategies contribute to the construction of reality in favor of elites and power groups by using one or more of the following linguistic tools: summary and/or explanation of parts of the law, question-and-answer sequences, narratives with dialogues, etc., often accompanied by visual aids, comic book stories, drawings and caricatures, graphics, colorful layout, special print formatting, etc.

NOTES
[1] I am indebted to Professors Angela Paiva Dionisio, Judith C. Hoffnagel, Carolyn R. Miller, Charles Bazerman and Débora de Carvalho Figueiredo for their critical reading, corrections and suggestions for this article.

[2] Getúlio Vargas was the president who governed the Brazilian Republic for the longest period of time. First, in his provisional government (1930-1934), then through an indirect election (1934-1937), followed by the "Estado Novo" (Portuguese for "New State," an authoritarian government installed by President Vargas) and afterwards through a direct election (1951-1954). Vargas took over after orchestrating the 1930 Revolution, bringing down Washington Luís' government. His 15 years in power—mainly during the New State dictatorial

phase—were characterized by authoritarianism, nationalism and populism, as well as the disregard of individual rights and democracy. Vargas was responsible for developing a kind of "legal hybrid" between the regimes of Mussolini's Italy and Salazar's Portuguese Estado Novo, copying repressive fascist strategies and conveying their same rejection of liberal capitalism, but attained power bearing few indications of his future quasi-fascist policies. In 1939, he created the Department of Press and Propaganda (DIP), an agency responsible for censorship and for the dissemination of his dictatorship's political ideals in mass media (TV, movies, music, books—and booklets).

[3] During the reign of John III (1502-1557), the Portuguese became the first Europeans to make contact with both China and Japan. He abandoned Muslim territories in North Africa in favor of trade with India and investments in Brazil. John III was responsible for the evangelization of the Far East and Brazil, in part through the introduction of Jesuit missions there. Both the Jesuits and the Portuguese Inquisition (introduced in 1536) were to become key institutions in Portugal and its Empire. John III considered the Jesuits particularly important for mediating Portuguese relations with native peoples, and the Inquisition served to spare Portugal from the civil upheavals of religious warfare of the sort that occurred in France and in other European nations during the 16th century (*Encyclopedia Britannica*).

[4] For Portugal, during the Portuguese Empirial period, the term *Metropolis*—from the Greek Metropolis "mother city" (polis being a city state, thus also used for any colonizing "mother country")—designated the European part of Portugal (Mainland Portugal plus the Azores and Madeira). The colonies in South America, Africa and Asia were called *Ultramar* (i.e., "overseas"). The word *Metropolis* was dropped from common usage in the mid-1970s when the last Portuguese colonies in Africa achieved independence (Webster, 2006).

[5] This is a traditional method of teaching reading and writing in Brazilian schools and adult literacy classes, as well as in many parts of the world. According to Chandrasekar (2002), the "synthetic method" begins by selecting the most common letters—those which can be easily written or which can be grouped on the basis of the similarity of their shapes. Then the students are taught to make words through the combination of the letters already learned (e.g., *pie, die, tie, lie*, etc.). The picture of an object is shown to the students and they are asked to pronounce the name of the object. Then their attention is drawn towards the sounds in the word they have pronounced and the letters representing those sounds are shown to them separately at first, and after that combined to make the word, which is printed next to the picture of the object. For a more detailed description of this methodology, see Cagliari (1998).

[6] Among the determinations of this Constitution, we can mention, for ex-

ample, the strengthening of the Executive Power (considered the "supreme State body"), the extinction of the post of Vice-President (the President was the "supreme authority in the country"), federal intervention in all States of the Union, the imposition of censorship, the extinction of political parties, the creation of a "political police," the extinction of state and municipal symbols and the consequent imposition of national symbols, the supreme authority of the State over the citizen (e.g., the institution of the death penalty and the "state of emergency," which allowed the President to suspend parliamentary immunities, invade households, arrest and exile opponents).

[7] Similarly, in spoken genres, the analysis of speech can no longer ignore gestures, intonations, facial expressions, etc., which are present in any verbal face-to-face exchange.

[8] Due to the limitations of space, I will present only some aspects of a couple of legal booklets. For the whole analysis of all my corpus and the complete theoretical framework and methodological strategies used (particularly regarding Multimodal and Critical Discourse Analysis), see Mozdzenski, 2006.

REFERENCES

Algranti, L. M. (2004). *Livros de devoção, atos de censura: Ensaios de história do livro e da leitura na América portuguesa (1750-1821)*. São Paulo: Hucitec/Fapesp.

Almeida, A. F. (1940). *A Constituição de 10 de Novembro explicada ao povo*. Rio de Janeiro: Imprensa Nacional/DIP.

Associação dos Magistrados Brasileiros. (1999). *Cartilha da justiça em quadrinhos*. Rio de Janeiro: Imprensa Oficial do Estado do Rio de Janeiro.

Bazerman, C. (2005). Cartas e a base social de gêneros diferenciados. In A. P. Dionisio & J. C. Hoffnagel (Eds.), *Charles Bazerman: Gêneros textuais, tipificação e interação* (J. C. Hoffnagel, Trans.) (pp. 83-99). São Paulo: Cortez.

Bhatia, V. K. (1993). *Analysing genre: Language use in professional settings*. New York: Longman.

Briggs, A., & Burke, P. (2004). *Uma história social da mídia* (M. C. P. Dias, Trans.). Rio de Janeiro: Zahar.

Brown, J. A. C. (1971). *Técnicas de persuasão: Da propaganda à lavagem cerebral* (O. A. Velho, Trans.). Rio de Janeiro: Zahar.

Cagliari, L. C. (1998). *Alfabetizando sem o bá-bé-bi-bó-bu*. São Paulo: Scipione.

Chandrasekar, R. (2002, August 13). *Nitty-gritty of teaching & learning* [Eletronic version]. Retrieved December 10, 2007, from http://www.hinduonnet.com

Daher, A. (1998). Escrita e conversão: A gramática tupi e os catecismos bilíngües no Brasil do século XVI. *Revista Brasileira de Educação, 8,* 31-43.

Dionisio, A. P. (2005). Gêneros multimodais e multiletramento. In A. M. Karwoski, B. Gaydeczka, & K. S. Brito (Eds.), *Gêneros textuais: Reflexões e ensino* (pp. 159-177). União da Vitória, Paraná, Brazil: Kaygangue.

Fairclough, N. (2001). *Discurso e mudança social* (I. Magalhães, Trans.). Brasília, Distritio Federal, Brazil: UnB.

Ferreira, C. L. L., & Mesquita Neto, T. (2004). *Manual de conduta do preso.* Rio de Janeiro: Forense.

Freire, P. (1987). *Pedagogia do oprimido.* Rio de Janeiro: Paz e Terra.

Garcia, N. J. (1982). *O Estado Novo: Ideologia e propaganda política.* São Paulo: Loyola.

Gomes, M. C. A. (2003). *A prática sócio-institucional do licenciamento ambiental: A tensão entre os gêneros discursivos, discursos e vozes.* Unpublished doctoral thesis, Federal University of Minas Gerais, Belo Horizonte, Brazil.

Houaiss, A. (2004). *Dicionário Houaiss de língua portuguesa.* Rio de Janeiro: Objetiva.

Jewitt, C., & Kress, G. (2003). *Multimodal literacy: New literacies and digital epistemologies.* Oxford: Peter Lang.

Kress, G., & van Leeuwen, T. (1996). *Reading images: The grammar of visual design.* New York: Routledge.

Kress, G., & van Leeuwen, T. (2001). *Multimodal discourse: The modes and media of contemporary communication.* New York: Oxford University Press.

Lemke, J. L. (2002). Travels in hypermodality. *Visual communication, 1*(3), 299-325.

Lessa, O. (1973). *Getúlio Vargas na literatura de cordel.* Rio de Janeiro: Documentário.

Lustosa, I. (2000). *Insultos impressos: A guerra dos jornalistas na independência (1821-1823).* São Paulo: Companhia das Letras.

Marcuschi, L. A. (2003). *O papel da atividade discursiva no exercício do controle social.* Paper presented at the Conference of the 55th Annual Reunion of the SBPC-ABRALIN, Federal University of Pernambuco, Pernambuco, Recife, Brazil.

Matos, M. (1987). Humanismo e evangelização no Oriente no século XVI. *Revista ICALP, 7-8,* 41-72.

McGee, M. C. (1980). The "ideograph": A link between rhetoric and ideology. *The Quarterly Journal of Speech, 66*(1), 1-16.

Mendonça, M. (2004). Diz-me com que(m) andas e te direi quem és: A relação entre as histórias em quadrinhos e seus suportes. Proceedings of the 2nd National Conference of the Language Sciences Applied to Teaching, Federal University of Paraíba, Paraíba, Brazil 1,273-1,283.

Moisés, M. (1971). *A literatura brasileira através dos textos.* São Paulo: Cultrix.

Mott, L. (1997). Cotidiano e vivência religiosa: Entre a capela e o calundu. In L. Souza (Ed.), *Cotidiano e vida privada na América portuguesa* (pp. 163-170). São

Paulo: Companhia das Letras.

Mozdzenski, L. P. (2004). A linguagem jurídica revisitada. Unpublished monograph, Federal University of Pernambuco, Pernambuco, Recife, Brazil.

Mozdzenski, L. P. (2006). *A cartilha jurídica: Aspectos sócio-históricos, discursivos e multimodais.* Unpublished master's thesis, Universidade Federal de Pernambuco, Pernambuco, Recife, Brazil. Retrieved December 10, 2007, from UFPE website: http://www.ufpe.br/pgletras/2006/dissertaoes/diss-leonardo-mozdzenski.pdf.

Netto, J. (2003). *Ao encontro da lei: O novo Código Civil ao alcance de todos.* São Paulo: Academia Paulista de Magistrados/Imprensa Oficial do Estado.

Neves, L. (1999). A "guerra das penas": Os impressos políticos e a independência do Brasil. *Tempo, 8*(4), 41-65.

Neves, L. (2002). Cidadania e participação política na época da Independência do Brasil. *Cad. Cedes, 22*(58), 47-64.

Nicola, J. (1987). *Literatura brasileira: Das origens aos nossos dias.* São Paulo: Scipione.

Paine, T. (1989). *Os direitos do homem* (S. Lopes, Trans.). Petrópolis, Rio de Janeiro, Brazil: Vozes.

Romanelli, O. (2002). *História da educação no Brasil.* São Paulo: Vozes.

Schlickmann, M. S. P. (2001). As cartilhas no processo de alfabetização. *Linguagem em (Dis)curso, 2*(1), 143-158.

Swales, J. (1990). *Genre analysis: English in academic and research settings.* Cambridge: Cambridge University Press.

Warat, L. A. (1995). *O direito e sua linguagem* (2nd ed.). Porto Alegre, Rio Grande do Sul, Brazil: Safe.

Webster, A. (2006). *The debate on the rise of the British empire.* Manchester, United Kingdom: Manchester University Press.

7   Uptake and the Biomedical Subject

Kimberly K. Emmons

INTRODUCTION

Recent health information campaigns draw on the ideological power of genres as a means of imposing subjectivities and subsequently disposing individuals toward biomedical interventions into their lives[1]. Asking readers "Are you depressed?", an online depression screening quiz hosted by iVillage.com offers a medicalized genre—the quiz is touted as "developed by the National Mental Health Association"—as an appropriate response to its query. By responding, readers not only *take* a quiz, they *take up* a genre and *take on* an identity that has been readied for diagnosis. Freadman (1994) has viewed such discrete generic activities as "shots" within a socially and textually constructed "game" (p. 44). She uses the term "uptake" to name "the bidirectional relation that holds between" genres (2002, p. 40), and she goes on to describe the ideological functions of that relation as occuring when genres are taken up, or translated, across boundaries (p. 43). On the iVillage site, the symptoms checklist, a diagnostic genre developed for use in research and clinical settings, crosses into a new social space, namely, the privacy of a reader's home or office, and this crossing redefines private life as clinical experience. The symptoms quiz, a list of multiple choice questions, produces a "return shot" from the reader: the "answers." In turn, the answers impel further action (visiting a doctor's office), and thus the textual chain provides an important map of the subject's transition from *reader* to *patient*. Such a textual analysis ironically elides the physical bodies and subjective actors that are the objects of medical interventions. Therefore, a reanimation of uptake with the individuals who ultimately perform it appears both necessary and timely.

The close of the twentieth century brought patients and physicians unprecedented access to information about health and illness. From online patient support groups to direct-to-consumer advertising, from memoirs to Hollywood movies, depression itself became a key character in the US health narrative. Its ubiquity may be attributed to any number of contemporary factors: the discovery of a new class of "wonder drugs," the selective serotonin reuptake inhibitors such as Prozac˚, which was approved for use in the US in 1987; the relaxing of direct-to-consumer advertising restrictions by the US Food and Drug Administration in 1997; and the growth and popularity of online health reference services, such as WebMD˚. Each of these factors continues to generate its own systems of genres, and each contributes to the discursive construction of the illness. For example, pharmaceutical development and subsequent advertising encourages the medicalization of sadness and social disconnection; information delivery services create statistical portraits of the illness, informing us that each year, 14.8 million American adults experience a major depressive disorder, and that women are more likely to be depressed than men (NIMH, 2006). The current experience of depression is thus highly rhetorical in that it responds to these circulating discursive constructions, and it becomes visible through the patterns of the illness's expression. Individuals make use of these patterns as they come to inhabit healthy and ill subjectivities, taking on dispositions and subjective orientations as they take up the available genres and discourses[2].

Despite this potential to shape individual subjectivities, genre scholars have attended to uptake primarily as a necessary heuristic for understanding the ways texts and genres cohere within systems of social activity. The concept of uptake has made visible a bidirectional temporal/textual relation between, for example, a writing prompt and a student's essay in first-year composition[3]. Yet to the extent that uptake is a relation that attests to ideological processes, it needs complication not only in terms of the textual and generic chains it can help us apprehend, but also in its rhetorical preparation of the *subjects* who enact and receive utterances. Via the processes of uptake, these subjects become available for other kinds of interventions—subjective, even somatic ones. Outside of the courtroom, where the fates of subjects and their bodies are determined first rhetorically (in a sentence) and then materially (in an incarceration or an execution)[4], the medical context perhaps most dramatically illustrates the high stakes for the relations among genres, texts, and subjects[5]. Within medical encounters, embodied rhetorical moves become particularly urgent and consequential, and the roles individuals assume as they negotiate their medical-rhetorical contexts—in addition to the roles of texts and genres within those contexts—provide clues to the construction of biomedical subjects. In the following analysis, I examine a web of texts constituting the discourse of depression as mental illness in the United States, and I argue for a reanimation of uptake with individual subjectivities at the center of theoretical consideration.

REDEFINING UPTAKE

As Freadman (2002) articulates it, "uptake" is the linkage between *and* the process of linking genres within and across systems of social action. In her analysis, uptake naturalizes the connection of two (or more) generic texts in order to create a coherent sequence of activity[6]. Outside the courtroom, in which the state is officially sanctioned to dispose of bodies and subjects according to generic codes, the rituals of medicine display the crucial role uptake plays in translating textual phenomena (words and genres) into physical outcomes (pharmaceuticals and procedures). Language manifests itself within the body via a series of inter-generic translations: a consultation interprets patient *talk* as a series of *symptoms*; a diagnosis responds to *symptoms* with a *prescription*; a pharmacist transforms a *prescription* into a *medication*; and a patient ingests the *medication* in accordance with the *directives* on the bottle, thereby incorporating into the body a material response to an initial, purely rhetorical locution. In each of these translations, a process legitimizes the connections between genres; both context (the office, laboratory, and pharmacy) and convention (the textual forms of professional legitimacy and the social rituals of prescribing), for example, must sanction the doctor's ability to write a prescription, and the pharmacist's to fill it. Freadman's articulation of uptake draws our attention to this process, which, in the medical example, socially legitimizes and individually compels the taking of drugs.

There is, however, more to a series of medical encounters than the forward march of textual signification that ultimately acts upon a patient's (passive) body. Within these medical encounters, the subject rhetorically positions her-self[7]—via the mechanisms of uptake—within a specific social activity, and in the process complicates the discursive scene. The value of uptake in promoting smooth travels within the semiotic landscape of health and illness seems clear: without a doctor's uptake of *symptoms* as evidence for a *diagnosis*, a patient is unrecognizable within the medical system and unable to receive treatment. But, before deciding to visit a doctor's office, the individual must first take up experiences themselves as potential symptoms. Before the biomedical system can impose control or deliver treatment through medication, the patient must first acquire the habits of mind that comprehend experiences as symptoms, and then take up the genres of medical interaction which lead, ultimately, to the doctor's office and the pharmacist's counter. These preliminary activities operate on the boundaries of social systems; they provide evidence of indi-vidual struggles for discursive agency; they offer insight into the workings of social and discursive power.

In most scholarship on uptake, analysis focuses on sequences of texts at the expense of attending to individual, embodied subjectivities. While Freadman herself uses the legal world to display physical punishment effected via a series of instances of uptake, the body of the punished subject becomes a mere arti-fact, and its death one more sign available for uptake within political and cul-tural debate over capital punishment. In Freadman's articulation, each genre in a sequence is an uptake of a previous genre, and each uptake depends upon what she calls "memory" to make the sequence intelligible and consequential (2002, p. 42). By drawing attention to the interstices between genres, Freadman's theory of uptake has itself been taken up by scholars seeking to name a process that authorizes genres (Bawarshi, 2003), that precludes generic recognition (Roberts & Sarangi, 2003), or that opens a space for the performance of identity (Kill, 2006). In each of these uses of uptake, however, attention is focused on the social and interactional consequences of individual acts, without full consideration of the subjectivities constituted through the processes of uptake. If we are to account for the power, particularly the intimate, embodied power, of uptake, we must redefine uptake not as the relation between two (or more) genres, but as the disposition of subjects that results from that relation. Genres as social actions are powerful only when they direct or forestall human interaction.

In theories of performativity, what passes for identity is enacted through symbolic displays—whether writing, dress, speech, or other semiotic means[8]. The emphasis in such theories is often on how the performance creates the conditions for its recognition in the future by citing past performances. Such citations are certainly not individual innovations; they rely on their previous contexts for their present authority. In her analysis of the discourse of femininity and individuals' practices in relation to it, Dorothy Smith (1990) argues for women as "secret agents," performing beyond the public scene of discourse. Smith writes of "the subject-in-discourse [who is] is denied agency," but also of "another subject who is here speaking in her capacity as a knowledgeable practitioner of the discourse of femininity" (pp. 192-193). In other words, agency is available through a skillful articulation of circulating discourses, and agency need not—indeed cannot—be directed toward liberation from discourse *per se*. Instead, agency derives from the choices of citation made available to and taken up by individual subjects. Processes of uptake similarly cite previous genres, discourses, and situations to act within new scenes; agents represent themselves within the genres and discourses that are most likely to be recognized. Drawing on historical records, Solomon (2001) documents such adaptive behavior among seventeenth-century melancholics:

> Two-thirds of the aristocrats who came to [a physician] complained of melancholy humors; and these men and women were well informed, speaking not simply of waves of sadness but complaining quite specifically on the basis of the scientific knowledge and fashion of the time. One such patient was "desirous to have something to avoid the fumes arising from the spleen." (p. 300)

For these patients, the "scientific knowledge and fashion of the time" provided the language that made them recognizable to their physician. Their reproduction of that language enabled them to receive treatment, but it also signaled their incorporation into a social discourse that associated melancholy with "great depth, soulfulness, complexity, and even genius" (p. 300). Their performances, Solomon suggests, were motivated by the desire to embody a poetic sensibility, rather than by the experience of illness. Such discursive manipulation represents active agency on the part of the patients (they secure a doctor's uptake of their performance *as* melancholy, and they receive the treatments that they seek), but it also represents their submission to a fashionable identity which had them ingesting concoctions that included "lapis lazuli, hellebore, cloves, [and] licorice powder . . . dissolved in white wine" (p. 300). The ability to model locutions on past genres and discourses provides evidence for the processes of uptake, processes that entail subjective dispositions and naturalize additional rhetorical and material responses.

To account for these processes of uptake, I expand Dorothy Smith's concept of the "secret agent" who uses discourses for her own pleasure (as the seventeenth-century melancholic aristocrats also seem to have done) to encompass the "double agent" in Bawarshi's (2003) characterization of the student writer as "both an agent *of* his or her desires and actions and an agent *on behalf* of already existing desires and actions" (p. 50). This more expansive notion of agency works within circulating discourses (a patient must describe his pain in familiar ways) but that also has the ability to achieve individual ends (the patient secures the intervention that he seeks). Yet in these achievements, individuals produce personal dispositions that have significant physical consequences. Thus, the problem of uptake is the problem of what is *taken on* when an individual *takes up* particular genres and discourses.

To write or speak within a system of social activity is also to assume a variety of habits and dispositions that are commonplace to that system. This may be partly a conscious act, but it may also be the inevitable consequence of being recognized within the system. As Schryer (2002) notes:

> Each genre . . . has a different trajectory, a different potential for producing world views and representing human agency. In my view all genres operate in this fashion. They function as discourse formations or constellations of strategies that instantiate a "commonsense" understanding of time and space that can affect their writers or readers. We can become habituated to these constellations of resources and fail to see the possibilities for the constraints on human action that they enact. (p. 85)

This is the power inherent in choices of genre: to position subjects and to allow them to inhabit (only) particular social roles. To the extent that scholars have investigated the generic positioning of subjects, they have largely considered the selection and maintenance of group membership through the acquisition of genre knowledge (e.g., Schryer, 1994). Bazerman's (1988) analysis of the development of research genres and the organization of the personal (and, increasingly, public) interactions of those who came to view themselves as *scientists*, however, clearly demonstrates the stakes for individuals and communities. Confronted with the realities of scientific practice, scientists perceive a "situation and available alternatives and in their choices make and remake social structure[s]" (p. 129). Nevertheless, the thrust of Bazerman's analysis is toward the construction of *science*, and, though that necessarily also includes the construction of *scientists*, individual subjectivities beyond that of the professional scientist are not his primary concern. In the contemporary medical context of depression, individuals choose from alternatives that confer not social standing as Bazerman's scientists hope to achieve, but medical recognition and subsequently the regulation of their lived experiences. Such selections—by non-members of a professional community, with the purpose not of joining but of interacting with the professional community—draw attention to the discursive and bodily consequences of uptake.

FORMS OF UPTAKE

Uptake—redefined as the disposition(s) assumed through the use of genres—encompasses the effects of those generic choices upon individuals. Making uptake visible, however, requires a means of marking and referring to the textual traces of the process. In the following analysis, I distinguish between two kinds of activities, though I do not mean to imply that they operate separately. Rather, this division allows me to focus attention on distinct textual phenomena that illuminate the subjectivities available and contestable within processes of uptake. First, "generic uptake" describes the subject's selection and translation of forms of discourse (and the impositions of power those forms imply) into new speech situations. Drawing on the textual and rhetorical patterns of other genres, generic uptake, to borrow Austin's (1975) terms, makes "nonserious" use of the speech acts that the genres are meant to perform (p. 122). Yet these nonserious uses are not, therefore, powerless (as Austinian speech-act theory would predict, given their violation of the felicity conditions for their performance). Rather, they can have very serious consequences because the forms are not empty of social dispositions when they are taken up[9]. Generic uptake can be used to exert power across institutional and social boundaries. In Freadman (2002), just such a "nonserious" use of courtroom genres allows a politician to cast a dissenting judge in the role of state's witness, thereby "confirming the disempowerment of one jurisdiction [the court] and the power of the other [the government]" (p. 47). Thus, generic uptake involves the selection and translation of typified forms (e.g., testimony) and social roles (e.g., prosecutor, witness) into new discursive situations, thereby potentially restricting future uptake and the participants' possible subjectivities[10]. Instances of generic uptake focus our analytic attention on the organization of bodies and the persons they materially ground within a social scene.

"Discursive uptake" is a second kind of textual representation of the processes of uptake, where key phrases, rather than patterns of social organization or discursive form, are taken up in new situations[11]. Here again, the object selected must be recontextualized within its new speech situation. But, unlike those of generic uptake, the dispositional effects of discursive uptake are more individual than collective. Where generic uptake focuses attention on social organizations and roles available to multiple participants, discursive uptake provides clues to the positioning of the individual subject[12]. Political catch phrases do this extremely economically: a speaker need only use the single phrase "pro-choice" to find herself read as a particular kind of political subject. More importantly, her subjectivity is shaped by entailments within the larger "pro-choice" discourse when she takes up this single phrase. In this way, discursive uptake necessitates the assumption of particular attitudes and dispositions. In medical contexts, many of these dispositions are physical as well as rhetorical. In both forms of uptake, textual performances negotiate previous, current, and future utterances through the related practices of citation, articulation, and entailment. In generic uptake, these practices draw forward previous forms and social organizations that work to secure future roles and responses available to interlocutors. In discursive uptake, these practices draw forward previous key phrases and dispositions that work to position individuals within recognizable social systems.

As they encounter the discourse of depression, individuals use both forms of uptake as performative and interpretive acts. They draw on influential texts such as Kramer's (1997) reissued *Listening to Prozac,* which calls attention to the pharmaceutical treatments that modulate the experiences of individuals. That the revised edition of this text appears a mere four years after the original attests to the pubic appetite for such attention. Kramer's (1993) description of a "cosmetic psychopharmacology" that seemed to allow individuals to alter their *selves* in addition to treating their illnesses catalyzed a wide range of responses (p. xvi). Such responses include personal stories of depression (Casey, 2001), scholarly collections that debate the cultural repercussions of antidepressants (Elliott & Chambers, 2004), memoirs (Wurtzel, 1994; Danquah, 1998; J. Smith 1999), and monographs that analyze the psychiatric (Metzl, 2003) and pharmaceutical (Healy, 2004) communities. Many of these texts circulate without meriting much rhetorical analysis. Where such analysis has been directed, scholars have attended to the power of master documents such as the *Diagnostic and Statistical Manual of Mental Disorders* (DSM) to organize the social scene of therapy (McCarthy, 1990; Berkenkotter, 2001). While some studies consider the content and contexts of discursive repetitions (Ferrara, 1994; Ravotas & Berkenkotter, 1998; Berkenkotter & Ravotas, 2001, 2002) within therapeutic relationships, none have attended specifically to the paths that lead to such therapeutic interactions. Within the larger social discourse of depression—represented by the myriad texts listed above—individuals select and translate genres and terms that help them make sense of their own experiences. Within these selections and translations, they encounter and assume new subjectivities that ready them for medical intervention.

Textual traces of these processes include what I have defined as generic and discursive uptake. In the discourse of depression, a common generic form is the symptoms list, which defines the boundaries of the illness by enumerating the number of discrete symptoms that sufferers must experience to qualify for diagnosis. Generic uptake of this symptoms list, therefore, organizes social actors around the diagnostic moment. In addition, the biological shift in psychiatry has given rise to a biomedical discourse that further defines depression as a "chemical imbalance." Discursive uptake of this catch phrase shapes individual dispositions toward biomedical treatment models and responses to the illness. In the following examples, these processes operate in concert to shape the depressed subject and her future responses to the illness. Traces of uptake within a variety of texts reveal the positioning of the depressed subject as a result of complex interactions among texts, genres, scenes, and individuals.

GENERIC UPTAKE OF THE SYMPTOMS LIST FOR DEPRESSION

According to the DSM, a "Major Depressive Disorder is characterized by one or more Major Depressive Episodes (i.e., at least 2 weeks of depressed mood or loss of interest accompanied by at least four additional symptoms of depression)" (APA, 2000, p. 345). First published in 1952, the DSM has rapidly become the governing document for psychiatric diagnoses in the US, and, therefore, it has come to regulate diverse systems of activity, from scientific research to health insurance reimbursement. The third edition of the DSM, published in 1980, contained the first sets of symptoms that were intended to classify distinct disorders[13]. These symptoms, in the form of a short checklist, were taken up from research instruments (e.g., Beck et al., 1961; Center, 1971), and they have subsequently been taken up in self-assessment tools (e.g., "The Zung Assessment Tool" available online at www.Prozac.com). In the current DSM-IV (2000), the symptoms for depression include:

- depressed mood
- diminished interest/pleasure in activities

- significant weight loss or gain
- insomnia or hypersomnia
- psychomotor agitation or retardation
- fatigue or loss of energy
- feelings of worthlessness or excessive guilt
- diminished ability to think or concentrate
- recurrent thoughts of death or suicidal ideation (p. 356)

Originating from contexts of empirical research and acquiring medical authority through its reproduction in the DSM, the symptoms list positions expertise in the interpretive act of "scoring" the quiz or checklist. Users of the genre have either experience of the symptoms (patients) or knowledge of the meaning of combinations of those symptoms (researchers/doctors). By completing a questionnaire or checklist, an individual literally submits the form and herself to a medical interpretation. Via the genre, personal experience becomes the property of diagnostic readings, and the ability to interpret such experiences moves outside of the individual's purview.

Examining texts that display generic uptake of the symptoms list for depression, we can see the social roles of users being manipulated and redefined. One of the most productive sites of such uptake is the direct-to-consumer pharmaceutical advertisement in the US. A 2001 Zoloft' advertisement transforms the symptoms list into a series of second-person imperatives:

- You know when you're not feeling like yourself.
- You're tired all the time.
- You may feel sad, hopeless . . . and lose interest in things you once loved.
- You may feel anxious and can't even sleep.
- Your daily activities and relationships suffer.
- You know when you just don't feel right.

In this case, the diagnostic outcome is tied to an apparently authoritative reader who is encouraged to accept diagnostic certainty—she *knows* when things "just don't feel right." Nevertheless, her masquerade is revealed by the advertisement's subsequent reinstatement of traditional medical authority: "[o]nly your doctor can diagnose depression." The campaign's tagline—"When you know more about what's wrong, you can help make it right"—places the reader in the grammatical subject position, suggesting a repositioning of the actors in typical diagnostic settings. The reader (who "knows") and the pharmaceutical manufacturer (who provides information) assume more active and assertive roles, but those roles travel only as far as the doctor's office, where the reader is commanded to "Talk to your doctor about ZOLOFT." Even the empowered consumer has limited options for responding to the disorder. The generic uptake in this advertisement instantiates the social organization of acts of diagnosis, and even though the reader is encouraged to play the role of her own doctor initially, she is reinstated as the recipient of medical authority within the larger context of the advertisement. Serial acts of generic uptake accomplish this medicalization of experience: first, the DSM takes up the genre of the symptoms list from the clinical research community; then, the advertisement takes up the genre and translates it into a persuasive appeal; and, finally, the reader takes up the genre and the implicit subjectivity of an empowered *consumer* whose knowledge prepares her to submit herself to medical intervention.

In her memoir, *Undercurrents*, Martha Manning (1995) discusses her own struggle to accept a diagnosis of depression. A psychologist herself, she turns to the familiar genre of the symptoms list to persuade herself that what she is feeling *cannot* be depression:

> I pull out my manual and flip to the section on major depression. I want a second opinion. I do this in those quizzes in women's magazines with the little tests that will answer questions like, "Are you keeping your man satisfied in bed?" or "what does your closet say about your personality." I love those stupid quizzes. I fill them out, add up my score, and then quickly turn to the section that gives me my rating. If I don't like the results, I automatically turn back to the test and take it over. I change answers that were only marginally true, or ones that I've rationalized aren't really true at all, trying to get my score into a more acceptable range. I do that now. But as I work my way down the list, there are no marginal answers, not a single area in which I can "massage the data." . . . I am rattled for the rest of the day. (p. 73)

In her description, Manning seeks "a second opinion" from the genre contained within her diagnostic manual, and she initially assumes that she has control over her performance within that genre, likening it to "those stupid quizzes" in women's magazines[14]. Here, Manning performs a generic uptake that attempts to reconcile two genres that appear similar in their positioning of herself as a respondent. The diagnostic symptoms list, however, resists the revisions Manning customarily performs on the more frivolous personality quizzes. In her admission of being "rattled" by her inability to "massage the data" in her response to the symptoms list, Manning demonstrates her awareness of a received identity, a suddenly medicalized persona that has been entailed by her uptake of the symptoms list. Thus, generic uptake positions social actors (Manning as a respondent, the text as a representative of medical authority) and they entail particular subjectivities (in this case an uncomfortable reception of a patient identity for Manning).

Beyond published examples of generic uptake, the implications of taking on the subjectivities encoded in the symptoms list are clearly visible in the talk of women experiencing mild to moderate symptoms of depression. In 2002, I conducted two semi-structured group interviews with university students to capture some of this talk about mental health and illness. The subjects in my study were recruited via a flyer that mimicked the symptoms list (e.g., Are you feeling blue?), and to qualify, they had to complete a diagnostic survey (I used the CES-D [Center, 1971]) and score within a range that would classify them as "sub-clinical." As such, these women represent the "worried well," a group that scholars argue is particularly affected by biomedical discourses (Eade & Bradshaw, 1995, p. 61). In the conversations excerpted here, I highlight moments of discussion about completing the study materials. For the women in my interviews, the questionnaire was at first troubling, but quickly became an important determiner of their health status. In one group, I invited the women to "tell me a little bit about [their] reaction[s]" to the study screening materials[15]. The answers below occur within roughly five minutes of conversation:

> Stephanie: I wanted to check between the boxes. Like, okay, last week this happened. Oh that's not quite the same as 3 or 4; it was kind of 2 and 3. I probably tried, but I've kind of forced them into categories for simplicity's sake.

Here, Stephanie refers to the choices available on the CES-D, which require respondents to indicate how often in the past week they have experienced various symptoms of depression. A few turns later, Jennifer responds to my initial question, and Mei and Stephanie elaborate on their experiences of completing the study materials:

> Jennifer: Yeah, I don't really remember. The only thing I remember, um, filling that out is, "Oh, am I going to be picked for this study?" ((laughs)) . . . .

> Mei: Well I just I guess it was just nice . . . . If you asked me to write it out, I might not have written all the symptoms, but then checking the box was like: "Yeah, yeah, I do have that" ((laughs)) . . .

Stephanie: It was kind of a convenient compartmentalizing experience. "Oh, yes, this is what this is. Oh, wow, other people feel—[this]. This is so validating."

For Stephanie, the experience of completing the CES-D was "a convenient compartmentalizing experience" that allowed her to validate her feelings; she assumes the categories on the form represent others' experiences. Significantly, however, she first describes how her uptake of the CES-D was not immediately validating: she "wanted to check between the boxes." In these few minutes of conversation, Stephanie's self-presentation moves quickly from that of an individual whose experiences are *not* congruent with the genre to one whose experiences are validated and recognizable within the genre. Mei, too, finds the genre comforting, and implies that the genre itself helped her to identify symptoms that she "might not have written" had I asked simply for a narrative. For Stephanie and Mei, and indeed for others I spoke with, the genre is viewed as a tool for producing a particular identity, first as someone qualified for my study (as Jennifer suggests above), and also, often, as someone who is depressed.

The women's reception of an identity contained within the CES-D, namely, the identity of a depressed person, is striking because none of the women in my study technically qualified for a clinical diagnosis of depression. The power of the genre to help Mei recognize her symptoms and to validate Stephanie's experiences implies that the generic uptake helps translate experiences into symptoms, and therefore helps move individual bodies into the biomedical system. Despite all of my precautions—explaining that this was a study only of the language of depression, selecting only women who were not clinically depressed—several of my participants seemed to expect medical intervention or outcomes, a byproduct, I believe, of their generic uptake of my screening materials. The practice of generic uptake entails interacting with and through a form that encodes particular identities; once the form has been accepted, the medicalized identity necessarily follows.

DISCURSIVE UPTAKE OF THE BIOMEDICAL MODEL

Discursive uptake draws upon the stock phrases and dispositions of specific communities. For example, the biomedical discourse on depression is best represented by the current popularity of "brain chemistry" as source and possible cure for mental disorders. In this discourse, depression is a treatable "imbalance" of chemicals, essentially a mechanical problem that requires (most often) a pharmaceutical intervention. Poet Chase Twichell (2001), writing about her experiences with depression, relies heavily on the biomedical discourse of mechanics and brain chemistry. She writes:

> The biochemical chain reaction that results [in depression] is extremely complicated, much of it still hypothetical. What is known is that certain neurotransmitters (especially serotonin and norepinephrine) do not work properly, causing a disruption in the flow of information between nerve cells. It's like a game of telephone; the message gets lost as it travels, eventually affecting cellular metabolism, hormone balance, and the circadian system, the clock that determines cycles of rest and activity. (p. 23)

In Twichell's description, qualities of the biomedical discourse include the use of chemical names, for example, "serotonin" and "norepinephrine," and the reliance on mechanical and systemic metaphors. Twichell uses the images of a chain reaction, information flow, a game of telephone, and the notion that a clock regulates bodily activity to describe the mechanisms of depression. Importantly, she notes that what is wrong is that something "do[es] not work properly." This idea of *working* is key to the mechanical metaphor that sits at the root of the biomedical discourse; if something does not work, the solution is to fix or replace the faulty mechanism[16]. Thus, discursive uptake regulates dispositions—here Twichell understands her own depression as a malfunctioning system in need of repair—and enables particular responses to material realities. The biomedical discourse influences the research, treatment, and ideological models for depression.

Pharmaceutical companies are, obviously, very invested in this biomedical discourse; they are uniquely positioned to offer solutions to these mechanical problems. Advertisements for many antidepressants use the idea of levels of serotonin in their explanations of depression. In the words of one Prozac ad, "When you're clinically depressed, one thing that can happen is the level of serotonin (a chemical in your body) may drop." Similarly, in a Zoloft advertisement, the text asserts, "While the cause is unknown, depression may be related to an imbalance of naturally occurring chemicals in the brain." In both cases, the pharmaceutical companies are very careful to use mitigating language such as the modals *can* and *may*. Nevertheless, these markers of uncertainty do not detract from the power of the biomedical discourse. Implicit in such talk of "levels" and "balances" is the assurance that there is an optimal level, a "fill line," for serotonin or other neurotransmitters[17]. New York writer and teacher Joshua Wolf Shenk (2001) describes the reliance on the mechanical models of depression as a means of lessening uncertainties and "provok[ing] the least fear of the unknown." He writes:

Phrases like "running out of gas," "neurotransmitter deficits," "biochemical malfunctions," and "biological brain disease" are terribly common, and are favored by well-intentioned activists who seek parity between emotional and somatic illnesses. Pharmaceutical companies also like machine imagery, since they manufacture the oils, coolants, and fuels that are supposed to make us run without knocks or stalls. This language not only reflects, but constructs our reality. (p. 247)

Here, Shenk recognizes the power of discursive uptake to "construct our reality." In this discourse, depression is essentially a mechanical problem—an imbalance of chemicals—and, as such, it is easily resolved with pharmaceuticals that rebalance the system. Individuals who take up the biomedical discourse, often through citation of the catch-phrase "chemical imbalance," ready themselves for such pharmaceutical interventions. The simplicity of a mechanical metaphor holds explanatory power for such individuals, and leads them to discount other possible causes of and responses to depression. Such reliance produces subjectivities that are then doubly vulnerable to a common pharmaceutical "poop-out" phenomenon. Lauren Slater (1998) describes the betrayal: "As fast as Prozac had once, like a sexy firefighter, doused the flames of pain, the flames now flared back up, angrier than ever, and my potent pill could do nothing to quell the conflagration" (p. 116). Having come to rely on the "sexy firefighter"—a gendering of cure as telling as the gendering of the disease itself—Slater cannot reconcile her returned symptoms with her original conceptual framework. She writes, "Prozac never again made me as well as it once had" (p. 127).

The conceptual value of the biomedical explanation is clear to the women in my interviews. The women remember pharmaceutical advertisements as key disseminators of this information:

Paige: Zoloft has a commercial with the little guy who bounces around and—

Claire: Yeah, and explains the, you know, chemical imbalance. How it works—

KE: What do you think of that commercial?

Claire: It made sense to me for some reason.

KE: The diagram, or the little guy?

Claire: The diagram. I was like, "Okay there's not really anything go-
            ing on in my mind that I should be this depressed about. You
            know . . . I have it going really well right now, so why do I feel
            sad? Maybe it's a chemical imbalance."

Here, the key feature, for Claire at least, is the explanation of the "chemical
imbalance, how it works." This discursive uptake serves an important function
for Claire's self-identity. She signals her acceptance of this concept in her final
turn, saying, "I have it going really well right now . . . Maybe it's a chemical imbalance." In this example, Claire has taken up the phrase "chemical imbalance"
and actively applied it to herself. She is uncritical of the advertisement ("It made
sense to me for some reason"), and seems to be particularly persuaded by the
diagram—which offers a "dramatization" of neurotransmitters with and without
Zoloft—that organizes her understanding of her own emotions. In this case, her
discursive uptake disposes Claire to see her experiences as the result of her own
faulty brain chemistry.

Similarly, in other moments, the discursive uptake of a biomedical discourse
might be seen as readying the women's bodies for medical intervention. When I
asked the women (after several mentions of the phrase) how they might know if
they had a "chemical imbalance," they were quick to disavow any ability to diagnose themselves, but they seemed to assume that the imbalance was nevertheless
specifically quantifiable:

KE: So, how would you know if you had a chemical imbalance?
Mei: I don't know how to diagnose it ((laughs)). I don't know, I mean
        aren't there tests they could do? Or I mean? I'm sure 'cause
        ((pause)) actually yeah, I don't know.

In this excerpt, Mei performs the subject position that may well have been entailed by her generic uptake of the symptoms list (see above): she disavows an
ability to "diagnose it" and questions whether "they" could do tests to confirm
a "chemical imbalance." In this moment, she is a patient, and the third-person
pronoun indicates a medical authority; Mei is no longer validated by the genres
and discourses of depression, she is subjecting herself to a medical model. Further, the notion that there should be "tests" that could confirm an imbalance
demonstrates the entailments of her discursive uptake. She has not simply taken
up the catch-phrase, she has also taken on the implied mechanical model of
depression as well. Ultimately, this uptake seeks the translation of her body into
the medical system via diagnostic tests and eventual pharmaceutical intervention. This desire for a precise diagnosis is echoed by patients in sociologist David

Karp's (1996) *Speaking of Sadness*. One man's diagnosis "became clear to him after 'they gave me a blood test and said, "You're depressed." And I believed them.'" Karp's informant experiences a series of hospitalizations following this conversion, and Karp describes the moment as "the beginning of his licit drug therapy" (p. 84). The discursive uptake of the biomedical model for depression clearly has consequences that play out within and upon patients' bodies.

CONCLUSION: THE CONSEQUENCES OF UPTAKE

In the preceding examples, generic and discursive uptake provide evidence for the shaping of individual dispositions toward experiences that come to constitute the mental illness depression. Scholars are quite good at identifying the power of discourse to structure lived experience, so my analysis of discursive uptake should be relatively familiar. However, the consequences of generic uptake seem less well understood, and, further, the interactions *between* generic and discursive uptake—such as the yoking of the genre of the symptoms list to the biomedical explanation for depression in the Zoloft advertisement—have not been adequately theorized among medical rhetoricians. In the discourse of depression, generic and discursive uptake operate in a wide variety of textual locations, requiring that we attend to social scenes more diverse and dispersed than traditional therapeutic settings. News reporting, popular self-help literature, and, even more ephemeral, word-of-mouth practices provide the environment for individual uptake, by which I mean the disposition of the self in relation to biomedical realities.

Generic uptake of the symptoms list for depression has become so commonplace that it begins to resemble discursive uptake. In a 1999 interview with *Newsweek* magazine, US Second Lady Tipper Gore talks candidly about her depression, which began after her son was injured in an accident:

> I think I can say this in generic terms: one's mind plays tricks with oneself. It's a very insidious kind of disease because you don't know you have it and you think . . . that the world would be better off without you. That is very serious . . . . There are a number of signs and symptoms of depression [including gaining weight, changes in sleep habits, lack of energy and feelings of low self-esteem]; if you read down the list and two to four of those apply to you for more than two weeks, you should see a mental-health professional. That's what I did. I know so much about this—I have a master's degree, I was going into family counseling—so in a way, I quickly knew. I looked it up and went, OK, this time I'm calling my friend not as a friend but professionally. (Rosenberg, 1999, p. 51)

Here, Gore describes depression "in generic terms," by which she means terms applicable to everyone, but by which her text also implies the diagnostic genre itself. "There are a number of signs and symptoms of depression," Gore relates, but the specific symptoms must be inserted by *Newsweek* itself. The habits and social organizations of the genre, however, are preserved in Gore's description: "if . . . two to four of those [symptoms] apply to you for more than two weeks, you should see a mental-health professional." Here, Gore positions the expertise outside of herself and, importantly, outside of her readers as well. The reduction of the genre to a mere reference implies a thorough acceptance of its entailments, not only of a patient subjectivity, but also of dispositions toward one's body and experiences. These include a reliance on quantifiable symptoms ("two to four") and rapid diagnostic decisions ("I quickly knew"). As a news story, Gore's description of her depression is a performance that anticipates its own citation and repetition by its readers; it expects uptake.

In one of my group interviews, Claire, a graduate student, describes a recent visit to the campus health center:

Claire: I went to Campus Health and talked to a woman in there. She asked me questions, and I told her my symptoms, which are all on the list, and ((pause)) she didn't, you know, say "You're depressed," she said it sounded that way and recommended counseling and medication.

In this excerpt, and at the time of the interview itself, Claire seems unsure of how to respond to her visit. She is both antagonistic toward the "woman in there," who, presumably, has at least some medical training, though I suspect was not a physician or psychologist, and also anxious to conform to the diagnostic scene, which compels her to describe her "symptoms" rather than to provide "answers" to the questions she is asked. Claire has already translated her experiences into symptoms, and has determined for herself that those symptoms are "all on the list." She seems frustrated that the health professional does not offer explicit diagnosis, and she remains ambivalent about whether she will take up the recommended therapeutic response. This generic uptake, I believe, mirrors Mei's assumption that there are "tests" that can determine whether an individual has a "chemical imbalance." In both cases, the women have already adopted subjectivities that position them as patients with limited responsibilities and options. They have done so at least in part through processes of generic and discursive uptake within the circulating discourse of depression. Yet their hesitation and self-doubt shows them to be at least partially aware of the restrictions encoded within instances of uptake: the women in my study held open the possibility of "going that route," by which they meant taking antidepressants, but they were not yet willing to assume a biomedical subjectivity completely. Acting as double agents within the discourse of depression, these women inhabit complicated subjectivities and authorities in relation to their own bodies and selves. They are both acting as their own agents, claiming the power to choose the pharmaceutical "route" or not, depending on their own definitions of health and illness, and they are also acting as agents of the biomedical discourse, relinquishing their rights to the diagnostic interpretation of their experiences.

For genre studies, then, the complementary dynamics of generic and discursive uptake reveal much about the formation of subjectivities in relation to professional communities and larger social networks[18]. Because the dispositions entailed by instances of uptake shape the future performances of individuals for themselves (Gore identifies herself as depressed and seeks therapy) and for others (the Second Lady demonstrates the responsibility of depressed women), attention to uptake promises to yield a clearer understanding of how *experiences* become *symptoms* and how *individuals* become *patients*. Moving beyond the textual performances occasioned by generic production, attention to uptake allows us to follow individuals through their interactions with multiple genre systems. As individuals navigate the many systems to which they belong and with which they must interact, they inevitably take up both the positions implied by generic coordination and the dispositions implied by discursive construction. Beyond exploring the textual connections within such systems, attention to the dynamics of uptake illuminates the formation of subjectivities in and through genres, and thus explicates the complex relationships individuals cultivate with biomedical and other powerful institutions.

NOTES

[1] I wish to express my gratitude to the participants in my research interviews for their willingness to share their experiences. I also very gratefully acknowledge the generous and thoughtful commentary on earlier drafts of this essay, provided by Kurt Koenigsberger and by the editors of this volume, particularly Charles Bazerman. This work additionally benefited from the comments of participants in the 4th International Symposium on Genre Studies, my travel to which was funded, in part, through the auspices of the Foreign Travel Grant program of the Baker-Nord Center for the Humanities, Case Western Reserve University.

[2] Segal (2007) makes a similar claim for the power of conventional narratives to constrain the potential subjectivities available to breast cancer survivors.

[3] This classroom application of uptake is given fullest description by Bawarshi (2003, pp. 135-141).

[4] Freadman (1999) provides a detailed account of the circulation and uptake of legal and cultural genres in relation to the case of Ronald Ryan, whose execu-

tion in 1967 marks the last imposition of capital punishment in Australia.

[5] For a more broadly rhetorical analysis of healthcare genres and interactions, see Segal (2005).

[6] Miller (1994) argues for a notion of genre that accounts for it as "social action." Freadman's work suggests that such action occurs *only* when a particular genre secures its own uptake. In Freadman's conception, it is genre itself that has agency and accomplishes social action, and individual subjects are relegated to a role in which they produce texts that are recognizable (i.e., can secure uptake) within appropriate generic systems. I am arguing that subjective agency ought to be returned to individuals in relation to "social action"—not only do speaking subjects' acts of textual production have significant effects within social systems, but also upon the shapes and trajectories of their own and others' individual subjectivities.

[7] The use of the feminine pronoun here is intentional—depression is commonly believed to be a "woman's disease" and many of the texts that encourage self-diagnosis and treatment target women in the US.

[8] See, for example, Butler's (1990) description of gender as a performance. In addition, Butler (1997) argues that the performative act is recognized less through individual intention than through successful "*repetition or citation of a prior and authoritative set of practices*" (p. 51). This definition emphasizes the role of citation within successful performative acts, and it parallels Freadman's (2002) sense of uptake as a process that derives legitimacy from gesturing backwards to previous utterances before enabling future texts (p. 42).

[9] This analysis is drawn in large part from Freadman (2002).

[10] In processes of translation, generic uptake opens the possibility for revision of forms and subjectivities. Thieme (2006) argues that, within journalistic responses to women's suffrage in Canada, the genre of direct political action (militancy) is cited (Freadman's "selection") in various ways, but that it is also redefined (Freadman's "translation") as unnecessary and unfeminine within the Canadian context. In my terms, the journalistic responses perform the generic uptake that shapes material realities and gendered identities for suffragists in Canada.

[11] Theories of intertextuality (Foucault, 1972; Kristeva, 1980; Worton & Still, 1990; Fairclough, 1992), and heteroglossia (Bakhtin, 1986) are important foundations for my concept of "discursive uptake." In addition, Wells (2003) provides a provocative discussion of repetition and interdisciplinary translation of both discourse and genre.

[12] Something like discursive uptake is the process that Bawarshi (2006) identifies in his response to a special issue of *College English* on language diversity. Reading essays by leading scholars on World Englishes, Bawarshi notes that student discursive choices—what I would call their discursive uptake—can often

seem dissonant or insincere to instructors within school-sponsored activities. Bawarshi calls for closer attention to such moments of uptake for what they can tell us about students' and instructors' attitudes and ideologies.

[13] Critiques of the DSM, including its history and authorship, add additional insight to this analysis (see Kirk & Kutchins, 1992; Kutchins & Kirk, 1997; Reynolds, Mair & Fisher, 1992).

[14] I have argued elsewhere that the overlap of diagnostic and personality quizzes is an important generic blend that specifically targets women (Emmons, 2007).

[15] I have changed names and identifying details to protect the privacy of the women who participated in my study. In addition, I have edited the excerpts for clarity, primarily by deleting false-starts and adding some punctuation; deletions of more than a single word and all additions are enclosed in square brackets.

[16] The mechanical metaphors for depression are often explicitly gendered, and this further complicates their discursive uptake. For example, in *Women and Depression*, Rosenthal (2000) explains that the "system of brain chemistry exchange is like a washing machine" (p. 157).

[17] In a telling critique of the biomedical model of serotonin imbalance, Lacasse and Leo (2005) write, "The take-home message for consumers viewing SSRI advertisements is probably that SSRIs work by normalizing neurotransmitters that have gone awry. This was a hopeful notion 30 years ago, but is not an accurate reflection of present-day scientific evidence" (p. 1214).

[18] Gender plays an important role in these processes, as I have noted above. See also Bazerman (1999) for an investigation of the gendered roles made available through the new genres.

REFERENCES

American Psychiatric Association. (2000). *Diagnostic and statistical manual of mental disorders* (4th ed.). Washington, D.C.: American Psychiatric Association.

Are you depressed? (n.d.). iVillage Total Health. Retrieved November 1, 2007, from http://quiz.ivillage.com/health/tests/depression.htm.

Austin, J. L. (1975). How to do things with words: the William James Lectures delivered at Harvard University in 1955 (J.O. Urmson, & M. Sbisà, Eds.) (2nd ed.). Cambridge, Massachusetts: Harvard University Press.

Bakhtin, M. (1986). *Speech genres and other late essays* (C. Emerson & M. Holquist, Eds., V.W. McGee, Trans.). Austin: University of Texas Press.

Bawarshi, A. (2003). *Genre and the invention of the writer.* Logan: Utah State University Press.

Bawarshi, A. (2006). Response: Taking up language differences in composition. *College English, 68*(6), 652-656.

Bazerman, C. (1988). Literate acts and the emergent social structure of science. In C. Bazerman, *Shaping written knowledge* (pp. 128-150). Madison: University of Wisconsin Press.

Bazerman, C. (1999). The language of flowers: Domesticating electric light. In C. Bazerman, *The languages of Edison's light* (pp. 313-331). Cambridge, Massachusetts: MIT Press.

Beck, A.T., Ward, C. H., Mendelson, M., Mock, J., & Erbaugh, J. (1961). An inventory for measuring depression. *Archives of General Psychiatry, 4,* 561-571.

Berkenkotter, C. (2001). Genre systems at work: DSM-IV and rhetorical recontextualization in psychotherapy paperwork. *Written communication, 18*(3), 326-349.

Berkenkotter, C. & Ravotas, D. J. (2001). New research strategies in genre analysis: Reported speech as recontextualization in a psychotherapist's notes and psychosocial assessment. In E. Barton & G. Stygall (Eds.), *Discourse studies and composition studies* (pp. 223-249). Cresskill, New Jersey: Hampton Press.

Berkenkotter, C. & Ravotas, D. J. (2002). Psychotherapists as authors: Microlevel analysis of therapists' written reports. In J. Z. Sadler (Ed.), *Descriptions and prescriptions: Values, mental disorders, and the DSMs* (pp. 251-268). Baltimore: Johns Hopkins University Press.

Butler, J. (1990). *Gender trouble: Feminism and the subversion of identity.* New York: Routledge.

Butler, J. (1997). *Excitable speech: A politics of the performative.* New York: Routledge.

Casey, N. (2001). *Unholy ghost: Writers on depression.* New York: William Morrow.

Center for Epidemiologic Studies, National Institute of Mental Health. (1971). *Center for epidemiologic studies depression scale (CES-D).* Rockville, Maryland: National Institute of Mental Health.

Danquah, M. N. (1998). *Willow weep for me: A black woman's journey through depression.* New York: Ballantine.

Eade, G., & Bradhsaw, J. (1995). Understanding discourses of the worried well. *Australian and New Zealand Journal of Mental Health Nursing, 4,* 61-69.

Elliott, C., & Chambers, T. (Eds.). (2004). *Prozac as a way of life.* Chapel Hill: University of North Carolina Press.

Emmons, K. (2007). "All on the list": Uptake in talk about depression. In B. Heifferon & S. Brown (Eds.), *The rhetoric of healthcare.* Cresskill, New Jersey: Hampton Press.

Fairclough, N. (1992). *Discourse and social change.* Cambridge: Polity Press.

Ferrara, K. W. (1994). *Therapeutic ways with words.* New York: Oxford University Press.

Foucault, M. (1972). *The archaeology of knowledge and the discourse on language* (A.

M. Smith, Trans.). New York: Pantheon Books.

Freadman, A. (1994). Anyone for tennis? In A. Freedman & P. Medway (Eds.), *Genre and the new rhetoric* (pp. 43-66). London: Taylor & Francis.

Freadman, A. (1999). The green tarpaulin: Another story of the Ryan hanging. *UTS Review, 5*(2), 1-67.

Freadman, A. (2002). Uptake. In R. Coe, L. Lingard, & T. Teslenko (Eds.), *The rhetoric and ideology of genre: Strategies for stability and change* (pp. 39-53). Cresskill, New Jersey: Hampton Press.

Healy, D. (2004). *Let them eat Prozac: The unhealthy relationship between the pharmaceutical industry and depression.* New York: New York University Press.

Karp, D. A. (1996). *Speaking of sadness: Depression, disconnection, and the meanings of illness.* New York: Oxford University Press.

Kill, M. (2006). Acknowledging the rough edges of resistance: Negotiation of identities for first-year composition. *CCC, 58*(2), 213-235.

Kirk, S. A. & Kutchins, H. (1992). *The selling of DSM: The rhetoric of science in psychiatry.* New York: Aldine de Gruyter.

Kramer, P. (1993). *Listening to Prozac: A psychiatrist explores antidepressant drugs and the remaking of the self.* New York: Penguin Books.

Kramer, P. (1997). *Listening to Prozac: The landmark book about antidepressant drugs and the remaking of the self.* (Rev. ed.). New York: Penguin Books.

Kristeva, J. (1980). *Desire in language: A semiotic approach to literature and art* (L. Roudiez, Ed., T. Gora, A. Jardine, & L. Roudiez, Trans.). New York: Columbia University Press.

Kutchins, H., & Kirk, S. A. (1997). *Making us crazy: DSM, the psychiatric bible and the creation of mental disorders.* New York: The Free Press.

Lacasse, J. R., & Leo, J. (2005). Serotonin and depression: A disconnect between the advertisements and the scientific literature. *PLoS Med, 2*(12), 1211-1216.

Manning, M. (1995). *Undercurrents: A life beneath the surface.* San Francisco: HarperCollins.

McCarthy, L. P. (1990). A psychiatrist using DSM-III: The influence of a charter document in psychiatry. In C. Bazerman & J. Paradis (Eds.), *Textual dynamics of the professions: Historical and contemporary studies of writing in professional communities* (pp. 358-378). Madison: University of Wisconsin Press.

Metzl, J. M. (2003). *Prozac on the couch: Prescribing gender in the era of wonder drugs.* Durham, North Carolina: Duke University Press.

Miller, C. R. (1994). Genre as social action. In A. Freedman & P. Medway (Eds.), *Genre and the new rhetoric* (pp. 23-42). London: Taylor & Francis.

National Institute of Mental Health. (2006, March). *The numbers count: Mental disorders in America.* Retrieved March 27, 2007, from http://

www.nimh.nih.gov/publicat/numbers.cfm

Prozac. (1998, February 9). Advertisement. *Time*, 98.

Ravotas, D. & Berkenkotter, C. (1998). Voices in the text: Varieties of reported speech in psychotherapists' initial assessments. *Text: An Interdisciplinary Journal for the Study of Discourse, 18*(2), 211-239.

Reynolds, J. F., Mair, D. C., & Fisher, P. C. (1992). *Writing and reading mental health records: Issues and analysis*. Newbury Park, CA: SAGE Publications.

Roberts, C., & Sarangi, S. (2003). Uptake of discourse research in interprofessional settings: Reporting from medical consultancy. *Applied Linguistics, 24*(3), 338-59.

Rosenberg, D. (1999, May 24). My ambivalence is pretty normal. *Newsweek*, 51.

Rosenthal, M. S. (2000). *Women and depression*. Los Angeles: Lowell House.

Schyrer, C. F. (1994). The lab vs. the clinic: Sites of competing genres. In A. Freedman & P. Medway (Eds.), *Genre and the new rhetoric* (pp. 105-124). Bristol, Pennsylvania: Taylor & Francis.

Schryer, C. F. (2002). Genre and power: A chronotopic analysis. In R. Coe, L. Lingard & T. Teslenko (Eds.), *The rhetoric and ideology of genre: Strategies for stability and change* (pp. 73-98). Cresskill, New Jersey: Hampton Press.

Segal, J. Z. (2005). *Health and the rhetoric of medicine*. Carbondale: Southern Illinois University Press.

Segal, J. Z. (2007). What is a story of breast cancer? In A. Bonini, D. de Carvalho Figueiredo, & F. J. Rauen (Eds.), *Proceedings of the 4th international symposium on genre studies*. University of Southern Santa Catarina, Turbão, Brazil, 158-163.

Shenk, J. W. (2001). A melancholy of mine own. In N. Casey (Ed.), *Unholy ghost: Writers on depression* (pp. 242-255). New York: William Morrow.

Slater, L. (1998). *Prozac diary*. New York: Penguin Books.

Smith, D. (1990). *Texts, facts, and femininity: Exploring the relations of ruling*. London: Routledge.

Smith, J. (1999). *Where the roots reach for water*. New York: North Point Press.

Solomon, A. (2001). *Noonday demon: An atlas of depression*. New York: Scribner.

Thieme, K. (2006). Uptake and genre: The Canadian reception of suffrage militancy. *Women's Studies International Forum, 29*, 279-88.

Twichell, C. (2001) Toys in the attic: An *ars poetica* under the influence. In N. Casey (Ed.), *Unholy ghost: Writers on depression* (pp. 21-28). New York: William Morrow.

Wells, S. (2003). Freud's rat man and the case study: Genre in three keys. *New Literary History, 34*, 353-366.

Worton, M., & Still, J. (Eds.). (1990). *Intertextuality: Theories and practices*.

Manchester, United Kingdom: Manchester University Press.

Wurtzel, E. (1994). *Prozac nation: Young and depressed in America*. New York: Houghton Mifflin.

Zoloft. (2001, June 25). Advertisement. *Newsweek*, 58.

8 Stories of Becoming: A Study of Novice Engineers Learning Genres of Their Profession

Natasha Artemeva

INTRODUCTION[1]

The study presented in this chapter was prompted by some conclusions drawn from the research into the university-to-workplace transition that was conducted and published in the 1990s through the early 2000s. Some researchers (e.g., Anson & Forsberg, 1990/2003; Dias & Paré, 2000; Dias, Freedman, Medway, & Paré, 1999; Freedman & Adam, 2000a; Freedman, Adam, & Smart, 1994; Mackinnon, 1993/2003) expressed suspicion of the efficacy of traditional professional communication classrooms and raised questions of the portability of genres taught in such classes (Artemeva, 2005). In a more recent debate, Downs and Wardle (2007), Fogarty (2007), and Kutney (2007) continued to discuss the portability of rhetorical strategies between first-year composition courses and "other writing situations" (Kutney, p. 277), with Kutney "echoing Downs and Wardle's . . . concerns about the lack of research on transfer in writing" (p. 278).

In an attempt to further explore the processes of genre learning and the role of the formal classroom instruction in these processes, I designed a longitudinal study that sought answers to the following research questions: (1) What does it mean to master domain-specific—that is, both academic and professional—genres, and in particular, the genres of engineering? (2) Is it possible to teach domain-specific communication strategies apart from the local contexts in which they occur? (cf. Artemeva, 2005). In order to locate answers to these questions, I relied on a theoretical framework (Artemeva, 2008) that I had developed on the basis of the integration of Rhetorical Genre Studies (RGS), also known as North American genre theory (e.g., Artemeva & Freedman, 2006; Bakhtin, 1986; Devitt, 2004; Miller, 1984/1994; Freedman & Medway, 1994a, 1994b; Schryer, 1993, 2000), Activity Theory (AT) (e.g., Engeström, 1987; Leont'ev, 1981; Vygotsky, 1978, 1981), and situated learning (Lave & Wenger, 1991; Wenger, 1998).

This chapter begins with a discussion of the integrated theoretical framework. Next, it describes the design of an engineering communication course that I developed and taught at a Canadian university. Then, it presents four case studies of novice engineers who had taken that course and whom I later observed for several years, following their trajectories in learning genres of engineering. The case studies provide illustrations of the integrated theoretical framework's applications to the study of genre learning by novice professionals. The chapter ends with a discussion of *genre knowledge ingredients* (Artemeva, 2005, in press) that allow novices to become successful in using genres of their profession.

INTEGRATED THEORETICAL FRAMEWORK

In the past fifteen years or so many studies of workplace learning and school-to-work transition have relied on Rhetorical Genre Studies as the theoretical framework (e.g., Coe, Lingard, & Teslenko, 2002; Dias et al., 1999; Dias & Paré, 2000). Within the RGS framework, genre is viewed as typified social action (Miller, 1984/1994). RGS allows researchers to expand the study of genre beyond the exploration of its textual features to the analysis of recurrent social contexts that give rise to and shape genres and, at the same time, are shaped by genres (Bawarshi, 2000, 2003; Freedman & Medway, 1994a, 1994b; Miller, 1984/1994; Smart & Paré, 1994). Thus, RGS serves as a useful theoretical framework for research into genre development, learning, and use. For the purposes of my study I have adopted Schryer's (2000) definition of genre as a constellation "of regulated, improvisational strategies triggered by the interaction between individual socialization . . . and an organization" (p. 450). Particularly important for my study is Schryer's (1993) view of genre as stabilized only for now, flexible, allowing for change, and forming the rhetor's behavior, while the rhetor reconstructs genre.

RGS provides us with a social perspective on how individuals learn and use genres. In order to better flesh out relationships between the individual and the social (cf. Berger & Luckmann, 1967), and between agency and structure (cf. Giddens, 1984; Schryer, 2000; 2002) some researchers have successfully complemented RGS with such social theories of learning as Activity Theory, situated learning, and other theoretical perspectives (e.g., Artemeva & Freedman, 2001; Bazerman & Russell, 2003; Freedman & Adam, 2000b; Freedman & Smart, 1997; Dias et al., 1999; Le Maistre & Paré, 2004; Russell, 1997; Schryer, 2000, 2002, 2005; Winsor, 2001). In this chapter, I rely on a complex theoretical framework that integrates RGS with both AT and situated learning (Artemeva, 2008). This integrated framework allows for a close analysis of the interplay between the individual and the social in the study of genre learning in the process of novices' university-to-work transition. However, before presenting this integrated theoretical perspective for the study of genre learning and use, it is necessary to demonstrate that the theories it is based on *are* compatible and *can* be integrated both philosophically and methodologically.

First of all, I would like to stress the inherent dialogism (e.g., Bakhtin, 1986) of both AT (Engeström, 1987) and the concept of communities of practice (CoP) used in the situated learning perspective (Lave & Wenger, 1991; Wenger, 1998). The so-called "third generation" version of AT (Engeström & Miettinen, 1999) attempts to understand interactions between several activity systems, each of them with multiple perspectives and voices, thus bringing the notion of dialogue to the centre of the analysis of human activity. Lave and Wenger's (1991; Wenger, 1998) view of CoP, where newcomers, working on authentic activities with oldtimers, gradually move towards the full participation state, reflects the dialogic nature of the apprentice-master relationship in the context of an authentic activity. These dialogic features of both theories indicate their strong connection with the RGS notions of dialogue and dialogism as conceived by Bakhtin (1986). Other processes and concepts addressed in RGS, such as the dynamics of genre learning activity during a novice's transition from the classroom to workplace context, genre learning in communities of practice, and the concept of identity can be successfully explored and expanded with the use of AT and situated learning.

When studying a novice's learning trajectory in her learning of domain-specific genres as she moves from the university context into workplace CoPs, it is crucial to understand the processes through which this learning occurs. AT provides us with the lens necessary for such an analysis. Human activity in this model is represented as consisting of mutually dependent and connected levels, with constant mutual transformations taking place at each level and among the levels: level 1 (the highest), *need* and *motive* and the corresponding—often collective—*activity*; level 2 (intermediate), *goal* and the corresponding—collective or individual—*action*; and level 3 (the lowest), *conditions* that are necessary to achieve the goal and the corresponding automatic *operations* (Leont'ev, 1981). AT supplies a view of human activity as always mediated through the mediational means, be it physical tools (e.g., a hammer or a pen) or language and other sign systems (Vygotsky, 1978). These AT premises indicate that the theory can be productively applied to research into genre learning. For example, generally, when university course instructors design specific exercises to provide input to students' learning, they perceive these exercises as connected, sequenced, and forming a coherent series of pedagogical tools. For the instructor, completing such exercises is, most probably, closer to the level of operations: the instructor can do them almost automatically. As the three-level model of human activity suggests, an inexperienced student does not and cannot do these exercises at the operation level. We can compare this student with a novice driver learning to drive a car (cf. Leont'ev's famous example): every "exercise" for her has its own *goal* and becomes an *action* that requires full conscious attention. That is, an exercise that for the instructor is a mediational artifact for conveying course content, for a student becomes an object.

Another example of the AT application to the study of the university-to-workplace transition was provided by Le Maistre and Paré (2004) who successfully combined RGS and AT in order to develop a model of different activities in which their participants were involved as students in classroom settings and as novice members of a CoP (interns working in the workplace). Le Maistre and Paré suggested that when a student becomes involved in the professional practice, the objects of "the learning activity in the school (the theories, laws, methods, tools, and other artifacts of the profession) become 'mediational means' in the workplace" (p. 45).

To elaborate how individuals learn genres, Legitimate Peripheral Participation (LPP), an analytical perspective on learning in CoP provided by the situated learning perspective (Lave & Wenger, 1991), directs our attention to local situations and participants. In this respect the notion of communities of practice allows researchers to analyze learning "that is most personally transformative" (Wenger, 1998, p. 6). Each community of practice is constituted by distinct intellectual and social conventions. These conventions are shared assumptions about the roles of the audience, the rhetor, and the social purposes for communicating, which makes these conventions remarkably similar to the notion of rhetorical genre.

A discussion of community as one of the central RGS notions would be incomplete without a discussion of the formation of a professional identity in novices entering professional communities of practice. In order to understand the role of the agent, it is important to investigate the notion of identity from the perspective of the proposed theoretical framework. The notion of identity is particularly important for RGS because genre "is largely constitutive of the identities we assume within and in relation to discourse" (Bawarshi, 2000, p. 343). Multiple studies of the development and formation of identities through participation in the systems of genres (e.g., Bazerman, 2002) have demonstrated that social action and identity construction are both mediated through and constituted by genres (Hirsh, as cited in Bawarshi, 2000, p. 343). Genres provide social codes of behavior for both interlocutors—the speaker and the listener, the writer and the reader—involved in a dialogic exchange (Bawarshi, 2000, 2003; Voloshinov, 1930/1983). Particularly important in the recent literature on RGS has been the formation of a professional identity of a novice who moves into the workplace after years of academic and professional training. The development of a professional identity is inextricably linked to participating in the workplace genres and "learning one's professional location in the power relations of institutional life" (Paré, 2002, p. 69). From this perspective, identity formation is linked to socialization into, the resistance to, or subversion by, local genres, which may occur either without one's conscious involvement or through a critical analysis of the organization.

Working within the framework of situated learning, Lave (1991) and Lave and Wenger (1996) introduced the notion of a *knowledgeably skilled identity*, which, as Smart and Brown (2002) observed, is closely linked to a growing novice's sense of professional competence. Learning to communicate in a particular professional situation is part of becoming a legitimate member of a CoP. As Dias et al. (1999) and Smart and Brown noted, learning to become an accepted and functioning member of a particular workplace situation does not involve a simple transfer of knowledge and skills acquired in an academic setting directly to a professional setting. Smart and Brown commented that a growing sense of a novice as a competent professional, that is, the development of her professional identity, contributes to her ability to act as an expert and enhances her capacity to learn in the workplace.

The integrated theoretical perspective based on the combination of AT, the situated learning perspective, and RGS allowed me to analyze both social and individual aspects of genre learning within activity systems and communities of practice. In addition, in my analysis of novices' learning trajectories, I used the concepts of *kairos* (2005) as the right timing and proportion, and *kairotic* opportunities (see Consigny, 1974; Kinneavy, 1986; Miller, 1992) as both "emerging from the communicative activities of . . . rhetors and audiences . . . in specific situations (e.g., institutional context, task, place, and chronological time)" and "enacted, arising when socially situated rhetors choose and/or craft an opportune time to interact with a particular audience in a particular way within particular circumstances" (Yates & Orlikowski, 2002, p. 108).

At the same time, Bourdieu's theory of social practice (1972) provided me with the notions of agency and social capital, in particular, cultural capital as a form of culturally authorized values (Artemeva, 2005). Bourdieu's theory has been recently used by rhetorical genre researchers (e.g., Dias et al., 1999; Paré, 2002; Schryer, 2000, 2002, 2003; Winsor, 2003) to complement RGS and illuminate the role of social agents and texts within organizations which, according to Giddens (1984), represent complex social structures. As Winsor (2003) explained, for Bourdieu, capital exists in different forms that are not necessarily "reducible to money" (p. 17). Bourdieu's capital may take both material and non-material forms that can be converted into each other (e.g., monetary capital may be used to pay for, or be converted into, education, and vice versa). Among other forms of capital, Bourdieu introduced social capital (e.g., hierarchical positions within an organization) and cultural capital (i.e., particular cultural knowledge, such as engineering knowledge, or competency, such as professional engineering competency).

Cultural capital is the key form of capital in Bourdieu's theory. It is defined as "a form of values associated with culturally authorized tastes, consumption patterns, attributes, skills and awards" (Webb, Schirato, & Danaher, 2002, p. x) and, thus, includes, for example, the ways people communicate within particular situations or, in other words, use certain genres (e.g., engineering genres). People can acquire cultural capital without a conscious effort, from their family or social contexts (e.g., school, workplace apprenticeships); they then possess such capital for life. In Bourdieu's view, we would be wrong to think that by deliberately learning components of relevant cultural capital, a person who was brought up in a family with limited relevant cultural capital could acquire as much of it as a person brought up in a family with rich relevant cultural capital. People's appropriation of this type of capital depends both on the sum of cultural capital that their family possesses and on when, how, and in what forms this capital is implicitly transmitted to them from their family and surroundings. Cultural capital can be converted into social capital: for example, a person's education and background in a particular discipline can lead to, or be converted into, her higher position within an organization.

In discussing various other notions integral to Bourdieu's theory, Bourdieu and Wacquant (1992) observed that an adequate theory of social practice requires a theory of social agents. Human agents and the notion of agency, defined as humans' capacity for freedom of action, understanding, and control of their own behavior (Holland, Lahicote, Skinner, & Cain, 1998; Schryer, 2002; Webb, Schirato, & Danaher, 2002), thus play particularly important roles in Bourdieu's theory. As Archer (2002) puts it, we need to conceptualize human agents as being both formed by their "sociality" (p. 11) and able to effect a change in society (Artemeva, 2005).

The concepts of *kairos* and the notion of agency are directly linked. If we see *kairos* as objectively given and then discovered, and as constructed by humans, then the rhetor's ability to select and/or create an opportune moment and act proportionally implies agency. Bourdieu's (1972) theory of social practice provides insights into the acquisition and effect of cultural capital and the role of agency that are invaluable for analyzing an individual's rhetorical behavior within the context of the chosen discipline or profession.

THE FOUNDATIONS OF THE ENGINEERING COMMUNICATION COURSE DESIGN

The engineering communication course (ECC) that I designed and taught (see Artemeva, 2005; Artemeva, Logie, & St-Martin, 1999) served as the starting point for my study. The theoretical foundations of the course design were provided by RGS and the situated learning perspective. In other words, in the

ECC design I attempted to establish an engineering context that would allow students immersed in it to (a) experience genres of engineering communication as an integral part of any project rather than learn *about* genres and (b) be introduced to the idea of genre flexibility that depends on the requirements of a particular situation.

The ECC unfolds around a student project on a topic that each student—or a small student group—chooses from an engineering course(s) that each student is taking concurrently with the ECC. The project may involve conducting a small-scale research study on the chosen topic; performing a laboratory experiment and discussing it on the basis of relevant theoretical literature; designing (and sometimes building) an engineering device and providing a discussion of the theoretical engineering concepts on which the design is based, and so on. I ask students to select topics from their engineering courses according to their interests, and then individually discuss each topic with the student, or a small group of students working on the same project. The project is designed to allow the students to experience the communication course as situated within the engineering curriculum, thus not only allowing students to familiarize themselves with engineering genres but also facilitating their learning in engineering courses. Students are asked to provide a series of project documents as they are progressing in their work: a statement of intent, progress report, oral progress report, completion report, and others. The genres relevant to engineering projects are discussed in class, but it is expected that the task of adapting them to the individual projects will be completed by the students. Every project document/assignment in the sequence is based on and connected to the previous assignment. Students receive both peer and instructor feedback on drafts of each written assignment. All course assignments and feedback received from peers and the instructor form the ECC project genre system (Bazerman, 1994). The project gradually unfolds over the term.

The aim of the project design is to provide students with the opportunity to develop a genuine motivation to adapt the genres they are learning in the ECC for the purposes of their projects, thus experiencing the need to use genres in order to appropriately respond to a particular rhetorical situation. Students experience genres as regulated, improvisational strategies (cf. Schryer, 2000; Zachry, 2007), hence developing an initial rhetorical flexibility. The accuracy of the engineering content is particularly important for the communication course project, as it seems futile to separate rhetorical expertise from domain content expertise (cf. Geisler, 1994). In my assessment of the accuracy of the engineering content of students' projects I rely on the knowledge accumulated over the years of my previous career as a metallurgical engineer and on my ongoing research into the teaching and practice of engineering.

METHODOLOGY OF THE STUDY

The study had an emergent design: at the beginning it was designed as an assessment of the pedagogical approach used in the ECC, and then it gradually developed into a qualitative, longitudinal exploration of former ECC students' trajectories in learning genres of engineering. The data analysis in the study is based on Charmaz's (2000, 2002, 2006) constructivist version of grounded theory (see Strauss & Corbin, 1998). In this study, I used a purposive self-selective sample of convenience (cf. Miles & Huberman, 1994; Patton, 1990) of ten volunteers from among my former ECC students (from the 1997-1998 and 1998-1999 engineering cohorts). The case study approach that I used in my research allowed for "progressive focusing" (Stake, 1995, p. 8); that is, it allowed me to reconsider and develop research questions through data collection and analysis. I collected data over the span of eight years (1997-2005), while engaging in a concurrent and recursive data analysis. The study received ethics approval.

I collected data through in-class questionnaires administered as part of the engineering communication course, electronic questionnaires regularly emailed to the participants, individual follow-up email messages sent for clarification of particular responses, one-on-one qualitative interviews, field notes, and samples of the participants' academic and workplace writing. I used the constant comparative method for categorization (coding) (e.g., Miles & Huberman, 1994) and complemented it with the analysis of the context, or connecting strategies (i.e., case studies and narrative summaries) (e.g., Charmaz, 2000, 2002, 2006; Maxwell, 2005; Maxwell & Miller, 1992, 2002). For the purposes of my study, I decided to adapt the form of representation known as Individual Case Synopsis (ICS) (Fischer & Wertz, 1979) to present an *individual* participant's learning trajectory in her learning of engineering genres, with a focus on change through time. Such ICS were developed for four study participants who provided me with a particularly detailed and complete body of data. For the remaining six study participants, an overall summary of experience was written.

The study used multiple ways of triangulation: (a) data triangulation, provided by the use of multiple study participants and a variety of data sources in a study; (b) theory triangulation, achieved through a combination of multiple theoretical perspectives used to interpret data, complemented with the theory building from the data; (c) methodological triangulation, achieved through the combination of categorizing and connecting strategies. I also employed member checks (e.g., Stake, 1995, 2000; Winsor, 1996) to ensure that study participants had an opportunity to verify my interpretation of the data collected from them. All ten participants provided me with member checks. The use of member checks assisted me in creating the ownership of the study that was shared by my participants and myself. The use of various triangulation strategies and the multicase design allowed me to verify the interpretation of the data, and thus, to further validate the study.

Stories of Becoming: Four Individual Case Synopses

Four out of ten participants—Bill, Sami, Rebecca, and Moe (the participants are identified by pseudonyms)—supplied me with a large body of data, over 50 sources of data each. These participants' stories are presented in the abbreviated Individual Case Synopses below (for complete ICS see Artemeva, 2006).

Sami's and Bill's fathers were engineers (for a detailed discussion of Sami's case, see Artemeva, 2005). Sami and Bill (Bill's case was also discussed in Artemeva, 2008) grew up surrounded by "war stories" (Lave & Wenger, 1991)—that is, oldtimer's stories about the practices of the engineering profession. They both had various engineering-related experiences through the years before and at the university and had an opportunity to work under the supervision of mentors who had helped them to enter engineering communities of practice. For example, Sami, who was a third-generation engineer, often referred to his father as a major influence in his life. Thus, he once noted, "I became an engineer because my father is one" (16 September 2003). Bill's father helped him to obtain a co-operative placement at an engineering company when Bill was a high school student. This had allowed Bill to enter an engineering CoP very early, and to work under the mentorship of experienced oldtimers for a few years before he entered an academic engineering program. In other words, both Bill and Sami had acquired their families' cultural capital related to the engineering profession at a very early age, and, thus, had been socialized into the engineering practices even before they formally entered the world of engineering (Artemeva, 2005, 2008).

Shortly after graduating from university, both Sami and Bill were able not only to join engineering companies and work productively, but also to change communication practices of their companies. For example, Sami, shortly after being hired by an engineering company, encountered a situation in which his immediate supervisor was asked to propose a solution to an engineering problem. Sami seized this *kairotic* moment and proposed his own solution. He wrote a proposal by using—as he explained in an interview—everything that he had learned in the ECC. For example, he went to the company's library and studied backgrounds of all committee members who would evaluate the proposals in order to learn how much background knowledge and technical details to provide in the proposal so that each of the committee members could understand it. The genre of the proposal that Sami used, as he observed, was based on his learning experiences in the ECC, rather than on the genres traditionally used in the company. (Please note that none of the study participants ever used the term *genre* in their responses). Even though the genre of the proposal that Sami introduced differed from the genres used by the company, engineers and managers recognized the effectiveness of the new genre, accepted his engineering solution over the proposal that a company's oldtimer presented, and quickly promoted him (Artemeva, 2005).

Bill continued his engineering studies in a graduate program. After finishing his Master's degree he was hired by a small start-up company. In the new workplace, Bill discovered that, in his opinion, many of the communication practices used by the company were inefficient. In an e-mail, he commented that the company employees "are not doing any record keeping at all. Because the people [who are] doing the design work are two or three people. They talk at lunch" (05 March 2002). On his own initiative, Bill was able to gradually introduce more efficient ways of internal communication and communication with customers. The new communication strategies that he proposed on the basis of the ECC and his previous engineering workplace experiences were accepted by the company and included in its genre system (Artemeva, 2008).

In other words, the new communication practices that Sami and Bill had introduced were recognized as acceptable and approved by oldtimers in their engineering CoPs. Both Sami and Bill referred to the engineering communication course and their other engineering-related experiences as the sources of their understanding of how professional genres work. In other words, their audience awareness, relevant cultural capital, the ECC and workplace experiences, understanding of engineering genres as allowing for flexibility, engineering knowledge, and the ability to seize and create a *kairotic* moment and respond to it proportionally allowed them to enact genres in such a way that these genres, though changed and/or not developed locally, remained not only recognizable by professionals but also were acceptable as best practices (Artemeva, 2005, 2008). Sami's and Bill's stories illustrate the crucial role of cultural capital, domain content expertise, and agency in a rhetor's ability to both seize and create *kairotic* moments in the chronological flux of time and respond to them in a proportional manner. These stories also underline the importance of the rhetor's understanding of the improvisational qualities of genre.

Another participant in my study, Rebecca, unlike Sami and Bill, initially lacked knowledge and understanding of what the engineering profession entailed. In the first year of university she felt confused and could not understand practical applications of the courses she was taking. In response to the question that I asked all students at the end of the communication course, "Have you learned any useful communication strategies in [the ECC]?" Rebecca responded, "No." A term later, in response to the same question, she wrote in an email,

Yes, actually [I have]. . . . [The ECC] . . . provided a basis of knowledge for . . . [new types of] reports [that students are required to write in second-year courses] since they are not based on what was learned on writing reports in the first year courses. These lab write-ups include an extensive amount of documentation and written work. . . . Most of the concepts presented in the [ECC] are quite useful. (25 March 1998)

A year later, after she had worked in an engineering firm for a few months, Rebecca's response to the question "Did [the ECC] help you in your engineering course work?" was, "There was theoretical value in . . . [the ECC] . . . such as organization of long projects. . . . The great thing that I found quite worthwhile was the final report, and the orals/abstracts/proposal that went along with it" (30 October 1998).

Leont'ev's three-level model of activity (activity; action; operation) as a theoretical tool allowed me to unpack changes in Rebecca's perceptions of the ECC usefulness for her engineering studies and work. When Rebecca had reacted negatively to the whole course at the end of the term because, as she noted retrospectively, at that time a lot of course activities seemed to have lacked "a 'point' or a foreseeable goal" (21 April 2002), she was providing me with a fairly common novice's perception of an academic course in an unfamiliar discipline. Rebecca's cultural capital did not appear to include familiarity with the expectations of the engineering profession, and she had not been exposed to the field before taking the ECC. She took the communication course at the very beginning of her engineering studies when her domain content knowledge was practically non-existent. All these factors made it unfair and unrealistic to expect that she would gain the understanding of the integral role of communication in engineering from an introductory communication course.

Only with time and after having experienced situations that required the use of strategies learned in the ECC for other purposes, that is, other courses and/ or work, Rebecca began to realize that discrete course exercises had not been as randomly discrete as it had appeared while she was enrolled in the course (as Rebecca demonstrated in the third response). It is significant that, as time passed and as Rebecca became more involved in the context of engineering—both as an academic discipline and as a profession—her view of the effects of the ECC changed from the abrupt "No" in her first response, to the recognition of the usefulness of particular course activities in the second response, and to the view of the course as a whole in which all discrete activities finally found their place (in the third response). Several years later, when Rebecca was working in an engineering workplace and felt very comfortable communicating professionally, she noted, "I'm lucky that I get to do the same work [in the workplace] as what I took in University—I'm using the vast majority of my education to help me with my job" (18 September 2003). In other words, to learn a genre, as Dias et al. (1999) observed, one needs to use it *to get things done* with a particular purpose in an authentic setting.

Rebecca's story indicates that her mastery of engineering genres occurred later than in Sami's and Bill's cases and was based on her academic experiences in engineering classes, the ECC, and workplace experiences in the various workplaces where she worked throughout the years of her academic studies. By the time she graduated from the university, she was also able to develop her own communication strategies that helped her integrate into an engineering community of practice. The fact that she had lacked relevant cultural capital made her learning of engineering genres and developing her own rhetorical strategies slower than in Bill's and Sami's cases; however, she was able to learn from the ECC, other academic experiences, and the workplace environment and use what she learned in her workplace to develop successful rhetorical strategies.

The fourth study participant, Moe, enrolled in the engineering program expecting to be able to make much money after graduation (for a detailed discussion of Moe's case, see Artemeva, 2008). Moe lacked the relevant cultural capital and private intention (Miller, 1984/1994) to develop into a professional engineer: he did not know much about the profession when he started his studies, did not know any engineers, was not particularly interested in the engineering program, and was soon discouraged. He explained his motivation to choose an engineering university program by saying that "at the time, engineers were in demand and made very good salaries" (25 July 2003). Unlike Sami, for example, who constantly referred to what he had learned in the ECC, Moe repeatedly commented in the interviews that he had taken the ECC in the first year and "because I took it way back . . . I don't remember anything" (12 February 2001). He often mentioned that because he could not remember "anything" from the communication course, he had avoided writing tasks at the University (e.g., he would say, "I was doing the lab and my friend was doing the writing") and relied on other students, the "guys [who] are better than me in that" (12 February 2001). Unfortunately, university practices seemed to allow him to avoid the few opportunities to engage in engineering writing that the engineering program offered.

Paré & Le Maistre (2006) observed that higher education often creates passive learners who wait for knowledge to be imparted to them; such learners may miss the chances that wait for them outside of academic institutions. For example, at first, Moe could not find any full-time engineering employment, and later, he developed an ambition to become an entrepreneur rather than an engineer. He began by participating in business proposal competitions for young entrepreneurs that the University offered in partnership with local businesses and a government program. However, none of his attempts to secure funding for his enterprises was successful. He repeatedly included unrealistic budgets (hundreds of millions of dollars for a small start-up business) in his business plans and nearly missed deadlines for grant application submissions—*kairotic* moments—by writing his business plans at the last minute. It does not appear that Moe's sensitivity to professional genres and, in particular, to the genre of the business grant proposal, developed in any way, even after several attempts to apply for funding. Moe's repeated failures to secure an engineering job and to obtain funding in young entrepreneurs' competitions indicates that in his case, learning of relevant genres did not occur to the same extent as in Sami's, Bill's, and even Rebecca's cases (Artemeva, 2005, 2008).

Bereiter and Scardamalia's (1983) metaphor of high road and low road in learning to write seems appropriate in the discussion of Moe's learning trajectory as compared to those of Sami's, Bill's, and Rebecca's. According to Bereiter and Scardamalia, "The high road is characterized by struggling to master the art of writing in all its complexities. . . . The low road is characterized by striving to avoid or minimize the burden of those same complexities" (p. 24). Their main objection to the choice of the low road is that "it keeps writing from having a role in a person's mental life. . . . people who know only the low road of writing do not have a mental life in the same sense that people on the high road do" (p. 28). It appears from the Individual Case Synopses that Sami and Bill chose the high road, and Rebecca, though she had struggled at the beginning, did eventually develop communication strategies that eased her integration into the workplace context, while Moe was following the low road. The choice of the high or low road may also be dictated by private intention: while Sami, Bill, and Rebecca either before or during their university studies made a decision to become engineers, Moe was not happy about his choice of the discipline. His dominant motive, according to him, was to make as much money as possible, which is a legitimate but very different motivation. It might have caused him to look for faster ways of achieving his goal, which, in the context of my study, may appear closer to the "low road." It is clear from his ICS that his strategies did not lead to the immediate success because none of his proposals won the competitions and he had to finance his enterprise himself. Moe's story provides evidence that his difficulties in learning and using appropriate communication strategies might have been caused by his lack of relevant cultural capital, inability to recognize, seize, and respond proportionally to *kairotic* moments, and his markedly different private intention (to make a lot of money rather than to become a professional engineer).

Nearing the end of my study, I asked for the participants' views on the effects of the study on the development of their ability to reflect on their own professional communication practices. Sami observed, "[the study] allowed me to verbalize certain situations leading me to better understand what had happened [to me] and why" (23 May 2005). Bill responded, "your interest in my communication experience has caused me to reflect on my progression, and I've definitely learned something about myself through this process" (21 May 2005), while Rebecca added, "participation in the study has provided a time capsule for myself. Reading the [ICS] has shown how much I've changed from my educational career to my working career" (16 May 2005). These responses provide evidence that the qualitative methodology used in the study did not only allow for the collection of rich data and their multidimensional analysis, but also involved the participants in a reflective practice. Their last comments, in a sense, validated the study even further and suggested that the ownership of the study has indeed become shared between my participants and myself.

CONCLUSIONS

The four Individual Case Synopses presented in this chapter illustrate some possible applications of the integrated theoretical perspective to the analysis of genre learning in transitional contexts (Artemeva, 2008). They indicate that RGS, AT, and situated learning *can* be integrated into one theoretical framework which can allow professional communication researchers to focus on the roles of the knowledgeably skilled identity and individual agency, and the tension between agency and the social forces that affect the processes of professional genre learning.

The four ICS presented in this chapter shed light on the first question that I raised at the beginning of the chapter: what does it mean to master domain-specific genres, and in particular, the genres of engineering? The study allowed me to uncover the ingredients of genre knowledge and provided evidence that learning professional genres does not occur in a smooth, uninterrupted way which starts in the communication classroom and continues throughout the engineering program (Artemeva, 2008). Novices accumulate these ingredients throughout their lives from different experiences and encounters. The novices' cultural capital and private intentions appear to have a profound effect on their development as professional communicators. These ingredients, once acquired, help novices to become sophisticated users of professional genres.

A related question that I posed at the beginning of this chapter was: is it possible to teach domain-specific communication practices apart from the local contexts in which they occur? In other words, if we teach, for example, engineering communication strategies in a university course, are these strategies at all portable to workplace contexts? Can they be productively used by novices beyond the classroom context and would these strategies be accepted by oldtimers as legitimate professional rhetorical practices? While Moe's story indicates that the low road he had chosen in learning engineering communication practices and his narrow understanding of what "learning" of professional communication entails might not have lead him to successful genre learning and implementation (cf. Julie's case in Freedman & Adam, 2000b), Sami's, Bill's, and Rebecca's stories demonstrate that such practices *can* be taught in carefully designed communication courses, and thus provide evidence that academia and the workplace may not always be "worlds apart," to use Dias et al.'s (1999) phrase. That is, the findings of the study indicate that we may be able to teach domain-specific communication strategies apart from the local contexts, and that such teaching, if carefully constructed and theoretically grounded, can serve as *one* of the ingredients of professional genre knowledge.

As I observed, genre knowledge in those novices who had exhibited the ability to use engineering genres successfully—and even changed some and/or introduced new workplace genres—was a result of a summative effect of various genre knowledge ingredients accumulated from different sources at different time periods. The various sources of such genre knowledge ingredients included, but were not limited to, the classroom and workplace practices. The interpretation of the data suggests that, in addition to the knowledge of genre conventions and understanding of the audience's expectations, the following ingredients contribute to the formation of professional genre knowledge:

(a) agency, as reflected in the novice's ability to both seize and create *kairotic* moments in the chronological flux of time, respond to them proportionally, and enact genres in the ways that are recognizable by the community of practice;
(b) cultural capital;
(c) domain content expertise;
(d) formal education;
(e) private intention;
(f) understanding of the improvisational qualities of genre; and
(g) workplace experiences.

All these ingredients of genre knowledge helped the novices to understand the intricacies of domain-specific engineering genres (Artemeva, 2005, 2008).

It is notable that, contrary to the findings of some previous studies on the university-to-workplace transition (e.g., Anson & Forsberg, 1990/2003; Dias &

Paré, 2000; Dias et al., 1999) and more recent work on academic writing in the disciplines (e.g., Fogarty, 2007), neither Bill nor Sami or Rebecca had difficulties drawing on genres learned in the classroom context when applying them in the workplace context.

Even though the study presented in this chapter suggests that some ingredients of genre knowledge *can be* taught in a classroom context like the one provided in the ECC, for the genre knowledge to become active and for the individuals to be able to apply this knowledge successfully, it needs to be complemented by other genre knowledge ingredients accumulated elsewhere. In other words, the findings of the study again raise a question of the portability of rhetorical strategies across contexts, but from a different perspective. It appears that rhetorical strategies *may* be portable but only if a novice *already* possesses a combination of particular genre knowledge ingredients (Artemeva, 2005, 2008). This research once again indicates that our understanding of the processes of professional genre learning is far from complete and that the teaching of professional communication must be firmly grounded in empirical research in order to be of use to our students. More research is needed to further explore the complex processes of professional genre learning.

NOTES
[1] I would like to thank Chuck Bazerman, Anthony Paré, Bob Bracewell, Lynn Butler-Kisber, Aviva Freedman, Janna Fox, and Graham Smart for their comments on previous versions of this chapter. I am grateful to the anonymous reviewers for their suggestions.

REFERENCES
Anson, C. M. & Forsberg, L. (2003). Moving beyond the academic community: Transitional stages in professional writing. In T. Peeples (Ed.), *Professional writing and rhetoric: Readings from the field* (pp. 388-410). New York: Longman. (Reprinted from *Written Communication, 7,* 1990, 200-231).

Archer, M. (2002). The problem of agency. *Journal of Critical Realism, 5,* 11-20.

Artemeva, N. (2005). A time to speak, a time to act: A rhetorical genre analysis of the calculated risk-taking by a novice engineer. *Journal of Business and Technical Communication, 19* (4), 389-421.

Artemeva, N. (2006). *Becoming an engineering communicator: A study of novices' trajectories in learning genres of their profession.* Unpublished doctoral dissertation, McGill University, Montreal, Quebec, Canada.

Artemeva, N. (2008). Toward a unified theory of genre learning. *Journal of Business and Technical Communication, 22* (2), 160-185.

Artemeva, N. & Freedman, A. (2006). "Just the boys playing on computers": An activity theory analysis of differences in the cultures of two engineering firms. *Journal of Business and Technical Writing,* *15*(2), 164-194.

Artemeva, N., Logie, S., & St-Martin, J. (1999). From page to stage: How theories of genre and situated learning help introduce engineering students to discipline-specific communication. *Technical Communication Quarterly, 8*(3), 301-316.

Bakhtin, M. M. (1986). The problem of speech genres. In Emerson, C. & Holquist, M. (Eds.), (V. W. McGee, Trans.). *Speech genres and other late essays* (pp. 60-102.) Austin, TX: University of Texas Press.

Bawarshi, A. (2000). The genre function. *College English, 62*(3), 335-360.

Bawarshi, A. (2003). *Genre and the invention of the writer: Reconsidering the place of invention in composition.* Logan, UT: Utah State University Press.

Bazerman, C. (1994). Systems of genres and the enactment of social intentions. In A. Freedman & P. Medway (Eds.), *Genre and the new rhetoric* (pp. 79-101). London: Taylor & Francis.

Bazerman, C. (1997). The life of genres, the life in the classroom. In W. Bishop & H. Ostrom (Eds.), *Genre and writing: Issues, arguments, alternatives* (pp. 19-26). Portsmouth, New Hampshire: Boynton/Cook.

Bazerman, C. (2002). Genre and identity: Citizenship in the age of the Internet and the age of global capitalism. In R. Coe, L. Lingard, & T. Teslenko (Eds.), *The rhetoric and ideology of genre* (pp. 13-37). Cresskill, New Jersey: Hampton Press.

Bazerman, C. & Russell, D. R. (2003). *Writing selves/writing societies: Research from activity theory perspectives.* Retrieved July 15, 2007, from Colorado State University, WAC Clearinghouse and Mind, Culture, and Activity: http://wac.colostate.edu/books/selves_societies/

Berger, P. L. & Luckmann, T. (1967). *The social construction of reality: A treatise in the sociology of knowledge.* Garden City, New York: Anchor Books.

Bourdieu, P. (1972). *Outline of a theory of practice* (R. Nice, Trans.). Cambridge: Cambridge University Press.

Bourdieu, P., & Wacquant, L. (1992). *An invitation to reflexive sociology.* Chicago: University of Chicago Press.

Charmaz, K. (2000). Grounded theory: Objectivist and constructivist methods. In N. Denzin & Y. S. Lincoln (Eds.), *Handbook of qualitative research* (2nd ed., pp. 509-535). Thousand Oaks, California: Sage.

Charmaz, K. (2002). Qualitative interviewing and grounded theory analysis. In J. F. Gubrium & J. A. Holstein (Eds.), *Handbook of interview research: Context and method* (pp. 675-693). Thousand Oaks, California: Sage.

Charmaz, K. (2006). *Constructing grounded theory: A practical guide through qualitative analysis.* London: Sage.

Coe, R., Lingard, L., & Teslenko, T. (Eds.). (2002). *The rhetoric and ideology of genre*. Cresskill, New Jersey: Hampton Press.

Consigny, S. (1974). Rhetoric and its situations. *Philosophy and Rhetoric, 7*(3), 175-186.

Devitt, A. J. (2004). *Writing genres*. Carbondale: Southern Illinois University Press.

Dias, P. (2000). Writing classrooms as activity systems. In P. Dias & A. Paré, (Eds.), *Transitions: Writing in academic and workplace settings* (pp. 11-29). Cresskill, New Jersey: Hampton Press.

Dias, P., Freedman, A., Medway, P., & Paré, A. (1999). *Worlds apart: Acting and writing in academic and workplace contexts*. Mahwah, New Jersey: Erlbaum.

Dias, P., & Paré, A. (Eds.). (2000). *Transitions: Writing in academic and workplace settings*. Cresskill, New Jersey: Hampton Press.

Downs, N. & Wardle, E. (2007). Teaching about writing, righting misconceptions: (Re)envisioning "first-year composition" as "introduction to writing studies." *College Composition and Communication, 58*(4), 552-584.

Engeström, Y. (1987). *Learning by expanding: An activity-theoretical approach to developmental research*. Helsinki: Orienta-Konsultit Oy.

Engeström, Y., & Miettinen, R. (1999). Introduction. In Y. Engeström, R. Miettinen, & R.-L. Punamäki (Eds.), *Perspectives on activity theory* (pp. 1-16). Cambridge: Cambridge University Press.

Fischer, C. T., & Wertz, F. J. (1979). Empirical phenomenological analyses of being criminally victimized. In A. Giori & D. Smith (Eds.), *Duquesne studies in phenomenological psychology: Vol. 3.* (pp. 135 –153). Pittsburgh, Pennsylvania: Duquesne University Press.

Fogarty, J. (2007, November). *Students writing in a general education learning community linking composition and history: An activity/genre theory analysis*. Paper presented at the 12th Annual National Learning Communities Conference, Students at the Centre, Indianapolis, Indiana.

Freedman, A. (1994). "Do as I say": The relationship between teaching and learning new genres. In A. Freedman & P. Medway (Eds.), *Genre and the new rhetoric* (pp. 191-210). London: Taylor & Francis.

Freedman, A. (2006a). Interactions between theory and research: RGS and a study of students and professionals working "in computers." In N. Artemeva & A. Freedman (Eds.), *Rhetorical genres studies and beyond* (pp. 101-120). Winnipeg, Manitoba, Canada: Inkshed Publications.

Freedman, A. (2006b). Pushing the envelope: Expanding the model of RGS theory. In N. Artemeva & A. Freedman (Eds.), *Rhetorical genres studies and beyond* (pp. 121-141). Winnipeg, Manitoba, Canada: Inkshed Publications.

Freedman, A., & Adam, C. (2000a). Bridging the gap: University-based writing that is more than simulation. In P. Dias & A. Paré (Eds.), *Transitions: Writing in academic and workplace settings* (pp. 129-144). Cresskill, New Jersey: Hampton Press.

Freedman, A., & Adam, C. (2000b). Write where you are: Situating learning to write in university and workplace settings. In P. Dias & A. Paré (Eds.), *Transitions: Writing in academic and workplace settings* (pp. 31 – 60). Cresskills, New Jersey: Hampton Press.

Freedman, A., Adam, C., & Smart, G. (1994). Wearing suits to class: Simulating genres and simulations as genre. *Written Communication, 11*(2), 193-226.

Freedman, A., & Medway, P. (Eds.). (1994a). *Learning and teaching genre.* Portsmouth, New Hampshire: Boynton/Cook.

Freedman, A., & Medway, P. (Eds.). (1994b). *Genre and the new rhetoric.* London: Taylor & Francis.

Freedman, A., & Smart, G. (1997). Navigating the current of economic policy: Written genres and the distribution of cognitive work at a financial institution. *Mind, Culture, and Activity, 4*(4), 238-255.

Geisler, C. (1994). *Academic literacy and the nature of expertise: Reading, writing, and knowing in academic philosophy.* Hillsdale, New Jersey: Erlbaum.

Giddens, A. (1984). *The constitution of society: Outline of the theory of structuration.* Berkeley: University of California Press.

Holland, D., Lachicotte, W. Jr., Skinner, D., & Cain, C. (1998). *Identity and agency in cultural worlds.* Cambridge, Massachusetts: Harvard University Press.

Kinneavy, J. L. (1986). Kairos: A neglected concept in classical rhetoric. In J. Dietz Moss (Ed.), *Rhetoric and praxis: The contribution of classical rhetoric to practical reasoning* (pp. 79-105). Washington, D.C.: The Catholic University of America Press.

Kutney, J. P. (2007). Will writing awareness transfer to writing performance? Response to D. Downs and E. Wardle, "Teaching about writing, righting misconceptions." *College Composition and Communication, 59*(2), 276-279.

Lave, J. (1991). Situating learning in communities of practice. In L. B. Resnik, J. M. Levine, & S. D. Teasley (Eds.), *Perspectives on socially shared cognition* (pp. 63-82). Washington, D.C.: American Psychological Association.

Lave, J., & Wenger, E. (1991). *Situated learning: Legitimate peripheral participation.* Cambridge: Cambridge University Press.

Le Maistre, C., & Paré, A. (2004). Learning in two communities: The challenges for universities and workplaces. *Journal of Workplace Learning, 16* (1/2), 44-52.

Leont'ev, A. N. (1981). The problem of activity in psychology. In J. V. Wertsch (Ed.), *The concept of activity in Soviet psychology* (pp. 37-71). Armonk, New York: Sharpe.

Mackinnon, J. (2003). Becoming a rhetor: Developing writing ability in a mature, writing-intensive organization. In T. Peeples (Ed.), *Professional writing and rhetoric: Readings from the field* (pp. 411-422). New York: Longman. (Reprinted from *Writing in the workplace: New research perspectives*, pp. 41-55, by R. Spilka, Ed., 1993, Carbondale, IL: Southern Illinois University Press)

Maxwell, J. A. (2005). *Qualitative research design: An interactive approach* (2nd ed., pp. 96-99). Thousand Oaks, California: Sage.

Maxwell, J. A., & Miller, B. A. (1992). *Two aspects of thought and two components of qualitative data analysis.* Unpublished manuscript, Harvard University, Cambridge, Massachusetts.

Maxwell, J. A., & Miller, B. A. (2002). *Categorizing and connecting as components of qualitative data analysis.* Unpublished manuscript, George Mason University, Fairfax, Virginia.

Miles, M. B., & Huberman, A. M. (1994). *An expanded sourcebook: Qualitative data analysis* (2nd ed.). Thousand Oaks, California: Sage.

Miller, C. (1992). Kairos in the rhetoric of science. In S. P. Witte, N. Nakadate, & R. D. Cherry (Eds.), *A rhetoric of doing: Essay on written discourse in honor of James L. Kinneavy* (pp. 310-327). Carbondale: Southern Illinois University Press.

Miller, C. (1994) Genre as social action. In A. Freedman & P. Medway (Eds.), *Genre and the new rhetoric* (pp. 23–42). London: Taylor & Francis.

Paré, A. (2002). Genre and identity: Individuals, institutions, and ideology. In R. Coe, L. Lingard, & T. Teslenko (Eds.), *The rhetoric and ideology of genre* (pp. 57 -71). Cresskill, New Jersey: Hampton Press.

Paré, A., & Le Maistre, C. (2006). Distributed mentoring in communities of practice. In P. Tynjälä, J. Välimaa, & G. Boulton-Lewis (Eds.), *Higher education and working life: Collaborations, confrontations and challenges* (pp. 129 -144). Amsterdam: Elsevier.

Russell, D. R. (1997). Rethinking genre in school and society: An activity theory analysis. *Written Communication, 14*, 504-554.

Schryer, C. F. (1993). Records as genre. *Written Communication, 10*(2), 200-234.

Schryer, C. F. (2000). Walking a fine line: Writing negative letters in an insurance company. *Journal of Business and Technical Communication, 14*(4), 445-497.

Schryer, C. F. (2002). Genre and power: A chronotopic analysis. In R. Coe, L. Lingard, & T. Teslenko (Eds.), *The rhetoric and ideology of genre* (pp. 73-102). Cresskill, New Jersey: Hampton Press.

Schryer, C. F. (2003, March). *Genre and techne in medical case presentations.* Paper presented at the Conference of College Composition and Communication, New York.

Schryer, C. (2005, April). *Genres and professional identity formation: A behind-the scenes exploration of a research program.* Paper presented at the Carleton University Speaker Series Seminar in Applied Language Studies, Ottawa,

Ontario, Canada.

Smart, G., & Brown, N. (2002). Learning transfer or transforming learning?: Student interns reinventing expert writing practices in the workplace. *Technostyle, 18*(1), 117-141.

Stake, R. E. (1995). *The art of case study research.* Thousand Oaks, California: Sage.

Stake, R. E. (2000). Case studies. In N. K. Denzin & Y. S. Lincoln (Eds.), *Handbook of qualitative research* (2nd ed., pp. 435-454). Thousand Oaks, California: Sage.

Strauss, A. L., & Corbin, J. (1998). *Basics of qualitative research: Techniques and procedures for developing grounded theory* (2nd ed.). Thousand Oaks, CA: Sage.

Voloshinov, V. N. (1983). Literary stylistics: The construction of the utterance. In A. Shukman (Ed.), *Bakhtin School papers* (N. Owen, Trans.). (pp. 114-138). Oxford: RPT Publications (abridged).

Vygotsky, L. S. (1978). *Mind in society: The development of higher psychological processes* (M. Cole, V. John-Steiner, S. Scribner, & E. Souberman, Eds.). Cambridge, Massachusetts: Harvard University Press.

Vygotsky, L. S. (1981). The genesis of higher mental functions. In J. V. Wertsch (Ed.), *The concept of activity in Soviet psychology* (pp. 144-188). Armonk, New York: Sharpe.

Webb, J., Schirato, T., & Danaher, G. (2002). *Understanding Bourdieu.* Thousand Oaks, California: Sage.

Wenger, E. (1998). *Communities of practice: Learning, meaning, and identity.* Cambridge: Cambridge University Press.

Winsor, D. (1996). *Writing like an engineer: A rhetorical education.* Mahwah, New Jersey: Erlbaum.

Winsor, D. (2001). Learning to do knowledge work in systems of distributed cognition. *Journal of Business and Technical Communication, 15*(1), 5-28.

Winsor, D. (2003). *Writing power: Communication in an engineering center.* Albany, New York: SUNY Press.

Yates, J., & Orlikowski, W. (2002). Genre systems: Chronos and kairos in communicative interaction. In R. Coe, L. Lingard, & T. Teslenko (Eds.), *The rhetoric and ideology of genre* (pp. 103-121). Cresskill, New Jersey: Erlbaum.

Zachry, M. (2007). Introduction: Regulation and communicative practices. In M. Zachry & C. Thralls (Eds.), *Communicative practices in workplaces and the professions* (pp. v-xi). Amityville, NY: Baywood Publishers.

9   The Dissertation as Multi-Genre: Many Readers, Many Readings

Anthony Paré
Doreen Starke-Meyerring
Lynn McAlpine

. . . I have found smart, accomplished colleagues in other disciplines who have little vocabulary for discussing writing beyond the corrective grammar they learned in high school. Although they have learned the genres of their profession and are successful in them, their reflective ability to manipulate them is limited because of a lack of linguistic and rhetorical vocabulary. (Bazerman, 2007, p. 46)

Since most academics have completed a dissertation, it is ironic that the genre is such an under-theorized, under-studied, and under-taught text (Rose & McClafferty, 2001; Lundell & Beach, 2002; Kamler & Thomson, 2006). Perhaps, like childbirth, it is best forgotten; more likely, as Bazerman's comment above suggests, the linguistic and rhetorical complexities of the dissertation are simply inexpressible for most academics. Unfortunately, doctoral students are often in desperate need of help with their dissertations, and yet, when Kamler and Thomson (2006) searched the literature, they found a "relative scarcity of well-theorized material about doctoral supervision and writing" and remarked that "doctoral writing was a kind of present absence in the landscape of doctoral education. It was something that everyone worried about, but about which there was too little systematic debate and discussion" (p. x). Our focus in this chapter is on the supervisory dyad and the collaborative relationship between doctoral students and their advisors. We see the dyad as a critical dynamic in the student's apprenticeship in disciplinary consciousness, identity, and discourse, and we set out to discover what occurred in supervisory sessions, especially when writing was the topic.

When we began the study reported here, we thought of the dissertation as a genre on the border between overlapping, sequential activities. On one hand, it is the ultimate student paper, the final school-based display of knowledge and ability. On the other hand, it is often—in whole or in part—the first significant contribution to a disciplinary conversation. We imagined the supervisor playing a dual role: as Bill Green (2005) has noted, "the supervisor represents, or stands in for, the Discipline itself, and also the Academy" (162). However, our research has helped us see the dissertation as even more complex than that—not just a double genre, but a multi-genre, responding to multiple exigencies, functioning in multiple rhetorical situations, addressing multiple readers. In itself, this recognition breaks no new ground. For many years, the technical writing literature has considered how different readers of the same text create rhetorical complexity in even simple institutional discourse (e.g., Mathes & Stevenson, 1976), and work in Writing Studies long ago fragmented a unitary notion of audience (e.g., Ede & Lunsford, 1984; Paré, 1991; Park, 1982). What our study does contribute is a first look at that multiplicity in the context of doctoral education—a look that explains some of the difficulties associated with writing and reading the dissertation. Not only does the dissertation contain variations on a number of distinct sub-genres (the literature review, the essay, the experimental article), it also responds to various exigencies and performs a range of social actions in several different contexts, including the supervisory dyad itself, the doctoral committee, the academic department, the disciplinary community, and the research setting. It is its simultaneous response to and service in these many settings that leads us to call the dissertation a multi-genre.

STUDYING THE DOCTORATE

The larger project of which this dissertation research is part is a multi-site, longitudinal study of the doctoral experience that seeks to determine the complex factors influencing the success and failure of students pursuing the PhD. We view the doctoral student as located within a series of nested contexts (McAlpine & Norton, 2006) that begin in the wider society and end in the small community of the student-supervisor dyad. According to Green (2005), "supervision is better conceived *ecosocially*, as a total environment within which postgraduate research activity ('study') is realised" (p. 153), and this image of nested contexts helps capture the complex ecology of the doctorate. Each context, each activity system—society, discipline, university, faculty, department—exerts an influence on the others. For example, national economic policies determine government research funding priorities that, in turn, raise or lower the status and viability of particular research agendas and their affiliated disciplines until, finally, individual university-based researchers can or cannot afford to support doctoral students. On our own campus, as on many others, the effects of these relations are manifest in concrete and steel: buildings devoted to research in certain sciences and technologies sprout, while arts and humanities colleagues work in cramped and decaying quarters.

At the time of writing, we are completing the first year of data collection from a variety of sources: student logs; interviews with students, supervisors, administrators, and others; focus group discussions; recorded supervisory sessions and follow-up interviews; policy and procedure documents related to the doctorate at various levels, from government funding agencies to departments; town hall meetings of students and faculty. Our design incorporates feedback loops because analysis is tested in seminars and workshops with doctoral students and supervisors; as a result, methods, questions, goals, and other aspects of the research continue to evolve.

SITUATED LEARNING, DISCIPLINARITY, AND GENRE

Our study of the dissertation follows and benefits from a rich tradition of research into the relationship between writing and disciplinarity (e.g., Bazerman, 1988; Bazerman & Paradis, 1990; Spilka, 1993; Geisler, 1994; Berkenkotter & Huckin, 1995; Winsor, 1996; Prior, 1998; Dias, Freedman, Medway, & Paré, 1999; Hyland, 2001; Bazerman & Russell, 2002); in addition, along with many others in Writing Studies, we have relied on such variations on cultural-historical theory as situated learning (e.g., Lave & Wenger, 1991; Wenger, 1998) and activity theory (e.g., Engeström, Miettinen, & Punamäki, 1999). When we turn our attention to texts and textual practices specifically, our chief theoretical lens has come from rhetorical genre studies (e.g., Miller, 1984; Freedman & Medway, 1994; Coe, Lingard, & Teslenko, 2002).

With her 1984 argument that "a rhetorically sound definition of genre must be centered not on the substance or form of discourse but on the action it is used to accomplish" (p. 151), Carolyn Miller gave writing researchers a powerful heuristic and a new agenda. Her insistence that we look beyond textual regularity to the consequences of repeated symbolic actions gave us our key questions: To what does a text respond? For what purpose or motive? As part of which situation or activity? To what effect? To understand texts or textual practices, we need first to know what a text *does*, what work it performs.

We see the dissertation as one genre within the doctoral genre set (Devitt, 1991)—a genre that students learn on the job, as it were, under the tutelage of a veteran scholar (and others). Learning to perform in or enact the dissertation genre is a critical part of the process of developing disciplinarity. As Carolyn Miller (1984) notes, "for the student, genres serve as keys to understanding how to participate in the actions of a community" (p. 165). This perspective on learning-to-write as a central dynamic in the development of disciplinary or professional identity and consciousness extends previous research that considered the transition from school to workplace and disciplinary writing (e.g., Dias, Freedman, Medway, & Paré, 1999; Dias & Paré, 2000).

Viewing the academic department as a workplace in which newcomers are inducted through apprenticeship has helped us make sense of what we are observing. Knowledge can be seen as a product of human labor and activity: we *make* knowledge in universities; or, more accurately, we deploy academic genres in order to make knowledge, and we apprentice doctoral students in that making process. That making then has consequences or outcomes; it performs social action. As Lave and Wenger (1991; Wenger, 1998) have demonstrated in varied contexts, workplace learning involves the gradual passage to full participation through increasingly more difficult tasks. That process, which they call "legitimate peripheral participation," consists of engaging the workplace newcomer in authentic and ever-more central workplace activity under the watchful eye of one or more veteran members of the collective. Doctoral students may follow a teaching trajectory that goes from tutoring to teaching assistantships to undergraduate teaching and a research trajectory that goes from research assistantships to postdoctoral fellowships.

Elsewhere (Paré, Starke-Meyerring, & McAlpine, 2006), we have compared our own sense of this gradual transformation to Prior's (1998) description of three modes of graduate student participation: "passing," "procedural display," and "deep participation" (pp. 100-103). Our conception of this growth has relied on different terms but charts a similar path toward membership:

> undergraduates are eavesdroppers, listening in on the disciplinary conversation and reporting it back to the professor (an actual member); Master's students are ventriloquists, able to sound like participants, but really only channelling the voices of the true members; doctoral students—if they are fortunate—find themselves increasingly involved as participants in work that matters, in work that will be public and that might affect others. Their access to and engagement in the range of practices that constitute the community's work results in the "deep participation" to which Prior refers. (Paré, Starke-Meyerring, & McAlpine, 2006, p. 10).

Likewise, the doctoral genre set (Devitt, 1991)—a series of rhetorical strategies that might include grant applications, course papers, comprehensive exams, dissertation proposals, and finally the dissertation itself—might be considered a movement toward deeper or more central participation in disciplinary discourse.

As in other workplace settings, we have noted a constant movement back and forth between planned and serendipitous learning in the academic department, and there is a wide range of teachers—a phenomenon we have called "distributed mentoring" (Paré & Le Maistre, 2006). In data collected so far, we have heard students describe the variety of support they have received—from supervisors, of course, but also from their committees, other faculty members, classmates, students in study and writing groups, administrators, and secretaries and other support staff. The lessons, too, are infinitely varied, from the highly pragmatic (when and how to apply for grants) to the ineffable and nearly inexpressible (the physical presentation of self during the oral comprehensive examination). Much of this appears to be taught and learned tacitly, an observation made by Parry (1998) about discipline-specific linguistic rules.

Academic workplaces, like many complex and multidisciplinary endeavors, are "laminations of activity" (Prior, 1998). The compressed nature of workplace activity captured by Prior's metaphor seems particularly apt to us. Doctoral students fill several subject positions simultaneously—student, teacher, researcher, classmate, colleague, university/faculty/department member, disciplinary apprentice—and all of that in addition to and interaction with their identities as parents, partners, members of affinity groups, and on and on. Even the descriptions of activity systems and the multi-triangular representations of those systems (e.g., Engeström, Miettinen, & Punamäki, 1999) do not capture that simultaneity. Consider how literacy theories, for example, might be simultaneously the doctoral student's objects of study (in the activity of learning) and mediational means (in the activity of teaching). Moreover, some of those concurrent and layered activity systems might be in conflict with each other; so, for example, a doctoral student whose disciplinary community favors qualitative research may find herself within a university department where a quantitative paradigm holds sway, or a student who wishes to conduct participatory action research might find himself in conflict with a research ethics committee that requires a detailed statement of methodology before research can commence.

Another similarity between university departments and other sites of on-the-job teaching and learning is the way in which the doctoral student's efforts reflect on the supervisor, and this may be no more apparent than with the dissertation. We hear supervisors refer to the dissertation as if it were a co-authored text, indicating what "we" need to do or how data support "our" argument. This seems to us a blatant reference to the induction into disciplinary culture that is the supervisory dyad's *raison d'être*. Our graduate students are highly visible products of our own knowledge work, and we have a vested interest in their successful passage to disciplinary membership.

These and other factors make a workplace perspective on academic units a productive way of seeing doctoral activity and the dissertation. However, in addition, there are certain aspects of the university department that makes it, if not unique, at least unusual. For one thing, the academic department, particularly in a multi-discipline like education, may be more of an institutional convenience than a community of like-minded scholars. The individual professor or doctoral student may actually be a member of a widely distributed disciplinary community, no other members of which are actually present on the university premises. As a result, the education department's specialist in literacy, for example, may publish in journals that none of her university colleagues even reads, and attend conferences where she is the only representative of her faculty. The result of that, and another distinguishing feature of the academic workplace, is that one's community of practice is first encountered textually, as a disembodied collective dispersed over time and space. In what other line of work might a long-dead colleague continue to influence the current conversation? Where else are one's fellow workers—those with whom one might interact (textually) every day—encountered face-to-face only once a year at an annual association meeting? The doctoral student seeking passage to disciplinary membership must locate herself in a textually constituted community.

SUPERVISION AND COMPOSITION

We will now return to the specific focus of this chapter—the function of the supervisory dyad in the writing of the dissertation. The dyad is perhaps the most intimate and high-stakes educational relationship, and the supervisor's role is complex and critical. As Kamler and Thomson (2006) put it, "the supervisor embodies and mediates institutional and disciplinary cultures, conditions and conventions" (p. 144). Stories of disaster in the relationship are legion, and assistance is rare. For this aspect of the project, we had these sorts of questions:

- What do people talk about during supervisory meetings? What topics and issues come up? What advice is given/taken? What strategies considered/deployed?
- What relationships are formed/enacted? What roles are played?
- What seems to work? What doesn't?
- What are supervisors/students thinking when they come to these meetings? What do they think/do after the meetings?

From the data we have collected to date, certain patterns have begun to emerge. For example, the bureaucratic logistics of departmental, faculty, and university practice are a clear focus of much anxiety and advice: deadlines, appropriate paperwork, number of committee members and external examiners required, binding and layout regulations, and so on. Another identifiable theme in the conversations consists of supervisors reassuring students that whatever they are experiencing is normal, often by recounting stories of their own work. This is how one supervisor put it: "It's hard. I know when I was doing my thesis, you're just so close to it. You can't see the forest anymore, you're looking at the bark." Another pattern, which might be labeled "tea and sympathy," consists of apparently non-dissertation related conversation about life outside the academy; based on our own experience as supervisors and on the work of our colleagues, we see these light chats about children or hobbies or current affairs as essential to creating working relationships. Finally, we have been much interested by supervisor and student commentary on organization and sequence in the dissertation, which depends heavily on spatial and design metaphors, but generally lacks explicit commentary on the rhetorical justification for the placement or order of ideas (more on this below).

READERS AND READINGS

In the remainder of this chapter, however, we would like to focus on an especially intriguing pattern, one that seems to us particularly revealing of the numerous exigencies to which the dissertation genre responds and the many social actions it seeks to perform. What distinguishes this pattern is the supervisor's performance as multiple readers and, as a result, her/his rendition or enactment of multiple readings. The pattern describes a variety of readers (and readings) from the general to the specific, the implied to the implicated—from the invisible and unmentioned reader, to the named reader for whom the dissertation could have serious consequences. In this pattern we see Prior's (1998) "laminations of activity" dramatized as the supervisor moves from one role/reading to another and, in the process, positions the student writer in different worlds. We have used the word "multirhetoricity" to describe the multiple locations, situations, and exigencies evoked by the supervisor and experienced by the student. For the moment, we have identified five readers/readings, although we recognize the categories as unstable and permeable.

The implied reader

Like Parry (1998) and Bazerman (2007), we have been struck by how implicit the teaching of disciplinary language conventions—linguistic and rhetorical—appears to be. Students are told to add to, reduce, move, and delete sections without clear reference to readers or to rhetorical justifications. For the researcher, the implied reader must be inferred, although it may be that both student and supervisor have a clear sense; sometimes it seems to be any reader (or everyreader, as we note below), at other times it appears the supervisor has a specific individual or type in mind. The reader lurks but does not emerge. Some examples[1]:

Larry: That's a very interesting phenomenon. You should, if you could,
           pursue that because I really think it's quite rampant.

* * *

Dennis: Because there is a section [in the dissertation] on critique of career theory and models; there's so many career theories and models. I mean, if you're going to criticize something, you will have to provide some information about those models before you do that.

Why "should" the topic be pursued? To whom, besides the supervisor, will it be "interesting"? Why does the writer "have to provide some information"? Again and again, we see examples in the data of this type of unexplained directive. They imply a reader and a rhetorical purpose—the information will make it possible, by someone's standards, for the writer to criticize "career theory and models." Claims must be supported, but when, why, and how? Again, the implied reader might be as general as a reader of English or as specific as a well known disciplinary expert on "career theory and models."

A similar but more explicit directive is apparent in a pattern we are calling Everyreader. The examples that follow do contain a reference to readers (or "us," in one case), but they seem to be *any* reader who happens to come across the text. With a reference to readers comes slightly more rhetorical justification:

Darlene: Here you sort of rapidly converge on something, and I don't have enough justification for what led you there. And then you need some sort of conclusion here: So, what does this tell us? Research in this field is fragmented? Underdeveloped? . . . So, you want to give a kind of sum-up. "Here's where things stand. Here's where I see the strengths and weaknesses of each."

    * * *

Juan: When you're writing a thesis, one of the things you need are road signs to guide the readers through the thesis [and] prepare them intellectually to expect what's coming. And, if you don't do that, then they get lost, they get confused, and they get pissed off.

Both of these excerpts also contain the pattern we mention above in which spatial or movement metaphors are used to describe textual organization. Road signs are required at points of convergence. Readers are noted, but they aren't identified as specialized readers, or readers with particular expectations for the structure or logic of arguments. However, we believe that the reader portrayed in these readings may be a member of the discipline, and that the reading being performed may be a specialized reading. These examples, we believe, demonstrate how knowledge becomes procedural without being declarable; students learn how to perform acts of disciplinary reading and writing without explicit instruction; genres become commonsense.

The absence of instruction becomes apparent when, in the rare event, a supervisor spells out reasons for injunctions, as in the following:

Wray: So for each study, make a grid like this; then you can identify the parts and what you'll see in the first study is that none of these things show up. . . . that will help the reader to see that they weren't there. Those steps weren't there. You had some other steps which will not appear in these—in [studies] two and three . . . . But to have the steps the same, because then you can see how much they overlap and that will make people see, "oh if you don't have these steps, it ain't process drama."

The grid or chart described is not presented as a disciplinary convention; it's simply a good way to represent data. However, Golde and Walker (2006) refer to a similar chart as "a tool familiar to educators" (p. 248), and we believe much of the advice offered by supervisors comes from a deep, discipline-specific, but inexpressible discourse knowledge. Although we are attempting to get colleagues to articulate the standards to which they hold their doctoral students, even the most experienced supervisors seem uncertain, as Bazerman notes in this chapter's epigraph. Consider this interview excerpt:

Lex: . . . it's a very formal exercise, undertaking research for a PhD, in presenting the work in the actual thesis, and so I need to sort of enforce certain conventions.

Interviewer: Right, and whose conventions are those? Where do those conventions come from?

Lex: Well I . . . that's an interesting question. I suppose they come to [student] filtered through me, so as a supervisor I suppose at the end of the day it's my view of what is a convention, and I suppose my view is formed partly by seeing other theses. But I'm not sure that's the answer. I'm not really sure where . . . . I'm not sure I can answer it. I have a view. Obviously it must come from somewhere. But I don't know where. I don't know where we decide how we do this.

The evoked reader

As the reader being portrayed or anticipated takes on an identity, the rhetorical justification for directives becomes more explicit. In the following excerpts, readers with defined expectations or needs are identified, and the provision of required information is thus justified. An unpersuaded or perplexed reader is evoked, and rhetorical action is recommended:

Lex: [Committee member] is bound to ask, "Well, okay, but you have all this data, so how's it going to help you out?" is the question. I mean, I know he'll ask it, if one of the others doesn't.

* * *

Lex: I would give them a few numbers about it. Remember we talked about possible external examiners. We've identified three possible external examiners and none of them are from Quebec. Two are from the States and one is from Canada. Apart from whoever might read your thesis in the future and might not know the details of how things are done in Quebec. . . . I mean how would somebody in the US know what a French immersion school is?

In the latter excerpt, some of the specific readers evoked are members of the discipline, but it is not their disciplinary knowledge that is at issue. They are being brought to mind, as it were, as any reader who "might read [the] thesis in the future and might not know the details of how things are done in Quebec." The supervisor is not trying to help the writer position herself vis à vis the field's current conversation; that takes a different sort of reader and reading.

The disciplinary reader

As we move our research into seminars and workshops for colleagues, there is one type of reader and reading we will be promoting: the disciplinary reader/reading—the one in which a discipline's rhetoric is laid bare. This is the type of reading that writing tutors are often trained to provide—the think-aloud reading that exposes the reader's meaning-making process, or the reading accompanied by commentary. In the three examples below, with varying degrees of explicitness, the supervisors help the students locate their texts in a community's ongoing conversation. In the first two, they offer rhetorical justifications for the inclusion of certain information; in the third, the supervisor states a blunt, rhetorical truth about disciplinary knowledge-making.

Frances: I think maybe what you should say is—have a footnote to say in that chapter—that some of this work has already been published in an international journal, or whatever, because that's gone through a peer review process, it's been published and [that] tells people that you've already got the seal of approval from your academic peers in an international journal.

* * *

Juan: A lot of adult education theory goes back to them [Gramsci and Freire]. So I think what you should do is figure out, when you read this again, just make sure that you've genuflected enough to them.

* * *

Juan: The thing is, with PhD theses, you've got to be careful about who you choose to be external examiners. Someone like [Prof. X], for example, might fail this [dissertation] because, you know, I mean, there's a bunch of people, of which [Prof. X] is part, and I think that she'd have huge problems with this, okay? There are other people who wouldn't. . . . And I think that's who we'll send it to. We'll put them down as the examiners. There's, if you like, a politics to it, right?

These comments begin to exhibit the type of rhetorical savvy that we believe supervisors and doctoral students need—not necessarily because they will learn better how to participate in their field's knowledge-making practices, since that seems to happen reasonably well without explicit instruction, but because we believe that a truly critical appreciation of those practices is not possible without a rhetorical perspective.

The implicated reader

In this final type of reader/reading, one we did not expect to find, we include comments about actual but non-disciplinary readers—those portrayed in the research or with a vested interest in its results. With the advent and increasing use of various action research approaches, this type of reader begins to figure more and more in disciplinary writing. The school, hospital, agency, community centre, or other research setting is also an activity system, one in which the doctoral student has taken a subject position, and in which the rhetorical stakes might be considerably higher than in the relative safety of the academy. Here we see most clearly the dissertation's multiple exigencies and outcomes, the "lamination of activities" to which Prior (1989) refers.

> Student: I'm feeling more pressure than I thought I would because it's not just my mom who's going to be reading this, and you. [The administration at the research site] is very interested in this work.

> * * *

> Larry: But you know what's going to be challenging as you write this, is that you have to do it in a way, first of all, you have to know that these teachers might read your thesis for one thing . . . .

> Student: Yeah, I know. I'm going to have to be careful. . . . I'm not going to write in the same bull-headed way that I'm speaking to you about it. Because I'm aware that they're going to read it and I know that it's going to go to the school board office.

Here, too, we see much need for work with our students and colleagues. When the workplace text leaves the workplace, it can be confusing, off-putting, alienating, and hurtful.

CONCLUSION

As we noted above, we do not see these categories as closed or clearly demarcated. We've described a variety of readers and readings which seem to lie on a continuum from the implicit to the explicit and from the general to the highly specific. In the next phase of our work, as we collect more supervisory conversations and post-conversation interviews, we hope to see and describe a clearer spectrum of readings and to ask colleagues to help us understand what is happening in those readings. One thing seems certain: when supervisors ventriloquate readers or perform various readings, rhetorical consciousness is raised, even without explicit explanations. As supervisors express confusion, critique interpretations, question claims, wonder aloud, and ask for more information—even when they do so in the role of unidentified readers—students are alerted to possible mis-readings. They do go away and revise; and many do move toward a text that actual readers find acceptable in different settings.

As we consider these multiple rhetorical demands on the dissertation writer, we are developing a greater appreciation of how much more complex the dissertation genre may be in the multiplicity of its rhetorical demands than perhaps anything else academics write. There are relatively few genres in which a writer negotiates university and departmental demands, criteria, and practices (including faculty from any disciplinary background attending comprehensive exams and thesis defences); committee demands that can reflect a disciplinary diversity and perhaps even incommensurable research paradigms (Kuhn, 1962) that would be rather unlikely to come together in the disciplinary forums in which the doctoral student will eventually settle; and the concerns of research participants who may read the dissertation because of their involvement and their stakes in the research results, but who often are not considered significant readers of specialized journal articles. Returning to Miller's observation about the key function of genre in learning how to participate in the work of a community, we see the dissertation as a highly complex multi-genre that not only locates the student in a particular disciplinary community, reproducing its "commonsense" ways of knowing, but also engages the student in its boundary work with other disciplinary communities (as represented by committee members or department demands) or practitioner communities (as represented by research participants). As a multi-genre, the dissertation thus becomes a rich and rhetorically challenging space for supervisors and students to enact the complexity of a widely distributed disciplinary and academic life in one text.

NOTES
[1] All excerpts, unless otherwise noted, are comments by supervisors from transcribed conversations with their doctoral students. Pseudonyms are used.

REFERENCES
Bazerman, C. (1988). *Shaping written knowledge: The genre and activity of the experimental article in science.* Madison: University of Wisconsin Press.
Bazerman, C. (2007). Writing and cognitive development: Beyond writing to learn. *Proceedings of the 4th International Symposium on Genre Studies* (pp. 38-49), University of Southern Santa Catarina, Tubarão, Santa Catarina, Brazil.
Bazerman, C., & Paradis, J. (Eds.). (1991). *Textual dynamics of the professions.* Madison: University of Wisconsin Press.
Bazerman, C. & Russell, D. (2002). *Writing selves/writing societies: research from activity perspectives.* Retrieved from Colorado State University, WAC Clearinghouse and Mind, Culture, and Activity: http://wac.colostate.edu/books/selves_societies/
Berkenkotter, C. & Huckin, T. (1995). *Genre knowledge in disciplinary communication: Cognition/culture/power.* Hillsdale, New Jersey: Erlbaum.
Coe, R., Lingard, L., and Teslenko, T. (Eds.). (2002). *The rhetoric and ideology of genre.* Cresskill, New Jersey: Hampton Press.
Devitt, A. (1991). Intertextuality in tax accounting. In C. Bazerman & J. Paradis

(Eds.), *Textual dynamics of the professions* (pp. 336-357). Madison: University of Wisconsin Press.

Dias, P., Freedman, A., Medway, P., & Paré, A. (1999). *Worlds apart: Acting and writing in academic and workplace contexts*. Mahwah, New Jersey: Erlbaum.

Dias, P. & Paré, A. (Eds.). (2000). *Transitions: Writing in academic and workplace settings*. Cresskill, New Jersey: Hampton Press.

Ede, L., & Lunsford, A. (1984). Audience addressed/audience invoked: The role of audience in composition theory and pedagogy. *College Composition and Communication, 35*(2), 155-171.

Engeström, Y., Miettinen, R., & Punamäki, R.-L. (Eds.) (1999). *Perspectives on activity theory*. Cambridge: Cambridge University Press.

Freedman, A. and Medway, P. (Eds.). (1994). *Genre and the new rhetoric*. London: Taylor & Francis.

Geisler, Cheryl. (1994). *Academic literacy and the nature of expertise: Reading, writing, and knowing in academic philosophy*. Hillsdale, New Jersey: Erlbaum.

Golde, C. M. & Walker, G. E. (Eds.). (2006). *Envisioning the future of doctoral education: Preparing stewards of the discipline*. San Francisco: Jossey-Bass.

Green, B. (2005). Unfinished business: Subjectivity and supervision. *Higher Education Research and Development, 24*(2), 151-163.

Hyland, K. (2004). *Disciplinary discourses: Social interactions in academic writing*. Ann Arbor: University of Michigan Press.

Kamler, B. & Thomson, P. (2006). *Helping doctoral students write: Pedagogies for supervision*. London: Routledge.

Kuhn, T. S. (1962). *The structure of scientific revolutions*. Chicago: University of Chicago Press.

Lave, J. & Wenger, E. (1991). *Situated learning: Legitimate peripheral participation*. Cambridge: Cambridge University Press.

Lundell, D. B. & Beach, R. (2002). Dissertation writers' negotiations with competing activity systems. In C. Bazerman & D. Russell (Eds.), *writing selves/ writing societies: research from activity perspectives* (pp. 483-514). Retrieved from Colorado State University, WAC Clearinghouse and Mind, Culture, and Activity: http://wac.colostate.edu/books/ selves_societies/

Mathes, J. & Stevenson, D. (1976). *Designing technical reports: Writing for audiences in organization*. Indianapolis, Indiana: Bobbs-Merrill.

McAlpine, L., & Norton, J. (2006). Reframing our approach to doctoral programs: A learning perspective. *Higher Education Research and Development, 25*(1), 3-17.

Miller, C. (1984). Genre as social action. *Quarterly Journal of Speech, 70*, 151-167.

Paré, A. (1991). Ushering "audience" out: From oration to conversation. *Textual*

Studies in Canada, 1(1), 45-64.

Paré, A., Starke-Meyerring, D., & McAlpine, A. (2006, April). *Entering the text: Learning doctoral rhetoric.* Paper presented at the annual meeting of the American Educational Research Association, San Francisco. Retrieved from http://doc-work.mcgill.ca/public-space/aera-2006-paper.doc/view

Paré, A. & Le Maistre, C. (2006). Distributed mentoring in communities of practice. In P. Tynjälä, J. Välimaa, & G. Boulton-Lewis (Eds.), *Higher education and working life: Collaborations, confrontations and challenges* (pp. 129-141). Amsterdam: Elsevier.

Park, D. (1982). The meanings of "audience." *College English, 44*, 247-257.

Parry, S. (1998). Disciplinary discourse in doctoral theses. *Higher Education, 36*, 273–299.

Prior, P. (1998). *Writing/disciplinarity: A sociohistoric account of literate activity in the academy.* Mahwah, New Jersey: Erlbaum.

Rose, M. & McClafferty, K. A. (2001). A call for the teaching of writing in graduate education . *Educational Researcher, 30*(2), 27-33.

Spilka, R. (Ed.) (1993). *Writing in the workplace: New research perspectives.* Carbondale: Southern Illinois University Press.

Wenger, E. (1998). *Communities of practice: Learning, meaning, and identity.* Cambridge: Cambridge University Press.

Winsor, D. (1996). *Writing like an engineer.* Mahwah, New Jersey: Erlbaum.

GENRE AND MEDIA

10   The Distinction Between News and
      Reportage in the Brazilian Journalistic
      Context: A Matter of Degree

      Adair Bonini

INTRODUCTION

In my previous researches on news and reportage (Bonini, 2003a, 2003b, 2006; Kindermann & Bonini, 2006) I have found it increasingly difficult to distinguish between exemplars of these two genres and in finding consistent and clear definitions for them in the literature, even though they are treated as distinct genres within Brazilian journalistic culture. Instead I have found that there is a continuum of genres with purer forms of news to reportage at the poles, with mixed forms in between.

This work is based on the new rhetoric approach to genre studies, more specifically on the view of genre as a social action as proposed by Miller (1984), and later developed by Swales (1990) and Bazerman (1994, 2004). The exemplars of news and reportage considered here were published in the Brazilian newspaper *Jornal do Brasil*, and therefore belong to a specific journalistic culture. Yet, even though focusing on a specific cultural environment, the research findings about the genres and practices focused here may lead to reflections on other journalistic contexts. Additionally, it allows us to think about the relation between genre and environment (systems, ecology) and between genre and practice.

In the following sections I present a brief explanation of the new rhetoric approach to genre studies; an analysis of the definitions of news and reportage currently available in the literature (considering especially technical, but also academic texts); the research methodology; and the results.

THE NEW RHETORIC APPROACH TO GENRE STUDIES

Miller (1984) proposes that a genre should be seen as a rhetorical action which recurs in a given social environment. She defines recurrence not as a material but as an intersubjective process, since it depends on the participants' interpretations and on the consequent sharing of these interpretations. This process of recurrent sharing of socially interpreted and signified situations establishes the types (of situations and actions), which serves as the common knowledge basis required for communication.

Swales (1990), in the same way as Miller, developed a concept of *genre* as a communicative event guided by purpose(s) and which occurs within a *discourse community* (a specific group, interested in certain activities and subjects). It was based on these two concepts that he developed his CARS (create a research space) model to explain research article introductions, through which he has proposed the rhetorical move analysis as a way to study genres. Regarding the organization of the research article, his study reveals the presence of movements, such as "establishing a territory," and steps that perform those movements, like "reviewing items of previous research" (p. 141).

Bazerman (1994), on the other hand, developed the concept of system of genres, defining it as "interrelated genres that interact with each other in specific settings" (p. 97). Within a system, a specific genre creates conditions and establishes requirements for the realization of a following genre. The systems of genres, in turn, operate within activities systems (Bazerman, 2004).

In the research I am reporting here I used Swales' (1990) rhetorical move analysis, so there is an implicit acceptance of his concepts of genre and discourse community. The hypothesis of a continuum between news and reportage, however, has been inspired by the idea of genres and activities systems (Bazerman, 1994, 2004), since the unclear border between both genres results, I believe, from the fact that they are part of the same newspaper activities system (an issue I will discuss in more detail at the end the article).

To review the definitions of news and reportage as they are presented in the literature on the subject, I considered four aspects: (1) the purpose; (2) aspects of the production, the reading and of the social roles involved; (3) the rhetorical organization; and (4) the nomenclature of these genres. The first and last criteria come from the Swales' (1990) concept of genre, the second and third, from the genre study methodology developed by Paré and Smart (1994). In their article, these last two authors tried to answer an intriguing question: "When conceived as social action, what, in addition to texts, are the observable constituent elements of a genre?" In this sense, they focus on four aspects: (1) textual features; (2) social roles; (3) the processes of composition; and (4) the practices of reading.

When trying to establish a critique of the existing definitions of news and reportage, I was faced by the same question raised by Paré and Smart (1994), because many aspects of Swales' (1990) genre concept, such as prototypicality, are not enough to achieve the objectives aimed here. Thus, I decided to combine Paré/Smart and Swales' explanations. Moreover, the choice of grouping several genre characteristics in the third item of my analytical categories is due to the fact that such aspects had been little explored in the literature on the genres considered here.

Many of the thoughts developed in this chapter depart from a project entitled

"Newspaper Genres," which my advisees and I have been developing since 2003, following the new rhetoric approach. This project has resulted, so far, in seven MA dissertations: Figueiredo (2003), Kindermann (2003), Simoni (2004), Innocente (2005), Cassarotti (2006), Borba (2007) and Caldeira (2007). What I am doing in this article, more specifically, is a review, and therefore a re-discussion, of two works we have done on the genre reportage: Kindermann (2003) and Kindermann and Bonini (2006).

NEWS AND REPORTAGE

In general terms, the literature from the area of journalism in Brazil makes it very hard to understand journalistic genres. This is due to two reasons: first, most of these works were produced prior to the debate on genre; second, such works lack linguistic theories that could allow us to determine which aspects are central to the definition of a genre.

In most cases genre definitions (coming up from the journalistic practice itself) are little theorized or linked to old and already crystallized debates. Even the authors who attempt to determine criteria to characterize a specific genre are hindered by this lack of a theoretical basis. To define the news Lage (1979), for example, claims that "The answer depends on a definition that could cover the appearance, aspect or form of the news in contemporary journalism, paving the way for a more rigorous approach to its content." His work, however, does not sufficiently justify why it would be important to focus on such characteristics. In relation to this literature, we must stress, however, that the definition of a specific genre is not an easy matter, even for those who have delved exclusively into this topic.

News as a genre

The definitions of news[1] are, in general, countless, inconsistent among themselves and very superficial, as pointed out by Lage (1979, p. 52). This does not seem to be at all a peculiarity of the Brazilian context since journalism in this country was early influenced by American manuals like Bond (1954). In addition to that, in Portugal, Cascais (2001, p. 140) makes similar claims to Lage's about the news definitions there.

This proliferation of superficial and inconsistent definitions may be related to the ambiguity of the word "news," as pointed out by Van Dijk (1988, pp. 3-4). The author states that "news may be understood as new information or as a news article but also as a TV program in which news is presented . . ." Considering Van Dijk's statement, I think it's possible to conclude that discerning news-fact from news-genre (the latter being the focus of this work) is perhaps the most productive way to build a consistent definition for that term.

Regarding the material consulted, I tried to center on those definitions which, in some way, focused on news as text. The quotes below, therefore, are organized in order of the least to the most consistent in terms of a definition based on the notion of genre, and say that news are:

(1) Report of facts or current events of interest and importance to the community, and capable of being understood by the audience. (Rabaça & Barbosa, 1978, p. 513)

(2) Pure recording of facts, without opinion. (*Folha de S. Paulo*, 1998, p. 157)

(3) . . . A report of a series of facts departing from the most important one, and then from its most important aspect. Thus, we reduce the field of discussion to what would be *important*, a word which summarizes abstract concepts such as *truth* or *human interest*. This allows us to regard the news as something which consists of two basic components: (a) a relatively stable organization, or the logical component; and (b) elements which are organized in the news, chosen according to essentially variable value criteria—the ideological component. (Lage, 1979, p. 54)

These definitions are very fragile from a logical point of view, because most of the features identified, in addition to being too general, apply to many other journalistic genres. The first of them, for example, is very fuzzy, characterizing the news as a report "of interest and importance to the community, and capable of being understood by the audience." It is difficult to understand such elements as defining aspects of the news because, in fact, they are present in virtually all written journalistic production. This particular definition also lacks scientific grounding, since the importance of information to the community, for example, is not something obvious. At the very least it is necessary to define what "important" means in this case. Moreover, we have here an acritical definition, one which focuses on the naturalized image of the press as a public service, capable of bringing to the reader the so-called "important" information.

In general, definitions like that are not helpful to the understanding of what constitutes the news as a journalistic genre. They do not tell us very much about the central aspects necessary to a genre based definition. Regarding the points which I tried to capture in this definition (the purpose of the genre; aspects of the production, the reading, and of the social roles involved; the rhetorical organization; and the nomenclature), almost nothing can be concluded about them. The last explanation is the only one that focuses, in a more consistent manner, on the generic elements of the news (aspects of the organization and production processes), although it also lacks theoretical grounding.

Reportage as a genre

Similarly to the news, reportage is also an ambiguous term in Brazilian journalistic literature, because at the same time that it names a genre it represents the work of information gathering which serves as a basis for several journalistic genres. This ambiguity is pointed out by Lage (1979, p. 51), but also by Sousa (2005, p. 188) in the Portuguese context. Often, the Brazilian definitions of reportage stops at this second aspect, as shown in the style guide of the newspaper *Folha de S. Paulo* (1998, p. 42), and in Rabaça and Barbosa's (1978) dictionary of communication. In the latter, the authors define the reportage as "A set of measures which is necessary to manufacture a journalistic news: coverage, investigation, data selection, interpretation and treatment, within certain techniques and requirements to articulate the informational journalistic text" (p. 638).

In the case of the reportage, on the whole it is very difficult to say, from the majority of the definitions found in the Brazilian literature, what characterizes this genre. Here again I present some definitions of reportage ranging from the less to the more coherent one in terms of a definition based on the concept of genre:

(1) The reportage can be considered the very essence of a newspaper, and differs from the news in the content, scope and depth. . . . Thus, it investigates not only the origins of the fact, but its reasons and effects. (*O Estado de S. Paulo*, 1990, p. 67)

(2) The reportage is the representation of a fact or event enriched by the author's intellectual capacity, careful observation, sensitivity, creativity, and fluent narrative. (Amaral, 1982, p. 133)

(3) [The reportage] ranges from a simple news complement—an expansion that contextualizes the fact in its more obvious relations with other preceding, succeeding and correlated facts—to an essay able to reveal, from the historical practice, contents of permanent interest, as it happens in Euclides da Cunha's report on the Canudos campaign (in his book *Rebellion in the Backlands*). (Lage, 1979, p. 115)

(4) The reportage is not directed at the coverage of a fact or a series of facts, but at the exploration of a subject from a pre-established angle. News deals with a government which has been deposed; regarding the same issue, reportages deal with the political-institutional, economic, and social crisis, with the configuration of international relations determined by the replacement of this government, with the conspiracy that led to the coup, with one or more characters involved in the episode, etc. (Lage, 1985, pp. 46-47)

Discarding the definitions which explain the reportage term only as journalistic activity, as reporting work, the four explanations above display two conceptions about the this genre, as pointed out by Kindermann (2003), and Kinderman and Bonini (2006). The reportage is conceived as an extension or deepening of the news in the first and second definitions, and as an independent genre in the last one. The third definition, however, consists of a mixed explanation.

In terms of the features considered here (the purpose of the genre; aspects of the production, the reading and of the social roles involved; the rhetorical organization; and the nomenclature) little can be raised from these definitions. Considering the whole explanation (and not only the definitions), the literature on the subject offers some details, but the interesting and relevant point to the issue discussed here is the nomenclature aspect.

In relation to the nomenclature for reportage, the Brazilian journalistic literature presents a set of discussions and proposals. I present these classifications below, also trying to display them from the least to the most consistent in terms of how they approximate to the notion of genre.

Sodré and Ferrari (1986) understand that the reportage occurs in three ways:

- Fact-story: "Involves the objective reporting of events, which follows in writing the inverted pyramid form. As in the news, the facts are narrated in sequence, in order of importance" (p. 45);
- Action-story: "It's a more or less stirring report, which always begins with the more attractive fact going down step by step to the exposure of the details. What matters in these reportages is the events being narrated in a personal way, next to the reader, who is involved with the visualization of the scenes, as if in a movie" (p. 52);
- Quote-story: "It is the documented report that presents elements in an objective manner, accompanied by quotations which supplement and clarify the subject. . . . It is expository and similar to a research. Sometimes, it has a denouncing character. But, in most cases, supported by data which grounds it, it acquires a pedagogical status, taking a stand about the subject in question" (p. 64).

It is, however, an explanation that does not distinguish the reportage from the news. It is too general, and does not characterize properly either of these two genres.

Lage (1979, p. 116) classifies the types of reportage according to journalistic paradigms as:

- Research type: "where one departs from one fact to show others more or less hidden facts and, through them, a situation whose profile is of interest to journalism (as in the Watergate case, or in the investigation of the My Lai episode during the Vietnam war)";
- Interpretative type: "where a set of facts is seen from the method-ological perspective of certain science (the most common interpre-tations are sociological and economic)"; and
- New journalism type: "investing exactly on the revelation of a non-theorized human-praxis, tries to capture the phenomenon's essence by using literary techniques to construct the narrated situations and episodes."

This classification also falls short of defining the reportage as a genre, since it overgeneralizes, focusing on journalistic techniques and thus remaining quite distant from the notion of text as social action.

Kindermann (2003) and Kindermann and Bonini (2006), from the analysis of 32 reportages coming from Jornal do Brasil's four sections collected in January 2000, propose a classification in four genres, which are:

- Deepening of the news: focusing on details, new data, and an over-view of the newsworthy fact;
- Reportage from interview: focusing on data from interviews with one or more defined themes (often, based on a fact);
- Research reportage: focusing on the investigation of several sources regarding a certain subject;
- Retrospective reportage: focusing on the sequence of facts which gave rise to a particular fact or on the history of a certain issue.

This classification, although built within a genre perspective, presents the problem of not being exhaustive. Few genre occurrences were analyzed, and the newspaper was not considered as whole.

The final classification considered here is that proposed by Chaparro (1998, pp. 94-96), which presents the following reportage genres:

- Profile reportage: it "reveals . . . the notoriety of people, cities, plac-es and institutions";
- Photographic reportage: it reports a fact or subject through photos and captions;

- Retrospective reportage: it has a "differentiated narrative structure to search, in the past, the contextual reasons for today's relevant journalistic events";
- Didactic reportage: it is "triggered by issues or situations which require certain behaviors (disease prevention, the enforcement of new laws, cooperation with campaigns, etc.) or which arouse the need for certain knowledge . . . .";
- Itinerary reportage—it is "very common in tourism supplements. . . . It has a descriptive text, with few citations of sources; it is logically ordered by some chronological, geographical or spatial criterion";
- Market reportage: "It is always related to the consumption of goods and to the consumers' tastes, or to the offer and demand for products, services, technologies and expertise. It is characterized by tone of usefulness and by a light and pleasant narration, in most cases with no critical purpose. But there are critical texts too, reporting on, for example, tests or experiments with products, conducted by the reporters, occasionally with the help of experts[2]."

This work, though very intuitive and presenting excessively synthetic descriptions, incorporates a genre perspective in the sense of social action. The genres raised by Chaparro (1998) seem to be fairly representative in terms of the reportage practices, and are, to a great extent, sustained by the corpus examined here.

The news to reportage continuum

The news and reportage, instead of two separated genres, seem to function as a continuum, which can serve as an explanation for the great difficulty that the Brazilian journalistic literature shows in trying to define both. This difficulty leads, sometimes, to the use of the word news applying to both genres, evidenced in, for example, the use of labels such as "planned or unexpected news, spontaneous or provoked news" (cited by Rabaça & Barbosa, 1978, p. 513). The same applies to the term reportage. According to the style guide of the newspaper *O Globo* (1999), reportage encompasses ". . . both the coverage of an everyday life's fact which has great impact (rains hitting the whole city, the announcement of a broad economic plan) and the exhaustive approach of a subject without a direct connection to the date of the edition (the state of public education, or the AIDS problem)" (p. 37).

The continuum between news and reportage is visible in the very manner the authors have defined this second genre, because (1) for Rabaça and Barbosa

(1978), the reportage does not exist as a genre, only the news; (2) for Amaral (1982), it consists in an in-depth news; and (3) for Lage (1985), the reportage is the opposite of the news, since it covers themes and not facts.

One compelling explanation for this continuum between both genres can be seen in the interest wave theory proposed by Lage (1979). According to this theory, a striking fact firstly generates news and, in the sequence, various reportages which deal with the most diverse topics related to this fact. Some time later, the interest in the fact tends to decrease and, consequently, so does the production of reportages. This author states that the "study of the reportage requires the consideration of what journalistic opportunity is," adding that "opportunity, in this case, refers specifically to an interest-generating fact" (p. 118).

Based on this explanation, the author seeks, therefore, to differentiate both genres. According to him, "the news distinguishes itself with some degree of subtlety from the reportage, which focuses on subjects, not necessarily on new facts; in the latter, what matters are the relations which update the facts, establishing a certain world view. The reportage is planned and follows an editorial line, a focus; the news does not" (Lage, 1979, p. 51). The author also exemplifies, saying that: "Even an unexpected fact (the collapse of a building) can be effectively complemented by some reportage (on building problems), while the journalistic industry develops rather fast techniques and processes for data collection and processing" (Lage, 1979, p. 116).

METHODOLOGY

The analysis reported here, which consisted of two phases, tried to map out reportage occurrences as a genre in all supplements of the newspaper. The news was taken as a departure point, from which the reportage occurrences were compared and allocated in order of distance.

In the first phase, the corpus was composed of 337 texts, corresponding to all news and reportage occurrences in three editions of *Jornal do Brasil*, which circulated on the 10th, 11th and 12th of January 2000. Additionally, as some supplements of this newspaper are published only once a week and others only every fortnight, these three collected editions did not include all of them. To make up for the absence of these supplements, I included copies of them published in other days (the 13th, 15th, 16th, 20th, 22nd, 23rd and 30th) of the same month and year (January 2000) in order to have a more complete view of the newspaper.

To reach this set of 337 texts, a survey was conducted of all genres presented in these three editions, and, after that, only the occurrences of the genres focused on were selected, as already reported in Bonini (2006).

To group these 337 texts in smaller sets, which corresponded to the several reportage manifestations, I used as criteria the text's objective, which could be inferred from the content of each examined text, and its rhetorical organization, viewed still in a superficial way.

In the second research phase, 10 texts were selected from each of the nine groupings for a more detailed rhetorical move analysis. However, one of these groups (the product reportages) had only four copies. As a consequence, in this phase only 84 texts were analyzed.

To carry out the move survey, I used Swales' (1990) CARS model. In this kind of analysis, the researcher seeks to determine what types of rhetorical action the text producer performs during the writing of a particular genre. In this research, however, I have adapted Swales' model, focusing only on the rhetorical moves, not considering the rhetorical step as an analytical category.

FINDINGS

The results from the analysis are presented here in two parts. The first one concerns a classification of the 337 texts into smaller groups (phase one), and the second presents a survey of the rhetorical organization of each group (phase two).

News and reportage within the newspaper

The classification of the 337 texts revealed nine groups, as can be seen in Table 1, which shows the identified purpose in each genre. According to the continuum hypothesis defended here, the several reportage manifestations are being understood as correlated genres, and not as reportage subgenres, although this does not imply the denial or impossibility of explaining the reportage as a single genre composed of variants.

GROUP	GENRE	PURPOSE
Factual	News	Reporting a fact or an event
	Retrospective reportage	Explaining the fact origin
	Opinion reportage	Approaching a fact or subject through surveyed opinion(s)
	Profile reportage	Describing a person or institution related to a fact, a current theme, socially prestigious or famous theme
	Coverage reportage	Reporting the day-to-day of an institution, big event/feast, or a lasting fact
Thematic	Product reportage	Describing a new product
	Research reportage	Presenting data on the interpretation of a current problem or on social behavior tendency
	Didactic reportage	Explaining a subject, troubled situation or service
	Itinerary reportage	Presenting tour possibilities

TABLE 1: NEWS AND REPORTAGE PURPOSES[3]

Following the continuum perspective, the texts were divided into two larger groups, in terms of being close to or distant from newsworthy facts. The factual texts group is composed of either news genre occurrences or reportages occurrences exploiting some news aspect (whether of a fact's history, the reactions to it, its characters, or the sequence of events). It must be emphasized, however, that the opinion and the profile reportages are often produced independently of a news fact, the former getting evidence from an interview with an expert in the theme, and the second, with a famous artist. The coverage reportage, although often confused with the news, has been placed as the last item in that group, since it is not the narration of a spontaneous fact, but the reporting of information constantly and deliberately surveyed.

The second group (the thematic) comprises the genres of more universal themes, therefore less linked to the occurrence of a fact. Nevertheless, the continuum remains, since the product reportage (which usually focuses on the launching of goods) is, for example, more connected with any theme in evidence than the itinerary reportage (which focuses on tour possibilities).

A percentage survey of the occurrences of such genres in the corpus was also conducted. The data in Table 2 allows the quite interesting conclusion that the main genre produced in a newspaper is not the news (22.25%), but the reportage (77.75%). The coverage reportage is the most frequent genre in the newspaper (33.23%), which seems natural, since spontaneous facts do not occur in sufficient numbers to fill in the daily editions. Therefore, the newspaper must have observers at strategic social points (Congress and Senate, the stock market, soccer teams, etc.) in order to bring certain events to the category of newsworthy facts, which is done by shedding light on some of them and, consequently, silencing others.

GROUP	GENRE	N.º	%
Factual	News	75	22.25
	Retrospective reportage	11	3.26
	Opinion reportage	34	10.08
	Profile reportage	10	2.96
	Coverage reportage	112	33.23
Thematic	Product reportage	4	1.18
	Research reportage	45	13.35
	Didactic reportage	35	10.38
	Itinerary reportage	11	3.26
Total		337	100

TABLE 2: TOTAL NUMBER OF OCCURRENCES IN THE *CORPUS*

News and reportage rhetorical structures

The survey of each genre's rhetorical organization, based on the analysis of 10 samples from each group, shows the content emphasis taken by each one of them. I will present them one by one, but, given the scope of this chapter, I will exemplify the four genres that seem most revealing both in terms of the continuum between these genres and of the features which distinguish them. The examples come from the news, and the coverage, the didactic and the itinerary reportages.

Van Dijk (1988) pointed out the following components of the news: headline, lead, main event, context, previous events, consequences/reactions, expectation and evaluation. The news rhetorical organization raised here (Table 3), although presented in a different formulation, reaffirms these elements, with the exception of the last two.

PARTS	MOVES
Title (And subtitle)	1. Citing the most evident aspect (optionally with complementation or specification of the information)
Lead	2. Summarizing the fact
Text's body	3. Narrating the fact 4. Describing details of the fact 5. Contextualizing in situational terms 6. Pointing out reactions to the fact 7. Contextualizing in historical terms 8. Pointing out related facts

TABLE 3: THE NEWS RHETORICAL STRUCTURE

The characteristic moves of this organization are (1) the fact summary with a lead form (answering who, what, when, where, how, and why questions) [move 2]; (2) the fact narration, which sometimes is replaced by a detailed description (when the lead has already enough information on the central action, and/or when the fact does not present a newsworthy action sequence) [move 3]; and (3) both the situational contextualization (which complements the narration) and the historical contextualization (mainly in order to show previous facts, which have possibly triggered the current one) [moves 5 and 7]. Example 1 enables the visualization of some of this genre's characteristic movements and serves as a comparison for the next three examples.

Policemen prevent Banespa's robbery	1. Citing the most evident aspect
São Paulo—Three men tried to rob, around 8:30 a.m. yesterday, the Banespa's agency located in the State Finance Department, São Paulo downtown. After exchanging shots with policemen who were at the	2. Summarizing the fact
site, Roberto Rocha dos Santos, Marcos dos Santos Vieira and Edson Felix Macedo escaped to the fourth floor, keeping six women as hostages for more than three hours. The Finance Department building was evacuated and at 11:15 a.m. only two hostages remained.	3. Narrating the fact
The robbers agreed to surrender after the arrival of a lawyer and the sister of one of them. Marcos Vieira was a prisoner serving a semi-closed custody sentence at an agricultural penal facility which he left yesterday morning to rob the bank.	7. Contextualizing in historical terms
Near the town of Vinhedo, 20 men robbed the Hopi Hari amusement park, on the Bandeirantes Highway kilometer 72. With machine guns, muskets and rifles, they kept 60 employees in a shed and took RS 500 thousand.	8. Pointing out related facts
(Jornal do Brasil, 11 Jan. 2000, Brasil, p. 5)	

EXAMPLE 1

The retrospective reportage (Table 4) is concerned with building the history of a fact reported in previous editions or in the same newspaper edition. In a certain way, it fulfills the function of contextualizing the news, but in an independent text, no longer in the form of a news text. Its most important moves are "recapping the news fact" and "contextualizing in historical terms."

The opinion reportage (Table 5), previously called "reportage from interview" by Kindermann (2003) and Kindermann and Bonini (2006), presents the characters' reactions to the fact and, in this sense, includes the voices of social actors who were not directly involved in the triggering of the event. As already mentioned, this kind of reportage can also report comments (from artists and experts) not linked to any current fact. Presenting these two forms of operation, this genre presents, therefore, two alternative introduction modes (recapping the

PARTS	MOVES
Title (and subtitle)	1. Citing the most evident aspect (optionally with complementation or specification of the information)
Introduction	2. Recapping the news fact
Text's body	3. Contextualizing in situational terms 4. Contextualizing in historical terms

TABLE 4: RETROSPECTIVE REPORTAGE RHETORICAL STRUCTURE

PARTS	MOVES
Title (and subtitle)	1. Citing the most evident aspect (optionally with complementation or specification of the information)
Introduction	2. Recapping the news fact 3. Pointing to a theme under current discussion
Text's body	4. Quoting the interviewee's speech 5. Giving extra information on the fact or theme 6. Contextualizing in situational terms 7. Contextualizing in historical terms

TABLE 5: OPINION REPORTAGE RHETORICAL STRUCTURE

The profile reportage (Table 6) presents the characterization of a person (artist, person in evidence, etc.) or a social institution (company, club, etc.), although the first case is the most common. One interesting aspect of this genre is its much more complex introduction if compared to the others, which is due to the fact that this part of the text summarizes key aspects of the text body, which has the same moves, but more extended. This introduction may contain one or more of the text body movements, but usually develops only one aspect in the form of an catchy sentence, as shown in the next example, which focuses on the character's way of thinking: "For the psychologist Cristina Versari, to know about sports is not only to know the rules of the game: it is, above all, to understand how athletes think" (Understanding athletes' minds. In *Jornal do Brasil*, 23 Jan. 2000, p. 5).

PARTS	MOVES
Title (and subtitle)	1. Citing the most evident aspect (optionally with complementation or specification of the information)
Introduction	2. Presenting the character's way of thinking 3. Presenting the character's way of acting 4. Giving credibility information about the character 5. Pointing out the character's involvement with the news fact 6. Presenting aspects of the character's personal history 7. Citing the character's name
Text's body	8. Presenting the character's professional history 9. Describing the character's noteworthy experiences 10. Presenting the character's life history 11. Pointing out credibility data about the character 12. Presenting the character's everyday life 13. Focusing on the character's personal life 14. Presenting the character's current activities 15. Presenting the character's perspectives on the future

TABLE 6: PROFILE REPORTAGE RHETORICAL STRUCTURE

The coverage reportage (Table 7) is one of the most significant in the analyzed corpus, since it is the most commonly mixed up with the news, even though it is quite different, as it reports facts that are searched for and not those which occur spontaneously with obvious news value[4]. It treats constant coverage themes, presenting three possibilities: (1) social environments seen as generators of important journalistic content (such as government departments); (2) large scale events (the Carnival in Rio, for example); and (3) indefinite duration facts (like the Iraq War).

Along with these three possibilities there are also three possible introductory forms: (1) to recap activities in progress (the Senate's latest facts, for example); (2) to recap the running (or organization) of an event (how the organization of the Rio Carnival is progressing, for example); and (3) to recap a fact in progress (the latest developments of the Iraq War, for example).

As it consists of a report of facts in their continuity, the following moves in the text body become relevant: "describing the latest activities" and "describing the foreseen agenda."

PARTS	MOVES
Title (and subtitle)	1. Citing the most evident aspect (optionally with complementation or specification of the information)
Introduction	2. Recapping activities in progress 3. Recapping the running (organization) of an event 4. Recapping fact in progress
Text's body	5. Presenting the event's noteworthy aspects 6. Describing the latest activities 7. Describing the foreseen agenda 8. Contextualizing in situational terms 9. Contextualizing in historical terms 10. Presenting perspectives 11. Quoting an expert position

TABLE 7: COVERAGE REPORTAGE RHETORICAL STRUCTURE

Example 2 explores a subject of constant coverage, soccer. One can notice that, although its introduction presents some news lead elements (who, what, when), it also signals that uninterrupted coverage with the phrase "today the pre-season activities have already begun," by which it recaps in-progress activities. Another aspect that underlines its difference from the news is that it does not include a fact narration, but rather the team's agenda specifications and an overview of recent events.

Physical trainings
 	
 Without Parreira, Flu improves physical conditioning in its pre-season
 	
    The Fluminense team reached the city of Vassouras yesterday and today has already begun its pre-season activities. The team will be in that town until the 17th, when it returns to Rio for the Fla-Flu game which opens the soccer season in the state of Rio de Janeiro. The game also will serve to distribute the sashes to the Brazilian Series C and Mercosul Cup champions. Meanwhile, the team works without their coach, Carlos Alberto Parreira, who is still in Rio to solve some personal problems. So, the physical coach, Moraci Santana, is commanding the training, and using that time to improve the players' form. The attacker Roni, who was eliminated from the Under-23 Selection due to a muscle injury in his right thigh, is receiving treatment.
    In Rio, the club's president David Fischel has promised reinforcement for the game on the 20th. "Flamengo will have Petkovic and we will also have someone to show. I can't name any names now."
 	
 (*Jornal do Brasil*, 12 Jan. 2000, p. 25)
	1. Citing the most evident aspect (optionally with complementation or specification of the information)
	 2. Recapping the activities in progress
	 7. Describing the foreseen agenda
	
	 6. Describing the latest activities

EXAMPLE 2

The product reportage (Table 8) is a kind of review of a new or recently launched product. However, as it usually does not present criticism on the product, it is also similar to a profile. The description of the product's aspects and main features is central to this genre's organization. This genre deserves more detailed descriptions, as only 4 occurrences were found in the analyzed corpus.

The research reportage (Table 9) has as its subject a behavior trend (enterprises' investment on the environment, for example) or a current problem (the difficulty of health professionals to deal with generic medicines, for example). The genre organization focuses on the data presentation, and most of the information generally comes from interviews with experts.

PARTS	MOVES
Title (and subtitle)	1. Citing the most evident aspect (optionally with complementation or specification of the information)
Introduction	2. Highlighting the central aspect 3. Pointing out the launching of the product
Text's body	4. Describing the product 5. Highlighting aspects of the product 6. Contextualizing in historical terms 7. Pointing out credibility data on the product 8. Comparing it to other products

TABLE 8: PRODUCT REPORTAGE RHETORICAL STRUCTURE

PARTS	MOVES
Title (and subtitle)	1. Citing the most evident aspect (optionally with complementation or specification of the information)
Introduction	2. Pointing out a behavior trend 3. Pointing out a current problem
Text's body	4. Giving evidence on the current problem 5. Quoting an expert position 6. Giving examples 7. Giving guidelines to those interested in the issue

TABLE 9: RESEARCH REPORTAGE RHETORICAL STRUCTURE

The didactic reportage (Table 10) is quite similar to the one above, since both of them focus on some knowledge object. In the case of the didactic reportage, the explanation, however, rather than bringing to light new knowledge, focuses on the already stabilized knowledge as a background to guidelines and tips (the advising move).

PARTS	MOVES
Title (and subtitle)	1. Citing the most evident aspect (optionally with complementation or specification of the information)
Introduction	2. Pointing out a knowledge object
Text's body	3. Giving an overview of the knowledge object 4. Giving the object definition 5. Describing aspects of the object 6. Giving examples of applied knowledge 7. Advising

TABLE 10: DIDACTIC REPORTAGE RHETORICAL STRUCTURE

This genre is completely different from the news, as one can see in the third example. A subject with quite distant relations to the facts reported in the newspaper enters into play here. Such reportage, therefore, may sometimes have been waiting in a drawer as a resource for days of little news content.

The final reportage is the itinerary one (Table 11), which is also similar, in some ways, to the review and profile reportages, since it has the description of a tourist attraction as its central feature. The introduction of this genre also presents a summary nature, recovering one or more aspects that its producer believes to be central or picturesque about that tourist attraction, in terms of the aspects presented in the text body.

The text body can be organized in three alternative ways, as its producer decides to describe aspects of the tourist attraction by themes (cooking, shopping, tours, etc.), by chronological order (what can be done firstly and subsequently), or in the order he/she followed him/herself (in this case, in the form of a first person narration).

Attitude is investment	1. Citing the most evident aspect
Professional self-development depends on the investment in learning and knowledge updating through courses, lectures, readings. The good relations established in the work environment are, in the same way, important.	2. Pointing out a knowledge object
The psychologist and consultant to companies Ricardo Montenegro—who teaches, in the MUDES Foundation, the courses *Recruitment and Selection* and *Leading and Leadership*—reminds the readers that the organizations are emphasizing a set of values which needs to be translated into behavior. According to Montenegro, regarding the job market, it is worth always keeping in mind some fundamental points.	3. Giving an overview of the knowledge object
Here are some tips from the consultant: (1) customers are all those who directly influence your conduct. This means that virtually all the people with whom relations are established (co-workers, bosses, subordinates, workers from other sectors of the company, family, friends, etc.) influence or are influenced by your work. . . . (5) to innovate, to challenge, to transform. To contribute with suggestions and to experiment with new processes. Even if the old method is not outdated, it is a good idea to learn a new system which benefits your performance and the organization's.	7. Advising
(*Jornal do Brasil*, 16 Jan. 2000, p. 2)	

EXAMPLE 3

PARTS	MOVES
Title (and subtitle)	1. Citing the most evident aspect (optionally with complementation or specification of the information)
Introduction	2. Pointing out the central aspect(s) of the tourist attraction
Text's body	3. Presenting an overview of attractive aspects 4. Describing tour possibilities by thematic order 5. Describing tour possibilities by chronological order 6. Describing tour possibilities by visited points 7. Giving guidelines for people interested in that tourist attraction

EXAMPLE 3

The fourth example shows one of the itinerary reportage organization forms, and also illustrates the way this genre is distant from the news factuality. At the same time, this example provides a view on how this kind of reportage is distinguished from the previous didactic reportage example. Although both of them have a utilitarian purpose, the itinerary reportage does not centre on a knowledge object that must be learned, but rather on a number of opportunities for action and culture consumption.

It is important to highlight, regarding this set of descriptions, that this is a didactic explanation. Much of the texts' complexity and difficulties in genre distinction is mitigated by this focus on the texts' regularities. The continuum described here is a working hypothesis, which may even show applied didactic value, but which should not be confused with the "truth" about these genres. What the data show, actually, is that the boundaries between these journalistic genres are quite blurred.

Apparently, newspaper production is guided by a system of activities which overlaps with a system of genres. Unlike many other social environments (such as the legal one), where the genre system marks the performance of the activities, in the journalistic environment the genre does not assume a guiding role; it is much more a final product, emerging from the activities. In this sense, there seems to be, in this environment, a language production pattern which is peculiar to it: texts are built from the available data and according to current editorial conditions. The blurring of genres can certainly be explained by the social dynamics of the journalistic environment and might be seen even as an ideological mechanism, but I will not explore this type of reflection here.

	1. Citing the most evident aspect (optionally with complementation or specification of the information)
Friburgo becomes an oasis in the summer **Fresh climate, diversified cuisine and good options for leisure attract visitors who flee from the suffocating heat**	
The summer season in Rio does not count only on scorching heat, lots of sunshine, beaches and very cold beer. To escape from overcrowded beaches and high temperatures, some people prefer going up to the mountains, to head to a place of cool climate, diversified cooking and good leisure options. Nova Friburgo, or just Friburgo to its close friends, attracts weekend tourists who wish to escape from the suffocating Rio summer.	2. Pointing out the central aspect(s) of the tourist attraction
The beautiful Friburgo has much more than the centenary and picturesque architecture, which recalls a small Swiss town. The charming nature, good restaurants and hotels, and the several options for ecological tourism—such as trekking—turn Friburgo into a place for all tastes.	3. Presenting an overview of attractive aspects
Those who are interested in *green* programs may visit the waterfalls in the region, such as Poço Feio (Ugly Well) and Poço Verde (Green Well), between Lumiar and São Pedro da Serra. The best thing to do is to visit this part of the city by car, which is half an hour from the Centre. Another unforgettable tourist point is the Parque das Furnas do Catete (Catete Cave Park), home to the famous Sitting Dog Stone . . . . The food is well diversified in Friburgo. International cuisine can be found in the city, in its Swiss, French, Japanese and even Arab restaurants. Those who enjoy night life have several options of bars and nightclubs, where the beer is as cool as in Rio's beaches.	4. Describing tour possibilities by thematic ordering
(*Jornal do Brasil*, 23 Jan. 2000, p. 8)	

EXAMPLE 4

From the way the genres treated above are organized, there is a repetition among them of many rhetorical moves. The "historical context" move appears, for example, in five of nine genres, and the "situational context" move, in four. This recurrence is a finding that can be taken as evidence, to some extent, of the hypothesis exposed here that the system of activities overlaps that of genres. The obtainment of information is a system of activities which is the basis of many of the genres that make up a newspaper. Often, the journalist does not know beforehand what genre will be produced from the data he/she collected, since it depends on a number of editorial decisions. A face-to-face interview, for example, may become a text of ping-pong or continued interview (Borba, 2007), or it can even serve as a basis for other newspaper genres (Sousa, 2005, p. 169).

In addition to the idea of system of genre, another concept which could be valuable to interpret this continuum between news and reportage is genre ecology, as proposed by Spinuzzi (2003a, 2003b). Genre ecologies tell us about the way people adapt themselves in certain environments through practices they perform and the genres they use; and, as Spinuzzi (2003b) explains: "Genre ecologies highlights idiosyncratic, divergent understandings and uses of artifacts and the practices that surround them as they develop within a given cultural-historical milieu" (p. 99).

From this perspective, we can say that genres exist in a complex ecology of gradual distinctions. Considering that the distinction between news and reportage does not seem to be really evident in the American context—as the Wikipedia's reportage entry allows us to conclude (Reportage, 2008)—we could affirm that there are different journalistic genre ecologies in the world. The fact that different genre names and distinctions are in circulation, however, does not allow us to conclude that genres and practices are in fact different in the Brazilian and the American contexts. This is a topic that needs additional research.

CONCLUDING REMARKS

The results presented here enable us to understand the news and reportage as genres immersed in a continuum. More than this, however, they represent a key for interpreting these genres, which can thus be viewed in terms of more prototypical points within this continuum, and not exactly as discrete units in opposition.

This interpretation, in my opinion, can exercise some role on the teaching of these genres' reading and production, as much in basic education as in journalism schools. Since the existing literature is not at all clear on what characterizes each of these genres, it is not an easy task to teach and learn the reading and writing practices assigned to both of them. In this case, the continuum hypothesis indicates that the intermediary genres (retrospective, opinion, profile and coverage reportage) are a hindrance to the student's development of specific representations of the news and the reportage. Early pedagogical work, in this sense, should focus on the prototypical news (that is, factual) and on the more thematic reportages (i.e., product, research, didactic and itinerary reportages).

NOTES

[1] It's necessary to emphasize that most news and reportage definitions considered here come from dictionaries, guides, and textbooks written for students of journalism and/or for popular audiences. There are only two scholarly works cited here: Lage (1979) and Chaparro (1998). The minor presence of research works is due to my focus on the most used literature in the field, but is also due to the fact that the notion of genre in journalistic academic debates in Brazil is still given little importance. It's also necessary to say that the material quoted here is translated from Portuguese.

[2] It's important to say that Chaparro was born in Portugal, and that this book was published there. However, although it should be considered as Portuguese journalistic literature, I placed this book among the Brazilian works because this author has been working in Brazil for a long time, and even got his PhD in this country.

[3] The photographic reportage was eliminated from this framework for two reasons: firstly, because it requires an exclusive study; secondly, because this genre didn't occur in the editions of Jornal do Brasil considered here.

[4] According to Galtung and Ruge (1973) it consists of assigning news value to a particular fact, basing it on certain criteria. The more recent or culturally closest to the newspaper region, the greater chance it has of being reported, for example.

REFERENCES

Amaral, L. (1982). *Jornalismo: Matéria de primeira página* (3rd ed.). Fortaleza, Ceará, Brazil: UFC.

Bazerman, C. (1994). Systems of genres and the enactment of social intentions. In A. Freedman & P. Medway (Eds.), *Genre and the new rhetoric* (pp. 79-101). London: Taylor & Francis.

Bazerman, C. (2004). Speech acts, genres, and activity systems: How texts organize activity and people. In C. Bazerman & P. Prior (Eds.), *What writing does and how it does it: An introduction to analyzing texts and textual practices* (pp. 309-339). Mahwah, New Jersey: Erlbaum.

Bond, F. F. (1954). *An introduction to journalism: A survey of the fourth estate in all its forms.* New York: Macmillan.

Bonini, A. (2003a). Os gêneros do jornal: o que aponta a literatura da área de comunicação no Brasil? *Linguagem em (Dis)curso*, 4(1), 205-231. Retrieved from http://www3.unisul.br/paginas/ensino/pos/linguagem/revista/revista.htm.

Bonini, A. (2003b). Veículo de comunicação e gênero textual: noções conflitantes. *D.E.L.T.A.*, *19*(1), 65-89. Retrieved from http://www.scielo.br/scielo. php?script=sci_home&lng=en&nrm=iso.

Bonini, A. (2006). Os gêneros do jornal: questões de pesquisa e ensino. In A. M. Karwoski, B. Gaydeczka, & K. S. Brito (Eds.), *Gêneros textuais: Reflexões e ensino* (2nd ed., pp. 57-71). Rio de Janeiro: Lucerna.

Borba, M. S. (2007). *A entrevista jornalística: Uma análise do gênero a partir de exemplares publicados no jornal Zero Hora.* Unpublished master's thesis, University of Southern Santa Catarina, Santa Catarina, Brazil. Retrieved from http://www3.unisul.br/paginas/ensino/pos/linguagem/disserta/index.htm.

Caldeira, A. B. (2007). *Chamada de capa: Análise do gênero jornalístico com abordagem sócio-retórica de Swales.* Unpublished master's thesis, University of Southern Santa Catarina, Santa Catarina, Brazil. Retrieved from http://www3. unisul.br/paginas/ensino/pos/linguagem/disserta/index.htm.

Cascais, F. (2001). *Dicionário de jornalismo: As palavras dos media.* Lisbon: Editorial Verbo.

Cassarotti, L. C. (2006). *Crítica de cinema no Jornal Folha de S. Paulo: Um estudo do gênero.* Unpublished master's thesis, University of Southern Santa Catarina, Santa Catarina, Brazil. Retrieved from http://www3.unisul.br/paginas/ensino/ pos/linguagem/disserta/index.htm.

Chaparro, M. C. (1998). *Sotaques d'aquém e d'além mar: Percursos e gêneros do jornalismo português e brasileiro.* Santarém, Portugal: Jortejo.

Figueiredo, L. F. (2003). *A nota jornalística no Jornal do Brasil: Um estudo do gênero textual e de sua função no jornal.* Unpublished master's thesis, University of Southern Santa Catarina, Santa Catarina, Brazil. Retrieved from http://www3. unisul.br/paginas/ensino/pos/linguagem/disserta/index.htm.

Folha de s. Paulo. (1998). *Novo manual da redação.* São Paulo: Folha de S. Paulo.

Galtung, J., & Ruge, M. (1973). Structuring and selecting news. In S. Cohen & J. Young (Eds.), *The manufacture of news: Social problems, deviance and the mass media* (pp. 62-72). London: Constable.

Innocente, L. G. (2005). *A tira de quadrinhos no Jornal do Brasil: Um estudo do gênero.* Unpublished master's thesis, University of Southern Santa Catarina, Santa Catarina, Brazil. Retrieved from http://www3.unisul.br/paginas/ensino/ pos/linguagem/disserta/index.htm.

Kindermann, C. A. (2003). *A reportagem jornalística no Jornal do Brasil: Desvendando as variantes do gênero.* Unpublished master's thesis, University of Southern Santa Catarina, Santa Catarina, Brazil. Retrieved from http://www3. unisul.br/paginas/ensino/pos/linguagem/disserta/index.htm.

Kindermann, C. A., & Bonini, A. (2006). A reportagem jornalística: uma caracterização inicial do gênero a partir de exemplares publicados no Jornal do Brasil. In D. Motta-Roth, N. C. A. Barros, & M. G. Richter (Eds.), *Linguagem, cultura e sociedade*. Santa Maria, Rio Grande do Sul, Brazil: Federal University of Santa Maria.

Lage, N. (1979). *Ideologia e técnica da notícia* (3rd ed.). Florianópolis, Santa Catarina, Brazil: Insular.

Lage, N. (1985). *Estrutura da notícia* (5th ed.). São Paulo: Ática.

Miller, C. R. (1984). Genre as social action. In A. Freedman & P. Medway (Eds.), *Genre and the new rhetoric* (pp. 23-42). London: Taylor & Francis.

O Estado de S. Paulo. (1990). *Manual de redação e estilo* (Eduardo Martins, Ed.). São Paulo: Moderna.

O Globo. (1999). *Manual de redação e estilo* (26th ed.). São Paulo: Globo.

Paré, A., & Smart, G. (1994). Observing genres in action: Toward a research methodology. In A. Freedman & P. Medway (Eds.), *Genre and the new rhetoric* (pp. 146–154). London: Taylor & Francis.

Rabaça, C. A. & Barbosa, G. G. (1978). *Dicionário de comunicação* (2nd ed.). Rio de Janeiro: Campus.

Reportage (2008). In *Wikipedia*. Retrieved March 23, 2008, from http://en.wikipedia.org/wiki/Reportage

Simoni, R. M. S. (2004). *Uma caracterização do gênero carta consulta nos jornais O Globo e Folha de S. Paulo*. Unpublished master's thesis, University of Southern Santa Catarina, Santa Catarina, Brazil. Retrieved from http://www3.unisul.br/paginas/ensino/pos/linguagem/disserta/index.htm.

Sodré, M., & Ferrari, M. H. (1986). *Técnica de reportagem: Notas sobre a narrativa jornalística*. São Paulo: Summus.

Sousa, J. P. (2005). *Elementos de jornalismo impresso*. Florianópolis, Santa Catarina, Brazil: Letras Contemporâneas.

Spinuzzi, C. (2003a). *Tracing genres through organizations: A sociocultural approach to information design*. Cambridge, Massachusetts: MIT Press.

Spinuzzi, C. (2003b). Compound mediation in software development: Using genre ecologies to study textual artifacts. In C. Bazerman & D. R. Russel (Eds.), *Writing selves/writing societies: Research from activity perspectives*. Retrieved from Colorado State University, WAC Clearinghouse and Mind, Culture, and Activity: http://wac.colostate.edu/books/selves_societies/

Swales, J. M. (1990). *Genre analysis: English in academic and research settings*. New York: Cambridge University Press.

Van Dijk, T. A. (1988). *News as discourse*. Hillsdale, New Jersey: Erlbaum.

11   The Organization and Functions of the Press *Dossier:* The Case of Media Discourse on the Environment in Portugal

Rui Ramos

INTRODUCTION[1]

This study aims to analyze and explain the macrotextual organization and the most relevant pragmatic-communicative dimensions of a dossier from a daily newspaper in the Portuguese press on the theme of climate change. The study therefore is placed within the theoretical framework of Discourse Analysis, or more precisely the interface of textual genre studies (focusing in particular on press discourse) and Linguistic Pragmatics.

The selected *corpus* is composed of texts from the November 30th, 1997 edition of *Público*, a recognised daily newspaper in the contemporary Portuguese press. This edition came out the day before the conference for the negotiation and signing of what would become known as the Kyoto Protocol. The conference was called to set limits and calendars for reducing the emission of gases that lead to the greenhouse effect and to climate change, and was therefore a moment of great social and political importance, both nationally and worldwide.

The choice of texts was dictated by their internal configuration and social function. The discussion of environmental issues commonly appears in the form of many different textual types and genres: among restricted groups of speakers or through public opinion forums; in private circles—family, professional and institutional; and between the young and old, and between men and women. The intention of the various texts may be descriptive, instrumental or combative. But not all of them manifest the relevant characteristics for analysis in the framework of this study. Those chosen for the purpose of this case study take the form of "publicly dominant discourse[s]" (J1ung, 2001, p. 271). These are texts/extended discourses understood as structured and delimited sequences of enunciations constituting a whole, in which the relationship between individuals and the context is publicly defined (namely, in the *media*). These discourses contribute to the interdiscursive flux of everyday verbal exchanges; providing the concepts, the terminology, the organizational modes, and, above all, creating the real.

THE *DOSSIER* UNIT

The *dossier* is a common designation in the journalistic sphere and in the context of linguistic analysis of press discourse. Charaudeau2 (1997) describes it as a collection of articles aimed at clarifying a question, as much from the point of view of the facts as from the commentaries included. This description underlines the heterogenic composition of the *dossier* with the suggestion of the cross-over between the pragmatic dimensions of the texts and the aspects of its sequential organization. Charaudeau approaches the *dossier* as a whole in recognition of its significance as a trans-textual unit: the *dossier* typically includes some parts (texts) that are more closely related to information discourse and others that are closer to opinion discourse; some texts are more neutral and others more personally informed; some organize themselves according to narrative models[2], and others according to argumentative, explicative, descriptive, or dialogued models[3].

Beacco5 (1992) designates such texts in a *dossier* as the *main text* and *satellite text(s)*, thus clearly establishing the hierarchical and complementary nature that characterizes them. He affirms that the former usually performs a descriptive/narrative function, while the other(s) assume an explicative/interpretative function.

The main text occupies a central position in the *dossier's* configuration, introducing the topic in question or referring to the core event, positioning itself as the point of reference for the remaining texts and presenting the information judged more relevant, by either the voice of the journalist or that (those) of the protagonist(s). Given that this type of text can be classified as reportage, it would be reasonable to expect the strong descriptive element which is characteristic of this discursive genre[4]. However, authors such as Revaz (1997) defend that reportage is typically narrative with the double mission of informing and explaining.

The satellite texts are complementary to the main text, providing technical information, defining the contours of specific parts of the problems, and offering background elements for an understanding of the central question discussed in the *dossier*. It is also the function of the satellite texts to create the effect of the real by providing the small details which may seem superfluous, but which in fact provide the general report with the necessary credibility. These details form the background for the development of the core event by registering it in a succession of happenings, or by associating it with other similar ones that happened in the past, or by evoking parallel histories. In the case of *dossiers* that deal with the core events in environmental issues, it is noticeable that the evoked voices are frequently those of the victims; however, specialists or representatives of different interests are also commonly evoked[5]. Finally, the satellite texts also work to construct a background or commentary for the explanation of certain phenomena, which is didactic in character[6].

It should be noted that there is a collection of other texts with different functions in the journalistic economy and in the mechanism of opening interaction with the reader. They are probably less relevant to the informative content of each *dossier*, but of real importance in the construction of the newspaper and in the appellative dimension of journalistic treatment. Adam (1997b) classifies them within the *peritext*[7], which is organized in the following way:

(a) at the level of the newspaper:
   i. name of newspaper;
   ii. indication section

(b) at the level of the article:
   i. verbal: headline, subtitle, presentation paragraph, internal titles;
   ii. iconographic: illustrations, captions.

It must be highlighted that these elements of the peritext have an effective distance from the journalistic texts they appear beside because they are characteristically not dependent on the author of those texts, but instead on "the editorship" (Adam, 1997b, p. 5), with the peritext thus having a different enunciative origin to the articles.

Charaudeau defines what he calls *"la titraille"* (1997, p. 220) (headlines, subtitles, leads), as an independent discursive genre that, together with the other elements of the graphical organization of the paper (first page, sections, photographs, graphics, tables, columns, etc.), responds to the newspaper's demands for visibility and together they play a triple role: *phatic*, by contact with the reader; *epiphanic*, by announcing the news; and *synoptic*, by orientating the visual path of the reader in the informative space of the newspaper.

In this way, these texts constitute an independent group, which bring other enunciators into the communicative media space. These enunciators are simultaneously readers/receptors of the journalistic articles and writers/producers of the modalized word and highly operative in the effort to capture the attention of the newspaper's addressee.

From the point of view of its communicative functioning, the *dossier*, in its whole, should respond in particular to two of the four demands that Adam (1997a) identifies in the way the press works: legibility and intelligibility[8].

The former obliges the written *media* to report the events taking place in the social sphere as clearly as possible, turning the *raw event*[9] into a *media event*, using textual forms such as informative articles, as well as short articles and other essentially expository texts; it also leads them towards an objectified enunciation (Moirand, 1999).

This study pinpoints three separate instances in the configuration of the media event: the reported event, which helps in the construction of a thematic space, and which is a result of the (essentially informative) mediatic treatment of the points of interest; the commentary of the event, or the construction of a problematized space; and the ensuing event, corresponding to the construction of a public debate space outside the *media*.

The demand for intelligibility refers primarily to the commentary produced from the facts or declarations on the reported event, which find their most prototypical concretization in the textual forms (genres) of the editorials, chronicles, analyses or commentaries.

Having looked at the design of the *dossier* unit and its respective explanation/ exemplification, it should be noted that the texts that constitute this precise grouping do not all present the same interests or the same internal structure. In order to understand how they are characterized, there now follows an analysis of some of the more salient aspects of the *dossier* which is the particular focus of this study.

THE *CORPUS*

The transtextual organization of the *dossier* under analysis (see annexes) is structured as follows: on the first page, a high impact title, with a photograph (Text 1); inside the newspaper, a group of seven texts, occupying its first pages (up to page six). There is an opening article, beginning on page two and continuing on page three. This text is complemented, for the purposes of scientific interest, by various others texts, written either by the same journalist, by a scientist or issuing from news agencies; then comes an opinion article. Finally, there is also a map and some information quantified in different graphics and presented schematically.

Even if the essentially iconic texts are excluded from the analysis and the analysis itself is restricted to those texts of (almost) exclusively linguistic formulation, these articles, as their simple enumeration allows us to suppose, present an obvious typological heterogeneity. In some cases, they show an equally notable composite heterogeneity (at the level of the sequential organization of each text).

The main text (Text 2) reveals the starting point of the event. Its textual organization is controlled by the narrative structure, but argumentative and explicative sequences can also be identified.

The first segment of the text is essentially a descriptive sequence, with the identifiable elements serving to position it temporally and referentially; this segment also reveals the aspectualisation of the text, according to the perspective the speaker adopts and the evaluation he makes in characterizing the overall scenario—not only as regards the actual negotiations, but equally as regards the fundamental questions of climate change. It incorporates argumentative dimensions and makes use of a regressive order between the arguments and the conclusions, beginning with a lapidary phrase which is later justified (definitively in the body of the text), making it more closely related to the model of discourse authorized by Science, with a demonstration of affirmations founded on an observation of the facts:

(1) It will be a battle against egoism. In Kyoto, starting tomorrow, the countries of the world will be judged by their willingness to prevent life on Earth collapsing under climate change. Not one of them wishes to abdicate their economic development. But the climate cannot wait. Portugal knows this, as do many other countries. Floods have brought chaos and pain, and people from Alentejo are already well aware of what it will be like to live in a dry and arid future. The Mediterranean is on the path to disaster, a foreseen catastrophe that was ignored by many. For years, the scientists have been sending out warnings, but recently, they issued their full condemnation of Man as the guilty party. We cannot postpone any longer. Nature simply cannot adapt to such drastic changes. This is not a question of alarmism, fundamentalism or any other *isms*. It is a question of survival. (Text 2)

The argument for the interpretation of the negotiations as a "struggle against egoism" is developed in later segments, where the desire for "economic development" of some is set up in opposition to the sustainability of life on Earth, at present at risk from "collapsing under climate change." In the same way, the confrontation between the opposing affirmations "Not one of them wishes to abdicate their economical development" and "But the climate cannot wait," linked by the connector of argumentative opposition "but," implies the conclusion that the second affirmation will prevail.

It should be noted that the argumentation herein developed does not begin from zero: there is a recurrent *doxa*, which is implicitly evoked in all discussions on the topic; this *doxa* is present in all social discourse from contemporary western societies, and is moreover so well recognised by the citizens of these societies that they have come to paraphrase it as "in the present models, economic development and protection of the environment are incompatible." This *doxa* is not generally disputed, but the multiple arguments which are evoked in association with it tend to result in divergent conclusions.

Nevertheless, the speaker is clearly aware that this can be understood as *one more* cry in defense of the environment, and that the listener may be displeased by such banalisation, under the facile label of just another *ism*. He recognizes it, but erases it, by anticipating this reaction and dramatizing the discourse to the limit: this, he contends, is a question of "survival." And models of development must be changed now before it is too late, "because Nature simply cannot adapt to such drastic changes." This is an argument that sustains the conclusion ultimately advanced, and explains the relation between the two (as identified by the explicative/argumentative connector "because").

It is therefore legitimate to describe this introductive segment as being dominated by a descriptive structure with some typical elements and, especially, with contextual indicators that determine this expectation. It must be pointed out that there is also a complex argumentative dimension developed throughout the descriptive and explicative segments, which, from the very beginning, heralds the heterogeneous structure that characterizes the text.

The same sequential organization runs through the whole text. Its first two paragraphs define the starting point of the event (the beginning of the negotiations), aspects of contextualization (the divergence between positions, particularly between the "rich and poor" is presented as "a given"), and its implications (either a treaty is signed or life on Earth "will be seriously threatened"). What follows, in the third paragraph, is an analeptic movement introducing a historical context (which has already been introduced at the beginning of the second paragraph, affirming that "climate change is the big question now at the end of this century"), which reinvokes the relation between policy makers and scientists regarding the importance of recognising the problem of climate change.

Next, various explicative segments appear. A brief illustration of the greenhouse effect is given, essentially in the form of imminent and tangible repercussions (right from the presentation paragraph all the way through). But an actual explanation of the phenomenon, given in more technical language, and approached in more depth, will appear only in Text 8, which is clearly divulgative in intention. In conjunction with the explicative segments, Text 8 underlines the incipient divulgative vocation of the main text, but it also testifies to a complementary relationship between the main text and the satellite texts, and a strong connection between the elements that form the *dossier*. This text refers to "climate change," or "the gas emissions that lead to the greenhouse effect," but other technical terms such as "carbon dioxide," "methane," "nitric oxide," "plerfluorcarbons," etc., including the chemical symbols or signs that identify them, only appear in the satellite texts.

In the same way, the main text points out some of the real consequences of the phenomenon, those within the scope of the readers' experience; but it is the task of Text 3 to develop the topic, evoking, to that effect, the voice of a "scientist" from the "Lisbon University Faculty of Sciences," and introducing other strong arguments voiced by various different sources.

There is also a segment that definitively explains the initial affirmation of the speaker, "It will be a struggle against egoism," although this explanation will only finally be completed at the very end of the article:

> (2) But national egocentrisms continue to prevail. The principal guilty party for the gas emissions creating the greenhouse effect does not want to sacrifice a penny of its actual economy to prevent the catastrophe. The USA arrived in Japan with an extremely modest proposal: to stabilize the emissions over the next 15 years at the levels registered in 1990. To this end, they demanded that the poorer countries, which aspired to a better life but at present were doing little to contribute to the problem of climate change, should also limit their emissions. The argument is valid—"they should not make the same mistakes as us"—but it will not be easily accepted by those who already have so little to lose. The scission has been created. (Text 2)

The opening statement of the paragraph, which re-emphasizes the initial affirmation of the article, is explained/justified in the propositions that follow, particularly regarding the standpoint of the USA. In this way, a subtle change is worked: from the "national egocentrisms" introduced initially, the discourse slides towards an explanation of only one of these egocentrisms, the North American. The US is thus the major opponent of those who "already have so little to lose," which is to say, the poorer countries—and, as was previously mentioned, this is a powerful artifice in the construction of a scenario that clearly privileges one of the sides in the conflict (notice the contrast between the "well-being" of the Americans and the scenario of "catastrophe").

What follows are three descriptive paragraphs tracing the positions of each country or group of countries. There are, again, explicative segments, such as the following:

> (3) Europe has decided to take a leading role and put an audacious proposal on the table, but it is one that will inevitably be rejected.

> Even before the meeting, the Japanese press published articles on the willingness of the Union to reduce its proposal for a 15% reduction in emissions to 10%, to be achieved by the year 2010, a tactical manuever designed to make the other countries accept the proposal. (Text 2)

The evaluation-conclusion is not explicitly present in this segment, but instead in the final paragraph of the text. This, in fact, takes the form of a conclusion of an argumentation that has been developed throughout the article: on the one hand, the problem is global and demands "global solutions" (treaties between all the countries in the world); on the other hand, each country has to "assume its responsibilities," without egoisms.

In this way, the composite heterogeneity of this main text is clearly established; likewise its descriptive functions (of a state of things) and technical divulgations to a wide public are also demonstrated. The main text's vocation in the economy of the *dossier's* is to build a complete scenario: this includes the central action and the main characters, whose motivations, characterization and movements should be summarily drawn, thus leaving space for complementary information, evaluation, background scenery, props and the extras brought on in the satellite texts.

It was mentioned previously that Text 8 in this *dossier* is characterized by divulgative intentions. Text 4 can be characterized in the same terms:

> (4) This phenomenon is called "greenhouse effect" because it is exactly this that provides the heat felt in greenhouses used in agriculture. Why is it that the light (and the heat) can pass through the atmosphere when they come from space, and yet cannot pass through when they are reflected up from the earth's surface? Because, after having struck the land or the sea, the rays of light suffer an alteration in their wavelength (in their colour) and the atmosphere is less transparent to this new light." (Text 4)

> (5) **What is the greenhouse effect?**
> Life on Earth is hugely dependent on the greenhouse effect. The carbon dioxide, . . .

> **What is climate change?**
> Because the heat remains trapped next to the Earth, the Climate automatically changes . . . .

> **How do we release the gases with a greenhouse effect?**

The principal gases with a greenhouse effect are carbon dioxide (CO_2) . . . . (Text 8)

Various segments of these texts of scientific divulgation are constructed by imitating, as closely as possible, the precise interaction between speaker and audience: this is the case of Texts 4 and 8, the latter being organized as "Questions and answers on climate change" (this being its actual title) and taking up an interactional dialogue comprised of the didactic texts, or of the many segments with interrogative structures, reproducing the organization of the multiparty texts and the shared intervention of the audience in the definition of the discursive model.

The explicative segments are dominant, almost exclusive in some texts (as segments (4) and (5) show); their aim is to be accessible to the common reader, who is unspecialized or uninitiated in these matters and without the scientific fundaments which would allow him to understand the questions and take an informed position, explicitly activating the scheme of the explicative sequence as Adam (1997a) describes it.

Regarding the definition of the contours of discourse on the environment, it is possible to point out how some texts work as a mechanism of adaptation/ re-contextualization of the scientific articles originally produced within the parameters and procedures of scientific communication (that is to say, in restricted communities, already initiated in the subject matter and dependent on specific rules). In this way, Text 4 is an adaptation of a scientific article that originally appeared in *Science* magazine, published nine days before (November 11th, 1997); Text 6, composed essentially of maps and scientific data from the same *dossier,* is co-authored by the Hadley Centre[10], a research unit on climate change at the British Institute of Meteorology.

What is first identified then is the sudden entry of the discourse of Science into the discourse on the environment, manifested by the identification of sources and authors of articles. Likewise, there is an alteration in the original discourses through the presence of the "adaptation" to which they were subjected in order to support and fulfill the different functions performed in the newspaper. Thus, they take the form of an explicit intertextual dialogism (M2oirand, 1999).

On the other hand, the inclusion of these texts in the *dossier* reinforces its definition as a heterogenic construction. Besides the already mentioned text types, texts with a very strong iconic component (maps and graphics) now also appear.

Text 3, dominated by descriptive and explicative structures, characterizes Portugal's situation in the face of the risks of climate change, underlining the precise negative consequences. The macro-proposition of the topic anchor, pointed out by Adam (1997a) as a characteristic of the descriptive sequences[11], develops in the first paragraph of the text:

> (6) Being a coastal country is rapidly becoming a disadvantage. With a coastline of 800 kilometres, Portugal will be one of the first to suffer from one of the major consequences of climate change: the rising of the sea level. But the problems do not end there. The lack of drinking water will be acutely felt, desertification will advance in the interior and the floods, downpours and storms will come to stay. (Text 3)

The macro-proposition of aspectualisation is immediately identified in this first paragraph as having an indisputable orientation: the dramatization of the present and future realities (by their enumeration, but also by the characterisation of the rising sea levels as one of the "problems") will work as a strong argument for justifying the necessity of an international treaty on emissions.

But the macro-proposition of relation, by which are established metonymic relations with the global problem, is also found throughout the whole text. This begins in this initial paragraph until the second part of the article, separated by an internal title ("The Disadvantages of South Europe") which explicitly introduces the Portuguese problem (and the countries from the Mediterranean basin) into the global picture. In this way, the specific national circumstances are inscribed in a larger scenario—that of global climate change. Thus, the internal manifestations of the problem appear as a mirror image of that which affects the entire world.

The explicative function is important in bringing home the actual significance, in experimental consequences, of a problem that is invisible to the common citizen. This mechanism of reification is also patent in the first paragraph of the text, but takes no less recognisable forms in the fifth paragraph with precise quantifications, technical terminology and demonstration of palpable consequences, while evoking the authorized voice of Science:

> (7) What is certain is that what is happening in this country is exactly in line with what has been observed and predicted on a global scale. The 1995 report from the Intergovernmental Panel on Climate Change (IPCC), comprising a large group of scientists and technicians from the whole world, predicts that the South of Europe will experience a temperature increase of between 1.5 and 4.5 degrees centigrade if the emissions of carbon dioxide double. Furthermore, the report shows that there will be a decrease in precipitation in the whole of the Mediterranean and, therefore, a decrease in river volumes. (Texto 3)

Once again, the final paragraphs reveal the argumentative orientation behind this descriptive and explicative construction, urging study and action "in anticipation"—even though the rhetorical question that closes the article suggests that there are doubts concerning Portugal's capacity to respond favourably to this demand, a fact that increases the general climate of unavoidable catastrophe.

> (8) In the face of this evidence, there are only two options: do nothing, hoping that those most responsible for the carbon dioxide emissions agree to reduce pollution at the Kyoto Summit—Portugal will not have to make great sacrifices to reduce its emissions because the national contribution stands at about 1.5% within the Union, and, according to the national report for Kyoto, it could still increase this by 40%—or begin to prepare the country to be able to face the increase in frequency of these floods, storms, and the lack of water. The key to success is to study the question and act in advance. But, would the country be capable of such planning? (Text 3)

The suggestion of the possibility of choice in the penultimate paragraph is rhetorical, delimitating a possibility that is presented as convenient in the short term but unacceptable because of its mid- to long-term consequences, a fact which naturally orientates the reading of the text in only one direction.

Essentially, these segments concisely recover the whole scenario laid out throughout the text and present it as undeniable, paraphrasing it as "the evidence," in a final movement of authorization of the previous discourse. They apparently admit two possible directions for Portugal.

The first direction corresponds to the "do nothing" and in general terms, again takes up the not-guilty and convenient arguments of some of the politicians responsible, grouped together under the "national report for Kyoto" umbrella. This is all in keeping with a common sentiment held by the Portuguese, which implicitly evokes Lusitanian smallness—geographically, economically, politically, and, as is to be expected, in terms of responsibility for the gas emissions that lead to the greenhouse effect. As in many other aspects of community life, the report suggests that the responsibility and onus for change falls on the heads of others.

The second, directly opposite path to follow (as the structure marked by the disjunctive connector "or" shows), will prepare the country to face the environmental catastrophe. This makes the second path inevitable in the case of the first possibility of action not being followed. Thus, this structure is configured with a conditional value: if Portugal and "those most responsible for the carbon dioxide emissions" reduce their emissions, it won't be necessary to prepare the country to face the cataclysm. The cause-effect connection between the emissions and environmental catastrophe is presented as a given, thus avoiding a direct declaration which might (more easily) be refuted by the listener. The text closes with a challenge issued in the form of the rhetorical question at the end. The challenge is strong, in part because of the importance of the questions in play and in part because of the suggestion of failure (or of strong doubt that the speaker seems to feel) marked by the future modal: "would."

Despite being dominated by descriptive and explicative sequential structures, a favorable argumentative line regarding the signing of the Kyoto Treaty runs all the way through Text 3, thus influencing public opinion to this end.

The opinion article (denominated as "Commentary"), intergrated in the *dossier*, which also belongs to the group of satellite texts, is dominated by narrative and argumentative sequences (mostly the latter). Here appearing as Text 5, this article is authored by the director of the newspaper and begins with a descriptive structure:

> (9) While we go around dazed by reshufflings and other minor episodes here, on the other side of the planet a Summit is being organised which is undoubtedly much more important for our future than the numbers of "Cardinal" Pina Moura or the resurrection of the eternal Veiga Simão. Meanwhile, in Kyoto they will try to invert an evolution that is leading our planet towards catastrophe. (Text 5)

This first paragraph of the text outlines the entire scenario, highlighting the point in discussion: the Kyoto Summit. This is an operation of referential anchorage. A second macro–proposition of aspectualisation runs parallel to this in the form of an evaluation of the state of things, which incorporates equally a movement of convergence and of divergence.

The movement of convergence establishes a link between the speaker and the listener, by the use of "we" in "go around." Furthermore, this use of the first person, which appears in exclusivity in the opinion articles, is witness to the speaker's subjectivity. This subjectivity is indicated by the peritextual elements that perform a preliminary contextualization of the text; the suggested complicity puts the commentator on the side of the reader—or, preferably, the reader on the side of the commentator, sharing his point of view about the state of things being analyzed and commented upon in the article.

The movement of divergence resides in the critique developed by the speaker:

the Portuguese people "go around dazed by reshufflings and other minor episodes." From the semantics of "go around dazed" comes

- the referred critique but also, by pragmatic implication, a call for a change of behaviour;
- the confrontation, at an implicit level, between the essential and the accessory, with the focus of attention being on the latter to the detriment of the former.

The cross-over of the two previous items results in a call for a change in focus of the Portuguese, which is explicit in the text: the accessory is the "reshufflings (of government) and other minor episodes," while the essential corresponds to "a summit which is undoubtedly much more important for our future" than the mentioned "episodes." In both cases, the adjectives stand out: the first being a comparative of inferiority and the second a comparative of superiority (intensified by the adverb "much"), thus stretching the extreme limits of the scale of values portrayed.

The macro–proposition of relation is also activated by the evocation of what is known by the listener (he who likewise goes around in a daze), as the economic reference to the episodes of Portuguese political life confirm—the "reshufflings" and the other "minor episodes," co-referenced with expressions like "the numbers of "Cardinal" Pina Moura or the resurrection of the eternal Veiga Simão." It is to be noted that this co-referentiality is not explicitly affirmed but rather suggested to the listener. The listener will recognize it in a movement of interpretative cooperation which will only happen if, in fact, there is some kind of sharing of knowledge between the speaker and the listener. This supposition of sharing of universes and encyclopedia makes it evident which profile the journalist idealizes in his readers.

Finally, this descriptive segment is taken up by the actual speaker to fulfill an argumentative function, as can be verified by the connector "meanwhile" at the beginning of the second paragraph, justifying the affirmation produced in the first, in a regressive argumentative order. This justification clarifies the topic indicated at the beginning of the text, making it clear that it's about the summit and not about the "minor episodes" of internal politics. It serves equally for an extreme dramatization, recurrent in the *corpus*, of the projected "catastrophe" scenario, a scenario that is coherent with the contrast between the essential and accessory mentioned above. This is in agreement with the affirmations of Masuy (1997) on the argumentative dimensions supported by the descriptive segments, that which Adam (1997a) describes as "the heterogeneity of type [dominant sequence > dominated sequence]."

The text continues with a narrative segment, corresponding to the next paragraph, in which two lines of organization evolve, in parallel and mutually supported; one is temporal and the other argumentative:

> (10) At the beginning of the 80s, when the discussions on climate change, the greenhouse effect and global warming first began, there were many who looked disbelievingly at the scientists who placed the blame on human activity. Five years ago, in Rio de Janeiro, at the Eco-92, the amount of scientific proof was already sufficient to take measures—but there was no political will. Now it's no longer possible to ignore the problem. This problem, essentially, puts into question the models of development of the last century and a half in human evolution. Quite simply, the origin of the problem is carbon dioxide, CO_2 which industrialized societies produce on a large scale. (Text 5)

The narrative structure is tripartite, with three almost overlapping temporal indicators: "At the beginning of the 80s," "five years ago," and "now."

Besides these, there are further argumentative axes of increasing scientific certainty about the causes of global warming: "there were many who looked disbelievingly at the scientists who placed the blame on human activity," "the amount of scientific proof was already sufficient to take measures," "Now it's no longer possible to ignore the problem."

This temporal and scientific evolution subscribes to the generalized conviction that conceives of scientific progress as an undeniable fact and of contemporary societies as more scientifically and technologically evolved than in the past, in a line of constant and unidirectional progress. However, alongside the recognition of the importance of Science and of technology in occidental societies and in the real life of modern man, coexists the notion of the limits, the fragilities and the blank spaces in Science; it too, just like many other aspects of social life, is the object of doubt and polemic. If the unstoppable march of time goes unquestioned and is therefore difficult to prove, the same is not true of the affirmations of Science. In this way, the association of those two realities offers a greater credibility to its fragile side: the inscription of the growing scientific conviction in the axes of time acquires a growing force of truth. Of course, this effect stems equally, as paradoxical as it may seem, from the confession of doubts, even if distance in time is supplanted by scientific progress (and by the progress of scientific certainty), about the role of human activities in the global warming of the earth's atmosphere. Moreover, the speaker lists a group of facts to offer as testimony to the previous affirmations, in a model of argumentation in regressive order. This is an insistent option in the *corpus,* which ultimately also proves the argumentivity of the affirmations produced.

What has to be underlined at this point is the overlapping of the narrative and argumentative structures, with the supremacy of the pragmatic objectives sought by the latter.

Text 5 also shows indicators of composite heterogeneity into which explicative and argumentative sequences intervene:

> (11) The scientific evidence has begun to be imperative: if the gas emissions that lead to the greenhouse effect continue to grow at this rate, within one century we will be traveling by boat in Terreiro do Paço and by camel in the Alentejo, or we will be fighting malaria in the Minho valleys. Is this an exaggeration? Perhaps not. It could all in fact be worse. One of the possibilities that scares the scientists is that warming of the atmosphere could eventually provoke a global change of the maritime currents—a kind of "El Niño" on a global scale—a change capable of totally upending our climates and provoking the complete ruin of agriculture production. At present, no one can foresee this phenomenon, but there is an image that is sometimes used: the elasticity image. In reality, all the studies start from more or less linear models, the same linearity with which elastic is stretched: we can say how far it will stretch depending on the force used. However, none of the models can respond to what would happen if there was a qualitative alteration, that is, if the elastic should break. The same could happen with our climates. (Text 5)

The sequential explicative organizational model starts from an affirmation that is afterwards explained, as is clearly indicated with the marker of reformulation "that is," the segment "a kind of," and also the express reference to the "image" that the speaker constructs to explain a reality not immediately accessible (from his point of view) to the understanding of the listener. However, it can be clearly stated that this segment is not one of scientific explanation. Rather it is one of argumentation; the presentation of all the data and affirmations of the qualified enunciators ("the scientists") confirms the affirmation made in the first of these paragraphs (again, in a regressive argumentative form).

Consequently, this explanation seems to equally sustain the structure and the dominant objective of the text, of the argumentative domain. This dominant objective is revealed in the last paragraph:

(12) What are the ways out (for the environmental problems)? It's important to continue to study the climatic phenomena and to put pressure on the governments. In spite of everything, the evolution since Eco-92 has been great. (Text 5)

This conclusion of the text concretizes the directive dimension developed in the argumentation and configures the text as *circular*: the only way out will be to "continue to study the climatic phenomena and to put pressure on the governments." This is the conclusion strategically anticipated from the very beginning by the organisation of the text, in particular by the drawing up of the eventual scenarios of future environmental calamity if the "way out" presented here at the end should be refused. Accordingly, the macro-textual complex in study can be understood as an organization orientated to a make-believe and make-accept (the speaker's points of view) at the service of a make-make (support/demand the study of solutions from the scientific community and put pressure on the policy makers to take favourable decisions from Kyoto), with the composite heterogeneity being subordinate to those dominant pragmatic objectives. From the speaker's point of view, the fact that the Portuguese were going around "dazed" by banalities gives the warning an added urgency. This obvious criticism of the Portuguese, with its implicit call for change, is affirmed at the beginning of the article; the possible response/solution is found at the end.

FINAL REMARKS

It can be said that, in the same way as this opinion article, the *dossier*'s organization is also circular: from the predominately informative text, to the explicative texts, and finally the opinion text, the facts and arguments evoked by the conflicting parts support the mobilising speech of the newspaper's director. This fact confers a great coherence to the group of texts, which are mobilised in the same ideological orientation and the same perlocutionary objectives. The *dossier* thus appears as a complex of elements united by a strong connection, which goes beyond the thematic confluence and encounters a new pertinence in the pragmatic objectives sought.

APPENDIX A: IMAGES

FIGURE 1: TEXT 1

FIGURE 2: TEXTS 2-5

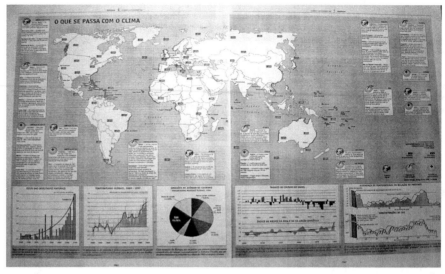

FIGURE 3: TEXT 6

FIGURE 4: TEXTS 7 AND 8

APPENDIX B: IDENTIFICATION OF THE *CORPUS*

TEXT	PAGE	TITLE
1	1	Climate in danger. What is changing. What can we do.
2	2-3	The future of the climate is at stake now
3	2-3	Portugal: a country that has everything to lose
4	3	What we already know and what we only imagine
5	3	The way of Kyoto
6	4-5	What is happening to the climate
7	6	1997 is the hottest year
8	6	Questions and answers on climate change

NOTES

[1] This article is the result of research carried out in the ambit of the project "The politics of climate change: discourses and representations", financed by the Portuguese Foundation for Science and Technology. (POCTI/COM/56973/2004)

[2] See Adam (1997a).

[3] Journalistic manuals commonly divide the identifiable genres in the written media into *information* and *commentary*, based on the following criteria: (a) semantic (the topic); (b) argumentative and pragmatic (the illocutionary objective—to inform and explain); and (c) enunciative (position of the journalist to his discourse or his sources). But this organisation is not consensual and, according to Adam (1997b), it corresponds more to the position of the enunciator regarding the informational contents than to a real division of genres. In this, the position of Moirand (1999) coincides with Adam when she refers to genres of subjectivized enunciation as presenting indicators of either explicit or identifiable subjectivity, and which are defined as such (e.g., opinion, editorial, etc.) and the genres of objectivized enunciation as being without indicators of the speaker's subjectivity or with these signs significantly hidden (e.g., news, reportage, brief, scientific article, etc.).

[4] See Masuy (1997).

[5] See Ramos (2005).

[6] See Cicurel (1994) and Adam (1997b).

[7] Adam (1997b) criticises the notion of *genre* sometimes being applied to the title or lead (which are nothing if not peritextual units) of journalistic texts. The

same consideration is extended to the operation of reformulation of earlier texts and communications emitted by the news agencies. In this case, we are dealing with criteria external to the textual material, which depend only on conditions of production.

[8] The third and fourth of these demands are visibility and dramatization, respectively.

[9] See Charaudeau (1997).

[10] The Hadley Centre for Climate Prediction and Research.

[11] According to Adam (1997a), the remaining macro-propositions are aspectualisation, relation and organisation according to sub-topics.

REFERENCES

Adam, J.-M. (1997a). *Les textes: Types et prototypes. Récit, description, argumentation, explication et dialogue.* Paris: Nathan.

Adam, J.-M. (1997b). Unités rédactionnelles et genres discursifs: Cadre général pour une approche de la presse écrite. *Pratiques, 94,* 3-18.

Beacco, J.-C. (1992). L'explication d'orientation encyclopédique: Remarques sur un régime discursif. *Les Carnets du CEDISCOR, 1,* 33-54.

Charaudeau, P. (1997). *Le discours d'information médiatique: La construction du miroir social.* Paris: Nathan.

Cicurel, F. (1994). Les scénarios d'information dans la presse quotidienne. *Le Français dans le Monde, Numéro Spécial Recherches et Applications: Médias Faits et Effets,* 91-102.

Jung, M. (2001). Ecological criticism of language. In A. Fill & P. Mühlhäusler (Eds.), *The ecolinguistics reader. Language, ecology and environment* (pp. 270-285). London: Continuum.

Masuy, C. (1997). Description et hypotypose dans l'écriture journalistique de l'ambiance. *Pratiques, 94,* 35-48.

Moirand, S. (1999). Les indices dialogiques de contextualisation dans la presse ordinaire. *Cahiers de Praxématique, 33,* 145-184.

Ramos, R. (2006). *Aspectos do discurso do ambientalismo nos media escritos.* Unpublished doctoral thesis, University of Porto, Porto, Portugal.

Revaz, F. (1997). Le récit dans la presse écrite. *Pratiques, 94,* 19-33.

12   Multi-semiotic Communication in an Australian Broadsheet: A New News Story Genre

Helen Caple

INTRODUCTION[1]

In exploring the rhetoric of science, Miller (1992) introduced the notion of "kairos" (often translated as "the right time" [p. 312]) as the critical occasion for decision or action. But kairos also has a spatial dimension with the notion of "opening" or "opportunity" being at its heart, thus giving us the notion of being in the right place at the right time. An organisation that I believe has in recent years recognised one such critical occasion, thus showing a clear understanding of the business of news dissemination, has been Fairfax Media Limited, a newspaper company that publishes *The Sydney Morning Herald* in Sydney, New South Wales, Australia. There is no doubting the fact that the newspaper industry is in decline. Circulation has been falling all around the world, including Australia (Who Killed The Newspaper?, 2006), and the steady uptake of online consumption of news, especially among the younger generations, is hastening this decline. However, *The Sydney Morning Herald* (hereafter *SMH*) appears to have anticipated these changing winds through their strategic manipulation of the news story genre to now include news stories that rely heavily on visual stimulation. By this I mean that they now publish news stories that make use of a dominant news photograph with a heading and only a short caption. This new genre is termed the "image-nuclear news story" (Caple, 2008). As complete and independent texts in themselves, such news stories differ both in their function and structure from other more traditionally presented news stories. In fact, this new genre appears to be very much like the "newsbites" (p. 20) in the online version of *SMH*, as described by John Knox (2007) in his research into visual-verbal communication on online newspaper home pages. He describes newsbites as

> operating as independent texts in their unique cotextual environment to construe actors and events according to the institutional goals and ideologies of the newspaper . . . newsbites function to highlight the stories valued by the institution of the newspaper as most important on a given day. Their social purpose is to present

the focal point of a news story with immediacy and impact. They afford the institutional authors of the newspaper the means by which to visually evaluate stories in terms of their comparative importance (including by size, relative positioning, headline font size and colour and inclusion of optional structural elements such as images), and are designed to attract readers to navigate to story pages in order to access longer (and/or modally different) versions of the "same" story. (Knox, 2007, p. 26)

Like newsbites then, image-nuclear news stories do also reflect the ideological position of the news organisation towards the stories and how they are valued as news. Unlike newsbites, though, image-nuclear news stories are independent stories in themselves and do not point to other news stories elsewhere in the newspaper. Thus, along with other design changes in the newspaper as a whole, *SMH* has demonstrated the rhetorical savvy necessary to position their newspaper within this new media field. At the same time, *SMH* has used this new news story genre to express cultural and social solidarity with its readers; a solidarity that *SMH* is exploiting to ensure that circulation figures are maintained.

In this paper I shall firstly outline the genesis of image-nuclear news stories and then explore how this news story genre has helped to provide *SMH* with a means of retaining an interested and stimulated reading public.

THE EVOLUTION OF THE NEWS STORY GENRE

It is a commonly held belief within socio-cognitive theories of genre that genres are sites of contention between stability and change (Berkenkotter & Huckin, 1995). One such site of contention is the news story genre. During the last two centuries the newspaper industry has witnessed remarkable social and technological changes that have had an enormous impact upon how and what is disseminated as news to the public. In the 1920s, radio was predicted to decimate the circulation of newspapers, and then in the 1950s it was the turn of the television to kill off both radio and newspapers. Yet all three media platforms have prospered, albeit in somewhat more specialised roles, and have continued into the 21st century where they have been joined by the digital revolution and the rise of the internet. At the same time, the news story genre has evolved and has been shaped to better serve the needs of the contexts in which it is consumed.

The constant in the news story genre is the fact that it has existed since the inception of Australian newspapers and has always served the basic purpose of informing the reading public of the major happenings within a particular society. The change has been seen not only in the text stages and language features of the news story genre, but also in the way that the story engages the reader interpersonally. In this section I shall briefly review the evolution of the news story genre in relation to one Australian broadsheet newspaper, *The Sydney Morning Herald.*

Since its inception in 1831, *SMH* has made use of the news story. At that time the generic structure resembled the narrative story structure, with the crisis event and orientation as macro-Theme coming at the beginning of the story, followed by a sequence of events that eventually led to the resolution of the event as a form of closure. The social purpose of these early news stories appeared to be to inform the reading public of the major events happening in the community. Thus, such stories were firmly entrenched in the ideational content, where the narrativisation of the event was driven by causation and temporality.

In the middle of the 19th century, the telegraph gave us the ability to electronically transmit the news around the globe. Because this was initially a somewhat unreliable technology, the telegraph forced journalists to re-order the information they gave over the wire so that the crux of the story could be gained before the transmission broke down. This ensured that the main idea of the story was captured. The details could be filled in later. However, whether or not this had a direct impact on the generic structure of the news story in newsprint is an area that is still contested today (see Pöttker, 2003). Nevertheless, changes in the news story structure were certainly occurring, especially towards the end of the century.

In the case of Australian news reporting, it was not until the end of the 19th century that the hard news story genre became entrenched as a distinct news story genre (Iedema, Feez, & White, 1994). Within the academic discipline of Journalism Studies, this news story structure is described as the inverted pyramid structure (Bell, 1991; Pöttker, 2003; Fulton, Huisman, Murphet, & Dunn, 2005; Conley & Lamble, 2006). Within Systemic Functional Linguistic circles, however, the hard news story structure is described as an orbital structure, centred on the notion of the nucleus^satellite structure (Iedema, Feez, & White, 1994; Iedema, 1997; White, 1997). It is the latter of these two perspectives that I shall focus on in this paper.

In the hard news story genre events are nuclearised and logical relations are disrupted (Iedema, 1997; White, 1997). The laying out of events leading up to the crisis point becomes more optional in the story, meaning that causation and temporality become less important organising principles. Rather, the news story now centres on a crisis point established in the headline and lead[2] (the nucleus), which then becomes the platform from which we leap into the remainder of the story. As Barnhurst and Nerone (2001) point out, headlines no longer functioned as titles or labels directing readers to the stories on the page, rather they became a "pointed summary of the news" (p. 198), carrying "deeply embedded codes of news values and cultural values . . . ranging from the unusual and the timely to the powerful and the moral" (p. 198). Thus for the most part, the nucleus works to direct the reader towards the news values underpinning the inclusion of that story in the news, which also reflects the ideological position- ing of the newspaper towards the events being covered. It is, then, the nucleus that attracts the reader into the story, and readers are now hooked into the story through the amplification of the ideational content.

Iedema, Feez and White (1994) also draw a distinction between news story types in that they describe both the hard news story and the soft news story. Soft news stories tend to deal in events that have a re-stabilising focus. They also make a distinction between different types of soft news story, depending on their social purpose. Media Exemplum is mainly concerned with exemplifying social and moral values; Media Anecdote with remarkable or unusual events that may challenge our sense of expectation; and Media Observation, with stories which record the passing of time, or events that reflect the established social order (Ie- dema et al., 1994).

Berkenkotter & Huckin (1995) make the assertion that all acts of commu- nication necessarily build on prior texts and that "no act of communication springs out of nothing" (p. 17). As far as the news story genre is concerned, I believe that it is out of both of these generic histories mentioned above that a new news story genre has evolved, one that exploits the functional structure of the hard news story and that also incorporates the social purpose of the soft news story, Media Observation in particular. In the year 2000, *SMH* underwent a ma- jor redesign. More white spaces between news stories were introduced, captions were sometimes moved to the sides of photographs, rather than underneath them and in general, larger more aesthetically motivated photographs were used. It is after this redesign that a particular kind of story started to emerge and began to develop a unique social purpose of its own. A greater number of large photo- graphs were to be seen on news pages, sometimes taking up three quarters of the page, with a short caption under the picture or to the side of the picture. The following story, for example, appeared on page 8 of *SMH* on August 4th, 2003 (see Figure 1 and Appendix 1).

Just necking . . . mother giraffe Shani stands over her newborn calf, Shaba, at San Diego Wild Animal Park. The park in southern California is home to two sub-species of giraffe, the reticulated giraffe and the baringo giraffe. Shaba is the 87th baringo giraffe to be born in the park. Photo: AFP

FIGURE 1: *SYDNEY MORNING HERALD*, 04/08/2003, P. 8

The caption reads:

> *Just necking . . . mother giraffe Shani stands over her newborn calf Shaba, at San Diego Wild Animal Park. The park in southern California is home to two sub-species of giraffe, the reticulated giraffe and the baringo giraffe. Shaba is the 87th baringo giraffe to be born in the park.*

This would be viewed as a fairly standard Media Observation, where the story is told through a salient, aesthetically motivated image and a caption that expands upon the story/event described. However, at the start of the caption there is a short, witty phrase "*Just necking . . .*" that is separated from the rest of the caption through the use of ellipsis. Here, the more common phrase "just checking" has been manipulated and as a result enters into a playful relationship with the image participants and the posture of the giraffes. So we could read the playful meaning in the extended neck of the mother giraffe or we could also read the protective gesture implied in "just checking" as the mother watches over her calf.

By 2004, the short abstraction that appeared at the beginning of the caption had moved to the position of heading[3] above the image and the font type, condensed interstate—a sans serif font used for the heading—became unique to these stories[4]. Figure 2, a story from page 11 of *SMH* on June 24th, 2004 (see Appendix 2), clearly exemplifies the changes now evident in such stories.

Give the lady a big hand

A visitor to the Contemporary Art Museum in the French city of Lyons looks at a sculpture by Chinese artist Sui Jianguo that represents the arm of Mao Zedong. Photo: AFP/Fred Dufour

FIGURE 2: *SYDNEY MORNING HERALD*, 24/06/2004, P. 11

Since June 2004, I have systematically collected all image-nuclear news stories that have appeared in *SMH*, and my corpus currently stands at 1000 analysed stories. In the twelve months between June 2004 and June 2005 480 stories were presented as image-nuclear news stories. The average per month during this period was 40, with March 2005 having the highest number in any single month, which was 61. This meant that each day's edition had on average two such stories on the news pages. Of the 480 stories, 473 (98.5 per cent) made use of the heading and of those headings 440 (93 per cent) included an element of play between the heading and the image. It is to this notion of play that I would now like to turn.

What is noticeable in these stories is the relationship that developed between the heading and the photograph. The majority of the headings in image-nuclear news stories (95 per cent of the total number of 1000 in the corpus) rely on the manipulation of common idiomatic expressions to fit the content of the photograph, as in the example in Figure 2. In this photograph we see a very large sculpture of the hand and arm of Chairman Mao, and a woman standing beneath the sculpture looking up towards the hand, giving us an idea of the size of this artwork. In using the heading *"Give the lady a big hand"* the author of this text has also availed himself of the literal meaning of the words used in this idiom. This interplay between the literal and the figurative has the effect of creating quite a humorous relationship between the verbiage and the image. Such play between image and heading can also extend to all manner of intertextual references, including cultural allusions, that the creators of the stories expect their readers to know and be able to decode.

What has also been an interesting development with this genre has been the kinds of events that have been portrayed in this playful manner. More and more stories dealing with essentially destabilising hard news events have also been presented in this format. In the total corpus, 14 per cent of the stories are what I would traditionally term hard news stories. In fact, many of these were also reported in other newspapers published in the same metropolitan area using the more traditional news story structure, centred on a verbiage nucleus between the headline and lead. Of that 14 per cent of hard news stories in my corpus, 77.8 per cent include a playful relationship between the heading and image. Figure 3 is an example of one such story (see Appendix 3).

In the story in Figure 3, the heading makes reference to the sporting discourse of swimming, manipulating technical terminology such as (swimming) coach, the swim stroke front crawl and the marking out of the swimming pool into lanes, with the middle lane usually being the lane that the fastest swimmer will swim from in a competition. There is also another meaning that can be drawn from this heading and image in that given the dangerous conditions portrayed, the bus probably is driving along quite slowly. Thus we can also infer that the bus is carefully "crawling" along the street. The tone set up between heading and image is one established in play and humour. The caption, however, does not reflect this tone at all, and quickly moves into the destabilising nature of this event and the death and destruction that came with it. The caption reads:

Coach does the crawl in middle lane

A bus eases its way along a Manila road flooded by monsoon rains that closed schools and offices yesterday. Elsewhere in the region a typhoon brought floods and landslides to northern Taiwan, where thousands were forced to flee their homes. Nine people were reported dead as Typhoon Aere passed through Japan and Taiwan before turning towards China. Mudslides buried a church in the Taiwanese county of Hsinchu, killing a man and his daughter and leaving four others missing. Another four were washed away by floods in central Taiwan. Photo: AP/Aaron Favila

FIGURE 3: *SYDNEY MORNING HERALD*, 26/08/2004, P. 16

A bus eases its way along a Manila road flooded by monsoon rains that closed schools and offices in the Philippine capital yesterday. Elsewhere in the region, Typhoon Aere brought floods and landslides to northern

> *Taiwan, where thousands were forced to flee their homes. Mudslides buried a church in the county of Hsinchu, killing a man and his daughter and leaving four others missing. Another four were washed away by floods in central Taiwan.*

There is certainly nothing humorous about the events being described in this caption. Thus, the initial stance towards the story established in the heading and image stands in stark contrast to the actual events being described in the caption. This relationship will be dealt with more fully in the next section.

In this manner, then, I believe that *SMH* has developed a new news story genre over the past six or seven years and, as a reader of *SMH*, I feel that I have been guided through a period of enculturation into the genre. It started out as the increased use of striking and somewhat aesthetically motivated images that dealt primarily with soft news events. Then with the playful abstraction at the beginning of the caption moving to the position of heading, a much closer relationship between the heading and image was established. Finally, having been apprenticed into this special playfulness, what was initially reserved for soft news events was also applied to hard news events; such stories began appearing from July 2004 onwards.

If we examine the functional structure of this news story, we can see how I came to term this new news story genre the image-nuclear news story. It is a news story in which the heading and image usually combine in a playful manner, in that the heading often manipulates common idiomatic expressions in a way that enables the reader to decode the layers of meaning through the image, the verbiage or through both. Then the caption elaborates on the news value behind the story. By foregrounding this relationship between the heading and the image, in what I am calling the nucleus, this new news story genre generates a playful stance towards the event that has important implications for the interpersonal management of the text. This is because of the evaluative stance it establishes towards the news event. (Figure 4 shows the generic structure of an image-nuclear news story.) Furthermore, by deliberately manipulating the discourse, the newspaper is assuming knowledge on the part of the reader of the cultural allusions of the idioms, which in turn, enables the newspaper to express cultural and social solidarity with the readers.

HOW INTERTEXTUALITY BREEDS SOLIDARITY

The organising principle of the image-nuclear news story is that the nucleus establishes a playful orientation to the event being reported. In my corpus of 1000 image nuclear news stories, 95 per cent of them enter into a verbal-visual play in the nucleus. The photograph and the heading work together to draw out

Heading: Dry hard with a vengeance

Nucleus
Image

Caption: Workers walk across the dried bed of the Hongyashan reservoir in Minqin, northwestern China. The reservoir, which is the largest in Asia and was held 98 million cubic metres of water, dried up last month for the first time since 1958, bringing hardship to the thousands of families depending on it. Photo/ AP

FIGURE 4: FUNCTIONAL STRUCTURE OF THE IMAGE-NUCLEAR
NEWS STORY

intertextual references that not only draw on the reader's knowledge of idioms but also call for a wide-ranging cultural and world knowledge to unpack the play not only in the verbiage but also in the image. It is to this playful relationship that we turn in this section and to how this nuclear function helps to build a community with the readers of the newspaper.

According to Chang (2004), an idiom is a "conventionalised multiword expression whose syntactic, lexical and phonological form is to a greater or lesser degree fixed, and whose semantics and discoursal functions are opaque or specialised, also to a greater or lesser degree" (Chang, 2004, p. 9). His definition also covers cultural allusions which may appear in the form of quotations, catch phrases, slogans and proverbs that are instantly recognisable within a particular cultural context. It is these idiomatic expressions making direct cultural allusions that have important implications in the interpersonal management of image-nuclear news stories.

By deliberately manipulating such idioms for stylistic effects to fit the context in which they are used, the text producer is, then, assuming that the reader has knowledge of the cultural allusions of the idioms. Thus, it is a certain kind of reader—one that has extensive cultural, general and linguistic knowledge and is able to engage with the multiple layers of play and meaning potential in these texts—that *SMH* is attempting to attract. As McCarthy states, "idioms are communal tokens that enable speakers to express cultural and social solidarity" (1998, p. 145, cited in Chang, 2004, p. 76). Punning or wordplay serves to membership the readers into "belonging to a community with shared linguistic and cultural values" (Grauberg, 1989, cited in Chang, 2004, p. 105). Of course, an important effect of being able to form such a community of readers is that *SMH* can then articulate quite accurately the demographic that is its readership to advertisers.

Another important effect of this manipulation of heading and image is that *SMH* can use this playful stance towards the story to establish the newspaper's ideological or evaluative stance towards the news, one that it expects the readers to share. By invoking both the literal and metaphorical meanings in the heading, the newspaper editors who write these stories hope to share with their readers this value-added re-reading of the heading, and it is through the sharing of this evaluation of the news and appreciation of the play that these two groups bond. This can be further argued from the point of view that the nucleus, that is, the heading and image, in image-nuclear news stories can be construed as the hyper-Theme (Martin, 1993, 2001) of the whole text. The notion of hyper-Theme comes from the work of Martin (1993, 2001) in investigating how interpersonal meaning is negotiated in multimodal texts. Martin argues for a correlation between higher order Theme and New and evaluation and what is placed in the position of hyper-Theme establishes the method of development of the rest of the text, which he labels higher order interpersonal Theme. In the case of image-nuclear news stories, the hyper-Theme can be thought of interpersonally as well as textually because this textual peak of dominant image and playful heading at the front of the story affords the interpersonal. With this playful evaluation of the news dominating the first take on this story, we then view the rest of the story from this position of evaluative stance. Thus, as texture, the image and heading function as an evaluative Theme, naturalising the stance from which the ensuing verbiage can be read.

CONCLUSION

Newspapers along with magazines, radio and television have long been posited as the media of the public sphere (Habermas, 1974), a sphere which "mediates between society and state, in which the public organises itself as the bearer of public opinion" (p. 50). Indeed, newspapers are seen as the "bearers and leaders of public opinion" (Habermas, 1994, p. 53). Thus they carry enormous influence over how and what the public thinks. In *SMH*, a news story genre has emerged in which a news event is couched in an evaluative Theme that has strong implications for how that story should be read. It attracts a certain kind of reader, one who not only appreciates the aesthetic in good press photography, but also who wants to be challenged in the way that he/she reads the news. By introducing such news stories to the editorial pages, *SMH* has demonstrated great awareness of the potential of the internet and other media platforms to threaten its future. It is also a newspaper that realises the importance of maintaining a loyal readership, one that can share in and can exchange with other readers this common approach to how the news is viewed. In the last three years, *SMH* has enjoyed increasing circulation (Fairfax Media, 2007), which is no mean feat given that newspapers across the world are in decline. Clearly, this is a newspaper that knows the essence of good timing.

NOTES
[1] I would like to sincerely thank Sam North, Managing Editor of *The Sydney Morning Herald*, for his continuing support of my research and for graciously granting copyright access to the pages used in this paper.

[2] In the UK, this is known as the "intro"; in America and Australia, the lead.

[3] I have used the term "heading" rather than "headline" to distinguish this news story genre from the other more established news story genres.

[4] In more recent times, however, this font has also been used for other headlines, in particular in sub-headlines on other stories.

REFERENCES
Barnhurst, K., & Nerone, J. (2001). *The form of news: A history*. New York: Guilford.

Bell, A. (1991). *The language of news media*. Oxford: Blackwell.

Berkenkotter, C., & Huckin, T. N. (1995). *Genre knowledge in disciplinary communication: Cognition/culture/power*. Mahwah, New Jersey: Erlbaum.

Caple, H. (2008). Intermodal relations in image nuclear news stories. In L. Unsworth (Ed.), *Multimodal semiotics: Functional analysis in contexts of education*. London: Continuum: 125-138.

Caple, H. (in press). What you see and what you get: The evolving role of news photographs in an Australian broadsheet. In V. Rupar (Ed.), *Journalism and sense-making: reading the newspaper*. Cresskill, New Jersey: Hampton Press.

Chang, C. G. (2004). *English idioms and interpersonal meaning*. Guangzhou, Guangdong, China: Sun Yak-sen University Press.

Conley, D., & Lamble, S. (2006). *The daily miracle: An introduction to Journalism* (3rd ed.). Melbourne: Oxford University Press.

Fairfax Media (2007). *Fairfax media publications circulation and readership results for newspapers, inserted magazines and websites—to June 2007*. Retrieved 21st October, 2007, from www.fxj.com.au

Fulton, H., Huisman, R., Murphet, J., & Dunn, A. (2005). *Narrative and media*. Melbourne: Cambridge University Press.

Habermas, J. (1974). The public sphere: An encyclopaedia article. *New German Critique, 3*(3), 49-55.

Halliday, M. A. K. (1978). *Language as social eemiotic*. London: Edward Arnold.

Iedema, R. (1997). The history of the accident news story. *Australian Review of Applied Linguistics, 20*(2), 95-119.

Iedema, R., Feez, S., & White, P. (1994). *Stage two: Media literacy. A report for the Write it Right Literacy in Industry Research Project by the Disadvantaged Schools Program, N.S.W.* New South Wales, Australia: Department of School Education.

Knox, J. (2007). Visual–verbal communication on online newspaper home pages. *Visual Communication, 6*(1), 19-53.

Kress, G., & van Leeuwen, T. (2006). *Reading images: The grammar of visual design* (2nd ed.). London: Routledge.

Martin, J. R. (1993). Life as a noun. In M. A. K. Halliday & J. R. Martin (Eds.), *Writing science: Literacy and discursive power.* London: Falmer: 221-267.

Martin, J. R. (1996). Types of structure: Deconstructing notions of constituency in clause and text. In E. H. Hovy & D. R. Scott (Eds.), *Computational and conversational discourse: Burning issues—an interdisciplinary account.* Heidelberg, Germany: Springer: 39-66.

Martin, J. R. (2001). Fair trade: Negotiating meaning in multimodal texts. In P. Coppock (Ed.), *The semiotics of writing: Transdisciplinary perspectives on the technology of writing. Semiotic and Cognitive Studies, 10,* 311-338.

Martin, J. R. & Rose, D. (2003). *Working with discourse: Meaning beyond the clause.* London: Continuum.

Martin, J. R. & White, P. R. R. (2005). *The language of evaluation: Appraisal in English.* New York: Palgrave Macmillan.

Miller, C. R. (1984). Genre as social action. *Quarterly Journal of Speech, 70,* 151-167.

Miller, C. R. (1992) Kairos in the rhetoric of science. In S. P. Witte, N. Nakadate, and R. D. Cherry (Eds), *A rhetoric of doing: Essays on written discourse in honor of James L. Kinneavy* (pp. 310-327). Carbondale: Southern Illinois University Press.

More Media, Less News (Special Report). (2006). *Economist.* Retrieved August 26 2006, from http://www.economist.com/opinion/ displaystory.cfm? story_id=7827135

Pöttker, H. (2003). News and its communicative quality: The inverted pyramid—when and why did it appear? *Journalism Studies, 4*(4), 501-511.

Who Killed The Newspaper? (2006). *Economist.* Retrieved August 24 2006, from http://www.economist.com/opinion/displaystory. cfm? story_id=7830218

White, P. (1997). Death, disruption and the moral order: The narrative impulse in mass "hard news" reporting. In F. Christie & J. R. Martin (Eds.), *Genres and institutions: Social processes in the workplace and school.* London: Cassell: 101-133.

13 Narrative and Identity Formation: An Analysis of Media Personal Accounts from Patients of Cosmetic Plastic Surgery

Débora de Carvalho Figueiredo

INTRODUCTION

According to Woodward, of late years the concept of identity has come to matter, "both in terms of social and political concerns within the contemporary world and within academic discourses, where identity has been seen as conceptually important in offering explanations of social and cultural changes" (1997, p. 1). In late modernity, the concepts of identity and identity formation are inseparable from language and discourse. As scholars both in the area of linguistics and of social sciences affirm, identities are forged within discourse, more specifically within socially and institutionally situated discursive practices (Fairclough, 1992, 2003, 2006; Moita Lopes, 2001; Hall, 1996; Bruner, 1990, 2004; etc.).

Recent social phenomena/movements such as the liberation of women, of gays/lesbians, of blacks, etc., have helped to open up spaces for discussion and theorization about who we are in social life (Moita Lopes, 2001, p. 56). In late modernity, media discourses (of television, cinema, print media, the internet), by presenting human experience under multiple and plural forms, register and publicize the constant changes that are taking place in social life. However, as Moita Lopes (2001, p. 55) points out, there is an ever-present danger that information technologies, working for a neoliberal globalized discourse, might erase "the differences we are made of." This is precisely one of the points I want to explore in this article: the fact that, at the same time that the mass media offer us windows through which we can glance at different possibilities of being and living, they also work to impose hegemonic models of identity, be them in terms of gender, sexuality, human relations, or body design.

In this work I am interested in how female identities, especially in what concerns the intersection between self-identity and body shape, are construed and represented by certain genres endemic in glossy women's magazines, a highly popular mass media product whose pleasures are hard to resist. The attraction of women's magazines lies in the fact that they explore what it means to be a woman, and the problems typically faced by everyday women, in a light, colourful, superficial and easy-to-process way. In fact, they function as "manuals" of womanhood (especially the hegemonic model of womanhood, based on the typical white, neo-liberal, middle-class, heterosexual female reader), teaching and advising women on how to behave, especially in what concerns the most private aspects of their lives (love, their bodies and sex). If we were to consider women's magazines as a genre, we could say that the presence of fixed sections create textual expectations and help to build and define a loyal readership.

The glossy female magazines (in Brazil, *Claudia, Elle, Marie Claire, Desfile, Boa Forma, Corpo a Corpo*, etc.) seem to have incorporated some basic feminist values, such as the fact that women now work outside home and have careers. However, these values are construed, in the pages of these magazines, against the backdrop of conservative and misogynist notions of femininity, such as female passivity, the need for female beautification and body care, and the search for a permanent male partner as a woman's main "career" (Caldas-Coulthard, 1996).

In this article, based on the theoretical frameworks of Critical Discourse Analysis, Identity Studies, Narrative Studies and Genre Studies, I investigate how the identities of three women, especially in what concerns their body design, are construed in the genre "media personal account", in the present case of experiences of cosmetic plastic surgery published in two Brazilian glossy magazines, *Claudia* and *Plastic Surgery&Beauty (Plástica&Beleza)*. *Claudia* is a monthly publication addressed at adult women which covers a variety of themes ranging from love and family life, sex life, professional life, beautification and fashion. *Plastic Surgery&Beauty*, on the other hand, is a monthly publication which thematizes cosmetic and plastic procedures for women, and as such its advertising contents (ads for plastic surgery clinics, private surgeons, cosmetic clinics/spas, and cosmetic products) are much larger than that of *Claudia*. From these magazines, three personal sections of media personal accounts have been selected for analysis: from the November 2006 edition of *Plastic Surgery&Beauty*, the fixed sections "My diary—your story with the scalpel," in which a common reader relates her personal experience of a cosmetic plastic surgery (from now on CPS), and "Celebrity Cosmetic Surgery—the secret for a perfect shape," in which a current celebrity (from television, for instance) also relates her personal experience of CPS. From the October 2006 edition of *Claudia*, the selected section was called "Silicone Diary," which presented a personal account of a reader who underwent a breast enlargement surgery.

Personal account sections are endemic in women's magazines, especially the thematic ones (i.e., those addressed at specific topics such as dieting, exercise, fashion, plastic surgery, etc.). In terms of genre, these sections consist of a fixed title, the name of a journalist (optional), a lead, which contextualizes the personal story in question, photos of before and after, and the personal account itself. Even though media personal accounts could be viewed in themselves as personal experiences lived by "real" readers, it is important to point out that, by being introduced by the section's title, the journalist's name, and a lead, they are strongly framed and influenced by the journalist's voice, position and institutional point of view, realizing in this case a specific kind of media genre. In this sense, media personal accounts are similar to other media genres in which the voice of a "real" person from the "real" world is filtered, framed and recontextualized by the voice of a journalist, such as in reader's letters and interviews. My main contention in this work, in terms of genre, is that certain genres of the media (such as media personal accounts) perform the social action of creating idealized identities that interpellate and imbricate individuals by and into gendered narratives.

THEORETICAL BACKGROUND

Narrative and identity formation

According to researchers from different areas of the Social Sciences, narrative, as a discursive form of acting in the world, plays a central role in the construction of social identities (Bruner, 1990, 2004; Mishler, 1999; Schiffrin, 1996; Bamberg, 1997; Moita Lopes, 1998, 1999, 2001; Fabrício, 2006, etc.). These researchers share the view that "to tell stories is a way of making sense of life (Bruner, 1990) or of who we are and how we are formed in the social world" (Moita Lopes, 2001, p. 60). From that perspective, autobiography, such as in personal narratives, is seen as a "set of procedures for 'life making'" (Bruner, 2004, p. 692), that is, the ways of telling self-stories end up by shaping the very persons we become.

According to Bruner, for human beings lived time can only be described in narrative form. Life narratives are socio-cognitively constructed by human beings through language. In this sense, life itself is a socio-cognitive human construction. As the author puts it, "narrative imitates life, life imitates narrative. . . . There is no such thing as 'life itself.' At the very least, [life] is a selective achievement of memory recall; beyond that, recounting one's life is an interpretive feat" (Bruner, 2004, pp. 692-693).

The focus of scholars such as Bruner and Moita Lopes is the role of narrative as an organizing element of discourse and, by extension, of knowledge, identities and social relations. In that sense, many of these scholars (Moita Lopes, 1999; Bruner, 1990, 2004; Linde, 1997; Norrick, 1997; Duranti, 1986; Schiffrin, 1984; Fabrício, 2006) criticize the classic model of narrative analysis proposed by Labov and Waletsky (1967) and Labov (1972) due to its structuralist and determinist character which, they claim, does not allow for an adequate understanding of the social uses of language. However, I believe that a socio-discursive approach, such as CDA, can expand and complement the Labovian proposal, adding a social dimension to that form-oriented model.

Narratives are not just ways to build certain views of reality. As spaces of struggle for the legitimation of specific meanings and representations, they also represent forms of controlling and manipulating reality and the participants of discursive events. In identity terms, narratives legitimate and privilege certain forms of subjectivities while excluding others.

Moita Lopes sees "the thematization of the issue of identity formation by the Social Sciences as the result of macro-social factors related to recent historical changes, specifically the phenomenon of globalization and the technological developments which have been affecting everyday life and, thus, who we are becoming in the social world . . . ." (2001, p. 62). This view of discourse and identities "allows the analyses of narrative practices to be theoretically anchored in institutional life as a privileged space for identity studies, since institutions play a major role in our socialization into the types of people we are" (Moita Lopes, 2001, p. 62).

Narrative and genre

Fairclough defines genres as discursive aspects of the way people act and interact in social events (2003, p. 65). That is, genres are particular forms of social relations between social agents (individuals or organizations). From the point of view of CDA, therefore, genre analysis of texts focuses on the role played by genre in establishing social action/interactions in social events.

Fairclough's proposal for genre analysis is threefold: analysis of genre chains; analysis of genre mixtures in particular texts; and analysis of individual genres in a particular text. In this article, my focus is on the latter. The author points out two preliminary and basic features of genres: they are not stable, fixed or homogenized, and they lack an established terminology. This second point is the one I want to draw special attention to, since there is no consensus among academic authors regarding the appropriate nomenclature for personal narrative genres, or even for the status of narrative as a genre or not.

Fabrício (2006, p. 14), for instance, characterizes "the act of telling stories as a discursive genre," even though she is aware that her position is by no means pacific, since many genre analysts see narrative as a rhetorical form of discourse organization which is found in different genres (Bonini, 2001), while others see it as something broader than a mere type of discourse organization (Paltridge, 1996). Some authors refer to first-person narrative genres as "*personal narrative*" (Meurer, 2002), others as "*account*" or "*testimony*" (Sousa, 2003), and others still as "*narrative*" or "*first-person account*" (Caldas-Coulthard, 1996; Moita Lopes, 2001; Fabrício, 2006). In this work I shall use the term *personal account* to refer to a specific genre, the press stories told in the first person, published either in a section of a newspaper/magazine by themselves (as is the case of my data), or as part of a news story.

According to Fairclough (2003), one of the difficulties of dealing with the concept of genre is that it can generate definitions at different levels of abstraction. The author claims that some genres stand at a high level of abstraction, transcending particular networks of social practices. If we could call Narrative a genre, it would be located at this high level of abstraction, and it would take the form of different specific narrative genres in particular social practices (e.g., conversational narratives, accounts in the media, stories told in institutional settings such as therapy, legal depositions, etc.). However, if we believe that a genre is linked to a particular social practice or network of practices, then Narrative should not be called a genre, but a *pre-genre* (Swales, 1990).

That way, in this article I will adopt Fairclough's terminology to avoid confusion: I shall call "pre-genres" the most abstract categories (e.g., *narratives*), and "situated genres" the ones specific to a particular network of social practices (e.g., *media personal accounts*).

Another useful concept presented by Fairclough in his analysis of genre is that of "activity," which refers to "what people are doing discoursally" (2003, p. 70). The interest here is to distinguish, among social activities, those which are primarily discoursal (e.g., a lecture) and those in which discourse plays an ancillary role (e.g., fixing a machine, mowing the lawn). This notion is useful to understand genres because genres are commonly defined in terms of the purposes of the activity. According to Fairclough, purposes can be relatively explicit or implicit, and hierarchically ordered.

The texts under analysis in this article are probably part of a category of genres which could be called *personal stories* narrated in the first person. They are primarily discoursal, and their basic purpose is to give strength, vividness and credibility to an array of hegemonic discourses, sometimes in an openly promotional form (e.g., in websites of plastic surgery clinics which present personal accounts of ex-clients, always satisfied with the results of the cosmetic procedures/surgeries underwent), sometimes in a less overtly promotional form, aiming at circulating, strengthening and legitimizing a certain ideology (e.g., oral personal accounts given by participants of groups such as Weight Watchers, Alcoholics Anonymous, churches and religious sects). If we say that the main communicative purpose of personal accounts in general is, explicitly, to illustrate a certain point in a discussion, we could also claim that there is a secondary purpose (generally implicit) which gives these texts a strong ideological character: many of them are used for promotional aims, or as a way of adding vividness, legitimacy, veracity and credibility to the discourse where they occur (e.g., the discourse of women's magazines).

However, as Fairclough points out, there are problems in privileging purpose in the definition of a genre: "while some genres are clearly purposive, clearly tied to broadly recognized social purposes, this is not true of all genres" (2003, p. 71). Fairclough believes that this problem arises from a distinction between "communicative" and "strategic" action (Habermas, 1984). *Communicative action* takes place in interactions oriented to arriving at understanding (e.g., a personal chat with a friend), while *strategic action* takes place in interactions oriented to getting results (e.g., a sales encounter). The problem, according to Fairclough, is that:

> The modernization of social life involves the emergence of complex social systems whose rationality is "instrumental" (rather than communicative), in which interaction is predominantly strategic—which are, in short, oriented to efficiently producing results. Purpose-driven genres characterized by a determinate structure are a significant part of these instrumental social systems. (2003, p. 71)

Media personal accounts, though apparently communicative (i.e., aiming at transmitting someone's personal experience to the readers, and thus illustrating a point in an argument), are in fact strategic in the sense that they also help to "sell" specific ideas, products and services (in the present case, cosmetic procedures and surgeries advertised by the magazines). This can be seen as ideological since it legitimizes the "pathological" (Habermas, 1984) invasion of the lifeworld (the world of everyday experience) by systems and instrumental rationality (Fairclough, 2003). This blurring of communicative and strategic purposes in media personal accounts of CPS indicates that women's magazines mediate information on CPS between expert systems (doctors, clinics, pharmaceutical companies, who are their advertising clients) and the lay readers, thus shaping our knowledge of CPSs and gearing it towards market ends. Segal (2007) makes similar comments on the shaping of knowledge in narratives of breast cancer.

To sum up, the distinction between communicative and strategic purposes is not always clear-cut, and they frequently occur in combination. An evidence of the blurred purposes of certain activities is the strategic simulation of communicative interaction, a typical feature of media personal accounts. Therefore, genre studies need to take this distinction and this fuzziness into account in order to understand feminine narrative media genres (such as the media personal accounts analyzed here) and their impact on the female readers of women's magazines. In other words, to understand these genres, genre theory needs to

include perspectives from cultural and feminist studies and to incorporate tools
of critical discourse analysis within a genre frame.

ANALYTICAL PROCEDURES

In any mass media personal account, the text is supposedly a tale told by
a real person who, prior to the act of telling her story, has undergone some
personal experience worth telling and worth reading about. This is what Labov
and Waletsky (1967) called "reportability," that is, the success of any narrative
depends on it having a "point" and a reason to be told.

Labov proposed, in his 1972 essay, a structural model for the analysis of fully-
formed oral narratives, which I will apply to my data:

(1) **Abstract:** *What is the story about?*
(2) **Orientation:** *Who, when, where, what?*
(3) **Complicating action**: *Then what happened?*
(4) **Evaluation:** *So what, how is this interesting?*
(5) **Result or resolution:** *What finally happened?*
(6) **Coda:** *That's it, I've finished.*

However, it is important to point out here that while Labov's model was
proposed for oral narratives produced by a single narrator, I am applying his proposal to written media personal accounts, which, even though being presented
as the product of a single, "real-world" narrator, are constructed by a combination of two voices: that of the person who is relating a personal experience, and
that of the journalist in charge of the section of which the personal account is a
part. Therefore, some elements of the Labovian model are produced, in media
personal accounts, not by the person who lived the story herself, but by the
journalist in charge of the section. Another point is that, even though Labov's
model was not designed within the field of genre studies, I would like to argue,
by extension, that the elements he presents for a fully-formed narrative can be
seen as a basis from which we could raise the textual organization of the genre
"personal media account." Therefore, starting from Labov's model, I will use the
term "move" (Swales, 1990) to refer to each of the elements of his model, which,
from the analysis of the exemplars in my corpus, correspond to the organization
of the genre "media personal account."

In addition to the Labovian model described above, I am also applying to
the analysis of these narrative texts the macro-analytical model of "problem-
solution" developed by Hoey (1979, 1983), who viewed "narratives as linguistic
patterns organized in terms of a situation, a problem and a response (or solution), which can be evaluated positively or negatively" (Caldas-Coulthard, 1996,
p. 257).

Finally, to add a socio-discursive turn to the micro-analysis of my data, I am also making use of van Leeuwen's (1996) model for the analysis of social actors (coupled with some categories from Halliday's (2004) systemic functional grammar). In his model, van Leeuwen proposes a network of sociosemantic systems to investigate how social actors are represented in discourse.

Following the fact that discourses are situational, we can state that personal narrative genres are circumscribed by the contexts of the situations in which they occur, and by the contexts of culture which encompass specific discursive events. Among the institutional and socio-cultural restrictions that shape media personal accounts are the types of life valued and recognized by a given culture. In Bruner's words,

> Given their constructed nature and their dependence upon the cultural conventions and language usage, life narratives obviously reflect the prevailing theories about 'possible lives' that are part of one's culture. Indeed, one way of characterizing a culture is by the narrative models it makes available for describing the course of a life. (2004, p. 694)

As we will see below, the prevailing model of "possible lives" and "possible bodies" represented in the mass-media genre personal account of CPS is that of the slim, fit and young-looking body, a form of self-identity and of lifestyle sold in mass media texts as a guarantee of self-worth, personal balance, harmony and happiness (Figueiredo, forthcoming).

ANALYTICAL SECTION

Move I and II: Abstract and Orientation—who is really talking?

The genre of media personal accounts of CPS has a particular organizational pattern that gives a distinct structure to the story related, which then reinforces the cultural ideals expressed through them. That is precisely why I am stretching the notion of "element" from the Labovian model and comparing it to Swales' (1990) concept of "moves" that help organize the genre "media personal account," and also help to construe and disseminate ideological assumptions about women's identity. In terms of the first two elements (or moves) of Labov's narrative model (*abstract* and *orientation*), in *Claudia*'s narrative the lead fulfills the dual function of abstract (*What is the story about?*) and part of the orientation (*Who, when, where, what?*)

(1) **The advertiser and writer Magali Moraes** [orientation] **tells how life**

can change—in many senses—after an extra 225 milliliters in each breast [abstract] ("Silicon Diary," *Claudia*, Oct. 2006, p. 202)

In *Plastic Surgery&Beauty*, on the other hand, the section's name functions as abstract (*What is the story about?*), but not as orientation:

(2) **My diary—your story with the scalpel** By **Karine César** (*Plastic Surgery&Beauty*, Nov. 2006, p. 42)

(3) **Celebrity Cosmetic Surgery—the secret for a perfect shape By Suzana Ferreira** (*Plastic Surgery&Beauty*, Nov. 2006, p. 44)

In these two texts, part of the orientation (*Who, when, where, what?*) is presented in the lead:

(4) **The dancer and manager Ana Carolina Mattos, 25 years old** ("My diary—your story with the scalpel," *Plastic Surgery&Beauty*, Nov. 2006, p. 42)

(5) **The actress Mariana Guives, 25, [member of the cast] of the soap opera *Cristal*, from SBT.** ("Celebrity Cosmetic Surgery—the secret for a perfect shape," *Plastic Surgery&Beauty*, Nov. 2006, p. 44)

As we can see in these examples, the abstract and orientation are partially produced by the journalist who was/is responsible for the magazine section, and not by the first-person narrator, supposedly a "real" reader who wrote to the magazine recounting her personal experience of a CPS. In "Silicone Diary" (*Claudia*, Oct. 2006, p. 202), the journalist is not identified, in an example of what van Leeuwen calls "exclusion by backgrounding" (1996, p. 39). Even though we do not know the name of the journalist in charge of this reportage, we know, by the presence of a lead which introduces a quoted first-person account and which refers to the main narrator (and character) of this account (the "real" reader who is sharing her personal experience) in the third person (through nomination combined with functionalization and identification—*The advertiser and writer Magali Moraes*), that this text was at least partially produced (and certainly edited) by members of the magazine's editorial staff.

Different from *Claudia*'s article, in which the journalist is not mentioned, in *Plastic Surgery&Beauty* the journalists are semi-formally nominated (van Leeuwen, 1996, p. 39) right after the title of the section, that is, they are represented as having a unique identity through the combination of first name + surname, as we can see in examples 2 and 3 above.

In spite of this difference, in terms of authorial voices the three accounts share a common feature: all of them are textualized as quotations introduced by a journalist's voice. Caldas-Coulthard (1996) argues that quotations are a strategy used by journalists to seem detached from their texts, and at the same time to bring reader and character close together by mimicking a dialogue between them (confirming that these texts represent in fact strategic activities disguised as communicative ones). In her words, "the apparent 'factuality' is a fiction" (Caldas-Coulthard, 1996, p. 258). In this work, the media personal accounts of CPS, supposedly "factual," are introduced and recontextualized in such a way that represents the magazine's editorial voice and point of view.

In short, the media personal accounts analysed here are in fact examples of quoted accounts framed by a lead written by a journalist, which also fulfills the move of orientation, describing the first-person narrator by nomination + functionalization and identification (van Leeuwen, 1996). In *Plastic Surgery&Beauty*, the media personal accounts are even opened and closed by quotation marks. This produces what Caldas-Coulthard calls a "layered narration," in which the magazine, more specifically a journalist, occupies the powerful role of giving "the women voice to recount their personal experiences" (1996, p. 259).

Fairclough (2003) also raises the issue of selectivity and purpose in news stories genres (news, reportages [see Bonini, this volume], media personal accounts, profiles, etc.). Journalists, while composing media genres, include some things and exclude others (which means the inclusion/exclusion of certain voices), selecting and editing what was said by "real" life informants. In terms of purpose, basically news stories genres aim at telling people about things that have taken place in the world, but, if we consider the relationship between the areas of news media, politics, economics, and so forth, we could argue that news media is part of the apparatus of governance, and therefore that their aims are not merely informative but also political.

Move II: Orientation—Resources used in the narrators' "self" representation

In the media personal accounts analysed in this article, the identification of the main narrator, or character (part of the *orientation* in Labov's model), is textualized in the quoted accounts that follow the leads, either through the use of the first-person pronoun (**I**), through its ellipsis (**Ø**), or through other first-person references (**me, myself, mine, my**):

(6) **I** have danced ballet since I was four years old and during adolescence I began to consider myself fat. When **I** turned 23, I was far from my ideal weight. **My** self-esteem went down, my clothes didn't look good, and I

began to get mad at any little thing. . . . Last April **I** got engaged and we decided to get married next year. **I** started to analyze **my** situation and Ø realized that **I** couldn't get married with this body. ("My diary—your story with the scalpel," *Plastic Surgery&Beauty*, Nov. 2006, p. 42)

(7) Before thinking about changing **my** appearance, **I** used to eat anything. ("Celebrity Cosmetic Surgery—the secret for a perfect shape," *Plastic Surgery&Beauty*, Nov. 2006, p. 44)

(8) **I** am a Libra like *Cláudia*. When you read this anniversary edition, **I** will be enjoying the big present I gave **myself** for **my** 39th birthday: new boobs. ("Silicon Diary," *Claudia*, Oct. 2006, p. 202)

Since the theme of each of these media personal accounts is the main character's discontentment with her body shape, her representation requires a description of physical traits. This form of representation is what van Leeuwen calls *"physical identification,"* which depicts social actors "in terms of physical characteristics which uniquely identify them in a given context. It can be realized by nouns denoting physical characteristics . . . or by adjectives . . . or by prepositional phrases . . . ." (1996, p. 57). This is how the narrators supposedly described themselves physically:

(9) . . . during adolescence I began to consider myself **fat**. When I turned 23, I was **far from my ideal weight** . . . . ("My diary—your story with the scalpel," *Plastic Surgery&Beauty*, Nov. 2006, p. 42)

(10) But when I got the invitation from the [Cristal soap opera] production team, I started to worry about my **projecting tummy**. ("Celebrity Cosmetic Surgery—the secret for a perfect shape," *Plastic Surgery&Beauty*, Nov. 2006, p. 44)

(11) But, as my best friend said, what's the good of spending a week in Salvador with **a flat chest**? [But] after losing weight, **the little [breasts]** I had disappeared, and I started missing them, especially in summer. ("Silicon Diary," *Claudia*, Oct. 2006, p. 202)

Different from other forms of role allocation, physical identification is always overdetermined. In the excerpts above, this overdetermination is always negative, creating the image of the narrator's dissatisfaction with at least some aspect of her body shape. Van Leeuwen argues that "physical attributes tend to have connotations, and these can be used to obliquely classify or functionalise social actors" (1996, p. 58). The physical attributes focused on in the excerpts above legitimize and reinforce the hegemonic feminine model of the slim, fit and curvaceous body. In the excerpts, the women's bodies are fragmented, and some of their parts (the belly, the hips, the breasts) are given focal status as a part that epitomizes the ideal of female beauty and physical attractiveness: a flat belly, curvaceous hips (examples 9 and 10) and large, firm (or at least clearly visible) breasts (example 11). The use of physical identification is never neutral in the representation of social actors, and it can be used, as in *Claudia* and *Plastic Surgery&Beauty*'s media personal accounts of CPS, to focus the reader's attention on selected physical traits that objectify the narrators as sexual commodities. As van Leeuwen points out, "even when used for the purposes of classification, the category of physical identification remains distinct, because of its obliqueness, its overdetermination, and its apparent 'empirical innocence'" (1996, p. 58).

In the accounts analysed, most of the elements of the orientation move (the participants and the circumstances) follow the linear pattern of narrative genres, coming after the abstract and before the complicating action (Labov, 1972). Besides being described in terms of their physical traits, as we have seen above, another resource used by the narrators to refer to themselves is the representation of people around them. The women narrators, apart from the description of their bodies, are also identified through their relations with social actors from the private and the public spheres of their lives: friends, fiancé, husband, children, work colleagues, boss:

(12) Last April **I got engaged** and **we decided** to get married next year. I started to analyse my situation and Ø realized that **I couldn't get married with this body.** ("My diary—your story with the scalpel," *Plastic Surgery&Beauty*, Nov. 2006, p. 42)

(13) But when I got the invitation from **the [Cristal soap opera] production team**, I started to worry about my projecting tummy. ("Celebrity Cosmetic Surgery—the secret for a perfect shape," *Plastic Surgery&Beauty*, Nov. 2006, p. 44)

(14) I remember the first time that, half kidding, I talked to **my husband** [about the breast enlargement operation]. **Ricardo** gave me a big smile and surprised me with a nice "and why not?" If I had one motive, he **had** ulterior ones. . . . After that I could swear that every time **Ricardo** looked at me he saw a small sign saying: "Soon playground here." ("Silicon Diary," *Claudia*, Oct. 2006, p. 202)

(15) Talking about that, I still had to break the news [the decision to undergo a breast enlargement operation] to **two small men: my 10- and 6-year-old sons**. ("Silicon Diary," *Claudia*, Oct. 2006, p. 202)

The excerpts above are examples of "relational identification," usually possessivated, which "represents social actors in terms of their personal, kinship or work relations" (van Leeuwen 1996, p. 56). Husband, children, friends, colleagues are included but are referred to generically, through the use of a pronoun or article + general word (*the production team, my sons*). Only in one case is the husband identified (*Ricardo*—example 16). The main thing seems to be these social actors' relations to the narrators, and the way the narrators relate to their own bodies. The use of relational identification indicates that, even though the first-person female narrators are nominated and functionalized (their full names and professions are given), their social relations are also a central aspect of their identities, especially in what concerns their body shape, since it is through the impact of their images on others, through the gaze of the Other (especially a male Other) over their bodies, that they construct their self-identities. As Hall puts it, identities "have to do not so much with the questions 'who we are' or 'where we came from,' but much more with the questions 'who we can become,' 'how we have been represented,' and 'how this representation affects the way we can represent ourselves'" (1996, pp. 111-112). Notice that, in all of the examples above, the reactions of the social actors who surround the narrator (both privately and publicly) seem to have been essential in their decision to undertake a CPS, either as sources of encouragement and stimulation (*Ricardo gave me a big smile and surprised me with a nice "and why not?"*) or as representatives of the outside, hegemonic gaze that helps to shape and establish, even for the narrators themselves, the ideal of feminine beauty and bodily attraction (*I couldn't get married with this body; I could swear that every time Ricardo looked at me he saw a small sign saying: "Soon playground here"*).

The narrators also represented themselves in terms of their relations to the doctors who operated on them:

(16) I went to **a specialist in Aesthetic Medicine, Dr. Eliomar Jayme (RJ)** and I did a hydro-liposuction to remove some extra fat from my sides and abdomen. ("Celebrity Cosmetic Surgery—the secret for a perfect shape," *Plastic Surgery&Beauty*, Nov. 2006, p. 44)

(17) I went to **a plastic surgeon** and I liked him straight away . . . . ("My diary—your story with the scalpel," *Plastic Surgery&Beauty*, Nov. 2006, p. 42)

(18) Ah, the first appointment. Through the indication of a great friend, I already liked **the doctor** even before meeting her. But I didn't count on getting nervous . . . . Besides **a plastic surgeon and mastologist**, what did I expect? That she would be a psychologist too? Even though I loved her, I wanted to hear a second opinion. [I went to] another **surgeon, highly recommended, very competent** and . . . did he have to be so attractive too? ("Silicon Diary," *Claudia*, Oct. 2006, p. 202)

Only in one of the texts is the doctor nominated and functionalized (*a specialist in Aesthetic Medicine, Dr. Eliomar Jayme (RJ)*). In the other accounts the doctors are only functionalized (*a plastic surgeon; the doctor; a plastic surgeon and mastologist; another surgeon, highly recommended, very competent*), which indicates that these narratives do not aim at advertising the work of particular doctors, but rather at legitimizing the practice of CPS as a positive way of dealing with dissatisfactions with body shape, and of emphasizing the need to make use of the services provided by the experts in this area (plastic surgeons, specialists in aesthetic medicine, mastologists, etc.).

Move III: Complicating Action

The media personal accounts analysed in this article follow the formulaic pattern of beginning with a situation seen as problematic by the narrator (Hoey, 1979, 1983), corresponding to the Labovian move of *orientation*:

(19) I have danced ballet since I was four years old and during adolescence **I began to consider myself fat.** When I turned 23, **I was far from my ideal weight. My self-esteem went down, my clothes didn't look good, and I began to get mad at any little thing.** . . . Last April I got engaged and we decided to get married next year. **I started to analyze my situation and Ø realized that I couldn't get married with this body.** ("My diary—your story with the scalpel," *Plastic Surgery&Beauty*, Nov. 2006, p. 42)

(20) Before thinking about changing my appearance, I used to eat anything. But when I got the invitation from the [Cristal soap opera] production team, **I started to worry about my projecting tummy. As I had little time until the beginning of the shootings, there was no point in going to the gym because *the problem* wouldn't disappear overnight**" ("Celebrity Cosmetic Surgery—the secret for a perfect shape," *Plastic Surgery&Beauty*, Nov. 2006, p. 44)

(21) I am a Libra like *Cláudia*. When you read this anniversary edition, I will be enjoying the big present I gave myself for my 39th birthday: new boobs. Yes, I could have chosen a dress, a stock market, a trip. **But, as my best friend said, what's the good of spending a week in Salvador with a flat chest?** . . . . **after losing weight, the little [breasts] I had disappeared, and I started missing them, especially in summer. To use a metaphor, it was like redecorating the whole house and leaving a little corner out.** ("Silicon Diary," *Claudia*, Oct. 2006, p. 202)

The "problem" is always related to the fact that the narrator's figure did not conform, before the CPS, to the hegemonic model of the slim and curvaceous body. Notice that there are several clause-internal evaluative markers (Labov, 1972) dispersed through these "problematic" body situations, such as the use of epistemic modality coupled with the deictic intensifier "this" in example 19 (*I couldn't get married with this body*), the adjectives "*fat,*" "*far from my ideal weight,*" (example 19) and "*my projecting tummy*" (example 22), as well as a rhetorical question "*But, as my best friend said, what's the good of spending a week in Salvador with a flat chest?*" (example 21), which functions as an explanation and justification of why this narrator chose new "boobs" as a birthday present instead of a holiday trip. In example 21 the narrator also presents, along with the problem situation, the solution and its "positive" evaluation: the silicone implant that solved her lack of breasts—"*When you read this anniversary edition, I will be enjoying the big present I gave myself for my 39th birthday: new boobs.*"

The presentation of the problem is followed by the move complicating action (*Then what happened?*), which is the essence of the narrative (Labov, 1972). The problematic situation described by the narrators (their unhappiness with some aspect of their body shape) is dealt with through a series of actions:

(22) **I decided** to **do a liposuction on my abdomen and sides** to get faster and more efficient results. **I went to a plastic surgeon** and liked him immediately. . . . **I cleared all my doubts** before the surgery and **waited** for the day of the operation. . . . **I had no regrets** whatsoever. ("My diary—your story with the scalpel," *Plastic Surgery&Beauty*, Nov. 2006, p. 42)

(23) **I went to a specialist** in Aesthetic Medicine, Dr. Eliomar Jayme (RJ) and **I did a hydro-liposuction** to remove some extra fat from my sides and abdomen. ("Celebrity Cosmetic Surgery—the secret for a perfect

shape," *Plastic Surgery&Beauty*, Nov. 2006, p. 44)

(24) Surfing the web, **I discovered an array of possibilities**. . . . **I took that information in** and my brain gently transformed it into generous cleavages, tank tops, backless shirts. . . . **I decided to surrender myself to the scalpel** . . . . Oh, the first appointment. . . . The only thing I didn't expect was being nervous. . . . Finally the day arrived and **I was calm**. The surgery lasted less than two hours and **I went back home on the same day**. ("Silicon Diary," *Claudia*, Oct. 2006, p. 202)

In these actions the narrators represented themselves as "the active, dynamic forces in the activity," what van Leeuwen calls "*activation.*" In the excerpts above the narrator represents herself as actor in material processes (*I did a hydro-liposuction, I went to a plastic surgeon, I waited, I went back home*), sensor in mental processes (*I decided to do a liposuction, I cleared all my doubts, I had no regrets, I discovered an array of possibilities, I took that information in, I decided to surrender myself to the scalpel*), and carrier in a relational process (*I was calm*) (for more on the system of transitivity, see Halliday, 2004). Even though the narrators are actors of material processes, in semantic terms some of these processes are in fact carried out by other people, not by the narrator herself (such as in "*do a hydro-liposuction*" and even "*go to a plastic surgeon*"). In both these cases, the doctor is in fact the one who, once chosen by the patient, provides information on CPS and actually performs the operation. The mental processes (*I decided to do a liposuction, I decided to surrender myself to the scalpel, I discovered an array of possibilities, I took that information in*) seem to indicate that, even though the first-person narrator is the agent of these actions, they do not describe concrete actions in the "real" world, rather they represent a "master narrative" the narrator constructs for herself, a series of mental decisions that precede the surgical intervention and which have to do with how the narrator sees herself and wishes to be seen by others. These mental processes, coupled with the material processes which are in fact performed by others upon the narrators, represent the identity projected for each of these narrators: a woman who is concerned with her body shape, who concludes that her body is not "adequate" and, consequently, gives her body up into the hands of professionals (e.g., plastic surgeons) who can "correct," re-shape and align it with the hegemonic model of female beauty. In short, the first-person narrators construe themselves (or are construed) semiotically and symbolically, while others construct (or re-construct) them physically.

Move IV: Evaluation

Evaluation is a very important element in any type of narrative genre. From a critical perspective, the evaluative elements in narrative genres are extremely important because it is mainly through them that the narrator will express her ideological stance(s) towards the story she is recounting.

In the exemplars of media personal accounts analyzed here, all three narrators positively evaluate the surgical procedure they underwent:

(25) **The operation was great and I didn't feel any discomfort. I'm extremely happy** and anxious for the bikini test since this will be my first summer with my new silhouette! ("My diary—your story with the scalpel," *Plastic Surgery&Beauty*, Nov. 2006, p. 42)

(26) **To maintain the results,** I do sessions of lymphatic draining, in addition to modeling massage, endermology and carboxitherapy at the Vitalitá Clinic (SP). Besides, I work out an hour and a half everyday: I do the treadmill or spinning, yoga or Pilates. And my diet has changed completely! My meals are rich in salads, vegetables and fruit. **After my full recovery and as soon as I find some free time, I intend to have a breast enlargement surgery** ("Celebrity Cosmetic Surgery—the secret for a perfect shape," *Plastic Surgery&Beauty*, Nov. 2006, p. 44)

(27) It didn't hurt a bit. Of course the first thing I did when I woke up was to take a pip [at the breasts] in the recovery room . . . . **The difference was visible.** . . . I was only introduced officially to my new breasts 24 hours later, when I returned to take out the drain. When I opened the bra, they jumped out, happy and exultant. **Nice to meet you! And the pleasure was all mine** . . . . **Weighing everything, it was worth it. It's like having recovered something that was mine by right.** ("Silicon Diary," *Claudia*, Oct. 2006, p. 202)

The narrators talk about happiness and increased self-esteem after their bodies were better aligned with the thin and curvaceous hegemonic model. It is worth noticing the notion that a beautiful and attractive body is construed as a "right" of the female gender, as we can see in example 27 (*"It's like having recovered something that was mine by right"*). Also worthy of notice is the way this same narrator indicates that the gaze of the Other (usually Man) is an important measure of female beauty and value (*"I found out that size does matter"*): the premise here is that, to be beautiful and attractive, women have to be seen, and to be seen they have to possess the "right" physical proportions in the "right" places—curvaceous hips, small waist, large and firm breasts. Even the physical pain and discomfort of a CPS is represented as a small price to pay for this new and beautiful body form:

(28) **On the following day it felt like I had been hit by a truck. But I had no regrets whatsoever. I kept imagining the results. The first three days were the most difficult because the body is in a process of recovery. After that, you learn to move in such a way that you don't feel pain during your daily physical activities and everything gets better** ("My diary—your story with the scalpel," *Plastic Surgery&Beauty*, Nov. 2006, p. 42)

The new body is always measured against the old, as we can see below:

(29) **How nice to compare my before and after photos**! Mimicking that classic male concern, I found out that **size does matter**. ("Silicon Diary," *Claudia*, Oct. 2006, p. 202)

In certain cases, the verbal account is coupled with and strengthened by the combination of verbal and visual resources used to compare and contrast the "before" and "after" of CPS, as example 30 illustrates.

The evaluative utterances presented by the first-person narrators represent what Labov calls "external evaluation." In external evaluations "the narrator breaks the frame of the report to address the reader directly and interrupts the actions to express her general evaluation of the distant events" (Labov, 1992, p. 366). The lexical items chosen by these narrators are part of two lexical fields: a field of discontentment with their body form previous to the CPS (expressed by words such as *"fat," "far from my ideal weight," "projecting tummy," "flat chest"*), and a field of satisfaction, happiness and increased self-esteem after the surgical procedure (textualized through expressions such as *"the operation was great," "[no] discomfort," "extremely happy," "visible difference," "pleasure," "nice"*).

In these narratives evaluation is expressed not only by the women who actually underwent the CPSs, but also by the journalist in charge of the section. The title itself of one of the sections functions as a positive evaluation of CPS:

(31) *Celebrity Cosmetic Surgery—the secret for a perfect shape* (*Plastic Surgery&Beauty*, Nov. 2006, p. 44)

This title rests on two presupposed assumptions: first, that there is a pattern for the "perfect female figure" and that, because this imaginary figure is "perfect," every woman should aspire to it. Second, that CPS is the "secret" technique used by famous women to remain beautiful and sexy. Other examples of institutional evaluation of CPS present in the texts are:

EXAMPLE (30)

(32) **Glowing with the results of a liposuction** done three months ago, the dancer and manager Ana Carolina Mattos, 25 years old, **besides going down three numbers in her mannequin, reveals how she acquired the self-confidence she needed to change old habits** ("My diary—your story with the scalpel," *Plastic Surgery&Beauty*, Nov. 2006, p. 42)

(33) With humor and candidness, the advertiser and writer Magali Moraes tells **how life can change—in many senses—after an extra 225 millilitres in each breast.** ("Silicon Diary," *Claudia*, Oct. 2006, p. 202)

As we can see in examples 26 and 32 above, apart from promoting CPS as a way of achieving a "perfect figure," these media personal accounts also promote a series of other disciplinary techniques (physical exercises, dieting, cosmetic procedures, etc.) that, together with the CPS itself, are represented as legitimate ways to achieve and maintain the "perfect" body. In a nutshell, according to this genre, discipline (of habits, of body and of mind) is an integral and essential part of being a beautiful and attractive woman.

CONCLUDING REMARKS

In the cases of CPS addressed by the genre media personal accounts analysed in this paper, the narrators are nominated, functionalized and identified through the use of their full names and professions, which help to place them in recognizable social spaces. The professional glossing also seems to attach these narrators to the public rather than to the private world. This media genre seems to attempt to be more "realistic" and less fictionalized than other media narratives presented as part of larger reportages—e.g., as in Caldas-Coulthard's (1996) study of narratives of sex published by *Marie Claire*.

However, even though these first-person narrators are represented as professional women who occupy spaces in the public world, their physical appearance is seen as an important measure of their social worth. Their decision to undergo a cosmetic plastic surgery is also grounded on their relations to other social actors, such as partners, friends, colleagues and employers, who seem to function, to these narrators, both as a way of identifying themselves in terms of their network of social relations, and as sources of encouragement and rewards for making every possible effort to fit into the hegemonic model of female beauty and sex appeal.

Even though the genre organization of media personal accounts could allow different approaches to a certain issue (e.g., CPS), the exemplars analysed here are evidence that this genre is used to promote hegemonic models of female identity in women's magazines. The organization of media personal accounts, leading from a negative physical description of the narrators to their decision to undergo a CPS to a final positive evaluation of the results of such procedures, indicates that we are trained, through mechanisms of manipulation and control of media information, to distinguish between what can be thought and said in terms of our bodies and our identities, what should be silenced and excluded, and how to say what is socially acceptable, how to define/explain/understand ourselves and the world.

REFERENCES

Bamberg, M. G. W. (Ed.). (1997). Oral versions of personal experience: Three decades of narrative analysis [Special issue]. *Journal of Narrative and Life History*,

7(1-4).

Bonini, A. (2001). Ensino de gêneros textuais: A questão das escolhas teórica e metodológica. *Trabalhos em Lingüística Aplicada, 37,* 7-23.

Bruner, J. (1990). *Acts of meaning.* Cambridge, Massachusetts: Harvard University Press.

Bruner, J. (2004). Life as narrative. *Social Research,* 71(3).

Caldas-Coulthard, C. R. (1996). "Women who pay for sex. And enjoy it." Transgression versus morality in women's magazines. In C. R Caldas-Coulthard & M. Coulthard (Eds.), *Texts and practices: Readings in critical discourse analysis.* London: Routledge.

Duranti, A. (1986). The audience as co-author: An introduction. *Text,* 6, 239-47.

Fabrício, B. F. (2006). Narrativização da experiência: O triunfo da ordem sobre o acaso. In I. Magalhães, M. J. Coracini, & M. Grigoletto (Eds.), *Práticas Identitárias: Língua e Discurso.* São Carlos, São Paulo, Brazil: Claraluz.

Fairclough, N. (1992). *Discourse and social change.* Cambridge: Polity Press.

Fairclough, N. (2003). *Analysing discourse: Textual analysis for social research.* London: Routlege.

Fairclough, N. (2006). *Language and globalization.* London: Routledge.

Figueiredo, D.C. (2008). Identidades corporificadas nos discursos midiáticos pós-modernos: os discursos sobre o emagrecimento e a cirurgia plástica. In Matzenauer, C.L.B. et. al (Orgs), *Estudos da linguagem—VII Círculo de Estudos Lingüísticos do Sul.* Pelotas: Educat.

Habermas, J. (1984). *Theory of communicative action, vol. 1.* London: Heinemann.

Hall, S. (1996). Who needs identity? In S. Hall & P. Du Gay (Eds.), *Questions of identity.* London: Sage.

Hoey, M. P. (1979). *Signalling in discourse.* (Discourse Analysis Monographs No. 6). Birmingham, United Kingdom: University of Birmingham, English Language Research.

Hoey, M. P. (1983). *On the surface of discourse.* London: Allen & Unwin.

Labov, W. (1972). *Language in the inner city.* University Park: University of Pennsylvania Press.

Labov, W., & Waletsky, J. (1967). Narrative analysis: Oral versions of personal experience. In J. Helm (Ed.), *Essays on the verbal and visual arts.* Seattle: University of Washington Press.

Meurer, J. L. (2002). Reflexões sobre o ensino: Três perguntas não mistificadoras que você pode aplicar aos textos que traz para a sala de aula. In M. J. D Costa, M. E. Zipser, M. Zanatta, & A. Mendes (Orgs.), *Línguas: ensino e ações.* Florianópolis, Santa Catarina, Brazil: Editora da UFSC.

Mishler, E. (1999). *Storylines: Craftartists' narratives of identity.* Cambridge, Massachusetts: Harvard University Press.

Moita Lopes, L.P. (1998) Discursos de identidade em sala de aula de leitura de

L1: A construção da diferença. In I. Signorini (Org.), *Lingua(gem) e identidade*. Campinas, São Paulo, Brazil: Mercado de Letras.

Moita Lopes, L. P. (1999) Perceptions of language in L1 and L2 teacher-pupil interaction: The construction of readers' social identities. In C. Schaffner & A. Wenden (Eds.), *Language and peace*. Amsterdam: Harwood Academic Publishers.

Moita Lopes, L. P. (2001). Práticas narrativas como espaço de construção das identidades sociais: uma abordagem socioconstrucionista. In B. T. Ribeiro, C. C. Lima, & M. T. L. Dantas (Eds.), *Narrativa, identidade e clínica*. Rio de Janeiro: Edições IPUB-CUCA.

Norrick, N. R. (1997). Twice-told tales: Collaborative narration of familiar stories. *Language in Society*, *26*(2), 199-220.

Paltridge, B. (1996). Genre, text type, and all the language learning classroom. *ELT Journal*, *50*(3), 237-243.

Schiffrin, D. (1984). How a story says what it means and does. *Text*, *4*(4), 313-346.

Schiffrin, D. (1996). Narrative as self-portrait: sociolinguistic constructions of identity. *Language and Society Processes*, *25*(2), 167-203.

Segal, J. (2007). Breast cancer narratives as public rhetoric: Genre itself and the maintenance of ignorance. *Linguistics and the Human Sciences, 3*(1), 3-23.

Sousa (2003). Resistir, a que será que se resiste? O sujeito fora de si [Special issue]. *Linguagem em (Dis)curso, 3*, 37-54.

Swales, J. M. (1990). *Genre analysis: English in academic and research settings*. Cambridge: Cambridge University Pres.

Van Leeuwen, T. (1996). The representation of social actors. In C. R Caldas-Coulthard & M. Coulthard (Eds.), *Texts and practices: Readings in critical discourse analysis*. London: Routledge.

Woodward, K. (1997). Introduction. In K. Woodward (Ed.), *Identity and difference*. London: Sage.

GENRE IN TEACHING AND LEARNING

14 Genre and Cognitive Development: Beyond Writing to Learn

Charles Bazerman

As writers we all have had the experience of coming to a new perspective, seeing things differently, as the result of having written a paper, a report, an application or other text that has forced us to put together in a new way facts or ideas we previously have known. We are also aware that at times when we take on the task of writing a specific text our attention is engaged and focused until such time as we consider the problem of writing the paper solved—that is we find our thoughts sufficiently so that writing poses no new significant problems for us. When we emerge from these writing episodes we have solved problems novel for us, had thoughts new to us, and developed perspectives we may not have had before.

In these episodes the basic task we have taken on may have been quite familiar and no new fact may have come to our attention, yet at least the reconfiguration of the familiar helped us put the pieces in a new relation and think new thoughts. The autobiography and personal diary are widely recognized as creating new perspectives on the relations and events in our lives. Even such a mundane task as making a TO DO list can help us look more deeply and coherently at our activities and commitments.

Similarly, when we have gathered new facts or look more closely at texts, writing can help us move to a new stage of thinking. Sometimes, of course, we just learn new details from this exercise without changing our way of viewing things. Yet a fact or detail we gather in the process may help us see things in a different light—this addition changes the landscape in a significant way. Our old way of seeing things does not hold all the pieces together, and we have to do some fresh thinking and revisioning in reorganizing the big picture.

At every stage of my writing life, I know I struggled to write some texts—in middle school, in high school, as an undergraduate, as a graduate, and now as a published scholar. If pressed at the time of writing I could explain the coherence of the paper in a micro or mechanical way—for that was the way I was able to keep from drowning in material I was barely able to bring together. But I was not really sure what it all added up to; it wasn't until later—a week later, a month later, years later—that some observation reminded me of the essay, and I had the sense that now I understood what I had written earlier. Not only am I learning as I write, I learn from what I have written as the formulations I made rattle around in my mind and change the way I look at things afterward. It is that new way of looking which then reveals to me a deeper sense of what I had in fact been struggling to say. In the doctoral students I have supervised, as well, I have seen how the challenging work of the dissertation has that intellectually transformative effect.

As teachers we regularly work with this phenomenon. We notice when an assignment seems to bring out a higher level of thinking than we expect from a particular student. In fact we may design our writing assignments precisely to put students in a position where they need to combine information and ideas in ways new to them, or which requires them to consider issues from an unfamiliar stance. Although students somehow find ways to fulfill the letter and not the spirit of assignments, if we have guessed right about what the next step students were ready to take, we can create an occasion for intellectual growth for some students who get what the assignment is about.

WRITING TO LEARN

This phenomenon of cognitive refiguration stands behind much of the intuitive appeal of the Writing to Learn (WTL) movement, an enthusiasm that reaches beyond recognition that writing can serve more modest roles in learning through articulating understanding and rehearsing material to fix it in memory. We can find many allusions to the more dramatic cognitive impact of writing in the foundational literature in writing process (such as Emig, 1971, 1977) and Writing Across the Curriculum (Britton 1970). Yet when Durst and Newell (1989) looked at the prior research literature on WTL, they found attention directed toward more basic memory-focused forms of learning through rehearsal, consolidation and retention of material in note-taking, review questioning and summarizing. This memory-focused writing to learn was evidenced by improved performance on content examinations. The few studies that examine more ambitious forms of learning (Newell, 1984; Newell & Winograd, 1989) take a very broad approach contrasting the connective and global planning aspects of essay writing with memory enhancement from note-taking. Bereiter and Scardamelia's (1987) findings about growth in student writing strategies from knowledge telling to knowledge transforming also point in the same direction. Langer and Applebee (1987) move one step further in noting that different kinds of writing activity lead students to focus on different information. The idea that the kind of writing you did mattered was further substantiated by Cooper and MacDonald (1992) who noted that students who kept academic journals framed by academic questions performed better on their essays than students who wrote dialogic response journals or wrote no journals. Ackermann (1993), in reviewing studies until then found that studies in total were inconclusive with no robust learning gains running across all studies, suggested that it was not simply the act of writing that lead to learning. Rather the great variation in the results of the studies, which employed many different writing tasks in many different situations, suggested that learning through writing was a matter of task and genre choice under appropriate conditions. Discipline and genre specific applications have continued to flourish as teachers have found them useful to foster discipline specific learning and thought development (Bazerman et al., 2005). Boscolo and Mason (2001), in a particularly interesting study, provide evidence of how engagement with writing deepens conceptual understanding within subject matter and which transfers to other subject areas. The volume in which this study appears (Tynjala, Mason, & Lonka, 2001) contains several other studies that provide other evidence of higher cognitive development through writing.

Klein (1999) examines the WTL literature to sort out suggested mechanisms by which writing might affect learning and examines the published data that might support each. He focuses attention not so much on the character of the produced text as on the practices that are engaged as one produces the text—that is he looks at cognitive mechanisms engaged in the writing process. He clusters the mechanisms suggested in previous literature in four groups:

- versions of Britton's "shaping at the point of utterance" that find cognitive gain in the act of formulating and transcribing text;
- forward search hypotheses, placing emphasis on how the externalized text supports review and reformulation;
- genre-related hypotheses, focusing on how genres require the writer to search for and organize knowledge, to link ideas, to structure relationships with audiences, and to create stances toward material;
- backward search hypotheses, concerning the elaboration and structuring of text to be able to be intelligible by others at a distance (what some in an oversimplification call the decontextualization of text, obscuring the new contexts mediated by texts).

He finds some evidence for each, but generally finds them under-investigated, with genre hypotheses being the most tested and supported to that date. I point out that the genre distinctions in that literature, which I have also reviewed above, are rather general and form based. They are not tied to activities beyond generalized classroom practice—such as journals, study questions, and essays. The effects seem to be associated with the specific nature of tasks, with study questions leading to increased recall and essays associated with connecting ideas (see also Newell, 2006; McCutcheon, 2007). This pattern is reminiscent of Scribner and Cole's (1981) finding that the cognitive effects of literacy were varied and tied to the institutionally embedded practices which literacy was used for. Looking at cognitive practices in different forms of writing means considering writing processes as multiple and varied, depending not just on personal characteristics of the writer but on the genre, situation, and social activity system within which the writing is taking place and which support the writing in various ways. For example, though there may be variation among the writing processes of students writing an impromptu essay in their class, that same group of students will engage a different set of processes when they are at work on the student newspaper, and a different set of processes when they are filling out forms the next morning in the registrar's office. Even within the individual variations of students in each situation, there will be commonalities of most students in the situation that will contrast with the commonalities of the other situations. (Newell (2006) in reviewing the WTL literature follows this path in pointing toward the necessity of studying writing within disciplinary cultures in the K-12 settings, as I had begun examining in higher education settings in 1981.)

Klein notes that all four cognitive hypotheses he finds in the writing to learn literature are on a spectrum of problem solving around producing, planning, reflecting on, and structuring text—and thus are not mutually exclusive nor fully independent. I would point out, further, that the specific situations and associated genres would influence planning, structuring, reviewing, and audience accommodation, so that perception of a situation and a genre decision might affect them all. In a related study of students in grades 4, 6 and 8 writing about a science experiment, Klein (2000) found elements of all four kinds of cognitive mechanisms contributing to learning among various students, but he also noted that the mechanisms required various depths of compositional knowledge to be put into effect, with shaping at the point of utterance requiring the least, and genre and text structuring requiring the most. While much evidence suggests that emergent writers early on exhibit some genre knowledge (Donovan & Smolkin, 2006; Sandbank, 2001), Klein's finding suggests a possibility that a more explicit knowledge of genre and text structuring may incorporate, reframe, and direct the other kinds of cognitive activity triggered by writing that may affect learning—in an instance of sublation or *aufhebung* which we will discuss below.

Bangert-Drowns, Hurley, & Wilkinson (2004) in a metanalysis of 48 WTL studies noted small but significant genre effects on writing to learn, as measured by conventional measures of academic achievement at all levels of education from elementary to higher education, with the exception of grades 6-8 where writing to learn tasks had a cumulative negative effect size. The authors speculate that the negative effect in middle school may have to do with the restructuring of education around separate subjects, and the introduction to differing forms of writing, so that the genre learning interfered with the learning of material through that genre. The authors also noted that frequent (two or three times a week), shorter (under ten minutes) assignments done over a longer period (a term or longer) had more positive effects than longer writing tasks, done less frequently, for a shorter period. While there was no attempt to consider the effect of particular genres, it was noted that prompts which had a metacognitive component, such as reflection on topics one was confused about, were associated with greater effect sizes. This again suggests the possibility that the cognitive task and practices associated with the production of genres may be related to their potential for supporting various forms of learning.

VYGOTSKY ON LEARNING AND DEVELOPMENT

In the remainder of this essay I want to lay out a theoretical view of how genre might interact with both learning and development, using a Vygotskian lens, considering genres as tools of cognition. The connection between Vygotskian socio-cognitive theory and genre theory has been implicit in almost all the work from the North American Genre theory perspective, and explicit in my work, although not always centrally foregrounded. Here I will lay out some of the reasoning more explicitly and coherently so as to suggest a renewed sociocognitive research program in writing to learn and as a heuristic for pedagogic practice.

To develop a more refined view of writing to learn and its relation to cognitive development it is first useful to consider more carefully one of the Vygotsky's core distinctions, between learning and development. While this distinction has not yet become part of the writing to learn discussion, one can see its shadow on the distinction between the effects of notetaking or study question writing and the effects of analytic essay writing.

Psychologists, educational researchers, and writing theorists have pursued Vygotsky's association of cognitive development with children learning cultural tools to regulate their activities and thoughts. Within the North American genre group interest in the historical emergence of these tools and their relation to a Hegelian history of consciousness has been combined in activity-based genre studies with Schutz's ideas about typification in the life world, pointing to the differentiation of modern activity systems and the associated cognition. Much of the research in writing in the disciplines and professions follows this perspective. But this literature has not yet made much of a distinction between learning and development, although Vygotsky in *Thought and Language* explicitly distinguishes between learning and development, arguing that learning leads development (Vygotsky, 1987).

Vygotsky's view contrasts with Piaget's, which treats development as a precondition to learning; development happens outside of learning, and makes learning possible as the learner is made ready to engage in new forms of learning. Development is not influenced by learning, but learning is not possible without development. From this perspective you might say writing to learn is precisely just writing to learn: an opportunity to identify, rehearse, organize and reinforce memory of new material. One must have all the developmental preconditions of writing, including physical ability to record letters, cognitive abilities to code and decode, and the characteristics of short and long term memory needed to write, in order to engage in WTL. Already having attained the appropriate intellectual level to carry out the WTL task, one would not particularly develop a new way of thought in the activity. One would only learn the content of the writing one was rehearsing, and connect it to other things of a similar sort one had already learned. At most, if one was at an appropriate developmental level to reflect on what one had written, one could become more aware of the cognitive processes one was engaged in, but this too would be a learning that one was already developmentally prepared to take part in. WTL studies of note taking and study questions would comfortably fit within this view.

Vygotsky's view also stands in contrast to views which treat learning and development as happening simultaneously, with development being just the accumulation of smaller acts of learning. From this perspective WTL would allow for the accumulation of knowledge as well as new skills of thinking introduced in relation to the assignment and practiced in fulfilling the assignment. This view does allow for intellectual growth through explicit teaching and practice, as one learns to carry out new cognitive tasks. This view, accordingly, does allow us to think of genres as sociocultural cognitive tools which can be transmitted to the student. This brings us part of the way to Vygotsky's views, but not entirely. For example, the research on analytic essay writing as a tool of WTL does measure cognitive change that occurs through the organization, synthesis, and stance taking that are part of this school genre, as revealed through standard school measures and text evaluation. Similarly (but in greater ethnographic detail linking situated activity with text production and text produced), research on writing in the disciplines, workplace, and community (such as the work of Swales & Najjar, 1987; Bazerman & Paradis, 1991; Medway, 1994, 1996; Dias et al., 1999; Swales, 1998; Smart, 1998; Beaufort, 2000; Bazerman & Russell, 2002) demonstrates learning of new forms of situated cognition by learning to write in the disciplinary, professional, and community genres.

Vygotsky's view, however, posits that learning prepares the learner for new stages of development, where at some point the learned material becomes more than the sum of its parts, but is rather added up, reorganized, and reintegrated at a different level, so it becomes seen in a different light. This enables reflection on knowledge, perception, and understanding from a new perspective.

Learned material and new stages of development can influence and restructure what one has previously learned in different ways and in different domains. A new functional system of knowledge and thought has developed within which parts take on new significance. This concept of reformulated functional systems may be seen as an instance of Hegel's *aufhebung* or sublation, where concepts are transformed by the appearance of a new conceptual term. Marx extends this to consider how the transformation in material conditions also transforms conceptual meanings, and changes in conceptual orientation in turn changes our perception and engagement with the material. For Vygotsky, Luria (1970), and others in this tradition, each new set of cognitive practices is learned through social interaction, moving by internalization from the interpersonal plane to the intrapersonal. These internalized social tools have the potential for refiguring prior engagements with the material and social worlds. The incorporation of the new tools integrates with and reformulates existing practices. That is, the new practice is first learned as a separate task to be mastered as an absorbing activity in itself, but as it becomes less of a focal challenge, it may interact with other tasks and practices. (Leontyev, 1979, reformulated this insight in distinguishing among activity, act, and operation.)

One consequence of this perspective is that development need not be seen only as a phenomenon of childhood, with adults fully developed with only new learning but no development ahead of them. In the Vygotskian view, development is possible whenever one enters new domains that offer pathways for restructuring and reintegration of thought. Even in pursuing a single domain one can develop as one gains access to higher levels of understanding, perception, and decisions. While these adult forms of development may be more scaffolded by the vocational, community, and recreational activities and structures rather than those of schooling, and thus offer a wider range of possibilities and greater engagement with the activities of the world, their mechanisms of cognitive reformulation are no different than that of children moving through the challenges of different levels of schooling and subject learning.

The most prominent example of how learning leads development in Vygotsky's work is his account of early language learning. In the earliest period of language learning, Vygotsky sees little impact of the language on preexisting cognition based on material relations with the world, although language learning does include a heightened and expanded relation to the world and expanded domains of shared attention with one's interlocutors. But this expansion is all interpersonal, part of the social relation of communicating and learning to communicate with the others around one. Gradually, however, the child starts to engage in private speech, echoing to oneself the community attentions and relations embedded in language interaction. This internalization leads the child to self-regulation of attention and action. At this moment individual cognition begins to change, with a new linguistically based, symbolic rationality developing in the child. Whereas previously the child's cognition was directly related to the material experience and relations to the world and others, now that relation begins to be mediated by the child's internalized symbolic repertoire—a repertoire that not only names the world, but regulates behavior and gives directions, takes stances, and makes plans. At this point language moves from simply a newly acquired but separate functional system—a means of communicating and interacting with others—into reconfiguring previously acquired functional systems. It remakes the old as something new, and one finds it increasingly hard to recover what it felt and thought like to live in a pre-linguistic world. This is a qualitative change in the nature of thought and perception, which we might call a developmental leap.

DEVELOPING A DISCIPLINED VIEW OF LANGUAGE

While the internalization of speech and its functional reorganization of consciousness around age three is perhaps the most dramatic and foundational of the transformations, turning us into deeply symbolic and linguistic creatures, these transformations may continue to occur in smaller, more local ways that are nonetheless consequential throughout our life. One such example occurs in every one of us that has become a professional language instructor or researcher at the point at which we learn the formulations of prescriptive grammar, language structure, rhetorical analysis, genre analysis, or whatever techne of language that brought us from a direct expressive sense of language to a technical one. At first we learn these technes in our schooling somewhat cumbersomely in interaction, with scaffolded definition, identification, application, and practical use. These themselves are embedded within particular genres of rules, explanations, textbooks, and school exercises. In pursuing these tasks and accomplishing the genres associated with assignments, students must engage in all four sorts of the cognitive mechanisms that Klein saw hypothesized in the literature: putting together of sentences about the material and ideas (shaping at the point of utterance); forward searching (examining what you have already accomplished to see how to extend it forward); genre based searching for relevant knowledge and bringing the knowledge together in patterned discourse; and backward searching to elaborate and organize the text to be comprehensible for others. At first these are carried out in a fairly contained learning practice, tied to an instructional situation.

At some point we can carry this mode of thought on our own outside of the support of classrooms and tutors, and we are able to struggle through homework, or we even remember the rules and concepts totally outside of school-centered activities. At some point these technical tools of language then start interacting with our own writing and even speaking practices, perhaps starting to flower in our secondary or tertiary education. We use these technes to solve our personal linguistic problems, and if we are ever stuck in mid-sentence we can remember the trace of a rule or bit of advice to carry us on. At some point we spontaneously note these technical matters everywhere as we come to see all the words of others not just as a bunch of directly communicated meanings, but a complex linguistic environment. Our perception of language has been transformed into a new functional system and we come to process our hearing and reading in a different way. While there may be moments that hail us back to our earlier more naïve stance towards language, for the most part we find it hard to remember what language felt like before we incorporated our technical sense of it. We notice and are frustrated when our students don't have that same relation to language that we do, not seeing it the way we want them to see it, not identifying language practices how we would like them to, not able to make language choices on the basis of the principles that now seem natural to us.

We have good evidence that direct instruction in prescriptive grammar and doing drill exercises or related practices such as labeling parts of speech and diagramming sentences does not translate into direct improvements in grammatical correctness in produced sentences in the short term—that is in close enough proximity to be measured without so much intervening complexity that we can make no association (Hillocks, 1986). Accordingly many, including myself, have diminished the role of direct grammatical instruction within writing pedagogy, and have come to rely on students' ability to create meaningful utterances and gradually expand them through modeling. Insofar as we teach grammar and syntax it tends to be *in situ*, in revision, in correction comments, or in individualized conference—that is at the point of practical need. Yet we still cannot fully wean ourselves and others from the belief that explicit knowledge of grammar and syntax is an important part of the writer's craft, as well as the editor's. As experienced writers we regularly use prescriptive grammatical knowledge to correct, revise and even produce sentences. We use morphological and syntactic abstractions to diagnose difficult sentences as well as to consider phrasing alternatives. We use prescriptive syntax to orient ourselves when we get lost in a tumble of phrases. As we become language experts, it even becomes part of our fundamental understanding of the system of language (although the grammars change and become intellectually more sophisticated). What is at first learned as a concrete set of literate practices is at first used only in the concrete practice of exercises. But at a certain point, for some, it integrates with our perception of sentences, our activities of revision, and construction of sentences. At this point it reshapes our perceptions of language and processes of making meaning. Yet, if we have not reached that point of sublation, the grammatical knowledge has little to do with composing. I frequently have had the experience of working in individual conference with fairly fluent writers, and when I ask them to think about a technical problem in the construction of the sentence or consider an alternative syntax, they respond only at the level of meaning: they say, "What I am trying to say is . . ." and then repeat the existing sentence. The meaning is tied to the phrasing, which cannot yet be seen as a technical construct to be manipulated for different meaning potentials, despite students' ability to complete grammar exercises correctly as a discrete practice.

Thus writing at the sentence and subsentence level goes through many transformations as we integrate new forms and levels of understanding of the texts we and others produce. What those transition moments are, what threshold of knowledge and internalization is necessary, what triggers the change—I leave as open questions. The point here is that learning concrete literate practices within the context of the genres of grammatical instruction—including rules, exercises, and diagrams—at first seems to have no transfer value into functional use in writing and revision. Later, however, these integrate with the meaning making aspects of writing to create a new functional system of writing. We may also say something similar happens with reflective understanding of other levels of composing, such as text structuring devices, genre expectations, audience and situation concerns, and activity consequences within larger social systems.

DEVELOPMENT OF DISCIPLINARY COGNITION

There are close parallels in this relation between technical vocabularies and deeper understanding in every field that names and taxonomizes fundamental parts. Learning the names of trees and their distinctive features only becomes part of creative thinking about botany and evolution after the scheme has become internalized, to reshape perception, which allows for fresh observation and fresh thought. Learning taxonomies through repeating, applying, or identifying taxonomic items, can be a kind of rote writing to learn. Yet the internal logics within the taxonomies and distinctions to be comprehended once it has internalized the parts provides the basis for a new disciplined way of seeing and thinking once one has internalized the system—so that one sees and thinks within the systematic relations of the system. Names of felines invoke not only the names of other felines, but distinctions from canines in characteristics and ways of life. They also invoke understandings of mammalian forms of life, relations to all other fauna and flora, as well as creating the potential for integrating concepts of ecology at some later date. We come to know these relations not just by the lexicon, but by the kinds of discourses within which these taxonomized terms and the objects they represent are discussed.

Beyond learning to read and reproduce the taxonomies, there are in most fields genres of identification, application, inquiry, analysis, synthesis, planning, and coordination using those terms and concepts embedded in the namings of the field. There are also genres that repeat, interpret, synthesize and deploy the collective literature of the field to communicate knowledge, address specific tasks, identify new findings, deal with conceptual struggles, and lay out collective research and action agendas. These genres do not begin to exhaust the kinds of tasks carried out by texts in the field, texts that at first are carried out with great struggle, but then become ways of expression, thinking, seeing, and ultimately remaking one's prior knowledge of the field and prior knowledge of the world. In this way one learns to think and act as a member of one's profession or discipline—internalizing a view of the world that pervades not only what one has learned and done in the field, but how one relates to others and the world.

Each field is different in its cognitive consequences, as you know when you have an informal conversation with a sociologist, or a lawyer, or a medical doctor. Each profession shapes a distinct view of the world that lends unique perspectives to the conversation. Each distinct professional perspective may not be fully transparent to other participants from other professions. As I started to hang out with sociologists for a while, at some point I began to see things more sociologically in a way that went beyond the formulas I learned in the first-year introductory course. And in talking to students I can start to notice who has some of that sociological vision and who does not, just as I can notice who has developed some sophistication about language. In doing work in language across the curriculum and in the disciplines, I have found some accomplished colleagues who have become very thoughtful about writing in their field, have read a lot in language as well as the sociology and history of science—they are articulate about their writing and how they mentor their students in writing, and approach those tasks in a self-conscious professional way. On the other hand I have found smart, accomplished colleagues in other disciplines who have little vocabulary for discussing writing beyond the corrective grammar they learned in high school. Although they have learned the genres of their profession and are successful in them, their reflective ability to manipulate them is limited because of a lack of linguistic and rhetorical vocabulary and analytical methods. Their fairly developed language practice has not been professionalized or transformed through internalizing those disciplinary knowledges which would provide them a more sophisticated stance. This patterned variation in cognition around the literate practices of disciplines and professions suggests how pervasive the effects of writing have been. The emergence of differentiated written genres within differentiated activity systems have shaped the practices of knowledge, thought, and reasoning in the world since the introduction of literacy five thousand years ago (Bazerman, 2006; Bazerman & Rogers, 2008a, 2008b).

Each domain of learning provides opportunities to learn in the genres of the classroom and profession through which we rehearse the typical objects, relations, and reasoning of the field. We then learn not just to talk but to learn the forms of attention and reasoning which the language points us toward. The words of the field become associated with practices and perceptions, changing our systems of operating within the world and writing others. These ways of being and seeing may then interact with other functional systems within us, transforming them as well. We may view the process of being socialized into a literate domain not just as a set of social learnings, but as a cognitive apprenticeship (Brown, Collins, & Duguid, 1989) with punctuated periods of marked development where the learnings become integrated with other existing or parallel developed functional systems to create new functional systems. The learnings are organized into the genres of presentation and practice, each requiring a particular repertoire of cognitive practices and work for their reception and production. The line of reasoning presented here perhaps can provide a means of specifying the various ideas that have aggregated around schema theory.

In this punctuated process, previous learning that developed around the spontaneous concepts of everyday life (as Vygotsky described them) becomes reorganized and reintegrated within "scientific concepts," as Vygotsky called them, that are introduced and practiced through the genres of schooling, disciplines, and professions. This development of new ways of thinking, of approaching experience, of adopting new stances and engaging new experiences occurs within culturally and institutionally shaped Zones of Proximal Development (ZPD) (*not* Zones of Proximal Learning) that Vygotsky identified (Vygotsky, 1978). These ZPDs occur in the collaborative participation of typified activities and discursive forms familiar to the instructor, adult or more skilled peer, but at which the learner is not yet adept. No doubt that interaction with peers or others may lead to spontaneous learning and formulation, but it appears that Vygotsky had in mind these more structured interactions built around discursive activities familiar to one of the participants. In this ZPD the learner becomes familiar with the orientations, language, and practices in the domain, which at some point become familiar enough and internalized enough that they can be integrated into perception, thought, and activity, as well as the reformulation of capacities already developed. This developmental process is deeply tied to creating reflective structures of understanding, perception, and action, and thus self-regulation.

This Hegelian understanding of development, with a new synthesis reformulating earlier material within a new functional system, helps us understand the familiar experience of writers, that writing helps them reorganize their thoughts and reintegrate their knowledge into a more comprehensive picture. Further, if we see these integration tasks as accomplished within the genres and activity systems of school, disciplinary, and professional work, we have the mechanism by which students develop into disciplined and disciplinary thinkers, learning how to locate and inscribe subject-relevant facts and data in ways appropriate to the schooled versions of the field and fitting the chronotope of the genres they are writing in (Bakhtin, 1982). Students learn how to produce the kinds of thoughts appropriate to the assigned genres, using the concepts and discursive tools expected in the genres, and they learn how to locate their findings, analysis, and thought within the communal project of academic learnings. Further, we find in integrative genres a mechanism by which fully socialized professionals develop the leading edge of the field, moving the field onto the next level of work, influencing both group cognition and the cognition of participating individuals. There is an interaction between learning to write in more advanced, new, or hybrid forms and cognitive growth for both individual and community or "thought collective" (Fleck, 1979).

In all these instances, whatever the level of cognitive activity required, genres identify a problem space for the developing writer to work in as well as provide the form of the solution the writer seeks and particular tools useful in the solution. Taking up the challenge of a genre casts you into the problem space and the typified structures and practices of the genre provide the means of solution. The greater the challenge of the solution, the greater the possibilities of cognitive growth occurring in the wake of the process of solution. Thus in school and in the professions the interaction between group and individual cognitive development can be seen as mediated by activity system-specific genres.

REFERENCES

Ackermann, J. M. (1993). The promise of writing to learn. *Written Communication, 10,* 334-370.

Bangert-Drowns, R. L., Hurley, M. M., & Wilkinson, B. (2004). The effects of school-based writing-to-learn interventions on academic achievement: A meta-analysis. *Review of Educational Research, 74,* 29-58.

Bakhtin, M. (1982). Forms of time and of the chronotope in the novel. In M. Bakhtin, *The dialogic imagination: Four essays* (M. Holquist & V. Liapunov, Eds., V. Liapunov & K. Brostrom, Trans.). Austin: University of Texas Press.

Bazerman, C. (1981). What written knowledge does: Three examples of academic discourse. *Philosophy of the Social Sciences 11*(3), 361-88.

Bazerman, C. (2006). The writing of social organization and the literate situating of cognition: Extending Goody's social implications of writing. In D. Olson & M. Cole, (Eds.), *Technology, literacy and the evolution of society: Implications of the work of Jack Goody.* Mahwah, New Jersey: Erlbaum.

Bazerman, C., Little, J., Chavkin, T., Fouquette, D., Bethel, L., & Garufis, J. (2005). *Writing across the curriculum.* Retrieved from Colorado State University, Reference Guides to Rhetoric and Composition, Parlor Press and WAC Clearinghouse: http://wac.colostate.edu/books/bazerman_wac/

Bazerman, C., & Paradis, J. (Eds). (1991). *Textual dynamics of the professions.* Madison: University of Wisconsin Press.

Bazerman, C., & Rogers, P. (2008a). Writing and secular knowledge. In C. Bazerman (Ed), *Handbook of research on writing.* Mahwah, New Jersey: Erlbaum.

Bazerman, C., & Rogers, P. (2008b). Writing and secular knowledge. In C. Bazerman (Ed.), *Handbook of research on writing.* Mahwah, New Jersey: Erlbaum.

Bazerman, C., & Russell, D. (Eds.). (2002). *Writing selves/writing society.* Retrieved from Colorado State University, WAC Clearinghouse: http://wac.colostate.edu/books/selves_society/

Beaufort, A. Learning the trade. *Written Communication 17*(2), 185-223.

Bereiter, C., & Scardamalia, M. (1987). *The psychology of written composition.* Hillsdale, New Jersey: Erlbaum.

Boscolo, P., & Mason, L. (2001) Writing to learn, writing to transfer. In P. Tynjala, L. Mason, & K. Lonka (Eds.), *Writing as a learning tool: Integrating theory and practice.* Dordrecht, The Netherlands: Kluwer Academic.

Britton, J. (1970). *Language and learning.* London: Penguin,

Britton, J., Burgess, T., Martin, N., McLeod, A., & Rosen, H. (1975). *School councils research studies: The development of writing abilities.* London: McMillan.

Brown, J. S., Collins, A., & Duguid, P. (1989). Situated cognition and the culture of learning. *Educational Researcher, 18,* 32-42.

Dias, P., Freedman, A., Medway, P., & Paré, P. A. (1999). *Worlds apart: Acting and writing in academic and workplace settings.* Mahwah, New Jersey: Erlbaum.

Donovan, C., & Smolkin, L. (2006). Children's understanding of genre and writing development. In C. A. MacArthur, S. Graham, & J. Fitzgerald (Eds.), *Handbook of writing research.* New York: Guilford Press.

Durst, R. K., & Newell, G. E. (1989). The uses of function: James Britton's category system and research on writing. *Review of Educational Research, 59*(4), 375-394.

Emig, J. (1977). Writing as a mode of learning. *College Composition and Communication, 28,* 122-128.

Fleck, L. (1979). *The genesis and development of a scientific fact.* Chicago: University of Chicago Press.

Hillocks, G. (1986). *Research on written composition.* Urbana, Illinois: National

Council of Teachers of English.

Klein, P. D. (1999). Reopening inquiry into cognitive processes in writing-to-learn. *Educational Psychology Review, 11*(3), 203-270.

Klein, P. D. (2000). Elementary students' strategies for writing-to-learn in science. *Cognition and Instruction, 18*(3), 317-348.

Langer, J., & Applebee, A. (1987). *How writing shapes thinking: A study of teaching and learning.* Urbana, Illinois: National Council of Teachers of English.

Leontyev, A. N. (1979). The problem of activity in psychology. In J. V. Wertsch (Ed.), *The concept of activity in Soviet psychology.* Armonk, New York: Sharpe.

Luria, A. R. (1970). The functional organization of the brain. *Scientific American, 222*(3), 66-78.

MacDonald, S. P., & Cooper, C. (1992). Contributions of academic and dialogic journals to writing about literature. In A. Herrington & C. Moran (Eds.), *Writing teaching and learning in the disciplines.* New York: MLA.

McCutcheon, D. (2008). Writing and cognition: Implications of the cognitive architecture for learning to write and writing to learn. In C. Bazerman (Ed.), *Handbook of research on writing.* Mahwah, New Jersey: Erlbaum.

Medway, P. (1994). The language component in technological capability: Lessons from architecture. *Journal,* 85-107

Medway, P. (1996). Virtual and material buildings: construction and constructivism in architecture and writing. *Written Communication, 13*(4), 473-514.

Newell, G. E. (1984). Learning from writing in two content areas: A case study/protocol analysis. *Research in the Teaching of English, 18,* 265-287.

Newell, G. E. (2006). Writing to learn: How alternative theories of school writing account for student performance. In C. A. MacArthur, S. Graham, & J. Fitzgerald (Eds.), *Handbook of writing research.* New York: Guilford Press.

Newell, G. E., & Winograd, P. (1989). Writing about and learning from history texts: The effects of task and academic ability. *Research in the Teaching of English, 29,* 133-163.

Sandbank, A. (2001). On the interplay of genre and writing. In L. Tolchinsky (Ed.), *Developmental aspects in learning to write.* Dordrecht, The Netherlands: Kluwer Academic.

Schutz, A. (1967). *The problem of social reality.* The Hague, The Netherlands: Martinus Nijhoff.

Scribner, S., & Cole, M. (1981). *The psychology of literacy.* Cambridge, Massachusetts: Harvard University Press.

Smart, G. (1998). Mapping conceptual worlds: Using interpretive ethnography to explore knowledge-making in a professional community. *Journal of Business Communication, 35*(1), 111-127.

Swales, J. (1998). *Other floors, other voices: A textography of a small university building.* Mahwah, New Jersey: Erlbaum.

Swales, J., & Najjar, H. (1987). The writing of research article introductions. *Written Communication, 4*(2), 175-191.

Tynjala, P., Mason, L., & Lonka, K. (Eds.). (2001). *Writing as a learning tool: Integrating theory and practice.* Dordrecht, The Netherlands: Kluwer Academic.

Vygotsky, L. (1978). *Mind in society: The development of higher psychological processes.* Cambridge, Massachusetts: Harvard University Press.

Vygotsky, L. (1986). *Thought and language.* Cambridge, Massachusetts: MIT Press.

15 Bakhtin Circle's Speech Genres Theory: Tools for a Transdisciplinary Analysis of Utterances in Didactic Practices

Roxane Helena Rodrigues Rojo

APPLIED LINGUISTICS AND LANGUAGE TEACHING—INTER OR TRANSDISCIPLINARY APPROACH?

According to Bhatia (2004, p. 202), theories of speech genres raise a number of important themes and questions for research in Applied Linguistics (AL). Bhatia first asks "To what extent should pedagogical practices reflect or account for the realities of the world of discourse?" He later asks about research implications: "To what extent should the *analytical procedures* account for the *full realities of the world* of discourse?"

Recent debates about AL's research practices (Signorini & Cavalcanti, 1998a; Moita-Lopes, 2006a) have elaborated on such themes, which are so relevant to the applied linguists who work upon language teaching. These debates in particular (a) define the *primary interest* of research/studies in the field (AL) (Evensen, 1996); (b) discuss the *type of research objects* selected; and (c) debate the *inter or transdisciplinary*[1] nature of the studies carried out in this field (Evensen, 1996; Moita-Lopes, 1998, 2006b; Celani, 1998; Signorini, 1998; Rojo, 2006). According to Rojo (2006), there seems to be a consensus among authors as far as the first two aspects are concerned, that is, the primary research interest and the selected type of research objects/tools, while there is a conflict of positions (and definitions) regarding the inter, multi, pluri or transdisciplinary nature of the studies.

Several authors point out a *prospective* primary research interest among applied linguists in the last decade rather than a retrospective one. That is to say that, in high modernity[2], AL is interested in "understanding, explaining or solving problems," aiming at creating or "improving existing solutions" (Eversen, 1996, p. 91)—as well as several other research fields, applied (or not), on social or nature studies. According to Eversen (1996, p. 96), "the problem-oriented approach has gradually replaced theoretical orientation in AL."

To Rojo (2006), this is about examining problems of discourse and language use which are related to the concept of *suffered deprivation* (Calvino, 1988)[3], that is to say, that is a matter of looking into social problems that have social relevance and are contextualized, in order to construct useful knowledge to situated social actors. To the author,

> The main question is: it is not about "any" problem theoretical-
> ly defined, but it is about problems which are socially relevant
> enough to demand theoretical responses that bring improvement
> to social practices and its participants, in the sense of a better qual-
> ity of life, in an ecological sense. (Rojo, 2006, p. 258)[4]

Quoting Moita-Lopes (1998, p. 121), the *social responsibility* in academic research influences the choice of "what is worth studying, as well as the very structure of the research." Therefore, this primary research interest brings about more and more changes in the choice of research objects and the approach to them. Authors are unanimous in characterizing these research objects as problems of communication, of discourse, of contextualized language use in situated practices. Among them, we identify the use of language at school, the didactic discourses.

One of these problems is, for instance, this paper's opening question, which was brought to light by Bhatia (2004): to what extent should pedagogical discourses and practices at school represent the real functioning of discourses in society? The answer to this question surely demands another whole paper, but it is worth pointing out that it has already been outlined in the Brazilian Parameters for Basic Education (PCN, PCNEM, PCN+, OCEM)[5]: the contemporary school, the school of high or late modernity, has to account for the various discursive practices of the plural spheres of citizens' action in society.

It is at this point that the speech genres theory of the Bakhtin Circle (especially as exposed in Bakhtin/Voloshinov (1926, 1929), Bakhtin/Medvedev (1928) and Bakhtin (1952-53/1979, 1934-35/1975)) first appears in this discussion, impacting the Brazilian Educational Parameters when AL's research and academic knowledge proposes *speech genres* as the main object of reference to teach native language (Portuguese, in this case). This is one of the ways in which the primary research interest, that is, a specific social problem that demands solution—here, the problem announced by Bhatia—has an impact on the research object: the *speech genres* as objects of reference to teach and learn native languages.

Signorini (1998, pp. 101-103) calls our attention to the fact that, at the beginning of AL development as a research field, that is, in its applicationist phase, the research object is approached in a *residual* manner, in a Procustean way: AL focus lies on a disciplinary theoretical problem (of Linguistics, of Cognitive Psychology), so that the integrity of the conceptual and theoretical-methodological apparatus can be maintained. AL therefore turns the research object into a residue, by simplifying its complexity, by "disentangling the web lines," by purifying an object of hybrid nature.

To the author, the AL of the last decades progressively gives up this residual approach as it starts changing its primary research interest and turns its focus to the "search and creation of new concepts and new theoretical-methodological alternatives from the redefinition of research objects." This redefinition

> Reflects a movement of leaning over what Latour (1994) has named as the "mixture that weaves the world," or the "single material of the natures-cultures," that is, the hybrid elements that weave the world of the objects and the world of the subjects, involved in the same woof or web by a fragile thread that the analytical tradition slices in "little specific compartments," so that in each of them we cannot mingle with the knowledge of things, the interest, the desire, the power, the human politics. (Signorini, 1998, p. 101)

Consequently, this is about studying the real language in its situated use, the utterances and discourses, the language practices in specific contexts, trying not to break this fragile thread that maintains the vision of the web, of the woof, of the multiplicity and the complexity of the objects-subjects in their practices. In a certain way, this perspective answers the second question placed by Bhatia (2004): "To what extent should the *analytical procedures* account for the *full realities of the world* of discourse?" Although the answer may sound simple, it is not: in the best possible way and in the broadest possible measure, it could happen by our "trying not to pull the object out of the tissue of its roots" (Signorini, 1998, p. 101). At this point, the Bakhtin Circle's enunciation and speech genres theories appears for the second time in this text, as a way of approaching the *full realities of the discourse world* that makes it possible not to break the threads of the woof.

All this consequently and necessarily implies a non-disciplinary treatment of the object. Nevertheless, the authors that have written about AL's contemporary research practices show divergence regarding such an approach.

Moita-Lopes (1998) following Eversen (1996), for instance, initially prefers the concept of *interdisciplinary approach* to describe the work of the researcher in the AL field, but they also discuss the possibility of the (non)development of AL as a *transdiscipline*. To Moita-Lopes (1998, p. 114), the applied linguist "seeks bases in several disciplines that can theoretically light up the focused question." According to Celani (1998, pp. 131-132), as well, "in a multi/pluri/interdisciplinary perspective, plural disciplines collaborate to the study of an object, a field, a goal (Durand, 1993), in an *integrated* way."

However, differently from Eversen and Celani, Moita-Lopes (1998) states that we cannot see AL as a transdiscipline:

> We cannot work in AL in a transdisciplinary way. However, applied linguists can work with research groups of transdisciplinary nature that are studying a problem in a specific applied context and to which comprehension the internal visions of the applied linguist can be useful. (Moita-Lopes, 1998, p. 122)

Apparently, the author does not believe a field or domain of research itself can function in a trandisciplinary way, but prefers to reserve this qualification to transdisciplinary research teams which involves the participation of actors of different social spheres—not only of academic or scientific spheres (Gibbons et al., 1995). So, at first (1998), the author prefers to characterize AL as an *interdisciplinary* field and, in a later phase (2006), as an *indisciplinary* one.

On the other hand, Celani (1998) understands the transdisciplinarity of AL differently. Although she mentions "the active researchers' participation of involved fields" suggesting multidisciplinary teams, she also defines a transdisciplinary research perspective:

> However, a transdisciplinary perspective tries to highlight a *connecting thread* at the disciplinary collaboration and even an epistemological philosophy—the discovering "philosophy" . . . . A transdisciplinary approach involves more than juxtaposing some knowledge fields. It involves the *coexistence* in a *dynamic interaction* state that Portella (1993) named *spheres of cohabitation* . . . . New knowledge spaces are created, leading the researcher from disciplinary interaction to concepts interaction and then to methodologies interaction. (Celani, 1998, pp. 132-133)

Therefore, to Celani, it is the *dynamic interaction* between disciplinary concepts and methods seeking to solve a linguistic-discursive problem at a language practice that characterizes the transdisciplinary approach in AL. This dynamic interaction due to the research object complexity rescues the *connecting thread* of the discovery.

According to Signorini (1998), this complexity or hybridism of language practices defines the object as a *multiple* or *complex* one. Otherwise, I prefer to reserve the term *multiple* to inter or multidisciplinary studies and the term *complex*—in its etymological sense and not in its common sense as "complicated, difficult[6]"—to transdisciplinary studies. It means that interdisciplinary research practices focus on the object from *multiple* disciplinary perspectives, with or without interaction between these perspectives, but they do not reshape the object in the AL's research field making them "complex," that is, they do not reshape and make them "as a sort of coherent whole, whose components keep a number of relations of interdependency or subordination among themselves."

The "transdisciplinary research routes, in their turn, create their own theoretical-methodological configurations, non-coincident or non-reducible to the contributions of its original disciplines" (Signorini & Cavalacanti, 1998b, p. 13). To the authors, this move implies "the required (re)constitution of the object in the applied field through its reinsertion in the web of practices, tools and institutions that make it meaningful in the social world" (Signorini & Cavalcanti, 1998b, p. 13).

Therefore, it can be said that transdisciplinary research routes produce theory—and not merely consume it—in the applied field. It is exactly what has nowadays happened within the AL field as far as the New Literacy Studies (NLS) or the applied research about identities, subjectivities and cultures are concerned, for instance.

Based on Bakhtinian concepts, Rojo (2006) adds two comments to the considerations placed by Signorini. The first is that what determines the (re)configuration of the object in the applied research field is the *evaluative appreciation* of the applied linguist from his social and academic position. The second is that, in this context, the disciplinary theories may function as a *vision surplus*[7] concerning the theoretical reconfiguration produced. As the author says:

> Even though these new theoretical-methodological configurations are dialogic, they are "of one's own" . . . . That is to say they are *articulated* from a unique point of view or *evaluative appreciation* towards the research object . . . in relation to which the configurations of disciplinary theories or knowledge may function as *a vision surplus* . . . in Bakhtinian terms. And it is exactly to articulate this point of view and this evaluative appreciation towards the problem or object that we need this *thinking lightness*[8] anchored on the *object weight*, which we call "transdisciplinary approach." (Rojo, 2006, p. 261)

Having stated these initial discussions about the contemporary applied linguist's procedures, we will go on, in the remaining parts, to carry out a transdisciplinary task, which consists of taking the "dialogic class[9]" as the object of analysis in order to show how the *multiple* contributions of several disciplines (conversational analysis, speech ethnography, interactional sociolinguistics, enunciation theories, education, didactics, psychology of learning) can be reconfigured when based on an approach of classroom interaction as a *complex whole*, allowing us to articulate, at one time, the object, the theoretical concepts and the analytical methodology. This exercise will be mainly based on the contributions of enunciation and speech genres theories of the Bakhtin Circle and will take the dialogic class as a school speech genre.

We will end the paper discussing how the Bakhtinian concepts themselves are reinterpreted in this transdisciplinary enterprise.

THE BAKHTIN CIRCLE—CONCEPTUAL AND METHOD-OLOGICAL TOOLS FOR THE ANALYSIS OF UTTERANCES IN DIDACTIC PRACTICES AND DEVICES

At this point, we will use some Bakhtinian conceptual tools to study situated utterances, especially the concepts of *sphere, speech genres,* their dimensions (*theme, thematic content, compositional form, architectural form, style*) and some other important related concepts, useful to detect the generic flexibility of utterances, as well as their ideological reflection/refraction, like: *dialogism, multilingualism, polyphony, voices, quoted discourse* and *active reply.* Because of that, in what follows, we present a brief and superficial definition of these terms, trying to make the analysis in the next sections more comprehensible to the reader. As stated in other papers (Rojo, 2005, 2006, 2007; Bunzen & Rojo, 2005), there is a historic process of construction of the concept of *speech genres* in the Circle's work and it is regrettable that the major part of AL's academic texts about the topic should be based exclusively on Bakhtin (1952-53/1979). Already in 1929, in "Marxism and Philosophy of Language[10]," the Circle announces that:

> Later, in connection with the problem of enunciation and dialog, we will face also the problem of *linguistic genres.* Regarding this, we will simply make the following observation: each period and each social group has its repertory of *discursive forms in the socio-ideological communication.* To each group of forms belonging to the same genre, that is, to each *form of social discourse* there is a corresponding group of *themes.* (Bakhtin/Voloshinov, 1929, p. 42, added emphasis)

In this quotation, we can note the primitive state of elaboration of speech genre's concept, imprecisely named as *linguistic genres* and imprecisely defined as "discursive forms in the socio-ideological communication." On the other hand, we can also see that the concept is already present and complemented by what later will be its conceptual pair: *sphere of communication* ("each period and each social group").

In fact, the elaboration of the concept seems to begin at Bakhtin/Medvedev's (1928) work, where the Circle confronts Russian Formalism. In this work, the Circle approaches *literary or poetic genres* and begins to extend the concept to other discursive spheres[11], suggesting the idea of *speech genres*. In the book, the Circle already sustains the central role of the concept of genre[12] and already distinguishes their definition and the Russian formalist one[13], describing genre by its double dialogic orientation towards reality and life:

> An artistic whole of any type, i.e., of any *genre*, has a two-fold orientation in reality, and the characteristics of this orientation determine the type of the whole, i.e., its *genre*.
>
> In the first place, the work is oriented toward the listener and perceiver, and toward the definite conditions of performance and perception. In the second place, the work is oriented in life, from within, one might say, by its thematic content . . . .
>
> Thus the work enters life and comes into contact with various aspects of its environment. It does so in the process of its actual realization as something performed, heard, read at a definite time, in a definite place, under definite conditions. It . . . occupies a definite place in life. It takes a position between people organized in some way. The varieties of the dramatic, lyrical, and epic genres are determined by this direct orientation of the word as fact, or, more precisely, by the word as a historic achievement in its surrounding environment. (Bakhtin/Medvedev, 1928, pp. 130-131, added emphasis)

Consequently, in the late 20s, the Circle's concept of speech genres shows already some of the main theoretical characteristics defined in 1952-53/1979: its relation to the concept of *sphere of ideological creativity;* its *two-fold dialogic orientation* which determines the genre as well as the generic utterances; the central role of *themes* to the *forms*, especially to its *completion*. In this basic text, Bakhtin (1952-53/1986, p. 60) reaffirms these characteristics that assume the form of the definition we can read everywhere: "each sphere in which language is used develops its own *relatively stable types* of these utterances. These we may call *speech genres.*"

Regrettably, similarly to what happened in Russian Formalism and to what was contested by the Circle, it is the genres' *stability* and *regularity* that people often emphasize in this definition, despite its relative nature, ignoring the *het-*

erogeneity that is emphatically pointed out through the same part of Bakhtinian text:

> The wealth and diversity of speech genres are boundless because the various possibilities of human activity are inexhaustible, and because each sphere of activity contains an entire repertoire of speech genres that differentiate and grow as the particular sphere develops and become complex. Special emphasis should be placed on the extreme *heterogeneity* of speech genres (oral and written). (Bakhtin, 1952-53/1986, p. 60)

Nevertheless, people focus on the stable and regular aspects of speech genres, and do not pay attention to the previous contributions of the Circle to speech genre theory, especially the text "Discourse in the novel" (1934-35/1981). In this text, Bakhtin points out two very important processes to generic heterogeneity, flexibility and richness: *hybridism*, not only of voices, intonations and styles but also of genres, and the phenomenon of *incorporated genres* (insertion of genres in the novel). The author defines *hybrid constructions* or *hybridism* in the novel as:

> An utterance that belongs, by its grammatical (syntactic) and compositional markers, to a single speaker, but that actually contains mixed within it two utterances, two speech manners, two styles, two "languages."' two semantic and axiological be-lief systems. We repeat, there is no formal—compositional and syntactic—boundary between these utterances, styles, languages, belief systems; the division of voices and languages takes place within the limits of a single syntactic whole[14], often within the limits of a simple sentence. It frequently happens that even one and the same word will belong simultaneously to two languages, two belief systems that intersect in a hybrid construction—and, consequently, the word has two contradictory meanings, two ac-cents[15] .... (Bakhtin, 1934-35/1981, pp. 304-305)

Another generic way to echo different voices and ideological perspectives is *incorporated genres,* for instance, letters, journals, confession in the novel. To Bakhtin (1934-35/1981, p. 320) this way is "one of the most basic and fun-damental forms for incorporating and organizing heteroglossia in the novel." In the case of *incorporated genres*, the boundary between the genres is compo-sitionally and syntactically marked.

> Such incorporated genres usually preserve within the novel their own structural integrity and independence, as well as their own linguistic and stylistic peculiarities. (Bakhtin, 1934-35/1981, p. 321)

Because of that they are able to resound heteroglossically and multi-vocalically.

It is therefore the *heteroglossia* and the *double-voiced* nature of an utterance within a genre that enables it to echo different ideological perspectives, sometimes *polyphonically*. Bakhtin defines heteroglossia as "*another's speech in another's language*, serving to express authorial intentions but in a refracted way." To him,

> Such speech constitutes a special type of *double-voiced discourse*. It serves two speakers at the same time and expresses simultaneously two different intentions . . . . In such discourse there are two voices[16], two meanings and two expressions. And all the while these two voices are dialogically interrelated, they—as it were—know about each other (just as two exchanges in a dialog know of each other and are structured in this mutual knowledge of each other); it is as if they actually hold a conversation with each other. Double-voiced discourse is always internally dialogized[17]. (Bakhtin, 1934-35/1981, p. 324)

Consequently, according to Bakhtin, generic and enunciative flexibility, creative forms and refraction of senses are due not only to the *style*, i.e., the "selection of the lexical, phraseological and grammatical resources of the language" (as stated in Bakhtin, 1952-53/1986, p. 60), but also by the heteroglot forms in utterances, a greatly varied and complex phenomenon.

Also, since 1924/1975, Bakhtin insisted on distinguishing between genres' *compositional form* and the *architectural forms*[18], the first having the characteristic of stability, being "practical," "teleological"—although "restless"—"available to realize the architectural task." On the other hand, *architectural forms*

> are the forms of moral and physical values of the aesthetic man, the forms of nature as his environment, the forms of happenings in his aspect of particular, social, historical life, etc. . . . are the forms of aesthetical being in its singularity. . . . Architectural form determines the choice of compositional form[19]. (Bakhtin, 1924/1975, p. 25)

It also determines the choice of the forms of introduction of multilingualism, even when they cause breaks to the stability of compositional form.

In the same way, the author treats the concept of *theme*. To Bakhtin, "theme" is not merely the topic of the discourse or the main idea of an utterance. The theme of an utterance or a word is unique, non-repeatable, exactly because it is its meaning plus its ideology or point of view. So, the theme of a word like "negro" is not the mere meaning of the word, referring to "black color," but it is its meaning plus the speaker's ideology, appreciation or point of view: depending on his/her ideology, it can carry prejudice or not to the utterance. Also, in the same direction as the distinction between architectural and compositional forms, Bakhtin also distinguishes thematic contents and themes: the theme is the concrete and situated significance of an utterance whereas the thematic contents are the possible allowed contents that the ideological field of a specific sphere of human activity admits. Thus, thematic contents are predictable whereas themes are situated and irreproducible.

Having explored, though briefly and superficially, some key-concepts of the Bakhtin Circle that will be used to describe the dialogic class as a school genre in the next sections, it is important to point out that this exercise will not be realized as a new application of the Circle theory to a new object, but will be developed in a transdisciplinary way, trying to unify, in a complex whole, a number of theoretical artifacts of different disciplines that study the dialogical class as a didactic space. To do so, we will adopt the *sociological method of utterances analysis* proposed by Bakhtin/Voloshinov (1929, p. 124).

AN INTERDISCIPLINARY APPROACH TO A DIALOGIC UNDERSTANDING OF CLASSROOM SPEECH GENRES

Rojo (2007, p. 339) suggests an interdisciplinary approach to a dialogic understanding of classroom interactions and justifies this approach:

> Classroom talk is described by researchers either as a didactic activity (Educational Sociology, Psychology of Learning, and so on) or as a specific type of face-to-face interaction or conversation (Ethnographic Sociolinguistics, Micro-Ethnography of Speech, for instance). In the first approach, researchers focus on the objects and teaching methods, its organization and its impact on learning. In the second, the interactional patterns, the participation structures, the conversational interchanges in classrooms are described. Thus, the tendency is to put aside the analyses of the themes and the

formal (conversational) organization of classroom interaction . . . .

This misleads data interpretation to analysts whose main presupposition is that language and discourse are basic materials to the teaching-learning activity in classrooms.

In the paper, the author tries

To create tools and analytical devices able to surpass this division and this partial focus, based on previous studies (especially Batista, 1997; Schneuwly et al., 2005), on Bazerman's (2005) approach to classrooms interaction as activity systems and genre systems, as well as on the Bakhtin Circle's theory of enunciation as a reference for data interpretation. (Rojo, 2007, p. 339)

Figure 1 exhibits the main disciplinary concepts suggested by the author, adopting an interdisciplinary approach that presupposes dynamic interaction between these disciplinary concepts and methods:

Figure 1 assumes the *synopsis* shape, a methodological tool to analyze classes developed by Schneuwly et al. (2005), trying to focus, in a systematic way, on the teaching objects constructed in classes (*teaching objects*). In this model, didactic activities are viewed as *founding professional gestures* of the teacher, who *elementarizes* the teaching object[20] by focusing on some of its aspects and, as a result, constituting the object effectively taught in classrooms. So, the synopsis tries to reproduce the essential didactic moves in class and allows for a whole vision of the teaching object. In the synopsis, the highest level of analysis (1.) corresponds to *didactic activities* carried out by the teacher and the students defined by its goals. In a certain way, the concepts of didactic activity are remotely related to the concept of *speech event* or *episode*[21] proposed by Gumperz (1982) and adopted by the interactional sociolinguistic and the ethnography of speech applied to classroom interaction. If we consider the thematic progression of speech events as aspects of the teaching object focused in class, the two approaches may be viewed in a complementary way.

However, Rojo (2007) chooses to divide language action into didactic activities not only by considering the aspects of teaching objects focused, which can lead us to ignore and eliminate other themes brought to class, but also by accounting for the *themes*[22] carried out in interactions. She adopts the notion of *global sequence* (Batista, 1997) to define the thematic progression (level 1.1.) and of *local sequence* (Batista, 1997) to focus on the existing turn taking/utterances (level 1.1.1.). The author suggests that this approach/model should also take

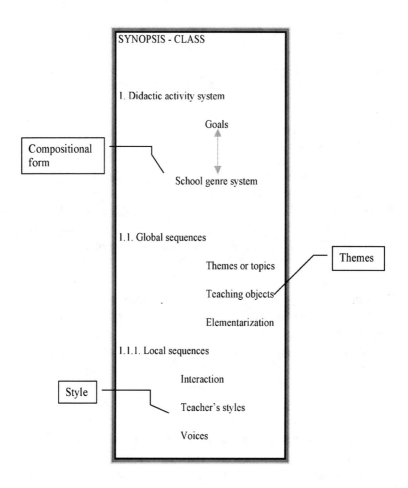

FIGURE 1: ANALYSIS PROPOSAL (ROJO, 2007)

into account and therefore be shaped by the *teachers' styles* (Mortimer & Scott, 2000, based on Bakhtin, 1934-35/1975) and by the *voices* (Bakhtin, 1934-35/1975) mobilized in class.

Additionally, Rojo (2007) sees the sequence of didactic activities of class not as a linear sequence, one placed after the other, but as a *system* of articulated activities, which calls for a specific *genre system* to function, according to Bazerman (2004, p. 23), who states, "in classroom, the teacher's work often serves to define genres and activities and, in so doing creates learning opportunities and expectations[23]."

Thus, Rojo (2007) in large part adopts Bazerman's vision of class as an articulated communication *activity system* of the educational sphere, in which *specific* non-random genres are also needed for its functioning. As far as the concept of genre itself is concerned, however, Rojo (2007) prefers to adopt the discursive/enunciative approach of the Bakhtin Circle rather than Bazerman's view, which is more pragmatic and socio-cognitive.

Nevertheless, it is important to point out that Rojo's (2007) suggestion has an interdisciplinary nature instead of a transdisciplinary one, in the sense discussed at the beginning of this paper, since the author uses a number of dynamically interrelated concepts and definitions of various disciplines (theory of enunciation, language didactics, interactional sociolinguistics, communication ethnography, education) to compose a multiple and more complete vision of class. However, she does not redefine or recreate the enunciative object of dialogic class in the AL field, as demanded by the definition of transdisciplinary approach adopted in this paper. The next section aims at fulfilling this intent.

THE DIALOGIC CLASSROOM DIALOGUE AS GENRE AND AS A COMPLEX ENUNCIATIVE CHAIN—A TRANSDISCIPLINARY APPROACH

In a transdisciplinary approach of dialogic classroom dialogue, we can first describe it as a discursive school genre—a complex secondary genre that merges other genres and presents a hybridism of voices and social languages.

To describe class as a genre, we will adopt the methodological social order proposed by Bakhtin/Voloshinov (1929, p. 124), which at first leads us to focus on the functioning of the school activity sphere, that is, "the forms and types of verbal interaction related to the concrete conditions under which they take place."

School as a social institution is a sphere of activity with a particular way of functioning. It functions by using secondary speech genres exactly because it is a sphere of the social superstructure related to the official ideology, as well as to the establishment and reproduction of ideologies. According to Bourdieu & Passeron (1977), school provides a pedagogical work which, by means of the appropriation of a "cultural arbitrary," produces a "habitus" that is perpetuated in the practices out of school.

School originates from the division between work and non-work as "skole"—"study leisure" to the Greeks—that is, the time free from work and politics dedicated to intellectual activity. It means that it is a specialized social space detached of other social spaces where these other spaces become objects to be studied, which are, in their turn, objectified, made literate and open to contemplation, analysis, comparison (Schneuwly, 2005; Lahire et al., 1994).

School as we know it today was created in the 19th century while Nation-

States developed. It happened mostly because of the constitution of new social forms of relations that Lahire et al. (1994) named "school forms," which implies a rupture with daily life ("skole") and turns knowledge into something objective and literate, so that it can be taken as explicit teaching objects (in parameters, syllabus, school books). These objects will then be "elementarized," analysed, and divided into unities to be accessible to learning. These unities or elements are then progressively arranged in *cursus*[24], syllabus and disciplines. Disciplines are, thus, at the same time an organization of knowledge (teaching objects) and of ways to teach it. Additionally, according to Chervel (1990, pp. 178-180), the word "discipline" is related to the idea of "intellectual gymnastics," aiming at "disciplining the children's intelligence," imposing rules to approach "the different domains of reasoning, knowledge and art." Therefore, by aiming at "disciplining" minds and the world, school forms and their "habitus" establishes and perpetuates several practices, activities and their own forms of didactic discourse—the school genres.

In spite of such a brief and almost schematic presentation of the forms of functioning of the school sphere, it is possible to see that the themes of the school utterances are not disconnected, incoherent or random. The thematic content of the majority of school utterances is related to the elementarized teaching object made concrete in the discourses (of the teacher, of school books) and determined by an enunciative intention or will—a discursive project that in didactics we refer to as "didactic goals." For instance, in a class aiming at producing a dissertation, the teacher, according to his/her evaluative perception of this object (dissertation) and about the capacities and knowledge of his/her interlocutors (the students), can construct a discursive project that includes (a) providing, elaborating and discussing possible topics to be developed (text content); (b) providing some information about dissertation structure; (c) asking for the text production (procedure); and (d) revising collectively the text, focusing on structure, spelling and content. This teaching project is also a discursive project determined by an enunciative will to teach and produce a dissertation. This enunciative choice is also determined by an ideology about the speech genre "dissertation" and its relevance to teaching writing, which includes ideas like "text is form and content," "texts may obey norms of standard language," "dissertation disciplines logical reasoning" and so on.

In this sense, we can view these five activities—with their global sequences (Batista, 1997) that elementarize the teaching object and use several ways to teach—as an "activity system" (Bazerman, 2005a) articulated to fulfill an enunciative will, and not simply as sequential activities as suggested by Gumperz. From the perspective of the Bakhtin Circle, this way of organizing class as genre, the architectonic that selects this specific compositional form to class, will also select the incorporated genres (instruction, request, order, question-answer, genres of the texts people read, dissertation) and the hybrid voices (of Science, of the author of school book, of the teacher, of students) that will integrate the compositional form of the class and its themes.

At this point, we are at the second moment of the Bakhtinian sociological method, when we describe

> The forms of different utterances, of the isolated speech acts strictly related to the interaction of which they are elements, that is, the categories of speech acts in life and in ideological creation that are determined by verbal interaction. (Bakhtin/Voloshinov, 1929, p. 124)

It is important to highlight that themes, their meaning effects and compositional forms of class are central to the appropriation of discourses that students can make in the learning process, because they correspond to the ways of teaching and to the ideological refraction about the teaching object determined by the different voices that are present in utterances. The *style* of the *genres* and of the *authors* of utterances (authors of school books, the teacher, the students) are also very important to the meaning effects. In this sense, the choice of genres that teachers have made to merge in dialogic class is not a neutral one, as nothing is neutral in language use. To choose orders and instructions in local sequences (Batista, 1997) is to adopt a genre style similar to military style, which demands a reception attitude of acceptance, of obedience, of revoicing, i.e., an *authoritative style*. On the other hand, the adjacent pair question-answer often viewed by the interaction research as an authoritative style (I-R-A pattern), depending on the type of question we make and on the type of answer we induce, can adopt an *internally persuasive style* that suggests an active reply of the students. For instance, WH-questions ("who?", "when?", where?") tend to induce revoicing whereas questions or instructions like "how?", "why?", "explain," "justify" tend to induce active reply. At this point, we are at the third moment of analytical method suggested by Bakhtin/Voloshinov (1929, p. 124): "the examination of linguistic forms in its common interpretation."

In spite of the shortness of the analysis we believe we have presented, considering the limits of this paper, we hope we have succeeded in showing how the interdisciplinary analysis of dialogic class previously shown can be reconfigured and articulated in an object, not multiple, but complex on the grounds of the Circle's speech genre theory. In the following and last section, we will conclude this paper discussing why this type of analysis is a transdisciplinary one, from an internal and an external point of view.

CONCLUSION—TRANSDISCIPLINARY APPROACH AS A *VISION SURPLUS*

From an internal point of view, the presented analysis can be first called transdisciplinary, as already stated, because viewing class as a complex enunciative chain which brings in an also complex genre makes it possible for us to reconstruct the vision of the object in the AL field based on a specific *language* theory capable of examining *language in use* in *discursive school practices*. The selected theory—understanding the ideological echoes in didactic utterances—is powerful enough to be applied to reduce "suffering deprivation" at school, to make quality of life better there. So, by allowing the reconstruction of the object in the specific field of AL, the theory keeps the dialog with the constructs of other disciplines, but also produces its own knowledge.

Changing now to an external perspective, able to reach a *vision surplus*, we ask: why and where is this analysis not a mere application of Bakhtinian concepts to a new object? Why is it not a mere applicationist exercise of "ordinary science"?

A simple—but not simplistic—answer calls for pointing to the fact that the Circle had never examined the genres of this sphere of activity and that, as a result, in the Circle's work there are very few passages where they mention school utterances, genres or discourse. Because it is a simple answer, it is not sufficient. A stronger answer may be suggesting that the analysis of school dialog or dialogic class, i.e., of classroom conversation (Interactional Sociolinguistics, Ethnography of Communication), can increase or even review the Bakhtinian approach of dialog as genre. Consequently, it is powerful enough even to reconfigure some Bakhtinian analysis.

Usually, when early Circle's works refer to dialog, they are either referring to the broader "social dialog" between utterances as it is configured in dialogism or dealing with the concept of daily dialog, which at this time begins to be studied[25]. Bakhtin/Voloshinov (1929), for instance, sustains that "the replies [of dialog] are grammatically separated rather than integrated in a unique context" (p. 147), or that

> There are no grammatical ties between them [the units of internal speech], as well as between the replies of a dialog; ties of another order rule them. . . . They are tied and subsequent not by the rules of logic or grammar, but following the laws of *appreciative convergence* (emotional), of *dialog concatenation*, etc. . . . in a narrow dependency on social situation historical conditions and on all the pragmatic course of existence. (Bakhtin/Voloshinov, 1929,

pp. 63-64)

Therefore, in 1929, the Circle tends to view indistinctly the replies of the dialog and the dialog itself as genre; it is not very clear how they are related. In the text of 1952-53/1986, the approach of dialog moves forward:

> Because of its simplicity and clarity, dialogue is a classic form of speech communication. Each rejoinder, regardless of how brief and abrupt, has a specific quality of completion that expresses a particular position of the speaker, to which one may respond or may assume, with respect to it, a *responsive position* . . . . But at the same time rejoinders are all linked to one another. (p. 72)

Nevertheless, they do not make explicit the type of existing relation between different replies and they do not even view these replies as integrated or merged in a complex genre—the dialog. They only exemplify these relations as "relations between question and answer, assertion and objection, assertion and agreement, suggestion and acceptance, order and execution, and so forth" (p. 72).

As a result, as affirmed by Bakhtin/Voloshinov (1929) himself, it seems that the study of the forms of dialog in different spheres of activity and ranges can bring new theoretical elaborations that are of interest to the Bakhtinian enunciative theory itself.

Therefore, to see how dialogic class chains together rejoinders-utterances that, however, are organized in a form and a style that attend to a unifying enunciative project or will can theoretically contribute in a new and productive way to the disciplinary theory adopted. Further, this perspective shows how the will is related to the sphere's determinations and is also a determining factor of an architectonic that suffers a returning influence of form and style, constituting a complex genre—the classroom dialogue or the dialogic class.

NOTES

[1] As Moita-Lopes (2006) says, *indisciplinary.*

[2] In the sense of Giddens (1991). The author does not follow the orientation of some others that name contemporary society "postmodern" or "post-industrial." On the contrary, he prefers the terms "high or late modernity," to indicate that the dynamic principles of modernity are still present in actual reality. So, high modernity, late modernity or reflexive modernity are defined by the author as a post-traditional order that instead of disrupting modern parameters makes their basic characteristics more radical and enhanced.

[3] Italo Calvino speaks about the nexus between *desired levitation* and *deprivation suffered* as an anthropological constant in societies.

[4] All translations of Brazilian authors from Portuguese to English are my

responsibility.

[5] In its 90th year, the Brazilian Ministry of Education has redefined its orientation for Basic Education, publishing some official documents—the National Curriculum Parameters—addressed to Primary (PCN) and Secondary Education (High School, PCNEM). The latter, the documents addressed to Secondary Education (High School) were complemented by some explanatory documents and orientations (OCEM, PCN+), due to its concise nature.

[6] In Latin *complexus*, past participle of *complecti* means "to comprise, to enclose, to understand." "It applies to a group/collection of parts, viewed as a more or less coherent whole, whose components function in a number of relations of interdependency or subordination which are very often difficult to understand and that generally present multiple aspects" (Houaiss, 2001, p. 776).

[7] Obviously, disciplinary theories only can function as a *vision surplus* if there are ethical relations. "The interdisciplinary approach involves interest and respect for the other's voice, interest to listen to what the other says in order to see how his ideas match with one's own perspectives. As Tannen (w/d) says, at university, the most common practice is to listen the other to destruct his argument as we do in private life when we are upset with someone" (Moita-Lopes, 1998, p. 117).

[8] Calvino (1988).

[9] "Dialogic class" here refers initially to the classroom interaction shaped in speech turns. Later, we will redefine "dialogic class" as the classroom discourse constituted by a complex set of genres packaged as a larger genre or a genre system. Evidently, with the "expository class" we need another type of analysis, closer to the "academic conference" analysis (see Rojo & Schneuwly, 2006).

[10] All translations of this text from Portuguese to English are my responsibility.

[11] For instance, when they compare the completion of poetic genres and of the utterances of other ideological spheres as the scientific or religious one (Bakhtin/Medvedev, 1928, pp. 129-130).

[12] "Poetics should really begin with *genre*, not end with it. For *genre* is the typical form of the whole work, the whole utterance" (Bakhtin/Medvedev, 1928, p. 129, added emphasis).

[13] "The formalists usually define genre as a certain constant, specific grouping of devices with a defined dominant. Since the basic devices had already been defined, genre was mechanically seen as being composed of devices. Therefore, the formalists did not understand the real meaning of genre" (Bakhtin/Medvedev, 1928, p. 129).

[14] Later in the same text, the author will show that also *quoted discourse*, i.e., "the forms to transmit the character discourses," is able to cause this same

hybridism and mix of accents and voices, but in this case showing formal and syntactic marks of the frontiers between the utterances of each speaker (Bakhtin, 1935-35/1981, p. 320).

[15] A good example of generic hybrid construction that resounds different accents and voices is popular songs. For instance, "My dear friend" by Chico Buarque de Hollanda (1976), which is, at the same time and without frontiers or rupture between utterances, a letter, a poem, lyrics and a song.

[16] According to Bakhtin, *voices* are always ideological perspectives, index of evaluative appreciation.

[17] To Bakhtin, this double-voiced discourse only is *polyphonic* if there is ideological conflict between voices.

[18] He does also the same kind of distinction between *theme* and *thematic content*.

[19] Our translation.

[20] *Elementarization* is defined as the process to divide complex objects into small and simple parts to simplify the teaching topics and constitutes the lower levels of didactic activities' analysis in the synopsis (1.1., 1.1.1.).

[21] To Gumperz (*apud* Prevignano & Di Luzio, 1995, pp. 7-10), *speech events* are defined as "interactively constituted, culturally framed encounters, and not attempt to explain talk as directly reflecting the norms, beliefs and values of communities seen as disembodied, hypothetically uniform wholes. To look at talk as it occurs in speech events is to look at communicative practices. . . . [It is] sequentially bounded units, marked off from others in the recorded data by some degree of thematic coherence and by beginnings and ends detectable through co-occurring shifts in content, prosody, tempo or other formal markers."

[22] In the Bakhtinian sense of thematic content of utterances, not cleaned of its ideological refractions and reflections, of its evaluative accents.

[23] Our translation.

[24] In Latin: route, trip, march.

[25] For instance, by L. P. Iakubinski, "O dialoguítcheskoi rietchi" (About dialogic discourse), in *Rússkaia rietch* (The Russian speech), Petrograd, 1923.

REFERENCES

Bakhtin, M. M. (1926). *Discurso na vida e discurso na arte.* Tradução de Carlos Alberto Faraco & Cristóvão Tezza. Circulação restrita.

Bakhtin, M. M. (1975). O problema do conteúdo, do material e da forma na criação literária. In M. M. Bakhtin, *Questões de literatura e de estética: A teoria do romance* (pp. 13-70). São Paulo: Hucitec.

Bakhtin, M. M. (1981). Discourse in the novel. In M. Bakhtin, *The dialogic imagination: Four essays* (M. Holquist & V. Liapunov, Eds., V. Liapunov & K. Brostrom, Trans., pp. 259-422). Austin: University of Texas Press.

Bakhtin, M. M. (1986). The problem of speech genres. In C. Emerson & M. Holquist (Eds.), *Speech genres and other late essays* (pp. 60-102). Austin: University of Texas Press.

Bakhtin, M. M./Medvedev, P. N. (1928/1985). *The formal method in literary scholarship*. A critical introduction to sociological poetics. Cambridge, Massachusetts: Harvard University Press.

Bakhtin, M. M./Voloshinov, V. N. (1929/1981). *Marxismo e filosofia da linguagem* (2nd ed.). São Paulo: Hucitec.

Batista, A. A. G. (1997). *Aula de Português: Discurso e saberes escolares*. São Paulo: Martins Fontes.

Bazerman, C. (2005a). Atos de fala, gêneros textuais e sistemas de atividades: Como os textos organizam atividades e pessoas. In C. Bazerman, *Gêneros textuais, tipificação e interação* (A. P. Dionísio & J. C. Hoffnagel, Eds. & Trans., pp. 19-46). São Paulo: Cortez.

Bazerman, C. (2005b). Formas sociais como habitats para a ação. In C. Bazerman, *Gêneros textuais, tipificação e interação* (A. P. Dionísio & J. C. Hoffnagel, Eds. & Trans., pp. 47-62). São Paulo: Cortez.

Bhatia, V. K. (2004). *Worlds of written discourse: A genre-based view*. London: Continuum.

Bourdieu, P., & Passeron, J. C. (1977). *A reprodução*. Petrópolis, Rio de Janeiro, Brazil: Vozes.

Bunzen, C., & Rojo, R. H. R. (2005). Livro didático de língua Portuguesa como gênero do discurso: Autoria e estilo. In M. G. Costa Val & B. Marcuschi (Eds.), *Livros didáticos de língua Portuguesa: Letramento e cidadania* (pp. 73-118). Belo Horizonte, Minas Gerais, Brazil: Autêntica/CEALE.

Calvino, I. (1988/1994). *Seis Propostas para o próximo milênio* (2nd ed). São Paulo: Cia das Letras.

Celani, M. A. A. (1998). Transdisciplinaridade na lingüística aplicada no Brasil. In I. Signorini & M. Cavalcanti (Eds.), *Lingüística aplicada e transdisciplinaridade* (pp. 129-142). Campinas, São Paulo, Brazil: Mercado de Letras.

Chervel, A. (1990). A história das disciplinas escolares: Reflexões sobre um campo de pesquisa. *Teoria & Educação, 2.*

Evensen, L. S. (1998). A lingüística aplicada a partir de um arcabouço com princípios caracterizadores de disciplinas e transdisciplinas. In I. Signorini & M. Cavalcanti (Eds.), *Lingüística aplicada e transdisciplinaridade* (pp. 81-90). Campinas, São Paulo, Brazil: Mercado de Letras.

Gibbons, M., Limoges, C., Nowotny, H., Schwartzman, S., Scott, P., & Trow, M. (1995). *The new production of knowledge*. London: Sage.

Giddens, A. (1991). *Modernity and self-identity: Self and society in the late modern age.* Cambridge: Polity Press.

Gumperz, J. (1982). *Discourse strategies.* Cambridge: Cambridge University Press.

Houaiss, A., & Villar, M. S. (2001). *Dicionário houaiss de língua Portuguesa.* Rio de Janeiro: Objetiva.

Lahire, B., Thin, D., & Vincent, G. (1994). Sur l'histoire et la théorie de la forme scolaire. In G. Vincent (Ed.), *L'Education prisonnière de la forme scolaire? Scolarisation et socialisation dans les sociétés industrielles* (pp. 11-48). Lyon, France: Lyon University Pole.

Moita-Lopes, L. P. (1998). A transdisciplinaridade é possível em lingüística aplicada? In I. Signorini & M. Cavalcanti (Eds.), *Lingüística aplicada e transdisciplinaridade* (pp. 113-128). Campinas, São Paulo, Brazil: Mercado de Letras.

Moita-Lopes, L. P. (Ed.), (2006a). *Por uma lingüística aplicada indisciplinar.* São Paulo: Parábola.

Moita-Lopes, L. P. (2006b). Lingüística aplicada e vida contemporânea: Problematização dos construtos que têm orientado a pesquisa. In L. P. Moita-Lopes (Ed.), *Por uma lingüística aplicada indisciplinar* (pp. 85-107). São Paulo: Parábola.

Mortimer, E. F., & Scott, P. (2000). Analysing discourse in the science classroom. In R. Millar, J. Leach, & J. Osborne (Eds.), *Improving science education: The contribution of research.* Buckingham, United Kingdom: Oxford University Press.

Prevignano, C., & Di Luzio, A. (1995). *A discussion with John J. Gumperz's Bologna round table on dialogue analysis: Units, relations and strategies beyond the sentence.* Retrieved May 10 2007, from http://sunsite.berkeley.edu/Anthro/gumperz/gumpc.pdf.

Rojo, R. H. R. (2005). Gêneros do discurso e gêneros textuais: Questões teóricas e aplicadas. In J. L. Meurer, A. Bonini, & D. Motta-Roth, (Eds.), *Gêneros: Teorias, métodos e debates* (pp. 184-207). São Paulo: Parábola.

Rojo, R. H. R. (2006). Fazer lingüística aplicada em perspectiva sócio-histórica: Privação sofrida e leveza de pensamento. In L. P. Moita-Lopes (Ed.), *Por uma lingüística aplicada indisciplinar* (pp. 253-276). São Paulo: Parábola.

Rojo, R. H. R. (2007). Práticas de ensino em língua materna: Interação em sala de aula ou aula como cadeia enunciativa? In A. B. Kleiman & M. Cavalcanti (Eds.), *Lingüística aplicada, suas faces e interfaces* (pp. 339-360). Campinas, São Paulo, Brazil: Mercado de Letras.

Rojo, R. H. R., & Schneuwly, B. (2006). As relações oral/escrita nos gêneros orais formais e públicos: O caso da conferência acadêmica [Special issue]. *Linguagem em (Dis)curso, 6*(3), 463-493. Retrieved from www3.unisul.br/paginas/ensino/

pos/linguagem/revista/revista.htm

Schneuwly, B. (2005). *Genres oraux et genres écrits à l'école*. Lecture presented at Colóquio com Bernard Schneuwly. Campinas, São Paulo, Brazil.

Schneuwly, B., Cordeiro, G. S., & Dolz, J. (2005). *A la recherche de l'objet enseigné: une démarche multifocale*. (Manuscript submitted for publication)

Signorini, I. (1998). Do residual ao múltiplo e ao complexo: O objeto da pesquisa em lingüística aplicada. In I. Signorini & M. Cavalcanti (Eds.), *Lingüística aplicada e transdisciplinaridade* (pp. 99-110). Campinas, São Paulo, Brazil: Mercado de Letras.

Signorini, I., & Cavalcanti, M. (Eds.). (1998a). *Lingüística aplicada e transdisciplinaridade*. Campinas, São Paulo, Brazil: Mercado de Letras.

Signorini, I. & Cavalcanti, M. (1998b). Introdução. In I. Signorini & M. Cavalcanti (Eds.), *Lingüística aplicada e transdisciplinaridade* (pp. 7-19). Campinas, São Paulo, Brazil: Mercado de Letras.

16 The Role of Context in Academic Text Production and Writing Pedagogy

Désirée Motta-Roth

INTRODUCTION

The problem of text production in academic genres has been a challenge for undergraduate and graduate students as well as for writing teachers from different departments. Previous research has provided important results on the structural aspects of academic genres (Swales, 1990) and the discursive construction of identity in academic writing (Ivanic, 1998). However, few studies have concentrated on the contributions of exploration and reflection on context to actual teaching practices. From the perspective of Systemic-Functional Linguistics (SFL), in this paper I would like to focus on the reciprocal relationship between text and context, i.e., the way context can be recreated by analysis of text and vice versa. The aim is to point out some practical implications derived from the use of SFL principles in academic writing teaching and research through context exploration. The focus will be on writing activities that aim at fostering students' awareness about the connections between contextual features (activity, identity, relations as well as the role performed by text in the situation) and their respective linguistic realizations (expression of content, instantiation of relationships between interlocutors, and organization of text).

One of the main challenges in language education and research is to teach creative ways to negotiate the norms of the language system (grammar) within the academic culture: the set of meanings, rules, values, power relations and relevant genres that constitute the social practices of a community. Educating students about the uses of language in specific contexts depends on clear descriptions of the connections between text and context.

Public discourse on academic publication in Brazil is mainly issued by the Ministry of Education through its two main Research Funding Agencies, CAPES and CNPq, which hold quantitative and qualitative expectations about scholars' intellectual production but offer no substantial line of financial support for pedagogic research and course development. Thus full-fledged writing programs are seldom found in Brazilian universities. Very often what we find is some individual or collective teaching initiatives that have survived defying all the odds (e.g., lack of personnel and financial resources) situated in specific institutions.

In my context of pedagogic practice in academic writing at the Federal University of Santa Maria (UFSM), I personally started to offer a course on academic writing to graduate students in 1994. Since then, I have been offering the course to a multidisciplinary class, made up of Master's and PhD students. These newcomers to academia often feel that the task of writing research genres demands substantial and detailed formal instruction. My aim is to foster students' awareness of how the language system operates in different academic genres in terms of semantic field (content), interpersonal relations (effect), and text structure, so that they can engage in text production in order to appropriately perform relevant activities according to (a) their own interests and (b) the conditions and constraints of the cultural context in question. The pedagogical approach presented here is focused on students' situated practice and the cultural context of their discipline. I would like to think of it as a transformative practice.

In this paper I consider how theory works in practice, drawing practical implications, especially from Systemic-Functional Linguistics, to the teaching of academic writing and reflective thinking about the academic context. It differentiates itself from other previous texts that describe writing pedagogy approaches (as the several ones described in Zemliansky & Bishop, 2004) in that it identifies specific issues and questions that can be explored with students in order to develop their awareness about the discourse of science in their own disciplinary areas.

CHALLENGES IN THE ACADEMIC SETTING

In the academic context, the challenges in teaching writing to newcomers are many:

- Discourse events are dynamic linguistic activities that combine social and cognitive resources in meaning making, "complex dynamic systems in action, with people as agents in social systems, using other complex systems — of language and other semiotic means — in interaction with each other" (Larsen-Freeman & Cameron, 2008, pp. 161-162, 186)[1];
- Centripetal and Centrifugal forces interact in discourse (Bakhtin, 1986). In other words, genres are intersubjective representations of events that are constructed with reference to our shared experience of recurrent discursive situations. Thus they are relatively stable. At the same time, genres are social processes and thus dynamic, realized in different registers (Martin, 1992). The research article genre, for example, is differently realized in Applied Linguistics and Electrical Engineering concerning form and style, as different registers of the same genre;

- Novice writers must negotiate meaning considering the disciplinary culture they are new to (Swales, 1990; 1998) at the same time that they keep in perspective the existing power relations and tensions in their local disciplines and in academia as a broad cultural site (Ivanic, 1998); and
- Systemic knowledge is not enough to accomplish both of the above tasks, which depend on one's understanding of the meaning potentials that situations offer (Bakhtin, 1986).

These challenges seem more reasonable if we consider language learning as two interrelated steps: we learn to interact and thus learn the language that is constitutive of that interaction (Halliday, 1994).

In my own teaching practice, there are additional specific challenges:

- I teach a course that lasts 15 weeks, with weekly 100-minute meetings with a multidisciplinary and multilevel academic writing class (PhD and Master's students from Chemistry, Rural Sciences, Education, Law, English, among other areas), therefore we need to analyze the different discursive practices (processes of text production, distribution, and consumption, according to Fairclough, 1989) into which students must acculturate;
- Learners are usually novices or junior scholars with different experiences in writing (mostly master's students and PhD candidates)
- Learners' make different choices for genres in which to write their texts (research project, article, dissertation/thesis chapter).

These various challenges have to be considered and recontextualized in my teaching practice in order to answer a range of questions such as the following: How do we foster learners' textual production competencies? How can we teach learners to function within academic genres to engage in disciplinary discourse? And maybe even more importantly: how can we help them develop an academic identity as authors (Ivanic, 1998, pp. 26, 219, 341)?

In order to comment on possible approaches to these questions and challenges, first I will discuss the relationship between academic text and context, taking into account the concepts of genre and register. Secondly, I will explore the pedagogic approach that I call "Academic writing cycle" — an approach that I have developed throughout the years, based on previous research on academic genres and my own teaching practice with inexperienced academic writers. Finally, implications of this approach for academic writing teaching will be drawn.

In order to examine text production in the academic setting, language will be defined as a semiotic system with different planes of signification within the Systemic-Functional Linguistics (SFL) framework. In addition, discourse will be seen from a socio-historical perspective as an intersubjective, social and historical phenomenon, as expressed in the work of Mikhail Bakhtin (1986; 1929/1995).

THE RELATIONSHIP BETWEEN ACADEMIC TEXT AND CONTEXT

In SFL terms, the context in which a text is produced can be recreated by analysis of textual language, and the opposite is also true (Halliday, 1989). From that perspective, if genre is a socio-discursive process, then the teaching practice must develop learners' reflexivity about the relevant social context to use it as a scaffolding device to explore texts in a meaningful way.

Both text form and meaning are socially constructed and respond to demands of immediate circumstances and cultural tradition (Jamieson, 1975, pp. 414-415). Text and context are thus *mutually predictive* (Halliday & Martin, 1993, p. 22). As I will argue later, awareness about this bidirectionality (as dialectics in the work of Bakhtin, 1986; Fairclough, 1989) between text and context allows students to situate their text in the system of genres (Devitt, 1991; Bazerman, 2005) that structure academic interactions and thus helps them see the connection between the text they write and the research activity.

Definition of the academic context as a culture and disciplines as situations

My teaching practice has always included the analysis of students' text and the observation of their struggle and my own to write and become an academic writer. This teaching and writing experience finds expression in Charles Bazerman's words:

> I found that I could not understand what constituted an appropriate text in any discipline without considering the social and intellectual activity which the text was part in. (Bazerman, 1988, p. 4)

In order to define the "social and intellectual activity which the text was part in" I have resorted to SFL perspective on language, genre, register, and text[2].

Academic discourse, genre, register and text

Academic discourse can be described as the linguistic expression and construction of concepts, values and practices shared by members of an institution characterized by technical language and researching, teaching, learning and publishing practices that are constituted in different genres and registers. In SFL terms, language is a "system of meaning creation," that is, a system in which meaning is "the product of the interrelations among the parts" of the system of language and context (Martin, 1992, pp. 497-498). Both genre and register are oriented to the context.

In the broad "Context of Culture" (Halliday, 1989, p. 6), defined as the actions and the meanings (and the values attached to them) produced by the members of a social group, genres are these members' intersubjective representations of the types of situations and texts that recurrently co-occur in that social group and thus distinguish it from other social groups and their respective cultures.

In the "Context of Situation" (Halliday, 1989, p. 6), defined as the environment of the text, the set of meanings that is possible/probable (potentially available) in a given situation, register is "the configuration of semantic resources that the member of the culture associates with a situation type" (Martin, 1992, p. 498).

As an example, we can think of the research article as the *genre* (in opposition to the book review, the dissertation, etc.) that is consistently different in content, format and style when used to report a research in applied linguistics or in rural sciences, thus in two different *registers* (Motta-Roth, 2003). The *text* is the concrete realization of these social-linguistic processes of genre and register choices.

The relationship between context, discourse, genre, register and text can be visually represented in Figure 1 in terms of the several planes in the overall system of language.

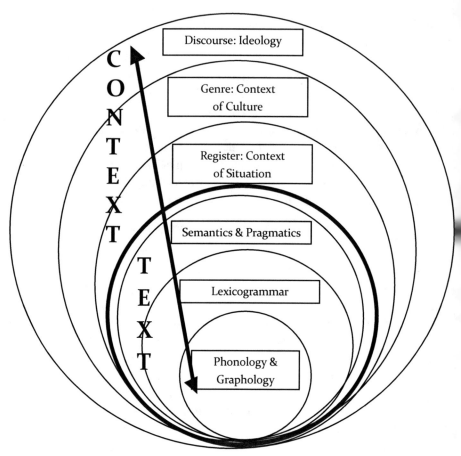

FIGURE 1: REPRESENTATION OF THE STRATIFICATION OF (LIN-
GUISTIC AND CONTEXTUAL) COMMUNICATIVE PLANES (ADAPT-
ED FROM MARTIN, 1992, P. 496; HENDGES, 2005, P. 6).

Text, register and genre are three levels of realization (or instantiation) of the language system. The genre — the most abstract one — is a staged, purpose-oriented set of actions in a discursive event recognized as such in a given Context of Culture (the research article in academia). The register is the configuration of meanings that realize the genre in the Context of Situation (the research article in applied linguistics for the Brazilian Journal of Applied Linguistics). The text is the immediate concrete plane of language instantiation (my article). It is this set of relations between planes of realization that the inexperienced writer will be working with to situate not only their own text but also their writing and reading practices.

In my particular teaching practice, academia is viewed as the "Context of

Culture": a set of concepts, values, and beliefs that typically go together, associated with university life, with which students, faculty and personnel interact through texts. Each individual student's experience of a discipline as a Context of Culture can be seen as a distinctive "Context of Situation" for texts. These "Contexts of Situation" can be defined in terms of three SFL variables that find correspondence with linguistic variables that define the register of the situation:

- Field — the nature of the social practice: the activity, the actions oriented towards a communicative aim by participants of a given situation/event (Bronckart, 1999; Vygotsky, 1986; Kuhn, 1970). It is represented by lexicogrammatical terms (verb, noun, adjective, adverb);

- Tenor — participant roles, relations and interactions: the nature of the connections between participants in the event, their roles and relations. It is represented by the Mood and modality features of the text;

- Mode — text organization: the nature of the semantic unit in use, its cohesion and coherence, the nature of the medium of transmission, its written/oral format.

Each genre then is realized in the form of a particular register that finds its concrete realization in a particular text. The identification of the context variables of academic practices within which we write is fundamental to become a producer and consumer of academic texts. If we want to get an insight into the configuration of a text, we must try to understand the nature of the social practice, of the activities occurring in the relevant context, the situation participants' roles and relations, and the way these conditions are construed in the text with a certain organization.

By presenting language as a socio-semiotic system that constitutes the practices of each social group (instead of a set of independent texts) we help inexperienced writers to get initiated in academic culture (a system of meanings to be understood).

NETWORKING THE WRITING PROCESS

Students learning how to write usually find helpful the "Academic writing cycle," which I developed based on previous research on academic writing and genres (Bazerman, 1988, 2005; Swales, 1990, 1998, 2004; Swales & Feak, 1994; Motta-Roth, 1998, 2001) and on my own teaching practice with inexperienced writers at UFSM since 1994.

This "Academic writing cycle" presupposes the idea that text and context are two sides of experience that must be pedagogically explored in writing courses in order to foster students' critical awareness of the *kairos* of a text (Bazerman, 2007, pp. 119-149), the adequacy in content, form and style of a text to a rhetorical moment. Thus lack of writing experience can be translated as lack of understanding of how text production fits a given context of situation.

Text and context as two sides of experience

Understanding how a text fits a rhetorical moment depends on awareness of how a text constructs an institutional context (law system, science, school/ university, business, etc.). Two simple (and to a certain extent obvious) arguments motivate the activities of the "Academic writing cycle": first, in order for students to become writers in their field, they need to become discourse analysts (to produce the texts that are adequate in the discipline, they must learn to read these texts, learn how they function by analyzing not only linguistic form and content, but the interactions that these texts construct and structure); and second, in a crossdisciplinary classroom, students from different fields need to realize how language works from a sociointeractionist perspective, that is, they need to understand that texts work differently in each field depending on the nature of the activities each area of study conducts and the kind of relations the participants maintain to produce knowledge.

Vygotsky (1986, 1984/2007) and Halliday (1994) both state that we learn the language we speak because we interact in the contexts that use that language to conduct social activities. I have synthesized this view in my own terms:

> As learners come to realize the social arrangements of their environment, they develop reflexivity upon the rules of grammatical operation and text structures. Learners need to *reflect on context and text*, on how texts contribute to context dynamics.

This view offers a set of implications for academic writing that can be summarized in three "Discourse-analytical principles" that guide my pedagogic practice:

(1) In order to understand the uses of formal elements in language, *learners must reflect upon their context*;

(2) To be able to write, *novice writers need to analyze the relationship between social practices and texts*, comparing what they have been able to deduct from their observation with the texts produced in this context (journals,

books, dissertations, book reviews, etc.), *focusing on how research activities, social roles and relations are constructed in texts*;

(3) *To learn a language, learners must learn to analyze discourse* (McCarthy & Carter, 1994, p. 134). By reading and deconstructing exemplars of published texts from a lexical, grammatical and discursive perspective, learners will learn to write, revise, and edit their own texts more effectively.

By adopting these three principles, learners develop discourse-analytical abilities that will help them fine-tune their text form and content to a projected audience, thus avoiding the "writing-in-the-vacuum syndrome" (writing without a purpose and an audience in mind) that might arise when taking a text-focused or process-focused writing course.

Based on these three principles, I elaborated a writing cycle that encompasses three sets of activities:

(1) Context Exploration involves learning to interact with the environment in order to learn the language, observe research practices and understand the role of language in knowledge production practices;

(2) Text Exploration involves experiencing analytically the relationship between text and context, how language appropriately constructs the context and vice versa, by analyzing genre systems and genre sets;

(3) Text Production, Revising and Editing involves becoming a discourse analyst by writing, revising and editing one's text as well as other classmates', focusing on how linguistic resources are used for engagement and participation in social and discursive academic practices.

The objective in educating novice writers to think of writing as a cycle of context and text exploration-text production-text revising-text editing is to take these writers from the actual stage of accomplished development in their writing competencies (in Vygotskyan terms, their Zone of Real Development) to a richer, more informed and elaborated stage (their Zone of Potential Development) in which they are able to write with a certain amount of autonomy to exert their authorship. This process is done with the help of the teacher and of the participants of the disciplinary context in which these novice writers want to participate (as a Zone of Proximal Development, where the tasks are performed with the help of a more experienced partner) (Vygotsky, 1984/2007). The observation of the context functions as a scaffolding device to help novice writers project the kind of text that may interact with the relevant context.

The activities in the writing cycle (context and text exploration-text production-text revising-text editing) are arranged as an academic writing network of three sets of questions and tasks (Motta-Roth, 2007) presented in the following section.

The Academic Writing Network

Activity 1: Context Exploration
To understand the uses of formal elements in language, learners must reflect upon their context, the social conditions under which texts are produced and consumed.

This first set of activities is geared towards students' learning of how to interact in academia in order to learn the language. In the first class, I ask learners to observe research and social practices in their environment (laboratories, research groups, project teams, etc.) and to reflect upon the role of language in knowledge production practices. Before reflecting about grammatical rules or basic text structures, learners *observe the activities and interview participants* in laboratories, offices, meeting rooms, etc., about their research and writing practices. In addition, learners search for reference material (books, research articles, book reviews, dissertations, theses, short communications, etc.) that is valued in their academic context.

Students are given a set of exploratory questions they should try to answer, acting as ethnographers that are curious about a community and their social and discursive practices:

(a) Which research practices are used in your area? Which research projects are presently being developed in your research lab/group?
(b) Which research concepts and problems are practiced in your area? Which are the relevant research topics for the people in your lab/group?
(c) Which approach to a specific topic seems more interesting?
(d) Which preliminary readings were you advised to do?
(e) Which are the renowned journals in your area?
(f) Which genres are relevant in your context?
(g) Who publishes where? Who reads what?
(h) Do you intend to publish your text? How can you do that?

Usually, the class takes two meetings to discuss the results of their survey, to learn how to look for journals available in their area more effectively and to search through these journals more productively. After starting to write, the learner's attention will be called to different sections/genres in the journals in their areas and the different functions they perform, how to browse more efficiently through a text in order to decide if it is worth reading it extensively. The result of this activity is that students get aware of the main genres available to them and delineate their writing focus, determining the journal to which they will submit their papers, therefore avoiding the "writing-in-the-vacuum syndrome" again.

As they identify certain topics that seem to be of greater interest to them, we start delineating the semantic map for each student's text by using key-words, as seen in one student's example in Figure 2.

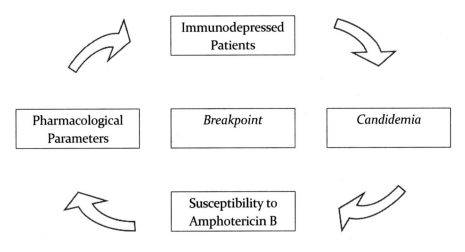

FIGURE 2: SEMANTIC MAP FOR A STUDENT'S ARTICLE

The example in Figure 2 was constructed by one of my students as a plan for a paper about the research he was conducting on the susceptibility to Amphotericin B of immunodepressed patients suffering from Candidemia and the pharmacological parameters that should be established in order to identify the breakpoint in treatments with the drug[3].

Similar semantic structures are used as general frameworks for students' plan for their research article in order to help them keep track of the basic what's (topic), why's (objective), and how's (methodology) of their studies.

Activity 2: Text Exploration
> **To understand how language appropriately articulates itself in a given context and to revise their text more efficiently, novice writers need to analyze the relationship between social and discursive practices.**

Phase 1: Genre systems and genre sets
> **Learners observe the activities and texts in the laboratories, offices, meeting rooms, etc.**

This first set of text exploration activities involves the analysis of genre systems and genre sets. Genre systems instantiate participation of various parts in the process of knowledge production: researchers, peers, students, department heads, editors, book shops, libraries, target audience, etc. (Bhatia, 2004, p. 54). The system indicates the importance of interaction in various (oral and written) texts such as research proposals, advising sessions, talks, articles, books and book reviews, for the establishment and functioning of specific communities (Devitt, 1991, p. 340). In addition, the concept of genre systems is diachronically important because it helps us realize the way various genres result from former texts and influence future texts (Devitt, 1991, pp. 353-354). That is, interrelated genres may "follow upon another in particular settings, because the success conditions of the discursive actions of each require various states of affairs to exist" so the intervention of each of the follow-up genres will have consequences for other genres and corresponding speech acts that follow in the enactment of social intentions (Bazerman, 1994, p. 98).

I believe that students can write more effectively if they can visualize how their research article occupies a position in the network of academic genres that structure the life of their research group, as the example shown in Figure 3 of the genre system that articulates the social interactions and activities at the Reading and Writing Teaching and Research Laboratory (ReWriTe Lab) where I work at UFSM.

Within this system of genres that define a social group, there are also the sets of genres that are instantiated in the everyday life of the group, the texts that structure the daily routine of a research community (Bhatia, 2004, p. 53). Throughout the day, abstracts, book reviews, articles, research proposals, books, chapters, proceedings, etc. are produced in part or whole inside an academic group whose members share interests and aims. Novice as well as experienced writers must develop awareness of how these genre systems and sets structure their experience in the academic context.

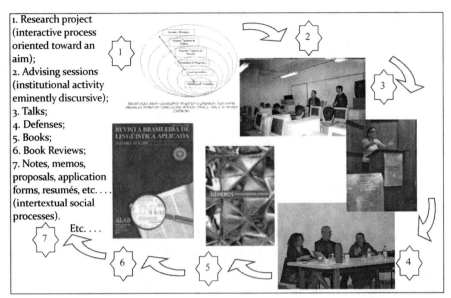

1. Research project (interactive process oriented toward an aim);
2. Advising sessions (institutional activity eminently discursive);
3. Talks;
4. Defenses;
5. Books;
6. Book Reviews;
7. Notes, memos, proposals, application forms, resumés, etc. . . . (intertextual social processes).

Etc. . . .

FIGURE 3: GENRE SYSTEM AT THE READING AND WRITING TEACHING AND RESEARCH LABORATORY (REWRITE LAB) AT FEDERAL UNIVERSITY OF SANTA MARIA, BRAZIL

Phase 2: Text and context relationships
Learners compare lab activities to the texts produced in that context, focusing on how research activities, social roles and relations are constructed in language.

The second set of activities — studying the relationship between text and context — is an attempt to develop students' reflexivity on the relationship between discursive practices and social practices.

Some of the questions the students have to research about are:

(a) Find exemplars of a relevant published genre (a well-succeeded interaction) in your disciplinary context. What is their usual extension in pages? How are they structured/divided?
(b) What type of information is recurrently found?
(c) What information seems central to you?
(d) Which text stages are frequently found? Which speech acts are performed (statement, questioning, promise, order, etc.)
(e) What semantic fields do the texts cover/refer to (plants, people, animals, objects, texts, etc.)?
(f) Is it possible to identify patterns in the lexicogrammatical choices, i.e.,

processes (verbs), participants (nouns), circumstances (adverbs), etc.?

(g) What research processes, participants, and circumstances are referred to?

(h) How do you define the author's *persona* (distinctive personal style in writing)? Are the ideas stated in a straightforward way or does the author use hedging to make statements? How?

(i) Are there signs of dialogism or polyphony? Does the author acknowledge the reader in the text? Is the text open to difference of opinion? How?

(j) Are there signs of intertextuality? Do you recognize vestiges of other previous texts? How?

(k) How do you think academic writers should project their identities in their texts?

These questions bring the learner from the contextual to the textual space, fostering their curiosity and critical eye about how texts are essentially related to the social practices of a given context, recreating it, recontextualizing it, in a resemiotization of previous experience.

The aim here is to make an "ethnographer" out of a novice researcher/writer. Usually, the class takes two meetings to discuss the results of their text exploration, to take a look at the exemplars of genres they have collected in their community. The result of this activity is that students develop textual awareness, identifying linguistic elements that realize certain functions at certain parts of the text (as in Swales, 1990; Swales & Feak, 1994; Motta-Roth, 2001; 2007).

Activity 3: Text Production, Revising and Editing
Learning a language means learning to analyze discourse.

The third set of activities — becoming a discourse analytic producer of texts — is focused on the writing process itself. At this point learners will concentrate on textual features as they write, revise and edit their texts and those of their classmates. They analyze discourse as they are producing text or as they read it.

The starting point is often the analysis of a published text in order to develop learners' sensitivity to linguistic features, analytical competencies of textual language. The awareness gained by these exercises can be used in text production in terms of the writing itself and of the revision stages.

Questions to guide the development of analytical competencies in writing and revising are:

(a) How are the sentences connected in the text? What is the basic text structure?

(b) Which element is in initial and final position in each sentence?

(c) Can you identify text stages that correlate with steps in the research process?

(d) Are there expressions that signal text organization (theme/rheme, conjuncts, subordinators, lexical signaling)?

(e) Do the connectors express addition, opposition, cause, consequence, etc.? What kind of connector can be found in each text stage?

(f) Do concepts get defined? How?

(g) Are research steps described? How? Is the vocabulary more emotional or objective, more descriptive or more argumentative?

(h) Which actions are represented in the text? Which processes are reported by which verbs/verbal phrases?

(i) Are there "action" verbs that suggest material processes (e.g., "catch," "emerge," "develop," "dissolve," "increase")? Or that suggest mental processes (e.g., "think," "predict," "plan") or verbal (e.g., "declare," "suggest," "indicate")? Are there processes that establish relations, classify or identify entities (relational processes, expressed by verbs such as "be," "become," "have," "seem")? Or processes that express existence or behavior (associated with the senses or body functions)? How are they used in the review of the literature or in the methodological sections, for example?

(j) Who are the participants in the actions represented in the text (expressed by noun phrases)? Can you identify the relationship among them (author-reader, researcher-object-phenomenon)? What tone is used by the author, e.g., symmetry/asymmetry (expert/expert, expert/lay person), friendship, impersonality, informality, formality, etc.?

(k) Which nouns and adjectivals can be associated with the circumstances described in the methodology, for example?

(l) Which interdiscursive elements are in the text, i.e., that simulate conversation, self-promotion, recommendation, etc.?

(m) Does the author make self-reference, reference to the reader or other groups? Which words or pronouns are used for that?

(n) Which verb tenses are used? Is there verbal, nominal or adverbial modalization? What kind of modalization is used, epistemic or deontic?

(o) When is passive or active voice used? Are the agents of the actions explicitly mentioned in the text?

(p) Which among these linguistic features do you think fit to adopt in your own paper?

These questions (and their paraphrases) focus learners' attention on the lexicogrammatical features of the texts they read and write. The aim here is to develop learners' awareness of the linguistic system and its uses, the text structure, content and style.

Usually, two-thirds of the twelve classes are dedicated to revising, criticizing and rewriting the texts of three or four students each day. Each week the class debates a section of the paper, its function and textual configuration, linguistic features, etc., so that at the end of the twelve weeks, each student has a complete paper that has been developed along the course.

The sets of activities in the "Academic writing cycle" are represented in Figure 4.

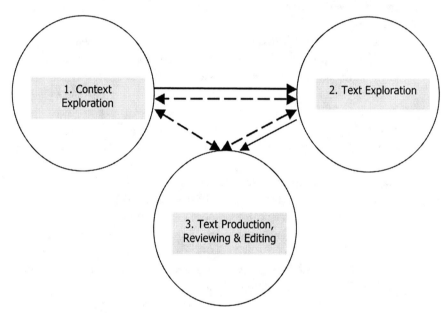

FIGURE 4: "ACADEMIC WRITING CYCLE" (BASED ON MOTTA-ROTH, 2001)

The figure shows a writing cycle as an activity network. The first phase of the cycle starts with the unidirectional arrows, with activity 1 leading to activities 2 and 3. This phase is completed with learners' first attempt to write a text relevant to the context they have in mind. The subsequent phases change the cycle into a network, because learners can continue from any activity at any moment, and any activity can occur at any time, lead to any next activity and even occur at the same time of other activities. Thus learners can go back and read more about the chosen topic before revising their text, or can revise the text before looking for more information, or can revise the text as they rewrite it.

In the following section, I will project some implications of the present approach for the teaching of academic writing.

IMPLICATIONS FOR ACADEMIC WRITING TEACHING

Awareness of how the language system operates in terms of semantic field, interpersonal relations and text structure can help students appropriate the system to serve their own interests according to the conditions they identify in their immediate research context. We can help novice academic writers develop writing abilities by leading them to explore social and discursive practices within their disciplinary culture. As novice writers learn to write, they need to consider contextual regulations (in Bakhtin's terms (1986) "centripetal force") as well as social, and therefore dynamic, collective discursive practices ("centrifugal forces").

With Bazerman's initial quote in mind (one needs to comprehend the activity to understand the text), students' first task is to observe their actual academic environment in order to build a framework to better understand how academic discourse and knowledge production practices are dialectically constructed. Texts are then seen as socio-rhetorical processes and artifacts, i.e., tools writers use to realize goals and carry out activities within a complex set of social relationships constrained by the goals sanctioned by the disciplinary community (Haas, 1994, p. 44).

Novice writers can be educated to develop an academic identity by helping them to decide what to write, to whom, and for what purpose.

From a critical perspective, the class should work with the concept of authorship so that learners can become authors themselves, writing texts that hold connection with the activities of their daily academic life (Halliday, 1991, p. 13). "Authorship" is the writer's prerogative and responsibility to choose the aim, the content and style, the readership of the text (Ivanic, 1998, pp. 26, 219, 341).

Observation of genre systems and sets (activities, roles and relations that mediate language) in specific contexts (lab activities, classes, office hours, research group meetings, etc.) should inform language pedagogy.

Genre pedagogy involves a debate over the production, distribution and consumption of texts. It is important that learners and teachers get to know (or learn to explore) the social situation of the relevant genres of each target-community, by asking questions such as the ones listed here.

Educating students about the uses of language in specific academic contexts depends on clear identification of the connections between text and their surrounding circumstances. There seems to be three great challenges in academic writing teaching that genre pedagogy can respond to: novice writers need to understand what genre is and how it functions, teachers have to effectively teach someone how to engage in the genres that constitute academic life, and novice writers must take part in the discourse of science.

NOTES

This work was supported by grant nº 304256/2004-8 from the Brazilian Research Funding Agency (CNPq). The idea for this work resulted from my participation in the panel "Challenges in genre analysis and genre teaching," at the ABRAPUI International Conference, Universidade Federal de Minas Gerais, Belo Horizonte, MG, Brazil, June 4th, 2007; and in the Writing Research Across Borders Conference, University of California Santa Barbara, CA, USA, February 24, 2008. Parts of this work have appeared in Motta-Roth (2007).

[1] I thank my colleague Vera Menezes de Oliveira e Paiva from the Federal University of Minas Gerais, Brazil, for calling my attention to this point.

[2] I should point out that Bazerman does not see the linkage between text and context as determinative and tight as Halliday and Martin do (see "mutually predictive" cited above). For him, text and context are dynamically interactive, so one needs to understand both in order to understand either fully. Predictability of course does increase with the stability and pervasiveness of particular practices of text and situation typification, but always creativity, novelty and locality of meaning, and polysemiousness work against simple predictivity in either direction. The situation does not define exactly what to say and whatever is said always modifies the situation, as does the uptake. (Bazerman, personal communication, July 27, 2008)

[3] *Immunodepressed:* Patient whose immunologic system has been effected by disease or treatment. *Candidemia:* Yeast infection. *Amphotericin B:* Fungicide agent, a powerful antibiotic drug used in yeast infection treatments. *Pharmacological Parameters:* Dimensions or ways of measuring or predicting the response of a patient to the properties and actions of a drug. *Breakpoint:* Condition(s) that determine(s) when a treatment must be interrupted. Source: *The On-line Medical Dictionary* (http://cancerweb.ncl.ac.uk/omd/); *Stedman's Online Medical Dictionary*, 27th Edition (http://steadmans.com/), retrieved on June 14, 2006.

REFERENCES

Bakhtin, M. M./Voloshinov, V. N. (1929/1995). *Marxismo e filosofia da linguagem.* São Paulo: Editora Hucitec.

Bakhtin, M. M. (1986). *Speech genres and other late essays.* Austin: University of

Texas Press.

Bazerman, C. (1988). *Shaping written knowledge*. Madison: University of Wisconsin Press.

Bazerman, C. (1994). Systems of genre and the enactment of social intentions. In A. Freedman & P. Medway (Eds.), *Genre and the new rhetoric* (pp. 79-101). London: Taylor & Francis.

Bazerman, C. (2005). *Gêneros textuais, tipificação e interação* (A. P. Dionísio & J. C. Hoffnagel, Eds. & Trans.). São Paulo: Cortez.

Bazerman, C. (2007). *Escrita, gênero e interação social.* (A. P. Dionísio & J. C. Hoffnagel, Eds. & Trans.). São Paulo: Cortez.

Bhatia, V. K. (2004). *Worlds of written discourse: A genre-based view.* London: Continuum.

Bronckart, J.-P. (1999). *Atividades de linguagem, textos e discursos: Por um interacionismo sócio-discursivo*. São Paulo: EDUC.

Devitt, A. J. (1991). Intertextuality in tax accounting: Generic, referential, and functional. In C. Bazerman & J. Paradis (Eds.), *Textual dynamics of the professions: Historical and contemporary studies of writing in professional communities* (pp. 336-357). Madison: University of Wisconsin Press.

Fairclough, N. (1989). *Language and power.* London: Longman.

Haas, C. (1994). Learning to read biology: One student's rhetorical development in college. *Written Communication, 11*(1), 43-84.

Halliday, M.A.K. (1989). Part A. In: M.A.K. Halliday & R. Hasan *Language, context, and text: Aspects of language in a social-semiotic perspective* (pp.1-49). Oxford: Oxford University Press.

Halliday, M. A. K. (1991). The notion of "context" in language education. In T. Lê & M. McCausland (Eds.), *Language education: Interaction & development. Proceedings of the International Conference on Language Education held in Ho Chi Mihn City, Vietnam* (pp. 1-26). Tasmania, Australia: University of Tasmania at Lauceston.

Halliday, M. A. K. (1994). *An introduction to functional grammar* (2nd ed.). London: Edward Arnold.

Halliday, M. A. K. & Martin, J. R. (1993). *Writing science: Literacy and discursive power.* Pittsburgh: University of Pittsburgh Press.

Hendges, G. R. (2005). *A genre and register analysis of electronic research articles from a systemic functional perspective: New medium, new meanings.* Unpublished doctoral thesis, Federal University of Santa Catarina, Santa Catarina, Brazil.

Ivanic, R. (1998). *Writing and identity: The discoursal construction of identity in academic writing.* Amsterdam: John Benjamins.

Jamieson, K. M. (1975). Antecedent genre as rhetorical constraint. *Quarterly Journal of Speech, 61,* 405-415.

Kuhn, T. S. (1970). *The structure of scientific revolution.* (2nd ed. expanded). Chicago: The University of Chicago Press.

Larsen-Freeman, D., & Cameron, L. (2008). *Complex systems and applied linguistics.* Oxford: Oxford University Press.

McCarthy, M., & Carter, R. (1994). *Language as discourse: Perspectives for language teaching.* London: Longman.

Martin, J. R. (1992). *English text: System and structure.* Philadelphia: John Benjamins.

Motta-Roth, D. (1998). Discourse analysis and academic book reviews: A study of text and disciplinary cultures. In J. F. Coll, I. Fortanet, J. C. Palmer, & S. Posteguillo (Eds.), *Genre studies in English for academic purposes* (pp. 29-48). Castellón, Spain: Universitat Jaume I.

Motta-Roth, D. (Org.) (2001). *Redação acadêmica: Princípios básicos.* Santa Maria, Rio Grande do Sul, Brazil: Imprensa Universitária, UFSM.

Motta-Roth, D. (2003). A dinâmica de produção de conhecimento: Teorias e dados, pesquisador e pesquisados. *The Brazilian Journal of Applied Linguistics, 3*(1), 165-177. Belo Horizonte, Minas Gerais, Brazil: Associação Brasileira de Lingüística Aplicada.

Motta-Roth, D. (2007). Escrevendo no contexto: Contribuições da LSF para o ensino de redação acadêmica. In L. Barbara & T. Berber Sardinha (Eds.), *Proceedings of the 33rd International Systemic Functional Congress* (pp. 828-860). São Paulo: LAEL/PUCSP. Retrieved October 22 2007, from http://www.pucsp.br/isfc

Swales, J. M. (1990). *Genre analysis: English in academic and research settings.* Cambridge: Cambridge University Press.

Swales, J. M. (1998). *Other floors, other voices: A textography of a small university building.* Mahwah, New Jersey: Erlbaum.

Swales, J. M. (2004). *Research genres: Exploration and applications.* Cambridge: Cambridge University Press.

Swales, J. M., & Feak, C. B. (1994). *Academic writing for graduate students.* Ann Arbor: University of Michigan Press.

Vygotsky, L. S. (1984/2007). Interação entre aprendizado e desenvolvimento. In L. S. Vygotsky, *A formação social da mente* (pp. 87-105). São Paulo: Martins Fontes.

Vygotsky, L. S. (1986). *Thought and language* (Rev. ed., A. Kozulin, Ed.). Cambridge, Massachusetts: MIT Press.

Zemlinsky, P., & Bishop, W. (2004). *Research writing revisited: A sourcebook for teachers.* Portsmouth, New Hampshire: Boynton/Cook.

17   Teaching Critical Genre Awareness

Amy Devitt

Outside the field of genre studies, writers, scholars, and teachers often think of genres as formulaic and constraining. Even within composition, teachers often see the power of genres to inhibit creativity more than the power of genres to reveal constraint. Genre teaching can indeed be formulaic and constraining, if genres are taught as forms without social or cultural meaning. Genre teaching can also be enlightening and freeing, if genres are taught as part of a larger critical awareness. I argue in this chapter for a genre pedagogy that recognizes the limitations of explicit genre teaching and exploits the ideological nature of genre to enable students' critical understanding. Genres will impact students as they read, write, and move about their worlds. Teaching critical genre awareness will help students perceive that impact and make deliberate generic choices.

Fears that writing instruction can encourage accommodation and assimilation extend beyond genre instruction. Teaching academic writing can privilege academic values if not taught critically (see Bizzell, 1993 for an extended discussion). Teaching literacy uncritically can minimize oral traditions and place negative labels on the less literate (see, for example, Barton, 1999). Teaching disciplinary discourse can promote acceptance of the disciplines' assumptions and existing power structures. Victor Villanueva worries that Writing Across the Curriculum is assimilationist, "a political state of mind more repressive than mere accommodation," (2001) in his responding to Donna LeCourt's argument that WAC can foster critical consciousness, using the pedagogy of Paulo Freire (1996). Villanueva seeks a way of fostering critical consciousness in genres other than the personal narrative (which LeCourt recommends). While Villanueva queries whether there is another "genre of engagement," he most wants to help students "maintain the critical and one's sense of identity and agency" (173). Although he might well accuse me of asserting an ideal, a Platonic "Good" (169), I suggest that critical genre awareness, rather than multiple genres of engagement, can help students maintain a critical stance and their own agency in the face of disciplinary discourses, academic writing, and other realms of literacy. I see critical genre awareness as a means to problem posing for students, not just as a way to encompass other genres, even potential genres of engagement.

The genre awareness I argue for is a type of rhetorical awareness, and others have posited that rhetorical awareness can lead to critical awareness and to more deliberate action. Charles Bazerman has summarized how rhetorical awareness "is precisely critical: rhetorical perception used as a means to distance ourselves from the everyday practice of the world's business in order to reveal and evaluate the hidden mechanisms of life" (1992). Such rhetorical awareness leads to greater agency: "The more precisely we learn how the symbols by which we live have come into place, how they function, whose interests they serve, and how we may exert leverage on them to reform the world, the more we may act meaningfully upon our social desires" ("Cultural"). Bazerman notes that action must follow awareness: "Criticism, however, is only the beginning of action. Action is a participation, not a disengagement" ("Cultural"). Armed with genre awareness, I would argue, students can distance themselves from the everyday practices of the genres that surround them but also can act, can participate in those genres. Unlike scholars merely studying genre, students wishing to participate in the academy or discipline or profession cannot simply disengage but must follow that distancing with enlightened participation.

In the rest of this chapter, I will acknowledge the limitations of explicitly teaching specific genres, suggest an alternative in teaching antecedent genres, and add a proposal for teaching genre awareness. Although I merely outline these three approaches to teaching genres in this piece, I plan to explore in future work how all three might work together to develop a fuller critical genre literacy. We will need such pedagogies if we are to help students gain critical access to literate worlds constituted through genres.

TEACHING PARTICULAR GENRES

The ideological nature and power of genres has become obvious to genre scholars today, as, for example, the articles in the collection *The Rhetoric and Ideology of Genre* (2002) attest. With genres understood today as actions in social contexts (based on Carolyn Miller's (1984) oft-cited article and the ensuing North American genre scholarship), genres become embedded in the assumptions, values, and beliefs of the groups in power as any genre emerges, develops, and changes. To teach a particular genre is to teach that genre's context. On the good side, that means we teach genres as rhetorical, with conventions that have rhetorical purpose and that can be used to achieve rhetorical aims in rhetorical situations. The result is a much richer teaching of writing than teaching, say, the arhetorical forms of a five-paragraph theme. Rather than teaching a three-part thesis, where to place that thesis, or how to add a transition at the beginning of each paragraph, for example, teachers can teach even the five-paragraph theme as rhetorically situated, with purposes of demonstrating understanding of a subject, audiences who value direct statements and logical connections, and an ethos that gains credibility through reasoning and distance. On the bad side, the contexts that genres carry include ideologies, norms and values that come to seem unquestioned, common sense—an unquestioned approach to acting through language that runs counter to our academic desire to question the existing. When writers take up a genre, they take up that genre's ideology. If they do it unawares, then the genre reinforces that ideology. When teachers select genres to use in the classroom, then, they are selecting ideologies that those genres will instill in students, for good and bad. Using five-paragraph themes or analysis papers, for example, reinforces apparent objectivity and distance from the subject and Western logic, and it minimizes personal engagement with the subject, emotional appeals, and an understanding of subjects having complexity that's irreducible to parts. Using personal narratives in the classroom, for a different example, reinforces apparent subjectivity and engagement with the subject, and it reduces personal experiences to 3-page stories, requires students to believe that sharing intimate life experiences is healthy and appropriate, and usually values emotional trauma over quotidian reality. In disciplinary discourses, too, particular genres carry their ideological as well as rhetorical contexts. Charles Bazerman and Joseph Little examine the internal rhetorical critiques in the fields of chemistry, anthropology, sociology, and economics, for one such example. Every genre carries with it such exchanges of beliefs and values that we might wish to promote and ones we might think are unfortunate.

Yet we all must teach using genres, in the texts we have students read and in the assignments we have students write. Whether we use genres consciously in the classroom or not, the genres we assign promote particular worldviews just as the topics we have them read about do. The first and most important genre pedagogy, then, is the teacher's genre awareness: the teacher being conscious of the genre decisions he or she makes and what those decisions will teach students.

More explicit teaching of genres, as I've been discussing it so far and as most people think of it, involves teaching students how to write or read particular genres—analysis papers, literacy narratives, sonnets, magical realism. But teaching particular genres explicitly is not the only way to teach genres, and it's a way that has some real controversy to it. Aviva Freedman, in her article "Show and Tell?" (1993), doubted that explicit instruction in genres was necessary or necessarily effective. Freedman's argument that explicit instruction is inadequate was based primarily on theories of and research into second language acquisition, and others have responded to Freedman's argument (most immediately, responses by Jeanne Fahnestock (1993) and by Joseph Williams and Gregory Colomb (1993)). Freedman's article received such attention not only because it was so thoroughly researched and well argued but also because it tapped into many of our fears about as well as desires for using genre studies in the classroom. As Freedman pointed out, writing teachers cannot possibly possess insider knowledge of all the genres students want or need to learn, so their instruction in particular genres will always be incomplete, no matter how much they want to help students gain access to important genres. Freedman was especially concerned with writing teachers instructing students in genres that they would need later in life, either in other courses or in workplaces. No one, no matter how knowledgeable, Freedman argued, can possibly articulate for novices all the expectations and fine details that mark the texts of experienced genre users. I can teach students about colon titles on academic papers, for example, but I can't teach them exactly which ones will be successful and which fall flat. I can teach students the emphasis on logical evidence in analysis papers, but I can't teach all the expectations for convincing evidence in history analysis papers and in philosophy analysis papers. Removed from the contexts in which people acquire new genres—that is, learning analysis papers in writing classes rather than in history or philosophy classes or, to use Freedman's examples, learning business genres in technical writing courses rather than in actual workplaces—the removed genres that are learned seem too easily reduced from the rhetorical to the formulaic.

Even within their originating contexts, genres entail qualities laden with fears for teachers. As discourse types that evolve within social contexts to serve groups' aims, genres seem too heavily embedded in the aims of the ruling powers for teacher comfort. As rhetorical forms that come to feel normal, genres seem too thoroughly ideological to be taught in classrooms that aim to enable students to create their own universes within their existing political and social structures. I would add, too, that teachers cannot possibly tease out all the ideological import of a genre, both because of the impossibility of that venture and because teachers themselves are wrapped in ideologies.

It is not enough simply to add critique to our explicit teaching of specific genres. Our critical awareness of any particular genre or even discipline can be as limited and incomplete as our knowledge and teaching of a particular genre. Bazerman points out that "Rhetorical criticism, especially if it is carried out with broad sweeps of condemnation missing the detailed processes of rhetorical struggle, may make disciplines seem purveyors of hegemonic univocality rather than the locales of heteroglossic contention that they are" ("Cultural"). To do justice to the genres of a discipline requires far more than any teacher or curriculum could teach. Note the complexity of the analysis Bazerman describes in his positive comment on what rhetorical criticism can achieve:

> Rhetorical analysis of the actual communications of the disciplines opens up and makes more visible these suppressed issues of the dynamics and evolving knowledge production of the disciplines.

> Rhetorical analysis can make visible the complexity of mutual par-
> ticipation of many people necessary to maintain the large projects
> of the disciplines, the recognition of the kinds of linguistic prac-
> tice developed in consonance with the goals of the disciplinary
> projects, the constant struggle between competing formulations,
> and the constant innovative edge that keeps the discourse alive.
> Rhetorical analysis can also open up exclusions and enclosures of
> discourse to see how and why they are deployed and to question
> their necessity in any particular case. ("Cultural")

In a course on writing in a particular discipline, perhaps such complex analysis
could be achieved for a few select genres. But, as Bazerman writes, "disciplines
are not games for beginners" (2002, 2006, p. 24).

Theoretically and pedagogically, then, our desires to give students access to
important genres face our fears of generic formula and inculcation. Practically,
though, teachers cannot escape genres, even if they want to. Even if we try to ignore genres in our reading and writing assignments, students will use the genres
they know as they try to interpret what we ask of them. Ask students to write
about the current candidates for president or to apply feminist theory to a literary work, and many will write five-paragraph themes. Ask students to write an
op-ed piece on the candidate of their choice, and they still might draw on the
five-paragraph theme, but they're more likely to try to adjust what they know
to a different situation. Teach them the nature and strategies of the op-ed genre,
and they'll be even more likely to make conscious and deliberate rhetorical decisions. So genre will affect our students' learning whether we teach genres explicitly or not. We also need to recognize that knowing particular genres is necessary
in the academy, disciplines, and professions. Ignoring that fact leaves knowledge
of specific genres as part of the hidden curriculum, as Frances Christie (1985)
argues. If we teach a genre explicitly, we will inevitably teach it incompletely, but
students will understand more about it than they would have if we had taught
them nothing about it at all.

The fears about and criticisms of genre pedagogy that Freedman and others
have examined, though, stem from only one type of genre pedagogy: teaching
particular genres explicitly to students so that they gain access to and can later
use those same genres. I would argue that two other genre pedagogies are at
least as important and escape or at least reduce many of the dangers and weaknesses of explicitly teaching specific genres. I will offer an alternative to teaching a particular genre for its own sake in teaching antecedent genres, and I will
describe how I teach genre awareness, a critical perspective on genre that I gear

toward transfer to other situations. All three pedagogical uses of genre theory—explicitly teaching particular genres, teaching antecedent genres, and teaching critical genre awareness—can work together to develop a theoretically sound genre pedagogy that can contribute to our writing assignments or structure our writing courses.

FROM GENRE THEORY TO GENRE PEDAGOGY

Although the move from theory to pedagogy is never a transparent one, pedagogy always moves within a theoretical context. Current genre pedagogies in general have moved within substantial theoretical frameworks. Yet different theoretical claims about genre lead to different pedagogies, and those differences have not always been noticed. All thoughtful genre pedagogies share an understanding of genres as socially and culturally as well as linguistically embedded. All genre pedagogies appear to share the same larger goal: to give students access to language, structures, and institutions that are important for their individual, academic, and professional development. Different genre pedagogies result, though, from emphasizing different theoretical concerns.

As I delineate some of the theoretical underpinnings of genre pedagogies, I make no claim to comprehensiveness. These five claims seem to me, at this point in genre studies, to be some essential ones and are the ones around which I base my own genre pedagogy.

- Genres are social and rhetorical actions: they develop their languages and forms out of rhetorical aims and contexts shared by groups of users.

- The spread of a genre creates shared aims and social structures.

- As new users acquire genres, that process reinforces existing aims and structures.

- Existing genres reinforce institutional and cultural norms and ideologies.

- To change genres, individually or historically, is to change shared aims, structures, and norms.

Although teachers may share these theoretical understandings, specific pedagogies emphasize different components at different levels. One might emphasize the languages and forms that develop, or the shared aims and social structures, or the process of reinforcement, or the ability to change. Focusing on different theoretical underpinnings leads to focusing on different pedagogical responses. Thus, different pedagogical responses to shared theoretical understandings emerge with different goals for learners.

- If genres are rhetorical actions, then learners can gain rhetorical understanding by gaining access to the language and forms of genres.

- If genres are social actions, then accessing genre forms can give learners insight into and agency within groups' aims and structures.

- If genres reinforce existing structures and ideologies, then gaining consciousness of genres can help learners reduce the reinforcement and propagation of existing norms and ideologies.

- If changing genres changes existing norms and ideologies, then learners who change genres can change a group's aims, structures, and norms.

These pedagogical goals overlap, of course, and one curriculum can pursue more than one pedagogical response. Each represents a potential genre pedagogy, though, with significant differences of emphasis. Focusing on the rhetorically contextualized language and forms of a genre may lead to giving access to particular genres. Focusing on the ways genres develop out of groups' shared aims may lead to focusing on giving access to those groups. Focusing on existing genres as ideological reinforcers may lead to focusing on critiquing genres. And focusing on norms and change may lead to focusing on how individuals might affect those norms and effect change.

Each of these pedagogical responses has potential pitfalls. For a start, as discussed in the previous section, Freedman and others have questioned whether learners could in fact gain full access to the languages and forms of genres. If even experienced users can never fully articulate generic traits, how can teachers help students learn more than a small portion of the languages and forms of a genre? Genre pedagogies need to continue to explain why less than full articulation is sufficient to their aims of giving access to particular genres. The second response, moving from seeing generic form to understanding generic purpose within social contexts, requires cognitive abilities that may be beyond children until a certain level of development has been reached. Genre curricula at different levels, of course, will necessarily address the cognitive abilities at those levels. The third response requires other cognitive abilities, and some quite reasonably question whether such consciousness is at all possible. Can teachers, much less learners, step outside their own ideological frames to see those within which genres exist? Even if they can, that step outside must be maintained in order to resist the existing ideologies. Finally, genres can be quite resistant to change, as institutions and cultures can resist change. The ability of individuals to subvert an existing genre even temporarily, in a single text, depends on others understanding and accepting that change so that communication has not broken down. Even if individuals manage change in an individual text, that change may have little impact on existing structures and norms if others do not take it up. The pedagogical responses we might wish to make to our genre theories are fraught with challenges and complexities. If we wish our pedagogy and our theory to support one another, we need to confront those challenges and design pedagogies with sufficient complexity to be theoretically sound.

One way to build a more complex genre pedagogy is to build a curriculum that addresses multiple approaches. Genres are languages and forms; and they are processes of developing, spreading, and learning; and they are ideologically embedded constructs. This perspective on genres as things, processes, and contexts draws from an old metaphor from physics applied to language-use by Kenneth Pike and developed for writing by Pike, Richard Young, and Alton Becker (Young, 1970): looking at genre pedagogies through the heuristic lens of particle, wave, and field. Loosely and metaphorically defined, this metaphor requires examining genre as a particle (a thing unto itself), a wave (a process), and a field (a context). Genres are things, with language and form and components that can be analyzed. Genres emerge through a process of development over time, and individuals acquire genres through their own learning processes. And genres exist in multiple contexts, as parts of social, institutional, and cultural contexts, and within ideological frames. I see our common theories of genre and our different pedagogical responses to those theories leading to three approaches to teaching based in genre studies—one that focuses on genre as a particle or thing, one that focuses on genre as a process, and one that focuses on genre in its contexts. Each is valid, important, and has the potential to help learners gain access to sources of power, success, and insight. But each is different from the others and merits consideration for what it can offer to learners.

The table below sketches the three pedagogies and how each treats genre as a particle/thing, wave/process, and field/context. The metaphor is meant to be clarifying but not delimiting. While the metaphor equates teaching particular genres as teaching genre as a thing, for example, the field/context aspect of that pedagogy would teach these genres in larger contexts of genre sets and social settings. While the field approach teaches genres in larger contexts, that pedagogy still involves teaching generic forms/things to explore and critique.

Teaching Genres as Particles/Things: Particular Genres	Teaching Genres as Waves/Processes: Antecedents	Teaching Genres as Fields/Contexts: Awareness
Goal: to learn to write particular genres	Goal: to learn how to build on prior genres when learning new genres	Goal: to learn how to critique and change existing genres
Particle/Thing: What relevant genres exist? How can they best be categorized?	Particle/Thing: What genres serve as antecedents for other genres?	Particle/Thing: What are the components of critical awareness? How do they apply to genres?
What genres do these novices need to learn?	What genres best establish potential antecedents?	Which genres lend themselves to developing critical awareness?
What are the components of those genres?		What components of genres lend themselves to developing critical awareness?
Wave/Process: How have these forms changed over time?	Wave/Process: How do people draw on known genres when encountering less familiar genres?	Wave/Process: How do conscious writers critique and change genres?
How do experts acquire these genres?	Which parts of these processes can be made explicit and taught?	What experiences do writers need to have to develop genre awareness?
How can novices learn these genres?		How can genres be changed? How can novices participate in that change?

Field/Context: What are the genre sets these novices need to use?	Field/Context: What future genres might these writers need antecedents for?	Field/Context: How will developing genre awareness affect writers' interactions with existing genre users?
What genres do they already know?	What genres do the writers already know as potential antecedents?	
How will learning these new genres affect their interactions with the larger context/culture?	How will learning these antecedents affect the writers' interactions in future contexts?	

TABLE 1: THREE PEDAGOGIES

ONE PEDAGOGICAL APPROACH

Each of these genre pedagogies, like all pedagogies, has its own advantages and pitfalls. Each genre curriculum, in combining these pedagogies, takes on both advantages and pitfalls and develops its own strengths and weaknesses. To exemplify how these pedagogies lead to specific practices, I will describe one I have developed for my own use, based on my theoretical preferences and classroom experiences and designed for college-level students in writing classes, at both the first-year and advanced levels. My approach combines teaching particular genres, how to use those genres as antecedents, and how to critique and potentially change genres.

Beginning with genre as particle, I note again that any genre pedagogy must use some particular genres, at least as examples. My goal in choosing and using particular genres, though, is not to teach any particular genre fully and thoroughly so that students have acquired the genres. Rather, I aim to give students enough experiences with those genres that at least some elements of those genres might serve as antecedents when students acquire unfamiliar genres in the future. I agree with Bazerman and Little that we have a "pedagogic responsibility" "to teach students to speak and write for academic purposes in first and second languages" (2005). While teaching academic purposes and academic registers, however, we cannot possibly teach all of the specific academic genres that students may need in academia. Although we cannot teach students a specific genre fully, the genres that we do teach and use in the classroom can serve as scaffolding for later genre acquisition, as these partially learned genres act as antecedents for other genres (see Chapter 7 of my *Writing Genres* for a fuller discussion of antecedent genres (2004)). In treating particular genres as antecedents for learning future genres, this pedagogy shifts from genre as particle to genres as wave or process.

Students in my first-year composition courses, for example, often have encountered in previous schooling the genres specified in the benchmarks from the Kansas State Department of Education, genres labeled narrative, expository, persuasive, and technical. The expository and persuasive papers for high school students involve benchmarks for using thesis statements and different kinds of details with an emphasis on meeting the readers' needs. I can see their prior experience with these genre elements in the early writing they do in my class, and I can build on those antecedents as I help students learn to develop more complex theses, integrate logical reasoning with personal experience, and serve the needs of different readers as well as their own needs. When I assign particular new genres, like the analysis paper, I intend to give students other writing experiences that can transfer to the writing they do in their major classes or in their workplaces. When I assign public genres like pamphlets, brochures, and organization websites, I aim to add public audiences and purposes to their generic repertoire so that they have more non-academic rhetorical antecedents to draw from in their political lives. I assign genres that supplement the genres they already know in ways that might serve as antecedents when they go on to other courses and other writing situations. I do not expect students to master any of these genres. I hope instead to have given them generic material from which to draw when encountering new genres. In my current teaching work, I am focusing on how to help students with other important parts of the process: helping them learn how to transfer from one set of genre material to new writing tasks. Whether any pedagogy can be successful at achieving such transfer from one genre to another is a question for more research.

My use of particular genres itself has a further purpose, treating genre as field: I want students not only to add to their repertoire but also to learn to critique the genres they know and encounter, with an end possibility of changing the genres that need to change to better serve their needs. The end goal is a critical consciousness of genre, a genre awareness—a conscious attention to genres and their potential influences on people and the ability to consider acting differently within genres. Some evidence does support that students can develop genre awareness and that it can transfer to new contexts. Sunny Hyon found, when she studied the reading of second-language students, that students did develop a general genre awareness out of instruction in particular genres; that genre awareness then transferred to reading and writing other genres as well (2002). Focusing on critical genre awareness with my own students is a major way I fight my own fears of teaching genre. Rather than just inculcating students with existing ideologies through established genres, I work to help them become more aware of the shaping influence of genres on their thinking and communicating. Without developing their genre awareness, people are more at the mercy of existing genres and existing power structures and dynamics. With a more highly developed genre awareness, people have a better chance of seeing how genres act upon them and of affecting those actions.

Developing genre awareness is no easier than developing any other kind of critical consciousness. I structure my curriculum around the same tagmemics heuristic, of helping students see genres as things, then as processes, and within larger contexts. Rhetorical analysis is a start, as Bazerman argued earlier. Seeing genres as things, with elements that have purposes rather than rules, opens students to see genres as created by people to achieve aims, not just as pre-existing and irrevocable constructs into which they must fit. Seeing genres as processes, which emerge and change, is a second component of the curriculum. And seeing genres as serving the aims of groups, institutions, and cultures is the third component. Combined, these three elements help students to understand genres as created, dynamic, and ideological constructs. When they learn a new, antecedent genre, I hope they thereafter learn it with some consciousness of genres' rhetorical nature and of their potential for adapting to writers' particular purposes and situations.

To help students understand genres both intellectually and experientially, I lead students through a series of assignments that have them analyze, write, critique, and change or rewrite genres, a series of assignments that gives some idea of how my conceptualization of genre pedagogy translates into practices. I juggle my selection of particular genres to include both genres that might serve as antecedent genres for students and genres that might help them step aside from their ideological contexts. As Heather Bastian argued at the 2007 Conference on College Composition and Communication, students more easily perceive genres' constructed nature in genres with which they are less familiar. She suggests having students analyze first a genre outside of their own culture or time—genres from the past that no longer exist or have been dramatically altered—or genres from other cultures, countries, or unfamiliar institutions. Analyzing such unfamiliar genres helps students to see that all genres serve groups and reinforce particular ways of viewing the world. When they return, next, to more familiar genres, they are better prepared to accept that their genres, too, represent particular viewpoints that shape their experience of the world. The process through which I ask students to approach these particular genres leads them through analyzing, writing, critiquing, and then changing genres, what I call rewriting genres. Cycling through these processes multiple times reinforces that genre analysis is not meant to stop at accommodation or assimilation but move to critique and change. Both particular genres and processes are perpetually embedded within larger contexts since I define genres from the start as rhetorical and social actions developing within particular social and cultural contexts.

This sequence of assignments, sketched below, includes genre as particle, wave, and field and aims toward helping students gain a critical genre aware-ness. Of course, these projects expand and condense, and constitute smaller or larger assignments, depending on the length of the course and the levels of the students.

- Project 1: analyzing a familiar, everyday genre as a class, learning the techniques of rhetorical analysis
- Project 2: writing that familiar genre differently, with a major shift in treatment of purpose, audience, subject, or setting
- Project 3: analyzing a genre from another culture or time, working in groups to gather samples, analyze the genre, and learn about the historical or cultural context
- Project 4: analyzing an academic genre chosen as a potential ante-cedent genre, working as a class on a common genre
- Project 5: writing that academic genre within a specific writing task for this class
- Project 6: critiquing that genre and recommending specific changes that might better meet each student's needs
- Project 7: analyzing, critiquing, and writing flexibly another poten-tial antecedent genre, chosen individually to serve the individuals' needs (depending on the group, either a public genre or a future major or workplace genre)

What I intend to achieve through these experiences is to start the process of enlightening students about genres. As they move from familiar to unfamiliar, back to familiar contexts and on to less familiar contexts, they have the chance to discover how contexts shape genres. As they move from analyzing to writing within to critiquing to writing with changes, they have the chance to discover how genres shape them and how they might shape genres. The results can be writers with expanded genre repertoires, including more potential antecedent genres, and writers with expanded genre awareness, including heightened sensi-tivity when they encounter new genres in the future.

Like all curricula, of course, this one slips in practice as it encounters real students with real intentions and reactions. It works for some better than others. I have not done the research required to claim effectiveness for this curriculum. And I am certainly not claiming any part of what I am teaching is unique or necessarily original. What I do intend is to contribute to the discussion of how genre theory can translate into sound and effective pedagogy by offering my own conceptualization and curriculum that derive directly from my knowledge of theory.

If we can teach genres in ways that acknowledge our inability to teach any genre thoroughly or completely and that help students to question as well as follow generic expectations, then we will come much closer to easing our well-founded fears of genres' power. Genre pedagogies can become part of a larger critical education, with the full powers of genre recognized and students' powers enhanced. As teachers of writing, we must use genres, but we must use them knowingly and deliberately. As scholars of genre, we know enough to achieve that critical awareness—of genres and of our fears of genres.

REFERENCES

Barton, D. (1999). *Situated literacies: Reading and writing in context.* London: Routledge.

Bastian, H. (2007). *Rethinking identity through generic agency.* Paper presented at the Conference on College Composition and Communication, New York.

Bazerman, C. (1992). From cultural criticism to disciplinary participation: Living with powerful words. In Charles Moran and A. Herrington (Eds.), *Writing, teaching, and learning in the disciplines* (pp. 61-68). New York: Modern Language Association.

Bazerman, C. (2006). Distanced and refined selves: Educational tensions in writing with the power of knowledge. In M. Hewings (Ed.), *Academic writing in context: Implications and applications. Papers in honour of Tony Dudley-Evans* (Rev. ed., pp. 23-29). Birmingham, United Kingdom: University of Birmingham Press.

Bazerman, C., & Little, J. (2005). Knowing academic languages. In H. Melander (Ed.), *Text/arbete/text at work* (pp. 261-269). Upsalla, Sweden: Upsalla University.

Bizzell, P. (1993). *Academic discourse and critical consciousness.* Pittsburgh: University of Pittsburgh Press.

Christie, F. (1985). Language and schooling. In S. Tchudi (Ed.), *Language, schooling and society* (pp. 21-40). Upper Montclair, New Jersey: Boynton.

Coe, R., Lingard, L., & and Teslenko, T. (Eds.). (2002). *The rhetoric and ideology of genre.* Cresskill, New Jersey: Hampton Press.

Devitt, A. J. (2004). *Writing genres.* Carbondale: Southern Illinois University Press.

Fahnestock, J. (1993). Genre and rhetorical craft. *Research in the Teaching of English, 27,* 265-271.

Freedman, A. (1993). Show and tell? The role of explicit teaching in the learning of new genres. *Research in the Teaching of English, 27,* 222-251.

Hyon, S. (2002). Genre and ESL reading: A classroom study. In A. M. Johns (Ed.), *Genre in the classroom: Multiple perspectives* (pp. 121-141). Mahwah, New Jersey: Erlbaum.

LeCourt, D. (1996). WAC as critical pedagogy: The third stage? *JAC: A Journal of*

Composition Theory, 16, 389-405.

Miller, C. R. (1984). Genre as social action. *Quarterly Journal of Speech, 70*, 151-167.

Villanueva, V. (2001). The politics of literacy across the curriculum. In S. H. McLeod, et al. (Eds.), *WAC for the new millennium: Strategies for continuing writing-across-the-curriculum programs* (pp. 165-178). Urbana, Illinois: National Council of Teachers of English.

Williams, J., & Colomb, G. (1993). The case for explicit teaching: Why what you don't know won't help you. *Research in the Teaching of English, 27*, 252-264.

Young, R. E., Becker, A. L., & Pike, K. L. (1970). *Rhetoric: Discovery and change.* New York: Harcourt Brace Jovanovich.

18 Curricular Proposal of Santa Catarina State: Assessing the Route, Opening Paths

Maria Marta Furlanetto

INTRODUCTION[1]

In this essay I propose a reflexive and evaluative synthesis of prior studies focused on discursive issues related to genres under Bakhtin's philosophical and theoretical approach. The essay's institutional context is the Curricular Proposal of the state of Santa Catarina (1998)[2], a document which establishes philosophical, linguistic and psychological principles, including Vygotsky's notions of historical-cultural psychology related to teaching-learning, and objectives and guidelines for L1 teaching at state schools. I try to summarize and trace relevant theoretical articulations for dealing with language practices related to genres at the school environment and their connections to the social world.

Such an approach is related to the current pedagogical relations based on directives of a political-educational character, which also influence the mediations related to teacher training. In short, this article shall deal with:

(a) the basic document that guides teaching and learning (Curricular Proposal) in the state of Santa Catarina;
(b) the interacting subjects;
(c) the learning tools.

In spite of the proposal's solid theoretical framework and of the numberless successful results obtained in the state of Santa Catarina, difficulties have arisen in several schools, as we cannot avoid the gap between an educational proposal and its corresponding practices. One should also consider the understanding one has of the teaching object—genres—and the didactic unity—the text—which demands from the individuals involved that they improve their practice as interlocutors, as readers, and as writers. In addition to the necessary involvement of teacher training (a training that demands an enormous increase in the teachers' range of knowledge), this issue also involves the conflicting relation between academic researchers and teachers (who, in contrast, are not devoted to research on a regular basis): how do they establish a cooperative mode in which the work of one group can become the knowledge and practice of the other?

These clashes are foreseen by Bakhtinian theory, which offers us a frame to understand how we can overcome such difficulties, and our ethical responsibility concerning them.

In order to complement and reflect upon the route of the Curricular Proposal (CP) in the state, I raise, as a counterpoint, a synthesis of my personal experience as a consultant to Florianópolis' Municipal Department of Education[3], from October to December 2006. Florianópolis' Curricular Proposal is similar to the state Curricular Proposal in its construction and theoretical basis. Fifty hours were devoted to what came to be known as "Resignifying the Curricular Proposal for the city of Florianópolis." The project sought to complement the basic Proposal (Florianópolis, 1996) by discussion and formulation of a document to advance understanding of genres, and by providing support for the selection of genres for elementary/junior high school (especially from the 5th grade on, since there was another group concerned with primary school literacy).

I shall begin by presenting a synthetic history of the preparation of the state's Curricular Proposal; next, I will propose a general evaluation of the efforts made to implement the directives pointed out in the document (more specific documents were released from 1998 on); after that, I will point out some critical elements and a review of the directives based on the conflicts resulting from its interpretation and the school practice; in addition, I will synthesize the work done by the Municipal Secretary of Education; finally, I will consider some philosophical and theoretical aspects crucial both for researchers and for those who are interacting daily with the students, and for the human relations resulting from this collective work.

Such considerations are based on the assumption that our experiences, from the simplest ones to the more intellectually elaborated, evoke those questions and reflections raised by Bakhtin. More explicitly, I think of Bakhtin's "architectonics of responsibility"—on every ethical act "the responsibility we have for our unique place in existence and for the media through which we relate such a singular event to the rest of the world, which is different from it" (Clark & Holquist, 1998, p. 90)[4]. I think the relationships with *others* need to be shaped into a "coherent performance," without excluding the idea that each one is building, through every act, in every thought, what Bakhtin called the *self*— something that only makes sense in the dimension of otherness.

THE PHILOSOPHICAL AND THEORETICAL MAKINGS OF THE CURRICULAR PROPOSAL OF SANTA CATARINA

The version of the Curricular Proposal under study was elaborated from 1995 to 1997 by a multidisciplinary group, and officially published in 1998[5]. It includes three volumes: curricular disciplines, multidisciplinary themes, and preparation for the teaching profession. The theoretical and methodological frame of the CP articulates a culturally and historically oriented psychology (the one elaborated by Vygotsky) with a philosophy of language (by Bakhtin) centered on the enunciative event (verbal interaction). The contents are delineated as a set of practices that have as organizing axes *speech/listening, reading/writing* and *linguistic analysis* (Santa Catarina, 1998, p. 73); the *genres* are presented as recurrent enunciations in characteristic situations, associated with social spheres, occurring either in an everyday language register or in a more formal one. In principle, all verbal manifestations occur as a *genre*, even if in a process of formation or transformation, since these genres are marked not only in thematic terms but also in their *organizational* and *stylist* aspects.

A basic premise was that the work with discursive practices would be congruent with the learning conception integrated into the project—a conception of a cultural and historical nature—focusing on the role of social interactions in the formation of superior psychological ones. In such a context it is *mediation*, in learning, that enables each individual to reach the necessary development to behave as a citizen. Thus the teacher holds a key role in the process: it is the teacher who, through his/her planning, creates activities that offer some challenges to the students; who, by guiding them, should always have in mind the goals of his/her work and the intended results; who assesses the student's performance, always challenging them to reach a level of independence. Such a process corresponds to Vygotsky's concept of zone of *proximal development* (1991). In its turn, such a notion deals with the transformation of common sense notions into educational ones[6].

Beyond the organizing axes referred to above, the contrast and the mutual dependence (dialectical relation) between *language-structure* and *language-event* was established. The *language-structure* dimension comprised the notational (conventional) and grammar studies as a necessary frame for communication; the *language-event* dimension focused on the discursive event, the teaching practices in their multiple goals. The intention of this configuration was to decentralize the teaching of grammar, showing how grammar is already integrated into the discursive production: it is to grammar that one refers when one talks of *reflection* and *linguistic analysis*.

The texts, units of the didactic work, circulate in the discursive communities as genre manifestations, with genres themselves taken as teaching objects. The diversity of genres should also take into consideration the physical medium of the text, that is, those elements that allow texts to circulate: books, newspapers, posters, TV and all kinds of possible mediations. "The mode of transportation and reception of the enunciation conditions the very constitution of the text, models the genre of discourse" (Maingueneau, 2001, p. 72). Thus, the media also allow for the characterization or identification of genres.

One assumes that to work with genres implies knowing the *procedures* employed in the flow of language, involving the development of specific abilities at school (some individuals teach, other individuals learn): How to produce a chronicle? How to prepare an interview? That implies a methodologically prepared teacher-mediator at the scene, with certain knowledge and abilities.

From Bakhtin's fundamental notions about the pedagogical paths, the main one adopted involves the recognition that there isn't *a* subject-teacher defined once and for all; to believe in a stable identity would be a delusion. All that appears or disappears in social life charges a subjective price in terms of the building of images and functions. The interactional process makes and unmakes objects, beliefs and values all around it.

GENERAL EVALUATION OF THE ROUTE OF THE CURRICULAR PROPOSAL—A CRITICAL REVIEW

In this section I call attention to specific points in the route of the CP, under the perspective of varying approaches and focusing on relevant themes from that document. On the one hand, I focus on research studies that describe cases of success obtained through practices oriented by the Curricular Proposal, on the discourse of the base-document, its structure and assumed function; on the other hand, I focus on how genres are treated as objects for school learning. I resort to that division with the aim to confront perspectives and to extract from them some lessons on social relations. The selected research works comprise a sample of the existing literature about this particular theme.

The Proposal in Practice: genre in school learning

Cardoso (2005) tried to describe and to analyze a pedagogical intervention based on non-school texts (and with non-verbal semioses), the packages of industrialized snacks, a genre that evidently gets around in the context of elementary school students. Having the CP as its background, she used as theoretical framework genre theory and the recent view on literacy.

The author believed that the study of snack packages as original genre vehicles, which circulate in the context of students and teachers, could be fruitful as a pedagogical, communicative and technological tool, in the sense of engaging a bigger interest and participation by the students. In that intervention, oral activities were carried out and a written questionnaire was applied with eleven open questions, answered by the 3rd graders of an elementary/junior high public state school. The questionnaire was part of an activity in the didactic sequence of the course planned, based on the reflections by the researcher produced with the pedagogical team and the teacher of that class.

After analyzing a primer adopted in 2004 by that school, Cardoso observed that

. . . in what relates to the work with genres and concepts, and the textual activities, the textbooks showed some progress, but still not enough to follow up the rhythm of society's development, of the communicative forms that are produced everyday. (Cardoso, 2005, p. 39)

The results of that experience made evident the increase in the quality of the pedagogical practice, both for teachers and students. In the conclusion of her dissertation the researcher stresses that the work with food packages as communicative pedagogical tools exhibits great potential to help in the literacy process, if its use in the school environment gives attention to the communicative purposes and senses present in the textual material—that is, its multitextuality.

When offering a workshop on text, Maieski (2005) integrated reading and linguistic analysis focusing on an opinion article (from the journalistic sphere) with results beyond what would be expected; the author's didactic proposal elaborated for reading, text production and linguistic analysis follows the directives of the Curricular Proposal of Santa Catarina (CP/SC), and the National Curricular Parameters (Parâmetros Curriculares Nacionais—PCNs). Using the methodology of action research, the author involved 20 elementary school students in an extracurricular activity, along 20 meetings. The students themselves pointed out the characteristics of the newspaper genre by means of analytical reading, moved on to text production and made the linguistic analysis.

Considering the importance of the procedures responsible for the success of that work, I now summarize the steps developed by Maieski (2005, pp. 97-98) for her practice:

(1)   Initial assessment about the students' knowledge of the selected genre and their registration on an internet provider;

(2)   Distribution of newspapers and magazines for reading and analysis/reflection on the genre;

(3)   Discussion of the socio-ideological functions of printed journalism: the appearance of journalism; media corporations; periodicity; publishing interests; dominant groups in that sphere; political and economic control of the press; social influences over the press; moral and ethical values; genres and their mode of manifestation (persuasion, public opinion formation, silencing, publishing criteria, etc.);

(4)   Reading and analysis of articles, integrating the reading/comprehen-

sion of the text-enunciation into the reading/analysis of the genre: who writes it, with what ends, to whom it is directed, how the theme appears; from where the authors speak (social place); how the author identifies him/herself; who else speaks through him/her; is the author a member of the newspaper's staff or someone invited by the newspaper; how the author builds the enunciations relative to what has already been said; what the author wants to show/prove/criticize/denounce; what are the author's arguments; what linguistic resources he/she uses; who are the intended interlocutors; who he/she imagines them to be; possible reactions-responses;

(5) Email contacts with newspaper writers whose articles would be read and analyzed;

(6) Discussion of varied themes in order to stimulate the students to take a standpoint and to give an evaluative answer;

(7) Textual production, based on events discussed during the workshop and related to the reality of the participants;

(8) Review, analysis and correction of the texts: readings by the teacher, reading/comprehension with students; assessment of difficulties; linguistic analyses made in pairs and in groups, oral and written; rewriting;

(9) Publishing of the articles.

Twenty-two articles were produced, which were circulated in a regional newspaper and on the internet. These texts show clear genre characteristics and, as important as that, the activities led the students to perceive texts as enunciations in the net of verbal communication. According to Maieski:

> The work with genre . . . leads the students to write and to position themselves from their social places, as authors of their texts. The production of the article (and of other argumentative genres) also allows the student to be an opinion maker . . . . As they position themselves, the students begin to get involved with the facts of their everyday life, not just watching passively what goes around them. (Maieski, 2005, p. 203)

Considering the practical results of his project, the author emphasizes the social function of writing at school, situating the teacher as that "who, above all, guides, and not only 'corrects,' those texts [produced] by the students" (p. 204). In relation to the students, the author observes their concern with the task of writing better, by understanding that rewriting is more than correcting mistakes: in such a task, the author points to the significance of linguistic analysis guided by a teacher with enough knowledge of that genre and of the teaching methodology:

> Linguistic analysis is an activity that, no doubt, leads the students to a more conscious reading of the text selected for reading, and afterwards, of the text produced [by them]. We believe that such a practice influences the textual production, both in relation to the adequacy to the genre and in relation to linguistic and textual aspects. However, such an activity requires a teacher who has some knowledge of the genre with which he/she is going to work in the Portuguese classes. (Maieski, 2005, pp. 204-205)

Luz (2005) worked with the genre *popular stories* in a 5th grade (elementary) class. Initially, the author observed and analyzed activities such as textual production, verifying if the verbal interactions occurring there helped to overcome the students' difficulties. Next, she planned and developed the classes in collaboration with the teacher, creating circumstances in which the students could perceive the significance of the use of language as interaction and human production. The results indicate that the proposal reached its goals: the subsequent textual production showed characteristics of the studied genre, and the students made progress in the understanding of the text as an enunciation in the chain of verbal communication.

The planning of the classes was made during an ongoing teacher training course offered by Luz in 2004. The popular stories produced would be part of an edition to circulate in the school, and which would later be donated to a senior citizen club in the community. Thus, a real audience was previously established. The work included the reading and questioning of a series of stories, followed by the discussion of the answers and evaluations. The next task was for the students to ask their parents and grandparents about interesting stories they had heard during their lives. After the narration of these stories in class, each student selected one to write it down.

One can see in such a situation the valuing and sharing of the student's social environment. In addition, with the research made by the students themselves, the notion of popular story came to be developed step-by-step. A work was being done in the *zone of proximal development*—that is, learning from challenges.

It was from there that the teacher-mediator began to call attention to the grammatical review of the text, based on what had been previously identified in the notebooks. The activities were mainly focused on those texts produced by the students. The next step was to intervene in the reviewing and rewriting of the texts. There were three versions. Below, I reproduce the first and the last version of the text selected by the author as an example in her work; even if further versions could improve the written production, the differences between the first and the last one are noteworthy.

A bola de Fogo	The ball of Fire
Minha vó contou que o pai dela trabalhava até a noite. Um dia quando o pai dela estava vindo do serviço apareceu uma enorme bola de fogo assustadora. Minha avó estava na porta da cozinha quando viu aquela enorme bola de fogo ela correu pra dentro de casa. Minha vó era uma moça bonita mais muito medrosa. O Pai dela era bem gordo por isso; não consegui correr da bola de fogo. A minha avó abriu a porta para o pai dela entrar o nome dele era Pedro. Ele entrou a bola de fogo foi embora e assustou todos que ela via. Minha vó chorou muito. Então eles foram dormir com muito medo. E é isso que minha vó conto até hoje. (VERSION 1)	My granny told me that her father worked till night. One day when her father was coming from work a huge frightening ball of fire appeared. My grandmother was at the kitchen door when she saw that enormous ball of fire she ran into the house. My granny was a pretty girl but a coward. Her Father was very fat; thus he couldn't run from the ball of fire. My grandmother opened the door for her father, his name was Pedro. He went in the ball of fire went away and scared everyone who saw it. My granny cried a lot. Then they went to bed scared. And this is what my granny tells up to this day[7].

A bola de Fogo	The ball of Fire
Era uma vez uma menina chamada Ida. Ela era uma moça muito bonita mais também muito medrosa. O seu pai se chamava Pedro. Ele era bem gordo e também medroso.	Once upon a time there was a girl called Ida. She was a very pretty girl but very scared. Her father was called Pedro. He was very fat and also scared. One day Pedro was coming back from work it was 11 p.m.
Um certo dia, Pedro estava voltando da roça era 23:00hs. Ele tinha muito medo de vim sozinho á noite. Naquela noite, ele estava muito cansado ele tinha trabalhado muito. Pedro que tinha uma luz muito forte em cima dele. Era uma enorme bola de fogo. Ele correu muito, mais sua casa era longe. A bola de fogo assustava todos que ela vissem, até os rebanhos de ovelhas. Pedro continuava correndo. Ida, viu seu pai correndo, então logo ela abriu a porta e seu pai entrou. Ele estava muito nervoso então ele disse: – Por favor minha filha! Não saia à noite sozinha! Ida disse: – ta bom pai! A bola de fogo estava rodiando a casa de Pedro. Então ele teve uma idéia, ele ligou ligou a mangueira e molhou a bola de fogo, ela se apagou e não pode assustar ninguém. (VERSION 3)	He was afraid to return alone at night. That night he was very tired he had worked a lot. Pedro had a very strong light over him. It was a huge ball of fire. He ran a lot, but his house was far. The ball of fire scared everyone who saw it, even the herd of sheep. Pedro kept running. Ida, saw her father running, so she opened the door quickly and her father went in. He was very excited so he said: "Please my daughter, don't go out alone at night!" Ida said: "Alright father!" The ball of fire was encircling Pedro's house. So he had an idea. He turned on turned on the hose and wetted the ball of fire, it went off and did not scare anybody else.

I call special attention to the following changes in Version 3: extension and inclusion of paragraphs; description of characters, their situation and their voices; script sophistication; improved syntactic construction and punctuation. These marks imply the work of reader guidance.

Many other research works, not always associated with the directives of the CP/SC[8], have shown that the perspective of working with genres not only leads to a better understanding of the social practices of language, but it also projects didactic experiences that depart from the traditional everyday school path. This is the case, just to point to an example, in the work by Haeser (2005).

In a private high school environment, with contents and methodologies conforming to didactic textbooks turned into printed material, Haeser (2005) successfully conducted a reading and written production experiment (using action research) in a workshop focused on the genre *reader's letter*. Based on Bakhtin, the author suggested a specific didactic elaboration, based on data from the selected genre researched *in sito* (that is, in a newspaper from Santa Catarina). The workshop was carried out along twelve meetings, promoting practices of social use of language (literacy). The results made evident the possibilities for innovative practices at school, working with the text under the perspective of genres.

> The ways one perceives a text involve specific knowledge in relation to what one intends [to do]. If the students can understand and, especially, recognize in the texts the social interactions referred to by the genres, for example, they come to have an innovative relation to what they read. (Haeser, 2005, p. 149)

In a private school, however, one must note that the selected didactic material may make it difficult to follow that path. In public schools the obstacles are usually of a different nature, but even there it is sometimes complicated to make an intervention integrated to the curricular grid.

The Discourse of the Proposal

In this section I present a critical view, produced by two researchers, of the CP discourse.

Dela Justina (2003), in a case study, raises a problem about language teachers that cannot be evaded: that of their poor reading skills. Her goal was to check the gap between the teachers' level of literacy (considering the reading of the Proposal) and those requirements established by the Proposal itself for a pedagogical practice. That research proves to be of fundamental significance, considering the double evaluation made: the teachers' level of literacy and the formulation of the Proposal.

Based on the CP and using questionnaires, interviews and the analysis of the school language course plans as research tools, she concluded that the teachers' level of literacy did not allow them to understand nor to discuss the document related to language teaching in the CP—for example, a basic distinction, that between genre and type, had not been understood. As a consequence, there was a significant distance between what the CP recommends and what the teacher does and says, making evident the difficulty of promoting the necessary didactic elaborations for pedagogical practices. Considering that there are substantial changes in the notion of language presented by the document in relation to the traditional notion teachers have worked with in the classroom, Dela Justina stresses that

> . . . that fact would be more of a problem than an alternative to increase the quality of language teaching in public schools, since the transformation of the suggested changes in the document into actual practice would depend, fundamentally, on the efficacy of the reading and ulterior writing on the teacher's work planning, something that s/he should carry out based on the Proposal. (2003, p. 12)

But as she pointed out concerning the teachers' literacy problems—blaming those problems partly on their immersion in a school culture in which reading and writing are not linked to social practices—Dela Justina turned back to the elaboration of the official document. The document—that is my interpretation and self-evaluation in what relates to my own participation in the making of that document—did not *address* its audience appropriately: according to her, the document assumed the profile of a homogeneous reader, prepared to read and understand it. Dela Justina, as a subject-researcher, had a "surplus vision" (Bakhtin, 2003) in relation to the group that produced the document, and thus pointed to conceptual gaps and some confusion between associated notions and eventual contradictions.

> Each aspect is discussed more at length, even if, many times, one still adheres to the scientificism characteristic of those more theoretical views, something that might have produced some resistance from the teachers . . . . (pp. 54-55)

> . . . the part that deals with the work with genres is small and insufficient to allow the teacher to decide, with the autonomy that the very document intends to give him/her, what genres are, which ones should be selected, what kind of approach should be employed. There is no clear definition about what is a genre and what

is a textual type, which, to use Bakhtin's notion of language, would necessarily demand an ampler debate. (p. 64)

Should one assume that teachers (the case in Dela Justina's study) could not have a satisfactory level of literacy?

The Curricular Proposal of Santa Catarina cannot be considered simple and easy reading, if compared to the materials mentioned by the teachers in the research as part of their reading habits. However, as it pertains to the teacher's work-sphere, it would not be reasonable to expect that such a material would be similar to magazines or newspapers, which belong to completely different genres. (Dela Justina, 2003, p. 115)

In the making of the CP an adequate level of reader literacy was indeed assumed, but one has to admit that the idea of undergraduate courses forming fully prepared teachers for the classroom is utterly unthinkable: why should an individual teacher be perfectly capacitated *before* the dialogical work of the classroom, a relevant factor in his/her formation? At a different level, and focusing on reading, one must acknowledge another aspect of that issue: what is evident for a researcher/specialist is not necessarily for the subject who experiences the classroom routine or who is still in training.

It is also known, even considering the courses of ongoing teacher education, that *reading* problems can persist, and that *writing* is not common in the teachers' routine, which should be a regulating factor of their own development and identification. Their role in the work environment is often that of *transmitters* of discourses and materials, even if these materials have been "selected" by others. At the end of the day, the prerogative of these teachers as educators is frustrated; their "mediation" is restricted to the task of mediating, without much reflection, official contents and materials prepared by someone else—basically what one has in textbooks. That can be verified, for instance, in Ferreira's (2000) research, conducted directly with teacher trainers.

Similarly to Dela Justina (2003), Prudêncio (2004) analyzes the CP in its discursive network and sociopolitical character, and stresses the clash between the pedagogical and the scientific discourse. The author also analyzes an (exemplary) text of discipline planning, showing the conflicts between the two documents, evidencing the distance between the two authors of these texts. The explanation for such a conflict is the clash between the functioning of the pedagogical discourse—circulating at school for specific practices—and that of the scientific discourse, here represented by the curricular document. Prudêncio concludes that the imaginary from which the authors[9] build the CP's subject-reader—again, it is a question of how to *address* the document's audience—is not that of the real reader, that is, teachers who do not belong to the scientific community, but of an ideal subject-reader member of the scientific community itself. Interpellated by the pedagogical discourse, the real-reader is unaware of that process of knowledge building. That, according to the author, would explain the inability of real teachers to give meaning to the Proposal's text.

Such aspects of Prudêncio's position (that perspective of the *other*) have the advantage of forcing a change of view and a detachment from the document (which is made easier, in this case, by the chronological distance from its production), simplifying its reevaluation. Prudêncio's comment reminds one of a passage by Bakhtin (2003), in which he speaks about genres and intimate styles, observing that they "base themselves on the maximal interior proximity of the speaker to the addressee of the discourse (at most, in the fusion of the two)" (p. 304). This makes clear how the speaker's style depends on how much he/she understands his/her addressee. In spite of the fact that no official document uses an intimate, informal style, Prudêncio (as well as Dela Justina) is calling attention to the excessive distance between the voice of the Curricular Proposal and the real-readers, the teachers, who end up by becoming secondary readers of something that was not addressed originally to them, and which does not seem to have anything to do with their realities.

The Curricular Proposal and the Teachers' Discourse

This section presents some research studies that provide evidence, from the teachers' discourse, of problems related to their familiarity with the Proposal and their difficulties in breaking away from their pedagogical routines.

Bonetti's work (2003), without focusing her analysis on the official document itself, aimed at verifying the level of knowledge, understanding, acceptance and applicability of the Curricular Proposal among Portuguese teachers (in this case, 12 subjects who answered a questionnaire), in addition to investigating if the CP was contributing to a reorientation of Portuguese teaching in elementary/junior high school.

Again the results indicated that the majority of the teachers did not have the necessary knowledge of the CP in order to follow its directives and to carry out the changes suggested by the document. The author concluded that it is necessary to create opportunities for studying and clarifying the document, as a way to assure ongoing teacher training, as proposed by the document itself.

Magnanti (2003), in order to investigate the theoretical-practical consistency of the epistemological and methodological principles found in the document, opted for hearing the evaluation of the Portuguese teachers themselves, who were following, satisfactorily or not, the directives of the CP. In order to collect the data, a questionnaire was used (with 40 teachers from 6 schools), an interview (with 3 teachers), and the observation of their practice (3 teachers). When looking at the data from a discursive perspective, a conflict becomes evident: the teachers' voices point to antagonistic discursive formations in theoretical terms and in the relation of theory to practice: the sociointeractionist discourse (the one they have been exposed to more recently) was mixed with images from a Positivist tradition, indicating a contradictory situation in which a democratic approach clashes with a hierarchical one. One should consider that even though the CP is the result of a work conducted under the approval of a governmental institution, it presents internal contradictions, working as a proposal not yet thoroughly recognized amid the traditional educational regulations. However, that research study showed that the teachers did contemplate the possibility of a rupture, of building educational projects according to the directives set out in the CP. The contradictory textualization of the discursive material analyzed has also allowed for a deep reflection of the researcher about her own work.

Luz (2005) reports on an 80-hour teacher education course offered by her, in 2004, for 31 elementary/junior high school teachers. The objective was to study the text (chapter) referring to the Portuguese language in the CP in order to make possible its pedagogical application. Six teachers had never attended an ongoing teacher education course, and only thirteen out of the twenty nine remaining Portuguese teachers had attended at least one. She carried out an assessment of the teachers' understanding of the terms *text* and *reading*. The majority wrote that text is structure, or a mechanism for the reproduction of ideas and for expressing ideas. Only one expressed the concept adopted by the CP; six mentioned the ability to translate and assimilate messages. In terms of the notion of reading there was a notable inversion: 22 expressed the notion proposed by the CP; six mentioned the ability to translate and to assimilate messages. In each case, three did not answer.

FLORIANÓPOLIS' CURRICULAR PROPOSAL—AN EXPERIMENT WITH GENRES

Against his background of positive and negative experiences based on the Curricular Proposals with Santa Catarina, at the end of 2006 I became a consultant for Florianópolis' Municipal Department of Education, for both Portuguese and foreign language teachers. My work attempted to overcome the kinds of difficulties discussed above in order to support teachers in more successfully implementing the CP of Santa Catarina and Florianopolis. I chose to present it here because a simpler context (involving a small number of individuals) dealing with the same thematic (the training of teachers with similar theoretical backgrounds) allowed me to make a fruitful comparison to the work developed by the state of Santa Catarina, which helped me in my own research at UNISUL to make observations and point out ruptures and flaws, as well as offer a general orientation for an educational policy and its eventual contrast[10].

Thus, similar to the State curricular document, the local proposal (Florianópolis 1996), published in 1996 under a left-wing administration[11], developed the fundamentals that make the two proposals similar in general lines.

The theoretical material on genres proposed by Bakhtin was elaborated along the development of the work to supplement the Curricular Proposal of Florianópolis and to help teachers to better understand the pertinent concepts. We discussed the significance of language in the life of communities and its heteroglossia; the principle of dialogism; the relations between enunciation/text; and the characterization of genres, stressing their ideological nature.

In order to guide the understanding of genre functions and the subsequent description and analysis of the genres to be selected, as well as the suggested didactic activities, I have used part of the dissertation by Barbosa (2001). Following Bakhtin's terminology, the methodological path suggested by her was the following:

(a) characterization of the sphere in which a genre circulates;
(b) study of the social-history of genre development, whenever possible;
(c) characterization of the context of production of the selected texts;
(d) analysis of the thematic content;
(e) analysis of the compositional construction;
(f) analysis of genre style;
(g) analysis of the author's style, whenever it was the case.

In order to show how to describe and analyze genres, the author presents a synthetic table referring to a corpus of the genre news—in this case, printed news, which is found in large newspapers—elaborated with the help of elementary school teachers. The analysis presents a considerable level of didactic elaboration (Barbosa, 2001, cap. 4). One can see that by observing the wide range of the approaches to the text, characterized not only by its visible organization but also by its emergence in the discursive context and in the wider-ranging elements of its institutional production (in a specific field).

To work with the teachers in Florianópolis, my work map included an attempt to suggest activities, which could be developed using examples of genres—integrating as much as possible oral tasks, reading, text production and linguistic analysis.

In addition, while taking into consideration a practice initiated by teachers in previous preparation activities, I explored to some extent the process of *didactization* of genres, proposed by the Geneva Group (Schneuwly & Dolz, 2004). This process consists in preparing didactic sequences related to social activities and genres aiming at transforming them in taught and learned knowledge—in our case, it was centered on the knowledge of genres in two dimensions: social and linguistic-discursive. At that stage, I also tried to make explicit how the work involving Vygotsky's learning theory would function, especially the key-concept of *zone of proximal development* (ZPD). The work with these teachers included a stage for experimenting with the elaborated didactic sequence, and also a stage for preparing didactic materials.

Barbosa (2001, p. 218) suggests the organization of two types of data banks, based on the teachers' work: one set would provide the school with descriptions and analyses of genres (including hypertexts) to be used directly by the teachers, while the other would be the didactic materials for the students. Such a concern has its justification, not only because it has already been included in the curricular proposals but also because of the need to link curricular contents to social practices, thematizing the many forms of language that everyday mediatic cultural products make use of: images, sound, movement, colors, etc.

Were there drawbacks along that path? Yes, there always are: in the relations we made within the teachers' community there was clearly good will, knowledge improvement and successful experiences, but also lack of hope, indifference and resistance. Within such a scene, when we face the national level of academic exams, which makes clear the general failure of the educational project for the country, we ask ourselves: what is our share in it?

The following section is an initial reflection on that question. The problems faced by the implementation of Santa Catarina's and Florianópolis' Curricular Proposals are similar, with the only difference that, in the case of the city of Florianópolis, the number of teachers is small, which facilitates the meetings and the understanding of these problems. On the other hand, some successful experiences have been carried out by MA and doctoral students, and deserve to be presented here. Understandably, their contact with the schools, even when they are not members of the school staff, allows for the socialization of knowledge and stimulates an investment on an alternative pedagogical proposal. I have observed that a considerable part of the success hangs on how the researcher or teacher acts towards and *with* the school teachers, and on how he/she reflects about the relations between scientific and pedagogical knowledge. This leads to the question of responsibility for the actions taken by the researchers in order to put his/her work in practice.

The following section is a reflection on this issue. In it, based on Bakhtin (2003), I deal with the notion of ethics in the social spheres under discussion here, its consequences and the notions related to it.

RECONSIDERING THE THEORETICAL BACKGROUND

The reflection I propose, given the partial conclusions presented above, is less related to genres and their immediate context in school than to the epistemological, historical and ideological senses entailed by the work with genres. This essay is about attitudes considered in terms of the very relations implied by the production, understanding and treatment of the thematized knowledge, in the ample social fabric, which brings us researchers closer to political and educational contexts as specialists who collaborate in the creation of educational policies. It is about understanding *where* we are, *from where* we speak and *how* we do it and *with whom*, grounded on what we believe we have learned from Bakhtin's philosophy of language, with his aesthetics and his architectonics—in sum, grounded on what we believe to have been his orientation for social life, including and privileging the school context. In order to undertake such an evaluation I need to present a few notions.

As we deal with texts (configured as genres) we find ourselves facing questions that Bakhtin faced every day in his studies: if every word is a bilateral act and if only through it we can make meaning, then what regulates the way meanings are shared within the context of language in each utterance? In the play of enunciation, vocabulary and grammar pre-exist each individual utterance, working as constraining elements (which, as such, allow a minimal framing for inter-understanding), but they occur to us in complex and singular contexts (in a multi-threaded net). The effect over the interlocutors is specific, in the same way that it is specific for the utterer him/herself (and I insist on that).

> The role of the *others*, for the person who builds the enunciation, is exceptionally large, as we already know. We have already said that these others, for whom my thought becomes for the first time a real thought (and, as such, also to myself), are not passive listeners, but active participants in the discursive communication. (Bakhtin, 2003, p. 301)

Here I am reconsidering the issue of the effects of utterances over the listeners/readers *and over the person who utters the utterance*, projected by its radically human dimension and its relevance in the role we play as researchers imbued with the significance of pedagogical practices, as well as trying to influence the (conflicting) pedagogical inter-relations between researchers and teachers.

As evident as the concepts we use routinely may seem to us, both in talking and in writing, the look that returns to the "same" words—always already said, written, revisited—suggests that we never know too well how far the *theme*, with the meanings that we also recreate, can take us, because within the singular context it is always about another sliding meaning, and because it is about a "self" which is constantly trying to signify itself.

It is by projecting such a background that I try to think of what is to come, in this area, during the subsequent stages of tasks framed within an ampler methodology (thinking about an "architectonics," under Bakhtin's perspective).

Our desire to say, the idea of an *address* for the uttered word, is substantial and deserves reflection at all levels of exchange: from the solitary research through the discussions we conduct in social practices and beyond: such an understanding becomes a fundamental content for dealing responsibly with the variety of texts (the genres) that we want students to handle appropriately. In fact, it is about the practical understanding of how subjectivity is built, the awareness that the "self" only builds itself in partnership with otherness.

The paradox of our political, economical and social situation lies in inducing one to think subjectively that the "self" can only subsist and win if he/she keeps the other in a subservient position. Even if we try to avoid it, the first reaction of many teachers to our arrival as researchers, consultants, "people from the academy," is influenced by the image of a poorly disguised hierarchy.

What we want to say is always in search of and demands an interpretation, which represents a move to a view of dialogue as understanding (a search for agreement). And here it is worth saying that our "intention" as writers/speakers can only be thought of as relative, since the "self," for Bakhtin, is always a function of an "us." Vygostsky (1991), too, insisted that consciousness only awakes after life in society, mediated by language—and self-consciousness, in its turn, corresponds to a more sophisticated level of reflexivity, of social maturity. Well now, dispersion is a reality: the apprehension and (re)construction of the *theme* in the communicative play may diverge largely from the intent of the utterance. And with that I can address the intention brought to the scene in the utterance of the CP and its counterpoint, which is the active response of its direct readers: the teachers.

Heteroglossia, a phenomenon of the dialogical order in Bakhtin's view, results from forces functioning in each communicative "encounter": the "same" and the different face each other. There are forces that align themselves to centralize meaning, leading to an inevitable structuring; there are other forces that feed the necessary diversity and dispersion by keeping open paths to the contextual, fluctuating world. Stratification and diversity compose heteroglossia—complementary moves among the demands of structuring, the floating and change of meanings. In that *continuum*, what connects them is the struggle between canonization and heteroglossia[12]. If meaning is always limited by contexts, contexts are unlimited. "The name of such non-limitation is 'heteroglossia'" (Clark & Holquist, 1998, p. 239).

In this field, each speaker/writer tries with some effort to make him/herself understood and to convince, to be accepted as a member of a community, to find an answer for his/her acts, and not just a lack of response. One tries, consciously or not, to work his/her *ethos* in order to obtain a self-satisfying reply.

A cornerstone in Bakhtin's philosophy, the concept of heteroglossia became also fundamental as a function of life itself (Clark & Holquist, 1998, p. 286). In the play between the trend to fixate and to disperse a society can harbor both the conservative and the tolerant in terms of language, with many overtones between these two extremes. This gives us an idea of how much such concepts and their practical understanding can weigh in pedagogical terms for all of the involved—beginning with ourselves.

How we create authorship is one of the facets of heteroglossia:

> We operate from a point of view and we mold values as forms. The way we do it is the medium through which we articulate what we are amid the heteroglossia of ideological possibilities open to us at any given moment. Bakhtin considers the values not as an abstract axiology, but as a practical work of construction. (Clark & Holquist, 1998, p. 37)

I want to associate the issue of authorship with the concept of superaddressee—the so-called "third," as Bakhtin explains (2003, pp. 379-380)—a kind of assurance that the effort to be understood is worthwhile. It is worth believing in that third, if to make sense is something that is only possible in a linguistic community, even if the danger of misunderstanding is always there. The superaddressee, beyond the *I* and the *you*, is something like a *him/her* (a third person) capable of understanding correctly what we are saying—that is, that entity who followed our *intention*, our will-to-say[13]. It is here that the intelligibility of saying, the idealized mode of communication, is safeguarded. It is also here, I think, that our delusion of the clearness of saying emerges: every enunciation unfolds as if there were a third character witnessing everything and understanding it all. He/she is "invisibly present."

Bakhtin explains how this "third" works in the context of understanding and interpretation. Understanding implies evaluation and surpasses the simple reproduction or repetition: it is active and creative. The third is thought of as an "objective position," analogous to a scientific knowledge, where the *I* and the *you* are neutralized, where they become replaceable:

. . . and that is only possible and justifiable in situations and in the solution to questions to which the integral and unique personality of man is not made necessary, that is, where man, so to speak, specializes himself, expressing only part of his personality separated from the whole, where he does not act as *himself*, but as "an engineer," as "a physicist," etc. (Bakhtin, 2003, p. 380)

It is here that the problems of *audience* and *address* in scientific discourse unfold. In other words, the discourse that should be directed to the teachers who we think and wish we are training. The superaddressee, idealized to function well in certain conditions, is not reached nor visualized by the concrete community to which we address ourselves—and that is apparently a paradox. We might be addressing our discourse to an abstract *teacher*, a third—talking *about the teacher* and not *to the teacher*—asking for understanding and acceptance, before any kind of negotiation[14], and that with the best of intentions. It is as if we were trying to juggle two relatively clashing guidelines.

To sum up, in the final section of this essay I will reopen a few questions.

EVALUATING THE ROUTE—OPENING PATHS

I have tried to reflect, along the directives of educational-political character, about the following pedagogical issues:

(a) the basic document that guides teaching and learning—in order to synthesize the its critiques and rethink the proposal;
(b) the interacting subjects—to reflect on processes and conflicts;
(c) the learning tools—to verify their pertinence.

All attitudes and actions taken in the past in connection with those issues that link the theoretical and the pedagogical order give considerable weight to the assessment of the results of works and to the concurrent reflections, which emerged within the process itself, to raise new questions, especially about the ruptures that we have let arise. At the end of each route (a collective experience, a chat, a course, a job consultancy), there remains something unfinished (there is no end) and the need to invest in the continued education—not merely for the teachers who are our target public today, but for the emergent "we" that was detected, and for each "I" that manifested him/herself in the utterances (voices, intonations, evaluations).

The best proposal in the world is still not a substantial political investment if it comes down to documents that cannot trigger the necessary drive to keep the discussion going. The materials that we prepare in the institutional context reflect much more than an educational policy—they bring the sign of the values we were imbued of; and certainly the way they *address* a specific audience is a social practice. That is why we always wait for a response. "From the start the utterer awaits their answer [from the addressees], awaits a responsive understanding" (Bakhtin, 2003, p. 301). However, we are not always capable of looking at our addressees from the right perspective.

Questions similar to the ones that were detected among the readers of the CP and by the self-evaluation procedures carried out by research studies appear in a number of works dealing with the National Curricular Parameters. This similarity makes it possible to better accept that an official text can become unreadable for its target public—in this case the teachers—a negative factor being the lack of knowledge of the theoretical sources for intertextual reconstruction of the text's meanings. That is what Silva (2006, p. 237), for example, stresses, and that is why the author points to the need to "reflect on the textual processes when circulating knowledge produced and discussed within the academic sphere among a non-specialized public" (p. 237).

Such a rethinking of the route assumes a permanent negotiation, a dialogical articulation—I see this as an ethical act of evaluation and responsibility within the set of social relations that mark us as subjects relatively situated towards others—"thy neighbors."

NOTES

[1] This paper was originally written in Portuguese and translated into English by Fernando S. Vugman, PhD.

[2] Santa Catarina is one of the states in the South Region of Brazil.

[3] Florianópolis is the capital of the state of Santa Catarina.

[4] The material quoted here is for the most part translated from Portuguese.

[5] Another substantial document was published in 2005, focusing on "thematic studies." However, it is not a review of the fundaments and methodology of the CP, but a "consolidation." In that case, the intent was to present alternatives to "(re)elaborate the systematized knowledge of the prior versions of the Curricular Proposal of Santa Catarina, which still demanded to be developed and applied in pedagogical practice, exerting the fundamental role of the School." (Santa Catarina, 2005, p. 15). The introduction of the new document advocates "a new school to the world," which should be in tune with the new information and communication technologies.

[6] One should remember that the activities cannot have a mechanical character, for mere entertainment; they must be significant in their mode of organization, in any field: in that of language it is essential to take into consideration their social functions (Moll, 1996).

[7] These translations try to reproduce the grammatical, stylistic and ortho-

graphical errors in the text, though absolute precision is impossible.

[8] Many interventions circulate within restricted contexts, and are not formally reported.

[9] The official author is the Secretaria de Estado da Educação (State Secretary of Education).

[10] Reciprocally, those studies undertaken in order to plan the state Proposal and the works carried out on the Proposal were relevant to the debate at the municipal level. My participation in the elaboration of both documents (the state and the local one) had, of course, some influence in the process.

[11] Sérgio José Grando (Communist Party) was Mayor of Florianópolis from 1993 to 1996.

[12] One of the facets of heteroglossia is the pure and simple mixture of different languages, cultures and class groups, or dialects, or modes of speaking, or records.

[13] Such an entity can acquire a concrete identity depending on the time and culture (God—as it happens in Descartes' philosophy—absolute truth, good judgment, the people, science, etc.).

[14] Analogously, those students who must produce a school *dissertation* may be in a process of assimilation by a homogenized figure named *student* (Furlanetto, 2006, p. 540).

REFERENCES

Bakhtin, M. (1979). *Marxismo e filosofia da linguagem*. São Paulo: Hucitec.

Bakhtin, M. (2003). *Estética da criação verbal* (4th ed., P. Bezerra, Trans.). São Paulo: Martins Fontes.

Barbosa, J. P. (2001). *Trabalhando com os gêneros do discurso: Uma perspectiva enunciativa para o ensino de língua portuguesa*. Unpublished thesis, Pontifical University of São Paulo, São Paulo, Brazil.

Bonetti, L. M. (2003). *proposta curricular de Santa Catarina: Língua Portuguesa— estudo de caso*. Unpublished thesis, University of Southern Santa Catarina, Tubarão, Santa Catarina, Brazil.

Cardoso, M. A. (2005). *Leitura de diferentes linguagens em suporte de texto não-escolar: O gênero embalagem de produtos alimentícios na atividade pedagógica*. Unpublished thesis, University of Southern Santa Catarina, Tubarão, Santa Catarina, Brazil.

Clark, K., & Holquist, M. (1998). *Mikhail Bakhtin*. São Paulo: Perspectiva.

Dela Justina, E. W. N. (2003). *A leitura da proposta curricular de Santa Catarina: Investigando os níveis de letramento*. Unpublished thesis, Federal University of Santa Catarina, Florianópolis, Santa Catarina, Brazil.

Ferreira, I. (2000). *Coerência, informatividade e ensino: Uma reflexão e estudo em textos de professores do Ensino Fundamental.* Unpublished thesis, Federal University of Santa Catarina, Florianópolis, Santa Catarina, Brazil.

Florianópolis. (1996). *Traduzindo em ações: Das diretrizes a uma proposta curricular.* Proposta Curricular para a rede municipal de ensino de Florianópolis. Florianópolis, Santa Catarina, Brazil: Secretaria Municipal de Educação.

Furlanetto, M. M. (2006). Argumentação e subjetividade no gênero: O papel dos topoi [Special issue]. *Linguagem em (Dis)curso, 6*(3), 519-546.

Haeser, M. E. (2005). *O ensino-aprendizagem da leitura no ensino médio: Uma proposta a partir de oficina com o gênero carta do leitor.* Unpublished thesis, Federal University of Santa Catarina, Florianópolis, Santa Catarina, Brazil.

Luz, V. T. (2005). *Do planejamento à prática: A construção da subjetividade no trabalho com gêneros do discurso em uma 5ª série.* Unpublished thesis, University of Southern Santa Catarina, Tubarão, Santa Catarina, Brazil.

Magnanti, C. I. (2003). *Vozes docentes: Avaliando a proposta curricular de Santa Catarina.* Unpublished thesis, University of Southern Santa Catarina, Tubarão, Santa Catarina, Brazil.

Maieski, M. N. (2005). *O gênero do discurso artigo como objeto de ensino-aprendizagem: Uma proposta de integração da prática de produção textual à leitura e análise lingüística.* Unpublished thesis, Federal University of Santa Catarina, Florianópolis, Santa Catarina, Brazil.

Maingueneau, D. (2001). *Análise de textos de comunicação.* São Paulo: Cortez.

Moll, L. C. (1996). Introdução. In L. C. Moll (Ed.), *Vygotsky e a educação: Implicações pedagógicas da psicologia sócio-histórica.* Porto Alegre, Rio Grande do Sul, Brazil: Artes Médicas.

Prudêncio, P. G. (2004). *Proposta curricular de Santa Catarina: Um lugar de confronto entre o discurso pedagógico e o discurso científico.* Unpublished thesis, University of Southern Santa Catarina, Tubarão, Santa Catarina, Brazil.

Santa Catarina. (1998). Secretaria de Estado da Educação e do Desporto. *Proposta Curricular de Santa Catarina: Educação infantil, ensino fundamental e médio.* Florianópolis, Santa Catarina, Brazil: COGEN.

Santa Catarina. (2005). Secretaria de Estado da Educação, Ciência e Tecnologia. *Proposta Curricular de Santa Catarina: Estudos temáticos.* Florianópolis, Santa Catarina, Brazil: IOESC.

Schneuwly, B., & Dolz, J. (2004). *Gêneros orais e escritos na escola.* Campinas, São Paulo, Brazil: Mercado de Letras.

Silva, S. B. (2006). A retextualização dos conceitos de letramento, texto, discurso e gêneros do discurso nos PCN de língua portuguesa. *Trabalhos em Lingüística Aplicada, 45,* 225-238.

Vygotsky, L. S. (1991). *A formação social da mente* (4th. ed). São Paulo: Martins Fontes.

19 Intertextual Analysis of Finnish EFL Textbooks: Genre Embedding as Recontextualization

Salla Lähdesmäki

INTRODUCTION

The EFL textbook may be described quite accurately through the concept of "complex genres" introduced by Bakhtin (1986) in his famous essay on speech genres. According to Bakhtin, many genres of arts and sciences, for instance, are complex or "secondary" genres which

> absorb and digest various primary (simple) genres that have taken form in unmediated speech communion. These primary genres are altered and assume a special character when they enter into complex ones. They lose their immediate relation to actual reality and the real utterances of others. (p. 62)

One of the most striking features of the contemporary Finnish EFL textbook is its textual and discursive heterogeneity. The textbook aims at representing language use in its full variety and therefore draws upon a wide array of different genres and discourse types. The attempt to provide a comprehensive selection of genres may be seen as one of the tasks of the EFL textbook as a genre. Indeed, one of the clearest trends in the development of the Finnish EFL textbook from its beginnings in the late 1890s till today has been the diversification of the genres presented. Certain traditional textbook genres such as transactional dialogues or highly informational, encyclopedic texts on "key" areas and subjects (such as important historical figures) have been supplemented with—and to some extent supplanted by—genres and conventions which are assumed to be more in tune with the lifeworld of the teenage readers and thus more salient and appealing to the intended readership.

This development may be attributed to different factors. The rise of the so-called communicative paradigm in language teaching, with its emphasis on authenticity and authentic materials, has undoubtedly been a major factor in this. Pedagogically motivated solutions have nonetheless been contingent upon other factors to a varying degree. From a material point of view, increased international mobility and technological development have meant that a wider range of authentic texts is easily accessible for textbook authors to draw upon. The changed role of English in Finland has enhanced this effect: as the English language has become a part of many communicative situations in Finland, increasing amounts of English-language textual material are available. From a technological point of view, advances in printing technology have made it possible to reproduce or recreate texts which *look* like real-life exemplars of the genres. This is significant as the visual outlook of texts, such as typical layout features, provides crucial cues in the recognition of genres in general as well as in the textbook context. Finally, the cultural context of the Finnish EFL textbook has changed significantly and with it the readers' expectations and, crucially, textbook authors' assumptions regarding those expectations. The typical Finnish teenager learning English at the turn of the millenium lives in a highly visual and remarkably text-saturated, mediatized and multi-modal world. As far as her use of English is concerned, she uses and encounters English in diverse everyday contexts without having to leave Finland (Leppänen, 2007). This profile is reflected in the ways in which contemporary Finnish EFL textbooks draw upon generic influences.

THE EFL TEXTBOOK AS AN OBJECT OF RESEARCH

Critical analyses of EFL materials have often attended to the socio-cultural content of textbooks. "Global" textbooks published by large multi-national companies, and used in diverse cultural and religious contexts around the world, have received attention in particular. Scholars have argued, for example, that textbooks typically represent values and worldviews which are highly culture-specific (and typically aligned with Anglo-American or "western" way of life) and which may be alien or even offensive to students of different cultural backgrounds (e.g., Alptekin, 1993; Colebrook, 1996; Gray, 2000). However, it has also been pointed out that recent policies, increasingly adopted by publishers, mandate cultural appropriateness and inclusivity, and this has resulted in textbooks being dominated by "aspirational" texts[2] or educationally appropriate informational texts dealing with, for example, social issues such as environmental problems (Colebrook, 1996; Gray, 2001; see also Jacobs & Goatley, 2000). EFL/ESL materials have also been looked at in terms of socialization, that is, in terms of what kinds of skills and competences they provide (Lesikin, 2001; Littlejohn, 1998). At the same time, some scholars have emphasized that analyses should focus increasingly on the role and the meaning of the textbook as a cultural artifact (Colebrooke, 1996) and the way in which textbook texts are dealt with in the classroom (Gray, 2000; Sunderland, Cowley, Abdul Rahim, Leonzakou, Shattuck, 2001).

Yet, despite the characteristic multi-genericness of the contemporary EFL textbook, the notion of genre does not feature prominently in the body of research on English language textbooks. Dendrinos (1992) is an important exception. She sees the EFL textbook as constructing a particular kind of social reality through the wide array of genres, or "discourse/text types," as she prefers to call them, which they (re)present. She ascribes to a view of genre which posits as a social practice implying particular ways of producing and interpreting texts (cf. Kress & Threadgold, 1988). While Dendrinos makes illuminating observations about how micro-level choices in instructional texts serve to position readers both as learners and as social subjects, her account fails to address the precise way in which textbook texts are linked to genres of out-of-school reality and, in particular, the generic and discursive hybridity which is evident in foreign language textbook texts. In my view, this is a crucial question in the analysis of foreign language textbook texts, which the concept of intertextuality can help elucidate.

This paper reports one part of an ongoing research project on the intertextuality of Finnish EFL textbooks. The research focuses on the manner in which textbooks draw upon generic influences. The data has been drawn from two series of Finnish EFL materials, published between the years 1995 and 2001. The books are intended for the grades 7-9 in the Finnish school system, which means that the texts have been written for 13- to 16-year-old pupils. The analysis focuses on the reading texts contained in the materials. Moreover, a body of secondary data has been collected, consisting of a selection of Finnish EFL textbooks from 1891 till the late 1980s, relevant policy documents (notably the National Framework Curriculum), and a body of authentic exemplars of genres from which textbook texts draw influences.

The specific aim of this paper is to argue for and to illustrate intertextual analysis as a viable model for the analysis of foreign language textbooks, which is warranted in the first instance by the characteristic generic heterogeneity of such textbooks. The paper focuses on the most obvious kind of intertextuality manifested by Finnish EFL textbooks, namely genre embedding. Of particular interest are the effects of the recontextualization of embedded generic formats in a textbook.

TEXTBOOK TEXTS AS HETEROGENEOUS ENTITIES

The prevalent approach to foreign language teaching in Finland, broadly based on the principles of communicative language teaching, lays emphasis on authenticity in language teaching. Despite this emphasis, contemporary EFL textbooks contain relatively few authentic texts, when an authentic text is seen as one which was originally produced for some other purpose and some other audience and which is incorporated into a textbook without adapting it in any significant measure[3]. Moreover, in the cases in which real texts *are* borrowed, they often come from educational magazines, such as *Senior Scholastic*, or from school textbooks in English for other subjects. As for other kinds of authentic texts, there are some literary extracts (e.g., from a Sherlock Holmes story and from *Romeo and Juliet*) and scattered instances of genres such as school regulations or graphs representing official statistics, to name a few, which are often appended to another text by way of illustrating or expanding its subject matter. Far more common, then, than bringing authentic texts into textbooks is for textbook authors to write original texts which draw influences from varied genres from out-of-school contexts.

EFL textbooks do not imitate or borrow genres in a consistent manner, but rather "absorb and digest" elements in varying ways and degrees. In some cases generic influences are drawn upon quite explicitly, so that a textbook text reproduces a genre text intact, adhering to the central conventions of the genre throughout the text. In other cases, generic influences appear more implicitly. The distinction between more explicit and more implicit incorporation of varied generic or discursive elements into a text has been referred to as the distinction between "embedded" and "mixed" intertextuality, respectively (Bhatia, 1997, 2004; Fairclough, 1992). The present paper focuses on the use of "embedded" generic influences in EFL textbooks.

Bhatia (1997, p. 191) defines "genre embedding" as cases in which "a particular generic form . . . [is] used as a template to give expression to another conventionally distinct generic form." He illustrates the definition with an example in which a job advertisement is written—and displayed—in the format of a poem. That the example comes from advertising is not a coincidence. Bhatia himself observes that genre embedding is very common in advertising. Bex (1996) discusses the same phenomenon, and notes that advertising tends to exploit such genres which are associated with a given section of population which is targeted by an advertisement. Embedded generic formats as employed in advertising thus serve to construct a specific target group *and* to construct that group as having shared needs, interests and concerns.

This is not unlike the case of the contemporary EFL textbook. The intertextual makeup of the EFL textbook, including its genre choices, is based particularly explicitly on assumptions regarding the literacy events and literacy practices in which young people engage in out-of-school contexts. That is, the EFL textbook will contain genres or conventions from genres which are assumed to be familiar to the teenage users of the books. Moreover, genres and generic conventions are often drawn upon in such a manner that they are easily recognized and may be identified. Embedded genres or genre formats are a case in point.

EMBEDDED GENRES AS RECONTEXTUALIZED GENRES

One central thought which emerges both from Bakhtin's (1986) discussion on secondary genres and Bhatia's (1997) definition of embedded genres is that when imported into a new context, a given genre will be altered. This is inherent in any process of "recontextualization." Linell (1998, p. 144) defines recontextualization as "the dynamic transfer-and-transformation of something from one discourse/text-in-context to another." Recontextualization as a concept has particular inflections in the context of educational research where it is mainly associated with the work of the educational sociologist Basil Bernstein (1996). According to Bernstein, "[p]edagogic discourse is constructed by a recontextualizing principle which selectively appropriates, relocates, refocuses and relates other discourse to constitute its own order" (p. 47). The various kinds of transformations which occur upon recontextualization are thus indicative of the practices and the values at stake in the particular social and textual site.

The question of recontextualization is germane to studies on intertextuality. It is particularly central, for example, in analyses of "intertextual chains" (Fairclough, 1992) or local "genre systems" (Devitt, 1991) which focus on the conventional ways in which texts (whether written or spoken) are recycled and reworked into new texts within or across institutions or professional settings (Berkenkotter 2001; Devitt, 1991; Solin, 2001). The process of recontextualization described in such studies is somewhat different qualitatively from the case of genre embedding. They focus mainly on the type of intertextual processes which Devitt describes as "referential intertextuality," which is a case of one text or set of texts functioning as the subject matter of subsequent text(s) and/or as an authority which is referred to in other texts.

As for the embedded generic formats featuring in the EFL textbook, the relationship between the textbook text and its intertext is imitative rather than referential. Thus, on the surface, it might seem that an embedded genre undergoes minimal transformation when relocated into a textbook. However, the situation is much more complex than that. As pointed out, for example, by Dendrinos (1992), the very relocation of a genre/text into the new site changes its nature irrevocably. A newspaper article occurring in a textbook will not trigger the same expectations in the reader when she encounters it in a textbook, as a pupil, as when she reads a similar text in a newspaper which she has bought or has a subscription to. One central feature of texts and genres imported into a textbook is that the relationship between the reader and the text is heavily mediated. Bakhtin (1986) and Bernstein (1996) both underscore the fact that upon relocation a genre or discourse loses its unmediated, "real" nature and, in Bernstein's words, becomes "imaginary" (p. 47).

Finally, it should be noted that recontextualization is a two-way process. Fairclough (1992, pp. 127-128) suggests that there are "constraints and rules of compatibility" between genres and discourses, albeit not nearly as conventional or as stable as between particular genres and compatible register choices, for example. An analysis of genre embedding thus also involves an examination of discourses potentially carried over into the textbook with the generic format. From the point of view of recontextualization, then, we need to focus our attention on the way in which a given genre is transformed upon recontextualization, but also on how the importing of elements from particular genres—and, crucially, not from others—into the textbook affects the textbook as a genre.

THE CASE OF "THE BLUNDERS LETTER"

In this section, I shall illustrate the above discussion empirically, with reference to data from a Finnish EFL textbook. The first subsection illustrates a typical case of genre embedding in my data, while the latter explicates the way in which genre embedding is an instance of recontextualization and what kinds of effects it has.

Genre embedding

The example which I am about to discuss is a text entitled *Dating disasters*[4] from a book called *This Way Up: Texts 2* (1999, pp. 54-55). The text poses as a spread from a teenage magazine, imitating a particular subgenre of readers' letters which is commonly found (and specific to) contemporary teenage magazines. These are letters in which readers recount and describe embarrassing events, arising from various kinds of social blunders they have committed themselves or witnessed. Magazines contain special sections for these letters. For want of a conventionalized genre label, I shall refer to these letters as "blunders letters[5]." The analysis below is informed by an examination of a sample of 64 authentic blunders letters from two Finnish and two North American teenage magazines.

There are a number of cues which guide the reader to construe the six personal narratives as readers' letters, albeit fictional, to a teenage magazine. Among the most obvious and explicit ones are self-referential verbal cues, that is, the name of a fictitious teenage magazine, *Young&Hip*, and the headings, *Your letters* and *Dating disasters*, which point to the genre and the more specific subgenre which are modeled in the text. Also crucial are different kinds of visual cues: the layout of the page, the use of colors, borders and photographs, as well as the use of different typefaces are all very similar to authentic exemplars. The text also displays textual and linguistic features which testify to its intertextual relation with teenage magazines' blunders letter sections. The overall structure of the text, consisting of heading(s) > a lead-in > a "colony" (cf. Hoey, 2001) of similar but independent short texts (followed by a signature) is conventional in the genre. The texts representing blunders letters are written in the first person singular, and they display a particular kind of narrative format which is characteristic of authentic exemplars. The letters fit both linguistically and structurally the definition of a storytelling genre which Eggins & Slade (1997), drawing upon Plum's (1988) typology, classify as an "anecdote."

What characterises anecdotes is a structure in which an "orientation" (a phase describing the setting of the events) is followed by some "remarkable event," that is, some unexpected and typically either embarrassing or amusing incident, which often represents or results in some kind of breach of social norms. An anecdote culminates in the "reaction" brought about by the remarkable event, that is, either the protagonist's own reactions or the reactions of others, which may be either psychological (e.g., mortification, disapproval) or physical (e.g., laughter, scream). As optional elements, anecdotes may open with an "abstract," which captures the gist of the story in a nutshell, and/or close with a "coda," which takes the narrator and the audience back to the "here and now" and comments on the significance of the events relayed. Linguistically, anecdotes are characterised by marked interpersonal involvement, manifested by the use of expressions which are evaluative and/or affective in nature. (For evaluative language, see, e.g., Thompson & Hunston, 2001.) Example 1, below, presents a structural analysis of one of the letters from *Dating disasters* as an anecdote.

> Example (1)
> From: *Dating disasters* (*This Way Up*, Otava 1999), reproduced with the permission of Otava Publishing house.

- **Orientation**
  I was out on a first date with a guy I had chased for so long. He took me to a really fancy little restaurant, which made me a bit uncomfortable.

- **Remarkable Event**
  During the dinner, as I was sipping my soda, he cracked some joke. I laughed so hard that the soda came out of my nose. I started choking.

- **Reaction**
  Everyone stared at us.

- **Coda**
  My date was really embarrassed and never called again.

Where anecdotes differ from "the classical narrative" as defined by Labov and Waletzky (1967), then, is that there is no explicit resolution (brought about by the protagonist's actions), nor do they necessarily contain an evaluation component, which spells out why the story was worth telling. It seems then that an anecdote presupposes more shared contextual information from the audience, that is, an audience that can appreciate why a particular incident is so amusing, embarrassing, and so forth. It is a type of story which is told among peers.

Recontextualization

In the above section I discussed one aspect of genre embedding, namely the way in which the conventions of one genre are drawn upon in order to create a template for the purposes of another genre. This section focuses on the way in which this template is put to work in the adoptive context. This involves examining, first, what sorts of features are carried over into the textbook from the original context of use of the embedded genre and, second, how it is modified or adapted in the new context.

The "blunders letter" is itself a recontextualization. It is the product of relocating the conventions of private (and perhaps primarily oral[6]) storytelling into a public genre. One particularly noteworthy feature of the "blunders letter" as a genre is its markedly gendered nature. Out of the 64 authentic "blunders letters" examined for purposes of comparison, 57 were written by females; in five cases the writer's pseudonym or the content of the letter did not unequivocally reveal the sex of the writer; and two letters were clearly written by males. This is explained to a large extent by the fact that this type of reader's letter is a constant feature of teenage magazines targeted at girls, which, of course, further reinforces its status as a gendered genre. However, even when it occurs in a gender-neutral magazine, most writers are girls and, interestingly, are *portrayed* as girls in humorous cartoon-like drawings employed to illustrate the letters (even in cases in which the sex of the writer is not apparent).

The gendered nature of the "blunders letter" is not surprising in light of the studies on oral storytelling, referred to by Eggins & Slade (1997). They point out that, based on the findings of Johnstone (1993) and Coates (1995), it seems that "stories in which speakers show themselves in fearful, embarrassing or humiliating situations are far more likely to be told by women than by men" (1997, p. 229). The appearance of the "blunders letter" in an EFL textbook is significant in that it is one example of several genres occurring in contemporary Finnish EFL textbooks which are typically associated with female readership. Such genres include notably media genres, such as horoscopes and personality tests, but also more private genres, such as diary entries. The fact that textbooks feature gendered genres has important consequences for the way in which textbooks position their readers. (For reader positioning, see Kress, 1985).

Besides the baggage of a gendered genre, however, the "blunders letter" as a genre affords a particular kind of meaning potential which may be deemed valuable from a pedagogic point of view. Storytelling does a lot of interpersonal work in conversation (Eggins & Slade, 1997), and it could be seen as being given similar functions in the language textbook. The anecdotes found in "blunders letters" are characteristically very involved: they are told in the first person; they are make extensive use of evaluative, affective language; and they present the narrator in a socially vulnerable position, but they are nonetheless humorous. It can be plausibly argued that an important function of the fictional "blunders letters" is to create proximity between the text and the student reader. Indeed, personal narratives and other kinds of stories are quite common in the EFL textbook generally.

What further attests to their perceived usability as elements of engaging pedagogic texts is the fact that narrative genres have a long history as textbook genres, going at least as far back as the time of the Reformation (C. Luke, 1989; see also Venetzky, 1987). Tales, jokes and anecdotes were also staple material in Finnish EFL textbooks from their beginnings in the 1890s for many decades. In textbooks from the early 1970s onwards, such storytelling genres have typically occurred within, or mixed with, generic formats from out-of-school contexts. In other words, the intertextual makeup of contemporary EFL textbooks is the product complex set of recontextualizations, with both synchronic and diachronic dimensions.

When entering a language textbook, texts undergo some fairly obvious changes. In the case of embedded generic formats, these changes could be seen as those features which immediately give away a text's status as a textbook text for all its genre-specific conventions. In *Dating disasters* such features include notably the chapter number, line numbering and the numbering of the letters. These are textbook conventions which have become naturalized owing to the purposes they serve in the totality of the discursive practices of schooling. Reading texts are numbered and often further categorized according to their centrality (e.g., "core" and "extra" materials) and/or the specific pedagogic purpose they are intended to serve ("listen," "find out," "study," "read," etc.). Moreover, the use of a text in the classroom is facilitated by providing line numbering and sometimes, as in this case, by numbering sections of the text. As C. Luke & A. Luke (1995) argue, such conventions arise out of the practices of a self-referential pedagogic "order of discourse" (see Fairclough, 1992), formed by a configuration of genres, discourses and practices such as the reading text, the adjunct exercises, the practices of the EFL classroom, and ultimately, for instance, the national curriculum and language pedagogic theory.

In addition to the overlay of textbook conventions, recontextualized generic formats in the EFL textbook are fitted into the school text in other ways as well. The recontextualization of the "blunders letter" into a textbook has brought about certain interesting "meaning shifts" (see Solin, 2004) in the way the genre is construed. Far from representing the blunders letter as a female genre, the writers of the fictitious letters in *Dating disasters* are predominantly male. It seems, then, that the textbook attempts to subvert the stereotype of men as incapable of telling stories about their blunders or foibles—and as not engaging in the writing of "blunders letters." Again, this is especially intriguing because it is not an isolated incident in my data: a similar shift occurs, for example, when another gendered genre, the pet magazine, is embedded into the textbook. This kind of adaptation of genre characteristics is likely to stem from (implicit or explicit) policies of textbook publishers to avoid texts or representations which could be potentially offensive (cf. Gray, 2001) and/or which are not in concordance with the value base of educational policies and official documents such as the national curriculum which emphasises, among other things, gender equity.

Modification of genre characteristics is also in evidence in the lead-in preceding the letters in *Dating disasters* (see Example 2, below).

Example (2)
From: *Dating disasters* (*This Way Up*, Otava 1999), reproduced with the permission of Otava Publishing house.

- Why is it that we always make fools of ourselves when somebody important is there to witness that terrible moment? The indescribable embarrassment makes your cheeks glow red-hot. You wish you had never been born. Don't fret! Read these stories and—what a relief!—your "disaster" wasn't that bad after all!

In authentic examples the lead-in dares the young readers to "expose themselves," as one magazine says, and to "entertain" other readers by sharing their grossest social blunders. The tone is almost celebratory, presenting blunders as something to boast about. (For example, in the *M Magazine*, blunders letters are tellingly referred to as *LOL stories*, where the three-letter acronym stands for "laughing out loud.") In the textbook version, on the other hand, the tone is rather more consoling than celebratory, and what is presented as the rationale for the publication of the letters is to show to the reader that other teenagers are equally fallible and that one's own disgraces may not even be that bad in comparison with those of others. To use the term from Bakhtin (1986), the lead-ins differ in terms of "addressivity," that is, they anticipate different kinds of readers and readings. Authentic examples address readers who are both able *and* willing to react to the lead-in by writing and sharing their own experiences. The textbook version, in turn, addresses a more passive audience who can only react emotionally, not physically and verbally by sharing their own stories. In other words, the lead-in implies a student-reader whose uptake of the text is controlled to a significant degree by the practices of the EFL classroom.

CONCLUSION

The *Dating disasters* text is an illustrative example of the way in which the EFL textbook attempts to engage and motivate its readers by incorporating generic influences from the domain of youth culture and particularly from the youth media. The characteristics of genre embedding in EFL textbooks may be usefully examined in light of the concept of "affinity" as formulated by Hodge & Kress (1988, p. 123). According to them, affinity is the expression of modality, a term conventionally used to refer to the truth value or the degree of obligation assigned to a verbal utterance. Hodge & Kress, however, extend the concept of modality, which they see as expressing commitment to representations of truth or "the real," and which may be constructed through different modalities. To give a few examples, a photo is regarded as being more "trustworthy" than a drawing; a news report is regarded as portraying reality more accurately than a fairy tale; and Tolstoy's *Anna Karenina* is probably regarded by most as saying something truer and more profound about human nature, love and relationships than a Barbara Cartland novel. From this perspective, the imitative intertextual linkages to salient genres can be seen as signaling "high" affinity in Hodge & Kress' terms. That is, the textbook aims at constructing a relationship of solidarity towards the reader by creating a textual environment which is "real" or "authentic" for the intended readership. In the case of *Dating disasters*, the specific generic features of the "blunders letter" enhance this effect. One of the most important functions of blunder stories, whether published in a teenage magazine or shared more privately in conversations or chatrooms, is surely the creation and maintenance of solidarity among peers.

However, the analysis of genre embedding in terms of recontextualization also underscores the complexities—and the challenges—involved in the embedding of such specific, situated genres into a textbook. Though not an entirely analogous case, Duff's (2004) study on pop culture references as an element of educational discourse is illuminating in this respect. What emerges from Duff's study is that the incorporation into classroom discourse of such intertextual elements is a strategy which relies heavily on an assumption of shared cultural knowledge and shared literacy practices and which, in the best of circumstances, may be empowering and engaging for students, but it also runs the risk of excluding those students who, for one reason or another, do not share the same resources. Such a concern is also relevant with respect to *Dating disasters* in that it models itself on a genre which is very strongly associated with gendered discourses and subjectivities. Despite the textbook's re-creation of the "blunders letter" as a gender-neutral genre, it retains its "social dispositions" (cf. Emmons, 2007, p. 192) as a gendered genre. Thus it might fail to engage male learners in the kind of discussion which the textbook authors seem to have intended, based on suggestions inscribed in the teacher's guide accompanying the book in question. Looked at from another angle, the case of *Dating disasters* exemplifies the way in which educational discourse "appropriates" genres and discourses under its own order, as suggested by Bernstein (1996) (see also Chouliaraki & Fairclough, 1999, p. 110). By rendering the "blunders letter" as educationally appropriate, as it were, the textbook text blurs the social and cultural anchorings of the genre, failing either to problematize the way in which media industries target and position girls (see below) or to validate the "blunders letter" as a resource for playful identity construction (primarily) for young girls.

Finally, the patterns of recontextualization evident in contemporary EFL textbooks provide an insight into the complex ways in which the textbook, as a culturally salient institutional text, is related to its social context. The notion of pedagogic discourse and, by extension, the school textbook as entities which are characterized to a large extent by the way in which they relocate discourses and genres, is not new. However, I have argued in this paper that the recontextualization of intertextual influences is particularly apparent in the contemporary EFL textbook. I also maintain that the intertextual features of the textbooks can be seen as indexing *the linguistic and discursive aspects of macro-level societal and cultural phenomena.* For example, the occurrence of gendered genres in textbooks should be addressed, besides as a choice made by textbook authors, in terms of what there is to choose from. In other words, the fact that the textbooks feature several media genres which are associated primarily or exclusively with female readership, while any distinctly "male" genres are hard to find, is partly connected to the way in which women and girls are targeted as readers (and consumers) by the print media. There is a proliferation of "general interest" women's and girls' magazines, while boys' tastes, it seems, are catered to by more specialized magazines. (And as a print genre, the magazine is easy to imitate in the printed textbook.) The prevalence of media genres and particularly their visual conventions in EFL textbooks could be interpreted in a similar vein, as reflecting the increased mediatization of communication, but also its increased visualization, in contemporary societies.

APPENDIX A: THE VERBAL TEXT OF *DATING DISASTERS*[7]

Your letters
Dating disasters

Why is it that we always make fools of ourselves when somebody important is there to witness that terrible moment? The indescribable embarrassment makes your cheeks glow red-hot. You wish you had never been born. Don't fret! Read these stories and—what a relief!—your "disaster" wasn't that bad after all!

(1) "I was out on a first date with a guy I had chased for so long. He took me to a really fancy little restaurant, which made me a bit uncomfortable. During the dinner, as I was sipping my soda, he cracked some joke. I laughed so hard that the soda came out of my nose. I started choking. Everyone stared at us. My date was really embarrassed and never called again." *Gina, 16* *Sacramento, CA*	(2) "I had the hots for this girl at school. I had asked her out and she'd said 'Yes'. I was on cloud nine and started showing off to my buddies. I'd always fancied myself as a good dancer, so I decided to show them how I would dance with my date. I was swinging my hips and doing a great routine in the school corridor. At first, the other guys were just grinning, but when my old belt broke and my pants went down to my ankles, they cracked, pointing their fingers behind my back. As I turned, I saw my date watching my show with a bunch of her friends." *Trevor, 16* *Baton Rouge, LA*	(3) "My boyfriend's parents went to the movies, but we decided to go and eat out in a Chinese restaurant. He ordered a meal which was large enough for an army: ribs, fried rice, soup and spring rolls. When the food arrived, he discovered he had no money. I had to pay the check! What really annoyed me was his parents' reaction. They thought it was funny and they didn't offer to pay for my boyfriend's share." *Ally, 18* *Bangor, ME*

(4) "My fourth date with a new girlfriend went fine until I accidentally called her by the name of my ex-girlfriend. That was the end of a promising relationship!" *Chas, 17* *Providence, RI*	(5) "My dating disaster happened at my senior prom. My girlfriend and I both still had braces on our teeth. While we were dancing cheek to cheek, we kissed every once in while. During one long kiss our braces somehow managed to get stuck! The whole school just stood there laughing their heads off." *Rob, 18* *Dallas, TX*	(6) "You would never expect to end up in a hospital on your first date—not even in your wildest dreams. It happened to me, and I wasn't the patient. My date wanted to teach me to bowl. She was really into bowling and good at it, whereas I was an absolute beginner. I dropped a bowling ball on her toe, so we spent a night in the not-so romantic emergency room of the hospital." *Theo, 14* *Detroit, MI*

APPENDIX B: AN IMAGE OF THE DATING DISASTERS TEXT[8]

Your letters

Dating disasters

Why is it that we always make fools of ourselves when somebody important is there to witness that terrible moment? The indescribable embarrassment makes your cheeks glow red-hot. You wish you had never been born. Don't fret! Read these stories and – what a relief! – your "disaster" wasn't that bad after all!

1 "I was out on a first date with a guy that I had chased for so long. He took me to a really fancy little restaurant, which made me a bit uncomfortable. During the dinner, as I was just sipping my soda, he cracked some joke. I laughed so hard that the soda came out of my nose. I started choking. Everyone stared at us. My date was really embarrassed and never called again."

Gina, 16, Sacramento, CA

2 "I had the hots for this girl at school. I had asked her out and she'd said 'Yes'. I was on cloud nine and started showing off to my buddies. I'd always thought of myself as a good dancer, so I decided to show them how I would dance with my date. I was swinging my hips and doing a great routine in the school corridor. At first, the other guys were just grinning, but when my old belt broke and my pants went down to my ankles, they cracked, pointing their fingers behind my back. As I turned, I saw my date watching my show with a bunch of her friends."

Trevor, 16, Baton Rouge, LA

3 "My boyfriend's parents went to the movies, but we decided to go and eat out in a Chinese restaurant. He ordered a meal which was large enough for an army: ribs, fried rice, soup and spring rolls. When the food arrived, he discovered that he had no money. I had to pay the check! What really annoyed me was his parents' reaction. They thought that it was funny and they didn't offer to pay for my boyfriend's share."

Ally, 18, Bangor, ME

4 "My fourth date with a new girlfriend went fine until I accidentally called her by the name of my ex-girlfriend. That was the end of a promising relationship!"

Chas, 17, Providence, RI

54 Young & HIP

389

NOTES

[1] The research reported was supported by the Academy of Finland Centre of Excellence funding for the Research Unit for Variation, Contacts and Change in English at the University of Helsinki and the University of Jyväskylä.

[2] Gray (2001) reports that EFL textbook publishers use the term "aspirational" to refer to content which centers around things which young people are assumed to find desirable and worth aspiring for, such as holidaying, shopping, etc.

[3] In other words, I am using the term here to refer to the provenance of texts. This is a conventional use of the term in much of language teaching literature. However, it should be noted that many authors emphasize that authenticity does not reside in texts. Widdowson (1991), for example, talks about the "genuineness" of texts when referring to their origin, distinguishing it from "authenticity" (or "inauthenticity"), which he reserves for describing the response to, or the uptake of, a text.

[4] The verbal component of the text is reproduced in Appendix A. An image of the text, displaying the visual conventions used, is provided in Appendix B.

[5] The names of "blunders letter" sections in Finnish and North American teenage magazines include: *Traumarama*, *Boy blunders*, "*Self-exposure*" (translated from Finnish), "*Blunders*" (translated from Finnish).

[6] It should be noted that the primacy of the oral mode might be challenged here on the grounds that young people, in particular, make extensive use of different electronic media and the written mode for private, informal interaction.

[7] From This Way Up. Texts 2, by T. Folland, M. Horwood, M. Lintujärvi, A. Nieminen & M. Tervaoja, 1999, Helsinki: Otava. Copyright 1999 by the authors and Otava publishing company. Reprinted by permission.

[8] From This Way Up. Texts 2, by T. Folland, M. Horwood, M. Lintujärvi, A. Nieminen & M. Tervaoja, 1999, Helsinki: Otava. Copyright 1999 by authors and Otava publishing company. Reprinted by permission.

REFERENCES

Alptekin, C. (1993). Target-language culture in EFL materials. *ELT Journal*, *47*(2), 136–143.

Bakhtin, M. (1986). *Speech genres and other late essays.* Austin: U of Texas Press.

Berkenkotter, C. (2001). Genre systems at work: DSM-IV and rhetorical recontextualization in psychotherapy paperwork. *Written Communication*, *18*(3), 326–349.

Bernstein, B. (1996). *Pedagogy, symbolic control and identity: Theory, research, critique.* London: Taylor & Francis.

Bex, T. (1996). *Variety in written English. Texts in society: Societies in texts.* London:

Routledge.

Bhatia, V. (1997). Genre-mixing in academic introductions. *English for Specific Purposes, 16*(3), 181–195.

Bhatia, V. (2004). *Worlds of written discourse: A genre-based view.* London: Continuum.

Chouliaraki, L., & Fairclough, N. (1999). *Discourse in the late modernity: Rethinking critical discourse analysis.* Edinburgh: Edinburgh University Press.

Coates, J. (1995). *The role of narrative in the talk of women friends.* Paper presented at the University of Technology, Sydney.

Colebrooke, R. (1996). *Semiotics and the EFL textbook.* Paper presented at the 11th World Congress of AILA, Jyväskylä, Finland.

Dendrinos, B. (1992). *The EFL textbook and ideology.* Athens: N. C. Grivas Publications.

Devitt, A. (1991). Intertextuality in tax accounting genres: Generic, referential, functional. In C. Bazerman & J. Paradis (Eds.), *Textual dynamics of the professions: Historical and contemporary studies of writing in professional communities* (pp. 336-357). Madison: University of Wisconsin Press.

Duff, P. (2004). Intertextuality and hybrid discourses: The infusion of pop culture in educational discourse. *Linguistics and Education, 14*, 231– 276.

Eggins, S., & Slade, D. (1997). *Analysing casual conversation.* London: Cassell.

Emmons, K. (2007). Uptake and the biomedical subject. In A. Bonini, D. Figueiredo, & F. Rauen (Eds.), *Proceedings from the 4th International Symposium on Genre Studies.* Retrieved from http://www3.unisul.br /paginas/ensino/pos/linguagem/cd/English/19i.pdf

Fairclough, N. (1992). *Discourse and social change.* Cambridge: Polity Press.

Gray, J. (2000). The ELT coursebook as a cultural artefact: How teachers censor and adapt. *ELT Journal, 54*(3), 274–283.

Gray, J. (2002). The global coursebook in English language teaching. In D. Block & D. Cameron (Eds.), *Globalization and language teaching* (pp. 151–167). London: Routledge.

Hodge, R., & Kress, G. (1988). *Social semiotics.* Cambridge: Polity Press.

Hoey, M. (2001). *Textual interaction: An introduction to written discourse analysis.* London: Routledge.

Jacobs, G., & Goatley, A. (2000). The treatment of ecological issues in ELT coursebooks. *ELT Journal, 54*(3), 256–264.

Johnstone, B. (1993). Community and contest: Midwestern men and women creating their worlds in conversational storytelling. In D. Tannen (Ed.), *Gender and conversational interaction* (pp. 62–80). New York: Oxford University Press.

Kress, G. (1985). *Linguistic processes in sociocultural practice.* Waurn Ponds, Victoria, Australia: Deakin University Press.

Kress, G., & Threadgold, T. (1988). Towards a social theory of genre. *Southern Review, 21*(3), 215–243.

Labov, W., & Waletzky, J. (1967). Narrative analysis: Oral versions of personal experiences. In J. Helm (Ed.), *Essays on the verbal and visual arts.* Seattle: University of Washington Press.

Leppänen, S. (2007). Youth language in media contexts: Insights into the functions of English in Finland. *World Englishes, 26*(2), 149–169.

Leppänen, S., & T. Nikula (in press). Diverse uses of English in Finnish society: Discourse-pragmatic insights from media, educational and business contexts. *Multilingua.*

Lesikin, J. (2001). Potential student decision-making in academic ESL textbooks. *Linguistics & Education, 12*(1), 25–49.

Linell, P. (1998). Discourse across boundaries: On recontextualizations and the blending of voices in professional discourse. *Text, 18*(2), 143–157.

Littlejohn, A. (1998). The analysis of language teaching materials: Inside the Trojan Horse. In B. Tomlinson (Ed.), *Materials development in language teaching* (pp. 190–216). Cambridge: Cambridge University Press.

Luke, C. (1989). *Pedagogy, printing, and protestanism: The discourse on childhood.* Albany: State University of New York Press.

Luke, C., & Luke, A. (1995). Just naming? Educational discourses and the politics of identity. In W. T. Pink & G. W. Noblit (Eds.), *Continuity and contradiction: The futures of the sociology of education* (pp. 357–380). Cresskill, New Jersey: Hampton Press.

Plum, G. A. (1988). Text and contextual conditioning in spoken English: A genre-based approach. Unpublished doctoral thesis, University of Sydney, Sydney, New South Wales, Australia.

Solin, A. (2001). *Tracing texts: Intertextuality in environmental discourse.* Helsinki: PIC Monographs.

Solin, A. (2004). Intertextuality as mediation: On the analysis of intertextual relations in public discourse. *Text, 24*(2), 267–296.

Sunderland, J., Cowley, M., Abdul Rahim, F., Leonzakou, C., & Shattuck, J. (2001). From bias "in the text" to "teacher talk around the text": An exploration of teacher discourse and gendered foreign language textbooks. *Language & Education, 11*(3), 251–286.

Thompson, G., & Hunston, S. (2001). Evaluation: An introduction. In S. Hunston & G. Thompson (Eds.), *Evaluation in text: Authorial stance and the construction of discourse* (pp. 1–27). Oxford: Oxford University Press.

Venetzky, R. (1987). A history of the American reading textbook. *Elementary School Journal, 87,* 247–265.

Widdowson, H. (1991). *Aspects of language teaching.* Oxford: Oxford Univ. Press.

GENRE IN WRITING ACROSS THE CURRICULUM

20 Exploring Notions of Genre in "Academic Literacies" and "Writing Across the Curriculum": Approaches Across Countries and Contexts

David R. Russell
Mary Lea
Jan Parker
Brian Street
Tiane Donahue

The SIGET IV panel on genre in Writing Across the Curriculum (WAC) and "academic literacies" (ACLITS) has set rolling a discussion of the similarities and differences in the two traditions, the former originating in the US in the early 1970s, the latter originating in England in the early 1990s. This paper maps out some elements of each in relation to the other and to genre, which we hope will set in motion further discussions and cross-fertilization.

At first glance, the two seem very different. As their respective titles suggest, one is about writing and the other about literacies. The term WAC means efforts to improve students' learning and writing (or learning through writing) in all university courses and departments (with some attention to school and adult education as well). The term "writing in the disciplines" (WID) is also used, somewhat synonymously, but suggests greater attention to the relation between writing and learning in a specific discipline. (For an overview and bibliography on WAC, see Bazerman, Joseph, Bethel, Chavkin, Fouquette, & Garufis, 2005.)

ACLITS is about *literacies* in higher education, primarily. In the UK, literacy has been more traditionally associated with school and adult learning, rather than the university. Indeed, there is still a strongly held belief amongst most UK university teachers that literacy needs to be attended to before students embark upon higher education studies (a view that is shared by many—perhaps most—US university teachers). ACLITS is working to change that view of literacy by taking social practices approaches to multiple and plural literacies, often associated with "New Literacy Studies" (Street, 1996).

WAC is twenty years older, and much larger and sprawling, encompassing many—and, often, dissenting—voices within it. Some 2400 articles and books on WAC have been published since 1975, with some 240 empirical studies. ACLITS is much younger, relatively smaller, and more focused and coherent. Though the object of both is similar—academic writing—the purposes are different. WAC is primarily a pedagogical reform movement. Despite being practitioner led, ACLITS has focused on research and theory thus far, describing practices and understanding them theoretically. It is just entering into large-scale pedagogy and reform efforts.

At first glance at least, the two also appear to come from rather different intellectual worlds. WAC comes out of US "rhetoric and composition," a field that arose out of the professionalization of teachers of first-year university general writing courses in the 1970s—with very much a humanities bent—and located in English departments primarily, with relatively little contact with linguistics. ACLITS comes primarily out of studies in language, literacy and ethnography, with a focus on descriptive studies of specific literacy practices, and has no particular disciplinary home.

These differences are magnified by the very different systems of higher education they inhabit. The US system emphasizes late specialization, with a period of "general education" in the first two years of university, and writing in several disciplines. In the UK students have tended to specialize early and write for one discipline, although recently "modular" courses have involved more "mix" of disciplines and therefore more switching of written genres (Lea & Street, 1998, 2006). In the UK assessments of students almost always involve extensive written work, whereas in the US assessments are often multiple choice. The primary difference is that the US has a ubiquitous, required general writing course in higher education, first-year composition, which deeply colors the whole enterprise of WAC.

Yet there are important similarities. Both ACLITS and WAC took their impetus from widening participation, as it is called in the UK, or admission of previously excluded groups in the US. The US has for decades had a system of mass education, whereas the UK is really only beginning "massification." So both WAC (in the 1970s) and ACLITS (in the 1990s) began as a response to an influx of new students.

Ideologically both are oppositional, attempting to reform higher education and make it more open. And both use writing/literacy to resist deeply entrenched attitudes about writing, and about students and disciplines. Both attempt to move beyond elementary skills (and thus remedial or deficit) models of writing to consider the complexity of communication in relation to learning.

And in terms of research, there is a strong element of ethnographic research in North America, that owes much to Dell Hymes and Shirley Brice Heath and that complements British traditions of anthropology and applied linguistics (see

Heath & Street, 2008). And ACLITS has from the beginning been influenced by North American WAC research by Bazerman, Bartholomae (1986), Russell and others.

And in the last 10 years, North American WAC programs have begun to speak of themselves in terms of multi-modal "communication across the curriculum" (CAC), in part a response to the New London Group and its interest in new media, which was also influential for ACLITS.

We organize this paper around parallel descriptions of each tradition under the headings historical origins, institutional positions, theory and research about genre, and finally pedagogy using genre. We conclude by drawing out a number of comparisons between the two for further dialog.

HISTORICAL ROOTS

ACLITS Origins

The notion of "academic literacies" has its roots in a body of practice-based research and literacy theory that became significant in the UK during the 1990s. Until this time little attention had been paid to issues of student writing, the general assumption—although rarely articulated—being that students would learn how to write through their tacit acculturation into the norms and conventions of single subject disciplinary frames (Ivanic & Lea, 2006). Hounsell (1988) had previously looked at problems students encountered when confronted with the unfamiliar discourses of the university. He identified academic discourse as "a particular kind of written world, with a set of conventions, or 'code,' of its own." He illustrated how students needed to be sensitive to different disciplinary ways of framing in their writing, and highlighted the tacit nature of academic discourse calling for its features to be made more explicit to students. (See also the Australian research of Ballard & Clanchy, 1988.) This focus on explicit acculturation into disciplinary codes and discourses shared much in common with the earlier work of Bizzell (1982) and Bartholomae (1986) in the US, which as we will see, grew out of the US WAC movement that began in the 1970s.

By the early 1990s, UK higher education was experiencing a fundamental change with unprecedented expansion in the sector and the consequences of the 1992 Education Act, which abolished the binary divide between polytechnics and universities, bringing them together for both administrative and funding purposes under one government funded body. In practical terms this meant increasing numbers of students and class sizes with no concomitant expansion in resources. One response was the creation of "study skills" and "learning support" centers, where students were able to receive one-on-one or small group support which their lecturers were no longer in a position to provide. It was among those practitioners working with students in such centers that the early roots of the field of academic literacies research began to emerge (much as in the US in the 1970s, the work of Mina Shaughnessey grew out of work with students identified as under-prepared and began serious interest in writing development). Increasingly frustrated with the limitations of simplistic surface- and skills-based models of student writing in their work with students, they began to look both for more workable and theorized explanations of the problems being encountered by student writers. As practitioner-researchers, they found themselves at the interface between theory and practice and their early publications often reflected this intersection (Ivanic 1998; Jones, Turner, & Street, 1999; Lea, 1994; Lea & Street, 1998, 1999; Lea & Stierer, 1999; Lillis, 1999, 2001).

The dearth of literature on student writing coming out of the UK at that time meant that these researcher/practitioners often looked to the US for theoretical framing for their work. Particularly influential was Bazerman's early work (1988). Although his concern had been with the texts produced by established academic writers, UK researchers found this a particularly useful framing with which to think about undergraduate student writing. In particular his claim that writing matters because the different choices around what and how we write results in different meanings, underpinned the framing for both research and practice with student writers. With the expansion of higher education and increasing numbers of adult students entering UK universities as "non-traditional" entrants in the early 1990s, Bazerman's analysis provided a fruitful way of exploring how these students brought their own knowledge and experience to the construction of the writing they were required to undertake for assessment (Lea, 1998). Examining the object under study, the literature of the field, the anticipated audience and the author's own self in the writing of mature students laid bare the ways in which engaging with academic knowledge could conflict with other more familiar "ways of knowing." For Ivanic and her colleagues at Lancaster University (Clark & Ivanic, 1991) adopting principles of critical language awareness provided a further theoretical orientation from which to view so called problems with student writing.

This backdrop provided a foundation for the contested approach which has become associated with academic literacies research during the last decade, examining in detail students' struggles with meaning making and the nature of power and authority in student writing (Ivanic, 1998; Lea, 1994; Lea & Street, 1998; Lillis, 1997). In part this was influenced by related developments in critical linguistics (Fairclough, 1989). Work on critical language awareness in schools (Fairclough, 1992) seemed particularly pertinent to the new higher education context. In 1996 Street published an innovative chapter on academic literacies which both challenged academic convention (by incorporating the original texts of others rather than integrating them into his own work with conventional referencing) and foregrounded questions of "academic literacies." The perspective taken by Street (1996) in this publication sat within a body of work that had become known as the "New Literacy Studies" (NLS). Street's seminal contribution to NLS had been made earlier when he distinguished between autonomous and ideological models of literacy (Street, 1984). He had argued that whereas an autonomous model of literacy suggests that literacy is a decontextualised skill, which once learned can be transferred with ease from one context to another, the ideological model highlights the contextual and social nature of literacy practices, and the relationships of power and authority which are implicit in any literacy event. Literacy, then, is not something that once acquired can be effortlessly applied to any context requiring mastery of the written word. Writing and reading practices are deeply social activities; familiarity with and understanding these practices takes place in specific social contexts, which are overlaid with ideological complexities, for example, with regard to the different values placed on particular genres of written texts. Following this perspective, NLS, with its roots in sociolinguistics and linguistic anthropology, conceptualizes writing and reading as contextualized social practices.

Until the mid-1990s New Literacy Studies had been concerned with school-based, community and work-place literacies, primarily of people in different cultural contexts, notably Iran, South Africa, and Latin America (Street, 2001) but had not paid any attention to literacies in the university "at home." Although the early work of, for example Lea (1994) and Lillis (1997), had conceptualized writing as contextualized social practice explicitly challenging deficit models of writing, neither at that time situated their work explicitly in the NLS tradition nor made reference to "academic literacies," as such. However, Lea (1994) did illustrate the multiplicity of discourses in the academy, an important distinction from the use of the term discourse in the singular. Ivanic also foregrounded the use of different and competing discourses in her study of mature students (Ivanic, 1998). Overall, what characterized this emerging body of work was its specific focus on student writing as social practice and recognition of the multiplicity of practices, whether these were conceptualized as discourses or literacies. The use of the term "literacies," rather than "discourses" (the framing more commonly provided by the US writers in the college composition field), gradually became more prevalent in the UK literature. This was not merely because of its association with a theoretical framing provided by the NLS, but because the focus of concern was student writing, rather than spoken language; the term discourse being associated more commonly with the use of spoken rather than written language at that time.

Research by Lea and Street (1998), building on the NLS methodological approach but also on Lea's practitioner experience, introduced new theoretical frames to a field which was, at the time, still predominantly influenced by psychological accounts of student learning (e.g., Gibbs, 1994). Rather than frame their work in terms of "good" and "poor" writing, Lea and Street suggested that any explanation needed to examine faculty and student expectations around writing without making any judgments about which practices were appropriate. Drawing on the findings from an empirical research project conducted in two very different universities, they examined student writing against a background of institutional practices, power relations and identities, with meanings being contested between faculty and students, and an emphasis on the different understandings and interpretations of the writing task. Findings from their research suggested fundamental gaps between students' and faculty understandings of the requirements of student writing, providing evidence at the level of epistemology, authority and contestation over knowledge, rather than at the level of technical skill, surface linguistic competence and cultural assimilation. Based on their analysis of their research data, they explicated three models of student writing. These they termed study skills, socialization, and academic literacies. The study skills model is based on the assumption that mastery of the correct rules of grammar and syntax, coupled with attention to punctuation and spelling, will ensure student competence in academic writing; it is, therefore, primarily concerned with the surface features of text. In contrast the academic socialization model assumes students need to be acculturated into the discourses and genres of particular disciplines and that making the features and requirements of these explicit to students will result in their becoming successful writers. In some respects the third model, academic literacies, subsumes many of the features of the other two; Lea and Street (1998) point out that the models are not presented as mutually exclusive. Nevertheless they argue that it is the academic literacies model which is best able to take account of the nature of student writing in relation to institutional practices, power relations and identities, in short to consider the complexity of meaning making which the other two models fail to provide.

The explication of the three models proposed by Lea and Street has been drawn upon very widely in the literature on teaching and learning across a range of HE contexts (see, e.g., Thesen & van Pletzen, 2006, on South Africa) and calls for a more in-depth understanding of student writing and its relationship to learning across the academy, thus offering an alternative to deficit models of learning and writing based on autonomous models of literacy.

WAC Origins

The WAC movement's origin in the US in the 1970s can only be understood in light of the century-old US tradition of university-level "composition" courses, required of almost all first year university students. These courses were taught in English departments and traditionally mixed the teaching of literary texts with skills-based instruction in writing, often with a remedial stigma attached (deficit model). In the late 1970s, composition teachers professionalized the teaching of writing, developing their own MA and PhD programs in rhetoric and composition (that is, the teaching of university-level writing). They developed several strands of research drawn from both the humanities (i.e., classical rhetoric) and the social sciences (e.g., education), and pushed composition teaching beyond literary analysis and "skills and drills."

As with ACLITS in the 1990s, the rise of the WAC movement in the late 1970s and early 1980s (Russell, 1991) was a response to the influx into higher education of previously excluded groups, through open admissions policies in public institutions. One response was to radically rethink the remedial or deficit model of writing and found writing centers, special curricula, and systematic research into the differences between student and teacher perceptions of error—much as with ACLITS research in the mid-1990s. Another approach was to enlist teachers from other disciplines to improve students' writing—and learning: the WAC movement.

The early theoretical inspiration for the WAC movement in the US came directly from a British educational theorist and reformer, James Britton, and his colleagues at the University of London Institute of Education, who coined the term WAC (Russell, 1991) as part of their efforts to improve writing in the disciplines in secondary education. Britton and his colleagues (1975) viewed writing (and talk) as a gradually developing accomplishment, thoroughly bound up with the particular intellectual goals and traditions of each discipline or profession, not as a single set of readily-generalizable skills learned once and for all. They also theorized writing in terms of disciplinary learning and personal development, not discrete, generalizable skills. And they used Vygotsky (among others) to theorize it. In Britain, the Language across the Curriculum or Language Awareness movements (as they were called) did not last long or have a great impact on secondary schools, and almost none in HE at the time (although see Ivanic, 2004, for more recent attention to Critical Language Awareness), but their ideas were picked up by the fledgling WAC movement in the US—mainly in higher education.

In the early 1980s, the dominant model of writing research was cognitive. But by the mid-1980s, a few US researchers began to use ethnographic methods to explore writing development as a cultural-historical phenomenon. As with the ACLITS in the late 1990s, the Ethnography of Communication was the inspiration. The seminal article was by Lucille McCarthy, a PhD student of Dell

Hymes. Her 1987 article "Strangers in Strange Lands" followed one student as he went to courses in four disciplines, and as the title suggests, McCarthy found that the differences in disciplinary writing practices and communities were much more important to the student than the similarities, a theme pursued by Lea and Street (1998) in their account of UK students' switching between courses in modular degrees.

Classroom practice in general composition courses began to change as well in the 1980s. "WAC textbooks" in first-year composition courses began to appear, which taught the genres of writing in the social and natural sciences—not as formulas to be followed, ordinarily, but as indices of the ways of knowing, the epistemology and social actions, of knowledge domains or disciplines.

Research into social dimensions of the disciplines and professions—how and why professionals write—complemented textual research. A large strand of research into the genres of professional and a academic research writing began (e.g., Bazerman, 1988; Berkenkotter & Huckin, 1995). Some compared student writing to that of professionals. For example, Geisler's (1994) work on expert and student texts in philosophy, Academic Literacy and the Nature of Expertise, exposed philosophers' ways of writing, thinking, and being, in relation to the discursive moves of students writing in philosophy courses. And an educational reform movement swept US HE.

INSTITUTIONAL POSITIONS

WAC Institutionally

Institutionally, WAC has been focused in programs within individual universities (and some secondary schools). It is a higher education reform movement, but without a centralized national organization, though it does have a loosely organized special interest group associated with the professional organization for composition, the Conference on College Composition and Communication (CCCC). Despite this, it has had wide influence in HE over the last 30 years. Perhaps one third of US institutions have some WAC program, in a vast number of forms (McLeod, 1992). Many WAC programs also include some curricular structure(s) to provide continuity. Institutions or departments often designate certain courses as "writing intensive" or "writing extensive" and require students to take certain ones (or a certain number of them) to graduate. Other universities have "linked" courses in which some or all of the students in a course in a discipline take a parallel course in writing, which uses the content of the disciplinary course and is planned in conjunction with it. More rarely, departments organize a sequence of writing tasks and student support that extends throughout their curriculum, from first year to last, to consciously develop students' writing (and often other communication modes). Some universities have required all departments to develop such a sequence. All these curricular forms are almost always in addition to first-year composition courses, though some universities require freshman "seminars" instead: a first-year writing course taught by staff in various disciplines with subjects for writing drawn from their disciplines (Monroe, 2006).

Almost all WAC programs include organized efforts to develop awareness of writing among teachers in the disciplines and their competence in supporting students in their writing. Many institutions have interdisciplinary workshops and seminars for academic teaching staff from all disciplines on writing development. There they not only discuss the particular needs and resources for their students' writing but also how writing works differently in each of their disciplines, how it brings students to deeper involvement with the unique ways of knowing in each—the epistemology of each—and how students can be helped to write to learn as they learn to write in a field (in Britton's famous phrase, now a slogan). Teaching staff learn to design and sequence assignments, communicate expectations, and give feedback. And since 1993 there has been a biennial national (now international) conference that draws about 500 faculty members from a great range of disciplines, institutions and countries.

Finally, WAC programs are often connected with or part of a writing center or centers (often attached to a student support unit). Tutors (graduate or undergraduate students, typically) give individual or small group help to students. Sometimes tutors are drawn from various disciplines. Sometimes there are discipline-specific writing centers. And sometimes there are tutors assigned to specific courses (usually large lectures) to help students with their writing and learning. These centers have tried to avoid the remedial or deficit model of writing by helping all students with their writing—and, in some centers, even teaching staff who are writing research articles.

All of these efforts struggle with a range of institutional attitudes and structures that militate against WAC: reductive and remedial concepts of student writing (particularly that writing is a set of general skills to be mastered in the ubiquitous first-year general writing courses), demands on faculty time for research, large enrollments in many courses, and so on (Walvoord, 1997). After 30 years, it is still an uphill battle, but because so many academics in the US have been exposed to the idea of WAC—through attending workshops or teaching writing-intensive courses, for example—WAC has become part of the institutional landscape of higher education in the US.

ACLITS Institutionally

In the UK, "writing-intensive" (though not writing conscious) undergraduate courses were traditionally the preserve of Oxford and Cambridge, where teaching was based on individual teaching by faculty members supervising student writing, or as it was perceived, student disciplinary learning, in weekly one-on-one sessions. The post-1992 expansion, entailing large class sizes and an increasingly diverse student body, and the growth of themed, interdisciplinary modular curricula resulted in more attention to writing as meaning making and as a social practice. This has led to movements such as Writing Development in Higher Education (biennial conferences since 1995) and more recently the WAC-influenced Thinking Writing project and new, US style, writing centers (for these and other examples see Ganobcsik-Williams, 2006).

ACLITS has influenced all of these efforts. However, as illustrated above, ACLITS, although primarily practitioner led, has tended to be more focused on theory and research. Indeed there have been questions raised in the literature about the value of the framing offered by academic literacies research for pedagogy. Lillis (2006) suggests that we need to develop an academic literacies pedagogy which places the nature of dialogue at its centre and that more specifically we should be thinking about how we can develop and validate alternative spaces for writing and meaning making in the academy. Lea (2004) suggests that the principles emerging from academic literacies research can be taken up in different institutional contexts. She illustrates this through a case study of a postgraduate course in teacher education delivered online.

From a practitioner perspective the provision of support based on any particular set of principles is unusual. Nevertheless, many practitioners do draw on the general framing offered by the academic literacies perspective, albeit not explicitly. The biennial Writing Development in Higher Education conference draws together those working across settings in the field of writing support, who are adopting a social practice model of writing. A number of institutions have pursued programs for supporting students and their teachers, often in relation to widening participation. These developments are frequently initiated by educational development units and supported by some form of student learning center. Although both these generally have a broad brief of which writing is only a part, taken together they are generally the most important institutional sites for writing development in the UK. While educational development units work directly supporting faculty with issues of teaching and learning, including student writing, the brief of most student learning centers is to work only with students. Coupled with the fact that the latter is often low status, hourly paid work and the academic credibility of the former is continually under threat as universities are increasingly reluctant to employ educational developers on academic contracts, the kinds of approaches suggested by Lillis and Lea are few and far between.

THEORY AND RESEARCH: THE ROLES OF GENRE

ACLITS Theory and Research Using Genre

Issues of genre are central to the three models of student writing outlined above (skills, socialization, and academic literacies). Each of these models is implicitly associated with a different orientation to the notion of genre. In terms of study skills, genre would be conceptualized primarily in relation to surface features and form; academic socialization would be associated with the conceptualization of genre in terms of established disciplinary norms for communication, given primarily by the texts written by academics within a disciplinary community. The empirically grounded academic literacies perspective is aligned with a view of genre as social practice rather than genre knowledge in terms of disciplinary communication per se, although this is by its very nature central to the social practice perspective.

Research in the field has uncovered the range of genres engaged in by students across the university, with variation evident not just in terms of the discipline or specific departmental or module requirements for student writers. For example, genre variation is evident in terms of the individual predispositions of individual university teachers and in relation to specific assignments (Lea & Street, 1998; see also Lea & Street, 1999, 2006). The contribution of the theoretical and methodological framing offered by social anthropology and applied linguistics is central to this understanding of genre types as they emerge in the detailed everyday encounters around writing in particular institutional contexts. Much of the research has been undertaken through an ethnographic lens which provides the opportunity to make the familiar strange, to approach everyday practices around student writing as an area of study without bringing to this judgments about the nature of that writing (see Heath & Street, 2008). Through such a lens a range of genres become visible and opened up for scrutiny, not just those that are given by either generic academic writing requirements or by the discipline. For example, researchers have examined feedback on students' written work and the implications for meaning making and issues of identity (Ivanic, 1998, 2004; Lea & Street, 1998; Lillis, 2001). Stierer (1997, 2000) has examined the nature of assignment questions for master's level students and the implications of the ways in which these are framed for students' understanding of assignment questions. Lea (2006) has explored the textual nature of online student debates and how students integrate these into their assignments. Street and colleagues have explored the issue of "genre switching" amongst pre-university students being prepared for university entry in Widening Participation courses at King's College London (Scalone & Street, 2006; Lea & Street, 2006—see below). The findings of the type of detailed research signaled above suggests, then, that genre questions arise in consideration of the range of texts and practices which are integral to any understanding of student writing—and how best to support it—rather than being merely concerned with disciplinary consider-ations, such as "how to write in History," "how to reference in Psychology," "how to develop an argument in English."

As we have already discussed above ACLITS has tended to focus on un-packing micro-social practices, such as "gaps" between student and lecturer per-ceptions of particular writing activities, often embedded deeply in traditions of essayist literacy and the assessment of writing. Researchers in this tradition have also focused on theorizing and researching new genres of writing in HE teaching, in different modes and media (see below) and on the ways in which students are called upon—often implicitly—to switch between different genres and modes (which also raises the more general issue of how genre and mode are theorized in relation to other traditions of genre analysis and multimodal studies). Arguably what distinguishes academic literacies research from WID is its tendency to focus at this micro level and also upon the different interpreta-tions and understandings of genres of the participants in any particular writ-ing encounter in the university. Drawing on the kind of framing provided by Berkenkotter and Huckin (1995), genres emerge in the relationship between the creation of texts and their associated practices in any particular context. Not only do they vary across disciplines, subjects and/or fields of study but also in text types (e.g., academic assignments, faculty feedback/marginalia, email).

This approach to genre draws a range of texts and practices into the academic literacies frame, rather than concentrating on student essay writing per se. The focus on the minutiae of texts and practices in understanding meaning mak-ing is given by the ethnographic roots of this field, and particularly Hymes' (1974) ethnography of communication, resulting in the foregrounding of an institutional perspective which takes precedence over a disciplinary or subject based focus. This may indeed be the most important distinction between the different traditions being explored in this chapter, despite their evidently com-mon theoretical and, in part, methodological roots. As the landscape of higher education has changed over the last decade, with increased emphasis on profes-sional rather than purely academic study and concomitant attention to new genres of writing in the academy, the theoretical framing offered by academic literacies research is becoming increasingly valuable in terms of both research and practice. For example, Creme (2008) is concerned with learning journals as transitional genres bridging a gap between students' personal worlds and the rigorous discipline based genres embedded in more conventional essay writing. (Student journal writing is also a strategy used by the Widening Participation Programme at King's College London, described below).

A number of practitioner researchers are also underpinning their work in new multimodal environments for learning with principles offered by academic literacies research. Walton & Archer (2004) illustrate the limitations of teaching web searching skills in a South African context, if teachers do not understand the explanations and interpretations that their students are bringing to reading the web. They suggest that students already have to be in command of subject discourses and understand the genres they encounter online in order to make their searching worthwhile; supporting students in using the web in their studies requires sensitivity to the students' background and prior experience. This perspective mirrors that offered by the early findings in the field but has application to online learning. McKenna (2006) examines how students' use of hypertext challenges the linear construction of argument in academic writing. She suggests that this environment offers students the possibility to take up new subject positions not possible in more conventional essayist genres. The focus is less upon disciplinary genre knowledge and more upon issues of subjectivity and agency and the ways in which these both rub up against and challenge and subvert conventional academic genres.

WAC Theory and Research Using Genre

WAC research has taken two complementary directions: one investigating the writing of professionals in various disciplines and professions; another focused on student writing in the disciplines—especially the role of writing in learning (Russell, 1997). Concepts of genre have been central in theory and research in both. (See Klein, 1999, and Newell, 2006, for reviews of quantitative studies of writing to learn; see Russell, 2001, and Bazerman et al., 2005, for reviews of qualitative studies of student writing in HE).

Some studies have viewed genre in traditional form-based terms, as collections of identifiable features and conventions (e.g., contrastive rhetoric; the genre studies reviewed in Klein, 1999). However, in the past two decades, new ways of thinking about genre in student writing—growing out of the study of the genre and activity of professional writing—emphasize the activity of genre (Bazerman, 1988). This approach is rooted in C. Miller's (1984, 1994) theory of genre as social action. Genres are "typified rhetorical actions based in recurrent situations" (1984, p. 159). The researcher's focus shifts from the text itself to the relationship between the text and the activity of people in situations where texts are used in regularized—typified—ways. Genres are not merely forms of words, but forms of life, socio-cultural regularities that stabilize-for-now (but never finally) our interactions (Schryer, 1993).

In the late 1980s, the concept of genre as social action was combined with Vygotskian cultural-historical activity theory, which sees the relation between thought and language (and learning and writing) in social as well as cognitive terms. Cultural tools such as speaking and writing mediate our interior thoughts as well as our external social interactions. Genres, as typified ways of interacting with tools, can be seen as ways of coordinating joint activity and regulating thought (Russell, 1997; Bazerman, this volume). For Bazerman and Russell (2003), as the signs on a page mediate between relationships and people, so do genres; texts are "attended to in the context of activities" and can only be studied in their "animating activities"—production, reception, meaning, and value, "embedded in people's uses and interpretations."

Quantitative studies of student writing using genre have tended to see genres in the older, form-based way, and to look at their effects in more strictly cognitive rather than social cognitive terms. They focus on the requirements genres pose for searching out and organizing information, structuring relationships among ideas and with audiences, and controlling stance toward content (Bazerman, this volume; Klein, 1999; Newell, 2006). These studies show that students engage in different processes when they have the expectations of one genre rather than another (student newspaper, in-class essay, registrar's form).

Qualitative studies of student writing have tended to take an activity or social action approach to genre as they describe student writing and students' writing and learning. In the last dozen years, theories of genre systems (Bazerman, 1994; Russell, 1997) or networks (Prior, this volume) or ecologies (Spinuzzi, 2003), informed by cultural historical activity theory, have been applied to understanding professional work and its relationship to education (e.g., Smart 2006; Winsor 2003). Contexts such as organizations or institutions are viewed as complex activity systems mediated by complex systems of intertextual genres, through which knowledge circulates and activity is mediated in intersubjective networks (Prior, this volume; Russell & Yañez, 2003). Research on genre has traced the relationships between academic writing/activity and the writing/activity of other systems, such as home, professions, hobbies, etc. (e.g., Prior, 1998; Russell & Yañez, 2003), and its effects on both writing and identity. Genre is seen as offering direction or motive to activity, as well pathways to new identities for participants. Indeed, longitudinal studies of students in HE (Beaufort, 2007; Wardle, forthcoming; Sommers, 2004; Donahue, 2008) have described the genres that students acquire as they learn in the disciplines, within various institutional contexts.

PEDAGOGY AND GENRE

WAC and Pedagogy

WAC pedagogical theory, research, and practice are well developed and take two basic directions: implicit and explicit. The most common view among teachers in the disciplines (and most WAC experts, very likely) is that students learn to write new genres primarily through writing in authentic contexts, such as their courses in the disciplines. And the focus of the WAC movement is on encouraging writing, feedback (teacher or peer), and revision or repetition. In this view, students learn to write by writing.

A strong theoretical argument for this view has been made by a group of Canadian researchers, and supported with a long series of qualitative studies that fail to show transfer of genre knowledge from academic to workplace contexts (Dias, Freedman, Medway, & Paré, 1999). They theorize that genre knowledge is tacit and only acquired unconsciously as part of some purposeful, communicative activity in the context where the genre is used. Students "pick it up" without being explicitly taught a genre.

There are three well-articulated approaches in North America to explicit teaching, which inform much teaching of writing and, often, WAC as well. The first might be termed "genre acquisition," teaching in an explicit (though not necessarily presentational) way certain generic "moves" or conventions of genres, derived from analysis of the genres (either textual or contextual or both). This is the most common approach in North American second language teaching (English for Special Purposes/English for Academic Purposes). The goal is to provide linguistic resources that students need. For example, Swales' analysis of the generic moves of academic research article introductions is taught to L2 graduate students explicitly, along with a good deal of reading and analysis of introductions, structured practice writing them, and so on. This approach has been used rather little in WAC or first language teaching, perhaps because there are fundamental differences between first and second language learners (see Carter, Ferzli, & Weibe, 2004). (A somewhat similar approach, Systemic Functional Linguistics, is even less common in North America.)

A second approach (Devitt, 2004; Bawarshi, 2003) is to teach "genre awareness" as distinct from (but related to) genre acquisition. Students first rhetorically analyze familiar genres whose contexts they have experienced, then move to less or unfamiliar genres that are related to them (antecedent genres, usually), studying both the form and aspects of the context, always trying to "keep form and context intertwined" (Devitt, 2004, p. 198). They then do "genre ethnography" of some context in which the genre is used (see Johns, 2002). Devitt argues that teaching genre awareness, rather than particular skills, will facilitate transfer, as previously learned genres become antecedent genres for further learning and practice of related genres (Devitt, p. 202ff). This approach has been used mainly in general writing courses (first-year composition, technical communication, etc.) where there are students from a variety of disciplines and the teacher is not expert in all of them. Students do research in the target context and its genres. The teacher helps them become good researchers into genre. But the teacher does not teach a specific genre to the students.

A third approach, sometimes termed "New Rhetorical," is to teach a genre explicitly, but in the process of performing a rhetorical action in its target context of use—which is the situation in disciplinary classrooms, typically. In the process of doing some discipline-specific learning activity, students also get explicit instruction in genre. But the instruction is not confined to teaching stages or moves or conventions; it also attempts to teach the logic of communication in terms of the logic of the learning/disciplinary activity—the "why" and "where" and "when" of a genre as well as the "what" and "how" of it. For example, Carter et al. (2004) developed an online tool for teaching the laboratory report genre in science and engineering education. LabWrite leads students through the process of doing and representing (textually, mathematically, and graphically) the laboratory activity as they are doing it. The goal of instruction is not to teach "the genre" or "writing" but to teach scientific concepts and scientific method using genre as a mediational means. The genre is a tool for doing and learning science in the context of the course-specific laboratory. A comparison group study found that students who used LabWrite wrote lab reports that chemistry teachers rated as "significantly more effective" in (1) learning the scientific concept of the lab and (2) learning to apply scientific reasoning. The students also (3) developed a significantly more positive attitude toward writing lab reports than the comparison group. This is the only comparison group study to show explicit instruction effective in teaching a genre to L1 adults.

The second question—genre's relationship to writing to learn—has been explored empirically primarily with younger students. Efforts to substantiate the claim that the act of writing per se improves learning were not successful. Instead, research found that the kinds (or genres) of writing students do and the conditions in which they do it matter a great deal. Cooper and MacDonald (1992) found that university literature students who kept academic journals structured by discipline-specific questions did better on exams than students who kept unstructured personal journals on their reading. Indeed, the largest literature review to date of controlled comparison studies of writing to learn, Klein (1999), found that the most effective approaches were those based on genre, but the studies are few and still inconclusive. Klein describes the theory of how genre supports learning thus: "writers use genre structures to organize relationships among elements of text, and thereby among elements of knowledge" (p. 203).

However, as noted above, these quantitative studies of student writing using genre have tended to see genres in the older, form-based way, and to look at their effects in more strictly cognitive rather than social cognitive terms. They look at study questions, journals, and essays, not discipline-specific tasks. And as Bazerman (this volume) points out, "The effects seem to be associated with the specific nature of tasks, with study questions leading to increased recall and essays associated with connecting ideas (see also Newell, 2006; McCutcheon, 2007). This pattern, as Bazerman points out, is reminiscent of Scribner and Cole's (1981) finding that the "cognitive effects of literacy were varied and tied to the institutionally embedded practices which literacy was used for." Bazerman goes on to theorize that Vygotsky's (1978, 1986) concept that learning precedes development may explain the way genre may facilitate the development of higher-level discipline-specific ways of knowing, as well as low-level task-specific knowledge (this volume).

Finally, critical pedagogy has also influenced WAC on genre. Beginning with Mahala (1991), some teachers and theorists have called for WAC to embrace the wider critical pedagogy movement, in various ways (see Bazerman et al., 2005 for a summary). One line of critique and reform calls WID "assimilationist" and emphasizes the importance of valuing students' non-academic language and genres, especially those drawn from ethnic or class backgrounds, which academic genres often exclude (Delpit, 1993; Villanueva, 2001; McCrary, 2001).

Another line of critique and reform emphasizes students' individual voice, and questions whether academic discourse in the disciplines provides students with the authority and stance they need to preserve and express a personal voice, to assert their authority over the disciplinary genres—and to resist simply reproducing the dominant ideologies of the disciplines (Mahala, 1991; Halasek, 1999; LeCourt, 1996). These arguments often call for students to write personal or non-academic genres in the disciplinary classrooms. Elbow (1998) even argues that students best develop an intellectual stance for writing academic discourse by writing non-academic genres. And in a broader sense, Malinowtz's (1998) feminist critique argues that WID should challenge the established boundaries of disciplines and genres of academic writing, as third wave feminism has done.

Responses to these critiques emphasize (1) that the very power of the disciplines makes it important to understand them—and understanding is a necessary precondition to intelligently critiquing and/or resisting them, (2) that learning new ways of thinking and acting can enrich and expand one's identity, and (3) that critiques of the disciplines from the point of view of the humanities prejudge what students will find most valuable for their ethical and personal development (Bazerman, 1992, 2002). McLeod and Maimon (2000) argue that WAC itself is "quietly subversive" as it resists the banking (transmission) model of education and encourages teachers to make students active and critical learners rather than passive recipients of knowledge. Finally, disciplines themselves are not monolithic and each contains critical elements with it, with which WAC can and does engage.

There is then lively theoretical debate and much pedagogical experimentation and research on genre in WAC pedagogy, and discussions of pedagogy and genre between ACLITS and WAC approaches seem a fertile ground for producing new strains of pedagogical thought and action.

ACLITS and Pedagogy

Although the development of a pedagogic dimension of academic literacies is still in its infancy, increasing attention is being paid to the pedagogical significance of the specific application of theory and research on academic literacies, in which genre is an explicit pedagogical consideration.

Indeed, the seminal work of the ACLITS researchers referred to above has brought some very basic issues—of academic identity, of the status of academic knowledge, of whether and which genres of academic writing should be distinguished and valued—into the wider pedagogical debate.

One such debate is over assessment practices and their effect on learning. In researching and questioning feedback practices and the setting and implementation of marking (grading) criteria, ACLITS has highlighted some interesting preconceptions and hidden agendas. Shay (forthcoming) suggests that seeing assessment as a social practice has masked deep disciplinary and sub-disciplinary divisions between ideas of whether knowledges, knowledge-making practices or disciplinary "insiderdom" are being judged. Several projects reported at the European Association of Teachers of Academic Writing 2007 (e.g., Wrigglesworth & McKeever on "Developing Academic Literacy in Context," and Coffin et al. on "Genre-based pedagogy for discipline-specific purposes") reported that teachers' attempts to make assessment criteria more explicit had concealed rather than revealed assessment practices. An ACLITS approach revealed the concealment, but more clearly needs to be done to change pedagogic practice.

Two basic premises about ACLITS research, however, are that we need to be concerned with all the texts in the academy, not just student writing, and that focus on student writing alone has masked the need to focus on the range of genres (in various and intertwined media), not just those written genres which are dominant in terms of assessment (see Lea & Street, 1998; Lea, 2004; Stierer, 1997, 2006).

A narrow focus on assessment glosses over the question of whether normative genres should be resisted. Both students and academics may resist genres that have become part of their context; whether they in practice can and do resist is an interesting question. For, if genres appear in particular contexts but then become themselves part of the context and can in fact be resisted, should we be teaching students to conform or resist? Lillis (2006) calls for dialogue and interaction around texts and suggests "exploring ways in which alternative meaning making practices in writing can be institutionally validated." Burke and Herm-serschmidt (2005) take a similar approach; Creme (2008) suggests something similar in her "transitional writing." But how do we then deal with the fact that new genres tend to get quickly drawn into the academy, e.g., assessing learning journals (see Creme & Hunt, 2002)?

Debates such as these have become particularly pertinent as new genres of writing are taking their place in the academy. These spaces have the potential to offer a range of possibilities for explicating academic literacies principles and empowering student writers in contrast to the more essayist genres. However, a word of caution is necessary in that institutions are constantly trying to tie down new genres for assessment. For example, UK HE, under mandate from the government, is developing rigid assessment criteria based on those which have been associated with essay writing and applying these uncritically to more personal and reflective genres of writing, which were originally conceptualized as formative writing spaces. ACLITS offers possibilities to resist this focus on writing for assessment, pointing to academic writing's potential to develop, e.g., academic identity, disciplinary meaning-making and pedagogic autonomy.

There are currently perhaps two generally accepted pedagogic models of aca-demic writing: in one, writing is regarded as a personal act of meaning making; the other sees writing as a demonstration of the acquisition of institutional, subject or disciplinary knowledge and insiderdom. The first is largely transfor-matory—certainly of the individual and potentially if communicated to the dis-ciplinary and academic community, of that community's meaning-making pro-cesses. The second is concerned with disciplined writing, in at least two senses: with the writing and the control of what John Bean (1996) called "expert insider prose." Whatever the possibilities of the first, academics work with institutional pressures at all levels to use the second, controlling, expert model. So feedback practices tend to a default "correction" model, while the student struggling to make and communicate meaning is seen as a problem; summative assessment criteria are linked to disciplinary and professional benchmarks and genre study used to identify dominant conventions, codes and criteria.

Students can indeed be taught both about genres and about how to resist them (Devitt, this volume). However, ACLITS research draws attention to aca-demic writing beyond the classroom, chiming with WAC's model of a contin-uum between student, doctoral and faculty writing (Monroe 2002). ACLITS research is perhaps more problematizing, showing that beyond the individual teacher's classroom, institutional pressures circumscribe and define what can be written—written, or a least accepted as "disciplined" for the purpose of being awarded a Masters or PhD and being published to the academic community. In Europe, South Africa and Australia, an academic performance culture has gone beyond the demand to publish to the demand that publication be in a "rigorous" journal—peer-reviewed, of course, but also one accepting the role of, and accepted as, disciplinary gatekeeper. (A pressure that some academic journals are publicly resisting, publishing "alternative" critical writing in its own right and as embedded in disciplinary journal articles—see Creme, 2008, and Creme & Hunt, 2002—publishing Essays and New Voices, and in Special Issue "Calls" welcoming "alternatives forms of writing and experimentation with form, and different ways of giving voice.")

At a time when UK and European university policy makers, research funding and assessment bodies seem to be demanding generic and normalized academic writing, ACLITS research illuminates both the pragmatics and problematics of genre and/in academic writing.

CONCLUSION: TOWARD FURTHER DIALOG

Comparisons are difficult, first because (as we said in the introduction) WAC and ACLITS are doing different things, and secondly because the US WAC moment is large and diverse, with so many currents and conflicting strands that it is difficult to make generalizations about it. But perhaps a good place to begin is with genre theory and research methods.

The ACLITS perspective, coming out of Ethnography of Communication and Applied Linguistics, views genre as social practice rather than genre knowledge in terms of disciplinary communication per se, and its analysis is meant to unpack micro-social practices, such as "gaps" between student and teacher perceptions of particular writing activities, often embedded deeply in traditions of essayist literacy and the assessment of writing. Ethnographic methods show how genre types emerge in the detailed everyday encounters around writing in particular institutional contexts and how genre switching may be a hidden feature of pedagogy.

Not surprisingly, the ACLITS perspective on genre is perhaps closest to the sorts of WAC research that come out of linguistic anthropology and ethnomethodology. This includes the work of Dell Hymes' student McCarthy (1987) and her work with Fishman (2000, 2002), Herrington and Moran's (2005) research on new genres, and most especially the work of Prior (1998) and his group, who unpack the "laminated" micro-processes of student writing through longitudinal text analysis combined with ethnographic observation. Prior (this volume), along with Spinuzzi (2003) and others (Prior, Hengst, Roozen, & Shipka, 2006; Prior & Shipka, 2003), look for the surprising ways writing is embedded in genres that do not reach official status or even, sometimes, conscious recognition, and that emerge in and out of the multi-modal spaces of composing (post-it notes, marginal drawings, and so on). And they look for pedagogical possibilities in these.

The dominant North American perspective sees genre not as social practice (from the point of view of the Ethnography of Communication) but as social action, from a rhetorical and speech act perspective (Bazerman, 2004). This has no counterpart in ACLITS, nor does the North American research on writing in the professions toward which students move. This research may sometimes use ethnographic methods, but may also use a range of other methods: content, discourse, intertextual, rhetorical, or speech act analysis—looking at texts (even large numbers of texts) in contexts that are often viewed in historical, rhetorical, or other sociological terms rather than anthropological or ethnographic terms.

One consistent tendency in genre research in both ACLITS and WAC (apart from cognitive research on writing-to-learn in psychology) is that both are concerned to go beyond a linguistic "needs analysis" and pedagogical provision of the kind that, for example, English for Academic Purposes (EAP) has emphasized (important as these are) and look further at the wider aspects of the learning situation, in terms not only of disciplinary epistemology and methods, but also of student identity, social positioning and resistance, gender, and so on, as well as in terms of wider institutional factors.

In terms of pedagogy, ACLITS, though it has a practitioner-led aspect, has tended to be more focused on theory and research, and the relationship of writing support and "academic literacies" approaches has been less defined and institutionalized than WAC in the US. The descriptive tendency (reserving judgment, as in the best ethnographic tradition) has only begun to enter the crucible of political change on the ground in teaching and in institutional politics. WAC, by contrast, has for three decades striven to work with individual faculty and courses, to influence departmental curricula and institutions. As ACLITS begins to expand and institutionalize its interactions with teaching staff in other disciplines, it will be mutually beneficial to compare notes.

As we noted, there have been repeated calls for WAC to resist institutional practices and traditions that limit student writing and learning, calls which resonate with Lillis' (2001) call for ACLITS to develop an academic literacies pedagogy which places the nature of dialogue at its centre and considers how to develop and validate alternative spaces for writing and meaning making in the academy. In WAC the ideological valences of writing pedagogies have been a source of controversy, as we noted, whereas it has been endemic to the ACLITS approach from the outset given its rooting in New Literacy Studies and the "ideological model" of literacy. Research on teachers who take an explicitly political approach in the WAC classroom have found resentment and counter-resistance among students (Seitz, 2004) and most WAC programs take a much more indirect approach to institutional change. (This explains why US WAC programs may appear to be "academic socialization," in Lea and Street's terms, but are in fact about much more.) Thus far, ACLITS seems to be taking a nuanced path, not fronting the political in the classroom or asking students themselves to directly challenge existing structures, generic or otherwise, but rather respecting their vulnerable institutional position, as in Street and colleagues' work with the King's College widening participation project. These experiments will give US advocates of critical pedagogy and their opponents something to think about. Similarly, the successes and failures of US critical pedagogy applied to the disciplines might prove instructive to ACLITS.

Future dialog might proceed on many issues and congruencies, but with healthy scholarly caution. Because WAC is older by two decades, North Americans may have to resist a feeling of déjà vu and consider both the institutional differences that lie behind findings and the ways in which findings are only superficially similar. For example, Crème's (2008) analysis of learning journals as transitional genres bridging personal and discipline-based genres sounds much like the decade-long US experiments with journals and learning logs (MacDonald & Cooper, 1992), but Crème's approach rests on rather different assumptions and a different HE system. Indeed, ACLITS approaches to journals might overcome a number of (in hindsight) naïve assumptions that led the move toward journals to fade, in large part, in WAC.

Similarly, the major efforts of ACLITS on assessment research, particularly "diversifying assessment" beyond the academic essay, resonate strongly with the major efforts in the US toward alternative assessment (in new or hybrid genres), which were pioneered in WAC research and practice, particularly in the mid-1990s in the journal *Assessing Writing*.

And the multi-modal, multi-literacies approach of ACLITS finds its counterpart in the Communications Across the Curriculum programs that emerged in the US in the last ten years, new versions of (or successors to) WAC programs (Hocks, 2001). But clearly there is a different valence to the concept of multi-literacies in the UK and CAC in the North America.

Similarly, there is much potential in terms of reaching beyond HE to other educational levels. ACLITS is now becoming much involved in what in the UK is called further education and what in the US is called adult education or life-long learning. WAC has not been much focused on this (despite much research on this in adult literacy in education departments), apart from some work in community colleges, and might learn much from the research of Ivanic and her colleagues, for example.

Both ACLITS and WAC have been interested in the transition from secondary to higher education, but have not developed major collaborative efforts with secondary schools, either for research or pedagogical experimentations, apart from some work in the 1990s in the US (Farrell-Childers, Gere, & Young, 1994) and some recent work on Widening Participation in the UK that has included support for pre-university students (see above). And perhaps most importantly, neither ACLITS nor WAC have much developed a dialog with the international EAP/ESP community of second language research and teaching, which has its own varied theories of genre and approaches to teaching, often existing side-by-side with first-language efforts in universities or even departments.

Finally, we hope that this mapping of ACLITS and WAC will further discussion, not only between the US and UK, but also with other countries. While both ACLITS and WAC treat genre in social and cultural terms, there are fundamental differences in approaches to and development of genre theory, research, and pedagogy, which deserve fuller exposition and continuing mutual reading of each others' work and dialog on it.

REFERENCES

Ballard, B., & Clanchy, J. (1988). Literacy in the university: An "anthropological" approach. In G. Taylor, B. Ballard, V. Beasley, H. K. Bock, J. Clanchy, & P. Nightingale (Eds.), *Literacy by Degrees* (pp. 7-23). Milton Keynes, United Kingdom: Society for Research into Higher Education/Open University Press.

Bartholomae, D. (1986). Inventing the university. In M. Rose (Ed.), *When a writer can't write: Studies in writer's block and other composing-process problems* (pp. 134-166). New York: Guilford Press.

Bawarshi, A. S. (2003). *Genre and the invention of the writer: Reconsidering the place of invention in composition.* Logan: Utah State University Press.

Bazerman, C. (1988). Shaping written knowledge: The genre and activity of the experimental article in science. Madison: University of Wisconsin Press.

Bazerman, C. (1992). From cultural criticism to disciplinary participation: Living with powerful words. In A. Herrington & C. Moran (Eds.), *Writing, Teaching, and Learning in the Disciplines* (pp. 61–68). New York: MLA.

Bazerman, C. (1994). *Constructing experience.* Carbondale: Southern Illinois University Press.

Bazerman, C. (2002). Distanced and refined selves: Educational tensions in writing with the power of knowledge. In M. Hewings (Ed.), *Academic writing in context* (pp. 23–29). Birmingham, United Kingdom: University of Birmingham Press.

Bazerman, C. (2004). Speech acts, genres, and activity systems: How texts organize activity and people. In C. Bazerman & P. Prior (Eds.), *What writing does and how it does it: An introduction to analyzing texts and textual practices* (pp. 309-339). Mahwah, New Jersey: Erlbaum.

Bazerman, C. (this volume). *Genre and cognitive development: Beyond writing to learn.*

Bazerman, C., Little, J., Bethel, L., Chavkin, T., Fouquette, D., & Garufis, J. (2005). reference guide to writing across the curriculum. West Lafayette, Indiana: Parlor Press.

Bazerman, C., & Russell, D. R. (Eds.). (2003). Writing selves/writing societies: Research from activity perspectives. Retrieved from Colorado State University, The WAC Clearinghouse and Mind, Culture, and Activity: http://wac.colostate.edu/books/selves_societies

Bean, J. C. (1996). *Engaging ideas: The professor's guide to integrating writing, critical thinking, and active learning in the classroom.* San Francisco: Jossey-Bass.

Beaufort, A. (2007). *College writing and beyond: A new framework for university writing instruction.* Logan: Utah State University Press.

Berkenkotter, C., & Huckin, T. N. (1995). *Genre knowledge in disciplinary communication: Cognition/culture/power.* Hillsdale, New Jersey: Erlbaum.

Bizzell, P. (1982). Cognition, convention, and certainty: What we need to know about writing. *PRE/TEXT, 3*(3), 213-244.

Britton, J., Burgess, T., Martin, N., McLeod, A., & Rosen, H. (1975). *The development of writing abilities 11-18.* London: Macmillan.

Burke, P., & Hermserschmidt, M. (2005). Decsonstructing academic practices through self-reflexive pedagogies. In B. Street (Ed.), *Literacies across educational contexts: Mediating learning and teaching* (pp. 346-367). Philadelphia: Caslon Press.

Campbell, P. (Ed.). (2008). Measures of success: Assessment and accountability in adult basic education. Edmonton, Alberta, Canada: Grass Roots Press.

Carter, M., Ferzli, M., & Weibe, E. (2004). Teaching genre to English first-language adults: A study of the laboratory report. *Research in the Teaching of English, 38*(4), 395-413.

Clark, R., & Ivanic, R. (1991). Consciousness-raising about the writing process. In C. James & P. Garrett (Eds.), *Language awareness in the classroom* (pp. 168-185). London: Longman.

Coffin, C. (in press). Genre-based pedagogy for discipline-specific purposes. *Proceedings of EATAW.*

Creme, P. (2008). A space for academic play: Student learning journals as transitional writing. *Arts and Humanities in Higher Education 7*(1), 49-64.

Creme, P., & Hunt, C. (2002). Creative participation in the essay writing process. *Arts and Humanities in Higher Education, 1*(2), 145-166.

Delpit, L. (1993). The politics of teaching literate discourse. In T. Perry & J. W. Fraser (Eds.), *Freedom's plough: Teaching in the multicultural classroom* (pp. 285–295). New York: Routledge.

Devitt, A. J. (2004). *Writing genres.* Carbondale: Southern Illinois University Press.

Dias, P., Freedman, A., Medway, P., & Paré, A. (1999). *Worlds apart: Acting and writing in academic and workplace contexts.* Mahwah, New Jersey: Erlbaum.

Donahue, C. (2008). *Ecrire à l'université: Analyse comparée.* Villeneuve d'Ascq, France: Presses Universitaires du Septentrion.

Fairclough, N. (1989). *Language and power.* London: Longman.

Fairclough, N. (Ed.). (1992). *Critical language awareness.* New York: Longman.

Farrell-Childers, P. B., Gere, A. R., & Young, A. P. (1994). *Programs and practices: Writing across the secondary school curriculum.* Portsmouth, New Hampshire: Boynton/Cook.

Fishman, S. M., & McCarthy, L. P. (2000). *Unplayed tapes.* New York: Teachers College Press.

Fishman, S. M., & McCarthy, L. P. (2002). *Whose goals? Whose aspirations? Learning to teach underprepared writers across the curriculum.* Logan: Utah State University Press.

Ganobcsik-Williams, L. (Ed). (2006). *Teaching academic writing in UK higher education: Theories, practice and models.* London: Palgrave/Macmillan.

Geisler, C. (1994). *Academic literacy and the nature of expertise: Reading, writing, and knowing in academic philosophy.* Hillsdale, New Jersey: Erlbaum.

Gibbs, G. (Ed.). (1994). *Improving student learning: Theory and practice.* Oxford: Oxford Centre for Staff Development.

Halasek, K. (1999). *A pedagogy of possibility: Bakhtinian perspectives on composition studies.* Carbondale: Southern Illinois University Press.

Heath, S. B., and Street, B. (2008). *On ethnography: Approaches to language and literacy research.* New York: Teachers College Press.

Herrington, A., & Moran, C. (Eds.). (2005). *Genre across the curriculum.* Logan: Utah State University Press.

Hocks, M. (2001). Using multimedia to teach communication across the curriculum. *WPA: Writing Program Administration, 25*(1-2), 25-43.

Hounsell, D. (1988). Towards an anatomy of academic discourse: Meaning and context in the undergraduate essay. In R. Saljo (Ed.), *The written world: Studies in literate thought and action* (pp. 161-177). Berlin: Springer-Verlag.

Hymes, D. H. (1974). *Foundations in sociolinguistics: An ethnographic approach.* Philadelphia: University of Pennsylvania Press.

Ivanic, R. (1998). *Writing and identity: The discoursal construction of identity in academic writing.* Amsterdam: John Benjamins.

Ivanic, R. (2004). Discourses of writing and learning to write. *Language and Education, 18*(3), 220-245.

Ivanic, R., & Lea, M. R. (2006). New contexts, new challenges: The teaching of writing in UK higher education. In L. Ganobcsik-Williams (Ed.), *Teaching academic writing in UK higher education: Theories, practice and models.* London: Palgrave/Macmillan.

Johns, A. M. (Ed.). (2002). *Genre in the classroom: Multiple perspectives.* Mahwah, New Jersey: Erlbaum.

Jones, C., Turner, J., & Street, B. (Eds.). (1999). *Students writing in the university: Cultural and epistemological issues.* Amsterdam: John Benjamins.

Klein, P. D. (1999). Reopening inquiry into cognitive processes in writing-to-learn. *Educational Psychology Review, 11*(3), 203-270.

Lea, M. R. (1994). "I thought I could write until I came here": Student writing in higher education. In G. Gibbs (Ed.), *Improving student learning: Theory and practice* (pp. 216-226). Oxford: Oxford Centre for Staff Development.

Lea, M. R. (1998). Academic literacies and learning in higher education: Constructing knowledge through texts and experience. *Studies in the Education of Adults, 30*(2), 156-171.

Lea, M. R. (2001). Computer conferencing and assessment: New ways of writing in higher education. *Studies in Higher Education, 26*(2), 163-182.

Lea, M. R., & Stierer, B. (1999). *Student writing in higher education: New contexts.* Buckingham, United Kingdom: Open University Press/SRHE.

Lea, M. R., & Stierer, B. (2007, December). *Writing as professional practice in the university as workplace.* Paper presented to the Society for Research into Higher Education Annual Conference, Brighton, United Kingdom.

Lea, M. R., & Street, B. (1998). Student writing in higher education: An academic literacies approach. *Studies in Higher Education, 23*(2), 157-172.

Lea, M. R., & Street, B. (1999) Writing as academic literacies: Understanding textual practices in higher education. In C. N. Candlin & K. Hyland (Eds.), *Writing: Texts, processes and practices* (pp. 62-81). London: Longman.

Lea, M. R., & Street, B. (2006). The "academic literacies" model: Theory and applications. *Theory into Practice, 45*(4), 368-377.

LeCourt, D. (1996). WAC as critical pedagogy: The third stage? *JAC: A Journal of Composition Theory, 16*(1), 389–405.

Lillis, T. M. (1999). Whose common sense? Essayist literacy and the institutional practice of mystery. In C. Jones, J. Turner, & B. Street (Eds.), *Student writing in university: Cultural and epistemological issues* (pp. 127-147). Amsterdam: John Benjamins.

Lillis, T. M. (2001). *Student writing: Access, regulation, desire.* London: Routledge.

Lillis, T. (1997). New voices in academia? The regulative nature of academic writing conventions. *Language and Education, 11*(3), 182-199.

MacDonald, S. P., & Cooper, C. M. (1992). Contributions of academic and dialogic journals to writing about literature. In A. Herrington & C. Moran (Eds.), *Writing, teaching, and learning in the disciplines* (pp. 137–155). New York: MLA.

Mahala, D. (1991). Writing utopias: Writing across the curriculum and the promise of reform. *College English, 53*(7), 773–789.

Malinowitz, H. (1998). A feminist critique of writing in the disciplines. In S. C. Jarratt & L. Worsham (Eds.), *Feminism and composition studies: In other words* (pp. 291-312). New York: MLA.

McCarthy, L. P. (1987). A stranger in strange lands: A college student writing across the curriculum. *Research in the Teaching of English, 21*(3), 233-65.

McCrary, D. (2001). Womanist theology and its efficacy for the writing classroom. *College Composition and Communication, 52*(4), 521–552.

McCutcheon, D. (2007). Writing and cognition: Implications of the cognitive architecture for learning to write and writing to learn. In C. Bazerman (Ed.), *Handbook of research on writing* (pp. 451-470). Mahwah, New Jersey: Erlbaum.

McKenna, C. (2005). Words, bridges and dialogue: Issues of audience and addressivity in online communication. In R. Land & S. Bayne (Eds.), *Education in cyberspace* (pp. 140-162). London: Routledge.

McLeod, S. H. (1988). *Strengthening programs for writing across the curriculum.* San Francisco: Jossey-Bass.

McLeod, S. H., & Soven, M. (1992). *Writing across the curriculum: A guide to developing programs.* Newbury Park, California: Sage.

McLeod, S. H., & Maimon, E. (2000). Clearing the air: WAC myths and realities. *College English, 62*(5), 573–583.

Miller, C. R. (1984). Genre as social action. *Quarterly Journal of Speech, 70*(2), 151-176.

Miller, C. R. (1994). Rhetorical community: The cultural basis of genre. In A. Freedman & P. Medway (Eds.), *Genre and the new rhetoric* (pp. 67–78). New York: Taylor & Francis.

Monroe, J. (Ed.). (2002). *Writing and revising the disciplines.* Ithaca, New York: Cornell University Press.

Monroe, J. (Ed.). (2006). *Local knowledges, local practices: Writing in the disciplines at Cornell.* Pittsburgh: University of Pittsburgh Press.

Newell, G. E. (2006). Writing to learn: How alternative theories of school writing account for student performance. In C. A. MacArthur, S. Graham, & J. Fitzgerald (Eds.), *Handbook of writing research* (pp. 235-247). New York: Guilford Press.

Prior, P. (1998). *Writing/disciplinarity: A sociohistoric account of literate activity in the academy.* Mahwah, New Jersey: Erlbaum.

Prior, P. (this volume). *From speech genres to mediated multi-modal genre systems: Bakhtin, Voloshinov, and the question of writing.*

Prior, P., Hengst, J., Roozen, K., & Shipka, J. (2006). "I'll be the sun": From reported speech to semiotic remediation practices. *Text and Talk, 26,* 733-766.

Russell, D. R. (1991). *Writing in the academic disciplines, 1870-1990: A curricular history.* Carbondale: Southern Illinois University Press.

Russell, D. R. (1997). Rethinking genre in school and society: An activity theory analysis. *Written Communication, 14*(4), 504-554.

Russell, D. R., & Yañez, A. (2003). "Big picture people rarely become historians": Genre systems and the contradictions of general education. In C. Bazerman & D. R. Russell (Eds.), *Writing selves/writing societies: Research from activity perspectives* (pp. 331-362). Retrieved from Colorado State University, The WAC Clearinghouse and Mind, Culture, and Activity: http://wac.colostate.edu/books/selves_societies

Scalone, P., & Street, B. (2006). Academic language development programme (widening participation). *British Studies in Applied Linguistics, 20,* 121-136.

Schryer, C. F. (1993). Records as genre. *Written Communication, 10*(2), 200-234.

Scribner, S., & Cole, M. (1981). The psychology of literacy. Cambridge, Massachusetts: Harvard University Press.

Seitz, D. (2004). *Who can afford critical consciousness? Practicing a pedagogy of humility.* Cresskill, New Jersey: Hampton Press.

Shay, S. (in press). Beyond social constructivist perspectives on assessment: The centering of knowledge. *Teaching in Higher Education.*

Smart, G. (2006). *Writing the economy: Activity, genre, and technology in the world of banking.* London: Equinox Publishing.

Sommers, N., & Saltz, L. (2004). The novice as expert: Writing the freshman year. *College Composition and Communication, 56*(4) 124-149.

Spinuzzi, C. (2003). *Tracing genres through organizations: A sociocultural approach to information design.* Cambridge, Massachusetts: MIT Press.

Street, B. (1984). *Literacy in theory and practice.* Cambridge: Cambridge University Press.

Street, B. (1996) Academic literacies. In D. Baker, C. Fox, & J. Clay (Eds.), *Challenging ways of knowing: Literacies, numeracies and sciences* (pp. 101-134). Brighton, United Kingdom: Falmer Press.

Street, B. (Ed.). (2001). *Literacy and development: Ethnographic perspectives.* Routledge: London.

Stierer, B. (1997). *Mastering education: A preliminary analysis of academic literacy practices within master-level courses.* Milton Keynes, United Kingdom: Education Centre for Language & Communications, Open University.

Stierer, B. (2000). Schoolteachers as students: Academic literacy and the construction of professional knowledge within master's courses in education. In M. R. Lea & B. Stierer (Eds.), *Student writing in higher education: New contexts* (pp. 179-195). Buckingham, United Kingdom: Society for Research into Higher Education/Open University Press.

Thesen, L., & van Pletzen, E. (Eds.). (2006). *Academic literacy and the languages of change*. London: Continuum.

Villanueva, V. (2001). The politics of literacy across the curriculum. In S. McLeod, E. Miraglia, M. Soven, & C. Thaiss (Eds.), *WAC for the new millennium* (165–178). Urbana, Illinois: NCTE.

Vygotsky, L. (1978). *Mind in society: The development of higher psychological processes*. Cambridge, Massachusetts: Harvard University Press.

Vygotsky, L. (1986). *Thought and language*. Cambridge, Massachusetts: MIT Press.

Walton, M., & Archer, A. (2004). The web and information literacy: Scaffolding the use of web sources in a project-based curriculum. *British Journal of Educational Technology, 35*(2), 173-186.

Walvoord, B. E. F. (1997). *In the long run: A study of faculty in three writing-across-the-curriculum programs*. Urbana, Illinois: National Council of Teachers of English.

Wardle, E. (in press). Understanding "transfer" as generalization from FYC: Preliminary results of a longitudinal study. *WPA Journal*.

Winsor, D. A. (2003). *Writing power: Communication in an engineering center*. Albany: State University of New York Press.

Wrigglesworth, J., & McKeever, M. (in press). Developing academic literacy in context. *Proceedings of EATAW*.

Tiane Donahue

INTRODUCTION

How genre is understood and configured in analyses of disciplinary texts and discourses is key to understanding the nature of student work in the disciplines. The question of genre is also intimately linked to what we know about expert texts in a discipline. These relationships have been studied for some time in France, first through traditional-formalist frames of text types and modes, more recently through understandings of genre in social, cultural, and disciplinary contexts. Proponents of both traditional and newer perspectives appear to agree on the usefulness of genre when researchers seek to classify texts to be studied, but take fundamentally different stances ("radical reconfigurations," to use the terms of Coe, Lingard and Teslenko, 2002) towards how that classification might be done, as well as what the relationships are among groups of texts, single texts, and the social and political situations in which textual production and reception are carried out. Currently, many of the French genre theorists in the field of *la didactique de l'écrit* (the field of discipline-based theory about the teaching and learning of writing) systematically explore disciplines and genres in higher education, using the frames of theories of didactic-disciplinary universes of writing, discourse communities, or generic reception theory. I will offer here a partial review of some of the more innovative paths being taken, showing how perspectives about genre have been evolving in both complementary and divergent ways as scholars explore the complex set of elements that make "genre" a usable research tool for studying students' writing in the disciplines. A current higher education research project in France, a first-of-its-kind study of students' writing and learning practices in four disciplines at three universities, will serve to highlight some of the ways in which current, complex notions of genre are being fruitfully brought into play in the study of student writing across disciplines.

WRITING IN THE DISCIPLINES IN THE FRENCH TEACHING CONTEXT

In France, writing as a mode of learning and assessment in every discipline has been integral to French education throughout its history at every educational level: writing as a tool for learning, for assessing learning, for processing thinking, for summarizing concisely, for responding, for developing texts in disciplinary work. But French scholars have only recently begun to focus on theorizing writing across the disciplines, as they fully recognize that writing, disciplinarity, and knowledge construction are inextricably embedded in each other. This research trend has had the effect of highlighting interest in writing in higher education, always already disciplinary even though perhaps only reductively so in the first or second year. Recent changes in higher education have also heightened awareness of student writing in general: the past decade or so of "massification" through wider access has brought new kinds of students to the University; the discipline of "French" has begun to resist being defined as the sole purveyor of writing instruction, and this, at every educational level; finally, research has identified students' difficulties in several areas of writing, including source integration, voice, and development, at the college level. Students work on some of these issues in middle school but only occasionally in high school (Donahue, 2004).

In French introductory courses, more unevenly offered at the start of post-secondary education, and often more focused on initiating students into both writing and research, issues in the discipline have been foregrounded, and the features of the text types students learn have thus been more discipline-specific[1]. The real initiation into the advanced writing of a field occurs when students begin what is called "researched writing" at the end of undergraduate studies and the beginning of graduate work. Researched writing is specifically defined as "any academic writing that includes a research question (*problématique*) and situates itself in the context of the discourse of others. Researched writing is thus a component of academic writing, a broader term that designates, for us, all of the written products a student must master in order to progress in his or her studies, to receive positive evaluations of his or her work, and so on" (Delcambre & Boch, 2006). Delcambre & Boch have suggested the following range of the most likely pieces students will produce before arriving at the researched writing that represents the discipline more fully:

- analysis of documents/commentary
- discussion of opinions/judgments
- essay based on a general statement
- essay based on a quote
- observation report
- case study
- book report/summary
- long final report
- multiple choice test

- question asked in class
- internship report
- theme to explore based on a general statement
- theme to explore based on a reading or a document
- theme to explore based on a quotation
- document synthesis
- text to be commented on (answering a set of questions)
- text to be commented on (based on a proposed theme)
- text to be commented on (no questions or theme)
- summary of a text
- theme to develop (subject provided in a couple of words)
- research work, studies

TRADITIONAL THEORIZING OF GENRE IN RELATION TO TEACHING AND RESEARCHING WRITING IN FRANCE

Earlier work exploring genres in different educational settings in France was based on traditional literary or rhetorical versions of genre. The literary versions of genre offered characterizations of different text types based on various schemes of classification (see for example the Russian formalists or E. Benveniste). The rhetorical approaches of the same time period, rooted in centuries of thinking about types of texts not necessarily seen as part of poetics, defined major types based on text function and the features associated with a function. These traditional perspectives have been reviewed—and critiqued—by many scholars, including Bakhtin (see, for example, "The Problem of Speech Genres" p. 61). The first phase of French linguist J.M. Adam's genre and text type work, in the 1970s and 80s, was key to the entrenched relationship between text types and writing instruction in France. Adam single-handedly set the parameters for describing, teaching, and thinking about text types and prototypes for years. He developed a language around the construction of genres in "textual sequences," defining texts as "complex hierarchical structures made up of N elliptical or complex sequences, of the same type or different types" (cited in Canvat, 1996, p. 4). Adam's system of classification included three levels: "genres" as sub-classes of discourse (literary discourse, for example), "text types" which are the components of discourses and genres (the "story" for example can be a component of advertising texts, literary texts, political texts, etc.), and finally "sequences," both prototypical and as components of a given text.

These distinctions allowed Adam to work on genres of discourse, textual genres or types of texts, and to account for textual heterogeneity, dominance of a particular sequence in a given text, or the occasional "pure" genre. His model includes identification of texts by their conventional schemas, each with its own rules of connection, development, continuity and so on. These conventional structures can be, he suggested, regrouped into "superstructures" that are learned through cultural exposure, such as the argumentative or narrative superstructure (Adam 1992). While Adam later reworked his perspective, shifting attention to the flexibility we need when talking about text typologies and the importance of seeing a text as only more or less typical of the prototype in a particular genre, his influence on French teaching of genres and types remained prevalent.

Genre work building on the "classificatory" role of genres across disciplines initially focused extensively on characterizing the features of various kinds of writing in order to help students to better understand how they might write in a given disciplinary context. This work has included the study of the classificatory act itself (see for example the special issue of *Recherches* 42, 2005, titled *Classer* and featuring articles about text typology and school activity around genre classifications) as well as prolonged and careful study of expert texts and student texts, such as the work by F. Boch, F. Grossmann, and F. Rinck, focused on academic articles in literature and linguistics and on research "*mémoires*" in linguistics and education at the graduate level. J. Swales is one of the anglo-saxon scholars cited in French analysis of writing in different disciplines (in particular in the sciences) in higher education, as is K. Hyland. These authors' frames are used to identify, through extensive and detailed analysis of expert texts, the conventions of certain kinds of written academic discourse, in order to concretize its features: introductory and concluding "formulas," useful schemas for organizing research writing, suggested verb tenses and other modalities.

Traditional genres as stable entities were also the bedrock of teaching writing at all school levels in the 1970s and 80s, and traces of the typologies of texts from those years are everywhere, in particular in teaching practices, school textbooks, and official curricula. The traditional genres are quite similar to those considered in the US scholarship, influenced by literary history and theory as well as by R. Jakobson's early division of texts into various functional types. Plane (2002) also discusses the evolution, during the 1990s, of text typologies in the discussion of genre in France. According to her introduction to a special issue of the journal *Repères*, attention remained focused on

> the definition of textual or discursive objects, imagined through the lens of teaching and learning, with two key hinges around which the research has gathered, the narrative text . . . and the argumentative text. We can see the evolution of these as objects of research unfolding through the special issues of the journal *Pratiques* (Masseron, 1992, 1997; Schnedecker 1994). On the fringes of these major themes, other relevant themes concerning

more limited objects became the object of specific research proj-
ects of their own in *la didactique de l'écriture*, such as the summary
(Charolles & Petitjean 1992), the explicative text (Petitjean 1986;
Garcia-Debanc 1990, *Repères* 69, 72, 77) or the descriptive text
(Petitjean 1987; Reuter 1998).

While these categories may sound familiar, one key organizing difference is the
long-standing classification, in French scholarship, of two meta-genres: *récit* and
discours (story and discourse), a distinction developed by E. Benveniste in his influential work on verb tense as indexical.

COMPLEXIFYING UNDERSTANDINGS OF GENRE AND DISCIPLINE IN FRANCE

While descriptions of genres in different disciplines as collections of identifiable features and conventions persist in both teaching and research about
writing in the disciplines in France (and in particular, in the research in contrastive rhetoric), and while in French school systems, pre-university, "text types"
remain solidly in place as teaching tools, new ways of thinking about genre
have influenced the study of student writing in different disciplines in the past
decade. I turn to these now in order to explore several paths in France and Switzerland that have been part of the "radical reconfiguration" of genre announced
by Coe, Lingard and Teslenko, genre theories that have begun to enable an understanding of both the sociality of genre and the ways in which individual texts
(and their authors and readers) negotiate, appropriate, and modify those genres.
French theorists have moved systematically towards understanding the disciplines in higher education, in particular in their socio-cultural forms, through
these recent evolutions.

The new genre work has some roots in the University of Geneva school in the
1990s. B. Schneuwly and J. Dolz (1997) introduced genre primarily as a psychological tool, a material and symbolic mediator between the student subject
who integrates the schema of use of the genre, and the situation. J.P. Bronckart
(1996) proposed that textual genres are sociolinguistic formations, organized
according to heterogeneous modalities related to heterogeneous determinations.
Discourses and texts were thus, for him, socially motivated and oriented. In this
frame, text typologies became interactive, taking into account extralinguistic parameters, surface textual features, and production operations. Genres as cultural
tools of teaching and learning could thus act as tools for entering a particular
discipline.

Concepts of disciplinarity through this lens thus began seeping in to the

French genre work focused on school and university settings in the late 1990s and early 2000s. Researchers identified in particular the interest in understanding how the classroom community in different disciplines can construct shared objects of study through particular discursive procedures. Research teams worked with the notion of "argument," for example, as shaped and produced differently in different disciplines. It might be, for example, "justification" for a process leading to an answer in mathematics, explication showing cause and effect in history, a form of plausibility and refutation in physics/chemistry, or a restricted set of moves grounded in Aristotelian logos in the discipline of French (Donahue, 2004).

The textual emphasis began to shift towards an emphasis on discursive communities in the late 1990s, which simultaneously encouraged another perspective on genres in different disciplines. M. Jaubert, M. Rebière and J.P. Bernié (2003), working at the Université de Bordeaux II, treated disciplines as discourse communities, each with its own social set of ways of thinking, speaking, and acting, although this research group was not working on writing at the university level[2]. In a move to reject structural linguistics and to differentiate themselves from the Genevan school, which they consider too focused on the formal aspects of genres rather than their nature as psychological activity (p. 71), Jaubert et al. reflected on school situations by working through a series of notions: context, tool, posture and genre—both discursive genre and genre of activity (2003, p. 51). They describe discourse genres as "recognized modes of expression" that "signal . . . belonging, inscription in a world of values, beliefs, practices, in a community that gives them meaning, . . . crystallizing values, enunciative positions, and specific social practices" (pp. 68, 71). For the Bordeaux group, the frames of primary (in the moment of production) and secondary genres (removed from the moment of production) as presented by Bakhtin are the key components for both the analysis of genres and the work of teaching writing in different disciplines. Jaubert et al. suggest, citing both Bakhtin and Voloshinov, that students must adopt positions of relative exteriorization that enable them to traverse various contexts through a continuous decontextualizing and recontextualizing of knowledge and know-how. Secondary genres are, in the Bordeaux team's perspective, the ones that do the work of a disciplinary discourse community, while primary genres are what students bring with them into school or disciplinary settings. The work of schools is not to teach students about what secondary genres look like or how to construct them, but to teach students the activity of secondarizing (p. 68).

Other French researchers followed and developed this path. The frame of discursive communities opened up discussions about the heterogeneity and conflicted nature of a given disciplinary "community," as researchers turned an eye to the intellectual, practical, and ideological negotiations carried out in their own research groups, inspired in part by the work of B. Latour. His work became quite influential in France in understanding disciplinary differences in the genre of argument in expert and student work. For example, J. Biseault's work (2003) applied Latour's description of professional science research groups to analysis of negotiations in classroom situations of knowledge construction, collaboration, and peer review. Biseault suggests that argument in the science classrooms he studied is not a text type but a social act of knowledge negotiation, and learning to "write science" is thus learning the social behaviors involved.

But most of the research about these disciplinary discursive communities in France focused on school-aged students and the ways in which students navigate the various groups and knowledge communities, described as heterogeneous because the scholars, teachers, and other practitioners of a discipline do not form a block of unified thinkers. Research about writing and academic discourse communities at the post-secondary level tends to cite non-French authors of reference such as J. Swales.

F. Boch, F. Grossmann, and F. Rinck have more recently studied students' difficulties entering a discipline's research community from a textual perspective, focused on academic articles in literature and linguistics and on students' research "*mémoires*" in linguistics and education. I. Delcambre and F. Boch note that

> . . . students must learn to position themselves as authors, express, nuance, or reinforce their point of view, make their place in the multiplicity of voices, orchestrate the polyphony, and learn to use the signals that guide readers through these texts. . . . [Boch and Grossmann] seek to describe the norms characterizing the different genres of research writing, in particular those that regulate enunciative dimensions (in the act of drawing on others' discourse). Boch and Grossmann's theoretical frame conceives of a student's entry into research writing in terms of acculturation into genres of research writing (Swales 1999), but their didactic frame draws them to taking into account students' specific writerly practices. For them, acculturation into research writing should not only be imagined in terms of mastery of a new genre. Students' specific practices contribute no doubt to the construction of a "researcher identity." (Proposal to the *Association Nationale de Recherches* 2006)

Of particular interest in this description is the suggestion that genres of writing and other *practices* are distinct. Some research groups in France, part of the research community of "*didacticiens*" whose focus is on theorizing the teaching and learning of disciplinary knowledge and know-how, have more recently theo-rized "genres" in relation to "practices": genre as the apprehension and categori-zation of objects and products, practices as the apprehension and categorization of activities, production, and doing. Genres are thus objects that regulate the interactions among actors and between actors and knowledge (Reuter 2007), while practices are (linguistic or non-linguistic) activities that do the same. For Reuter, genres constitute themselves as structural elements of key didactic func-tions through the relationships they have with practices. Genres are regulators in the learning process, organizing the work of didactic subjects, influencing teaching and evaluation (2007, p. 15).

In the disciplines in particular, for Reuter & Lahanier-Reuter (2008) genres become part of a set of frames used to analyze writing in a discipline that also includes the "disciplinary configurations" in which a text is constructed and the "disciplinary awareness" of the writer. A traditional picture of genre is thus destabilized by its entirely different set of features in different disciplinary set-tings as it works with different actors and knowledges. While the key goal of a "description," for example, might always be "to give the reader the impression that he can see" what is being described (Reuter 1998), the descriptive discourse activity involves different values, forms, and modes when it is used in scientific description, sociological accounts, or literary analysis; it has different intellectual and ideological purposes and is situated in a different network of other genres, activities, and recipients.

For Reuter & Lahanier-Reuter (2008),

> Genres are . . . discursive units, belonging to a given socio-cultural sphere, which determines and constrains (by its key components) the forms chosen. The components are:
> - its materiality (for example, in writing, the medium, the size, the ways it is presented);
> - its peritextual indicators (in the way Genette, 1982, 1987, de-scribes these, as for example any identification of the author, the recipient, the date . . .);
> - its linguistic actualization (lexical, syntactic, rhetorical . . .);
> - its enunciative markers (explicit or implicit control over the discourse, announced subjectivity or not, organization of con-tent through, for example, modes of linkage or hierarchization . . .);
> - the thematic domains and the "treatable" contents in those do-mains, in terms of specific conditions of production and recep-tion (categories of authors, relationships among these, implied

temporality, specs, functions, stakes, and types of evaluation in play . . .). (p. 32)

Genres thus format, for Reuter and his research group, what can be said and its shapes in a given social space. In this framework, "genre and practices function in interaction with each other in order to enable us to understand the diversity and the modalities of actualization of writing and of written texts" (Reuter 2007). Genre is, for Reuter, the constituting element of functions within didactic spaces; genre is in turn constituted by the interactions among the school system (institutions), the pedagogical system (teaching and learning forms), and the disciplines themselves (knowledge and know-how) (p. 16). Reuter (2007) does mention that school genres do not exist independently of extra-scholastic genres, in the scientific, private, or professional domains. In addition, he emphasizes the importance of characterizing genre in terms of its place in the didactic system, its disciplinary status, and its stability and history in relation to other genres (p. 13). In some ways this dynamic description does complement activity theory perspectives of genre, in particular in its insistence on genres as belonging to socio-cultural spheres, formatting the "sayable and its forms" (p. 14), and in its assertion that "genres exist only inasmuch as they take their place in systems, in a [disciplinary] configuration that determines their status" (p. 14).

But it also creates other distinctions and emphases. The list of characteristics Reuter (and, in another article, Reuter and Lahanier-Reuter) offers remains resolutely text-based and leaves minimal place for the sociality of genre in disciplinary work, including it only in "conditions of production and reception." And as much as this exploration of genre emphasizes generic heterogeneity, that heterogeneity is largely internal to the text's construction, even if in relation to factors of context and production. Finally, in every way, Reuter's theorization of genre considers practices as separate, as formatting genres and vice versa, interdependent but still separate (for analysis and for teaching and learning): "the genre . . . determines the practices that generate it; the practices produce the genre as both example and category" (p. 15).

Consider in contrast the exploration of genre provided by Bazerman (2004): an utterance embodies a speech act, a "meaningful social action being accomplished through language"; these acts are "carried out in patterned, typical, and therefore intelligible" genres, textual forms that are self-reinforcing because they are recognizable in a given setting. In this, activity theory perspectives on genre are closer to the Bordeaux team's construction than to Reuter's construction. Bazerman is careful to say, however, building again from Bakhtin, that genres typify not only textual forms but also social activities (or that at the very least we cannot separate these two). If we focus on the regularity of generic forms for carrying out similar tasks, a routine Russell (1997) first highlighted, we see that teaching writing in the disciplines can clearly be carried out as a method for introducing these regular forms and enabling students to practice them, but it can just as well be an exploration into the meaningful social actions being carried out, the sources of recognition, the purposes and situations of utterances, and so on. In fact, if "genre helps locate [a] text in some familiar social arrangements and activities" (Bazerman, Little, & Chavkin, 2003), we might suggest that teaching has more to do with making sure students are in fact familiar with the social arrangements and activities of a discipline or sub-discipline. In addition, there is room here for the student-utterer to modify or transform the genre, and its work as mediating artifact (Bazerman & Prior, 2005) in a context of shared expectations allows for a valuing of student discourse that we rarely find in the French scholarship.

Even with this framing, however, much of United States activity theory work in recent years has focused on production, on the social relationship between genre and context, in spite of its recognition of "texts in use" as the key to interpretation or identification. French genre theory in "*la didactique de l'écrit,*" as embodied by Reuter and his research team's analytic frame, has largely focused on research about the shapes of genre: the explanation, description, and analysis of textual objects in different contexts; the Bordeaux team has largely focused on the student-producer and his or her relationship to others in the community (students and teachers). All of these perspectives allow the role of the recipient of discursive acts to remain in the background, relatively unexplored in analysis even as it is acknowledged as central. I do not mean the recipient's role in the rhetorical sense (the writer considers the potential reader; the speaker considers the potential listener). Instead, I mean the role of the recipient in defining or redefining the genre of a text (always generic-specific in some form) based on its reception, its use for a particular recipient who is himself a generic-specific member of a particular context.

The genre of a text, in this case, exists only in the relationship between the reader or recipient and the text. That relationship is a dynamic activity of reception. The reception of a text is not, however, an arbitrary anything-goes. Readers or recipients are themselves constrained participants in any number of spheres of activity. We might explore, for example, the reception of a text by a participant in a discipline, but the specificity-heterogeneity of that participant constructs his or her "disciplinarity" and affects the nature of the relationship. In addition, a recipient is no more stable a member of a sphere of activity than a text is permanently identifiable as a genre.

This exploration of how texts are received and taken up is a far cry from the earlier depictions of texts as collections of fixed features, and is a complement to seeing genres as mediators, tools, and activities. In this frame, we have a rich repertory of genres that we practice, even though neither their use nor their acquisition is necessarily conscious, as Russell suggested in 1997. The monolithic sets of literary or rhetorical genres were the norm in France until their closed "set" nature was fragmented in the 1990s, partly through Bakhtin's assertions, widely taken up and far too briefly summarized here: "The wealth and diversity of speech genres are boundless because the various possibilities of human activity are inexhaustible, and because each sphere of activity contains an entire repertoire of speech genres that differentiate and grow as the particular sphere develops and becomes more complex" (1986, p. 60). What Bakhtin describes as the "extreme heterogeneity of speech genres" includes the most everyday category of utterance alongside the most literary or scientific, and allows for the study of language data from any context, in "typical forms of utterances," and with the potential for greater or lesser degrees of individual style depending on the sphere and its constraints (p. 63). But the fact that a text is produced in a sphere of activity does not prevent it from meaning something in another sphere. We rediscover in this way the zones of contact that meet up, intersect, or bump up against each other across spheres of activity, creating new "negotiating" genres that constitute neither one nor another set of features or typical forms.

The genre theory work done by Bazerman and Russell, as evoked above, has opened up new ways of working through these complex questions in the US. I turn now to another French scholar, linguist F. François, and his set of conceptual frames for considering the more fluid aspects of genre. He provides another way in to the complexity we need to both recognize and study. François, whose genre work has not evolved in a *"didactique"* vein but rather a broadly-applied analytic vein, develops the socio-discursive notion of *"reprise-modification"* as a way to pinpoint aspects of a dynamic understanding of the textual genres that we read and write, here applied to what students produce and professors read. He does this by positing "reprise-modification" (literally, re-taking-up-modifying) as the essential discursive act, whether in the production or reception (acts which cannot be separated) of an utterance. From the specific point of view of a text's reception, François (1998) distinguishes discourse, text, and corpus, with implications for how we might thus consider genres: discourses are the essential simple acts of language use (someone speaks to someone else as a social activity); texts are the "secondarized" versions of discourse, the versions in which an utterance moves from a Bakhtinian primary genre to a Bakhtinian secondary genre and are thus redefined by their modes of reading or reception; a corpus is a quasi-object, a set of utterances that have become (temporarily) objects of research study. What is particularly relevant to the discussion here is his insistence that a single utterance or group of utterances is, in the context of being in the world, constantly moving among these places. A given text, say a novel or a student paper, may be a corpus to analyze, but is a different text (in fact, a different *object*, if we consider Russell's point that a particular text might be, in another circumstance, a doorstop) in each of its multiple socially situated receptions. Both *producing* and *receiving* text are discursive acts of reprise-modification. François (1998) points out, "Fixing a genre is thus never an end to itself. It is a way to highlight the relationships that cannot be pure identity, among a general framework for uttering, a general form, and the variations of production and reception—the circulation." A focus on reception is not meant to imply a focus on "individual readers" in the way that reader-reception literary theory, for example, encouraged. On the contrary, the reader-recipient is a social entity who both shares common features with other readers/sets of readers and has a specific "style" in what he or she does with a text. This way of thinking "genre" in relation to disciplines in higher education has been, to date, less frequently explored.

A STUDY OF STUDENT WRITING ACROSS DISCIPLINES

A "school" text is, of course, most often received as such by the teacher, and so already we can study that particular relationship. The "disciplinary" school context is a slippery one, as students are both proving knowledge and trying on disciplinary discourse. The research project I will now describe is seeking a deeper understanding of these issues through the concrete texts it collects, the students' discourse about text and context, the faculty discourse about these, and the analyses being carried out by readers who are both teachers across disciplines and researchers representing disciplines. The objectives of the study can be read through the genre theory lenses we have seen thus far. The study focuses on writing in the disciplines in higher education, seeking to better understand the genres of writing students produce across years of study, and involving researchers who are themselves steeped in the ways of thinking and doing from a variety of disciplines.

The French project is titled *Les écrits à l'université: Inventaires, pratiques, modèles* (University Writing: Inventories, Practices, Models—EUIPM), and is led by researchers I. Delcambre (Université de Lille III) and F. Boch (Université de Grenoble II), each working with a team from her institution's research group, with input from two consulting teams, one from the US and the other from the UK. It uses surveys, follow-up interviews, student writing samples, and faculty focus groups as methods for collecting data. The project was initially developed to address two gaps in French research about writing in the disciplines in higher education. Delcambre and Boch (2006) report in their project proposal:

- There is little sustained, systematic knowledge about genres of writing in postsecondary education or about the relationship of these genres to the genres and genre expectations (implicit and explicit) students bring with them to the university or, finally, about the relationship of these genres to genre expectations (implicit and explicit) teachers offer students.
- There is no widely adopted theoretical model in France for conceptualizing writing at the university. There is an abundance of available work conceptualizing writing in primary and secondary school situations, work that proposes several models in confrontation: cognitive models, the model of "discourse community," the model of "literacy" and so on.

Delcambre and Boch hypothesize that writing difficulties are intrinsically linked to new discourse objects, the academic discourses themselves, that students discover at the university. They thus hypothesize that difficulties are associated with the content of discourse, but we might also consider the relationship between the content and the new genres. Research in what is named the "didactics" of writing supports the idea that

> writing difficulties can not be considered simple technical difficulties, but are tightly linked to writers' representations (their representations of writing and of themselves as writers, of academic expectations about the writing to be produced, etc.), to the expected text genres, and to the frames these genres propose for written production, in particular with respect to discourse content and types of knowledge, and finally to the forms of support and evaluation that accompany the learners' writing, forms that are themselves based on teachers' representations of writing and learning. (Delcambre & Boch, 2006)

Existing French research about university students' difficulties has largely not considered the discipline in which the writing was studied as a variable but as a given, a descriptive piece of the framing for the research; this project aims to consider the discipline, its ways of knowing, its content as key variables.

The study's preliminary stage is the traditional corpus-based task of cataloguing types of writing students produce in different disciplines, as defined largely by the task objective, the disciplinary course, and the external textual features; genres are being used to inventory shared or different types of writing in the different disciplines. Beyond this step, however, it seeks a deeper understanding of the dynamic social nature of the disciplinary work being done. This complicates at least two existing processes:

(1) Research methods for studying student writing across disciplines, and
(2) Approaches for teaching student-initiates the ways of working with text production and reception in a discipline. For this article, I am focusing on the first issue, but I will end with a few thoughts about implications for the second.

The research being done is leading to a systematic construction of the ways in which different texts are being produced and received in different contexts, and are in fact woven into these contexts and their knowledge bases. The interviewing, focus group work, and textual analysis provide multi-point sources of data for understanding how students and faculty in different disciplines use genre as what D. Russell (personal communication) reminds us is "both a constraining mould and an affording landscape for communication." The study gets at what Russell highlights as the strategic agency of participants, "who further their interests through mutually recognized, genred action, within the moments of utterance, though always constrained by the degree of congruence in their understandings, and always open to difference" (personal communication). This strategic—perhaps negotiating—agency exists for both the student participants and the teacher participants and, we might add, the researcher participants. That is, the "socially shared repertoire of genred actions" that Russell, building on Bazerman (2006), describes would seem to include all three sets of participants. The study explores aspects of how teachers, students, and researchers develop these repertoires.

As we look at this study, I would like to emphasize that what I report here can only be a partial accounting of what it offers. The French study seeks to understand texts produced by students in a particular discipline as situated in social and intellectual disciplinary activities. It does so by asking students and faculty to describe not only what texts they produce or require, but how each text fits into and negotiates the discipline's work. The study posits the genres it is inventorying as social institutions, as recurrent activities doing the work of the discipline, and in particular as activities by students who are at different stages: beginning to do the work of the discipline, nearing the end of undergraduate work, and in MA-level work. The student entering the discipline's sphere of activity and work is doing so through the specific activity of "researched writing" (the focus of the study's deeper analysis through follow-up interviews and text analysis) with its polyphony, its complexity, its intertextuality and modes of thinking. The interviews with French faculty to hear their accounting of successful writing in this context will produce variant "readings" of the same texts. Researchers analyze the disciplinary perspective but also hear their own expertise in studying and understanding language use. For current versions of genre, this is key. A discipline's members, as we are reminded by J. Monroe (2007), own the writing in the field, even as researchers might offer methods and insights for understanding the genres being studied. The French study's focus on both texts and practices helps to bring out the relationship between them.

A FEW CONCLUDING REMARKS

F. François offers "style" as an alternative term for the "genre" of an individual text when we explore the work it is doing, rather than seeking to fix its membership in a category. Style is, in this case, the intersection of specific-particular and shared-common textual movements. What does this mean for studying student writers? We see in their texts both existing (disciplinary) generic frames and individual texts that themselves both take up and don't take up the recognized regularities that are part of a genre. François proposes that student writing thus modifies the very constraints the genre might usually impose.

The French study explores that situatedness by using different disciplines as variables in the study and by involving students and faculty in collecting and discussing the work. The various sources of information collected and pulled together, layered, account for the animating activities around (student) production and (faculty) reception as specific to disciplinary contexts.

In this way, the study takes apart disciplinary genres, questions their homogeneity, angles to understand the ways in which the disciplinary sphere and its genres enable student work. The study represents students' work as part of the discipline, although only that part we see in schooling. But even this study does not, and in fact nor does any other study of which I am aware, consider fully the question of genres of reception. It is not focused on genre as the dynamic activity of reception (for example, reception by a teacher of a student's piece, or reception by a researcher of a text that is part of a corpus).

Bazerman, Little and Chavkin's rich example of a text as a piece of paper that can reappear in almost any situation anywhere and can, because of its genre, be located in "familiar social arrangements and activities" that enable meaning-making, does not directly explore what happens—textually—when a recipient does not recognize the genre but still uses the text. Where, that is, does the orienting genre come from? Considerations of intent might be particularly tricky in the academic situation of student writing, in which intent is a multilayered weave of student writer's intent, teacher-assigner's intent, institutional intent, and student "voice" as the carrier of these intents (and others not yet articulated). In a research situation, might we (in particular if we do not want to return to discussions of authorial intent or purpose as the source of "actual" meaning) consider the act of research as a genre destabilizer?

Perhaps the most encouraging feature of the EUIPM study is its resistance to rushing to pedagogical applications. Results of the analyses will likely complicate the teaching and learning relationship in higher education work in the disciplines: teaching students to "write a genre" promises to become more difficult than ever. In the current shifting French context of higher education, this is a critical point. Rather than acquiring conventional moves, learning disciplinary genres can be considered a progressive adopting-questioning-modifying that entails critical membership in the fullest sense of the term. Writing in the disciplines work needs to account for all of the ways genre is in play: as sets of recognizable features, as social and thus ideological acts to be adopted-resisted, as complement to activities, and as a relationship with a particular reader. In French higher education, teaching writing in the disciplines does not appear to take this complex critical approach to understanding disciplinary, genred writing. But the field of *la didactique* expressly resists "*applicationisme*" and so the work of research and theory is slow to influence practice, perhaps valuably slow. Both French and North American genre theories require us to account for multiple social, cultural, organizational, linguistic and textual phenomena that simply do not allow for understanding the genres of the disciplines as stable entities in stable fields into which students must be acculturated. In addition, the theoretical strands presented here offer insights in ways that become clear as we see how the French research project might benefit from North American genre theorists and vice versa in a fruitful exchange.

NOTES

[1] This is not uniformly true; the technical higher education tracks include required writing courses designed to improve students' abilities in reading and synthesizing material from multiple documents. In 2007, a new law was passed that will reform higher education in several ways, including focusing far more attention on student success in the undergraduate cycle. Campuses are already developing first-year composition courses, with a focus on skills and generic writing ability.

[2] In fact, the discussion about writing and disciplinary knowledge developed around primary and secondary education well before it became a subject of research interest in terms of university students in France.

REFERENCES
Adam, J.-M. (1992). *Les textes: Types et prototypes*. Paris: Nathan.

Adam, J.-M. (2005). La notion de typologie de textes en didactique du français: Une notion "dépassée"? *Recherches, 42,* 11-23.

Bakhtin, M. M. (1986). *Speech genres and other late essays* (V. McGee, Trans.). Austin: University of Texas Press.

Bazerman, C. (1994). *Constructing experience.* Carbondale: Southern Illinois University Press.

Bazerman, C. (2002). Genre and identity: Citizenship in the age of the internet and the age of global capitalism. In R. Coe, L. Lingard, & T. Teslenko (Eds.), *The rhetoric and ideology of genre* (pp. 13-37). Cresskill, New Jersey: Hampton Press.

Bazerman, C. (2006). The writing of social organization and the literate situating of cognition: Extending Goody's social implications of writing. In D. Olson & M. Cole (Eds.), *Technology, literacy and the evolution of society: Implications of the work of Jack Goody.* Mahwah, New Jersey: Erlbaum.

Bazerman, C., Little, J., & Chavkin, T. (2003). The production of information for genred activity spaces. *Written Communication, 20,* 455-477.

Bazerman, C., & Prior, P. (2005). Participating in emergent socio-literate worlds: Genre, disciplinarity, interdisciplinarity. In R. Beach and J. Green (Eds.), *Multidisciplinary perspectives on literacy research* (pp. 133-178). Cresskill, New Jersey: Hampton Press.

Beaufort, A. (2006). Writing in the professions. In P. Smagorinsky (Ed.), *Composition research: Multiple perspectives on two decades of change* (pp. 217-242). New York: Teachers College Press.

Biseault, J. (2003). Chercher, communiquer et apprendre en sciences à l'école primaire. In M. Jaubert, M. Rebière, & J. P. Bernié (Eds.), *Actes du colloque construction des connaissances et langage dans les disciplines d'enseignement.* [CD-Rom]

Bizzell, P. (1992). *Academic discourse and critical consciousness.* Pittsburgh: University of Pittsburgh Press.

Britton, J. (1992). *The development of writing abilities 11-18.* London: Macmillan.

Bronckart, J. P. (1996). Genres de texte, types de discours et opérations psycholinguistiques. *Voies Livres, 78,* 1-20.

Coe, R., Lingard, L., & Teslenko, T. (2002). Introduction. Genre as action, strategy, and différance: An introduction. In R. Coe, L. Lingard, & T. Teslenko (Eds.), *The rhetoric and ideology of genre* (pp. 1-10). Cresskill, New Jersey: Hampton Press.

Delcambre, I., & Boch, F. (2006). *Les écrits à l'université: Inventaires, pratiques, modeles.* Proposal to the Association Nationale de Recherches, France.

Donahue, T. (2004). Writing and teaching the disciplines in France: Current conversations and connections. *Arts and Humanities in Higher Education, 3,*

59-79.

Donahue, T. (2008). *Ecrire à l'université: Analyse comparee, France—Etats-Unis.* Lille, France: Presses Universitaires du Septentrion.

François, F. (1998). *Le discours et ses entours.* Paris: L'Harmattan.

Geisler, C. (1994). *Academic literacy and the nature of expertise: Reading, writing, and knowing in academic philosophy.* Hillsdale, New Jersey: Erlbaum.

Jakobson, R. (1963). *Essais de linguistique générale.* Paris: Minuit.

Jaubert, M., Rebière, M., & Bernié, J. P. (2003). L'hypothèse "communauté discursive": D'où vient-elle, ou va-t-elle? *Les cahiers THEODILE, 4,* 51-80.

Kinneavy, J. (1971). *A theory of discourse.* New York: W. W. Norton and Company.

Monroe, J. (2001). *Writing and revising the disciplines.* Ithaca, New York: Cornell University Press.

Monroe, J. (2008). Writing, assessment, and the authority of the disciplines. *L1 Educational Studies in Language and Literature, 7*(5).

Plane, S. (2002). La didactique du français, témoin et acteur de l'évolution du questionnement sur l'écriture et son apprentissage. *Repères, 22,* introduction.

Prior, P., & Bazerman, C. (Eds.). (2004). *What writing does and how it does it.* Mahwah, New Jersey: Erlbaum.

Recherches. (2005). Revue de didactique et de pédagogie du français. Lille, France: IUFM du Nord Pas de Calais.

Reuter, Y. (1998). Repenser la description? *Pratiques, 99,* 5-26.

Reuter, Y. (1999). Douze propositions pour construire la description. *Cahiers Pédagogiques, 54,* 11-13.

Reuter, Y. (2007). Statut et usages de la notion de genre en didactique(s). *Le Français Aujourd'hui, 159,* 11-18.

Reuter, Y., & Lahanier-Reuter, D. (2008). Presentation of a few concepts for analyzing writing in relation to academic disciplines. *L1 Educational Studies in Language and Literature, 7*(5).

Rogers, P. (2007). Methodological and developmental lessons from longitudinal studies of writing across the college span. (Unpublished manuscript)

Russell, D. (1997). Rethinking genre in school and society. *Written Communication, 14,* 504-554.

Schneuwly, B., & Dolz, J. (1997). Les genres scolaires: Des pratiques langagières aux objets d'enseignement. *Repères, 15,* 27-41.

Thaiss, C., & Zawacki, T. (2006). *Engaged writers, dynamic disciplines.* Portsmouth, New Hampshire: Heinemann.

Negotiating Genre: Lecturer's Awareness in Genre Across the Curriculum Project at the University Level

Estela Inés Moyano

INTRODUCTION

It has been said that genres created in each "area of human activity" (Bakhtin, 1953-54) or by "discourse communities" (Swales, 1990) **are shared** by "participants in these various areas" or "expert members of communities." However, at least in Argentina, researchers and post-graduate students are not fully familiar with the conventions of expected academic genres, as we have found in previous ethnological research (Moyano, 2000, 2001). Most new researchers realize they have difficulties in producing their scientific/academic texts, and MA and PhD students delay or do not complete their theses. Pre-university and undergraduate students, as well, show limited skills at solving writing tasks assigned by lecturers in Spanish as a mother tongue (Ezcurra, 1995; Ameijide, Murga, Padilla, & Douglas, 2000; Pereira & Di Stéfano, 2001; UNLu., 2001; Zalba, 2002; Cubo de Severino, 2002; Murga, Padilla, Douglas, & Ameijide, 2002; Moyano, 2003a).

It could be said, then, that this sharing of genres does not occur as a natural process, just by being in contact with them. As Swales (1990) suggests, new members of each community should be "initiated" by the experts. Or, as Martin and Rose (2007) emphasize, genres must be taught in the educational formal system or working places. According to these authors and other scholars of the Sydney School, teachers don't have genre consciousness. Then, the job of linguists is to identify and name the different kinds of texts that are found,

> looking closely at the kinds of meaning involved—using global patterns to distinguish one text type from another and more local patterns to distinguish stages within a text. Recurrent global patterns were recognized as genres, and given names. . . . Recurrent local patterns within genres were recognized as **schematic structures**, and also labeled. (Martin & Rose, 2007)

Martin defines genre as "a staged, goal-oriented, purposeful activity in which speakers engage as members of our culture" (1984), or "—more technically—as a particular configuration of register variables of field, tenor and mode" (Martin & Rose, 2003, 2007). "This means that genres are defined as a recurrent configuration of meanings and that they enact the social practices of a given culture."

So, the global patterns of academic, scientific and professional texts are related to human activities and meanings in each of these cultures. These specific practices with specific purposes are realised in texts according to the institutions and the field of knowledge, the participants involved and the role played by language. To be part of these social areas, where language is constitutive of the activities with some participation of multimodality, the students need to know what kind of practices, relationships between participants and different kind of texts take place in each area, and what resources of language are available to construe meaning. So, students need to be taught different genres in the academy and "how they relate to one another" (Martin & Rose, 2007) to be members of these cultures.

Academic activity across the curriculum demands more complex discursive practices while students reach a new step in their careers. These practices are related to disciplinary contents and research, technological development and professional life. So, they have to deal with theoretical concepts and produce texts in various genres. These activities are new for them, so they need to learn new genres, in which language is the main important resource: not only construing meaning (disciplinary concepts and their relations) but realising practices as social activities. In written and oral texts in these cultures, language is reflective and constitutive of the genre, with different kinds and degrees of multimodality. If students at the end of their career cannot manage this kind of text, they will be excluded from the University, scientific activities and/or working places.

José Luis Coraggio (1994) identifies two kinds of causes for the undergraduate educational crisis in Argentina: poor skills in learning from reading texts combined with a lack of abilities for solving problems, and frequent disruptions in studies and attrition from academic programs. These two factors, the academic difficulties and the individual lack of continuity of studies, might be related to each other.

ACADEMIC LITERACY IN ARGENTINA: A BRIEF REVIEW

There are different proposals about how to do the work of teaching academic literacy at the University: to offer writing courses outside the subjects (taught by linguistics lecturers); to teach academic literacy inside the subjects (taught by the subject lecturer as member of the discourse community); to give special training to advanced students who become tutors. These proposals were developed in the Writing Across the Curriculum movement, largely in the United States (McLeod & Soven, 1992; Marinkovich Ravena & Mirán Ramírez, 1998; Fullwiller & Young, 1982) and they are applied in some isolated practices in Argentina (UNLu, 2001). However, there are other approaches that focus on teaching genre in other traditions: ESP, applied especially in teaching academic literacy in English as a foreign language; and some SFL, applied in English in several universities and in Spanish in the Universidad Nacional de General Sarmiento (UNGS).

Despite these initiatives, Carlino (2003) has said that the universities in Argentina have the tendency to ignore that written activities affect knowledge acquisition and understanding. Professors only assign writing to evaluate learning, but not to develop the learning process. To reach this conclusion, Carlino carried out exploratory qualitative research, analyzing students' discourse, teaching programs and papers offered in education and literacy conferences. She found, as a result, that there are 30 universities where some professors teach academic literacy in their disciplinary classes, but without institutional support. These proposals—she says—are based on Writing Across the Curriculum movement (WAC), Process Pedagogy (Murray, 1982) and ESP (Dudley-Evans, 1994; Swales, 1990).

In a similar review, conclusions of "La lectura y la escritura como prácticas académicas universitarias" Conference (UNLu, 2001) identify two kinds of proposals in Argentina, which are represented by two groups, and remark too about the lack of institutional support for these initiatives. The first group includes remedial courses in pre-undergraduate studies or for freshmen, oriented to fill in the gaps left by "defective" schooling. This perspective implies that secondary schools have to teach "general abilities" for writing, rather than discourse abilities in context. The job is assigned to Spanish professors or reading and writing specialists. These proposals are based on theories of texts as autonomous objects, cognitive processes, pragmatics and rhetorical discourse, ESP and New Rhetoric—following Hyland's classification (2002).

The second group is formed by university professors of different disciplines, who conceive of reading and writing development as strongly related to each discipline's knowledge construction. They assign students very complex tasks of reading and writing, but they only teach the concepts of the discipline. Others try to combine teaching discipline and literacy practices as socialization into the community. Again following Hyland's classification (2002) they apply cognitive theories, expressivist views of writing, writing as cognitive process, knowledge telling and knowledge-transforming models.

Carlino's approach is that students get into disciplinary contents through reading and writing practices: they interpret, assimilate and engage other cognitive processes to understand a specific field. It follows, in her view, that the lecturer's duty is to work on academic literacy in their specific subject as a fundamental tool for learning (2005), but she lacks a linguist perspective to help students in this process.

However, it doesn't seem that disciplines' lecturers have got the tools for doing this job. In fact, although Carlino proposes very interesting and useful interventions and literacy practices with her students, it is obvious that her work needs more specific linguistic knowledge and specified techniques for consolidating student's learning in literacy.

THE PRODEAC PROGRAM

Taking into account students' limited literacy skills in Argentina—mentioned above—the Universidad Nacional de General Sarmiento (UNGS)[2] gives a compulsory introductory workshop in literacy for all students before they start their careers. Although the workshop lasts seven months, there is not enough time to teach all genres that students will face across the curriculum, nor is there time to develop a theoretically and technically grounded view of texts. So, we have selected to teach at this stage some "basic genres" that are often combined in academic macro-genres (Moyano, 2005) and a literature report (Pereira, Moyano, & Valente, 2005).

In the First Cycle of the curriculum, which lasts two and a half years, professors say that students have serious problems in reading literature recommended in their classes. This assumption is based on written examinations, in which students answer some questions about fundamental concepts and, sometimes, relationships between them. In the Second Cycle—2 and a half more years—lecturers complain about student's writing and oral skills in using academic language and structuring more complex texts. Therefore, in 2002, lecturers from the Instituto de Industria of the UNGS asked for our help as linguists, because professors have failed in helping students to improve their academic literacy[3].

Based on theoretical assumptions about genres, teaching and learning, and taking into account lecturers' complaints and requests from students, we have designed a Project to Develop Literacy Across the Curriculum (PRODEAC) to apply in the Second Cycle (Moyano & Natale, 2003)[4]. This project was refused twice by the *Consejo Superior*—the collegiated government organ of the University. This fact indicates the lack of institutional support for these kind of programs in Argentina (UNLu, 2001; Carlino, 2003, 2004, 2005), against the general consensus in other countries, especially in the Anglo-Saxon context, like Canada, US, Australia and the UK (Carlino, 2001a, 2001b, 2002, 2003, 2006; Marinkovich Ravena & Mirán Ramírez, 1998).

Finally, the project was only approved as a University Program in a revised version (Moyano and Natale, 2004) in 2005, after the three Institutes in charge of the Second Cycle of the diverse curricula joined to support and demand this project, under the condition that it had to be evaluated during its first application. In consequence, PRODEAC is the first Program of this kind in Argentina with institutional financial support necessary for its development.

The theoretical frame of this work is Genre & Register Theory, developed by Martin and the Sydney School in Systemic Functional Linguistics, and its pedagogical proposal (Martin & Rose, 2003, 2005, 2007; Eggins & Martin, 2001, 2003; Martin, 1993, 1999, 2000; Christie & Martin, 1997; Eggins, 1994; Martin & Rothery, 1993; Cope & Kalantzis, 1993; Halliday & Martin, 1993), adapted to our context and different educational levels in the course of research during 2004-2005. (Moyano & Natale, 2004; Moyano, 2007).

PRODEAC proposes that the joint work between language professors and professors in subject disciplines has central relevance in teaching academic/scientific and work place literacy. It could be said that this kind of joint work can guarantee the level of literacy development expected at the end of undergraduate studies. However, this multidisciplinary practice only can take place under some conditions:

(1) Language professors must have some specialization in scientific discourse and related linguistic and pedagogical theories.

(2) The scientific/academic and work place genres used need to be described and taught.

(3) The pedagogy has to be oriented to the academic or professional contexts, and must help students develop from heteronomy to autonomy.

(4) Disciplinary lecturers and linguists will work interdisciplinarily, sharing knowledge to design pedagogical activities for teaching genres, the teaching program, and evaluation and assessment.

This Program assumes that the students have to be introduced to common practices in the field by the expert members of the community. It allows, also, the improvement of communication via interaction between experts, to enrich the diversity of genres in the university. What's more, the modeling of joint-practice between experts of diverse disciplines could make a difference in the profile of graduating students who have the habit of working in inter or multi-disciplinary groups to produce knowledge in co-operative work.

For achieving these goals, we have created the figure of an "assistant linguistics professor" who has the role of accompanying the process of teaching literacy inside the subjects. This means that the linguist has to (a) negotiate with lecturers the genres they want students to produce; (b) intervene in classes teaching students not only genres' moves (Swales, 1990) or stages (Martin, 1992), but also the most relevant resources of scientific discourse; and (c) encourage students to deal with individual work, giving them the possibility of consulting in individual sessions. The texts produced are marked by both the linguist and the subject's professor in charge of the subject. This collaborative process provides a model for the specific subject's professor, so that they can do this job alone after three semesters of intervention, with the possibility of ongoing consultation with linguists.

Then, PRODEAC has three pedagogical goals:

(1) To guide the improvement of students' academic development through teaching genres and their realisation through language in relation to their activity as university fellows.
(2) To give assistance to specific subjects' lecturers in planning, assigning and evaluating written and oral tasks, in order to increase knowledge construed by their students about the field and academic and work place practices.
(3) To increase specific subjects' lecturers awareness of their disciplinary genres and guide them in teaching these genres.

NEGOTIATING GENRES

Before interacting with students, the linguists have to deal with the different levels of professors' genre awareness. They often lack consciousness about genres as activity in the university or in working contexts, about genres as constitutive of social action, and about the concept of language as a resource to construe reality or technical or scientific knowledge.

The way we found to work with lecturers is called "negotiation." By negotiation we understand the discussion between linguists and professors about the tasks they want to assign their students to write. These texts—following Genre & Register Theory—are instantiations of a genre, so are social activities with a clear purpose that members of a culture relate to another in a specific context or situation. These texts are developed by stages and phases which the students have to recognize, as well as their realisation by language. So, the lecturers need to be aware of these aspects of genre to formulate the assignments and to explain the usefulness of genre awareness in learning the subject and the academic or professional practice involved.

The negotiation begins with private encounters between the linguist and the lecturer participating in the Program. They talk about the subject and how teaching and evaluation will be developed. Then, they discuss the written or oral texts the lecturer will assign to their students.

The negotiation can develop in different ways, depending on the lecturer's consciousness. Some professors have changed their teaching program and the way of evaluation as soon as they have been notified that are going to participate in PRODEAC. Doing this, they show commitment with the Program. One of them said:

> Until the last semester, the evaluation of the regular course has been done through two individual writing exams, based on a few questions to answer. The student's mark in the subject was based on an oral examination, which consisted in an individual oral exposition about a special topic that integrates the contents of the subject at the end of the course. .

From the moment we started working with PRODEAC, this lecturer decided to change the strategies of evaluation: he assigned a written exam to do at home, a second one of the traditional type and a final written work to do at home with an oral defense. He expected to get written academic texts with characteristics similar to professional or scientific ones. Then, we could say he trusts in the action of the Program to improve the literacy abilities of his students.

Other professors showed high expectations about the goals their students could achieve, asking, as a final work, for texts for presentation in academic conferences or for publication. In this kind of work they expected the students to write a "scientific essay," using the course contents to solve a related issue.

It can be said, then, that some of the lecturers were very interested in the Program at the moment we started to work with them. Sometimes, their expectations were too high for the first time of application, but after several interventions through the semesters with the same group of students, they obtained some results that met those expectations.

EXPLORING NEGOTIATION

In this part of this paper, I will try to show the process of negotiation with different lecturers and to analyze their point of departure and their development through the 2nd semester of 2006[5].

Case 1

In this first case, the subject lecturer was a very experienced professor and researcher who was assisted by two very young graduated fellows. They wanted the students to write an academic text similar to a research article, based in field experiences and incorporating technical and scientific concepts included in literature. The first activity consisted in reading some literature and writing resumès, which they could do well at this level of the curriculum. Then, the second assignment—designed by one of these young assistants—consisted of determining, after observation, variables affecting an ecologic site and their indicators. When the assistant linguist asked the professor what he thought the students would write, he said "two lists linked by arrows." The assistant linguist didn't contradict the proposal.

In most cases the students made two lists of elements linked by arrows. The professors marked these resolutions with 7 points and appraised them very much. These products were evaluated considering only the content, such as two lists of elements related "in some way" by the arrows. But, what did those arrows mean? Why did they choose those variables and what did they mean? There was no explanation. The variables were well selected, as were the indicators and the links between them. But they weren't texts. Only a few students tried to write an introduction.

Then, the linguist suggested the professor ask students to transform this kind of schemata into a full and cohesive text, which could be a "case analysis." For this purpose, the linguist asked for an article that instantiated this genre, so that they could collaboratively analyze an example in order to identify the schematic structure, the register and discourse-semantics and lexico-grammar resources. But the professor couldn't identify a good example: he brought different articles about the same topic, but none was an instantiation of a "case analysis." This means that he couldn't recognize the genre, although this is one of the most common in this research area. The linguist, then, outlined by herself the schematic structure to show it to the subject's professors, who found it very adequate for the task. Finally, the linguist made the negotiation of genre with the students, in a joint construction of the schematic structure of the genre and the possibilities of choices the language system provides in that context, unless the students were not aware of scientific language or genres. As a result of these actions, they produced case analyses from 14 to 25 pages long, well enough written.

After this experience, during the second part of the subject course, the written examination was prepared by the second young assistant. As she made a sequence of tasks to guide a short research, the linguist suggested that the students could write a research article (RA). The subject professor suggested that the linguist give the students another schemata, but the linguist proposed that students themselves analyze an RA—oriented by the linguist herself —taking into account not only the schematic structure but also variables of register and some discursive and grammatical resources. Without conviction, the lecturer agreed to read with students a paper, which was jointly analyzed with active participation of the three subject professors especially about the discipline's conventions and topics.

For the last week of the semester, the students completed texts from 8 to 17 pages long. It's very important to say that in the past the students have never presented the final work on time, but this time they all did it. It's necessary to say here that one of the purposes of the Program is that students don't delay the final works, because it delays their graduation too.

Case 2

In previous meetings, the subject professor of this case showed his teaching program to the assistant linguist. Surprisingly, it included an uncommon assignment: a publishable paper. It could mean that this lecturer had some previous consciousness about the role of language in learning processes, or, at least, that the students need to acquire some writing resources before finishing undergraduate studies.

During the meetings, the linguist manifested worries about students' lack of enough information on the field's domain to write a publishable paper and their lack of training in writing RAs. This clearly shows that she doubted that genres may be learned without reflection, by just being in contact with them—in coincidence with Sydney School (Martin & Rose, 2007)—and that giving them brief instructions as in expert reviews is not enough to achieve the goal.

Then, the agreement between the professor and the assistant linguist was that they would do joint reading activities with the students and assign them a resumè, before choosing RAs to make a joint analysis. In this case, the assistant's intervention in the subject was facilitated by the professor, who worked with the linguist in joint analysis of the RA to help students in their approach to the genre and their specific characteristics in the discipline. They identified the IMDC structure and the linguistic resources to construe meaning in this genre as well as in multimodal forms: charts, maps and graphics. The students made their texts with linguist and lecturer assistance taking one by one the phases recognized during the analysis and including multimodal resources. The students had some difficulties during the process, but finally wrote texts very close to the genre, assisted by both the linguist and professor through email or consulting.

Finally, the professor suggested working with these students the next semester in the co-relative subject. At the same time, he decided to include in the bibliography of his teaching program more RAs to be read and analyzed by students from the beginning of the next course.

Case 3

Some lecturers believe that they cannot require more than one written assignment each semester because more writing would not leave students enough time to read the literature, which—they affirm—is the most important task in the course. However, in some cases writing is as important as reading, because through writing the students can relate concepts and apply them, as in a case analysis or a project.

One of these lecturers planned to assign what he called "report of changes in an enterprise." When the linguist asked if the students would visit companies to gather data for the report, the lecturer answered that they wouldn't. Then, the assistant linguist suggested the students could better make a *"project of change,"* if the professor gave them an example of a specific issue in context. Then, the lecturer understood the idea of the Program and accepted this change. He negotiated with the linguist the genre, defining stages and phases, taking into account his experience in this area of professional work. After that, both participants of the negotiation prepared the task. The "project of change" should be a text presented by a professional for a specific purpose, e.g., a change in the production system.

The process of negotiation was very difficult with the subject professor, who didn't trust in the capability of students to write this kind of text. The subject professor and the linguist looked for models, but couldn't find any, except those that have confidential information. So, the negotiation was made by designing the structure schemata:

PRELIMINARY GENRE DESIGN

Purpose of the text:
Suggesting to authorities of a Company a "Project for a Production Plan and Control."

Genre:
Project of Change in a Company

Hypothetical Participants:
(1) Writer: Industrial Engineer making a proposal.
(2) Readers: Company's directors, professionals, mechanics and workers.

Information given to students:
Characteristics of an actual or hypothetical Company.
Problems faced by the Company in a specific time in its trajectory.

Schematic Structure:
(1) Company's situational description at the moment of the Project presentation:
   • What's going wrong and why?

- Recognizing and describing problems/difficulties etc.
- Identifying possible causes.
- Identifying and describing possible present or future conse-quential problems.

(2) Proposal of Change:
- What kind of changes could solve the identified problems?
- Proposing changes for solving problems.
- Anticipating benefits those changes might produce.

After giving these schemata to students, the subject lecturer had to give some orientation for them. So, he proposed working with the *Just in Time* system, successfully applied in two actual companies. Then, the linguist suggested asking the students to define and describe the *Just in Time* system from the literature provided by the professor, which demanded changes in the first schemata:

RE-DESIGNING THE GENRE

Genre:
Project of Change in a Company

Social space:
Company work place

Hypothetical Participants:
(1) Writer: Industrial Engineer making a proposal.
(2) Readers: Company's directors, professionals, mechanics and employees.

Schematic Structure:
Introduction
- Anticipating the development of the text.

(1) *Just in Time* system
- *What's the Just in Time system?*
- Definition with application samples.

(2) Proposal for interaction between Company's sectors
- *How might the interaction be between productive and commercial sectors?*
- Factorial explanations and procedures.

(3) Benefits of applying the Just in Time system
   - *Why will this system benefit the Company?*
   - Exposition. The student has to mention the benefits and disadvantages.

Conclusion
   - Synthesis.

During the genre presentation class, the linguist explained the schematic structure and resources of discourse and different genres involved. The subject professor collaborated giving contextual information: the internal communication's relevance in a company, its style, the kind of relationship between the interactants, etc. This was a very useful resource for students. Although they delayed the presentation of the final text, at the end of the course after lot of work with the linguist in private encounters, they made proper texts.

Case 4

In another case, a professor assigned a "literature report" not giving time for negotiation with the linguist, nor between the linguist and the students. The students made separate resumès of each text, and the lecturer accepted these resumès as though they completed the task correctly. The linguist expressed the view that the genre was not realised, and the lecturer answered she didn't know indeed what a "literature report" was, that she had heard the name and decided to assign it to the students.

This was just one example of a professor's lack of commitment to the class and the university during two semesters' work. After that, this professor left the university, which might explain her lack of engagement, but we do not know this for certain.

This lecturer's lack of commitment was a negative influence for students, who didn't engage with the Program during this time. In other subjects involving PRODEAC, the more engaged the lecturer was, the more the students were engaged. However, if the students showed too much resistance, the lecturers were more reluctant to negotiate.

It is in this kind of situation that institutional support is very much needed. The university's strong commitment—in this case of the Instituto de Industria—led this conflict to a good ending: lecturers had to negotiate and students had to accept their participation in the Program.

Case 5

We will refer now to another subject professor, who gradually understood the

Program during her participation. Before starting, she was already enthusiastic about giving written activities to her students. These activities were proposed for closing units of the teaching program, to help students think about the concepts of the subject and to evaluate learning. She called these activities "fresh" or "spontaneous" writing, "not being exemplars of a genre."

The first step for negotiation was to make a diagnosis, asking students to make a resumè of a text from the literature given. Both the professor and the linguist marked these texts and found that the students could accomplish this activity very well, as they were used to writing them in the First Cycle of the curriculum. Problems in writing emerge when the professors assign the students to write a literature report or a more complex text.

The second activity in this first edition of the joint work was to expose briefly some concepts about tensions in economics and politics during the 70s, applying them especially to the Argentinean case. The subject professor didn't want to analyze a text of this kind, so the linguist tried to recover the experience in literacy the students had had in a previous course they took prior to their studies as university fellows. The linguist proposed a kind of schemata for the text to be elaborated. The results were not as the professor expected, so the linguist negotiated to do a joint-editing work in the class, to explain to the students the common difficulties they had with the assignment.

The third task was defined as a "case analysis." The students had to take from newspapers a case related to concepts in the literature and analyze it in a "proper way," with students developing criteria for applying concepts from the literature. The linguist suggested it was very difficult for students to develop their own criteria at the 6th semester of the curriculum, because they were never asked to do a similar task in the First Cycle. So, they needed some guide to develop a critical view of the literature and how to relate it to a case.

As the subject professor didn't provide a text for analysis and as she saw that the results of the first case analysis weren't as expected, she agreed to work with the linguist to develop a schematic structure of the genre and help the students to develop the criteria for literature application. In her class, the linguist made special emphasis on the plan for the text and the students had to present their plans to the group for discussion. Only after that they were allowed to write the text. The results were better than before, so the subject professor accepted the need to define the genre, describe it and guide the production at this level.

During the second application, in 2006, the subject professor was more open to the linguist's suggestions. She changed the teaching program, enlightened by the first experience, and had better results.

It's relevant to say that she gave support to PRODEAC in front of the students, so they were increasing their participation in classes and working harder with their texts. We can say, again, that this support is very important for the developing of the Program. As was said before, when the professor is engaged, the students are too. For every assignment of the second edition of this experience, the professor had a clear idea of the genre she was asking for. The students not only understood what genre they had to produce but also how to construe criteria for analyzing the case. So, both professors advanced in the description of genres, taking into account its schematic structure, register, discourse-semantics and lexico-grammar patterns.

Case 6

The process of negotiation with an economics professor will be analyzed now. At the beginning of the intervention, the professor said that natural language doesn't intervene in teaching this subject: he projected on the board some charts with economic data and selected some numbers to put into relation for making conclusions with the students. So, he agreed to participate in the Program with the idea that "he hasn't anything to offer to it." As can be seen in this assertion, the subject professor thought that he had to give something to the Program, instead of seeing it as a multidisciplinary activity which would affect the learning of his subject and the specialized literacy development of students.

The assistant linguist decided to be present in his classes just to observe them, and, after some, showed to the subject professor in private that he in fact used natural language to construe meaning from the related data of the chart. Finally, at the end of the semester, the lecturer understood how language functions in interpreting data to make conclusions. Then, he looked for some reports from the Center of Studies for Latin America (CEPAL) for analysis, and then the students produced a brief report as a final work for the course. It's important to say that this is one of the last subjects the students have to complete before graduation as economists, so they need to learn how to write professional genres.

In the second semester this professor worked with PRODEAC, he modified the teaching program, including activities of joint analysis to show how the expert writers use the economic data of charts to construe their texts as expositions, as the students will have to do as professionals. Then, the students wrote their own texts; the linguist could do the joint editing of one of them, and the students wrote another text of this kind as a final evaluation in the subject.

Case 7

The last case I will take for this paper is a subject from the Industrial Engineering curriculum, where the students must design an industrial product, justify its need for the society and make the product itself as a prototype. The negotiation with the lecturers in charge was very difficult, because they understood that they needed to change the goals of the subject to work with PRODEAC.

The assistant linguist made an effort to do this negotiation, and it was difficult, as she needed the assistance of the director of the Program.

First, she asked the lecturers if the students had to write any texts during the semester, and they said that students had to write weekly progress reports. After arguing that these texts varied greatly, the professors provided last semester's progress reports so that the linguist could study them.

After studying the texts, the assistant linguist proposed a complex schematic structure of the genre, because—as a macro-genre—it includes different types of texts: one to tell how the idea was generated; a second one to justify the need of the product in the market; a third one to describe the product and the materials used for making it. For designing the schematic structure of the genre, the linguist took into account the forms that professionals have to fill in to request finances for innovative projects in competitions organized by the government or companies. Finally, the linguist had to include in the schematic structure some elements asked for by the subject professors in order to evaluate the performance of students in the activity. The genre was called "designing a product project."

When the negotiation reached an agreement between the lecturers involved, the linguist had the opportunity to intervene in some classes to describe the genre and give some instructions to write it. In this case, the joint evaluation had the most relevant function, because it helped the students to work with their texts through final revisions.

Finally, the students were interested in oral presentations of the products, which required the linguist to teach how to make a Power Point presentation and how to give a talk supported by this resource. In this task, the academic evaluative aspects of the genre were removed, turning it into a professional one labeled "proposal of a new product." The presentations were made to the public—students and engineers who teach at the university—and were very well received.

This case was very interesting, because it represented a hard challenge: how to obtain an understanding about the genre within real material and social activity. The professors themselves increased their understanding and now ask assistance from linguists to make their own presentations to government or commercial competitions.

LECTURER'S EVOLUTION

To sum up, at the beginning of the Program, we have detected in the subjects' lecturers three degrees of awareness of the role of language in knowledge construction (Vigotsky, 1978) and the value of the conceptualization of genres as social activities (Martin, 1984):

(1) The first group appreciates language practices in science and recognizes some scientific genres, but doesn't have pedagogical resources to teach them. In general, they are experienced writers and researchers who have also guided post-graduate theses, so their consciousness about academic and working practices is high.

Negotiating with this group is not very difficult: the professors allow the linguist to assist the students through joint analyses of academic genres and/or joint editing of their texts. In cases in which it was not possible to find a text for analysis, the linguist made a schemata with students (based on previous consensus with the professors), to guide the production. This group of lecturers participate in the linguist's classes, making comments and explaining matters about the discipline and the way to make decisions about what kind of contents should be included in the texts and why. When the students have written their texts, the linguist, the lecturer and the students jointly revise one or two texts written by the students. Sometimes, this is the first text they have produced in the genre, so the next activity could be to produce the same genre about another topic as final evaluation. The linguists make suggestions to the students about possible solutions to the proposed task, or about what else might be needed in the final, more complex assignment.

The negotiation includes discussion of different points of view between linguists and lecturers, but in most cases they gradually agree. In these cases, for the second experience, the lecturers included in their teaching programs' literature texts to analyze and to make genres familiar to their students.

(2) The second group also appreciates language practices, but doesn't know clearly how they could help their students to learn better the subject's concepts nor what kind of texts they might assign students for achieving this purpose. They are not aware about the concept of genre, although they know the more complex ones which they, as academics or professionals, are used to writing.

This group is indeed the most difficult to work with. At the beginning, some lecturers were not very interested in our proposal because they thought that we were going to put the emphasis on norms and "beautiful writing." They presented some resistance but some of them (not all mentioned here) have grown in understanding of the purpose of the Program after the first application. As we have shown, some of them didn't collaborate at all. In one case, after the first participation, the professor decided to give up the Program. But one year later she asked to rejoin it because she found that the students produced better texts and learned the subject better when she worked with PRODEAC. At this moment, we are working again with her.

(3) The third group hasn't any awareness of the role of natural language in knowledge construction, whether they consider that "numbers speak on their own"—as some economists said—or, as some engineers said, they only teach "activity" or "how to do things" in professional life. But, after seeing the results, they appreciate the Program and propose other ways to work, like producing materials for students to reinforce what is done in classes. This is a job in progress now, and it will be extended to other subjects, through writing a book which will describe the genres used more frequently.

It is necessary to say that the evolution of the lecturers involved in the Program is not as fast as it looks in this presentation. It requires slow and subtle work from the linguist, since the proposal is not clearly understood from the beginning. Some of the professors feel the process is invasive, and put up barriers, avoiding encounters or being absent in the linguist's classes. But after a period of interaction, things change: the lecturers start to see how the Program can help the teaching-learning process and the help it gives to the students' texts for their university and future professional lives.

CONCLUSION

To sum up, the negotiation consists in guiding the lecturers to define clearly, in interaction with the assistant linguist, genres the students need to learn. They make explicit for each genre the stages and phases, and the linguists help them to be conscious about the kind of language that realise the meanings each genre construes, the kind of relationship between interactants in the text and its realisation, the organization of these meanings in a text, and the information flow as well as the function of multimodality, sometimes represented by the use of charts, schemata, graphics, maps, etc.

In consequence, the lecturers acquire consciousness of genre, generally in the second time participating in the Program, when they work positively from the first moment and make proposals as alternatives. They also grow in comprehension of the possibility of teaching genres and take the habit of working in this way, recognizing that the students' productions show deeper reflection about theoretical contents and their application.

Now we reach the moment to discuss if this negotiation procedure is theoretically acceptable. It is supposed that the members of a community share genres that achieve their own communicative purpose (Swales, 1990), or that in each area of activity the speakers-listeners know genres as they know the system of language (Bakhtin, 1952-53). The fact is that in the academy this is not automatic, as we try to show through the cases analyzed before. So, in the theoretical frame we have chosen (Sydney School's G&R Theory), it is possible to say that a linguist can increase the awareness about genres of the members of a certain social activity institution in a culture. Negotiation seems to be an adequate procedure for this purpose, as is shown in this paper.

The work of the linguist is, as Martin and Rose (2007) said, to detect genres, describe them in all the strata of language and context and label them. In the case of academic and workplace genres, the experience with the subject professors is very useful. They are not aware of this necessity but increase in comprehension and collaboration as they work with the associated linguist of the Program.

About the legitimacy of this practice I can say that almost all the university community has shown interest in this Program to accomplish the foundational purposes of the university. The professors increase their awareness about the importance of genre to teach academic literacy, and the role of language in construing knowledge. The students improve their skills in academic literacy and can manage better the concepts of the different subjects they study. Genres are negotiated from the perspective of professional and academic activities in each field, the interpersonal relationships and the role language plays in the process of writing and learning.

Of course, there are many things to do in order to realize the Program and its impact, but we are still starting this process: in 2005 we worked in six subjects and in the second semester of 2007 we are covering 20 with more success than before. Now professors and students ask to participate in PRODEAC, so we try to cover their requests in different ways.

I have to remark, finally, on the importance of institutional support, not only financial but also the administrative determination to expand the application of the Program. It's important to say that the University is helping to form a stable group of linguists to carry out the work, creating posts for this purpose and giving support for publications or other means to increase students' and subject professors' interest in participating.

During the last months of 2007, UNGS is extending the Program to provide linguists to work with advanced students who are writing grant proposals and making presentations of their research. This means one step forward and a new challenge to expand PRODEAC.

NOTES

[1] I want to thank especially Dr. Charles Bazerman for his patient reading and his valuable help.

[2] The *Universidad Nacional de General Sarmiento* is located in the *2° Cordón del Conurbano Bonaerense*, "the second line of Buenos Aires suburbs." The main population comes from disadvantaged schools and workers' families, so in terms of Bernstein, they have restricted codes.

[3] The use of language has been seen as a relevant practice in our University since its foundation (Coraggio, 1994).

[4] This doesn't mean that we don't think that this Program should be applied all across the curriculum, including the First Cycle, but political issues didn't allow us to do a complete design.

[5] These different cases recount the experiences of linguists working as assistant professors: Lucía Natale, Silvia Mateo, Elena Valente and Oscar Amaya.

REFERENCES

Amaya, O. D. (2005, May). *La lectura y escritura en la universidad: Prácticas, creencias y reconstrucción de los esquemas de conocimientos en la constitución de la identidad universitaria*. Lecture given at the 2nd Coloquio Argentino de International Association for Dialogue Analysis (IADA), National University of La Plata, La Plata, Argentina.

Ameijde, D., Murga, M., Padilla, C., & Douglas, S. (2000). Conceptualizaciones sobre el saber lingüístico en el discurso estudiantil. In S. Menéndez, A. Cortés, A. Menegotto, & A. Cócaro (Eds.), *Actas VIII Congreso de la Sociedad Argentina de Lingüística (SAL): Las teorías lingüísticas del nuevo milenio, National University of Mar del Plata, Mar del Plata, Argentina*. [CD-ROM ISBN 987-544-047-5]

Bakhtin, M. (1982). El problema de los géneros discursivos. In M. Bakhtin, *Estética de la creación verbal* (T. Bubnova, Trans., pp. 248-293). Mexico City, Mexico: Siglo XXI.

Bernstein, B. (1971). *Class, codes and control: Theoretical studies towards a sociology of language* (Vol. 1). London: Routledge.

Bernstein, B. (1981). Code modalities and the process of reproduction: A model. *Language and Society, 10,* 327-363.

Carlino, P. (2001a). Enseñar a escribir en la universidad: ¿Cómo lo hacen en EE. UU. y por qué? [Electronic version]. *O.E.I—Revista Iberoamericana de Educación, ISS,* 1681-5651. Retrieved from http//www.campus.oei.org/revista/

deloslectores/279carlino.pdf

Carlino, P. (2001b). *Hacerse cargo de la lectura y escritura en la enseñanza universitaria de las ciencias sociales y humanas.* Lecture given at the Jornadas sobre la Lectura y Escritura como Prácticas Académicas Universitarias, National University of Luján, Luján, Argentina. Retrieved from http//www.unlu.edu.ar/_redecom/

Carlino, P. (2002). *Enseñar a escribir en todas las materias: cómo hacerlo en la universidad.* Lecture given at the Seminario Internacional de Inauguración Subsede Cátedra UNESCO, Lectura y Escritura, National University of Cuyo, Mendoza, Argentina. Retrieved from http//www.educ.ar/educar/superior/biblioteca_digital/

Carlino, P. (2003a). Alfabetización académica: Un cambio necesario, algunas alternativas posibles. *EDUCERE, 6*(20), 409-420.

Carlino, P. (2003b). *Leer textos científicos y académicos en la educación superior: Obstáculos y bienvenidas a una cultura nueva.* Lecture given at the 6th Congreso Internacional de Promoción de la Lectura y el Libro, XIII Jornadas Internacionales de Educación, 29th Feria del Libro, Buenos Aires, Argentina. Retrieved from http//www.unlu.edu.ar/_redecom/

Carlino, P. (2004, July). *¿De qué modos incentivar en nuestras instituciones la responsabilidad compartida por cómo se lee y se escribe en la universidad/IFD?* Lecture given at the inaugural conference of the Simposio Leer y Escribir en la Educación Superior (Universidad e Institutos de Formación Docente), realizado dentro del Congreso Internacional Educación, Lenguaje y Sociedad Tensiones Educativas en América Latina, Instituto para el Estudio de la Educación, el Lenguaje y la Sociedad, Facultad de Ciencias Humanas, National University of La Pampa, Santa Rosa, La Pampa, Argentina.

Carlino, P. (2005). *Escribir, leer y aprender en la universidad: Una introducción a la alfabetización académica.* Buenos Aires: FCE.

Christie, F. (Ed.). (1999). *Pedagogy and the shaping of consciousness: Linguistic and social processes.* London: Continuum.

Christie, F., & Martin, J. R. (1997*). Genre and Institutions: Social processes in the workplace and school.* London: Cassell.

Christie, F., & Unsworth, L. (2000). Developing socially responsible language research. In L. Unsworth (Ed.), *Researching language in schools and communities: Functional linguistic perspectives* (pp. 1-26). London: Cassell.

Cope, B., & Kalantzis, M. (1993). *The powers of literacy: A genre approach to teaching writing.* London: The Falmer Press.

Coraggio, J. L. (1994). Reforma pedagógica: Eje de desarrollo de la enseñanza superior. In *Documentos de trabajo 1. Estudios de apoyo a la organización de la Universidad Nacional de General Sarmiento.* San Miguel, Argentina: UNGS.

Cubo de Severino, L. (2002). Evaluación de estrategias retóricas en la comprensión de manuales universitarios. *Revista del Instituto de Investigaciones Lingüísticas y Literarias Hispanoamericanas (RILL)*, 15, 69-84.

Eggins, S. (1994). *An introduction to systemic functional linguistics*. London: Cassell.

Eggins, S., & Martin, J. R. (2003). El contexto como género: Una perspectiva lingüístico-funcional. *Revista Signos*, 36(54), 185-205.

Ezcurra, A., Nogueira, S., & Pereira, M. C. (1995). *Competencias cognitivas de alumnos de primer ingreso universitario potencial (en actividades de comprensión y producción de textos de tipo expositivo y argumentativo de género académico)*. Informe de investigación no publicado de la Unidad Pedagógica Universitaria, National University of General Sarmiento, Los Polvorines, Argentina.

Fullwiler, T., & Young, A. (1982). *Language connections: Writing and reading across the curriculum* [Electronic version]. Urbana, Illinois: National Council of Teachers of English. Retrieved from http//wa.colostate.edu/books/

Halliday, M. A. K., & Martin, J. R. (1993). *Writing science: Literacy and discursive power*. Pittsburgh: University of Pittsburgh Press.

Hyland, K. (2002). *Teaching and researching writing*. London: Longman.

Hyon, S. (1996). Genre in three traditions: Implications for ESL. *TESOL Quaterly*, 30(4), 693-722.

Marinkovich Ravena, J., & Mirán Ramírez, P. (1998). La escritura a través del currículum. *Revista Signos*, 31(43–44), 165–171.

Martin, J. R. (1984). Language, register and genre. In F. Christie (Ed.), *Children writing: Reader* (pp. 21-29). Geelong, Victoria, Australia: Deakin University Press.

Martin, J. R. (1993). A contextual theory of language. In B. Cope & M. Kalantzis (Eds.), *The powers of literacy: A genre approach to teaching writing* (pp. 116-136). London: The Falmer Press.

Martin, J. R. (1997). Analysing genre: Functional parameters. In F. Christie & J. R. Martin (Eds.), *Genre and institutions: Social processes in the workplace and school* (pp. 3-39). London: Cassell.

Martin, J. R. (1999). Mentoring semogenesis: "Genre-based" literacy pedagogy. In F. Christie (Ed.), *Pedagogy and the shaping of consciousness: Linguistic and social processes* (pp. 123-155). London: Continuum.

Martin, J. R. (2000). *Grammar meets genre: Reflections on the Sydney school* [Electronic version]. Lecture given at the inaugural Sydney Association for the Arts. Retrieved from http://www2.ocn.ne.jp/~yamanobo/systemic_bibliography/other_systemists_work/inaugural_martin.html

Martin, J. R., & Rose, D. (2003). *Working with discourse: Meaning beyond the clause*. London: Continuum.

Martin, J. R., & Rose, D. (2007). *Genre relations: Mapping culture*. London: Equinox.

Martin, J. R., & Rothery, J. (1993). Grammar: Making meaning in writing. In B. Cope & M. Kalantzis (Eds.), *The powers of literacy: A genre approach to teaching writing* (pp. 137-154). London: The Falmer Press.

McLeod, S., & Soven, M. (1992). *Writing across the curriculum: A guide to developing programs* [Electronic version]. Newbury Park, California: Sage. Retrieved from http\\wa.colostate.edu/books/

Moyano, E. I. (2000). *Comunicar ciencia: El artículo científico y las presentaciones a congresos.* Lomas de Zamora, Buenos Aires, Argentina: UNLZ.

Moyano, E. I. (2001) Una clasificación de géneros científicos. In A. Moreno & V. Collwell (Eds.), *Perspectivas recientes sobre el discurso.* Asociación Española de Lingüística Aplicada (AESLA), University of León, Spain, Secretariado de Publicaciones y Medios Audiovisuales. [CD-Rom ISBN: 84-7719-984-1]

Moyano, E. I. (2003a). *Informe final de resultados: Evaluación diagnóstica sumativa del taller de lecto-escritura del curso de aprestamiento Universitario de la UNGS.* Publicación interna Secretaría Académica— Instituto del Desarrollo Humano, National University of General Sarmiento, Los Polvorines, Argentina.

Moyano, E. I. (2003b). *Desarrollo de habilidades de lectura y escritura avanzadas: Criterios teóricos para un diseño curricular.* Lecture given at the Primera Jornada del Taller de Lecto-Escritura del Curso de Aprestamiento Universitario, Instituto del Desarrollo Humano, Universidad de General Sarmiento, Los Polvorines, Argentina.

Moyano, E. I. (2005). Géneros que hablan de ciencia. In M. C. Pereira (Coord.), *La lectura y la escritura en el ciclo de pre-grado universitario* (pp. 83-214). Los Polvorines, Argentina: UNGS.

Moyano, E. (2007). Enseñanza de habilidades discursivas en español en contexto pre-universitario: Una aproximación desde la LSF. *Revista Signos, 40*(65) 573-608

Moyano, E. I., & Natale, L. (2003). *Programa para el desarrollo de habilidades de escritura a lo largo del curriculum (PRODEAC).* Proyecto presentado al Consejo Superior, National University of General Sarmiento, Los Polvorines, Argentina.

Moyano, E. I., & Natale, L.. (2004). *Programa para el desarrollo de habilidades de lectura y escritura a lo largo del curriculum (PRODEAC).* Proyecto presentado al Consejo Superior, National University of General Sarmiento, Los Polvorines, Argentina.

Murga de Uslenghi, M., Padilla de Zerdán, C., Douglas de Sirgo, S., & Ameijide, M. (2002). Discurso estudiantil: Representaciones acerca de las competencias discursivas. Análisis crítico del discurso estudiantil en el nivel universitario. Oralidad, lectura y escritura: Categorización de dificultades. *Revista del Instituto de Investigaciones Lingüísticas y Literarias Hispanoamericanas (RILL), 15*, 85-103.

Painter, C. (1986). The role of interaction in learning to speak and learning to write. In C. Painter & J. R. Martin (Eds.), *Writing to mean: Teaching genres across the curriculum* (pp. 62-97).

Painter, C. (1999). Preparing for school: Developing a semantic style for educational knowledge. In F. Christie (Ed.), *Pedagogy and the shaping of consciousness: Linguistic and social processes* (pp. 66-87). London: Continuum.

Pereira, M. C. (Coord.). (2005). *La lectura y la escritura en el ciclo de pre-grado universitario*. Los Polvorines, Argentina: UNGS.

Pereira, M. C., Moyano, E. I., & Valente, E. (2005). *Programa taller de lecto-escritura: curso de aprestamiento universitario*. Los Polvorines, Argentina: UNGS.

Perelman, C. (1997). *El imperio retórico*. Santa Fe de Bogotá, Colombia: Norma.

Perelman, C. (1988). *L'empire Rethorique*. París, Vrin.

Rogoff, B. (1997). Los tres planos de la actividad sociocultural: Apropiación participativa, participación guiada y aprendizaje. In J. V. Wertsch, P. del Río, & A. Álvarez (Eds.), *La mente sociocultural: Aproximaciones teóricas y aplicadas* (pp. 111-128). Madrid: Fundación Infancia y Aprendizaje.

Swales, J. (1990). *Genre analysis: English in academic and research settings*. Cambridge: Cambridge University Press.

UNLu. (2001). *La lectura y la escritura como prácticas académicas universitarias: Universidad Nacional de Luján* [Electronic version].Retrieved from www.unlu. edu.ar/~redecom/

Vygotsky, L. S. (1981). The genesis of higher mental functions. In J. V. Wertsch (Ed.), *The concept of activity in Soviet psychology*. New York: Sharpe.

Vygotsky, L. S. (1998). *Pensamiento y lenguaje*. Buenos Aires: Fausto.

Zalba, E. M. (2002). *La palabra interdicta: Problemas de producción discursiva en estudiantes universitarios*. Lecture given at the 1st Simposio Internacional de la Subsede Universidad Nacional de Cuyo de la Cátedra UNESCO, National University of Cuyo, Mendoza, Argentina. Retrieved from http:// www.educ.ar/educar/servlet/Downloads/S_BD_SIMPOSIO_LECTURA_Y_ ESCRITURA/ZALBAC4.PDF

23 The Development of a Genre-Based Writing Course for Graduate Students in Two Fields

Solange Aranha

INTRODUCTION

Published academic papers are generally seen as a key factor in sharing knowledge from research with peers, promoting researchers in their scientific communities and creating a proper environment for scientific discussion. However, one of the problems faced by novice researchers is how to master academic genres. Figueiredo and Bonini (2006), for instance, found out that although many of their students were part of a Master's program, they showed little or no familiarity with the effective use of scientific discourse. To deal with this shortcoming, the authors devised a course that aimed at developing the students' skills in academic writing in their mother tongue. The results showed that students benefited from the course in different aspects, such as acquiring a view of genres as social practices and the notion that genres circulate within an academic community. However, the data also showed that students still remained as novices in the academic discourse community and, thus, were not confident enough to reflect upon the discourse, the practices and the genres accepted within the academic community they aim to be members of.

It may be argued that the constraints of academic writing pose difficulties for authors of any language. No matter the language the text is written in, students have to negotiate the genre conventions, the knowledge and the values of academic writing in their struggle for a personal voice. On the one hand, novices want and need to have their papers published, and, on the other, they are aware neither of how the community conventions work nor of what may be done to develop their academic writing skills.

The need to master academic genres is unquestionable, but the means to achieve mastery seem to be limited. Graduate courses in Brazil do not include disciplines whose aims are to develop the students' writing skills, not even in their mother tongue (the course described by Figueiredo and Bonini is an exception, and is not part of the regular graduate program in which it was taught). However, students are supposed to publish the results of their investigations. Some programs even consider publication as part of the requirements for obtaining the degree. The programs considered in this paper, i.e., graduate courses in Dentistry and Genetics, require their students to publish papers in English by the time they are about to finish the program, that is, after two years in a

Master's program and after four years in a PhD program.

The students are supposed to have studied English earlier in their education, since they are expected to efficiently use English writing skills during their graduate program. According to Canagarajah (2002), "ESOL (English for Speakers of Other Languages) students are not aliens to the English language or Anglo-American culture anymore" (p. 10). However, the fact that a graduate student is not alien to a foreign language or its culture does not mean that he/she is able to write texts in that language; texts that are already difficult to produce in his/her own mother tongue, let alone in a foreign language. The gap between "not being alien to" English and being able to use it properly in academic writing is huge. Recognizing and reading academic texts proficiently is not a guarantee that one is able to produce texts according to the constraints of academic genres which are likely to be accepted by individual academic discourse communities.

This paper therefore presents a specific course in academic writing in English for graduate students devised to fit the students' background knowledge, needs and motivations to develop academic skills.

COURSE TEXT

Swales and Feak's *Academic Writing for Graduate Students* (1994) is a textbook that develops academic writing skills "for people who are not native speakers of English yet are studying for graduate degrees (at both masters and doctoral levels) through or partly through the medium of English" (p.1). The material is composed of eight units whose aim is to propose tasks, activities and discussions that range from small-scale language points to studying the discourse of a chosen discipline. The first three units are essentially preparatory while the others include genre-specific activities. The book was designed for non-native graduate students with a focus on making a good impression with academic writing and concerned with improving academic texts.

The units develop from the concepts of audience, purposes, strategies, organization, style and flow to the construction of an academic paper (units seven and eight), where the rhetorical proposal for writing introductions (CARS—Create a Research Space) (Swales, 1990, p. 141) is shown with some modifications (discussed in Aranha, 2004), especially concerned with the labels "moves" and "steps" and with obligatory and optional elements. The units also include a specific part on grammar aspects entitled "language focus" with detailed grammar rules of the most common linguistic features in academic texts (relative clauses, articles, passive voice, adverbial clauses, prepositions, reference, linkers, and nominal clauses, among others).

The authors use texts "from a wide range of disciplines—from mechanical engineering to musical theory" and avoid "laying down rules about what a member of a disciplinary community should (or should not) do in a particular writing situation" (p. 3). The tasks always require that students find examples from their fields, thus, it is implied that multidisciplinary classes are encouraged. Bhatia's work with academic abstracts (1993, pp. 78-79) widens and elucidates the discussions in Swales and Feak (pp. 210-217).

The potential instructors are likely to be experienced teachers of academic writing. According to Swales and Feak, they aimed for "a textbook that can be used selectively and that easily allows teachers to substitute activities and texts more suited to their own particular circumstances" (p. 5).

Although in the concepts that underlie a course syllabus the idea of "contact zone" model endorsed by Canagarajah (2002) might be considered, in practice we did not have sufficient time to allow students to strategically negotiate with the academic discursive conventions and create multivocal genres. Nor did we have time to create "safe houses" (p. 182) for our students to practice the discourses of their home communities or develop discourses oppositional to the dominant academic discourse.

METHODOLOGY AND RESULTS

The graduate courses in Genetics and Dentistry at UNESP (São Paulo State University) require students to have reading proficiency in English when they enter the program. This proficiency is measured by an exam which is part of the selection process. If the candidate is not approved at this level, he/she automatically fails.

Reading assignments in English are common for the two courses, once most of the bibliographical materials in those areas are in English. In these particular fields, even some Brazilian journals are published in English. Besides being able to read, at a certain stage of the course the students are also required to write in English in order to have the results of their research studies published.

In this context, a course that would suffice their writing needs was first demanded by the Dentistry faculty of UNESP-Araraquara to the Modern Language Department of that same University in 2004. The faculty needed a course that empowered students to write, and consequently, to publish the results of their research findings. The Dentistry faculty of Araraquara holds one of the most important courses in Brazil, with a level A graduate program. Professors from that university are usually granted with scholarships and their academic records depend upon their publications as well as upon their advisees'. Besides, Masters and Doctoral students are potential candidates for teaching positions in the several Dentistry schools in the country, which means that their CVs must display references to their published works.

Graduate subjects within the Dentistry program are allotted 32 hours per semester and I was given one semester to teach academic writing. A genre-based writing course was designed under the limitation of time, based on Swales and Feak's (1994) proposal, ESP needs analysis, and my own experience in teaching in private schools. The course also seemed to have the advantages pointed out by Hyland (2004, p. 10), i.e., the instructions were explicit, and the course contents were systematic, needs-based, supportive, empowering, critical and able to raise the students' consciousness.

The classes were distributed along eight weeks, with four hours of instructions per week, in total a 32-hour discipline. In order to apply for the course, students were required to be developing a paper for publication, so these students were in their last year either in the Masters or the Doctoral programs. Complete results were not necessary, but the research should be at an advanced stage and the methodology should be complete.

The group was composed of 17 students who had the characteristics required. The classes were taught every fortnight so that students would have time to prepare their homework.

The schedule was organized as follows:

First week	• A needs analysis questionnaire was applied in order to check if these particular students' previous language knowledge and needs were appropriate for the course. This stage was also important to verify if all the students who applied for the course had completed part of their investigations. • In order to make their background knowledge explicit, an activity which included parts from different sections was planned. The parts of papers were presented both in
	Portuguese and in English; the aim of the activity was to check if the students could recognize all of them, independently of the language. • The activity above created an environment for the presentation of the concepts of genre and discourse community, which were first introduced informally.

Second week	• The first chapter of Swales and Feak's book was presented so as to introduce ideas of audience, purpose and strategy, organization, style and flow. This activity was prepared in power point form and included the main parts of the chapter selected by the teacher. • Excerpts from their own fields were selected as examples. It is important to emphasize that the group was not multi-disciplinary and the fields only varied within the Dentistry area. The activity intended to make students recognize aspects of the ideas presented earlier in texts produced by their peers. At this point, both Portuguese and English texts were used, although Swales and Feak's chapter included only examples in English. It was assumed that the understanding of the ideas would be emphasized if both languages were taken into account. • Discussions of the rationale of academic genres were carried out at different times and awareness about academic constraints and expectations seemed to be rising. Formal definitions of genre and discourse communities were presented based on Swales (1990).
Third week	• A handout which covered the second chapter of Swales and Feak's book was prepared. The main purpose of this chapter is to work with different sorts of definitions which could be used in different parts of a paper, but mainly in the introduction. This material followed the authors' proposal and included texts from different fields to introduce the ideas of general/specific texts, different types of definitions and generalizations.
	• The follow-up activity was to make students write in English for the first time in the course, aiming at making them describe their field of study, specifically the one in which the research findings were to be published.

Fourth week	• All the paragraphs written by the students as homework were presented to the whole class as a way of acquainting everybody with the research papers being developed by the members of the group. • A second moment was devoted to brainstorming the parts of an academic paper. Students were aware of the standard parts of a paper and knew that different journals required specific items. As mentioned before, reading papers in English is a requirement in the course and most of the students accomplished this task very well. Besides, many of them had already submitted a paper, so they were aware of the section entitled "A notice to authors" present in journals. The activity was supported by their background knowledge and, in very few cases, introduced new information. It is important to mention that whatever was new came from peers and not from the instructor, which helped stress the notion of membership of a discourse community. • An activity which included sentences from the main parts of a research paper, i.e., abstract, introduction, methods, results and discussion, was developed. These parts, according to Swales and Feak (p. 155), compose a typical organization pattern named IMRD. Students were supposed to label sentences according to the parts of the research article where they were likely to have appeared. Only examples in English, from their own fields, were considered. • As homework, students were assigned to write the methods and the results of their papers.
Fifth week	• The methods and results sections previously assigned as homework were brought to class on a floppy disk to be used in the following class.

	• The idea of move analysis was introduced and the constraints of academic genres were once again discussed. The rhetorical moves proposed by Bhatia (1993, pp. 77-78) for abstracts were presented and verified in many published abstracts from their field. • As homework, students were supposed to bring the abstract of their papers in a disk.
Sixth week	• The methods and results sections were presented and discussed with the whole class. The teacher previously selected examples of difficulties at language and discourse levels, which were then discussed by the class. • Once the abstracts were brought in disks, the teacher presented them in power point, verified the presence or absence of the four moves presented earlier and discussed the rationale to the understanding of the whole paper. • Students were asked to make final arrangements in the sections already studied.
Seventh week	• The idea of moves was elucidated once again and the CARS model (Swales & Feak, 1994) was introduced. The 1994 model was preferred to the 1990 one based on the discussion in Aranha (2004, pp. 28-32). • Different introductions from their own field were discussed. They had been already published and did not present grammar problems. • As homework, students were supposed to bring the introductions of their own papers in a floppy disk.
Eighth week	• All the introductions were discussed in power point. Most of them did not present Move 2—establishing a niche. • Each introduction was discussed with its author in further individual meetings, not previously set by the program.

The first week was crucial in raising students' awareness about their background knowledge. Although they could not explain how they recognized the extracts presented both in Portuguese and in English, they did not present difficulties in labeling the different sections. This fact was used to show them how important it is to think about choices when writing their own papers, since in their case, their writing would probably be recognized by their peers in the future.

During the second week, students, especially from the doctorate program, brought papers of their own to share with their classmates. They were critical about them, although many had already been published. They even suggested changes that might have been made to improve the contents.

The third week of the course raised many questions about cross-disciplinary comparisons. First, when texts from other fields were presented, the students did not present the same level of background knowledge as they displayed in their own field. It was problematic to them to discuss issues of structure, purposes, points of view and organization in texts alien to their fields. The main problem seemed to be the content of these texts, not the language. Students did not have opinions to share when the subject was not common to them. Students also seemed to have low motivation to perform the tasks proposed.

The fourth week was crucial for students to analyze their own production. The students showed great interest concerning the subjects of works whose sentences they were supposed to label. The sentences displayed important information in their fields, which made the apathy of the previous class disappear. Although Swales and Feak mention the advantages of a multidisciplinary class over a monodisciplinary one (p. 3), i.e., rhetorical consciousness and lack of a competitive environment, our context showed that the latter has advantages in relation to students' motivation, theme relevance and material organization.

The activities of the fifth week emphasized the fact that some of their previous papers had not been adequately prepared and did not display the language nor fit the constraints of academic genres. Broad discussions were carried out and many examples were brought to class and evaluated by peers. The doctoral students were enthusiastic in re-evaluating their own production and the Master's students took advantage of the discussion so as not to make the same mistakes. Genre awareness seemed to be improving and students were very motivated.

According to Swales and Feak (2004, p. 159), "the methods is usually the easiest section to write and, in fact, it is often the section that the researchers write first." As this part of the research was supposed to have been carried out before applying for the course, it was assumed that students would not present difficulties. The methods and results sections presented by the students followed the rhetorical structure of the papers they were used to reading. Except for a few grammar inadequacies, such as lack of verb-agreement and the use of passive voice, the texts did not present problems that could impair reading comprehension. Because students were evaluating their own production, interest and participation were high.

Bhatia's model for abstract content includes four moves, i.e., introducing purposes, describing methodology, summarizing results and presenting conclusions. Abstracts from published papers presented these four in most of the cases, but the ones selected from the students' papers did not. For example, an abstract like the one below was considered thoroughly inadequate because it did not clearly show the purpose of the work (although it could be inferred that the purpose was to differentiate the insects using ⊠-amylase system) nor results or conclusions, only methodology. In addition, the number of grammar errors weakened understanding. Remedial grammar exercises as well as grammar consciousness raising and information about abstract rhetorical organization were necessary so that the student would improve her writing.

> In this work we used ⊠-amylase system to differentiation of *Drosophila melanogaster, D. simulans* and hybrids *and D. mulleri, D. arizonae* and hybrids. The analysis was realized by PAGE containing amylose solution to detect isozyme ⊠-amylase. In all parental lineages was observed an only one band amylase but with different mobility among these species. Two bands were observed in hybrids corresponding at sum of patterns verified in parental lineages, independently of cross direction. The staining method PAS (Periodic Acid Schiff) widely used in histological studies to detect glycoproteins was adapted to analysis in PAGE and make registry permanent of experiments.

After specific attention to grammar problems, direct instructions about the role of abstracts and the importance of this section to the whole paper, and many drafts, the student revised the abstract as follows:

> Our investigations suggest that the staining method PAS (Periodic Acid Schiff), widely used in histological studies to detect glycoproteins, can be a technique used in PAGE and become a permanent register of the experiments. These analysis were carried out to differentiate Drosophila melanogaster, D. simulans and hybrids; D. mulleri, D. arizonae and hybrids by PAGE containing amylose solution to detect isozyme ⊠-amylase. In all parental lineages, only one band amylase was observed but with different mobilities

among these species. Two bands were observed in hybrids corresponding to a sum of patterns verified in parental lineages, independently of cross direction.

It was also very common to find abstracts with contents proper to introductions—such as the establishment of the field—or with just the methodology move, as the one mentioned before. The example below shows that although the text does not present grammar problems, the beginning of the abstract could be omitted (as it was in the final version). The introduction of that paper began the same way, with exactly the same two sentences. Consciousness raising about text structure and rhetoric redefined places of information.

The occupational noises from equipment used during the dental treatment are extremely harmful to the health of the dentist, promote the reduction of the auditory capacity and also take professionals to stress, fatigue, irritability, nervousness, low productivity and blood pressure alteration. Due to the fact that such noises cannot be eliminated, the early awareness of the dentists about these risks in their work becomes important. The present work observes the perception of dentistry students concerning the exposure to the occupational noise. A questionnaire . . . (methodology and result follow).

The awareness of the different places for different information seemed to have helped students improve their own papers, since, at the end, most of the abstracts did present four moves and did not contain any relevant grammar mistakes.

According to the model proposed by Swales and Feak, an introduction of an academic paper has three moves[1], each comprised of different steps. The first move (M1) establishes the territory of the research and can be expressed by a review of previous research (considered obligatory to the realization of this move) or by showing that the research area is central, important, relevant (considered optional). The second move (M2) establishes the niche of the research and is expressed either by a gap, or questions, or by knowledge extension (all obligatory to the realization of the move, but one excluding the other). The third move (M3) establishes the occupation of the niche previously stated by indicating purposes or establishing the nature of the research being presented (obligatory) and by optional steps: announcing principal findings or indicating the structure of the paper. The model—Moves in Research Paper Introductions—as proposed by Swales and Feak (1994, p. 175), is described in Figure 1.

MOVE 1	**Establishing a research territory**
	(a) showing that the area of study is relevant, important, crucial or making general comments (optional) (b) introducing or reviewing items of previous research (obligatory)
MOVE 2	**Establishing a niche**
	(a) indicating a gap in previous research, raising questions about previous research, or expanding previous knowledge (obligatory)
MOVE 3	**Occupying the niche**
	(a) showing purposes or establishing the nature of the research (obligatory) (b) announcing principal findings (optional) (c) indicating the structure of the research paper (optional)

FIGURE 1: THE MODEL OF MOVES IN RESEARCH PAPER INTRO-
DUCTIONS (SWALES & FEAK, 1994, P. 175)

Move 2—establishing a niche—is considered the "hinge" that connects M1 (what has already been done) to M3 (what is going to be done by that specific paper) (Swales & Feak, 1994, p. 185). During the 7th class, the ideas developed by Aranha (2004), which assume that (a) M2 is the most difficult move in an introduction because it is not usually short (as suggested by Swales & Feak, 1994, p. 186); and (b) all the arguments in M1 and M3 depend upon the purpose of M2, i.e., whether M2 is introducing a gap or extending knowledge were discussed.

Swales and Feak's proposal states that most M2s create a niche by indicating a gap, i.e., by showing that the research story so far is not yet complete. This move is expressed by the use of contrastive linguistics devices (*however, but, nevertheless*), of some verbs or verb phrases (*failed to consider, lack, disregarded, ignored, misinterpreted, overlooked, be restricted to*), of some adjectives (*controversial, incomplete, questionable, scarce, inconclusive*), and some nouns (*limitation, failure*). Aranha analyses 30 introductions in Biology and shows some disagreement in relation to the size of M2 and the use of contrastive elements to indicate this move. From 30 introductions analyzed, 19 of them contained questions or knowledge extension and 11 contained a gap. This information is against Swales and Feak's statement about the greater number of gaps in M2. They also stated that most M2s are short:

> *Most Move 2s establish a niche by indicating a gap—by showing that the research story so far is not yet complete. Move 2s then are a particular kind of critique.*

> *Usually Move 2s are quite short, often consisting of no more than a sentence. Sometimes, however, Move 2s can be quite complicated.* (p. 186)

The size of M2 found in Aranha's (2004) data varies from one sentence to more than ten, which also contradicts the statement above. This may be due to the area of study chosen (Biology, cancer, cells) where researchers seek to broaden the existing knowledge and treatment alternatives. It is crucial to use other authors' findings to advance the research and to share results and information in search of a cure.

The conjunctions of opposition, such as *however, but* and *although,* are said to be used in M2s that show a gap in previous research. The data show that the occurrence of such conjunctions not only introduces a gap to be fulfilled by that paper but also points to gaps in the literature review of the area. These gaps remain after the publication of the paper and the reason to show them is to indicate that the authors are aware of the limitations of their work. The authors do not have the intention of filling the gaps. In these cases, the conjunctions occur in M1. The example below shows the use of *however* in M1, indicating a gap within the review. The M2 in this introduction expands previous knowledge.

> In humans (review*)² and rats (*), estrogen receptor (ER) is localized within a subpopulation of mammary epithelial cells, whereas ER is expressed in a subpopulation of both epithelial and stromal cells in the mouse mammary gland (*). In human breast, epithelial proliferation and expression of ER appear to be mutually exclusive (*). Similarly, ER is typically not expressed in proliferating mammary epithelial cells of mice (*) and rats (*); **however,** the relationship does not appear to be as clear as in human cells.

The M3 from this introduction derives from knowledge extension. The conjunction was used to establish a territory (M1) and presents a gap in the review which will not be fulfilled by that work. The gap will remain. The example below shows M3 of the same introduction.

The objective of this investigation was to ascertain patterns of mammary cell proliferation and duct formation by employing bromodeoxyuriden labeling and three-dimensional reconstruction, and to evaluate the relationship between expressions of ER and progesterone receptor (PR) and the proliferation of epithelial cells in the bovine mammary gland.

The aim of signaling an unfulfilled gap may be to show that the state of the arts still presents questionable facts or gaps partially fulfilled by other works. From 30 introductions analyzed by Aranha (2004), 20 occurrences of *however* were found in 11 introductions and the function was to establish a territory, not a niche. Other conjunctions—*although, yet, despite*—also appear in M1 in introductions whose M2 was knowledge extension and not a gap. Aranha (2004) shows that these conjunctions have more than one communicative purpose and not a single one of the initiating M2s indicate a gap. This distinction was pedagogically crucial in the context of the present paper.

It is important to notice that, especially for Masters' students, it is very complicated to question established previous research results, since they are novices in the discourse community and the risk of being linguistically and discursively naïve is high. It is safer to continue tradition. Another fact is that both graduate programs develop projects to which most of the students are related; the results of their papers are part of a broader project and, therefore, depend on the previous works developed by others on the same theme.

At the end of the course, students felt the need for more explicit grammar rules, although not many different problems were detected. The occurrences concentrate on specific linguistic features. Because the group was relatively large, students also felt the need for more individual attention. Most of them had the sections ready for publication after long individual discussions in the introduction sections, mainly considering the need for M2 and the implications of its presence in the introductory section. These discussions were carried out individually and lasted about an hour. They took place after the seventh and eighth classes.

Genre awareness increased a great deal with this individual work. Demand for more classes was mentioned by all students but they said they could feel improvement in the way they wrote and in the way they viewed the use of language for academic purposes. Unfortunately, there was no time to study the discussion section, although many students sent theirs by mail later and I corrected and suggested modifications. Needless to say, the 32 hours assigned for this course are far from being enough.

REVIEWING THE RESULTS

The ideal design of any course should take into account "what the students know, what they are able to do, and what they are interested in learning" (Hyland, 2004, p. 93). The first version of the course described in this paper considered this ideal. It was assumed that students were fully aware of the constraints of the academic genre in their mother tongue and partially in English, since they could recognize parts of different sections in academic papers. In short, it was assumed that they would be able to write academic texts, especially sections such as methodology because they have reproducible characteristics and do not display rhetoric effort or linguistic polish. It was also assumed that learners were interested in learning due to the pressure of publishing or perishing. Thus, the main objective of the course was to make them aware of the linguistic constraints of academic writing in a foreign language. In other words, we expected problems at the language level, in the realization of the moves through steps, and not at the level of academic genres. Besides, we believed that being able to recognize different parts of academic papers meant being likely to produce them.

Most of these assumptions were proved wrong, except the one concerning the students' interest in learning. However, these assumptions did not come out of the blue. They were based on a previous work that described workshops in which similar activities were used, i.e., activities which aimed at recognizing and labeling different sections of academic papers (Aranha, 2002). This previous experience showed us that students usually knew more than they thought but could not express this knowledge, maybe because of shyness, lack of confidence, or fear. In addition, the absence of foreign language proficiency seemed to prevent them even further from expressing themselves. The process of recognition and awareness raising made them more confident and served, at that time, as a positive start for deepening the study of academic texts.

Unfortunately, a clear separation between the academic discourse of proficient writers (the ones students were used to reading) and one's own (the one students were expected to produce) was evident after the end of the first course. Canagarajah (2005, p. 17) states that "ESOL writers have to be made reflexively aware of the medium they are using, developing a critical understanding of its potentialities and limitation as they appropriate and reconstruct the language to represent their interests." We realized that being aware did not mean being "reflexively aware"; therefore, it seemed that the reflexive part somehow depended upon considering academic discourse as part of their lives and not as something that belonged to proficient writers, i.e., the authors they were expected to read.

The following assumptions served as the basis for the reformulation of the course:

(a) The act of recognizing (reading) is different from the act of producing (writing) academic genre regardless of the language;

(b) Students needed more individual attention, as what they wanted to say or show of their research was crucial for the understanding of linguistic and discourse aspects;

(c) Students seemed to be at very different linguistic threshold levels, although all of them had been previously considered competent by an entrance test, so more grammar and vocabulary were essential for writing production.

In other words, the teaching experience indicated that their alleged background in reading was not the main factor concerning the quality of their written production, and different linguistic aspects needed specific attention, forms of correction and strategies for awareness raising.

Some improvements based on the results

After the first WAC experience with the course offered to the Dentistry Faculty of Araraquara in 2004, the course "Redação acadêmica em língua inglesa" (Academic writing in English) was offered as an elective subject for the graduate program in Genetics at the Instituto de Biociências, Letras e Ciências Exatas at UNESP, São José do Rio Preto, at the request of the course coordinator.

The original course schedule was maintained, with classes every other week. The first and second weeks were condensed into only one, since the needs analysis questionnaire was answered at home and sent by mail up to the end of the first week to serve as a guide for the following classes. Students were also asked to send their methodology section to be discussed in class, without previous explanation. The time allotted to this section was little as Dentistry students had showed very few problems with this section. Thus, it was assumed that this section would not contain basic mistakes. Moreover, it was also assumed that students' linguistic threshold level would allow them to write this section properly.

Once the questionnaires arrived, it was detected that this group presented lower linguistic knowledge than the one in Dentistry. Besides, they did not have as much contact with papers published in English as the other group. Therefore, their methodology section expressed exactly these differences, with mistakes that ranged from basic noun-verb agreement to complete unexpected syntax and vocabulary inadequacies, as in this example which contains errors of verb form, lexical choice and syntactic arrangement:

> *The Schiff's reactive were throw out and the gels washed with sodium*
> *metabissulfit at 0.5% overnight.*

In this example, a basic lack of noun-verb agreement can be detected in the use of *were* instead of *was* to agree with a singular subject. Besides, at the vocabulary level, the use of *throw out* instead of *discard* shows little or no awareness of academic constraints in relation to the proper register for an academic paper. Another point to be considered is the misplacement of the adverb *overnight*. Examples with the same types of mistakes were common.

After the analysis of the students' methodology sections, the following issues had to be considered before the course could continue:

(a) After the first class, it was noticed that students did not have a well enough developed level of English to start studying genre in that language. Genre, as a concept, would have to be introduced in texts in Portuguese.

(b) The twenty-eight remaining hours would be insufficient to develop a paper as a whole, although many of the students were in the last year and needed to have their papers done. It was clear that the proposal they applied for had to be changed.

(c) The grammar points which had been previously selected for this course, based on the requirements from the Dentistry students, would have to be expanded and more detailed, because a wider linguistic knowledge had to be achieved before the students could produce their final papers in English.

The second week began as a result of the evaluation of these issues. Students were made aware of the limitations of the course and the impossibility of having their papers ready for publication after finishing it due to lack of hours in the course. It was stated that they would have to spend more time on their papers than they had expected outside class. Although they had their research studies almost finished and were about to end the course, English and genre were subjects to be discussed and implemented before they risked submitting their papers to be published. It seemed that papers had just been translated from Portuguese into English, and as a consequence they did not look like academic papers, not even in students' mother tongue.

Activities to raise the students' awareness about genre were carried out with texts in Portuguese, in order to allow students to recognize the differences between the language they spoke and the language they were supposed to write in. Besides, much reading of papers was assigned and students were asked to find out characteristics that seemed singular to the genre "research article." What was considered unnecessary for the Dentistry students had to be emphasized for the Genetics ones.

The course contents for the following weeks suffered reformulation in terms of methodology as well. Two classes on grammar were planned and included items such as passive voice, prepositions, subject-verb agreement, countable and non-countable nouns, sentence order and parallelism. As far as possible, examples were taken from their own methodology sections sent in the first class. A selection was made based on the "language focus" sections from Swales and Feak (1994) and from Aranha's (2004) results about transitivity and verb usage.

The classes were divided into two moments: in the first, students presented questions and findings from the papers they read, and, in the second, the teacher presented the selected material. After three classes that concentrated mainly on awareness raising about genre and discourse communities and about how language plays a role in both, the students were asked to rewrite their methodology sections for the fourth class. It was expected that, by then, they would have realized how they could improve that particular section of their papers.

The notions of audience, purpose and strategy, organization, style and flow, formerly part of the second class, were only introduced in the fourth class, before each section was discussed and reviewed by all students. Style and flow could then be analyzed in their own texts. Students became more aware of their own production and of the need for improving their linguistic knowledge to start writing about their research. We also increased students' awareness of the requirements of specific genres and the importance of being heard by specific discourse communities.

The following classes (from the 5th to the 8th week) focused basically on two sections: abstracts and introductions. The students' productions were brought to class and served as examples for discussions about appropriateness, context and mutual understanding. The idea of background information required by different audiences was extensively discussed because selecting information was considered a crucial aspect by the whole group. Texts were rewritten many times and in some cases not only to meet the teacher's demands, but for reformulating papers considered inadequate by their own authors after discussions and awareness raising. The fact that students read and reread their own work contributed considerably to the final quality of the sections.

FINAL REMARKS

It is safe to say that, as a result of the two courses on academic writing offered to graduate students, there was an increase in their interest in genre studies in their specific academic contexts, as the concepts of genre and genre conventions improved the students' texts considerably. However, the boundaries between genre and register, or rather, between language appropriateness and information selection and organization are still open and need further research.

Another point to be emphasized is the fact that pedagogical genre potential may vary according to the proficiency level in the language texts are written in, but the awareness of the concept of genre does seem to help any novice scholar researcher to write and to increase his/her chances of getting published.

These two WAC experiences were successful and the course schedule and contents have been improved based on the results. In 2006, another course was given for Dentistry students in Araraquara and the Medical School in São José do Rio Preto has scheduled a course to begin in March, 2008.

NOTES

[1] Similarly to the model proposed in 1990 (cars), the 1994 model is explained by an ecological metaphor.

[2] The symbol means bibliography review.

REFERENCES

Aranha, S. (2002). A otimização da escrita acadêmica através da conscientização textual. *Estudos Lingüísticos, 31.* (CD-Rom)

Aranha, S. (2004). *Contribuições para a introdução acadêmica.* Unpublished doctoral thesis dissertation, Paulista State University, Campus of Araraquara, São Paulo, Brazil.

Bhatia, V. (1993). *Analyzing genre: Language use in professional settings.* London: Longman.

Canagarajah, A. S. (2002). *Critical academic writing and multilingual students.* Ann Arbor: The University of Michigan Press.

Figueiredo, D. C., & Bonini, A. (2006). Práticas discursivas e ensino do texto acadêmico: Concepções de alunos de mestrado sobre a escrita [Special issue]. *Linguagem em (Dis)curso, 6*(3), 413-446.

Hyland, K. (2004). *Genre and second language writing.* Ann Arbor: The University of Michigan Press.

Swales, J. (1990). *Genre analysis: English in academic and research settings.* Cambridge: Cambridge University Press.

Swales, J., & Feak, C. B. (1994). *Academic writing for graduate students.* Ann Arbor: The University of Michigan Press.

24 Written Genres in University Studies: Evidence from an Academic Corpus of Spanish in Four Disciplines

Giovanni Parodi

INTRODUCTION[1]

The past decades have witnessed a remarkable surge of attention to the research of language variation through the study of the texts employed in different scientific disciplines. This focus on diversity has begun to describe and explain the divergent construction of specialized knowledge within discourse communities. At the same time, there is a lack of research and available data, based on corpus linguistics principles, to fill the gap that exists between a general approach and a more specific one based on naturally occurring language use. This specific approach should be one that is situated, data-driven, dynamic, and pedagogical (Herrington & Moran, 2005; Thaiss & Zawacki, 2006; Beaufort, 2007; Bazerman, 2008).

Empirical research from diverse linguistic approaches has documented the relevance of analysis based on corpus as a way of describing linguistic and discourse variations in greater detail through the disciplines and through prototypical genres (Biber, 1988, 1994, 2005, 2006; Biber, Connor, & Upton, 2007; Martin & Veel, 1998; Wignell, 1998; Williams, 1998; Swales, 1990, 2004; Flowerdew, 2002; Parodi 2005, 2006, 2007a, 2007b). Based on these assumptions, this chapter describes a research project currently being carried out at the Pontificia Universidad Católica de Valparaíso, Chile. This project involves the collection, construction, and description of a corpus of written texts belonging to four disciplinary knowledge domains: Social Work, Psychology, Construction Engineering, and Industrial Chemistry. The first part of this chapter presents some theoretical background that frames the research. The second part establishes the parameters of the constitution of the academic corpus, and undertakes a general description of the nine genres that have been identified in these four disciplinary domains during the five-year university programs of study.

THEORETICAL FRAMEWORK

Our general research aims to describe the written discourse in some university settings and the corresponding professional workplaces by collecting and studying the written texts that university students read and which provide them with knowledge particular to their chosen discipline. We examine assigned student readings in four academic degree programs and the written texts that form the core of daily communication in the professional workplaces that correspond to these four disciplines.

It is relevant to state some fundamental assumptions for this research. The approach taken towards discourse is decidedly interdisciplinary and of a psycho-sociolinguistic nature (Parodi, 2005, 2006a, 2007b). Hence, the texts chosen are linguistic units immersed in a cognitive and social context, that is, whose function is determined cognitively and contextually. From this perspective, texts are linguistic units with closed meanings in virtue of producers/speakers and readers/hearers in particular contexts and with defined purposes, with prior knowledge constructed from human cognition in specific social contexts. In other words, the texts are conceived of as meaning processes and products of cognition and context, and, at the same time, as forming supports that, in part, help people construct their world and their environment.

Specialized discourse: academic and professional genres

The notion of specialized discourse (SD) embraces the research objects of study. Academic discourse (AD) and professional discourse (PD) are analyzed as part of SD. The use of the term "specialized discourse" is currently widely accepted by the majority of language researchers. However, from its initial use, it has been employed to express a variety of meanings. Hence, SD includes a varied set of discourse genres, but each with certain prototypical features. It is precisely this idea of heterogeneity of texts and genres within a scale of gradation that Parodi (2005) applies when approaching the notion of SD. According to this notion, SD must necessarily be understood as a continuum in which texts and the corresponding genres are aligned along a diversified gradient that runs from a high degree to a low degree of specialization. Thus, SD could be conceived of as a supercategory of AD and PD.

Parodi (2005) defines SD by using a series of characterizing co-occurring linguistic features. Many researchers also agree that there are a set of lexicogrammatical co-occurring features that identify SD and many of them consider that specialized lexicon is highly important (Cabré, 1993; Burdach, 2000; Cabré, Doménech, Morel, & Rodríguez, 2001; Ciapuscio, 2003; Cabré & Gómez, 2006). Academic and professional genres are made operational through a set of texts that can be organized along a *continuum* in which the texts are linked together, from general school discourse to university academic discourse, and to professional discourse in a workplace environment. This is presented graphically in Figure 1.

Figure 1 illustrates a conception of discourse in academic and professional fields along a continuum that follows a process of permanent updating and multiple interactions. SD, in part, comes from AD and, in turn, is linked to and interacts with PD. This distribution of specialized knowledge organization is mainly proposed from a student's perspective, i.e., one in which the discourse continuum is traced from a learner who faces the process of instruction. In other words, this is not a researcher's or university professor's point of view because interactions would be different. For example, if research articles are considered, it is clear they overlap in academic and professional life, given they are discourse genres employed in both fields.

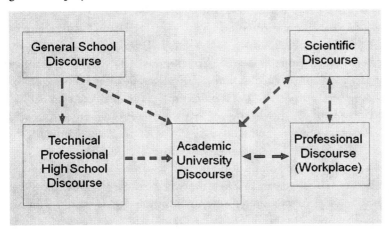

FIGURE 1: CONTINUUM OF DISCOURSES IN ACADEMIC AND PROFESSIONAL FIELDS

Academic discourse

There is no doubt that any newcomer to the study of AD will find a diversity of approaches, terminologies, and perspectives that makes an initial understanding of the field difficult. As Flowerdew (2002) suggests, there has been little systematic research into exactly what AD is. When one undertakes the study of this kind of discourse the following questions need to be addressed: (a) Are there any existing criteria that accurately define AD? If so, (b) what type of criteria are they? Below, three approaches to AD will be considered: (1) a functional communicative approach, (2) a contextual approach, and (3) a textual approach.

First, in functional communicative terms, AD is characterized by the predominance of one communicative macropurpose over another; in some varieties, more persuasive or didactic objectives are emphasized . Furthermore, AD carries with it credibility and prestige because of the writer's authority on a subject matter. Second, from the contextual criteria, AD is that which is used in academic contexts (Kennedy, 2001; Flowerdew, 2002; Dudley-Evans & St.

John, 2006). However, it is evident that academic settings are varied and not always easy to determine, which makes the criteria rather complex. This is due to the fact that AD does not have clear limits and may be confused or assimilated into other environments or nearby fields, such as technical-scientific, professional, pedagogic, or institutional ones (López, 2002; Flowerdew, 2004). Hyland (2000) argues that identifying the contexts and the participants involved in the interactions is indispensable. In other words, analyzing the texts as social practices is critical. This approach includes an analysis of the mediums in which these texts circulate and are used (Gunnarsson, 1997); so, AD is considered a manifestation of a specific community (Valle, 1997). Third, since AD is oriented towards the transmission of knowledge, generally through definitions, classifications, and explanations (Wignell, 1998), writers of AD use linguistic features that ensure clarity and conciseness. This manifests itself in an economy of words, an absence of empty adjectives, and the elimination of redundancy and repetition. It also has a more rigid and controlled syntax, and a higher proportion of nominalizations, than does non-academic discourse (Ciapuscio, 1992; Halliday, 1993; Lang, 1997; Gotti, 2003; Charaudeau, 2004; Parodi & Venegas, 2004; Cademártori, Parodi, & Venegas, 2006).

Multimodal resources frequently found in AD, such as chemical formulas, physics equations, virtual recreations, mathematical representations, and symbols, must also be play a fundamental role. In addition, items such as graphs, tables, figures, diagrams, and other graphic representations are relevant in this kind of discourse. In view of the above considerations, Lemke (1998) suggests that AD is a hybrid semiotic system, combining different kinds of verbal and non-verbal resources (Kress & van Leeuwen, 2001).

Professional discourse

Without a doubt, the problem that faces AD in its search for a strict characterization is similar to what occurs in the study of professional discourse (PD). This happens because in some cases these two terms tend to overlap, e.g., when the term PD is used in a general sense that includes AD, and vice versa. The current investigation will clearly separate these two discourses based on the environment in which the texts are collected. That is to say, PD will be that which is collected in contexts of professional use and circulation, while AD will be that which is collected in contexts of academic activities normally faced by university students. Nevertheless, there is an inevitable area of overlap or intersection between these two discourses. Therefore, our general research objectives include identifying and describing those texts that are used in both settings, and which form a nexus between the academic and professional worlds.

It is worth noting the work of Bazerman and Paradis (1991a) and their perspective on the notion of PD. These authors suggest that the structure of PD is founded on a textual dynamics that gives form to a profession. Bazerman and Paradis (1991b) review a series of related articles describing the way in which professional communities organize themselves based on their own relevant texts. PD, in this sense, is formed by those texts which bring together specific knowledge of the world, which, in turn, constitutes the purposes of the professional community (Berkenkotter, Huckin, & Ackerman, 1991; Doheny-Farina, 1991; Bathia, 1993, 2004; Christie & Martin, 1997).

Macrostructure and the superstructure have not been extensively examined by any analysis of PD. However, studies can be found that apply these categories to administrative language (MAP, 1995). López (2002) applies some rhetorical microstructures to the analysis of a text about economic policy, but there are no systematic studies with respect to how these rhetorical microstructures are distributed in each professional field. With regard to linguistic traits, the lexical level is the area that has received the greatest attention in academic studies, especially terminological analyses associated with particular professions (Ciapuscio, 2003). At the morphological level, an issue that has been extensively investigated is the role that nominalizations perform (Chafe, 1982, 1985; Biber, 1986; Ciapuscio, 1992; Halliday, 1993; Lang, 1997; Parodi & Venegas, 2004; García, Hall, & Marín, 2005; Cademártori, Parodi, & Venegas, 2006).

THE PRESENT RESEARCH: DESCRIBING THE ACADEMIC CORPUS PUCV-**2006**

This chapter will carry out a descriptive-comparative study of the genres identified in the academic domains of Basic Sciences and Engineering, as well as the Social Sciences and Humanities. This will be accomplished by collecting and examining an academic corpus following a methodology based on corpus linguistics principles (Sinclair, 1991; Leech, 1991; Stubbs, 1996, 2006; Tognini-Bonelli, 2001; Teubert, 2005; Parodi, 2006b, 2007a, 2007c). The academic corpus will be collected in a university setting, that correspond to the four university degree programs. The texts that comprise the corpus are collected following criteria that are highly representative and that accurately reflect the academic environment. Accordingly, the academic field will be defined by four degree programs offered by Pontificia Universidad Católica de Valparaíso, Chile: Industrial Chemistry, Construction Engineering, Social Work and Psychology.

This chapter will specifically describe the corpus collection processes as well as a quantitative and qualitative analysis of only the Academic Corpus PUCV-

2006. Special attention will be paid to the genre identifications emererging from the data collected in four university career programs in academic settings. Professional genres will not be described and analyzed in this study (see Parodi, 2008).

Constitution of the Academic Corpus PUCV-2006

As stated above, the aim is to collect as much required reading and reference material for the respective university degree programs as possible. The specific methodology of research is divided into different stages according to the status and focus of each corpus. Table 1 summarizes the general steps followed to collect and process the corpus.

Nine steps followed to collect and process the Academic Corpus PUCV 2006
Step 1: Construction of a database with the complete curricula of the four degree programs (including the syllabi of all required courses)
Step 2: Construction of a database with obligatory bibliographic references of all required courses
Step 3: Collection of complementary materials that all professors provide through prepared note files and photocopied materials
Step 4: Preparing a survey for all the professors of each of the four degree programs, which included a request for the complementary materials mentioned above
Step 5: Searching the internet to find those titles already available in digital format, thus minimizing time spent on digitalization
Step 6: Collecting the texts from the corresponding libraries and professors
Step 7: Photocopying each text in order to maintain a database in paper format
Step 8: Training a team of people to scan and compile all texts
Step 9: Processing all plain texts (*txt) through tagger and parser El Grial and uploading all texts in the web site http://www.elgrial.cl

TABLE I: STEPS USED TO CONDUCT THE CORPUS COLLECTION AND COMPUTER PROCESSING

By following these nine steps we were ensured the creation of a database that accurately reflects the written texts to which subjects were exposed to during their university programs. The steps outlined in Table 1 correspond to general procedural activities that help construct an online tagged corpus available at www.elgrial.cl. The corpus will be analyzed and described in detail in the following section of the chapter; also, from these texts the final discourse genre classification will emerge.

RESULTS AND DISCUSSION

In this section, we will define the Academic Corpus PUCV-2006 in quantitative terms as distributed among the academic disciplines and the four university degree programs. Also, a first genre classification that comprises the total Academic Corpus PUCV-2006 is given. This description identifies nine genres.

In Table 2, the figure 491 represents the total number of texts of the Academic Corpus PUCV-2006.

Scientific Field	University program	Number of texts
Basic Sciences and Engineering	Construction Engineering	69
	Industrial Chemistry	53
Social Sciences and Humanities	Social Work	142
	Psychology	227
Total of texts		491

TABLE 2: CONSTITUTION OF THE ACADEMIC CORPUS PUCV-2006: NUMBER OF TEXTS

Table 2 shows the high degree of diversity in the number of texts collected in each discipline. Moreover, there is a progressive increase in and a substantial difference between the quantity of texts in the fields of Basic Sciences and Engineering and Social Sciences and Humanities, as well as a considerable difference between the specific degree programs themselves. A preliminary interpretation might lead to believe that students in the Social Sciences and Humanities have to read much more than students in Basic Sciences and Engineering. Psychology students read up to four times the number of texts that Industrial Chemistry students read. However, an actual word count decreases the disparity, even though Psychology students still read more than twice the number of words as Industrial Chemistry students, as revealed by Table 3.

	Number of Texts	%	Number of Words	%
Psychology	227	46	22,163,379	39
Social Work	142	29	16,343,175	30
Construction Engineering	69	14	8,813,663	15
Industrial Chemistry	53	11	9,304,407	16
Total	491	100	56,624,624	100

TABLE 3: ACADEMIC CORPUS PUCV-2006: NUMBER OF WORDS AND PER-CENTAGES

Table 3 reveals students in Psychology and Social Work (39% and 30%) would read (in terms of number of words) more than two times as much as students in Industrial Chemistry and Construction Engineering (16% and 15%). This same comparison in terms of books is doubled, that is, it is almost four times. Therefore, as already pointed out by Parodi (2007d), there is a growing and progressive tendency based on the number of texts and the number of words, the university program, and the disciplinary domain to which they belong.

There is no other report of a written academic corpus available in the Spanish language of such dimension that is so representative and so thematically focused. A corpus of such size, close to 60 million words, in digital format, morphosyntactically tagged and parsed, organized by subject matter and genres, becomes a fundamental tool for cutting edge research in corpus linguistics and psycholinguistics in Spanish. Adding the Academic Corpus PUCV-2006 to those pre-existing corpora at www.elgrial.cl increases the amount of available diversified material for corpus research (more than 120,000 million words) (Parodi, 2007c).

A first attempt at a more in-depth analysis of the written material collected and a classification as to the genre types follows, using the communicative-functional and textual-discursive linguistic taxonomy, as proposed by Parodi, Venegas, Ibáñez & Gutiérrez (2008). Below, in Table 4, nine genres are identified along with their frequency of text occurrence.

Corpus Genres in the Academic Corpus PUCV-2006	Number of texts
Lecture	2
Didactic Guideline	40
Dictionary	2
Disciplinary Text	270
Regulation	13
Report	13
Research Article	23
Test	2
Textbook	126
Total	491

TABLE 4: DISTRIBUTION BY GENRE TYPES

The organization of the information in Table 4 follows the alphabetical order for the names applied to each genre. Simple, everyday names in Spanish were selected; names of rather easy accessibility and transparency in their usage for native academic speakers of Spanish. Definitions for each of the nine genres are presented in Table 5. Some of the variables involved in these definitions are macropurpose, participants, contents, organization discourse mode, and formats.

Genre	Definition
Lecture	Discourse genre whose macropurpose is to communicate a theoretical or empirical study, presented orally by a specialist (usually scholars of some standing) on a specific disciplinary topic or field; sometimes it is previously written. For the presentation, audio-visual resources may be employed.

Didactic Guideline	Discourse genre whose macropurpose is to instruct, produced by a teacher to help students to understand a specific topic on a subject matter under study. Normally it contains explanations and specifications, supported by didactic aids such as examples or evaluative activities in a paper or digital format.
Dictionary	Discourse genre whose macropurpose is to define concepts or procedures in a particular domain of knowledge of subject matter, written generally by a group of specialists. Its organization follows alphabetical or thematic principles and some of the definitions may include examples or images. Paper and digital formats are available.
Disciplinary Text	Discourse genre whose macropurpose is to present, to a specialized audience, one or more topics on a particular subject matter belonging to a field of study. Its main focus is argumentative. In some disciplines, few multimodal resources are employed. Paper and digital formats are available.
Regulation	Discourse genre whose macropurpose is to regulate behaviours or procedures. Normally it is written by an authority or a person in a higher rank position on a specialized subject matter. The content is organized as a list of prescriptions in a hierarchical order.
Report	Discourse genre whose macropurpose is to report about a situation, problem, or case. The main focus is on descriptions and the specification of variable relations that help support comments and conclusions. As for format, reports range from a simpler structure with headings to indicate topics, to more complex ones including charts, tables, hyperlinks, and references.
Research Article	Discourse genre whose macropurpose is to communicate a theoretical or empirical study, written by one or more specialists in a particular domain of knowledge. Normally it is published in a specialized journal in paper or digital format.

Test	Discourse genre whose macropurpose is to assess, by a specialist, the performance, knowledge or skills of a subject, procedure or material. The assessment is based on quantitative and qualitative criteria. Paper and digital formats are available.
Textbook	Discourse genre with a didactic macropurpose, written by one or more specialists in order to introduce or guide the access to newcomers or novices into a domain of knowledge. Normally, its macroorganization privileges explanations and descriptions about concepts or procedures. It is a teaching instrument with particular instructional aids including exercises, problem-solving activities, and multimodal resources.

TABLE 5: NINE ACADEMIC GENRES IN THE PUCV-2006 ACADEMIC COR-
PUS OF SPANISH

As it can be observed in Table 4, a quite heterogeneous panorama with clear concentrations emerges from the data presented. Two genres are by far the most frequent: Disciplinary Text (DT), with 270, and Textbook (TB), with 126. This provides an overall initial situation that combines, on the one hand, disciplinary knowledge as presented in subject matter books concentrating high thematic specialized knowledge in each domain (DT), sometimes with a high degree of discourse complexity; and, on the other hand, Textbooks, which, although oriented towards disciplinary knowledge, have a didactic and more disseminating character. TB generally uses more educational resources, such as graphs, tables, diagrams, etc., in a more systematic manner and incorporates exercises and other practical applications in order for readers to access, develop and test their knowledge.

Other genres are less common. For example, Didactic Guidelines (DG), although they are the third largest genre numerically, appear only at about a fifth the rate of the two largest. Perhaps even more surprising is the low representation of Research Articles (RA), which appear only about an eighth the rate of the Textbooks and the Disciplinary Texts. It is important to note that this discourse genre of transmitting specialized knowledge would have been expected to occupy a more prominent position, particularly in Basic Sciences and Engineering. So, the occurrence of only 23 RAs out of a total of 490 texts in the corpus indicates that it is not a common genre in undergraduate training. The genres identified in this corpus appear to be clearly concentrated in TB and DT. These findings reveal the two points of the continuum of genres, from general to specialized, as mentioned earlier. They do not, however, represent two extreme points. Both the TB and the DT are oriented towards greater specialization, but with a clear tendency towards mainstream dissemination of information. DG, which represents the extreme point of the generalized-specialized continuum, does not appear in sufficient number to be significant in the overall corpus.

As expected, the Textbook, irrespective of the discipline it is associated with, serves a clear common didactic purpose across academic settings. These kinds of texts disseminate discipline-based knowledge and are seen, in Hyland's words (2000), as "repositories of codified knowledge," which through some rhetorical structures may grant access to the most specialized professional communication. At the same time, these two text types interact with the audience in a writer-reader relationship that is appropriate to the educational and disseminating context; i.e., the writer acts as the specialist and the reader as the non-initiated student approaching a new knowledge and trying to become part of the discourse community.

Figure 2 compares the frequency of occurrence of each genre in the Social Sciences and Humanities. The resulting figure reveals a more in-depth analysis of the findings displayed in Table 4.

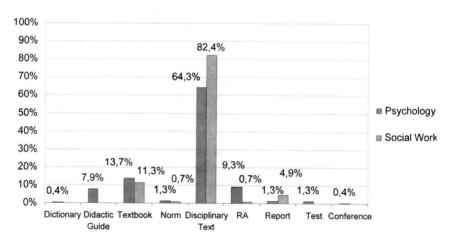

FIGURE 2: GENRES IN SOCIAL SCIENCES & HUMANITIES (PUCV-2006 ACADEMIC CORPUS)

As is obvious from these figures, only five common genres are detected in both university programs. It is indeed noteworthy that the area with the most genre types is Psychology (9), not only in Social Sciences and Humanities, but in the total corpus including Basic Sciences and Engineering (see Figure 3). Social Work presented only five of these genres (with an important concentration in two of them). DT and TB were the highest frequency genre types detected in both university areas of study, revealing themselves as the most common instruments of reading material students use while attending five-year academic programs. This distribution clearly reflects the kind of written texts through which students access discipline-specific knowledge. These texts are those which help students acquire professional expertise and become part of the academic community to which they will eventually belong. In the case of Psychology, seven genres show relatively low occurrence: Research Article (9.3%), Regulation (1.3%), Lecture (0.4%), Didactic Guideline (7.9%), Report (1.3%), Test (1.3%), and Dictionary (0.4%). Although they are part of the kind of readings students engage in during university life, they contribute in only a minor way to the students' discourse and knowledge training.

Similarly, we now compare the percentages of occurrence of genres in Basic Sciences and Engineering. Figure 3 shows the findings expressed in percentages.

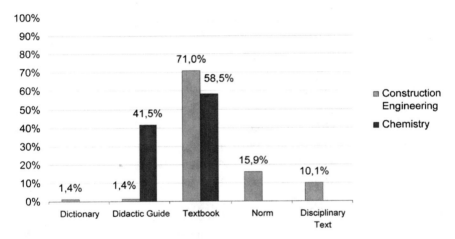

FIGURE 3: GENRES IN BASIC SCIENCES & ENGINEERING (PUCV-2006 ACADEMIC CORPUS)

This quantitative analysis reveals interesting differences of internal genre variability not found when comparing Social Sciences and Humanities. Not only are there fewer genres in Industrial Chemistry and Construction Engineering (as shown in Table 2), but there is less genre diversity, as seen in Figure 3.

Only five genres were identified in Construction Engineering, with TB dominating the distribution. There are four other genres that are part of the collected corpus: two are more closely related to the professional workplace (Regulation and DT), and two more typical of academic environments (DG and Dictionary). It is worth noting that in Industrial Chemistry only two genres were collected: DG and TB. This was unanticipated. There is a clear reader-oriented focus, recognizing the dialogic dimension of disciplinary instruction and directing readers to some action and understanding of the truths and facts under study.

These two genres represent important academic tools that open pathways to knowledge to novice students.

This variety of reading materials depicts the most common academic writings that students must encounter in their daily university discourse activities. The primary genre identified in this research is one oriented to disseminating knowledge. While this genre uses a disciplinary prose, it also combines instructional devices such as examples, diagrams, and problem solving exercises. TB is highly employed in Construction Engineering and Industrial Chemistry (71% and 58.5%), while DT appears most frequently in Social Work and Psychology (83% and 64.3%). This distinction between disciplinary domains in university settings is most revealing and constitutes a major finding of this research. There is an important difference in discourse interactions considering genre types in Social Sciences and Humanities and Basic Sciences and Engineering (for a detailed analysis of rhetorical and move analysis organization of TB and DT in both domains, see Parodi, 2008).

Figures 2 and 3 illustrate that the comparisons favored genres that disseminate knowledge (TB and DG), as well as more highly specialized genres (DT). Taken together, these figures reveal an important pattern of situating and distributing academic genres in these four university fields of study. This provides evidence that the social, cognitive and discourse interactions of members of these academic communities help shape their knowledge constructions and disciplinary representations, through this kind of written material. It also yields information about the way a university organizes its academic curricula.

FINAL REMARKS AND PROJECTIONS

In this chapter, we have described a corpus of 491 texts collected from four academic disciplines of study from two science branches. In addition, the emerging genre identification showed a distribution of nine types. The general results show some expected cross-discipline similarities, but most interesting are the inter-disciplinary variations, where, for example, Industrial Chemistry and Psychology are at the extreme poles of the continuum not only in the number of texts and words, but also in the variety of genres. In general, more disseminating reader-oriented genres were found in the fields of Basic Sciences and Engineering, with a particularly high frequency of DG and TB (especially in Industrial Chemistry). Social Sciences and Humanities showed a richer variety of genres, but with a major concentration in disciplinary-specific perspectives with less emphasis on didactic resources (important occurrence of DT).

With regard to the quantitative and qualitative analysis of the academic corpus PUCV-2006, the data presented in the areas of the Social Sciences and Humanities and in the Basic Sciences and Engineering reveal differences both in the number and variety of written genres identified. It is evident that Psychology and Social Work tend to employ a greater quantity of texts with a relatively more extensive range (at least in the number of words) during the course of their degree programs when compared to Industrial Chemistry and Construction Engineering, which use a smaller number of texts and more limited range of texts in terms of the number of words.

The current study identified an interesting heterogeneity of genres, which would confirm the validity of the idea of a continuum of genres between poles of higher discipline-specific complexity on one end and a focus on more teaching resources on the other.

We believe the corpus data collected is reliable in sketching a first approach to the study of genres across academic disciplines, in order to report and describe the actual genres that are read by students at four university programs. All of this has followed ecological and situated principles in particular contexts and in one particular tertiary institution in Chile.

From the findings presented in this chapter, we see that through corpus linguistics it is possible to provide rich, accurate descriptions of language use in institutionalized contexts; also, the findings have helped gain insights into the ways discourse practices vary across disciplines. Thus, we are beginning to realize and understand that the texts employed as reading material in one academic field (*hard sciences*) are not the same as in others (*soft sciences*). The data obtained from corpus-based research of written specialized discourse can provide valuable contributions in the areas of disciplinary reading and writing processes at university level and in specialized material development. The use of corpora allows researchers to explore complex issues related to disciplinary genres from ecological perspectives including large amounts of texts, and all this collected information can contribute to the knowledge-base used to shape better access and paths to disciplinary discourse communities and to help university readers engage in specific genres as part of their academic and professional lives.

NOTES

[1] Funded by Research Project FONDECYT N° 1060440

REFERENCES

Bazerman, C. (Ed.). (2008). *Handbook of research on writing: History, society, school, individual, text.* Mahwah, New Jersey: Erlbaum.

Bazerman, C., & Paradis, J. (1991a). Introduction. In C. Bazerman & J. Paradis (Eds.), *Textual dynamics of the professions* (pp. 3-12). Madison: The University of Wisconsin Press.

Bazerman, C., & Paradis, J. (1991b). *Textual dynamics of the professions.* Madison:

The University of Wisconsin Press.

Beaufort, A. (2007). *College writing and beyond.* Logan: Utah State University Press.

Berkenkotter, C., Huckin, T., & Ackerman, J. (1991). Social context and socially constructed texts: The initiation of a graduate student into a writing research community. In C. Bazerman & J. Paradis (Eds.), *Textual dynamics of the professions* (pp. 191-215). Madison: The University of Wisconsin Press.

Bhatia, V. (1993). *Analysing genre: Language use in professional settings.* London: Longman.

Bhatia, V. (2004). *Worlds of written discourse: A genre-based view.* London: Continuum.

Biber, D. (1986). Spoken and written textual dimensions in English: Resolving the contradictory findings. *Language, 63,* 384-414.

Biber, D. (1988). *Variation across speech and writing.* Cambridge: Cambridge University Press.

Biber, D. (1994). Using register-diversified corpora for general language studies. In S. Armstrong (Ed.), *Using large corpora* (pp. 180-201). Cambridge: MIT Press.

Biber, D. (2005). Paquetes léxicos en textos de estudio universitario: Variación entre disciplinas académicas. *Revista Signos. Estudios de Lingüística, 38,* 19-30.

Biber, D. (2006). *University language: A corpus-based of spoken and written registers.* Amsterdam: John Benjamins.

Biber, D., Connor, U., & Upton, T. (2007). *Discourse on the move: Using corpus analysis to describe discourse structure.* Amsterdam: John Benjamins.

Burdach, A. (2000). El léxico científico técnico: Un recurso publicitario persuasivo. *Onomazein, 6,* 189-208.

Cabré, M., Doménech, M., Morel, J., & Rodríguez, C. (2001). Las características del conocimiento especializado y la relación con el conocimiento general. In M. Cabré & J. Feliú (Eds.), *La terminología técnica y científica* (pp. 173-186). Barcelona: Instituto Universitario de Lingüística Aplicada.

Cabré, T. (1993). *La terminología: Teoría, metodología, aplicaciones.* Barcelona: Antártica/Empuréis.

Cabré, T., & Gómez, J. (2006). *La enseñanza de los lenguajes de especialidad: La simulación global.* Madrid: Gredos.

Cademártori, Y., Parodi, G., & Venegas, R. (2006). El discurso escrito y especializado: Caracterización y funciones de las nominalizaciones en los manuales técnicos. *Literatura y Lingüística, 10,* 243-265.

Chafe, W. (1982). Integration and involvement in speaking, writing and oral literature. In D. Tannen (Ed.), *Spoken and written language: Exploring orality and literacy* (pp. 35-53). Norwood, New Jersey: Ablex.

Chafe, W. (1985). Linguistic differences produced by differences between speaking and writing. In D. Olson, N. Torrence, & A. Hidyard (Eds.), *Literature, language and learning: The nature and consequences of reading and writing.* Cambridge: Cambridge University Press.

Charaudeau, P. (2004). La problemática de los géneros: De la situación a la construcción textual. *Revista Signos. Estudios de Lingüística, 37,* 23-39.

Christie, F., & Martin, J. (Eds.). (1997). *Genre and institutions: Social processes in the workplace and the school.* London: Continuum.

Ciapuscio, G. (1992). Impersonalidad y desagentivación en la divulgación científica. *Lingüística Española Actual, 14,* 183-205.

Ciaspucio, G. (2003). *Textos especializados y terminología.* Barcelona: Instituto Universitario de Lingüística Aplicada.

Doheny-Farina, S. (1991). Creating a text/creating a company: The role of a text in the rise and decline of a new organization. In C. Bazerman & J. Paradis (Eds.), *Textual dynamics of the professions* (pp. 306-335). Madison: The University of Wisconsin Press.

Dudley-Evans, T., & St. John, M. (2006). *Developments in English for academic purposes: A multidisciplinary approach.* Cambridge: Cambridge University Press.

Flowerdew, J. (Ed.). (2002). *Academic discourse.* Cambridge: Cambridge University Press.

Flowerdew, L. (2004). The argument for using English specialized corpora to understand academic and professional language. In U. Connor & T. Upton (Eds.), *Discourse in the professions: Perspectives from corpus linguistics* (pp. 11-33). Amsterdam: John Benjamins.

García, M., Hall, B., & Marín, M. (2005). Ambigüedad, abstracción y polifonía del discurso académico: Interpretación de las nominalizaciones. *Revista Signos. Estudios de Lingüística, 38,* 49-60.

Gotti, M. (2003). *Specialized discourse: Linguistic features and changing conventions.* Berne, Switzerland: Lang.

Gunnarsson, B. (1997). On the sociohistorical construction of scientific discourse. In B. Gunnarsson, P. Linell, & B. Nordberg (Eds.), *The construction of professional discourse* (pp. 99-126). Essex: Longman.

Halliday, M. (1993). On language and physical science. In M. Halliday & J. Martin (Eds.), *Writing science: Literacy and discursive power* (pp. 54-68). Pittsburgh: University of Pittsburgh Press.

Herrington, A., & Moran, C. (2005). *Genre across the curriculum.* Logan: Utah State University Press.

Hyland, K. (2000). *Disciplinary discourses: Social interactions in academic writing.* London: Longman.

Kennedy, J. (2001). Language use, language planning and EAP. In J. Flowerdew

& I. Peackoc (Eds.), *Research perspectives on English for academic purposes* (pp. 67-92). Cambridge: Cambridge University Press.

Kress, G., & van Leeuwen, T. (2001). *Multimodal discourse*. London: Arnold.

Lang, M. (1997). *Formación de palabras en español*. Madrid: Cátedra.

Leech, G. (1991). The state of the art in corpus linguistics. In K. Aijmer & B. Altenberg (Eds.), *English corpus linguistics: Studies in honor of Jan Svartvik* (pp. 8-29). London: Longman.

Lemke, J. (1998). Multiplying meaning: Visual and verbal semiotics in scientific text. In J. Martin & R. Veel (Eds.), *Reading science: Critical and functional perspectives on discourses of science* (pp. 132-149). London: Routledge.

López, C. (2002). Aproximación al análisis de los discursos profesionales. *Revista Signos, 35,* 195-215.

Martin, J., & Veel, R. (Eds.). (1998). *Reading science: Critical and functional perspectives on discourses of science*. London: Routledge.

Ministerio de Administraciones Públicas (MAP). (1995). *Manual de documentos administrativos*. Madrid: MAP.

Parodi, G. (Ed.). (2005). *Discurso especializado e instituciones formadoras*. Valparaíso, Valparaíso, Chile: EUV.

Parodi, G. (2006a). Reading-writing connections: Discourse-oriented research. *Reading & Writing Interdisciplinary Journal, 20,* 225-250.

Parodi, G. (2006b). Discurso especializado y lengua escrita: Foco y variación. *Estudios Filológicos, 52,* 165-204.

Parodi, G. (2007a). *Lingüística de corpus*. Buenos Aires: EUDEBA.

Parodi, G. (Ed.). (2007b). *Working with Spanish corpora*. London: Continuum.

Parodi, G. (2007c). El grial: Interfaz computacional para anotación e interrogación de corpus en español. In G. Parodi (Ed.), *Lingüística de corpus y discursos especializados: Puntos de mira* (pp. 31-52). Valparaíso, Valparaíso, Chile: EUV.

Parodi, G. (2007d). El discurso especializado escrito en el ámbito universitario y profesional: Constitución de un corpus de estudio. *Revista Signos. Estudios de Lingüística, 63,* 147-178.

Parodi, G. (Ed.) (2008). *Géneros académicos y géneros profesionales: Accesos discursivos para saber y hacer* (pp. 43-59). Valparaíso: EUV.

Parodi, G., & Venegas, R. (2004). BUCÓLICO: Aplicación computacional para el análisis de textos. Hacia un análisis de rasgos de la informatividad. *Lingüística y Literatura, 26,* 223-251.

Parodi, G., Venegas, R., Ibáñez, R. & Gutiérrez, R. (2008). Los géneros del discurso en el Corpus PUCV-2006: Criterios, definiciones y ejemplos. In G. Parodi (Ed.), *Géneros académicos y géneros profesionales: Accesos discursivos para saber y hacer* (pp. 43-59). Valparaíso: EUV.

Sinclair, J. (1991). *Corpus, concordance, collocation*. Oxford: Oxford University

Press.

Stubbs, M. (1996). *Text and corpus analysis*. Oxford: Blackwell.

Stubbs, M. (2006). Corpus analysis: The state of the art and three types of unanswered questions. In S. Hunston & G. Thompson (Eds.), *System and corpus: Exploring connections* (pp. 15-36). London: Equinox.

Swales, J. (1990). *Genre analysis: English in academic and research settings*. Cambridge: Cambridge University Press.

Swales, J. (2004). *Research genres: Explorations and applications*. Cambridge: Cambridge University Press.

Teubert, W. (2005). My version of corpus linguistics. *International Journal of Corpus Linguistics, 10,* 1-13.

Thaiss, C., & Zawacki, T. (2006). *Engaged writers, dynamic disciplines*. Portsmouth, New Hampshire: Boyton/Cook.

Tognini-Bonelli, E. (2001). *Corpus linguistics at work*. Amsterdam: John Benjamins.

Valle, E. (1997). A scientific community and its texts: A historical discourse study. In B. Gunnarsson, P. Linell, & B. Nordberg (Eds.), *The construction of professional discourse* (pp. 76-98). Essex: Longman.

Wignell, P. (1998). Technicality and abstraction in social science. In J. Martin & R. Veel (Eds.), *Reading science: Critical and functional perspectives on discourses of science* (pp. 297-326). London: Routledge.

Williams, I. (1998). Collocational networks: Interlocking patterns of lexis in a corpus of plant biology research articles. *International Journal of Corpus Linguistics, 3,* 151-171.

Author and Editor Institutional Affiliations

Solange Aranha, Department of Modern Languages, Universidade Estadual Paulista, Brazil

Natasha Artemeva, Carleton University, Canada

Nina Célia Barros, Department of Mother Language, Graduate Program in Language, Universidade Federal de Santa Maria, Brazil

Charles Bazerman, Department of Education, University of California Santa Barbara, USA

Adair Bonini, Graduate Program in Language Sciences, Universidade do Sul de Santa Catarina, Brazil

Helen Caple, University of Sydney Australia

Antonia Coutinho, Center for Linguistics, Universidade Nova de Lisboa (FCSH) / Centro de Linguística da Universidade Nova de Lisboa, Portugal

Amy Devitt , University of Kansas, USA

Tiane Donahue, Dartmouth University, USA

Kimberly Emmons, Case Western Reserve University, USA

Débora de Carvalho Figueiredo, Graduate Program in Language Sciences, Universidade do Sul de Santa Catarina, Brazil

Maria Marta Furlanetto, Graduate Program in Language Sciences, Universidade do Sul de Santa Catarina, Brazil

Cristiane Fuzer, Department of Mother Language, Graduate Program in Language, Universidade Federal de Santa Maria, Brazil

Salla Lähdesmäki, University of Helsinki, Finland

Mary Lea, The Open University, UK

Lynn McAlpine, McGill University, Canada

Florencia Miranda, Universidad Nacional de Rosario, Argentina; Center for Linguistics, Universidade Nova de Lisboa, Portugal

Désirée Motta-Roth, Department of Modern Foreign Languages, Graduate Program in Language, Universidade Federal de Santa Maria, Brazil

Estela Inés Moyano, Institute for Human Development, Universidad Nacional de General Sarmiento, Argentina

Jan Parker, The Open University, UK

Leonardo Pinheiro, Mozdzenski, Graduate Program in Language, Universidade Federal de Pernambuco, Brazil

Anthony Paré, McGill University, Canada

Giovanni Parodi, Graduate Program in Linguistics, Pontificia Universidad Católica de Valparaíso, Chile

Paul Prior, University of Illinois at Urbana-Champaign, USA

Rui Ramos, Institute of Child Studies, Universidade do Minho, Portugal

Fabio Rauen, Graduate Program in Language Sciences, Universidade do Sul de Santa Catarina, Brazil

Roxane Helena Rodrigues Rojo, Department of Applied Linguistics, Graduate Program in Applied Linguistics, Universidade Federal de Campines, Brazil

David Russell, Iowa State University, USA

Doreen Starke-Meyerring, McGill University, Canada

Brian Street, Kings College, UK

John M. Swales, The University of Michigan, USA

LaVergne, TN USA
11 December 2010
208379LV00005B/39/P